MASTER VISUALLY®

Web Design

Visual™

by Carrie F. Gatlin and Michael Toot

From
maranGraphics®

Wiley Publishing, Inc.

Best Selling Books • Digital Downloads • e-Books • Answer Networks • e-Newsletters • Branded Web Sites • e-Learning

New York, NY • Cleveland, OH • Indianapolis, IN

Master VISUALLY® FrontPage® 2002

Published by
Wiley Publishing, Inc.
909 Third Avenue
New York, NY 10022
www.wiley.com

Published simultaneously in Canada

Copyright © 2002 by Wiley Publishing, Inc., Indianapolis, Indiana

Certain illustrations and designs copyright © 1992–2002 maranGraphics, Inc., used with maranGraphics' permission.

maranGraphics, Inc.
5755 Coopers Avenue
Mississauga, Ontario, Canada
L4Z 1R9

Library of Congress Control Number: 2001092066

ISBN: 0-7645-3610-9

Manufactured in the United States of America

10 9 8 7 6 5 4 3 2

1V/RV/QX/QS/IN

Trademark Acknowledgments

Important Numbers

For U.S. corporate orders, please call maranGraphics at 800-469-6616 or fax 905-890-9434.

For general information on our other products and services or to obtain technical support please contact our Customer Care Department within the U.S. at 800-762-2974, outside the U.S. at 317-572-3993 or fax 317-572-4002.

Wiley also publishes its books in a variety of electronic formats. Some content that appears in print may not be available in electronic books.

Permissions

⑨**Wiley Publishing, Inc.** is a trademark of Wiley Publishing, Inc.

U.S. Corporate Sales	U.S. Trade Sales
Contact maranGraphics at (800) 469-6616 or fax (905) 890-9434.	Contact Wiley at (800) 762-2974 or fax (317) 572-4002.

Praise for Visual books...

"If you have to see it to believe it, this is the book for you!"

–*PC World*

"I would like to take this time to compliment maranGraphics on creating such great books. I work for a leading manufacturer of office products, and sometimes they tend to NOT give you the meat and potatoes of certain subjects, which causes great confusion. Thank you for making it clear. Keep up the good work."

–*Kirk Santoro (Burbank, CA)*

"I write to extend my thanks and appreciation for your books. They are clear, easy to follow, and straight to the point. Keep up the good work! I bought several of your books and they are just right! No regrets! I will always buy your books because they are the best."

–*Seward Kollie (Dakar, Senegal)*

"What fantastic teaching books you have produced! Congratulations to you and your staff."

–*Bruno Tonon (Melbourne, Australia)*

"Compliments To The Chef!! Your books are extraordinary! Or, simply put, Extra-Ordinary, meaning way above the rest! THANKYOUTHANKYOU THANKYOU! for creating these. They have saved me from serious mistakes, and showed me a right and simple way to do things. I buy them for friends, family, and colleagues."

–*Christine J. Manfrin (Castle Rock, CO)*

"A master tutorial/reference — from the leaders in visual learning!"

–*Infoworld*

"Your books are superior! An avid reader since childhood, I've consumed literally tens of thousands of books, a significant quantity in the learning/teaching category. Your series is the most precise, visually appealing and compelling to peruse. Kudos!"

–*Margaret Rose Chmilar (Edmonton, Alberta, Canada)*

"You're marvelous! I am greatly in your debt."

–*Patrick Baird (Lacey, WA)*

"Just wanted to say THANK YOU to your company for providing books which make learning fast, easy, and exciting! I learn visually so your books have helped me greatly – from Windows instruction to Web page development. I'm looking forward to using more of your Master Books series in the future as I am now a computer support specialist. Best wishes for continued success."

–*Angela J. Barker (Springfield, MO)*

"A publishing concept whose time has come!"

–*The Globe and Mail*

"I have over the last 10-15 years purchased $1000's worth of computer books but find your books the most easily read, best set out and most helpful and easily understood books on software and computers I have ever read. You produce the best computer books money can buy. Please keep up the good work."

–*John Gatt (Adamstown Heights, Australia)*

"The Greatest. This whole series is the best computer learning tool of any kind I've ever seen."

–*Joe Orr (Brooklyn, NY)*

maranGraphics is a family-run business
located near Toronto, Canada.

At maranGraphics, we believe in producing great computer books – one book at a time.

maranGraphics has been producing high-technology products for over 25 years, which enables us to offer the computer book community a unique communication process.

Our computer books use an integrated communication process, which is very different from the approach used in other computer books. Each spread is, in essence, a flow chart – the text and screen shots are totally incorporated into the layout of the spread. Introductory text and helpful tips complete the learning experience.

maranGraphics' approach encourages the left and right sides of the brain to work together – resulting in faster orientation and greater memory retention.

Above all, we are very proud of the handcrafted nature of our books. Our carefully-chosen writers are experts in their fields, and spend countless hours researching and organizing the content for each topic. Our artists rebuild every screen shot to provide the best clarity possible, making our screen shots the most precise and easiest to read in the industry. We strive for perfection, and believe that the time spent handcrafting each element results in the best computer books money can buy.

Thank you for purchasing this book. We hope you enjoy it!

Sincerely,

**Robert Maran
President
maranGraphics
Rob@maran.com
www.maran.com**

ABOUT THE AUTHORS

Carrie Gatlin is a Web producer, writer, and multimedia instructor in San Francisco, California. Over the course of her career, she has served as the principal Web producer for the Webby Awards and as a technical producer for CNET Builder.com. She remains a frequent contributor to CNET, authoring product reviews and features on Web design techniques.

Michael Toot is an author and software program manager in the Seattle area. He is an MCSE and MCP+I and has been involved with Microsoft operating systems since 1992. He has written a book on Windows 2000 Server and enjoys learning new programs and operating systems, even those not from Microsoft. When not working or writing books, he is reading, sailing, writing movie reviews, fiction, and nonfiction, and conducting adventures in home renovation and repair on his 93-year-old home.

AUTHORS' ACKNOWLEDGMENTS

First and foremost, I'd like to thank the people at Hungry Minds who worked on this project from beginning to end. Special thanks to Acquisitions Editor Jennifer Dorsey for getting this project off the ground and Editorial Manager Rev Mengle for his outstanding editing, guidance, and flexibility. Many thanks to Technical Editor Kyle Bowen, Permissions Editor Laura Moss, Copy Editor Jill Mazurczyk, Project Editor Dana Lesh, Jill Ann Proll, Mark Harris, David Gregory, Rhonda David-Burroughs, and to all of the other members of the Hungry Minds team responsible for editing, proofreading, designing the graphics and layout, and putting together the CD-ROM.

Thanks to the Web sites that allowed us to feature them in this book, and thanks to all of the companies that provided the software for the CD-ROM.

My heartfelt thanks to Sarahjane White for her continual encouragement, support, and creative input, and to Patrick Kane for sharing his technical expertise. Thanks to my former colleagues and mentors Paul Anderson and Maya Draisin for imparting their knowledge of this medium, and special thanks to Rachael Ann Siciliano for introducing me to Web development in the first place. Finally, thanks to my family for all of their love and support.

— Carrie Gatlin

A big "Thank you!" to my Acquisitions Editor Jennifer Dorsey and Project Editors Rev Mengle and Dana Lesh. You've all been a huge help in getting this book together and put to bed. Thanks are also due to the Hungry Minds and maranGraphics folks — copy editors, technical editors, graphics artists, and page layout wizards — who have worked hard behind the scenes to create a beautiful book. Although your names aren't known to me, you are warmly appreciated, and I hope to shake your hand some day. My deepest debt of love and gratitude is owed to my wife Victoria. What a wonderful adventure we're sharing together as the years go by — I wouldn't choose to spend it with anyone else but you!

— Michael Toot

DEDICATION

From Carrie Gatlin:

To Claire.

As long as there's something new to learn, the journey continues.

From Michael Toot:

To the memory of my father, Byron Toot, who passed away in March 2001. I hope you find the answers to your questions and your spirit is at peace.

WEB DESIGN

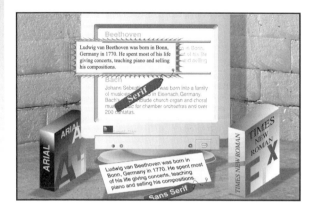

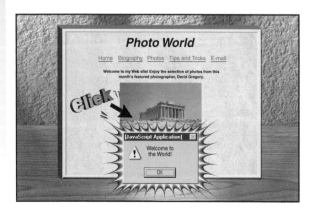

1

CONCEPTUALIZE YOUR WEB SITE

2

AUTHOR WEB PAGES

TABLE OF CONTENTS

4) CODE HTML FORMS

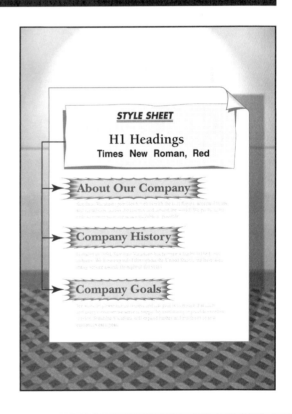

3

BUILD AN EFFECTIVE USER INTERFACE

7) DESIGN FOR USABILITY

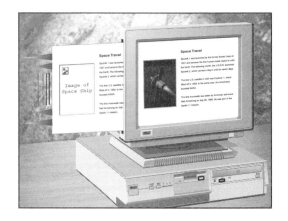

8) STRUCTURE INFORMATION

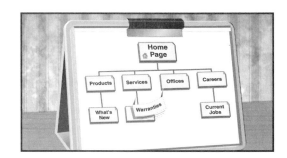

9) DESIGN NAVIGATIONAL SCHEMES

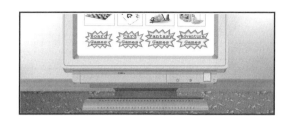

4

DESIGN A VISUAL INTERFACE

10) DESIGN PAGE LAYOUTS

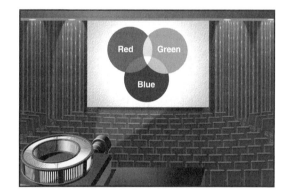

11) USING EFFECTIVE TYPOGRAPHY

TABLE OF CONTENTS

12) CREATE WEB GRAPHICS

13) USING NEW WEB GRAPHICS STANDARDS

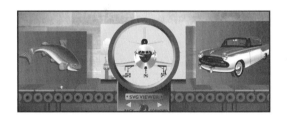

5

ADD INTERACTIVITY

14) MASTER JAVASCRIPT BASICS

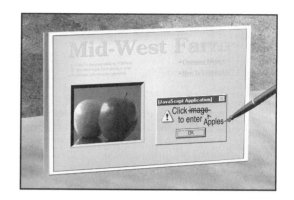

15) IMPLEMENT JAVASCRIPT APPLICATIONS

16) ADD MULTIMEDIA

TABLE OF CONTENTS

17) USING SYNCHRONIZED MEDIA

6

WORK WITH WEB SERVERS

18) ACCESS YOUR WEB SERVER

19) IMPLEMENT SERVER-SIDE SOLUTIONS

7 — EXPLORE EMERGING WEB TECHNOLOGIES

20) USING THE WIRELESS APPLICATION PROTOCOL

21) BUILD XML DOCUMENTS

TABLE OF CONTENTS

22) CODE PAGES IN XHTML

8

USING WEB DESIGN APPLICATIONS

23) CODE WEB PAGES WITH MACROMEDIA HOMESITE

24) DESIGN WEB PAGES WITH DREAMWEAVER

25) EDIT GRAPHICS WITH PHOTOSHOP

TABLE OF CONTENTS

Master VISUALLY Web Design is a visual reference for professionals and hobbyists who want to more completely understand the strategies and techniques that go into creating outstanding Web sites. Whether you are about to design your first Web site or you are a veteran Web site designer looking to increase the effectiveness of your pages, this book has tips, tricks, and instructions that will benefit you.

The Organization of the Book

This book is designed to help a reader receive quick access to any area of question. You can simply look up a subject within the Table of Contents or Index and go immediately to the topic of interest. The topics are arranged into self-contained units that walk you step-by-step through either a computer operation or the thought processes of a topic. Each topical unit, with rare exception, contains all the information you need regarding an area of interest.

Each computer operation task contains an introduction, a set of screen shots, and, if the task goes beyond one page, a set of tips. The introduction tells why you want to perform the task, the advantages and disadvantages of performing the task, and a general explanation of task procedures. The screens, located on the bottom half of each page, show a series of steps that you must complete to perform a given task. The tip section gives you an opportunity to further understand the task at hand, to learn about other related tasks in other areas of the book, or to apply more complicated or alternative methods.

Many of the chapters also contain illustrated groups of pages that either give you background information that you need to understand the tasks in a chapter or guide you through processes that do not necessarily require a computer.

The Sections and Chapters in This Book

Master VISUALLY Web Design has 25 chapters, divided into eight sections, and three appendixes. You do not have to read the chapters in order; you can simply look up a topic that interests you and dive right in. However, many of the early sections of the book contain important information on Web design, and we recommend that you look them over.

Section I, "Conceptualize Your Web Site," contains two chapters that put planning into perspective. We show you how to refine your Web strategy, from defining your goals and isolating your niche to putting yourself inside the mind of your user. We also give you a quick look at the principles of Web design and how you can build a Web site that answers your needs today—and tomorrow.

Section II, "Author Web Pages," focuses on the fundamentals of HTML and Cascading Style Sheets, the markup languages that you use to create pages for the Web.

Section III, "Build an Effective User Interface," explores three key principles of Web design: usability, information design, and navigation. These chapters show you how to build Web sites that are well-structured, easy to use, and accessible to everyone.

Section IV, "Design a Visual Interface," demonstrates techniques for designing Web pages that are visually compelling. Chapters show you how to develop page layouts, create and edit Web graphics, and effectively use typographical elements.

Section V, "Add Interactivity," contains four chapters that show you how to add interactive elements to your Web pages by using JavaScript, Java, Flash, and multimedia content.

Section VI, "Work with Web Servers," provides an introduction to the Web server environment and shows you how to perform common tasks such as transferring files to a Web server, using server-side includes for re-usable components, and working with both Windows NT and Unix servers.

Section VII, "Explore Emerging Web Technologies," introduces you to new standards and technologies on the horizon. Chapters focusing on XHTML, XML, and wireless Web applications give you a taste of the future of Web design and allow you to start building the Web sites of tomorrow today.

Section VIII, "Using Web Design Applications," shows you how to get the most out of today's most popular Web design applications. Chapters provide step by step instruction on common tasks in HomeSite, Dreamweaver, and Photoshop.

The Conventions in This Book

This book uses the following conventions to describe the actions you perform when using the mouse:

- **Click:** Press and release the left mouse button. You use a click to select an item on the screen.
- **Double-click:** Quickly press and release the left mouse button twice. You use a double-click to open a document or start a program.
- **Right-click:** Press and release the right mouse button. You use a right-click to display a shortcut menu, a list of commands specifically related to the selected item.
- **Click and Drag, and Release the Mouse:** Position the mouse pointer over an item on the screen and then press and hold down the left mouse button. Still holding down the button, move the mouse to where you want to place the item and then release the button. Dragging and dropping makes it easy to move an item to a new location.

A number of typographic and layout styles have been used throughout *Master VISUALLY Web Design* to distinguish different types of information.

- **Bold** indicates the information that you must type into a dialog box or code that you must type into the editing window.
- *Italics* indicates a new term being introduced and defined.
- Text in `monofont` indicates code. Italicized code indicates variables that you should replace. Capitalized code in Appendix B indicates the type of value that each property can accept.
- Slashes (/) are used in the steps to separate Windows and Macintosh commands, with Windows commands listed first. For example, the phrase "Ctrl/⌘ + F" means that you should press the Ctrl key and the F key simultaneously if you are working on a PC

operating Windows, and you should press the ⌘ key and the F key simultaneously if working on the Mac OS.

- Vertical bars (|) are used in the appendixes to separate different code options.

Regarding how the information is presented:

- Numbered steps indicate that you must perform these steps in order to successfully perform the task.
- Bulleted steps give you alternative methods, explain various options, or present what a program will do in response to the numbered steps.
- Notes in the steps give you additional information to help you complete a task. The purpose of a note is three-fold: It can explain special conditions that may occur during the course of the task, warn you of potentially dangerous situations, or refer you to tasks in the same or a different chapter. References to tasks within the chapter are indicated by the phrase "See the section..." followed by the name of the task. References to other chapters are indicated by "See Chapter..." followed by the chapter number.
- Icons in the steps indicate a button that you must press.

This book also makes two other assumptions:

- When you display a menu, a short version of the menu with the most recently used commands may appear. You can click the down arrows displayed at the bottom of the menu to display the complete list of commands. This book assumes that you are using full menus. If you do not see a particular command when following the steps in a task, click the arrows to list all commands.
- This book assumes the default toolbars settings unless otherwise indicated.

The screenshots and example figures used throughout this book provide visual examples based on the Windows operating system. If you are using a Macintosh operating system, expect slight variations in the appearance of software applications and task examples.

System Requirements

To perform the tasks in this book and use the contents of the CD-ROM, your computer must be equipped with the following hardware and software:

- A PC with a Pentium 133 MHz or faster processor, or a Mac OS computer with a 68040 or faster processor. A Pentium 200 MHz is recommended for working with Photoshop, an evaluation version of which is included on the CD-ROM.
- Microsoft Windows 95 or later, Windows NT 4 or later, or Mac OS system software 7.5.5 or later. Windows 98 or later and Mac OS 8.5, 8.6, or 9.0 are recommended for Photoshop.
- At least 16MB of total RAM, with 64MB recommended for working with Photoshop.
- A ten-speed (10x) or faster CD-ROM drive.
- A sound card for PCs.
- A monitor capable of displaying at least 800 x 600 resolution in 256 colors.
- A modem with a speed of at least 28.8 Kbps.

SECTION I

1) PLAN A WEB STRATEGY

2) AN INTRODUCTION TO WEB DESIGN PRINCIPLES

AN INTRODUCTION TO WEB STRATEGIES

Building successful Web sites is a complex process that incorporates a variety of distinct phases, from HTML and JavaScript coding to information architecture and usability. In their enthusiasm to begin crafting sites, Web designers often code pages or create visual layouts while overlooking the most important phase of all: the initial planning process. Even casual browsers of the Web can spot sites that have been designed and built without a coherent plan or strategy. These Web sites appear without structure or guiding principles, and produce confusion among visitors and customers who are unsure of the purpose of the site and are unable to accomplish their goals.

Before you start building your Web site, take the time to draft the strategic blueprints that provide a solid foundation on which to grow and develop your online property. Your blueprints should outline your purpose, define your unique selling point, and take into account who your visitors are and what they want to accomplish.

Understand Your Purpose

Understanding why you need a Web site is a fundamental element of online development that designers, site planners, and business managers alike often overlook. However, the ultimate success of your Web site depends on your ability to define and express the purpose of your online venture to partners, investors, and consumers. The "Craft a Mission Statement" section in this chapter demonstrates how to pinpoint and refine the purpose of your Web site.

Establish Measurements for Success

You need to understand how the Web site supports larger business goals and adds value in terms of revenue generation and brand building. Even Web designers building sites for non-commercial purposes should establish both general and specific goals for their site so they can measure the success of their venture.

Differentiate

The World Wide Web is a very crowded place these days. Literally millions of Web sites compete for attention online, and many of these sites offer a product similar to yours and share your target audience. Standing out from the crowd first depends on understanding your competition and isolating what it is that you can do differently. You can define your site's specialization in the "Isolate Your Niche" section later in this chapter.

Another way to get noticed is to develop a brand that resonates with users so that first-time visitors become return customers. Develop your site's personality and visual identity in the "Define Your Brand Identity" section later in this chapter.

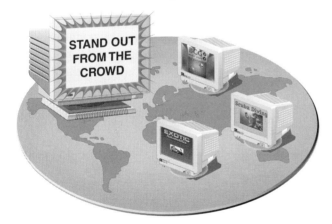

Know Your Audience

While you are laying out your own goals for your Web project, remember not to lose sight of your visitors' goals, which may be different from your own. You will only reach your goals for your site by first fulfilling your visitors' expectations. The first step in getting to know your audience is to understand who your users are and why they want to visit your site; these issues are explored in the "Define User Goals" section in this chapter. Then, explore ways in which fictional visitors might use your site by sketching characters and user sessions, outlined in the "Create User Personas" and "Create User Scenarios" sections.

Take Inventory

The last step in planning your site's development is to figure out exactly what content and technology your site will feature. The "Isolate Site Components" section of this chapter shows you how to develop a content wish list, take stock on the content you already have, and isolate the functionality requirements you should include in your plan.

CRAFT A MISSION STATEMENT

The first step in developing a Web strategy is to craft a mission statement that guides the development of your site from concept to launch and beyond. The mission statement that you develop is now the articulation of the "big picture" for your online property. Include a version of it on your site so visitors understand your primary purpose. Also include your mission statement in any press materials you develop for marketing your site, and use the mission statement whenever you communicate with prospective investors or business partners.

A mission statement should clearly express your site's primary purpose

and reasoning for being, whether it be to communicate with employees via a company intranet, display your personal work through an online portfolio, or educate and inform visitors. Your mission statement serves as both a means to communicate your purpose to others and a guide throughout the life cycle of your site. Each time you consider new opportunities and new directions to pursue, you should consult your mission statement to make sure every development is targeted directly to your primary purpose.

The worksheet at right and a similar Word document on the CD-ROM in the back of this book will help you develop your Web

site's mission statement. Use this worksheet to:

- brainstorm a list of products and services you want to offer on your site
- decide the relative importance of each product or service
- draft and revise your final mission statement

As you go through the process of developing your statement, be sure to consult with any other team members or colleagues who are involved in your Web project. You can also elicit advice from friends and family members to ensure that your mission statement is well-crafted and effective.

Where can I find examples of mission statements?

✔ Most commercial, corporate, or large-scale public sector sites post their mission statement or primary purpose. Look for a site's mission statement in content sections that feature information about the company or information targeted towards investors or partners. There are also numerous books published that list mission statements for successful corporations.

How long should a mission statement be?

✔ There is no hard and fast rule, but generally you should be able to clearly express your site's purpose in a single paragraph.

Should I target the mission statement to a specific audience or have one all-purpose statement?

✔ The primary purpose of your Web site should remain clear and consistent across the board, but you might tailor the language of your mission statement differently, depending on whether you are communicating with internal team members, prospective investors, or customers.

Plan a Web Strategy
Craft a Mission Statement

What products or services will your site provide? _____

_____

_____

What elements are of primary importance? _____

_____

_____

Indicate elements that are of secondary importance: _____

_____

_____

Write one or two sentences that summarize your site's purpose: _____

_____

_____

Craft those sentences into a rough mission statement: _____

_____

_____

Polish your mission statement: _____

_____

_____

DEFINE YOUR GOALS

For every Web site you design and build, you should define specific short-term and long-term goals for the project so that you can later measure the ultimate success of your venture.

Develop a specific list of goals for each individual area in which you want to measure success over time. Within each area, brainstorm specific short-term and long-term goals, such as leads and sales generated, increase in market share, or number of page views, new users, or e-mail newsletter subscriptions. Goals should always be quantitative and easily measurable. For example, rather than listing a goal such as "increase sales," list specific targets such as "increase sales by 5%" or "generate 100 transactions per day." You should also consider how you are going to be able to measure your success and how you are going to evaluate whether you have met your goals.

For goals such as number of page views, you can rely on your Web site statistics to measure success. However, for other goals, you might need additional functionality that helps you to determine how actions on the Web site translate to offline business leads. Be sure to address these elements when you outline your functionality requirements. See the "Isolate Site Components" section, later in the chapter, for more information.

When first launching a site, projecting target sales figures or site traffic numbers may be challenging. If you have access to media metrics for the Web, you can create a projection based on traffic at similar sites in your market space. Otherwise, monitor your site traffic during the initial launch phase to get a baseline figure, and then craft goals based on these numbers.

Where can I find information on Web traffic and media metrics?

✔ Many online companies such as www.mediametrix.com offer general traffic reports as well as more in-depth usage figures for a small fee.

How do I access statistics on my site traffic?

✔ Many commercial Web hosting companies offer some simple site traffic analysis for free. If you are running your own server, you can study the access log files where traffic statistics are stored, or you can purchase tools to perform more in-depth analyses.

When measuring Web site traffic, should I use hits, page views, or unique users?

✔ Page views and unique users are more accurate means of gauging traffic. A *hit* is any request the server receives for a file, including individual images.

Is there a way to convert hits into page views?

✔ There is no standard conversion, because the number of hits making up each Web page varies. You can estimate page views by assuming six to ten hits per page.

Define Your Goals

What are the areas in which you define goals?_____

_____

_____

_____

For each area, list your specific goals:_____

_____

_____

_____

What are the target dates for your goals?_____

_____

_____

_____

List the values for each of your long term and short term goals:_____

_____

_____

ISOLATE YOUR NICHE

Successful sites offer consumers and visitors something they cannot find elsewhere—a product, service, or unique content that serves to define the site's *niche*, or specialization, in an often crowded marketplace. If you do not define what makes your site unique and distinct from the competition, you run the risk of getting lost in the crowd. In addition, defining your specialization allows you to focus your efforts and excel in a single market.

Unlike the offline world, where geographical limitations enhance the appeal of one-stop shopping, Web visitors often prefer to visit specialty sites where they know that they can find greater selection

and a deeper level of expertise. Isolating your niche involves doing a competitive analysis of other sites offering similar fare, and then devising ways in which you can differentiate your site from your competitors and define your own specialized corner of the Web. The worksheet at right, which is also on the CD-ROM at the back of this book, will help you analyze your competition, identify gaps in products and services, and develop a positioning statement.

As you explore the competition, look for gaps or holes in the products they sell or the services they provide. A product gap can be something that is not offered anywhere else or an area that lacks

depth of coverage. A superstore Web site might seem to cover everything under the sun, but it probably lacks depth in key areas. Your specialty site can be geared toward the visitor who wants to dig deeper and explore a specific product or subject that your competitors only lightly cover.

Another way to establish your site's specialized focus is to target a slightly different audience than your competition. By defining the target audiences of competing sites, you can spot groups of potential visitors that your competition is not focusing on and specialize your site accordingly.

Is it better to appeal to a larger audience?

✔ If you try to appeal to a very large audience, you run the risk of diluting the message and purpose of your site, and in your attempt to please everyone, you may end up pleasing no one. In competitive markets, focusing your efforts is important.

How do I figure out the audience for a site if it is not apparent?

✔ You can get clues about the target audience from the content, editorial tone, and visual design of the site.

How do I find sites that I might consider competition?

✔ If you are unfamiliar with the market you are entering, try search engines or Web directories that include category listings of sites and online businesses, such as www.google.com or www.yahoo.com. After you locate the general category that corresponds to your site, drill down in the hierarchy until you find sites that offer services or content similar to your own.

What are some examples of audience segments?

✔ Audience segments might be broken down by age, gender, profession, income, and years of online experience.

Isolate Your Niche

Which sites do you consider to be competitors?_____

_____

_____

After exploring each competitor's site, list their strengths and weaknesses:_____

_____

_____

Are there any product gaps? If so, what are they?_____

_____

_____

What audience segment does each competitor serve?_____

_____

_____

Craft a positioning statement based on your feelings:_____

_____

_____

_____

DEFINE YOUR BRAND IDENTITY

You can differentiate your site from your competition by developing a unique brand identity.

Branding seeks to establish certain associations in the mind of the visitor, so that a logo, slogan, or other element consistently evokes both a clear message as well as a set of core attributes. The ultimate goal of developing a strong brand identity is to have new and returning customers think of your site first when they are in the market for the product or service you offer.

The attributes that define your brand should reflect the purpose of your site. For example, a Web site

for a bank or financial institution would probably be designed to convey the brand's sense of security, tradition, and stability, while an online journal writer might create a brand that evoked irreverence, wit, and intimacy. After you establish your site's essential "personality," consistently communicate these attributes through your site's color palette, typography, editorial voice, and marketing slogans.

Besides the design and editorial voice of your site, other important elements that both support your brand and help establish brand recognition include your company or Web site's name, Web address, and logo. Your name and Web

address should be simple, memorable, and descriptive, reflecting the core values of your brand identity. Be sure to choose a site name and corresponding Web address that no one else has registered. Remember that your brand also goes beyond elements such as recognizable colors, logos, and catchy slogans. Branding can also mean establishing a reputation for timely updates, authoritative and trusted commentary, or personalized customer service. The worksheet at right, included on the CD-ROM at the back of the book, will help you define these and other elements of your brand identity.

How do I find out if the domain name I want is taken?

✔ You can search available domain names at registration sites such as www. register.com. If the .com domain name you want is already taken, consider registering a site with an alternate extension such as .net, .tv, .ws, or one of the other new name extensions scheduled to be added in the near future. For more information on these extensions, visit www.icann.org.

How do I trademark my brand?

✔ Trademarks must be established separately for each country in which you do business. U.S. entrepreneurs can register a trademark and search for possible conflicts at the U.S. Patent and Trademark Office's Web site (www.uspto.gov).

How long does it take to build a successful brand?

✔ Building a successful brand does not happen overnight. Creating a unique brand identity is the first step, but fostering brand loyalty and establishing a lasting relationship with visitors takes time and depends on how your site delivers on users' expectations, such as timely order fulfillment, online customer service, and protection of visitors' privacy and security.

Define Your Brand Identity

Visit a commercial or large-scale commercial Web site. How is the logo integrated throughout the site?_____

_____

After isolating the color palette, identify any unique typography:_____

_____

Based on their branding effort, what do you consider the personality of the site to be?_____

_____

What adjectives describe your site's personality?_____

_____

Craft a site or company name that reflects your key attributes or site purpose:_____

_____

Designate a unique color palette for your brand. What does it look like?_____

_____

DEFINE USER GOALS

In order to meet your own goals for your site, you must first recognize and meet the goals of your users and visitors, which may be different from your own. Isolating your users' goals allows you to concentrate your efforts on creating products and content that address the visitor's needs as well as your own.

To define user goals, explore the types of visitors who may be interested in the content or product you have to offer, and what each audience group may want to accomplish on the site. For example, a site about Web design might attract a variety of visitors, from novices to professional developers. Novice designers might look for introductory tutorials while experienced developers might want advanced solutions and more in-depth coverage.

After brainstorming a list of users and their goals, consider the importance of each group in terms of your overall Web strategy. You may determine the relative importance of each segment based on the size or the revenue-generating potential of each audience. After you determine the relative importance of each audience segment, you can then isolate the group on which you should focus your efforts. In general, it is best to focus on one specific audience rather than attempting to cater to disparate users at once.

Understanding who your users are and what they want to accomplish can help you create the right content for your audience, and is also an important selling point when presenting your site to potential investors and partners.

How do I estimate the revenue-generating potential of an audience segment?

✔ You can estimate revenue-generating potential of audience segments by researching demographic information. Demographics provide general trends on the spending habits and income levels of various population groups. This information might be organized by geographical location, age group, gender, or other categories.

Where can I find research information for various audience segments?

✔ Plenty of free and easily-accessible market research data is available online at sites such as www.emarketer.com and www.cyberatlas.com. You can also view United States census data at the U.S. Census Bureau's Web site (www.census.gov).

Define User Goals

Make a list of potential user groups:

What tasks will the user want to accomplish for each group?

What is the most important site content for each user group?

List the relative importance of each user group:

CREATE USER PERSONAS

You can get a clear picture of the types of users who will be visiting your site by creating *user personas*, or fictional representations of various audience segments. By envisioning the personality and online habits of specific groups of users, you can target your content and visual design, as well as anticipate the most effective structure and navigation schemes for your site.

For each type of user or audience segment you think may visit your site, sketch out a detailed personality, including a name, profession, and any other hypothetical demographic information you feel may be relevant. Be sure to include details such as age, gender, years online, connection speed, operating system, and other Web sites the user might frequent.

Creating user personas is an important exercise in further understanding your potential audience, and serves as a catalyst for exploring the ways in which visitors may interact with your site. These personas also serve as useful conceptual guides if you decide to incorporate personalized content at a later date.

Create User Personas

Create one persona for each user group you anticipate:

What is the name and profession of each persona?

What are the relevant demographic details for each persona?

Are all possible user groups represented through your personas? If not, create more:

CREATE USER SCENARIOS

You can create *user scenarios*, or fictional narratives of user activity, to explore how real visitors will experience your site. By mapping out hypothetical user sessions, you can examine how the user might interact with content pieces and complete specific tasks. You may also want to refer back to these scenarios after you have built

out your site structure and navigation schemes (see Chapter 9) to see how the user scenarios translate to actual clickthrough paths.

When sketching out possible user scenarios, examine different ways in which people may interact with your site depending on what they

are trying to achieve. Some users may explore the site looking for something that catches their interest, while others come looking specifically for one particular product, service, or content piece. The user's browsing mode figures prominently into the behavior narratives you create.

Create User Scenarios

Sketch out a sample session for each persona:

How would the user go about completing specific tasks? Provide details:

ISOLATE SITE COMPONENTS

You can isolate the site components you need by developing a content inventory and functionality requirements document. The content inventory should list content pieces you want to include, existing content you already have, and the functionality you need to implement.

When you take inventory of the content you have, be sure to include pre-existing copy, brochures, and marketing materials. When using any non-original text or images, make sure

that you secure the rights to use the content and that you are not infringing on any copyrights or trademarks. For example, you can find artwork, graphics, and stock photography from many online sources, but most of these require that you pay a license fee and include trademark information. If you are unsure what types of other content pieces you should include on your site, browse other sites in your market space for ideas.

In addition to your content inventory, you should also outline the functionality requirements for

your site. Be sure to note any technology you are deploying, target browser and operating system support, and any plug-ins required. As you note the functionality your site will offer, include interactive components, such as multimedia games, message boards, chat rooms, or e-commerce shopping carts. Remember that the technology you deploy may limit the accessibility of your site if it is not cross-browser compatible or requires the user to download additional plug-ins.

Where can I find a list of browser plug-ins?

✔ Both Netscape and Internet Explorer users can visit Netscape's site for a complete listing of browser plug-ins. Besides the most widely-used plug-ins for Real media, Microsoft media, Quicktime, and Flash content, you can find dozens of multimedia, animation, and audio applications that require the use of specific plug-ins.

What are some examples of technologies that should be included in the functionality requirements document?

✔ Indicate both client-side technologies, such as JavaScript and DHTML, as well as any scripting solutions that require server support, including ASP, PHP, or CGI.

How do I determine what technologies my server supports?

✔ Contact your hosting service or system administrator to determine whether your server supports the type of technology you want to implement. Verify that you have enough bandwidth to handle the content you plan to provide.

Isolate Site Components

What is your initial content wish list?

Briefly, what is the purpose of each page?

List any existing content that can be used on the site:

What new content needs to be created?

What are the functionality requirements?

What technology will you be using?

What will the browser and OS support include? What plug-ins will be required?

Specify the server support needed:

BE INTERACTIVE

Unlike traditional media such as television, film, and print, the Web is fundamentally interactive. The Web is a two-way communication system where the user's input dictates the response.

When you browse the Web, think about the ways in which a site responds to your actions, whether they are mouse clicks, keystrokes, or even voice commands. Interactivity can be something as simple as clicking a link to load a new page, or having an image change in response to a mouse event. On some Web sites, interactive elements are highly complex, allowing visitors to decide exactly what content they want and how they want it formatted. As you design and implement your Web site, take advantage of the medium's capabilities by incorporating interactive elements that allow visitors to take an active role in their online experience.

Using Links for Interaction

The ways in which we navigate the Web are themselves interactive. For example, hypertext links, which form the backbone of the HTML language, allow users to jump to different pages with the click of a mouse. Add an element of basic interactivity to your site by including links to both internal pages and external Web sites. You can use hypertext links as navigation aids to help users find what they are looking for, or embed links within page content as a way of presenting supplemental information. Some Web sites use embedded links to take visitors to unexpected destinations. Learn how to add hypertext links to Web pages in Chapter 3.

React to User Events

A simple yet effective way of responding to user events is to have an image or link change when the user moves the mouse over it. *Mouseover*, or rollover, events that swap one image for another are often used in site navigation components. You can add this interactive element to Web pages by using JavaScript, a client-side scripting language. For more information on coding JavaScript rollovers, see Chapter 15.

In addition, Cascading Style Sheets allow you to apply a similar mouseover effect to regular text links. You can learn how to apply this effect in Chapter 6.

Respond to Input

Scripting languages such as JavaScript allow you to generate page content based on information the user enters via an online form. You can use JavaScript functionality to validate forms and generate messages, or create interactive quizzes, polls, and games. Explore these and other JavaScript applications in Chapter 15.

Interactivity and Multimedia

When implementing interactive elements on your site, remember that multimedia components such as audio, video, or Flash movies are not always interactive. These elements can create a richer user experience and provide compelling content, but they are only truly interactive if they invite input and respond to user actions. For more information on multimedia components such as audio, video, Flash movies, and Java applets, see Chapter 16.

Human Interaction

When Web interactivity is discussed, most of the time the discussion centers on how users interact with the content of the site or with the interface itself. However, one of the most powerful aspects of interactivity on the Web is the ability to communicate with other visitors and with the Web site author. You can provide visitors with the means to communicate with each other by implementing a message board, discussion forum, or chat component. At the very least, always give visitors the ability to interact with you via feedback forms and e-mail addresses. Learn more about using forms for feedback in Chapter 4.

USING CONSISTENT DESIGN ELEMENTS

Always use consistent design elements throughout your Web site. Every page of your site should rely on the same general layout, use consistent colors and font styles, and feature a uniform editorial voice. By establishing consistency through design, you can provide users with a clear understanding of your site's structure and purpose while establishing a coherent brand identity.

Keep a Consistent Page Layout

After you decide on the layout for your Web site, apply this structure consistently to each page of your site. Employing a consistent page layout helps visitors orient themselves and navigate your site more efficiently. For example, if your page layout uses a three-panel division with a header at the top of the page and links along the side, visitors expect to find these elements in the same location on each page. If you change the page layout and move the navigation elements, users must spend extra time locating links to other areas of your site. A consistent page layout helps visitors focus on the content of your site rather than figuring out the interface, so remember to be consistent in the following areas:

- Apply consistent page headers throughout the entire site. If your header contains elements such as a company or site logo, have these appear on every page to reinforce the structure of the site.

- Position navigation elements such as side navigation bars or tabs in the same location on each page of the site to prevent confusion.

- Organize text in main content areas consistently, using the same type of headings and subheadings on all pages.

Apply Colors and Type Consistently

You can use color and typography not simply for decoration, but to convey meaning and context. The color palette you choose is part of your brand identity, and visitors will come to associate your site with a particular set of colors that differentiate you from other similar sites. For this reason, always employing the same colors throughout your site is important. Both color and typography also convey contextual meaning, signaling to the user whether a particular portion of text is a heading, a footnote, or a clickable hyperlink to another document. One way to apply style elements consistently throughout your site is to use Cascading Style Sheets, explored in Chapter 6.

Keep a Consistent Editorial Voice

Use a consistent editorial style across your entire site to help establish your brand identity. Your editorial voice might be youthful and irreverent, or formal and authoritative, but it should always reflect the main purpose of your site. Without a consistent editorial style, visitors may have the impression that your site lacks coherence or does not understand its purpose or audience.

Use consistent functional colors and type for links and headings.

Use the same location for navigation elements.

Apply a consistent color palette throughout the site.

RELINQUISH CONTROL

When you design for the Web, you ultimately have no control over the appearance of your site. How your site appears to users depends on a variety of factors, including browser make and version, operating system, screen resolution, and individual preferences.

For example, when you set the typeface using <font> tags, you have no guarantee that all visitors see your text in the font you indicate. Some visitors do not have a large variety of fonts installed on their systems, and others choose to override font properties with their own browser preferences.

When you create Web pages, you are really only offering a suggestion of how information should be presented. Rather than agonizing over dictating specific fonts, colors, and pixel-precision layouts, realize that your site's appearance varies, and design with this variation in mind.

Test for Browser and Platform Differences

The variety of browser versions on the market creates discrepancies in how pages are rendered.

Do not assume that all users browse the Web with the latest version of Internet Explorer or Netscape. In fact, many people still use older versions of these popular browsers, while others use lesser known clients such as Opera, text-only browsers such as Lynx, or other alternative browsers for users with disabilities.

All of these browsers render pages slightly differently, and even among a particular browser make, there are differences in how pages appear depending on whether you are browsing on a PC, Macintosh, or Unix operating system.

For example, text often looks smaller on a Macintosh browser than on a PC browser, and the appearance of colors and HTML elements such as form controls can vary quite a bit. For this reason, testing your pages on as many browsers and platforms as you can in order to understand the variables at work is always a good idea.

Allow for User Control

Users can override your layout and design suggestions by applying their own formatting to documents or by disabling certain technologies.

Both Internet Explorer and Netscape allow users to set font and color preferences that override properties you set in your page. In addition, visitors can use the browser to increase or decrease the size of text, turn off image support, or disable technologies such as JavaScript and Java.

As you code your pages, experiment with your browser preferences to see how your site might look with user-selected colors and fonts.

Design for Variation

Even with the lack of control inherent in the medium, you can still apply good design principles and create visually pleasing layouts. However, rather than concentrating on imposing rigid design layouts and style rules, create pages that work well regardless of the browsing client or user preferences:

- When setting font properties, for example, provide a list of suggested fonts from which the browser can choose. Learn more about suggesting fonts in Chapter 11.

- In addition, consider using flexible table layouts to handle various screen resolutions. You can explore this technique in the section "Build for Flexibility."

- To ensure that your site works on both older browsers and alternative browsing clients, follow the guidelines in Chapter 7.

BUILD FOR FLEXIBILITY

An important variable to consider when designing Web sites is screen resolution, or the available space that the browser window occupies. Screen resolutions inevitably vary from visitor to visitor, but you can create flexible layouts that stretch or shrink to the available size of the browser window.

Using flexible designs rather than fixed width layouts allow you to avoid unsightly horizontal scroll bars on smaller resolutions and utilize the maximum space available on higher resolutions.

Understanding Variable Screen Resolutions

Screen resolution refers to the number of pixels a screen or monitor can accommodate. For example:

- A screen resolution of 640 x 480 means that the screen can accommodate 640 pixels horizontally and 480 pixels vertically. Although a 640 x 480 screen resolution is usually equal to the maximum space available on smaller computer monitors, screen resolution is actually independent of monitor size.

- Larger monitors have more maximum space available, and users can select their preferred screen resolution from a list of choices ranging from 640 x 480 to the maximum available space. Besides 640 x 480, common screen resolutions include 800 x 600, 1024 x 768, and 1280 x 1024, although users can resize browser windows to any resolution between the minimum and maximum possible.

- In addition to the wide variety of screen resolutions possible on computer monitors, Web designers should also take into account technologies such as WebTV, internet-capable handheld devices, and emerging internet appliances, all of which have varying screen resolutions.

Understanding Fixed-Width Layouts

This variety of screen resolutions creates a challenge for Web designers attempting to create fixed-width page layouts. Layouts built with a fixed width of 600 pixels appear fine on smaller computer monitors, but at higher resolutions, the content of the page is surrounded by hundreds of pixels of white space that is not being utilized.

Many Web designers choose to optimize their pages for 800 x 600 screen resolutions to utilize more of the available space. The main drawback of this approach is that visitors with lower resolutions end up with horizontal scrollbars across the bottom of the page. Both techniques are based on optimizing the layout for a single screen resolution, rather than creating an effective layout for all resolutions.

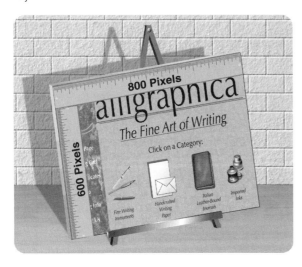

Solution: Using Flexible Layouts

To create effective designs for all screen resolutions, create flexible layouts that stretch or shrink depending on the available space. When using HTML tables for example, set the width of tables and cells to percentages rather than absolute pixels. A table width set to 100% occupies 100% of the available browser window, thus stretching to fill higher resolutions and shrinking to accommodate 640 x 480 screens.

Alternately, you can leave out global dimensions entirely and allow the page layout to be dictated by the amount of content on the page. Keep in mind, however, that flexible layouts inherently allow for less control over the final appearance of a page.

For more information on using tables for page layout, see Chapter 10.

USING ESTABLISHED BEHAVIOR PATTERNS

When you design your Web site, always take advantage of behavior patterns and conventions already established on the Web. Conventions are sets of practices and techniques that visitors learn once and can then apply in other situations. For example, frequent Web surfers know that clicking a link loads a new page, and that tabs allow them to jump to different categories or sections of a site. By relying on certain design conventions, you ensure that visitors to your site do not have to master an entirely new set of skills simply to accomplish their goals.

Balance Convention vs. Innovation

Web designers rely on conventions because they reduce the learning curve for the user, but that does not mean that every established convention is the most elegant or efficient solution. The Web is a young medium, and designers continue to explore creative approaches to common problems such as organization and navigation.

Depending on your site's main goal, bucking the system and experimenting with innovative approaches may be entirely appropriate. However, if you do decide to go against convention, take extra care to ensure that your interface is easy to use and matches the purpose of your site.

Using Consistent Link Conventions

One of the essential conventions on the Web is the appearance of hyperlinks. Every user knows that blue, underlined text means "click here."

By using HTML attributes you can alter the color of links, and with Cascading Style Sheets, you can create link text that is not underlined. However, when you change the appearance of links, you remove a vital clue that the visitor uses to identify clickable text.

If you do decide to alter link color or change the formatting of clickable text, be consistent throughout your site. In addition, do not underline non-clickable text on Web pages, because this can cause confusion for users.

For information on changing the appearance of links, see Chapters 3 and 6.

Plan for Structure and Navigation

Visitors on the Web are accustomed to seeing certain types of site structure and navigation, particularly side navigation bars, tabs, and category directories. News and zine Web sites often employ the left side navigation bar, where links to the site's subdirectories reside in a color band running the length of the page.

Originally, the side navigation bar was consistently positioned on the left side of the page layout, but more recently, Web designers have shifted the navigation bar to the right side of the page. This is a good example of slightly altering a convention while still taking advantage of an established behavior pattern.

Perhaps the most popular navigation convention is the tab-based interface that Amazon.com popularized. Tabs present an ideal way for users to toggle between product categories or different tasks, although they are often misused or poorly structured. For more information on side navigation and tab interfaces, see Chapter 9.

Another common convention is the category directory structure, often used in portal sites such as Yahoo! or other sites that have content in a wide variety of topic areas. In this organization model, the front door of the site presents a collection of links to top-level category pages. For each category, a handful of sub-category links are provided as well. This system is based on the convention of users clicking deeper into the site to reach increasingly specific categories. For more information on this and other organizational conventions, see Chapter 8.

As you design your Web site, explore other innovative approaches to structuring information and providing users with new ways to navigate the online space. However, before straying too far from established conventions, remember that any type of navigation that is unfamiliar might cause confusion and make it more difficult for users to find the information they seek.

KEEP IT SIMPLE

When you design Web sites, one of the primary challenges is taking complex structures and making them simple, clear, and comprehensible for the user. Simplicity in design does not mean that every Web site should embrace a minimalist approach. Simplicity on the Web translates to focused visual expression, easy-to-understand organizational structures, and clarity of purpose.

Keep a Focused Visual Design

Rather than distracting visitors from what they want to accomplish, your visual design should lead the user through the page, highlighting important elements and helping visitors achieve their goals. Every element of a visual design should serve a purpose, whether that purpose is to engage the user interactively, lead visitors through the components of a site, or establish a brand identity.

Visual elements that detract from rather than add to the design of a Web site include poorly selected color palettes and overuse of animated effects. Focused visual designs, on the other hand, use color, contrast, visual hierarchy, and white space to direct the user's attention. Learn more about these elements of design in Chapter 10.

Simplify Organizational Structures

Another design challenge is to organize information so that it is easy for users to find what they are looking for. Sophisticated information design takes complex information and successfully organizes it in a coherent fashion. Sometimes devising the right organizational structure means finding a balance between coherent organization and providing users with direct access to content.

This is particularly challenging for Web sites that feature large amounts of information, such as portals or directories. Portal content is often very deep, and users might have to click through several sub-levels to find what they are looking for. To compensate, portals and directories often bring more direct content links to the top level of the site. This approach makes it easier for users to access content, but it can also be visually overwhelming.

For more on designing effective information structures for your site's purpose, see Chapter 8.

Focus on Your Purpose

Clarify your Web site's purpose by focusing on your primary message or on the main task that users want to accomplish when coming to your site. If a visitor's goal is to find the latest news or content, make that the main element of the page. If visitors are using your site primarily to search the Web or the site itself, ensure that the search interface is easy to locate and easy to use. Always focus on what the user is trying to do and what message you are trying to convey.

SHOW VISITORS WHERE THEY ARE

You can ensure that visitors never feel lost or stranded on your site by providing landmarks and location guides on every page that you build. Landmarks should clearly tell the visitor where they are on the Web as well as where they are on the site itself.

Although the Web is a virtual space that defies geographical boundaries, users still think of the Web in terms of physical locations. Your site is a destination for visitors looking to purchase a product or gather information, but unlike customers in the physical world, visitors on the Web do not

always enter through the front door. They might arrive at a specific page from a search engine, a link from another site, or an e-mail newsletter, and the first thing visitors want to know is where they are on the Web.

Provide Landmarks

Perhaps the most effective way to communicate to visitors where they are is through your site's domain name. Your site's domain name, or Web address, provides a good landmark and can be a very effective branding tool, but you should always include additional site markers such as descriptive titles, logos, and other branding elements on every page you create. Including descriptive titles on your Web pages is particularly important, because the browser uses this information as a reference when visitors bookmark a site.

You can learn how to add descriptive titles to your page in Chapter 3.

Reinforce Location Within the Site

In addition to telling visitors where they are on the Web, each page should provide landmarks indicating the visitor's location within the site itself. Page titles should indicate not only the name of your site, but the name of the sub-directory and content page as well. Reinforce this placement by using guides and navigation aids such as bread crumb topic paths, on-state navigation buttons, and other visual markers.

For more information on helping visitors navigate your site structure, see Chapter 9.

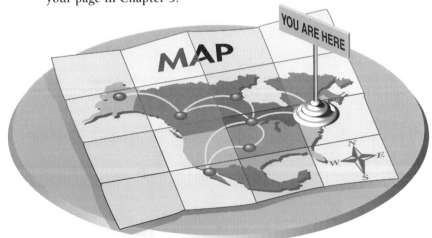

THINK GLOBALLY

The World Wide Web has no geographical boundaries, and depending on the purpose of your venture, international visitors may account for a significant portion of your audience. When you design your Web site, be sure to take into account the needs of international visitors, and ensure that they are able to access content, complete transactions, and participate in all the functionality your site has to offer.

Handle Language Barriers

The most obvious hurdle in creating internationally-accessible sites is language. If a significant portion of your audience does not speak English, the ideal solution is to create different versions of the site in various languages. Sites that use this approach usually decide on a default language while providing links to versions in other languages. The drawback of this approach is that it creates multiple versions of the same site that must be maintained simultaneously. For more information on the advantages and disadvantages of employing alternative language versions, see Chapter 7.

If you decide against various language versions of your site, you can still take measures to help non-native speakers understand your content. Try to simplify the language you use throughout your copy, avoiding slang, colloquialisms, and other dialectical elements that may be confusing to visitors outside of your local geographical region.

Clarify Times and Dates

The format of times and dates can create confusion, particularly for sites that feature live events such as chats and webcasts. When referring to specific times, always note the time zone and whether the time is AM or PM if you are using a 12-hour clock. When referencing dates, spelling out the month is always better than using number formatting such as 4/5. The date in this example could be interpreted as either April 5 or May 4, depending on your native language and cultural conventions.

Gather Information

One barrier for international users is the type of information you require when visitors complete forms. Drop-down menus for states and postal code entry fields are particularly problematic, because postal code formats vary from country to country, and only U.S. residents are able to select from drop-down menus with the 50 U.S. states as options. If you require these fields, many users will not be able to fill out your forms and complete online transactions.

If you must make certain fields required, the best solution is to have validation scripts that allow for different responses based on the country selected. For example, you can have a validation script that checks for the "state" value only when users select the United States as the country. In this case, include explicit instructions to assist users as they complete forms on your site. Instructions should include text stating that U.S. residents should fill out state and zip code, while international residents should type in a province.

For more information on using JavaScript to validate forms, see Chapter 15.

Know Product and Shipping Restrictions

If you are fulfilling product orders on your Web site, do not assume that your customers are in your local area or even in your country of business. Be sure to clearly note any geographical restrictions in delivery areas as well as additional shipping fees that may apply to international orders. Include this information at the beginning of the process so that customers outside of your service area do not waste time filling out forms only to discover at the end that they cannot complete the order.

In addition, carefully research any legal restrictions that may apply to product sales and delivery before embarking on an e-commerce venture. Both international and domestic laws restrict the types of goods that may be shipped from one location to another.

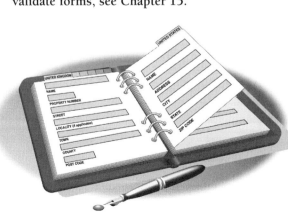

SECTION II

3) MASTER HTML BASICS

4) CODE HTML FORMS

5) CREATE HTML FRAMES

6) USING CASCADING STYLE SHEETS

AN INTRODUCTION TO HTML

When you create pages for the Web, you use a language called *HTML*, or *Hypertext Markup Language*, to build your pages. HTML is not a programming or scripting language. Rather, it is a document-layout language that tells a Web browser how to display the contents of a page. HTML also allows documents to be connected via *hypertext links*, which are clickable links imbedded within pages that allow users to retrieve other Web pages.

This book focuses on the HTML 4.01 specification and XHTML, the next generation markup language based on XML. For more information on XML, see Chapter 22. HTML specifications, or recommendations, are drafted by the World Wide Web Consortium (W3C), whose mission is to standardize Web technologies so that they function consistently across platforms and browsing clients.

Even with formal specifications in place, standardized HTML is more of a long-term goal than a reality. For years, the two major browser companies, Microsoft and Netscape, developed their own browser-specific HTML enhancements, and both have been slow to fully support the W3C's recommendations. With the latest releases of Netscape Navigator and Microsoft Internet Explorer, Web designers are closer than ever to having full cross-browser standardization, but there are still enough older browsers in use to create inconsistencies. In this text, any code that is specific to one browser or that has limited browser support is pointed out, but your best bet when coding is to use standardized, fully supported HTML and to test your pages on as many browser versions and platforms as possible.

HTML Case Sensitivity

HTML is a case insensitive markup language, meaning that <HTML>, <html>, and <HtMl> are treated the same by a browser. However, the newest incarnation of HTML, called XHTML, is case sensitive. In XHTML, all tags must be lowercase, so it is a good idea to start coding lowercase tags now in preparation for the transition.

HTML Elements

All HTML documents are collections of structure directions called *elements*, or *tags*, that have names enclosed within less than (<) and greater than (>) signs. Most HTML tags are content containers that have an *opening tag* (such as <html>) and a *closing tag* (such as </html>) that act as bookends for the enclosed content; *container tags* tell the browser how to display anything that occurs between the tags. Note that closing tags

include a slash before the tag name. A small number of tags are freestanding and do not require an end tag, such as the tag for a line break (<br>). For some container tags, you can omit the end tag, and the browser still renders the content properly, but it is a good idea to always include the end tag, even when it is optional. Not only does it stabilize your code, but in future versions of XHTML, all containers will require end tags to be well-formed.

Tag Attributes

Many tags can be modified with optional attributes that appear within the opening tag, usually in quotation marks.

Tag attributes allow you to specify properties such as

- color
- size
- name
- style

among other things.

According to the HTML specification, attribute values that are a single word or number do not need to be enclosed in quotation marks, but XHTML requires that all attributes appear within quotes.

```
<HTML>
<HEAD>
<TITLE>Foster City Zoo</TITLE>
</HEAD>
<BODY>
<FONT COLOR="#008000">
```

`<FONT COLOR="#008000">`

Nesting

HTML documents are composed of *nested tags*—that is, sets of tags occurring within other tags.

Keep in mind that you should always properly nest tags by ending the closest tag first, then each subsequent tag until you close the outermost tags.

The following code demonstrates how to correctly nest tags:

```
<body>

<p><b> This text is bold but
<i>this portion is bold and
italic</i>.</b></p>

</body>
```

Notice that the `<i>` tag is closed before the `<b>` tag, and the `<b>` tag is closed out before the `<p>` tag, according to proper nesting order.

```
<H1>Wendy's<i>COOL</i>Web Pages</H1>
```

The place to find to really cool web pages for fashion, entertainment and food!

VIEW HTML SOURCE CODE

One of the best ways to learn HTML and continue to expand your coding repertoire is to look under the hood of your favorite Web sites to sneak a peak at their HTML code. Unlike programming languages that are compiled or stored on a server, HTML code is public and viewable directly from a browser. When you view the HTML code for a Web

site, Netscape Navigator places the source code in a new window, while Internet Explorer loads the code into a text editor.

You can take advantage of the availability of source code to learn layout techniques and tricks of the trade. Feel free to copy and paste source code into an HTML editor, tinker with and retool it, and then

view the page in your own browser to see how it renders.

Be aware that while it is fine to use someone else's code as inspiration, you should never copy another Web designer's layout tag for tag. If you do, you may find yourself on the receiving end of an injunction or other legal action.

VIEW HTML SOURCE CODE

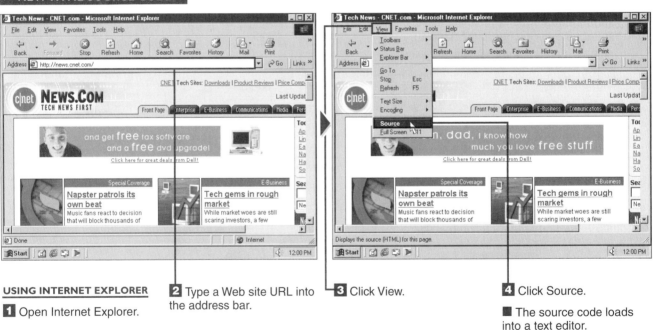

USING INTERNET EXPLORER

1 Open Internet Explorer.

2 Type a Web site URL into the address bar.

3 Click View.

4 Click Source.

■ The source code loads into a text editor.

Can I view code for other things besides HTML, such as JavaScript and Flash movies?

✔ JavaScript code and styles are often defined at the top of an HTML document, so you can view the code just like HTML. Other technologies, such as Java applets and Flash movies, are compiled or packaged by the author and only referenced as an object on the page, so you cannot see their source code.

How can I view the source code of documents contained in frames?

✔ If you try to view the source code for framed documents, all you see is the frameset code itself. To view the source code for the actual content within a frame, right-click, or click and hold, within the frame and select View Source in Internet Explorer or View Frame Source in Netscape Navigator.

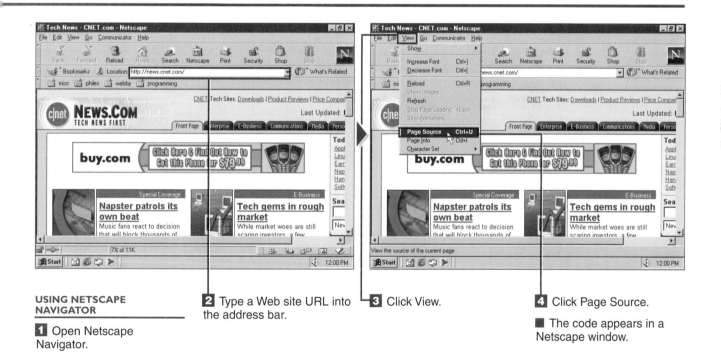

USING NETSCAPE NAVIGATOR

1 Open Netscape Navigator.

2 Type a Web site URL into the address bar.

3 Click View.

4 Click Page Source.

■ The code appears in a Netscape window.

CREATE AN HTML SKELETON

To create an HTML page, first set up the skeleton of the document. Every HTML document has a skeleton composed of a set of opening and closing <html> tags, a head, and a body. In addition, you should begin each HTML page with a document type declaration, a single line command that tells the browser that the HTML code conforms to a specific HTML standard.

The set of opening and closing <html> tags delineate the beginning and end of the HTML page and contain the document's <head> and <body> tags. In practice, the <html> tags themselves may be omitted, but it is good form to include them.

Within the document's <head> tags, you must include the <title> element. The text contained within the <title> tags appears in the user's browser window, usually in the window title bar above the standard buttons.

The document body houses all of the page's content, including text, images, and media files. Within the <body> tags, you can define global settings for the appearance of the document, including margins, link colors, and background properties.

CREATE AN HTML SKELETON

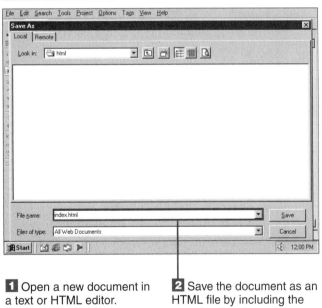

1 Open a new document in a text or HTML editor.

Note: For example, you can use Notepad, SimpleText, HomeSite, or BBEdit as HTML editors.

2 Save the document as an HTML file by including the .html extension.

3 Add the doctype declaration.

Note: The doctype declaration includes a reference to the HTML version in use and a URL pointing to the DTD document.

4 Add the opening and closing <html> tags.

Note: Remember to include a slash (/) before the tag name in the closing tag.

Do I have to be online to view my HTML document in a browser?

✔ No, you do not have to be online or connected to the Internet to view an HTML document. You can load and view HTML pages that are stored on your local drive while you are working offline. However, you must be online in order to test hyperlinks to external Web sites.

Can I save pages with an .htm extension?

✔ Yes. Web browsers recognize files with both the .html and the .htm extensions, used on Windows 3.1 operating systems. If your browser does not render files with the .htm extension, check with your server administrator to ensure that the MIME types are configured to render these files.

Can I use special characters or other HTML elements within the <title> tags?

✔ Browsers do not render any HTML formatting elements, such as bold or italic emphasis, that occur within the opening and closing <title> tags. To add special characters to the title content, see "Using Special Characters."

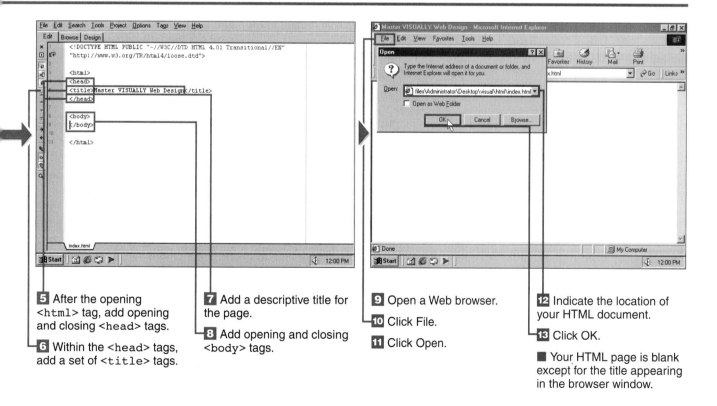

5 After the opening <html> tag, add opening and closing <head> tags.

6 Within the <head> tags, add a set of <title> tags.

7 Add a descriptive title for the page.

8 Add opening and closing <body> tags.

9 Open a Web browser.

10 Click File.

11 Click Open.

12 Indicate the location of your HTML document.

13 Click OK.

■ Your HTML page is blank except for the title appearing in the browser window.

SET MARGINS

Normally, a Web browser adds several pixels of margin space around the contents of a Web page, but you can set your own margin values by adding optional attributes to the <body> tag. Netscape Navigator and Internet Explorer support different attributes to control margins, but you can use both sets of attributes to cover all your bases.

Any attributes not supported by a particular browser are simply ignored.

Internet Explorer uses the `topmargin` and `leftmargin` attributes to control margin settings, and Netscape Navigator uses `marginheight` and `marginwidth`. Set all four attributes to zero (0) to have your

page run flush against the left and top browser window. In Netscape Navigator, you may still get a 10-pixel-wide margin on the right side of the browser window. This is to account for any necessary scroll bars and cannot be avoided.

You can also set margins using style sheet properties. For more information, see Chapter 6.

SET MARGINS

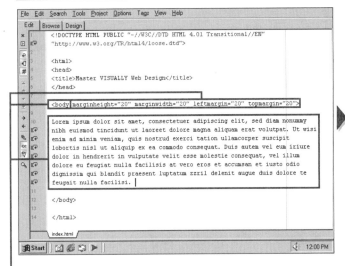

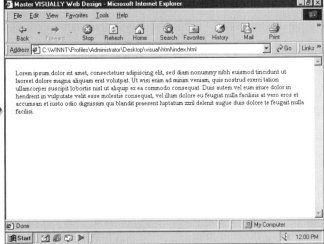

1 Open an HTML document in an HTML editor.

2 Add a <body> tag.

3 Add margin attributes and values.

4 Add text or other content.

Note: topmargin and marginheight control the horizontal space between the content and the browser's top edge. leftmargin and marginwidth control the vertical space on the left and right sides.

5 Open the HTML page in a Web browser.

■ The content of the page is offset by the margin values assigned.

DEFINE THE BACKGROUND

You can define the appearance of a Web page background by using the optional bgcolor and background attributes within the <body> tag.

The default background color for Web pages is either white or gray, depending on the browser, but you can use the bgcolor attribute to set a specific color for the page. Values for the bgcolor attribute can be either a color name or a

hexadecimal color value, a six-character sequence of letters and numbers. HTML supports only 16 color names, so most designers use hexadecimal codes when setting color properties, because they provide more variety. For more information on hexadecimal codes and the Web-safe color palette, see Chapter 10.

Rather than setting the background color, you can use the background

attribute with the <body> tag to designate an image that tiles, or repeats, in the background of your HTML page. The value for the background attribute is the location of the image file on the Web server. When using background images, make sure that the image does not interfere with the readability of your document's content.

DEFINE THE BACKGROUND

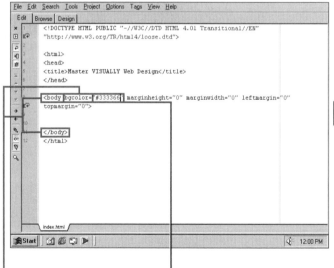

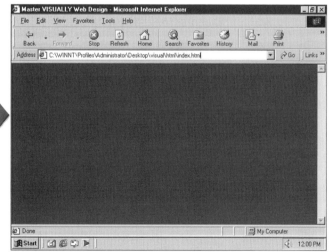

1 Open an HTML document in an HTML editor.

2 Add a set of <body> tags.

3 Add a bgcolor attribute to the <body> tag.

4 Assign a hexadecimal color value to the bgcolor attribute.

■ Alternately, add a background image using the background attribute and the image's file location.

Note: For more on color values, see Chapter 10.

5 Open the HTML page in a Web browser.

■ The background color of the page is the color set via the <body> tag.

CREATE PARAGRAPHS AND LINE BREAKS

You can break up text within the body of an HTML page by using the paragraph <p> tag and the line-break <br> tag. Unlike word processing documents, HTML documents do not recognize return characters, so you need to explicitly indicate line breaks and paragraph spacing.

Although the <p> element is a container tag with an opening tag

and a corresponding closing tag, the end tag </p> can be safely omitted. In fact, most coders use the opening tag on its own to insert white space between paragraphs. However, if you want your code to be compliant with the XHTML standard (see Chapter 21), you should enclose your paragraphs within both opening and closing <p> tags.

When a browser comes across a new <p> marker, it breaks the line and adds additional white space. If you just want a line of text to break and resume directly on the line below, use a line-break <br> tag. This tag simply tells the browser where a new line should begin and does not have a corresponding end tag.

CREATE PARAGRAPHS AND LINE BREAKS

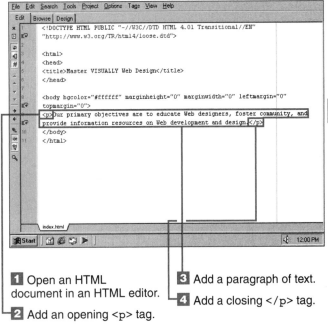

1 Open an HTML document in an HTML editor.

2 Add an opening <p> tag.

3 Add a paragraph of text.

4 Add a closing </p> tag.

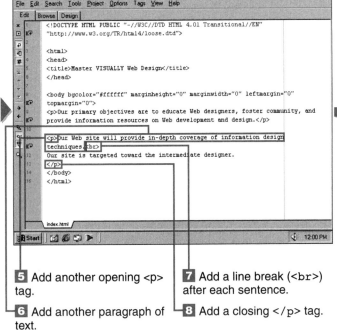

5 Add another opening <p> tag.

6 Add another paragraph of text.

7 Add a line break (<br>) after each sentence.

8 Add a closing </p> tag.

Can I control right text margins with line breaks?

✔ In a way. Normally a browser runs a line of text until it fills the width of the browser window or the containment element and then wraps the text to the next line. If you want your text to break at a specific width, you can insert explicit line breaks or use fixed width tables to contain your text. For more about tables, see the section "Create a Table."

How do I control the amount of space between paragraphs?

✔ There is no practical way to control the space between paragraphs. To reduce the space created with the <p> tag, you can use two consecutive <br> tags.

What happens if I include return characters in my HTML document?

✔ Under most circumstances, Web browsers do not render return characters, so they are visible only when you edit your code. However, if you try to seamlessly stack adjacent images, you may find that return characters in between the images produce a slight gap.

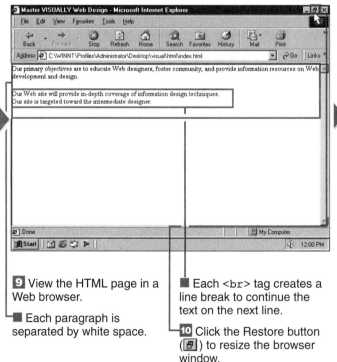

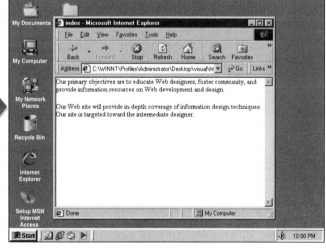

9 View the HTML page in a Web browser.

■ Each paragraph is separated by white space.

■ Each <br> tag creates a line break to continue the text on the next line.

10 Click the Restore button (⟦🗗⟧) to resize the browser window.

■ The text automatically resizes to fit the width of the current window, and the line and paragraph breaks are maintained.

ADD EMPHASIS TO TEXT

You can add emphasis to text by using either physical style tags or content-based style tags. Physical tags tell the browser exactly how the text should appear. Content-based style tags simply alert the browser that the enclosed text should be treated differently, but the output may vary from browser to browser.

To specify that text should appear bold, use the <b> tag and its corresponding end tag </b>. For italics, enclose the text within opening and closing <i> tags. The content-based equivalents of the physical <b> and <i> tags are the <strong> and <em> tags. Although these tags do not explicitly dictate how the text should be formatted, in practice most browsers bold any text within <strong> tags and italicize text within <em> tags.

The advantage of content-based tags is that they transmit contextual meaning to the browser rather than specific directions for appearance. For some browsing clients, such as those used by blind or otherwise disabled visitors, physical styles may have little meaning. These browsers instead look for contextual markers provided by content-based tags to render the text in an appropriate way.

ADD EMPHASIS TO TEXT

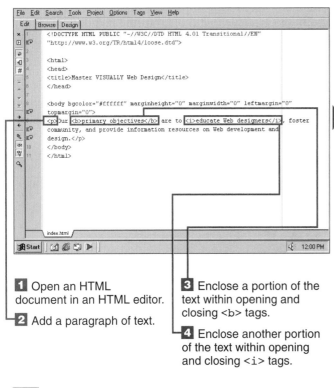

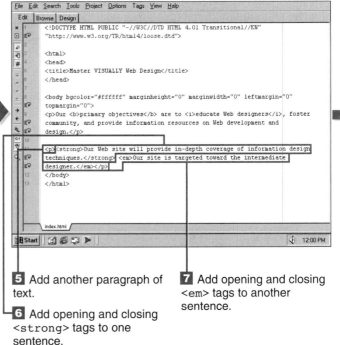

1 Open an HTML document in an HTML editor.

2 Add a paragraph of text.

3 Enclose a portion of the text within opening and closing <b> tags.

4 Enclose another portion of the text within opening and closing <i> tags.

5 Add another paragraph of text.

6 Add opening and closing <strong> tags to one sentence.

7 Add opening and closing <em> tags to another sentence.

MASTER IT

How do I underline text for emphasis?

✔ The physical style tag `<u>` and its corresponding end tag produce underlined text. However, the tag is deprecated, which means that it will eventually be eliminated. You can achieve the same effect by using style sheets (see Chapter 6), but keep in mind that underlined text normally signifies a hyperlink and confuses visitors if it is used only for emphasis.

Is there a tag to create a strikethrough effect?

✔ There are two physical style tags, `<s>` and `<strike>`, that put a line through the enclosed text. However, both tags are deprecated.

Is there a way to make text blink?

✔ Netscape Navigator supports the `<blink>` tag, which "blinks" the text on and off. This tag has never been part of the HTML standard and does little more than annoy your visitors. You should avoid it.

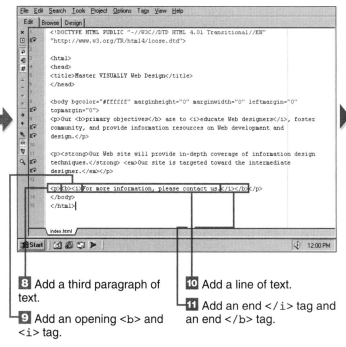

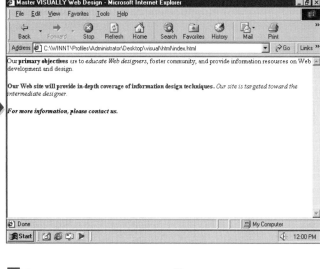

8 Add a third paragraph of text.

9 Add an opening `<b>` and `<i>` tag.

10 Add a line of text.

11 Add an end `</i>` tag and an end `</b>` tag.

12 Open the document in a Web browser.

■ The text appears both bold and italicized.

Note: In most browsers, bold and strong have the same effect, as do italic and emphasis.

SET FONT ATTRIBUTES

You can specify font attributes such as typeface, size, and color through the HTML `<font>` tag. The `<font>` tag is a deprecated element and is currently being phased out in favor of style sheet font properties. See Chapter 6 for more information.

You can set the font face for the text by using the `face` attribute of the `<font>` tag. The value of the

`face` attribute can be a single font name or a series of names separated by commas. The browser searches the list of font names until it finds one that the visitor's system supports.

You can indicate the relative size of text on a page by setting the `size` attribute of the `<font>` tag. To set the color of a font, use the `color` attribute.

Despite its precarious future, Web designers still use the `<font>` tag to achieve backward compliance with older browsers. You can continue to use the `<font>` tag as long as it is widely supported by browsers. If you are confident that your visitors are using CSS-compliant browsers, style sheet font properties are a better choice.

SET FONT ATTRIBUTES

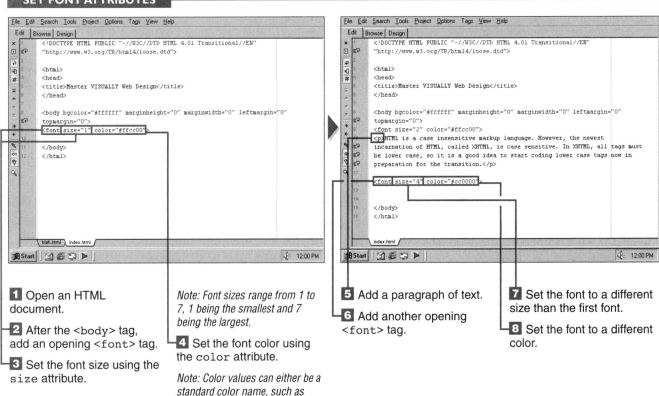

■1 Open an HTML document.

■2 After the `<body>` tag, add an opening `<font>` tag.

■3 Set the font size using the `size` attribute.

Note: Font sizes range from 1 to 7, 1 being the smallest and 7 being the largest.

■4 Set the font color using the `color` attribute.

Note: Color values can either be a standard color name, such as blue, or a 6-digit hexadecimal number.

■5 Add a paragraph of text.

■6 Add another opening `<font>` tag.

■7 Set the font to a different size than the first font.

■8 Set the font to a different color.

Is it necessary to set specific font attributes?

✔ No. In fact, many designers think it is a bad idea to override the users' own font preferences that they set via the browser's Options or Preferences panel.

Which fonts are used on the page if I do not set the font attributes?

✔ It depends on how the user has personalized his browser settings, but the default font is usually a serif typeface, such as Times or Time New Roman.

How do I set specific font sizes in points or pixels?

✔ HTML font sizes are relative rather than absolute, so there is no way to indicate sizes in points or pixels using the `<font>` tag. If you use style sheets, you can create font properties with sizes set to specific point or pixel values. For more information on style sheets, see Chapter 6.

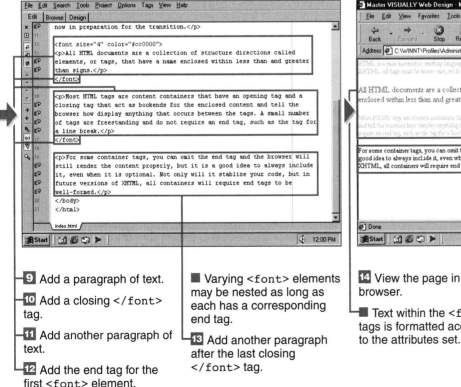

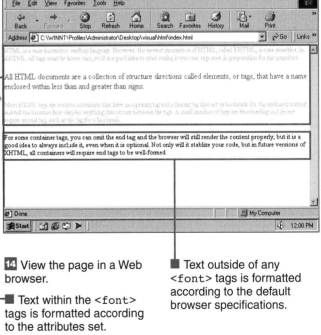

9 Add a paragraph of text.

10 Add a closing `</font>` tag.

11 Add another paragraph of text.

12 Add the end tag for the first `<font>` element.

■ Varying `<font>` elements may be nested as long as each has a corresponding end tag.

13 Add another paragraph after the last closing `</font>` tag.

14 View the page in a Web browser.

■ Text within the `<font>` tags is formatted according to the attributes set.

■ Text outside of any `<font>` tags is formatted according to the default browser specifications.

ADD HEADINGS

You can add headings to your HTML page with the six available heading tags, <h1> being the largest, top-level heading and <h6> being the smallest. Although the rendering of the heading text may vary from browser to browser, the text enclosed within a set of heading tags usually appears in bold.

On most browsers, a level four <h4> heading produces text that is the same size as the default body text. Level 1 headings are extremely large, while <h6>, the lowest heading level, is almost too small to be of use. Experiment with the middle range headings to find appropriate sizes for readability and visual design.

The advantage to using heading tags rather than formatting headings with the <font> tag is that the heading tags provide the browser with specific information about the content of the tag rather than just telling it how to format the text.

ADD HEADINGS

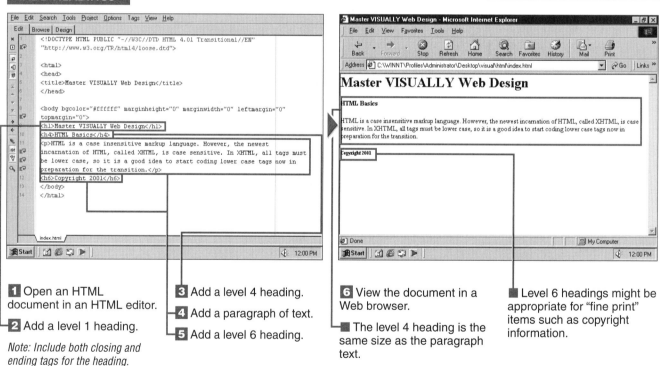

1 Open an HTML document in an HTML editor.

2 Add a level 1 heading.

Note: Include both closing and ending tags for the heading.

3 Add a level 4 heading.

4 Add a paragraph of text.

5 Add a level 6 heading.

6 View the document in a Web browser.

■ The level 4 heading is the same size as the paragraph text.

■ Level 6 headings might be appropriate for "fine print" items such as copyright information.

ADD A HORIZONTAL RULE

A simple way to visually indicate separate content sections on a Web page is to use the standalone horizontal rule <hr> tag. The <hr> tag has no corresponding end tag and simply tells the browser to break to a new line and insert a horizontal rule across the width of the page.

By default, the horizontal rule on most browsers is 3 pixels thick and appears with a slight 3D effect. You can add the noshade attribute to the <hr> tag to produce a plain horizontal line. You can also alter the thickness of a rule by using the size attribute. You can specify the width of the horizontal rule with the width attribute, which accepts

a value expressed in pixels or as a percent of the browser window.

Horizontal rules are helpful formatting tools that serve to break text into discrete, readable chunks. However, like any formatting element, excessive use of the <hr> tag clutters a page and distracts the visitor, so use it sparingly.

ADD A HORIZONTAL RULE

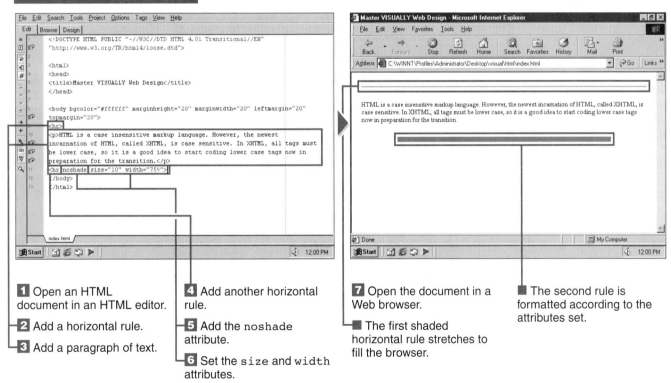

1 Open an HTML document in an HTML editor.

2 Add a horizontal rule.

3 Add a paragraph of text.

4 Add another horizontal rule.

5 Add the noshade attribute.

6 Set the size and width attributes.

7 Open the document in a Web browser.

■ The first shaded horizontal rule stretches to fill the browser.

■ The second rule is formatted according to the attributes set.

ADD HYPERLINKS AND MAILTOS

You can add hyperlinks to a Web page with the <a> tag and the href attribute. The value for the href attribute can be an HTTP or FTP URL on another server, the location of a page on your own server, or an e-mail address.

To provide a way for users to send you feedback, use a mailto URL

with the href attribute. When the user clicks the link, the browser opens her default e-mail client and fills in the To field with the indicated e-mail address.

To link to a Web site or Web page, simply add the URL to the href attribute. When the user clicks on the link, the site loads in the current browser window.

For links to other documents on your own server, you can use either absolute or relative URLs. Absolute URLs include the protocol (http://) and the server name in addition to the specific file location. With relative URLs, you indicate the file location in relation to the current document, and the browser automatically fills in the base URL.

ADD HYPERLINKS AND MAILTOS

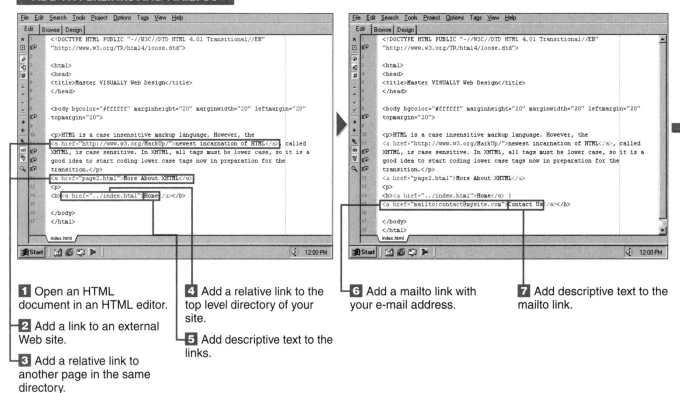

1 Open an HTML document in an HTML editor.

2 Add a link to an external Web site.

3 Add a relative link to another page in the same directory.

4 Add a relative link to the top level directory of your site.

5 Add descriptive text to the links.

6 Add a mailto link with your e-mail address.

7 Add descriptive text to the mailto link.

Can I link to newsgroups or newsgroup articles?

✔ Yes, you can use the news URL, which takes the form `news:newsgroup`, to link to an entire newsgroup or a specific article. However, your user's browser may not be correctly configured to read newsgroups, so you should probably avoid using news URLs.

How can I get a link to load into a new Web browser?

✔ If you want the site to load into a new browser window, add the `target="_blank"` attribute to the `<a>` tag. This causes the browser to launch a new window where the site loads.

Can I have the mailto link send to multiple recipients?

✔ Some browsers allow several recipients within the mailto URL. Separate each e-mail address with a comma and test on different browsers to ensure that it works correctly.

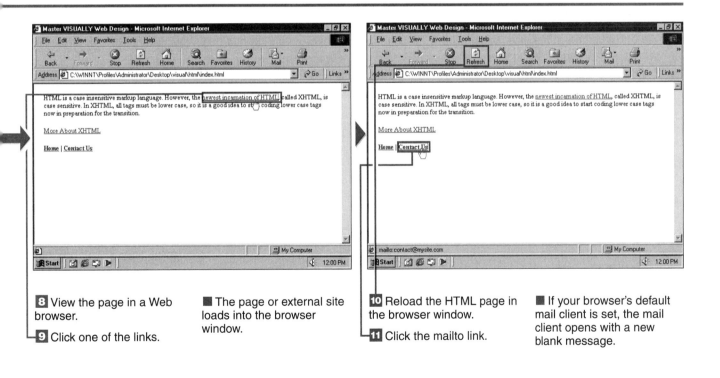

8 View the page in a Web browser.

9 Click one of the links.

■ The page or external site loads into the browser window.

10 Reload the HTML page in the browser window.

11 Click the mailto link.

■ If your browser's default mail client is set, the mail client opens with a new blank message.

CHANGE THE COLOR OF LINKS

Most browsers have default settings for how links on a Web page appear. Unless the user has altered the browser preferences, unvisited links are usually blue, while links to pages previously visited appear purple. To change the appearance of links on your Web site, use the link attributes associated with the <body> element.

There are three <body> attributes that control the appearance of the three link states:

- link
- alink
- vlink

All three attributes accept a color name or hexadecimal value. The link attribute sets the color of unvisited hyperlinks on the Web page, while the vlink attribute

sets the color of visited links. By default, the color for active links is red, but you can change this by setting the alink attribute.

Be aware that although you can set the link colors for your site, if the user sets specific preferences in her browser, these override the colors you set via the <body> tag attributes.

CHANGE THE COLOR OF LINKS

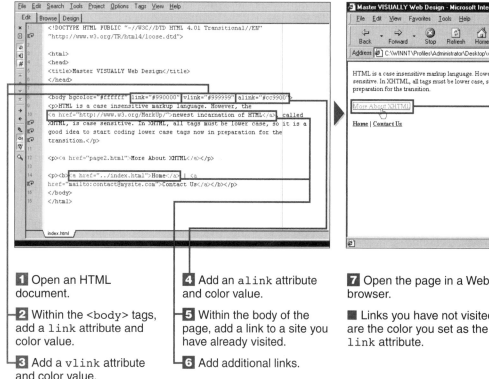

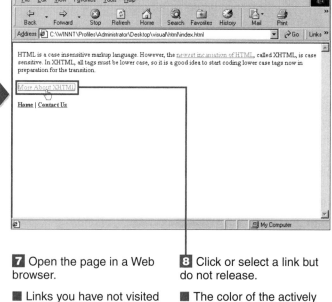

1 Open an HTML document.

2 Within the <body> tags, add a link attribute and color value.

3 Add a vlink attribute and color value.

4 Add an alink attribute and color value.

5 Within the body of the page, add a link to a site you have already visited.

6 Add additional links.

7 Open the page in a Web browser.

■ Links you have not visited are the color you set as the link attribute.

8 Click or select a link but do not release.

■ The color of the actively selected link is the alink color.

CREATE INTERNAL PAGE LINKS

Y ou can create a link to specific sections of a Web page by using the name attribute with the <a> tag.

Use the name attribute to identify sections of your page and then create links to these sections using regular <a href> tags. These internal links do not lead to additional pages, but rather direct

the user to sections of the current document.

When the <a> tag is used with the name attribute, the text contained within the tag does not display as a link but as regular text. When you want to link to named sections, use another <a> tag with the href attribute set to the section name preceded by a pound sign (#).

When visitors click the link, they go directly to the section with that name value.

By using internal page links, you can lead your visitors directly to the section of content they are looking for or provide a clickable table of contents at the top of a page.

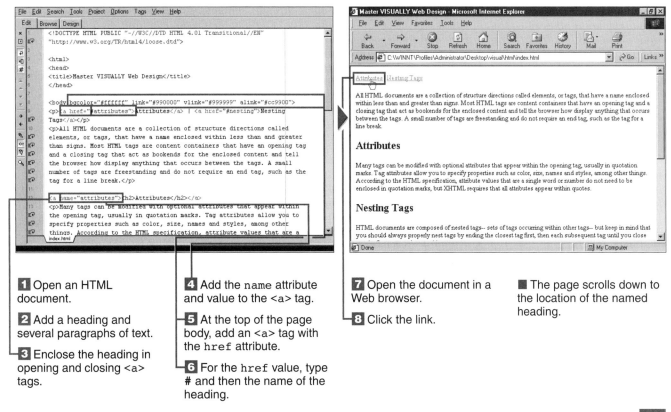

1 Open an HTML document.

2 Add a heading and several paragraphs of text.

3 Enclose the heading in opening and closing <a> tags.

4 Add the name attribute and value to the <a> tag.

5 At the top of the page body, add an <a> tag with the href attribute.

6 For the href value, type # and then the name of the heading.

7 Open the document in a Web browser.

8 Click the link.

■ The page scrolls down to the location of the named heading.

ADD AN IMAGE

You can add images to Web pages by using the standalone `<img>` tag with its required `src` attribute, which tells the browser where the image is located on your server.

In addition to the `src` attribute, there are several optional attributes you can use with the `<img>` tag, including `border`, `align`, `hspace`, and `vspace`. The three that you should always include are `height`, `width`, and `alt`.

You can indicate the actual pixel dimensions of the image with the `height` and `width` attributes. The `height` and `width` attributes are not required, but specifying the exact dimensions of your images can help reduce the time it takes for the browser to load your images into the page.

You should also include `alt` attributes with all images. `alt` attributes allow you to provide alternative text to describe the image and are important for disabled visitors or visitors with non-graphical browsers. Alternative text should be descriptive but very brief. For example, if the image is a company logo, use the company name as `alt` text.

ADD AN IMAGE

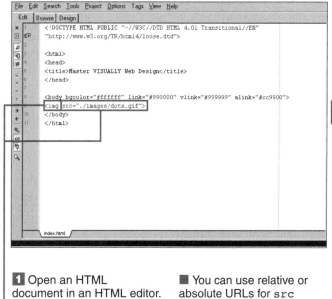

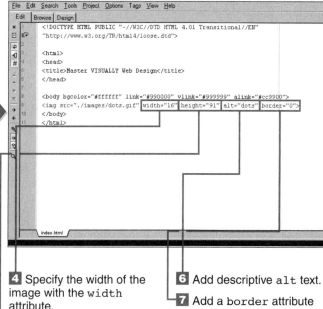

1 Open an HTML document in an HTML editor.

2 After the `<body>` tag, add an `<img>` tag.

3 Indicate the location of the image using the `src` attribute.

■ You can use relative or absolute URLs for `src` attributes.

Note: For more on URLs, see the section "Add Hyperlinks and Mailtos."

4 Specify the width of the image with the `width` attribute.

5 Specify the height of the image with the `height` attribute.

6 Add descriptive `alt` text.

7 Add a `border` attribute and value in pixels.

Note: The default border for images is 0. If the image is also a hyperlink, the default border is 2 pixels.

How do I make images clickable?

✔ To make images clickable, enclose the `<img>` tag within opening and closing `<a>` tags. For more information on creating hyperlinks with the `<a>` tag, see the section "Add Hyperlinks and Mailtos."

Do images have to be on my own server or can I link to images on other servers?

✔ You can link to images on other servers, but you should never reference images on other servers without first getting permission from the Webmaster.

Can I place one image against the right margin and another against the left and have the text appear in the middle?

✔ Yes. Use the `align` attribute with both images, setting one to `align="left"` and the other to `align="right"`. Directly after the second `<img>` tag, type your text. The text runs down the middle of the page between the two images.

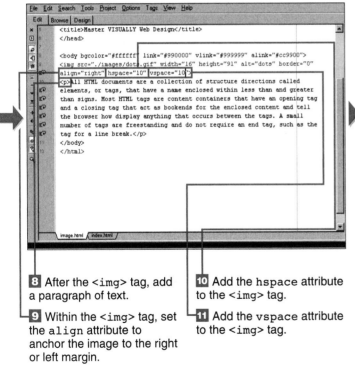

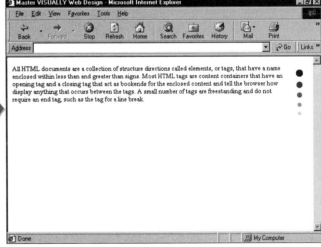

8 After the `<img>` tag, add a paragraph of text.

9 Within the `<img>` tag, set the `align` attribute to anchor the image to the right or left margin.

10 Add the `hspace` attribute to the `<img>` tag.

11 Add the `vspace` attribute to the `<img>` tag.

12 Open the document in a Web browser.

13 If the `align` attribute is set to `"left"` or `"right"`, the browser wraps the text around the image.

14 The `hspace` and `vspace` attributes provide padding around the image.

CREATE A LIST

You can create an indented list of items by using the <ul> and <ol> tags. The <ul> tag creates unordered, or bulleted, lists, while <ol> tags create numbered lists. Lists are useful formatting tools when you have groups of related information or step-by-step processes. They also allow users to quickly scan documents and get the information they need from the page.

A list is composed of list items, each enclosed within <li> tags. Most browsers allow you to omit the closing </li> tag, but it is better coding practice to include it.

You can also nest lists within other lists to create an outline organization of information. For bulleted lists, each time you nest an additional list, the bullet type reflects the nesting relationship by

alternating between solid disks, hollow circles, and squares. You can explicitly change the type of bullet for both nested and single lists by including the type attribute with <ul>, <ol>, and <li> elements, but this attribute is deprecated in favor of style sheet properties. For more information on CSS list properties, see Chapter 6.

CREATE A LIST

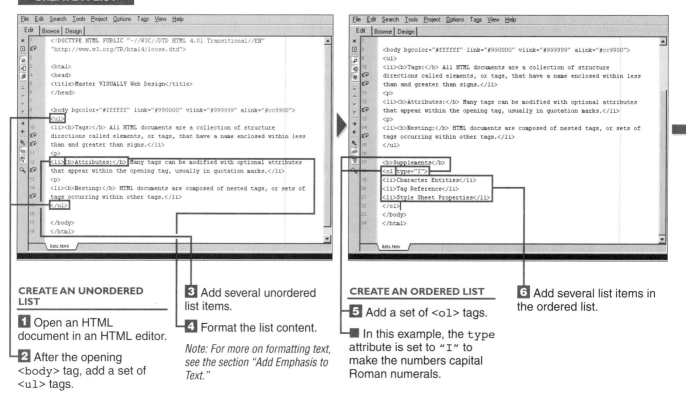

CREATE AN UNORDERED LIST

1 Open an HTML document in an HTML editor.

2 After the opening <body> tag, add a set of <ul> tags.

3 Add several unordered list items.

4 Format the list content.

Note: For more on formatting text, see the section "Add Emphasis to Text."

CREATE AN ORDERED LIST

5 Add a set of <ol> tags.

■ In this example, the type attribute is set to "I" to make the numbers capital Roman numerals.

6 Add several list items in the ordered list.

Do I need to set off a list with paragraph or line-break tags?

✔ No. When a browser encounters an opening list tag, it automatically provides space between the list and the preceding element. After the closing list tag, the browser inserts additional white space before rendering any remaining content on the page.

Can I set ordered lists to begin numbering items at a particular number?

✔ Yes. Add the start attribute to the opening <ol> tag and indicate the starting number for the listed items.

What bullet types are available for lists?

✔ There are three types of bullets for unordered lists: the disk, the standard bullet; the circle, a hollow bullet; or the square. For ordered lists, choose between capital letters (A), lowercase letters (a), capital Roman numerals (I), lowercase Roman numerals (i), or numbers (1).

How do I add space between list items?

✔ You can add white space between list items by inserting paragraph markers or multiple line-break elements between each <li> tag.

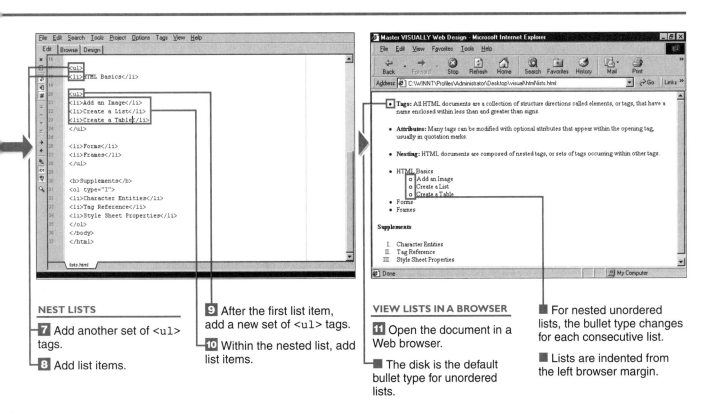

NEST LISTS

7 Add another set of <ul> tags.

8 Add list items.

9 After the first list item, add a new set of <ul> tags.

10 Within the nested list, add list items.

VIEW LISTS IN A BROWSER

11 Open the document in a Web browser.

■ The disk is the default bullet type for unordered lists.

■ For nested unordered lists, the bullet type changes for each consecutive list.

■ Lists are indented from the left browser margin.

CREATE A TABLE

You can create complex tables with the HTML <table>, <tr>, and <td> tags. Every table you create is composed of opening and closing <table> tags and one or more sets of table row <tr> tags. Within each table row, add table data cells using the <td> tags.

When you use the <table> tag without any optional attributes, the browser creates a borderless table

with a small amount of space between the table data cells and a small amount of padding within each cell. You can change these values by adding the optional border, cellspacing, and cellpadding attributes to the opening <table> tag. In addition, you can specify the width of the table using the width attribute, which you can set to a specific pixel value or a percentage of the browser window.

HTML tables, although not intended for layout purposes, offer a way to create stable, structured pages and more visually pleasing designs.

The other alternative for controlling page layout is to use style sheets (see Chapter 10). However, until more browsers offer full support of CSS, tables are the better solution.

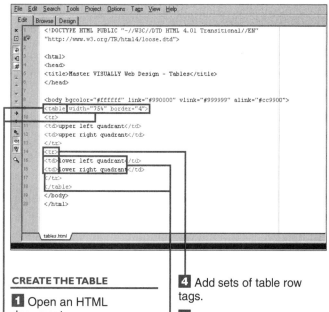

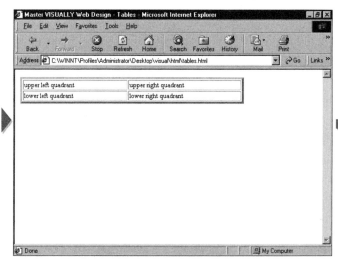

CREATE THE TABLE

1 Open an HTML document.

2 Add a set of opening and closing <table> tags.

3 Set the width and border attributes.

4 Add sets of table row tags.

5 Within each table row, insert table cells.

Note: Each row should contain the same number of table cells.

6 Place text within each cell.

7 Open the document in a Web browser.

■ The default cellspacing on the table is 2 pixels.

How do I get text to run along the side of a table?

✔ When the browser encounters a `<table>` tag, it breaks to a new line and renders the table. After the end `</table>` tag, the browser resumes any content on a new line. If you want text to continue on the side of the table, you can use the `align` attribute with the `<table>` tag to force the table to float to the left or right. If you align the table to the left, your text runs along the right side.

Can I put one table inside of another?

✔ Yes, you can nest tables within other tables. When nesting tables, insert the additional table inside a table data cell, just as you would insert text or an image into the table.

Do I have to include content in every table data cell?

✔ Yes. Tables with empty data cells are unstable and tend to collapse or render strangely on some browsers. If you do not want any visible content in the table cell, use a non-breaking space entity (` `) as a filler.

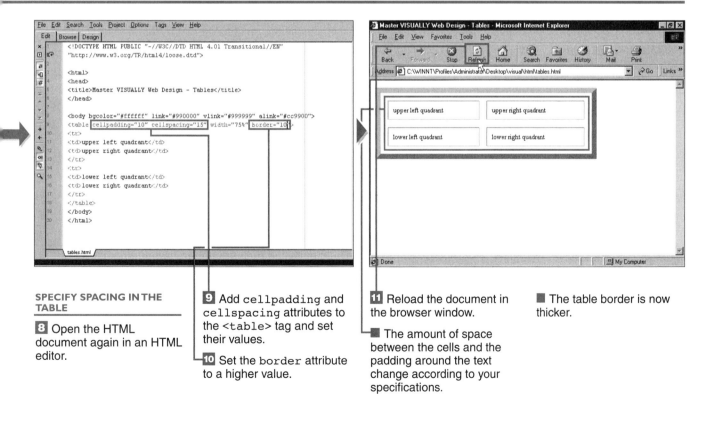

SPECIFY SPACING IN THE TABLE

8 Open the HTML document again in an HTML editor.

9 Add `cellpadding` and `cellspacing` attributes to the `<table>` tag and set their values.

10 Set the `border` attribute to a higher value.

11 Reload the document in the browser window.

■ The amount of space between the cells and the padding around the text change according to your specifications.

■ The table border is now thicker.

WORK WITH ROWS AND COLUMNS

You can control the structure and appearance of table content by adding various optional attributes to both the `<tr>` and `<td>` tags. You can set the background color of individual cells and rows, dictate height and width, and extend cells across several rows and columns to create complex page layouts.

Whether or not you use the table `bgcolor` attribute to change the color of the table, you can control the colors of individual cells by adding the `bgcolor` attribute to specific `<td>` tags. You can also set the height and width of table cells with the `height` and `width` attributes. If you prefer, you can use the `bgcolor` and `height` attributes

with the `<tr>` tag to set the appearance of an entire row of cells.

You can stretch the content of a cell across multiple columns or rows by including the `colspan` or `rowspan` attribute within the opening `<td>` tag. For example, if you want one cell to stretch across four columns, add a `colspan=4` attribute to that `<td>` tag.

WORK WITH ROWS AND COLUMNS

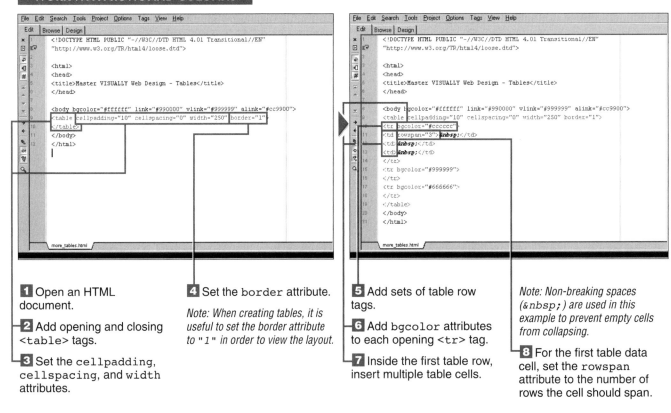

1 Open an HTML document.

2 Add opening and closing `<table>` tags.

3 Set the `cellpadding`, `cellspacing`, and `width` attributes.

4 Set the `border` attribute.

Note: When creating tables, it is useful to set the border attribute to "1" in order to view the layout.

5 Add sets of table row tags.

6 Add `bgcolor` attributes to each opening `<tr>` tag.

7 Inside the first table row, insert multiple table cells.

Note: Non-breaking spaces ( ) are used in this example to prevent empty cells from collapsing.

8 For the first table data cell, set the `rowspan` attribute to the number of rows the cell should span.

Can I apply cascading style properties to table rows and cells?

✔ Yes. You can use the id and class attributes with both <tr> and <td> tags in order to reference style properties. For more information on using cascading style sheets, see Chapter 6.

How do I define header cells within a table?

✔ Use <th> tags to define header cells. These tags are similar to <td> tags except that the browser renders the contained text in bold and may align the content differently.

Can I combine colspan and rowspan attributes within a single table data cell?

✔ Yes, you can include both colspan and rowspan attributes within the same opening <td> tag. This has the effect of extending a cell both vertically and horizontally so that it spans both rows and columns within the table.

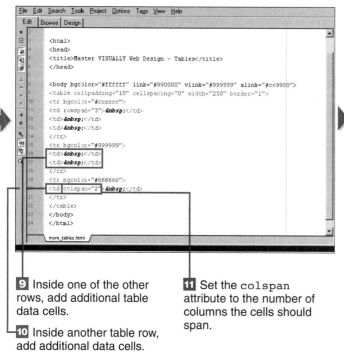

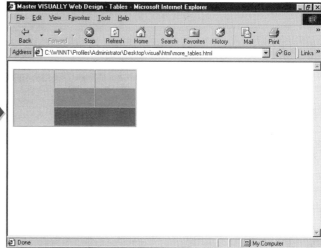

9 Inside one of the other rows, add additional table data cells.

10 Inside another table row, add additional data cells.

11 Set the colspan attribute to the number of columns the cells should span.

12 Open the document in a Web browser.

■ Cells with the rowspan attribute set span across multiple rows.

■ Cells with the colspan attribute set span across multiple columns.

ADD COMMENTS

You can include notes within Web pages by using HTML comments. HTML comments allow you to set off text that is not visible to the user via the Web browser window.

Comments occur within <!-- and --> indicators. You must include a space after the initial comment tag and another space before the end

tag. Use comments to include notes to yourself, such as where particular page elements begin and end. This is particularly useful if you have very complex pages and you work collaboratively with other designers or developers. You can also use comments to temporarily remove elements from a page without deleting the code entirely,

because browsers simply ignore any elements that you comment out.

Although browsers do not render anything within comment tags, the comments and enclosed elements are still part of the source code and accessible to any visitor who chooses to view your source.

ADD COMMENTS

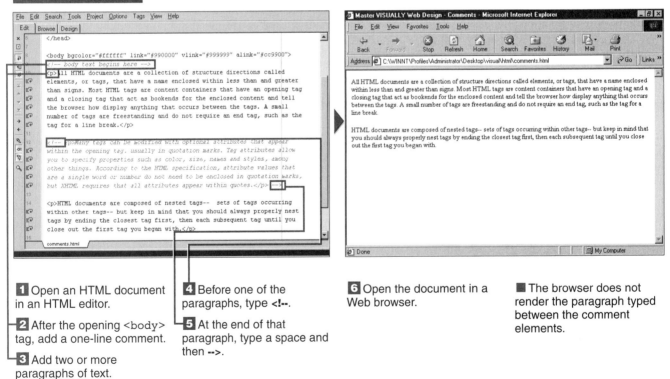

1 Open an HTML document in an HTML editor.

2 After the opening <body> tag, add a one-line comment.

3 Add two or more paragraphs of text.

4 Before one of the paragraphs, type <!--.

5 At the end of that paragraph, type a space and then -->.

6 Open the document in a Web browser.

■ The browser does not render the paragraph typed between the comment elements.

USING SPECIAL CHARACTERS

You can add certain characters such as greater than (>) and less than (<) signs, ampersands, and copyright symbols by using HTML character entities. You must use character entities for any characters that have special meaning in HTML documents or anything that is not standard text, such as symbols, signs, and foreign language characters.

Certain characters cannot be directly added to HTML pages because they are important parts of HTML code. For example, the browser normally interprets a less than sign (<) and greater than sign (>) as parts of an HTML tag. If you want the browser to actually render a less than sign, type **&#lt** or **&#060**;. Character entities always begin with an ampersand (&) and

end with a semicolon. Within the ampersand and semicolon, you can indicate entities using a pound sign (#) and its numeric entity, or in some cases a name entity.

A complete list of character entities is available in Appendix A.

USING SPECIAL CHARACTERS

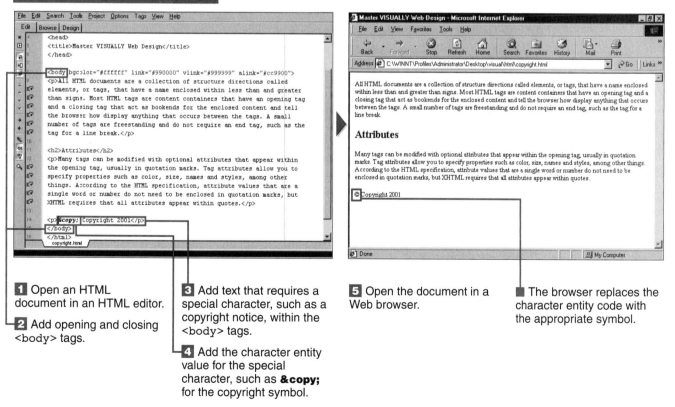

1 Open an HTML document in an HTML editor.

2 Add opening and closing <body> tags.

3 Add text that requires a special character, such as a copyright notice, within the <body> tags.

4 Add the character entity value for the special character, such as **©** for the copyright symbol.

5 Open the document in a Web browser.

■ The browser replaces the character entity code with the appropriate symbol.

ADD <META> TAGS

You can add important supplementary information to the head of an HTML document with <meta> tags. <meta> elements do not contain content that is rendered on the page by the Web browser. Rather, they provide *meta-information*, or information about information, to browsers or indexing search engines.

The two most common attributes for the <meta> tag are name and content. There are no predefined name values to accompany the name attribute, but two commonly used <meta> names are "keywords" and "description". When you use a <meta> tag with the keywords name, you can add a list of descriptive keywords, separated by commas, with the content attribute. When using the description <meta> name, you provide a brief sentence that describes the Web site itself. These descriptions can be up to 200 characters long or approximately 25 words.

You should always include <meta> tags for both keywords and a description of your site when coding pages. Their inclusion helps your site get indexed by search engines; without them, some indexing search engines might overlook your site entirely.

ADD <META> TAGS

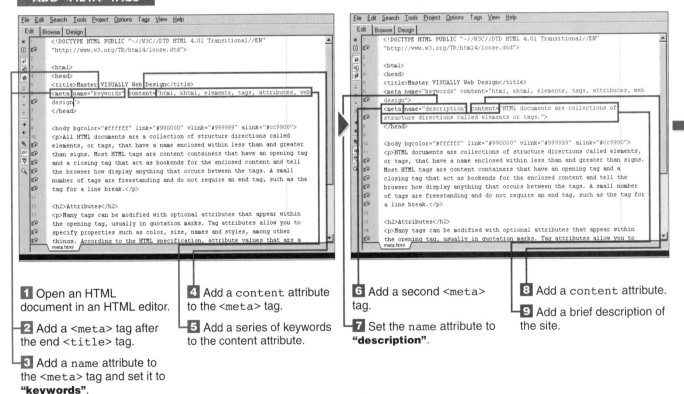

1 Open an HTML document in an HTML editor.

2 Add a <meta> tag after the end <title> tag.

3 Add a name attribute to the <meta> tag and set it to **"keywords"**.

4 Add a content attribute to the <meta> tag.

5 Add a series of keywords to the content attribute.

6 Add a second <meta> tag.

7 Set the name attribute to **"description"**.

8 Add a content attribute.

9 Add a brief description of the site.

What are some other \<meta\> attributes?

✔ \<meta\> tags also accept the http-equiv attribute, which sends additional information to the browser via the document header. If you set the http equiv attribute to "refresh" and indicate a time lapse and URL using the content attribute, the page automatically reloads or redirects to the new URL after the specified amount of time.

When I add keywords, should I include variations of spelling and capitalization?

✔ Include spelling variations for keywords that may be frequently misspelled, but in general it is not necessary to include variations based on capitalization.

Do all search engines use the information in \<meta\> tags?

✔ Some indexing search engines index only the keywords or the description content, while others bypass the \<meta\> tags entirely and index words within the actual body content of the page.

Can I prevent search engines from indexing certain pages?

✔ You can prevent some search engine robots from indexing pages by including meta name="robots" with the content value set to **noindex**.

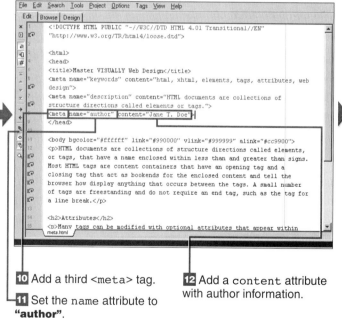

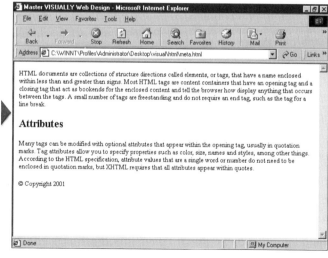

10 Add a third \<meta\> tag.

11 Set the name attribute to **"author"**.

12 Add a content attribute with author information.

13 Open the document in a Web browser.

■ The \<meta\> information does not affect the appearance of the page content.

AN INTRODUCTION TO FORMS

One of the primary ways visitors interact with Web sites is through forms. Forms are used to search the Web, send feedback, request information, post messages to bulletin boards, navigate sites, and make purchases, among other things. In many ways, forms are the perfect marriage of interactivity and functionality; they enable users to interact with your site while accomplishing specific goals. HTML forms, unlike other interactive elements such as in Flash and Java, require no additional plug-ins and work on almost all browsers.

HTML form controls are easy to implement and are extremely versatile. This chapter explores three basic types of form controls: text entry fields, including single-line fields and text boxes; multiple-choice elements, such as check boxes, radio buttons, and drop-down menus; and submission buttons. By combining these controls, you can create complex forms to handle almost any task.

Process Forms

There are several different ways to process the form data that a user submits.

If the form is being used for navigation or simple interactivity, you can use client-side scripting languages such as JavaScript to process the form and return values. For more information on JavaScript, see Chapter 14.

If you need to actually receive the form data, you can have the browser send values to an e-mail address or to a form-handling application on the server. The last section of this chapter, "Send Form Data to an E-mail Address," demonstrates how to deliver simple form data to an e-mail address, but for more robust form-handling, you should use server-side applications, such as ASP, PHP, or CGI programs. CGI programs are a popular way to process forms and are usually scripted in Perl, but they can also be written in other programming languages.

If you do not want to script your own server-side form applications, there are a number of online libraries where you can download scripts free of charge to use on your own site.

Some of the most popular online sources of ready-made scripts include cgi-resources.com, hotscripts.com, and scriptsearch.com. At these and other sites, you can often find scripts that are easy to use and can be customized to fit the forms you build for your site. Before installing scripts, make sure that your Web server or hosting company supports the technology that you are using. In many cases, you will also need to know how to change file and directory permissions. For more information on setting server permissions, see Chapter 19.

Secure Form Data

When implementing forms, carefully consider what level of security you need to implement. If you request private information from users, be sure to secure the transmission of the data from the user's browser to your Web server.

You can provide transfer security by using SSL, which stands for *Secure Sockets Layer*. This protocol encrypts data and then sends the data to the server via a secure connection. Visitors recognize sites that use SSL by the https:// protocol in the address bar. Consult your system administrator or Web hosting provider about using this protocol. In addition, you need to ensure that your Web server is adequately protected against malicious attacks. To find out what sort of security your server offers, talk to your system administrator or host provider.

Give Visitors Confirmation

HTML forms enable visitors to send feedback and process orders, but do not forget that communication on the Web is a two-way street. Each time visitors submit a form, they want to know that the transmission was successful and that you received their data.

Not only does confirmation improve the user's experience on the site, but in the case of online transactions, it is also a necessary element in establishing a reputation of trust and reliability. Confirmation can take the form of an e-mail response or a specific confirmation page that loads after the user submits the form. For forms that process online purchases, you should have both.

SET UP A FORM

You can add a form to your Web site with the HTML `<form>` tag. The opening and closing form tags contain all the form elements that you want to include, such as text entry boxes and buttons. You can also include other HTML elements within form tags so that you can properly lay out and format the form and provide text directions to help users.

There are two attributes that you must include with every opening `<form>` tag: the `action` attribute and the `method` attribute. Within the `action` attribute, indicate the location of the program that processes the form — for example, the cgi-bin directory for a CGI program.

The `method` attribute indicates how the browser sends the form data to the server. The value for the method attribute can be either `post` or `get`.

Choosing between `post` and `get` depends on a variety of factors, including the complexity of the form, the security of the transmission, and whether you need to pass parameters to the server. If your forms are fairly small and security is not an issue, use the `get` method.

SET UP A FORM

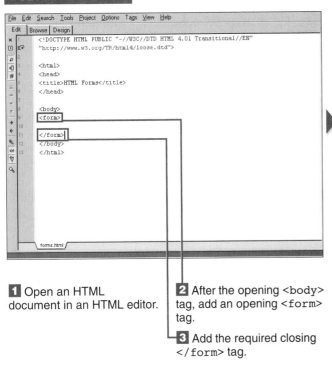

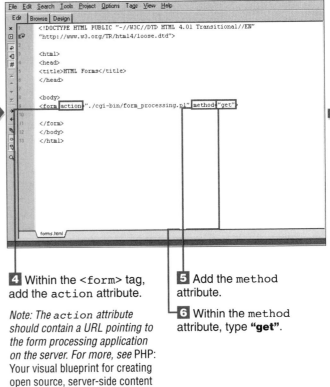

1 Open an HTML document in an HTML editor.

2 After the opening `<body>` tag, add an opening `<form>` tag.

3 Add the required closing `</form>` tag.

4 Within the `<form>` tag, add the `action` attribute.

Note: The `action` attribute should contain a URL pointing to the form processing application on the server. For more, see PHP: Your visual blueprint for creating open source, server-side content *(Hungry Minds, Inc.).*

5 Add the `method` attribute.

6 Within the `method` attribute, type **"get"**.

What does CGI stand for?
✔ CGI stands for Common Gateway Interface.

Can I send form data to an e-mail address?
✔ Yes. For more information, see the section "Send Form Data to an E-mail Address."

What is the difference between the post and get methods?
✔ The post method first contacts the server and then sends the data in a separate transmission. The get method contacts the server and sends the data in a single transmission with the data added on to the end of the action URL.

What optional attributes can be included within the form tag?
✔ Optional attributes include the enctype attribute, which indicates how the browser should encode the data, the lang attribute, which allows you to set the language used in the form, and the name attribute, supported by Netscape browsers. You can also include a variety of event handlers such as onSubmit. Event handlers are often used to invoke JavaScript functions to validate forms. For more information, see Chapter 15.

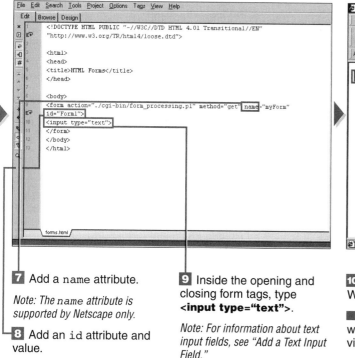

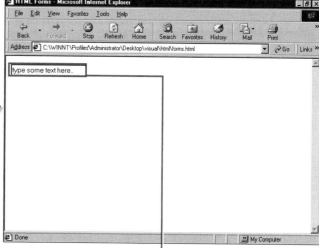

7 Add a name attribute.

Note: The name attribute is supported by Netscape only.

8 Add an id attribute and value.

Note: The id attribute allows you to assign a label to the form.

9 Inside the opening and closing form tags, type **<input type="text">**.

Note: For information about text input fields, see "Add a Text Input Field."

10 Open the document in a Web browser.

■ The input field contained within the form fields is visible.

11 Place your cursor within the input box.

12 Type a few words in the text box.

ADD A TEXT INPUT FIELD

Y ou can add single-line text fields with the `<input>` tag and the `type="text"` attribute.

Text fields are ideal when you need to prompt users for individual information such as a name or address. When adding a text input field, you must specify a name for the field by using the `name` attribute.

The size of the text input field varies from browser to browser, but you can indicate the character length of the visible field with the `size` attribute. Setting the `size` attribute to 2, for example, limits the visible space of the text input field to 2 characters. This is particularly useful when prompting visitors for information with specific character lengths, such as state abbreviations.

The `size` attribute controls only the appearance of the field, not the maximum number of characters the user may enter. If you want to make sure that users do not enter more characters than you want them to, add the `maxlength` attribute. If users type the maximum number of characters allowed, the browser prevents them from entering additional text.

ADD A TEXT INPUT FIELD

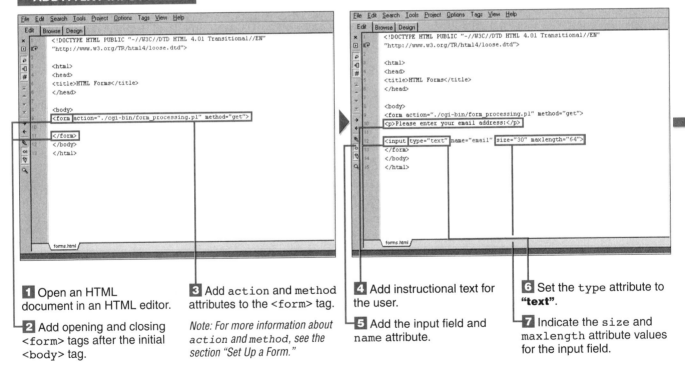

1 Open an HTML document in an HTML editor.

2 Add opening and closing `<form>` tags after the initial `<body>` tag.

3 Add `action` and `method` attributes to the `<form>` tag.

Note: For more information about `action` *and* `method`, *see the section "Set Up a Form."*

4 Add instructional text for the user.

5 Add the input field and name attribute.

6 Set the `type` attribute to **"text"**.

7 Indicate the `size` and `maxlength` attribute values for the input field.

What happens if I set the size to a specific value but the user types in additional characters?

✔ In this event, the input field scrolls to the left as the user continues to enter additional text.

What happens if the maxlength is smaller than the size of the input field?

✔ The size attribute still dictates the appearance of the form, but users are unable to type additional text after they have reached the maximum length allowed.

Is there a way to have text appear with the input field that the visitor can type over?

✔ Yes. Use the value attribute with text enclosed in quotation marks. The value you indicate appears within the input field. Even though the user must then erase the message in order to type in new text, prepopulated values on form fields can be a useful tool when guiding the user through the form process.

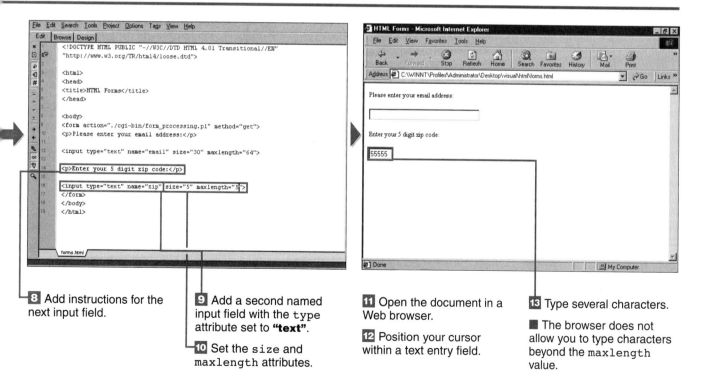

8 Add instructions for the next input field.

9 Add a second named input field with the type attribute set to **"text"**.

10 Set the size and maxlength attributes.

11 Open the document in a Web browser.

12 Position your cursor within a text entry field.

13 Type several characters.

■ The browser does not allow you to type characters beyond the maxlength value.

ADD A PASSWORD FIELD

You can add a form field that masks the text the user types by using the type="password" attribute. The password field is essentially the same as a regular single-line text entry field, except that the text characters appear obscured, usually as a series of asterisks.

All the attributes that apply to the text input field apply when you set the type to password, so be sure to include the required name attribute. In addition, you may use all the other optional attributes available to the input field, including size and maxlength.

You can use the password field in conjunction with a standard text entry field when you need users to enter a login and password to gain access to private or member

sections of your Web site.

Be aware, however, that the password type field only obscures the appearance of text on a browser window. It does not provide any additional security when the data is transmitted to the server.

ADD A PASSWORD FIELD

■1 Open an HTML document.

■2 Add opening and closing <form> tags after the initial <body> tag.

■3 Add action and method attributes to the <form> tag.

■4 Add text to prompt the user's password.

■5 Add a named input field.

■6 Set the type attribute to **"password"**.

■7 Indicate the size and maxlength values.

■8 Open the document in a Web browser.

■9 Type a password into the input field.

■ The text is obscured on the Web page.

ADD A TEXT BOX

To give your users the opportunity to submit feedback, use the `<textarea>` tag with your form. Unlike text type input fields that allow for only a single line of text, the `<textarea>` element creates a field with multiple lines so that users can enter entire paragraphs of text.

Set the visible size of the text box with the `rows` and `cols` attributes.

The `rows` attribute dictates the height of the box expressed as lines of text, and the `cols` attribute controls the width. A text box with `rows="4"` and `cols="30"` accommodates 4 lines of text with 30 characters in each line. If the user types additional text, the browser creates a vertical scroll bar to accommodate the additional rows.

The `<textarea>` element has both an opening and closing tag. You

must always include the closing tag.

Any text that you add between the opening and closing tags appears in the field as default text. You can use this text to prompt the user to enter specific information, but remember that your default text cannot contain any additional HTML formatting such as font or emphasis elements.

ADD A TEXT BOX

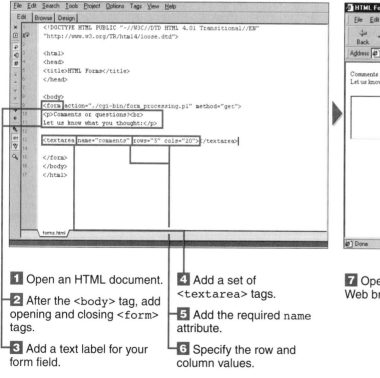

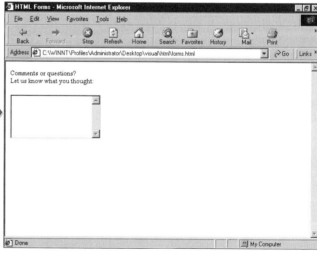

1 Open an HTML document.

2 After the `<body>` tag, add opening and closing `<form>` tags.

3 Add a text label for your form field.

4 Add a set of `<textarea>` tags.

5 Add the required `name` attribute.

6 Specify the row and column values.

7 Open the document in a Web browser.

■ The actual dimensions of the text box may vary from browser to browser.

ADD A SUBMIT BUTTON

The form fields that you include on your Web page are not of much use if your visitors cannot send the form data to you. To enable visitors to transmit form information, include a submit button. When the user clicks the submit button, the browser sends the data to the URL indicated in the form's action attribute.

To create a submit button, use the <input> tag and set the type attribute to **"submit"**. No additional attributes are required for the submit <input> tag, but you probably want to use both the name and value attributes.

Your form processing application uses the name attribute to identify which button the user clicks and the value attribute to control the button label that is visible to the user. If you do not include a customized value, the browser displays the button with the default "submit" label.

ADD A SUBMIT BUTTON

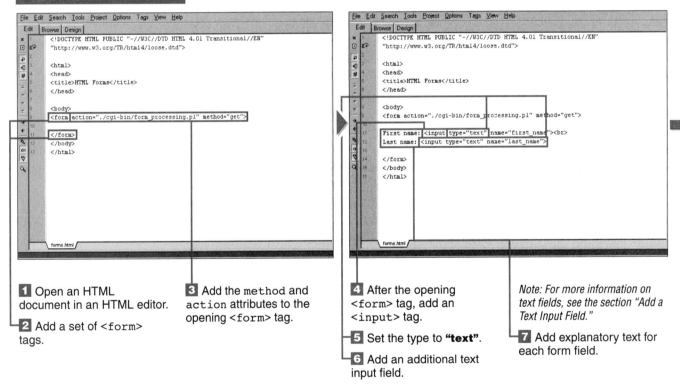

1 Open an HTML document in an HTML editor.

2 Add a set of <form> tags.

3 Add the method and action attributes to the opening <form> tag.

4 After the opening <form> tag, add an <input> tag.

5 Set the type to **"text"**.

6 Add an additional text input field.

Note: For more information on text fields, see the section "Add a Text Input Field."

7 Add explanatory text for each form field.

Can I include more than one submit button?

✔ Yes, you can include multiple submit buttons within the same form. For example, you might have distinct submit buttons for editing a certain field, saving to a shopping cart, or proceeding to checkout. If you include more than one submit button, give each button a unique name or value so that the processing application knows which button the user clicks.

Is there a way to create more customizable submit buttons?

✔ Yes. You can use the `<button></button>` tags. Set the `type` attribute to "submit" and include formatted text or images within the `<button>` tags. This content appears on top of a standard browser button. The `<button>` tag is not supported by older browsers.

Can I use an image as a submit button?

✔ Yes. The `<input>` tag accepts the `type="image"` attribute as well as `name` and `src`, which you use to indicate the location of the image file. When included within your form, the image appears as a clickable button.

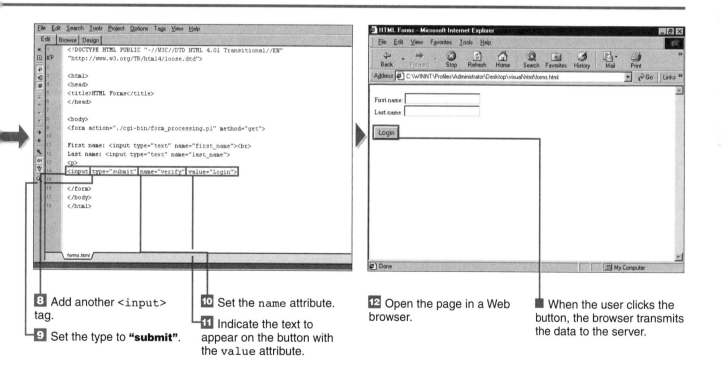

8 Add another `<input>` tag.

9 Set the type to **"submit"**.

10 Set the `name` attribute.

11 Indicate the text to appear on the button with the `value` attribute.

12 Open the page in a Web browser.

■ When the user clicks the button, the browser transmits the data to the server.

ADD CHECK BOXES

You can add check boxes to your form by using the `<input>` tag and setting the type attribute to **"check"**. Check boxes are useful when you want to present the visitor with multiple choices and enable them to select more than one option.

For each check box, include the name and value attributes. When you have a group of related check boxes, assign the same name to all the check boxes and then give each a specific attribute. For example, if you want visitors to indicate newsletter subscriptions, name all check boxes "subscriptions" and then make each value the specific name of a newsletter. When the user submits the form, the browser transmits any checked values associated with the check box name.

The value you indicate for each check box is not visible to the user, so you should include a label with each `<input>` tag. You can insert labeling text or images to the right or left of a check box. If there are no breaks between the label and the `<input>` tag, the elements are aligned vertically on the baseline.

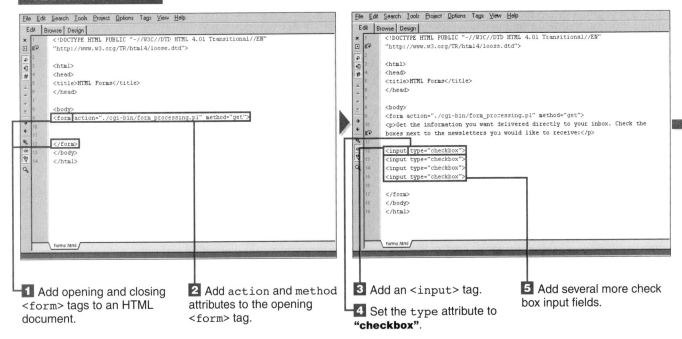

1 Add opening and closing `<form>` tags to an HTML document.

2 Add action and method attributes to the opening `<form>` tag.

3 Add an `<input>` tag.

4 Set the type attribute to **"checkbox"**.

5 Add several more check box input fields.

How do I prevent visitors from selecting more than one check box?

✔ Check boxes are designed to allow for multiple selections. If you want to have users select only one choice, use radio buttons instead. See the section "Add Radio Buttons."

How can I preselect certain check boxes?

✔ You can add the `checked` attribute to a check box to preselect an element. This is a good idea if your visitors are more likely to select one check box in the list than the others. The `checked` attribute is a standalone attribute that does not require any additional value.

How can I prevent users from selecting a particular check box?

✔ You can prevent users from selecting a check box by adding the `disabled` attribute to the `<input>` tag. You might want to do this for nested check boxes that are available only if other fields are selected. A disabled element does not allow user input, and the browser may change the appearance of the check box to signal that the option is unavailable.

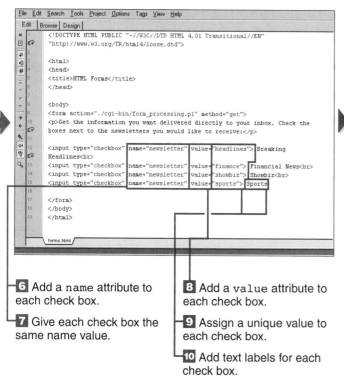

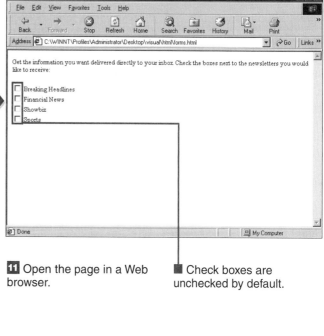

-6 Add a `name` attribute to each check box.

-7 Give each check box the same name value.

-8 Add a `value` attribute to each check box.

-9 Assign a unique value to each check box.

-10 Add text labels for each check box.

-11 Open the page in a Web browser.

■ Check boxes are unchecked by default.

ADD RADIO BUTTONS

When you want to offer multiple choices but allow users to select only a single choice, use radio buttons. *Radio buttons* are similar to check boxes, but only one choice may be selected at a time. Radio buttons are ideal when you need users to select between mutually exclusive choices or yes/no responses.

Add radio buttons with the <input> tag and the type attribute set to **"radio"**. For each radio button, you must include the name and value attributes. For each group of related radio buttons, the name you designate should be the same. However, each individual radio button should have a unique value.

For each radio button, include a descriptive label to the right or the left of the option. Like other form elements, there is no formatting inherently associated with radio buttons. You can use paragraph or line break tags to format buttons or place them within a table to further control the layout.

ADD RADIO BUTTONS

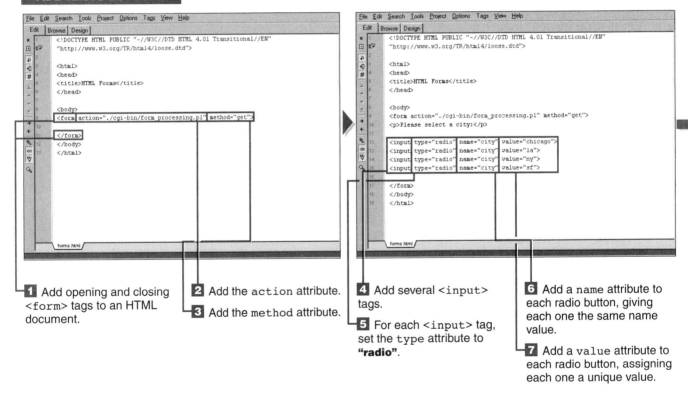

1 Add opening and closing <form> tags to an HTML document.

2 Add the action attribute.

3 Add the method attribute.

4 Add several <input> tags.

5 For each <input> tag, set the type attribute to **"radio"**.

6 Add a name attribute to each radio button, giving each one the same name value.

7 Add a value attribute to each radio button, assigning each one a unique value.

Can I use the checked attribute with radio buttons?

✔ Yes, you can use the `checked` attribute to preselect one option. Remember, though, that because radio buttons are mutually exclusive, you should never have more than one option checked.

Why are they called *radio buttons*?

✔ The term refers to the controls on a radio, particularly the traditional mechanical controls where pushing in one button selects a new station and causes the previously depressed button to pop out.

Can I change the color of radio buttons?

✔ Yes, you can change the background color of a radio button by using the `style` attribute with the `background-color` style property. Setting the `background-color` property to a hexadecimal value changes the color of the box that contains the radio button. For more information on using style sheets with form elements, see the section "Add Style to Form Elements."

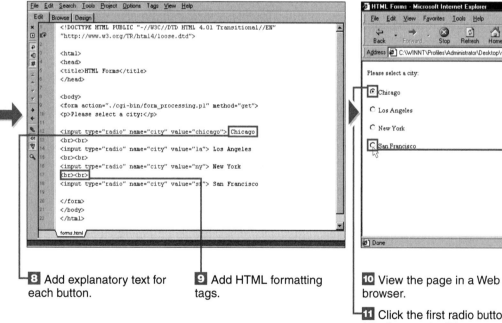

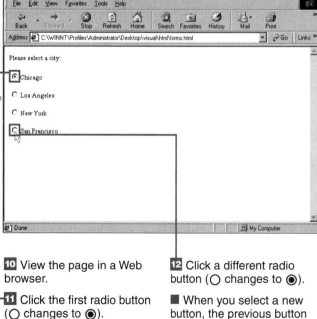

8 Add explanatory text for each button.

9 Add HTML formatting tags.

10 View the page in a Web browser.

11 Click the first radio button (○ changes to ◉).

12 Click a different radio button (○ changes to ◉).

■ When you select a new button, the previous button is automatically deselected.

CREATE A DROP-DOWN MENU

You can create a drop-down menu or scrolling list of options with the <select> tag.

For every menu you create, you must add the required name attribute to the opening <select> tag. In addition, you can use the multiple attribute to allow users to select more than one option at a time. To create a scrolling list with

several options visible, add the size attribute. Setting the size attribute to 5, for example, creates a list with the first 5 options visible.

Within the opening and closing <select> tags, add options using the <option> tag. The closing option </option> tag is not required and is often omitted. If you do not use the optional value

attribute with the <option> tag, the browser sets the value to the text content of the selection.

Use drop-down lists rather than check boxes or radio buttons in cases where you have a limited amount of space but want to provide the user with numerous options. Drop-down menus are a particularly good way to provide site navigation or search parameters.

CREATE A DROP-DOWN MENU

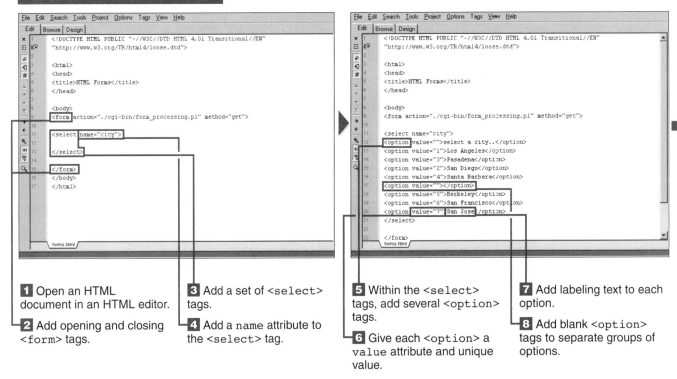

1 Open an HTML document in an HTML editor.

2 Add opening and closing <form> tags.

3 Add a set of <select> tags.

4 Add a name attribute to the <select> tag.

5 Within the <select> tags, add several <option> tags.

6 Give each <option> a value attribute and unique value.

7 Add labeling text to each option.

8 Add blank <option> tags to separate groups of options.

Can I have certain elements preselected in a drop-down menu?

✔ Yes. Add the `selected` attribute to an `<option>` tag to preselect that choice. If there are no `<option>` tags with the `selected` attribute, the browser displays the first option as the preselected choice.

How do I make the initial option a blank field?

✔ To make the initial option blank, add an additional `<option>` tag directly under the opening `<select>` tag, but do not assign it a value.

How do I control the width of drop-down menus?

✔ Most browsers expand the width of drop-down menus to accommodate the maximum number of characters presented in the option values. For example, if all your option values are 5 characters long and you add another option tag with a very long value, the menu expands to accommodate that longer string. The only way to exert some control over the width is to minimize the length of your option values.

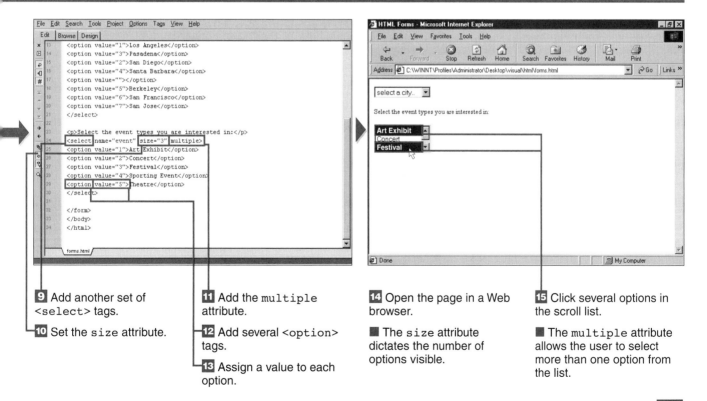

9 Add another set of `<select>` tags.

10 Set the `size` attribute.

11 Add the `multiple` attribute.

12 Add several `<option>` tags.

13 Assign a value to each option.

14 Open the page in a Web browser.

■ The `size` attribute dictates the number of options visible.

15 Click several options in the scroll list.

■ The `multiple` attribute allows the user to select more than one option from the list.

ADD STYLE TO FORM ELEMENTS

You can enhance the appearance of forms and specific form elements by using style properties. You can apply inline styles using the style attribute or reference style sheet classes through the class attribute.

To specify the background color for all form elements, include the style attribute and the

background-color property within the opening <form> tag. Or, you can use the style attribute with individual form fields, such as <input>, <select>, or <option> tags, to add color to specific elements. For example, to add color to an entire drop-down menu, add the style attribute with a specified color to the <select> tag. To have alternating colors for each choice, apply the style

attribute to each of the <option> tags with a different color for each option.

If you want to create global style settings that you can reference repeatedly, consider creating an internal or external style sheet with defined form selectors or classes. For more information on creating style sheets, see Chapter 6.

ADD STYLE TO FORM ELEMENTS

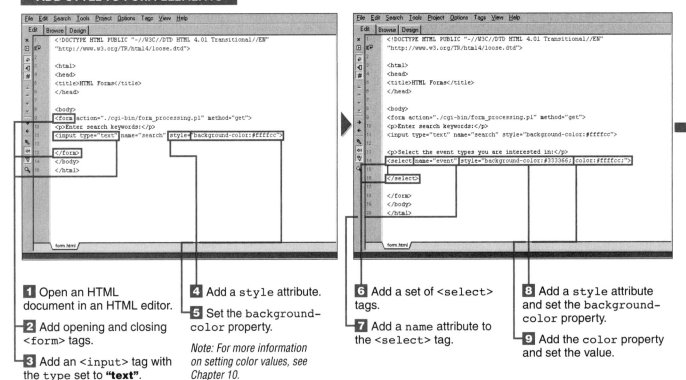

1 Open an HTML document in an HTML editor.

2 Add opening and closing <form> tags.

3 Add an <input> tag with the type set to **"text"**.

4 Add a style attribute.

5 Set the background-color property.

Note: For more information on setting color values, see Chapter 10.

6 Add a set of <select> tags.

7 Add a name attribute to the <select> tag.

8 Add a style attribute and set the background-color property.

9 Add the color property and set the value.

Can I apply style properties to the text that appears for each drop-down option?

✔ Yes. You can include font properties such as font-weight and font-size as well as the color property to change the appearance of text options. This is particularly useful if you change the background color of the <select> element or the individual <option> tags, because dark background colors effect the legibility of the option text.

Can I use style properties to affect the color of radio buttons and check boxes?

✔ You can use the background-color property to add color to the immediate area around a radio button. However, there is currently no way to change the color of the actual radio button or check box.

What happens if a browser does not support style sheets?

✔ If a browser does not support style sheets or certain style properties, it simply ignores the style attributes.

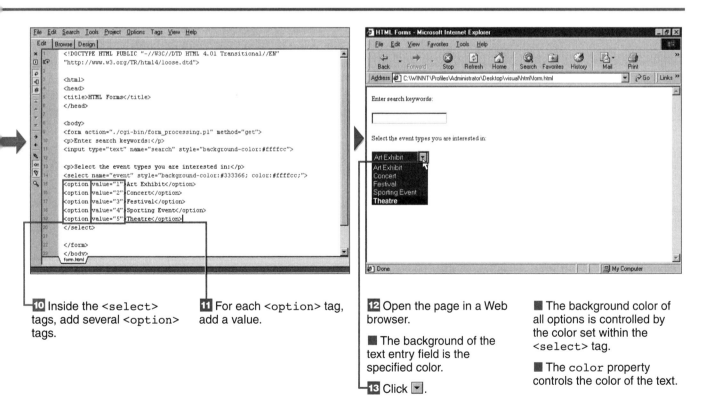

10 Inside the <select> tags, add several <option> tags.

11 For each <option> tag, add a value.

12 Open the page in a Web browser.

■ The background of the text entry field is the specified color.

13 Click ▾.

■ The background color of all options is controlled by the color set within the <select> tag.

■ The color property controls the color of the text.

USING FIELDSETS AND LEGENDS

You can organize related form elements by using `<fieldset>` and `<legend>` tags, two elements that were added to the HTML 4.0 specification. Fieldsets and legends provide additional contextual information for users who are vision-impaired, because they are specifically designed to work with language synthesizer components and improve accessibility via keyboard strokes. They also provide additional visual clues to show

relationships between form components.

To group a section of form components together, enclose the elements within opening and closing `<fieldset>` tags. The browser may render the fieldset differently, perhaps enclosing the elements within a border. You can add a label to the fieldset by including summary text within opening and closing `<legend>` tags. Neither the `<fieldset>` nor

the `<legend>` tags include any implicit formatting instructions, but you can apply style attributes to both. For information on using style sheets with forms, see the section "Add Style to Form Elements."

Older browsers do not recognize the `<fieldset>` and `<legend>` tags. That should not prevent you from implementing them, however, because browsers that do not support the tags simply ignore them and render the form elements normally.

USING FIELDSETS AND LEGENDS

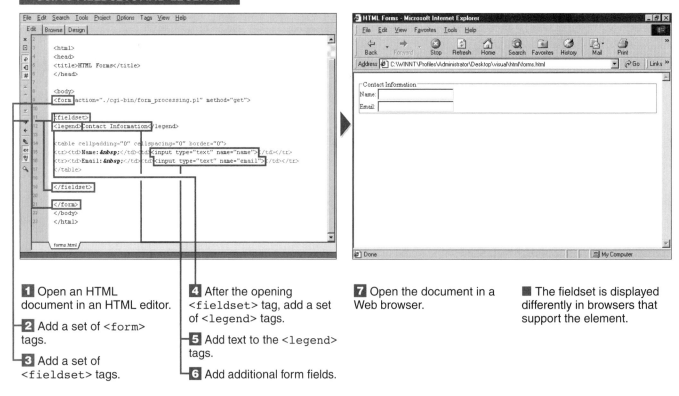

1 Open an HTML document in an HTML editor.

2 Add a set of `<form>` tags.

3 Add a set of `<fieldset>` tags.

4 After the opening `<fieldset>` tag, add a set of `<legend>` tags.

5 Add text to the `<legend>` tags.

6 Add additional form fields.

7 Open the document in a Web browser.

■ The fieldset is displayed differently in browsers that support the element.

USING LABELS

You can add labels to form elements with the <label> tag, part of the HTML 4.0 specification. Although you can provide standard text labels for form elements, the <label> tag offers two distinct advantages. First, it provides the browser with contextual information that associates the label text with a specific element. This is important for visually impaired visitors using special browsing agents. In addition, the <label> tag allows users to jump to specific form elements when the label text is selected. This can be a useful way of directing users to particular form fields.

The easiest way to add labels is to simply enclose your label text and form element within opening and closing <label> tags. You can also associate labels with form elements by using the for attribute with the <label> tag and the id attribute with the target form element. When the user selects the label text, the browser jumps to the form element that has the corresponding id value.

USING LABELS

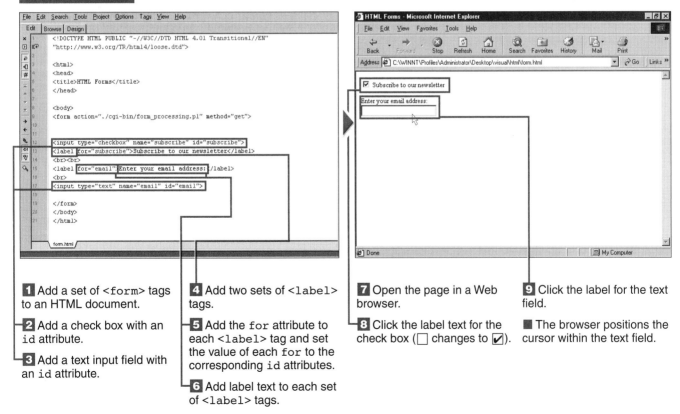

1 Add a set of <form> tags to an HTML document.

2 Add a check box with an id attribute.

3 Add a text input field with an id attribute.

4 Add two sets of <label> tags.

5 Add the for attribute to each <label> tag and set the value of each for to the corresponding id attributes.

6 Add label text to each set of <label> tags.

7 Open the page in a Web browser.

8 Click the label text for the check box (☐ changes to ☑).

9 Click the label for the text field.

■ The browser positions the cursor within the text field.

DISABLE FORM FIELDS

You can make form fields inaccessible to users through the `disabled` and `readonly` attributes. This is sometimes necessary when you want nested fields to be available only if the user has made a certain selection. When you disable form fields or designate them as read-only, the user cannot select the option or enter a new value, and the browser often displays the

fields differently, usually graying them out.

For selection-type form fields, such as check boxes, radio buttons, and drop-down menus, add the `disabled` attribute to the opening tag to prevent users from selecting the option. In the case of drop-down menus, you can disable the entire menu by adding the `disabled` attribute to the opening

`<select>` tag or disable specific options by adding it to an `<option>` tag.

For text input fields and text boxes, use the `readonly` attribute to prevent users from entering new text into the field. Because the visitor can still read the content of read-only fields, you can use them to provide rules or licensing agreements that you do not want the user to alter.

DISABLE FORM FIELDS

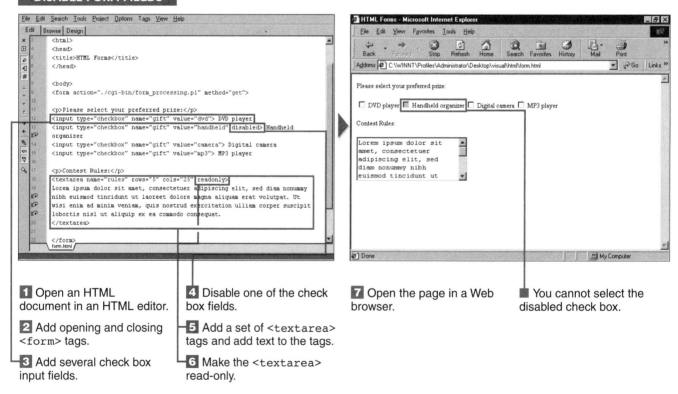

1 Open an HTML document in an HTML editor.

2 Add opening and closing `<form>` tags.

3 Add several check box input fields.

4 Disable one of the check box fields.

5 Add a set of `<textarea>` tags and add text to the tags.

6 Make the `<textarea>` read-only.

7 Open the page in a Web browser.

■ You cannot select the disabled check box.

USING HIDDEN FIELDS

When you need to include form fields in order to process a form but you do not want the user to alter or even view the information, you can use hidden fields.

Hidden fields are simple <input> elements with the type attribute set to **"hidden"**. For hidden fields, you must also include the name and value attributes.

Use hidden fields if your form processing application receives several different forms and you need to distinguish the processing action that should take place. For example, you might have an application that creates new records as well as updating existing ones. For forms with new record information, you might include a hidden field with the value set to

new. In another location, you might have another form with a hidden field where the value is set to update. Based on the hidden values transmitted, the form processing application decides how to handle the data.

USING HIDDEN FIELDS

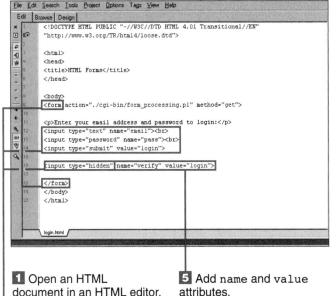

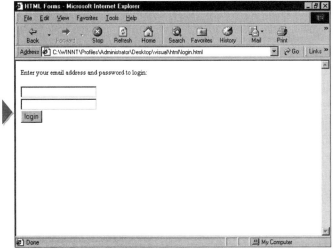

1 Open an HTML document in an HTML editor.

2 Add a set of <form> tags.

3 Add several form fields.

4 Add an <input> tag with the type set to **"hidden"**.

5 Add name and value attributes.

Note: The name and value should correspond to actions defined within your form handling application. When the program receives the hidden value, it executes specific code.

6 Open the page in a Web browser.

■ The hidden field is not visible to the user.

ALLOW USERS TO SEND ATTACHMENTS

You can give visitors the ability to send you attachments by using an `<input>` tag with the `type` set to "**file**". This creates both a text entry field where the user can enter in the path of a file as well as a button that allows users to browse their local drive and select a file to attach.

When using file selection input fields, you must include the `enctype` attribute within the opening `<form>` tag and set the value to "**multipart/form-data**". If you do not include this attribute, the form simply transmits the value entered into the text entry field, namely the location of the file on the user's drive. In addition, you must set the `method` attribute to "**post**".

How the file attachments are processed depends entirely on your form-handling application on the server. Because there is no way to verify the size or content of a file the user sends, make sure that your CGI or other application can cope with large files, a variety of formats, and possible file corruption.

ALLOW USERS TO SEND ATTACHMENTS

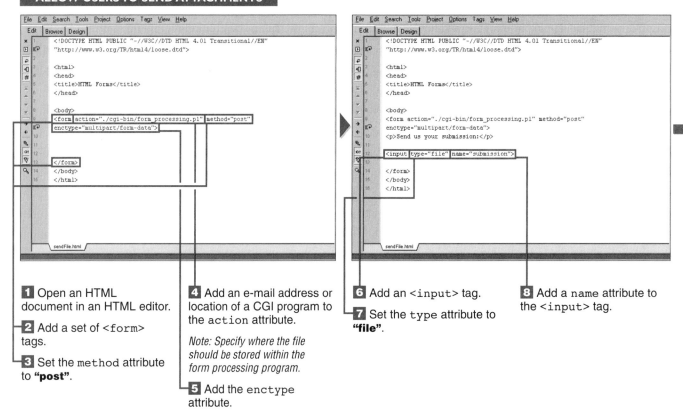

1 Open an HTML document in an HTML editor.

2 Add a set of `<form>` tags.

3 Set the `method` attribute to "**post**".

4 Add an e-mail address or location of a CGI program to the `action` attribute.

Note: Specify where the file should be stored within the form processing program.

5 Add the `enctype` attribute.

6 Add an `<input>` tag.

7 Set the `type` attribute to "**file**".

8 Add a `name` attribute to the `<input>` tag.

Can I limit the types of files that users can send?

✔ Yes. You can include the `accept` attribute within the `<input>` tag to restrict the types of files that users may attach. The value of the `accept` attribute should be specific MIME types. To limit the file selection to images, set the value of the `accept` attribute to "**image**/*". The asterisk tells the browser to accept all file formats with the `image` MIME type. To limit the selection to text files, include the "`text/*`" MIME type.

Can I have file attachments sent to an e-mail address rather than a CGI program?

✔ You can try. In theory, you can include a `mailto:` URL within the form's `action` attribute to send attachments to an e-mail address. However, in practice, this is not a very reliable way to process file attachments.

How do I indicate where the file should be stored on my server?

✔ This directive should be part of your form-processing application. For more on form processing, pick up a copy of *PHP: Your visual blueprint for creating open source, server-side content* (Hungry Minds, Inc.).

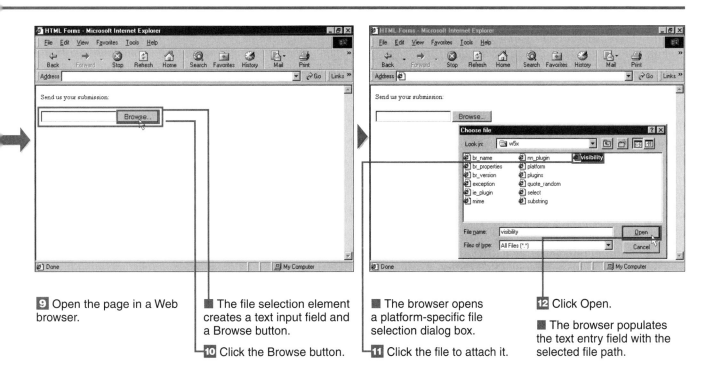

9 Open the page in a Web browser.

■ The file selection element creates a text input field and a Browse button.

10 Click the Browse button.

■ The browser opens a platform-specific file selection dialog box.

11 Click the file to attach it.

12 Click Open.

■ The browser populates the text entry field with the selected file path.

SEND FORM DATA TO AN E-MAIL ADDRESS

I f you do not have access to CGI programs to process forms, you can have form data sent directly to your e-mail address by including a mailto URL within the form's action attribute.

When you send form data to an e-mail address, you should include the enctype attribute inside the opening <form> tag. Set the enctype value to **"text/plain"** or

"multipart/form-data", in which case the browser transmits the form values as a separate file. If you do not indicate the enctype, the values are encoded and sent as a string of words and character entities, making the data difficult to decipher.

Because e-mail is extremely insecure, you should never use this method to transmit any secure

data, such as credit card numbers or other personal information from the user. If you are asking users to submit secure information, you should use SSL (Secure Sockets Layer) encryption. For more information on Web servers, see Chapter 18. In addition, sending form data via e-mail often requires that the users have their e-mail preferences set in the Web browser.

SEND FORM DATA TO AN E-MAIL ADDRESS

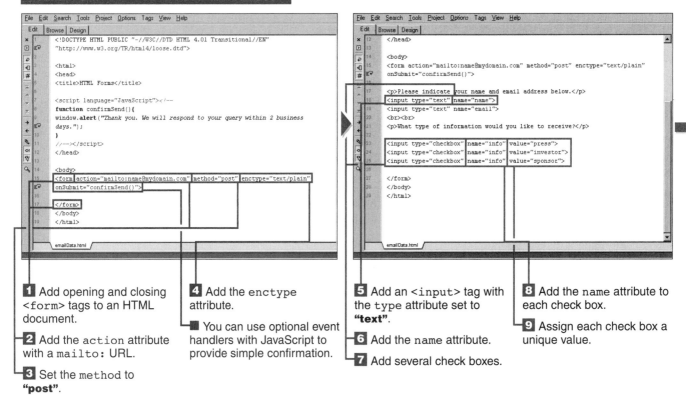

1 Add opening and closing <form> tags to an HTML document.

2 Add the action attribute with a mailto: URL.

3 Set the method to **"post"**.

4 Add the enctype attribute.

■ You can use optional event handlers with JavaScript to provide simple confirmation.

5 Add an <input> tag with the type attribute set to **"text"**.

6 Add the name attribute.

7 Add several check boxes.

8 Add the name attribute to each check box.

9 Assign each check box a unique value.

Can I send the user an automated e-mail confirmation?

✔ There is no way to automatically send an e-mail confirmation when sending form data via e-mail. If you want to send confirmation, consider using a form-processing application such as a CGI.

What exactly is SSL?

✔ SSL is a way of transmitting encrypted data from a browser to a Web server. You can recognize SSL-enabled servers by the `https` protocol in the address line of your browser.

Besides indicating a mailto URL in the form's `action` attribute, is there any other way to have form results sent via e-mail?

✔ You can program a CGI to send data to an e-mail address. If you do not want to create or adapt your own programs, most commercial Web hosting companies offer access to simple form-handling applications that send data to your e-mail address. These applications are usually CGI that allow you to customize a confirmation e-mail and direct users to a specific HTML page on submit.

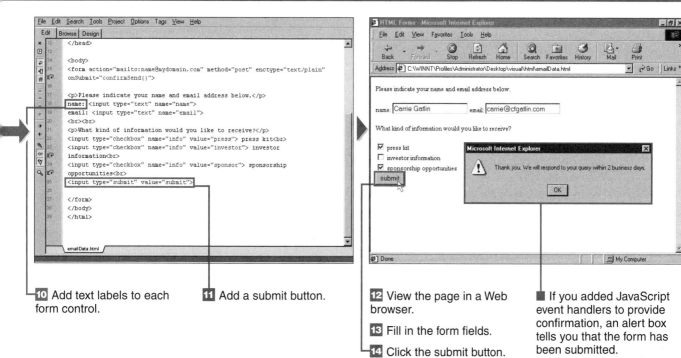

■10 Add text labels to each form control.

■11 Add a submit button.

■12 View the page in a Web browser.

■13 Fill in the form fields.

■14 Click the submit button.

■ If you added JavaScript event handlers to provide confirmation, an alert box tells you that the form has been submitted.

Note: For more on using JavaScript, see Chapter 14.

AN INTRODUCTION TO FRAMES

HTML frames are a way of dividing up Web pages into independent sections that each have their own source document. For example, you could have five different HTML documents load into the same window by creating a frameset with five frames. You could then have content load into a specific frame without changing the other framed content on the page.

Frames are easy to implement and require the use of only three tags: <frameset>, <frame>, and <noframes>. The <frameset> and <frame> tags are used to define the layout of your frame document, while the <noframes> tag provides alternative content for browsers that do not support frames or do not have frames enabled. In addition, Internet Explorer and Netscape Navigator 6 support the <iframe> tag, which embeds inline frames directly into the content of a standard HTML document. You can combine these tags and apply optional attributes to create simple or complex frame layouts.

Using Frames

Although framed documents are not as widespread as they used to be on the Web, you can still find them on some sites being used to isolate navigation components or separate banner advertisements from main content areas. Both uses of frames are addressed later in this chapter in the sections "Using Frames for Navigation" and "Using Frames for Banner Ads." In addition, frames are sometimes used in interactive elements where there is a need to use languages such as JavaScript to maintain state or store variables. For more information on JavaScript and frames, see Chapter 15.

Advantages to Using Frames

One advantage to using frames is that they are easier to maintain if you regularly update your site and add new directories or content pieces. For example, if your site navigation elements are contained within a single file on a frame-based site, you can update that single file rather than having to go through each page and edit the navigation elements. Be aware that you can accomplish the same thing and avoid the disadvantages of frames by using server side includes (see Chapter 19). Another advantage to using frames is that they introduce a level of interactivity to static pages. You can use inline frames to easily implement a slideshow presentation, for example.

Disadvantages to Using Frames

There are several disadvantages to using frames. First, when your site content is contained within a frameset, visitors cannot bookmark individual pages, only the top level document containing the frameset. In addition, many search engine robots are unable to index framed pages, so your site may not be returned in search results.

Further, if you choose to use frames to separate your site navigation from your content, you are not able to alter the navigation on each page to add position reinforcement elements such as "on-state" images, or images that appear differently depending on which page is currently loaded.

You should also consider that by devoting a portion of your page real estate to one frame, you reduce the available window space for the remaining portion of your content.

The Great Frame Debate

Almost immediately after frames were introduced with Netscape 2.0, Web designers began debating the merits of framed documents. Besides the notable disadvantages to using frames that are outlined previously, many designers object to the ways in which some Web sites use frames with little consideration for clear design and good usability. After all, just because you can create a page with ten frames does not mean that you should. On

the other hand, there is no reason to avoid frames completely when they may be the best solution for your needs.

Before implementing frames on your site, consider the advantages and disadvantages and evaluate whether frames are really the best way to accomplish your goal.

USING <NOFRAMES> TAGS

You can provide alternative content for browsers that do not support frames by including the <noframes> tags in your frame document. If you do not provide alternative content with the <noframes> tags, browsers that do not support frames display a blank page in lieu of your frame content.

You should place the set of opening and closing <noframes> tags

within the <frameset> tags. If you have nested frames on your page, put the <noframes> tags within the top-level or outermost frameset. There are no required attributes for <noframes> tags, but you can include optional class and style attributes for use with style sheets.

Within the <noframes> tags, be sure to include a direct link to your

site's main content frame in addition to a message. Of course, if portions of your site, such as the navigation elements, are contained within another frame, your non-frame visitors miss a vital piece of functionality. For this reason, it is a good idea to repeat essential navigation within the body of the main content pages.

USING <NOFRAMES> TAGS

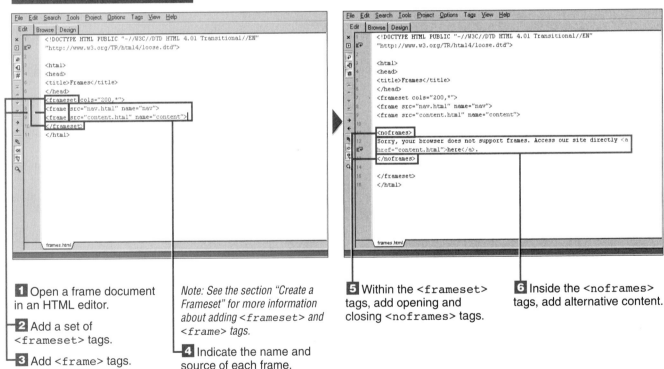

1 Open a frame document in an HTML editor.

2 Add a set of <frameset> tags.

3 Add <frame> tags.

Note: See the section "Create a Frameset" for more information about adding <frameset> and <frame> tags.

4 Indicate the name and source of each frame.

5 Within the <frameset> tags, add opening and closing <noframes> tags.

6 Inside the <noframes> tags, add alternative content.

Which browsers do not support frames?

✔ Netscape versions lower than 2.0 do not support frames. Lynx, a UNIX-based text browser, provides some limited support for frames, rendering the source for each frame as a link so that the user can access the content. In addition, some alternative browsers used by disabled visitors may not support frames.

Can I include any content within the <noframes> tags?

✔ You can include any content that you would normally include within HTML <body> tags, including text, links, and images.

Can I use the <noframes> tags with inline frames?

✔ No. Use the <noframes> tags only within <frameset> tags. To provide alternative content for inline frames, simply include the content between the opening and closing <iframe> tags. For more information about using inline frames, see the section "Create an Inline Frame."

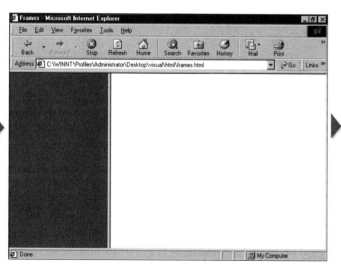

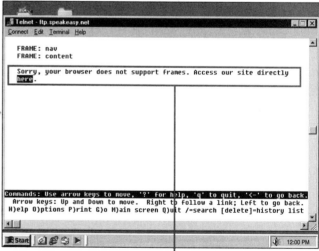

7 Open the document in a frame-enabled Web browser.

■ The content within the <noframes> tags is not rendered.

8 View the page in a browser that does not render frames.

■ The content of the <noframes> tags is displayed.

CREATE A FRAMESET

To create a frameset, you need only two tags — the <frameset> tag and the <frame> tag. The frameset sets up the collection of frames that compose the page. Do not use <body> tags on the frameset page: Simply include the frameset directly after the closing </head> tag. The <frameset> tag must include either the rows or cols attribute, which indicates the number and size of rows or columns contained in the frameset. You can employ both attributes together to create a grid format.

Within the <frameset> tags, use the <frame> tags to define the pages that make up the frameset. Each <frame> tag must have an src attribute that indicates the location of the page loaded within the frame.

For each <frame> tag, you may include an optional name attribute and a unique name. After you have assigned each frame a unique name, you can then include links throughout your site and have content load in specific frames. For more information on targeting content using frame names, see the section "Target Frames."

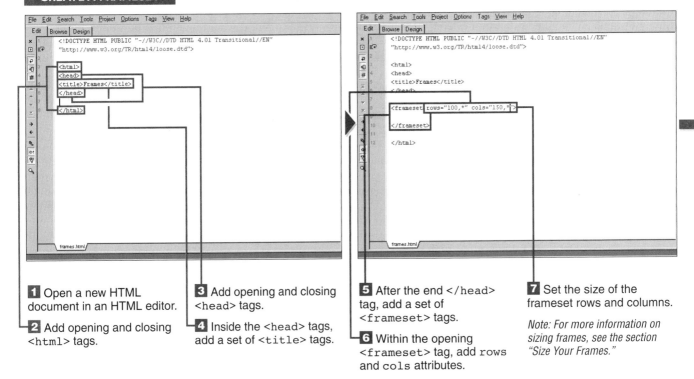

1 Open a new HTML document in an HTML editor.

2 Add opening and closing <html> tags.

3 Add opening and closing <head> tags.

4 Inside the <head> tags, add a set of <title> tags.

5 After the end </head> tag, add a set of <frameset> tags.

6 Within the opening <frameset> tag, add rows and cols attributes.

7 Set the size of the frameset rows and columns.

Note: For more information on sizing frames, see the section "Size Your Frames."

Can any other HTML tags occur within the frame document?

✔ Only <head> and <frameset> content should occur in a frame document. Within the outermost <frameset> tags, you may include the <noframes> tags that may contain standard HTML content. For more on using <noframes> tags, see the section "Using <noframes> Tags."

Can I have one frame load another framed document?

✔ Yes, the source of one frame can be the location of another frame document with its own frameset and frames.

Do all browsers support frames?

✔ Most browsers in use today support frames, but there are a few that do not. Most notably, Netscape versions older than 2.0 do not support frames. In addition, there may be alternative browsing devices used by disabled visitors that do not support frames.

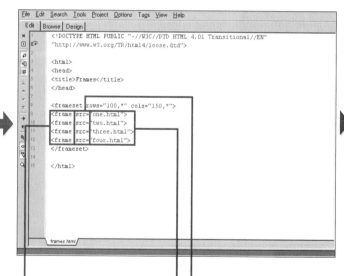

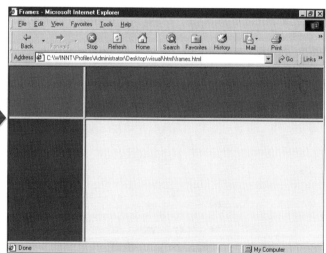

8 Add a <frame> tag for each segment of your framed document.

Note: The number of frames you need is determined by how many rows and columns you set.

9 For each frame, add the src attribute.

10 Indicate the file location of each frame source document.

Note: The src attribute should include the file location of the HTML page that will occupy the frame.

11 Open the page in a Web browser.

■ Each of the source documents is loaded into an individual frame.

SIZE YOUR FRAMES

You can set the size of each frame by indicating a value for the cols and rows attributes of the <frameset> tag.

When you set the size of rows or frame columns, you can use either fixed pixel dimensions or percentages of the current window. You can also use an asterisk in combination with pixel or percentage dimensions. This tells the browser to assign the remaining space in the window to the frame in question.

In addition, you can use the asterisk value to divide the available space proportionally. For example, for a page with two frame columns where one column is three times the width of the other, set the cols attribute to "3*,*".

When your source document for a particular frame contains more content than the amount of visible space you have assigned to it, the browser creates a scrollbar within that particular frame so that the user can scroll and see the rest of the content.

SIZE YOUR FRAMES

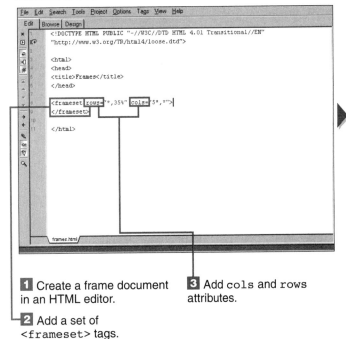

1 Create a frame document in an HTML editor.

2 Add a set of <frameset> tags.

3 Add cols and rows attributes.

4 Set the sizes of the rows and columns.

*Note: In this example, *,35% sets the second row to 35% of the window while the first row fills the rest of the available space. 5*,* sets the column size of the first column to 5 times the size of the second column.*

Can users alter the size of frame columns and rows?

✔ Yes. Users can position the cursor over a frame border and dynamically alter the dimensions of columns and rows. The exception is inline frames, which cannot be resized by the user. You can prevent the user from resizing frames by adding the `noresize` attribute to a `<frame>` tag.

How do I prevent scrollbars from showing up?

✔ Use the scrolling attribute with the `<frame>` tag and set the value to "no." This prevents the browser from adding scrollbars, even if there is enough content to warrant them. If you choose to explicitly turn off scrollbars, keep in mind that if your content goes beyond the dimensions of the frame, there is no way for your user to access that content.

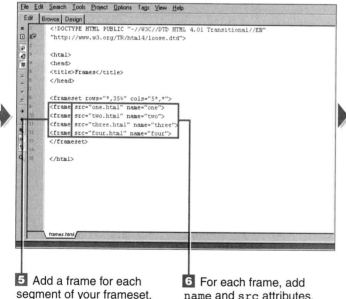

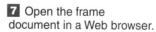

5 Add a frame for each segment of your frameset.

6 For each frame, add `name` and `src` attributes.

7 Open the frame document in a Web browser.

■ The size of each frame is determined by the values set for the `rows` and `cols` attributes.

CONTROL FRAME BORDERS

Unless you specify the borders you want to appear between frames, browsers display a 3D border between frames. You can add attributes to both the <frameset> and <frame> tags to control the size and visibility of these borders.

Add the frameborder attribute to the individual <frame> tags to explicitly turn borders on or off. Technically, Netscape Navigator

and Internet Explorer accept different values for the frameborder attribute, but each supports the other's attribute value. To turn frames off, set the value to either "0" or "no." To explicitly turn them on, set the value to "1" or "yes."

In theory, the frameborder attributes should give you all the control you need. In practice, some browsers may still display borders

even when you have the frame borders set to zero. You can add additional proprietary attributes to ensure that borders are rendered correctly. Internet Explorer supports the framespacing attribute for the <frameset> tag. This attribute sets the space between frames to a specific number of pixels. Netscape Navigator uses the border attribute with the <frameset> tag for the same purpose.

CONTROL FRAME BORDERS

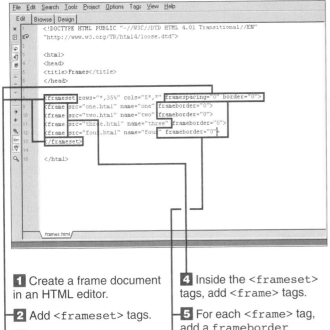

1 Create a frame document in an HTML editor.

2 Add <frameset> tags.

3 Set the framespacing and border attributes to **"0"**.

4 Inside the <frameset> tags, add <frame> tags.

5 For each <frame> tag, add a frameborder attribute.

6 Set each frameborder attribute to **"0"**.

7 Open the page in a Web browser.

■ There are no visible borders between the individual frames.

NEST FRAMES

By nesting framesets within other framesets, you can create more complex frame layouts. Defining rows and columns within a single frameset creates a grid layout, while nesting frames can create rows and columns that span the length of the page or have varying numbers of frames contained within particular rows or columns.

When using nested frames, you still set the rows or columns using the top-level <frameset> tag. Then, include additional framesets to add further sublevel divisions. These sublevel framesets define the rows or columns you set in the top level frame. By creating a nested frameset for each top-level row or column, you can have varying numbers of frames in each

segment, such as one row with two frames and another row with three.

Another option is to use nested framesets in combination with top-level frames. If you create a top-level frameset with two rows and then add one frame and a nested frameset, the single frame spans the width of the nested frameset.

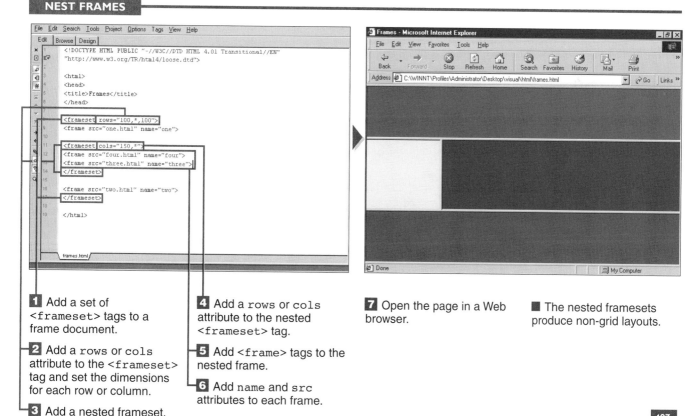

1 Add a set of <frameset> tags to a frame document.

2 Add a rows or cols attribute to the <frameset> tag and set the dimensions for each row or column.

3 Add a nested frameset.

4 Add a rows or cols attribute to the nested <frameset> tag.

5 Add <frame> tags to the nested frame.

6 Add name and src attributes to each frame.

7 Open the page in a Web browser.

■ The nested framesets produce non-grid layouts.

CREATE AN INLINE FRAME

You can create an inline frame by using the `<iframe>` tag. Unlike regular frame documents, inline frames occur within the body of a regular HTML document like any other embedded object.

Indicate the URL of the frame's content with the `src` attribute. You can use the optional `frameborder` attribute to explicitly turn the frame border on or off. In addition, you can control the height and width of the inline frame with the `height` and `width` attributes, which accept pixel values.

Inline frames are part of the HTML 4.0 specification and are supported by Internet Explorer and Netscape Navigator 6. Because most Netscape browsers do not support inline frames, be sure to provide alternative content. Instead of using the `<noframes>` tag as you would with regular frames, simply include your alternative content inside the opening and closing `<iframe>` tags.

CREATE AN INLINE FRAME

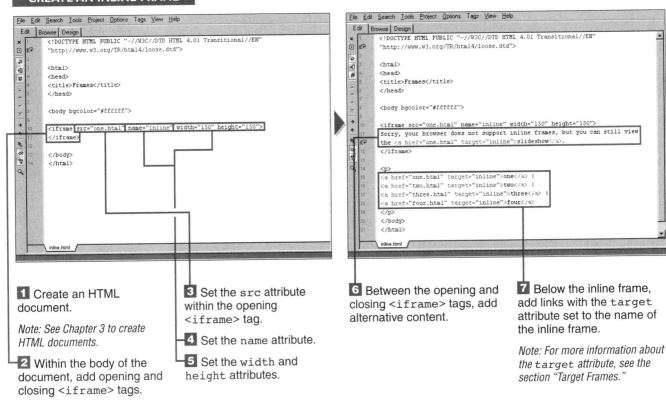

1 Create an HTML document.

Note: See Chapter 3 to create HTML documents.

2 Within the body of the document, add opening and closing `<iframe>` tags.

3 Set the `src` attribute within the opening `<iframe>` tag.

4 Set the `name` attribute.

5 Set the `width` and `height` attributes.

6 Between the opening and closing `<iframe>` tags, add alternative content.

7 Below the inline frame, add links with the `target` attribute set to the name of the inline frame.

Note: For more information about the `target` attribute, see the section "Target Frames."

MASTER IT

Can inline frames be resized by the user?

✔ No, unlike regular frames, users cannot resize inline frames.

Can I prevent scrollbars from occurring within inline frames?

✔ Yes, you can explicitly prevent scrollbars by adding the optional `scrolling` attribute and setting the value to "no." Other possible values are "yes" and "auto," which supplies scrollbars when necessary.

How can I get text to flow around an inline frame?

✔ To have text flow to the left or right of an inline frame, use the `align` attribute and set the value to `left` or `right`. With the frame aligned to the right side of the browser window, text flows to the left, and vice versa. Other values for the `align` attribute are `top`, `middle`, and `bottom`, and serve to align the frame with any adjacent text.

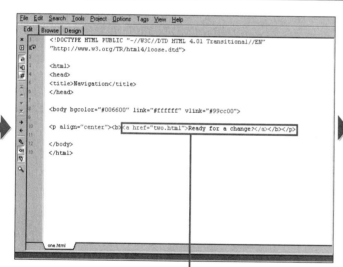

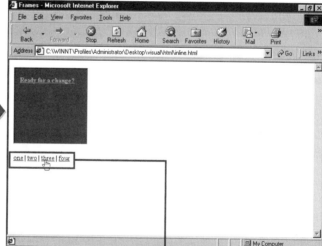

8 Create the HTML document that loads into the inline frame.

Note: Make sure to give the document the same file name you assigned as the `src` attribute in step 3.

9 Add links to additional pages.

■ Create additional optional HTML documents to load into the inline frame.

10 View the page in a Web browser that supports inline frames.

Note: If you view the page in a Web browser that does not support inline frames, the content you added in step 6 is displayed.

■ The browser renders the inline frame with the initial frame content.

11 Click a hyperlink you added below the inline frame.

■ The new content loads into the frame.

TARGET FRAMES

Y ou can have content load into specific frames by using the target attribute with <a> tags. For the value of the target attribute, use the name that you assign to the frame within your initial frameset.

Use the target attribute when you have specific frames for navigation

and content segments. For all the links within the navigation frame, set the target to the name of the content frame in order to have content load into that segment of the page. For links within the content documents themselves, there is no need to set the target attribute. Without an explicit

target, the browser loads any new content within the current frame.

If the target that you indicate does not correspond to any frame or window you have previously named, the browser opens a new window, assigns it the target name, and loads the content inside the window.

TARGET FRAMES

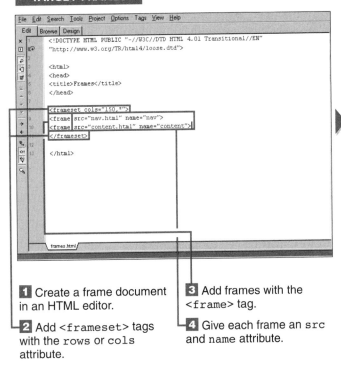

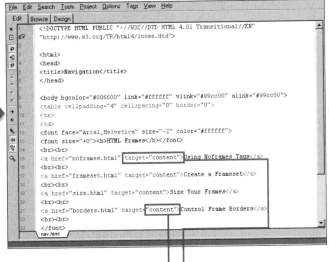

1 Create a frame document in an HTML editor.

2 Add <frameset> tags with the rows or cols attribute.

3 Add frames with the <frame> tag.

4 Give each frame an src and name attribute.

5 Create the source documents for each frame.

Note: Make sure to give the documents the file names you assigned in step 4 with the src attribute.

6 For each hyperlink you add to secondary frames, include the target attribute.

7 Set the value of the target attribute for the frame where you want the content to load.

What other values can I use with the target attribute?

✔ Besides the name of a specific frame or window, the `target` attribute accepts `_blank`, `_parent`, and `_top`. The `_blank` value loads the content into a new, unnamed window. The `_parent` value causes the content to load in the frameset that contains the frame in question. The `_top` attribute causes the document to load into the main browser window. If your principal frame document contains only one frameset, the `_parent` and `_top` values cause the same behavior. But if you have nested framesets, `_parent` indicates the immediate, nested frameset, and `_top` indicates the outermost frameset.

Can I use the target attribute to change the content of multiple frames at once?

✔ No, the `target` attribute accepts only one frame name. However, you can create functions with JavaScript that change the content of multiple frames at once. For more information on JavaScript, see Chapter 15.

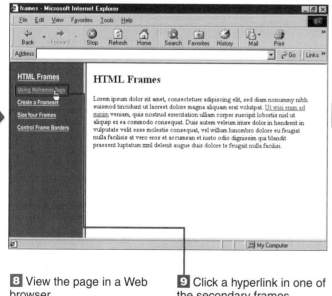

8 View the page in a Web browser.

9 Click a hyperlink in one of the secondary frames.

■ The content loads into the main content frame.

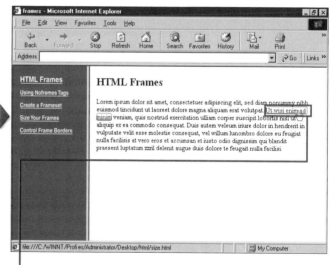

10 Click a link within the main content frame.

■ Without the `target` attribute set, the content is loaded into the currently active frame.

DEFINE A BASE TARGET

I f you have numerous links that you want to load into the same frame, you can save yourself the trouble of adding a target attribute and frame name value to every link on your page. To set a global target for all links on a page, simply add the standalone <base> tag with the target attribute to

your document. With the base target set, every link on the page loads into the specified frame.

Add the <base> tag within the opening and closing <head> tags of your document, directly after the <title> tag. The <base> tag must include an href attribute,

which specifies the base URL for the relative links on the page. For the value of the target attribute, indicate the name of the target frame just as you would for individual <a> tags. The base target is then applied to every link on the page that does not have a defined target.

DEFINE A BASE TARGET

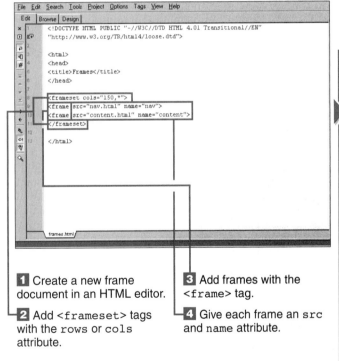

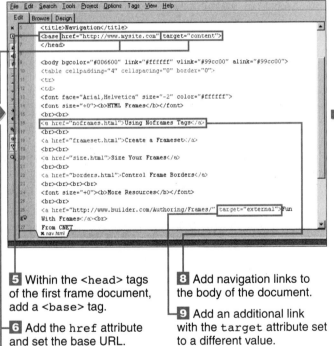

1 Create a new frame document in an HTML editor.

2 Add <frameset> tags with the rows or cols attribute.

3 Add frames with the <frame> tag.

4 Give each frame an src and name attribute.

5 Within the <head> tags of the first frame document, add a <base> tag.

6 Add the href attribute and set the base URL.

7 Add the target attribute with the name of the main content frame.

8 Add navigation links to the body of the document.

9 Add an additional link with the target attribute set to a different value.

Can I still use the target attribute with <a> tags when I have the base target set?

✔ Yes, you can still use the target attribute with individual hyperlinks when you want content to load into a frame other than the one indicated via the base target.

How do I make sure that links to external sites get loaded into a new window?

✔ To ensure that external links load into a new window, include the target attribute within the <a> tag for any external links. Set the value to _blank to launch a new unnamed window, or create a new named window by setting the target value to a name you have not yet used. Then, use that name as a target value for all external links to have them load into the same secondary window.

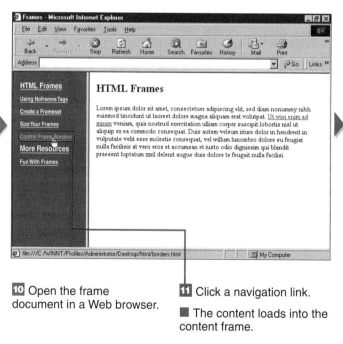

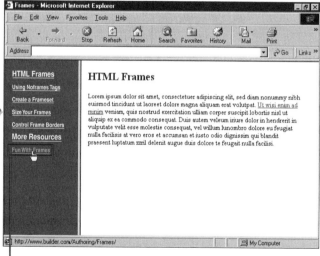

10 Open the frame document in a Web browser.

11 Click a navigation link.

■ The content loads into the content frame.

12 Click the link for which you assigned a different target value.

■ Because there is no frame with that name, the browser creates a new window and loads the content into it.

USING FRAMES FOR NAVIGATION

One common application of frames is to have one frame contain your site navigation and another frame contain the content of your site. As visitors use the navigation frame to explore your site, only the main content frame changes, and the navigation frame remains static. Thus one of the advantages to frame-based navigation is that users do not have to wait for the navigation page to

download each time a new content page loads. In addition, navigation frames are easy for Web designers to maintain, because edits to a single HTML file affect the entire site.

To create a site navigation frame, set your frameset to two columns and create two frames, one for navigation and one for content. Within the source document for the

navigation column, include links to other content areas of your site. Each link should have the `target` attribute set to the name of the content frame.

Although there are advantages to using framed navigation panels, keep in mind that users are unable to bookmark individual framed content pages.

USING FRAMES FOR NAVIGATION

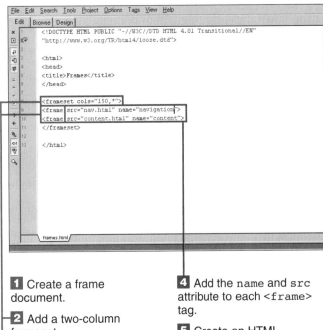

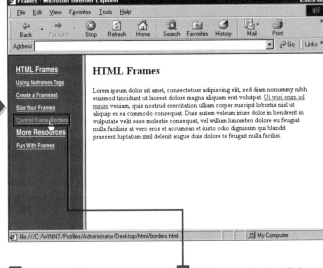

1 Create a frame document.

2 Add a two-column frameset.

3 Within the <frameset> tags, add two <frame> tags.

4 Add the `name` and `src` attribute to each <frame> tag.

5 Create an HTML document to house the navigation elements.

Note: Within the navigation document, all links should target the main content frame.

6 Open the frame document in a Web browser.

■ The navigation document occupies one of the columns.

7 Click a navigation link.

■ Content loads into the content frame.

USING FRAMES FOR BANNER ADS

A common application of frames is to have a separate frame on your site dedicated to banner advertisements. You may encounter this if you visit personal sites hosted on ISP member servers or networks composed of many independently run sites.

To create a separate frame for a banner ad, define a two row frameset as you normally would.

For the source of the banner frame, indicate the URL of the HTML document containing the banner ad.

When you code banner ads directly into regular HTML pages, you have the ability to serve a new banner ad each time the visitor loads a new page. Five page views on your site can yield five banner impressions, for example. However, when you place a banner ad within an

independent frame, the banner rotation is independent of the content page views because the frame containing the banner does not reload each time the user visits a new page. To control banner impressions, you can use a <meta> tag with a refresh attribute or create a script that rotates ads at specific intervals.

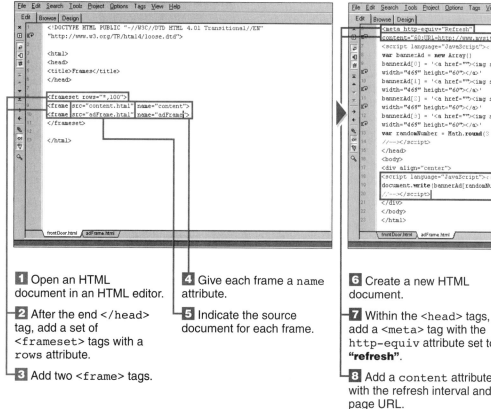

1 Open an HTML document in an HTML editor.

2 After the end </head> tag, add a set of <frameset> tags with a rows attribute.

3 Add two <frame> tags.

4 Give each frame a name attribute.

5 Indicate the source document for each frame.

6 Create a new HTML document.

7 Within the <head> tags, add a <meta> tag with the http-equiv attribute set to **"refresh"**.

8 Add a content attribute with the refresh interval and page URL.

9 Add a script to change the banner image on every page reload (see Chapter 15).

■ A random banner ad is served each time the page loads.

AN INTRODUCTION TO CASCADING STYLE SHEETS

Cascading style sheets provide authors with the means to apply style to HTML documents. Although it is certainly possible to create complex presentations using HTML, it is important to remember that HTML is a markup language focused primarily on content rather than style. HTML tells the browser which portions of the page are paragraphs, which portions are tables, and so on, but it has limited capabilities when it comes to controlling style and presentation. Cascading style sheets fill that void, allowing you to apply styles to fonts, margins, borders, and every element on a Web page.

More importantly, style sheets allow you to separate presentation from content. When style elements are contained in a separate document, they can be applied to any number of pages or across multiple sites, increasing design consistency and facilitating global alterations. In addition, by separating style from content, you create portable documents to which different styles and presentations can be applied depending on the destination of the pages.

The Cascade

There are three ways to implement style sheets: You can create an external style sheet, create a document-level style sheet within the head of an HTML document, or apply styles to individual tags using a `style` attribute. All three techniques can be used simultaneously, with the styles being applied in a cascading effect. Styles applied directly to a tag using a `style` attribute override conflicting rules declared at the document level. In turn, these document-level styles take precedence over conflicting rules in linked external style sheets.

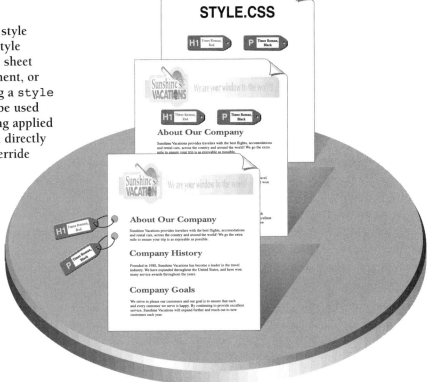

Define Rules

When you define styles, you create a selector rule and include appropriate style properties and values. These rules take the form of `selector [and]`. Within the curly braces of a style rule, you can add multiple properties as long as they are separated with semicolons. The selector portion of the rule can be a single HTML tag, a series of HTML tags, or a period-defined class name. Both tag slectors and style classes are explored in this chapter, in the sections "Using Tag Selectors" and "Define Classes."

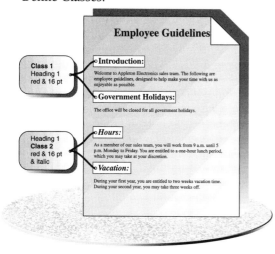

CSS Browser Support

Implementing style sheets presents a real challenge for Web designers, since very few browsers fully support the W3C's CSS specification. Version 4 of the two major browsers (Microsoft Internet Explorer and Netscape Navigator) featured some degree of support for style sheets, with each new version offering increased support. In fact, the latest release of the Netscape Navigator browser, version 6, offers full compliance with the CSS specification and renders style sheets correctly on both Windows and Macintosh platforms. However, there are still

many visitors using legacy browsers that offer little or no support for style sheets. Before you implement CSS, be sure to consider how to handle presentation on non-compliant browsers.

The CSS Box Model

Cascading style sheets use a simple box model to format elements on a Web page. When you apply style sheets to HTML pages, think of every piece of content, from a paragraph of text to a list, as a box with padding, borders, margins, and dimensions that you can control via style sheet attributes. Later in this chapter, in the sections "Position Page Elements," "Layer Elements with Z-Index," and "Control Visibility," you will see how you can use this model to position elements on a page, overlap divisions, and control the visibility of boxes.

DEFINE INLINE STYLE ATTRIBUTES

One way to apply styles is to associate inline styles with individual HTML tags in your document. To define inline styles, use the `style` attribute with the HTML tag.

Within the opening tag of an element, add the `style` attribute with a list of style properties and corresponding values. For example, you can change the color of an individual hyperlink by adding the `style` attribute and `color` property to the opening `<a>` tag.

There are not many advantages to using inline style attributes. Unlike style rules defined in document-level and external style sheets, inline styles cannot be applied to multiple elements. In addition, if you want to change the style attributes, you must edit each individual tag rather than alter a single global style rule. For these reasons, inline style attributes do not offer all the benefits of document-level or external style sheets.

DEFINE INLINE STYLE ATTRIBUTES

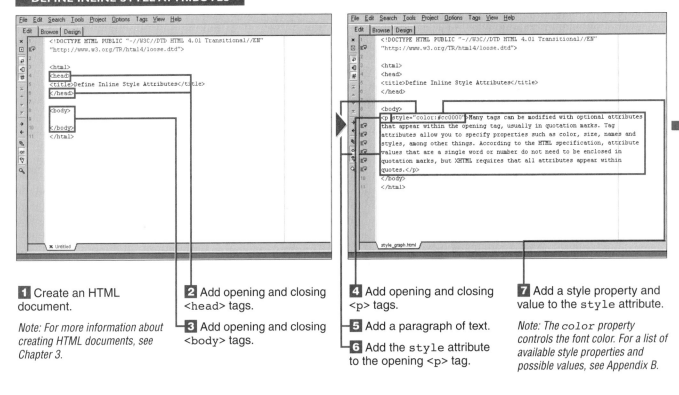

1 Create an HTML document.

Note: For more information about creating HTML documents, see Chapter 3.

2 Add opening and closing `<head>` tags.

3 Add opening and closing `<body>` tags.

4 Add opening and closing `<p>` tags.

5 Add a paragraph of text.

6 Add the `style` attribute to the opening `<p>` tag.

7 Add a style property and value to the `style` attribute.

Note: The `color` property controls the font color. For a list of available style properties and possible values, see Appendix B.

If I use inline style attributes with <a> tags, does that override link color attributes I set via the <body> tag?

✔ Yes, for that specific hyperlink, the style applied overrides global link colors. Keep in mind that the color you apply to the link using inline attributes also overrides visited and active link colors.

Can I use both inline style attributes and standard HTML tags to affect appearance?

✔ Yes. For instance, you might apply font colors and weights using both standard HTML tags and styles. This way, browsers that do not support style sheets or attributes can still format elements as you intended.

If I use both style properties and HTML formatting tags, do the style properties override the HTML formatting?

✔ In most cases style properties take precedence over HTML formatting in browsers that support CSS. However, there are instances where HTML formatting will be applied rather than conflicting style rules. For instance, if you set the alignment of an <img> tag using the HTML align attribute, this often overrides alignments set in style sheets.

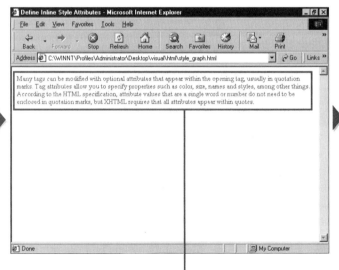

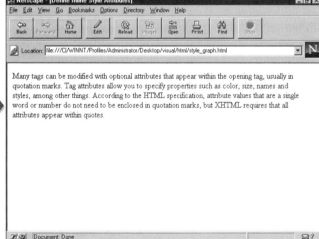

8 Save the document, and then view the page in a Web browser that supports style sheets.

■ The paragraph is formatted according to the inline style attribute.

9 View the page in a Web browser that does not support style sheets.

■ Older browsers and browsers that are not CSS compliant ignore the style attribute.

CREATE A DOCUMENT-LEVEL STYLE SHEET

Y ou can set style properties for an entire Web page by using document-level style sheets. You define document-level style sheets within the head of the HTML page. Style rules that you define this way can then be applied to multiple elements throughout the page, and when you need to alter the style, you only have to edit the style sheet rather than each occurrence.

When you create document-level style sheets, all style rules that you define appear within opening and closing <style> tags in the document's head. Style rules should be enclosed within HTML comment indicators so that older browsers that do not support the <style> tags do not render style rules as regular content. Newer browsers that support the <style> tag process the CSS rules correctly and ignore these HTML comments.

You can define style rules for particular HTML elements, such as headings or paragraphs, or create named classes that can be applied to tags via the class attribute. For more information about classes, see the section "Define Classes."

CREATE A DOCUMENT-LEVEL STYLE SHEET

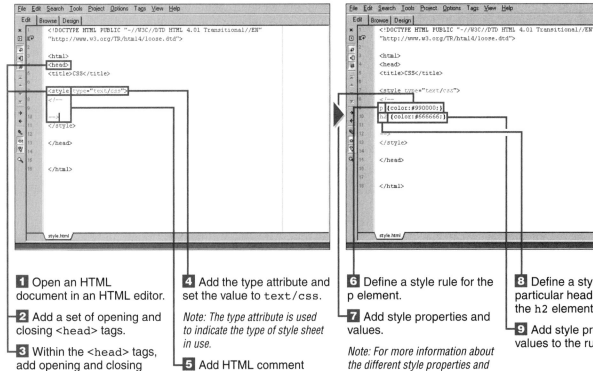

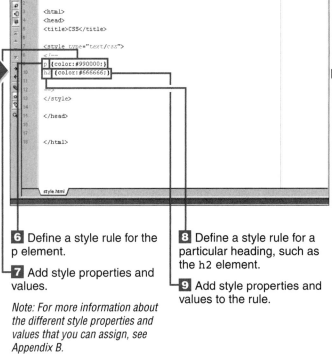

■1 Open an HTML document in an HTML editor.

■2 Add a set of opening and closing <head> tags.

■3 Within the <head> tags, add opening and closing <style> tags.

■4 Add the type attribute and set the value to text/css.

Note: The type attribute is used to indicate the type of style sheet in use.

■5 Add HTML comment indicators to hide style rules from older browsers.

■6 Define a style rule for the p element.

■7 Add style properties and values.

Note: For more information about the different style properties and values that you can assign, see Appendix B.

■8 Define a style rule for a particular heading, such as the h2 element.

■9 Add style properties and values to the rule.

Can I use document-level styles along with inline style attributes?

✔ Yes, you can combine document-level style sheets with inline styles. Any inline styles you apply to individual HTML elements override global styles set at the document level.

Besides text/css, what other values are there for the type attribute?

✔ Currently, the only other value you might use within the type attribute is "text/javascript". This style type refers to JavaScript style sheets supported by some Netscape browsers.

What attributes can be applied to <style> tags?

✔ Optional attributes for the <style> tag include title, media, dir, and lang. Use the media attribute to indicate the type of display for which the style sheet is intended. Possible media values include screen, tty (teletype), tv, projection, handheld, print, braille, aural, and all. The dir attribute is used to indicate the direction of any text set with the title attribute, and can be set to either ltr (left-to-right) or rtl (right-to-left). The lang attribute specifies the language used for the <style> tag title and accepts two-character ISO language names, such as "en" for English.

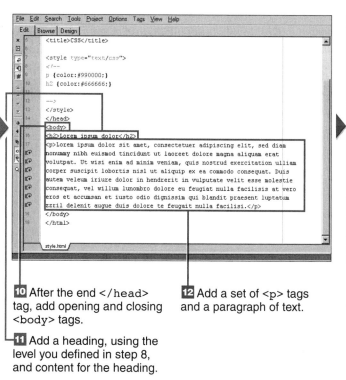

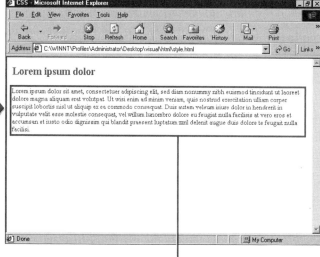

10 After the end </head> tag, add opening and closing <body> tags.

11 Add a heading, using the level you defined in step 8, and content for the heading.

12 Add a set of <p> tags and a paragraph of text.

13 Save the document, and then view the page in a CSS-compliant Web browser.

■ The style rules defined in the document are applied to the content in the body of the page.

CREATE AN EXTERNAL STYLE SHEET

You can define style rules and apply them to multiple Web pages by creating an external style sheet. External style sheets are text documents with a .css file extension that contain all of the style rules you choose to define.

You specify external style sheets within the head of an HTML document using the <link> tag. Within the <link> tag, include the href attribute and indicate the

location of the style sheet on the Web server. In addition, you should include the type="text/css" attribute and the rel="stylesheet" attribute with the <link> tag. The rel attribute indicates the relationship of the linked document to the HTML page.

External style sheets offer several advantages over document-level style sheets. As previously noted,

external style sheets can be applied to any number of Web pages. When you need to change the style rules, you only need to edit a single document to affect changes throughout your site. In addition, you can theoretically link to several different style sheets and offer the user the opportunity to choose a preferred style.

CREATE AN EXTERNAL STYLE SHEET

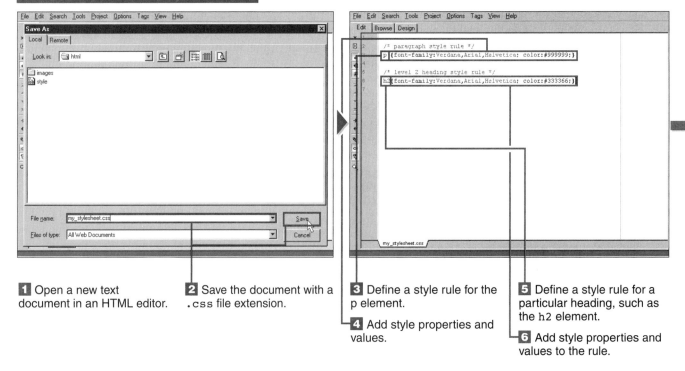

1 Open a new text document in an HTML editor.

2 Save the document with a .css file extension.

3 Define a style rule for the p element.

4 Add style properties and values.

5 Define a style rule for a particular heading, such as the h2 element.

6 Add style properties and values to the rule.

Can I use HTML comments within external style sheets?

✔ No. To add comments, you must use special style comments. For more information, see the section "Comment within Style Sheets."

Can I link to more than one external style sheet?

✔ Yes. According to the CSS standard, you can link to more than one style sheet to have the browser present the user with the choice of which style sheet to use. In practice, however, some browsers simply load multiple style sheets and have style rules in the last sheet override previously defined styles.

Is there more than one way to load external style sheets?

✔ Yes. In addition to the `<link>` tag, you can use the `@import url` command within the `<style>` tags to load an external style sheet. This command takes the form of `@import url(style.css)`, where `style.css` is the path of the style sheet.

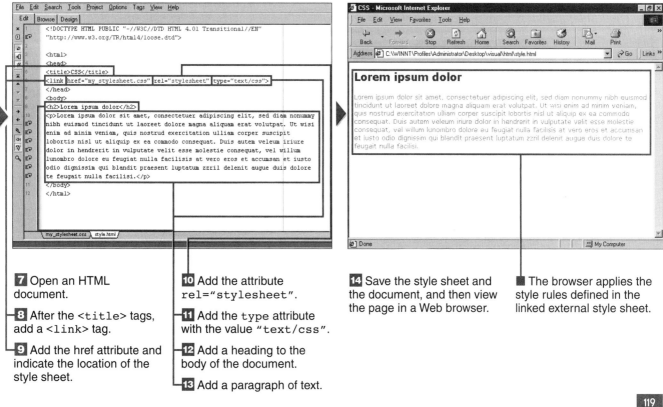

7 Open an HTML document.

8 After the `<title>` tags, add a `<link>` tag.

9 Add the href attribute and indicate the location of the style sheet.

10 Add the attribute `rel="stylesheet"`.

11 Add the `type` attribute with the value `"text/css"`.

12 Add a heading to the body of the document.

13 Add a paragraph of text.

14 Save the style sheet and the document, and then view the page in a Web browser.

■ The browser applies the style rules defined in the linked external style sheet.

USING TAG SELECTORS

You can apply styles to a particular HTML tag by creating a style rule associated with a tag selector. When you use tag selectors in your style rules, the style properties are applied to every instance of that tag throughout the HTML document.

A tag selector style rule is defined by the name of the HTML tag, or the characters contained within an opening tag of an element. For instance, you define rules for paragraphs by using the <p> tag selector followed by style properties and values enclosed within a set of curly braces ({ }). You can include multiple style properties within the braces as long as they are separated by semicolons.

You can apply styles to multiple HTML tags by defining a list of selectors. For example, to apply the same style to multiple levels of headings, list the heading tags for which you want the style to apply, including a comma between each tag. You can also create contextual style rules that apply a style to a tag when it occurs in conjunction with another tag.

USING TAG SELECTORS

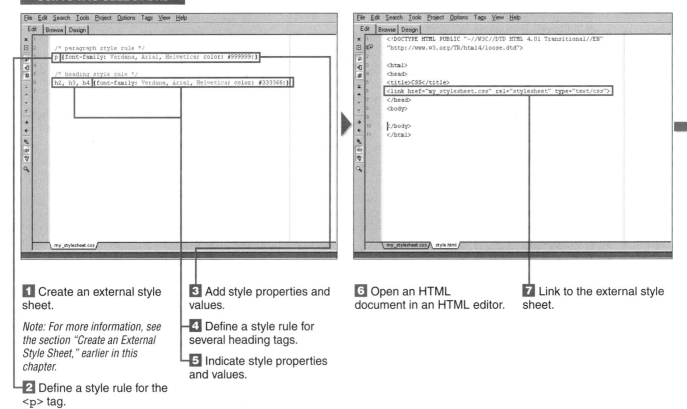

1 Create an external style sheet.

Note: For more information, see the section "Create an External Style Sheet," earlier in this chapter.

2 Define a style rule for the <p> tag.

3 Add style properties and values.

4 Define a style rule for several heading tags.

5 Indicate style properties and values.

6 Open an HTML document in an HTML editor.

7 Link to the external style sheet.

Are there guidelines about letter case when creating style rules?

✔ No, browsers that support style sheets ignore whether style rules are uppercase or lowercase, but for consistency and readability, it is better to choose a case convention and use it consistently throughout your style sheets.

Can any HTML tag be used as a style selector?

✔ Yes, style selectors can be defined for any HTML tag.

When using contextual selectors, do the HTML tags have to exactly match what is indicated in the style selector?

✔ No. In your HTML document, you can have tags nested within others and still have the contextual selector apply. For instance, the tag sequence P UL SPAN would still match the pattern in a contextual selector defined for P SPAN.

When defining multiple rules for the same tag, which style rule is applied?

✔ The style rule that is closer to the tag takes precedence—that is, a rule defined internally takes precedence over an externally defined style rule. If the location is the same, the more specific contextual selector is applied over a more general tag selector.

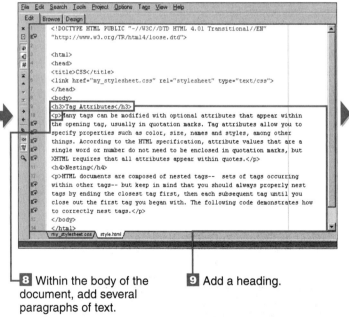

8 Within the body of the document, add several paragraphs of text.

9 Add a heading.

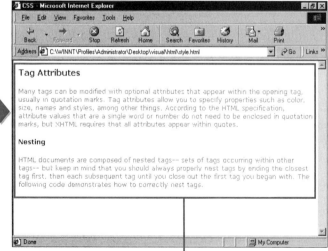

10 Save the style sheet and the document, and then view the page in a Web browser.

■ Styles are applied to the tags for which you created rules.

DEFINE CLASSES

You can define several different styles for the same tag or create generic classes that can be applied to a variety of HTML tags.

Unlike style rules associated with tag selectors, style classes are not automatically applied to every instance of an HTML tag. Rather, you reference classes explicitly by

adding the class attribute to the opening tag of an HTML element.

To define classes to be used with a specific tag, indicate the tag selector and then add a period and a class name. For generic classes not associated with a particular tag, simply start with the period and add the name.

Within the opening tag of the HTML element, add the class attribute and set the value to the name of the class. Class names can contain letters, numbers, and hyphens, but they must always begin with a letter.

DEFINE CLASSES

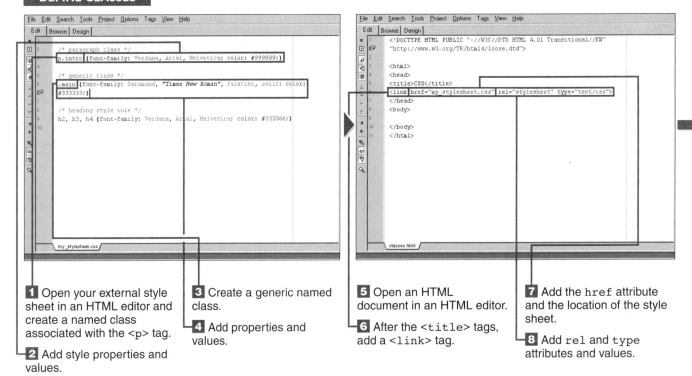

1 Open your external style sheet in an HTML editor and create a named class associated with the <p> tag.

2 Add style properties and values.

3 Create a generic named class.

4 Add properties and values.

5 Open an HTML document in an HTML editor.

6 After the <title> tags, add a <link> tag.

7 Add the href attribute and the location of the style sheet.

8 Add rel and type attributes and values.

Can I define nested class names?

✔ No, class names cannot be nested. For instance, you cannot create a class called `p.main` and a nested class called `p.main.bold`. Instead, you should create a second class and list all the appropriate properties and values.

Can I set up classes in both document-level and external style sheets?

✔ Yes, you can define classes at the document level and in external style sheets.

If I create a style rule for an HTML tag and then create classes for the tag, are the style rules for the tag applied to the classes?

✔ Yes. Classes inherit the style rules defined in the main tag rule. For instance, if you define the `color` property for the p element, this color carries over to any p classes you create. However, you can override this inheritance by specifying different property values within the class itself.

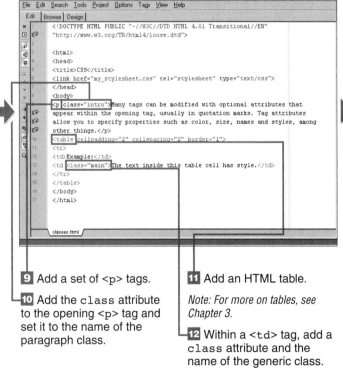

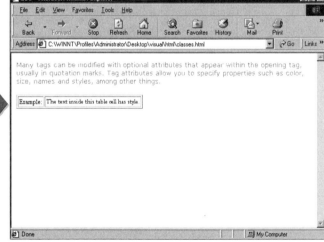

9 Add a set of <p> tags.

10 Add the `class` attribute to the opening <p> tag and set it to the name of the paragraph class.

11 Add an HTML table.

Note: For more on tables, see Chapter 3.

12 Within a <td> tag, add a `class` attribute and the name of the generic class.

13 Save the style sheet and the document, and then view the page in a Web browser.

■ The properties for the generic class are applied to the table content.

■ The properties for the paragraph class are applied to the paragraph.

DEFINE ID ATTRIBUTES

In addition to regular style classes, you can also create ID classes and apply them to an individual tag by using the id attribute.

ID classes are similar in form to regular classes, except that instead of using a period to define a class name, you use a pound (#) character. For instance, you might

define a body ID class such as body#about {background-color: #cc9900}. You would then include the id attribute within the <body> tag and set the value to "**about**" to apply this class to the document.

ID values within a document are supposed to be unique to a specific tag, so in theory you cannot apply

an ID-defined class name to multiple tags. In practice, some browsers allow you to apply the same ID class name to multiple tags while others do not.

If you use ID classes, apply them to tags that only appear once in a document. In most cases, standard period-defined classes are a better solution.

DEFINE ID ATTRIBUTES

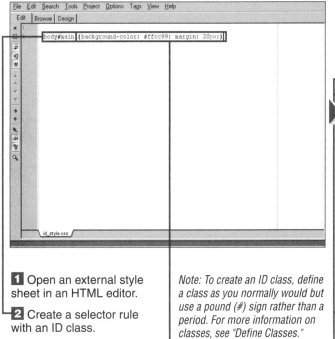

1 Open an external style sheet in an HTML editor.

2 Create a selector rule with an ID class.

Note: To create an ID class, define a class as you normally would but use a pound (#) sign rather than a period. For more information on classes, see "Define Classes."

3 Add properties and attributes.

4 Open an HTML document in an HTML editor.

5 Reference the style sheet using the <link> tag.

6 Add an id attribute to the tag for which you created the style rule.

7 For the value of the id attribute, indicate the name of the ID class.

■ When you view the page in a browser, the ID class is applied to the HTML tag.

SET STYLE PROPERTIES WITH <DIV> AND <SPAN> TAGS

You can apply styles to divisions of text rather than specific HTML elements through the <div> and <span> tags. When style classes are applied using the class attribute, you can control the presentation of sections of the page rather than content associated with specific formatting tags.

The <div> element divides an HTML page into organizational pieces the way you might divide an article into a headline, byline, lead paragraph, and body sections. You can use <div> tags to organize a Web page in a similar fashion and then apply styles to each division by adding the class attribute to the opening <div> tag.

<span> elements are used to set off a specific portion of text so that you can alter the appearance of just that segment. For instance, you might want to apply a different style to one sentence or a few words rather than an entire paragraph. You can accomplish this by setting off the text with <span> tags and then referencing a style class via the class attribute. You can even nest <span> tags within other <span> tags.

SET STYLE PROPERTIES WITH <DIV> AND <SPAN> TAGS

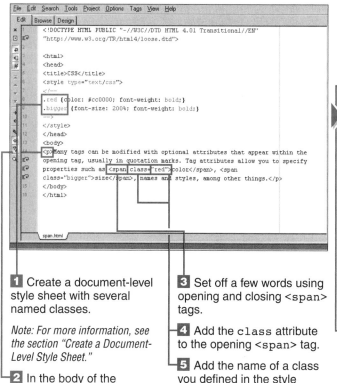

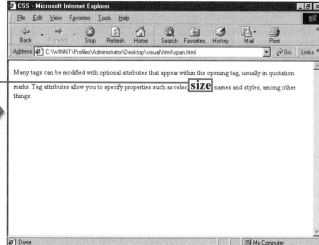

1 Create a document-level style sheet with several named classes.

Note: For more information, see the section "Create a Document-Level Style Sheet."

2 In the body of the document, add a paragraph of text.

3 Set off a few words using opening and closing <span> tags.

4 Add the class attribute to the opening <span> tag.

5 Add the name of a class you defined in the style sheet.

6 Save the style sheet, and then view the page in a Web browser.

■ The style is applied only to the text contained within the <span> tags.

Note: You can apply styles to <div> tags in the same way, using either the class attribute or the id attribute with ID classes. For more on ID classes, see "Define ID Attributes."

COMMENT WITHIN STYLE SHEETS

You can add production notes and comments to document-level and external style sheets by using special style comments.

Style comments, like those used in C programming, begin with a forward slash and an asterisk (/*) and end with another asterisk and forward slash (*/). Any text occurring within style comments is treated as white space and not processed by the browser.

Browsers that recognize styles ignore HTML comments within `<style>` tags, so you can use them to "hide" your style rules from older browsers (see the section "Create a Document Level Style Sheet"). However, you cannot use HTML comments within external style sheets.

You can use comments to organize your style rules and provide additional notation to explain how you are implementing individual styles. If you define several classes, note how each class should be applied within the HTML document. This is particularly helpful when you have multiple designers collaborating on the same project.

COMMENT WITHIN STYLE SHEETS

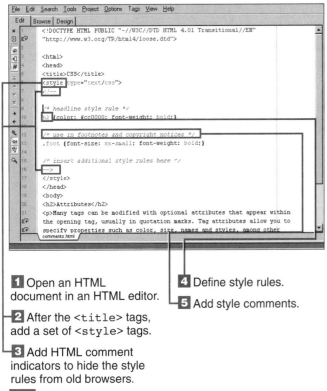

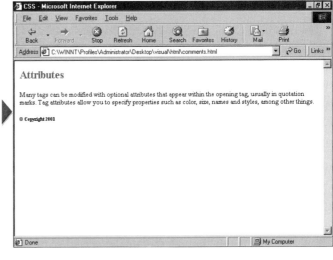

1 Open an HTML document in an HTML editor.

2 After the `<title>` tags, add a set of `<style>` tags.

3 Add HTML comment indicators to hide the style rules from old browsers.

4 Define style rules.

5 Add style comments.

6 Save the document, and then open the page in a Web browser.

■ Style comments are not rendered by the browser.

SET PAGE MARGINS

You can set the margins of a Web page using style sheet margin properties. Unlike HTML margin attributes for the <body> tag, style sheets have properties to control each of the four margins individually so that you can set specific values for the top, right, bottom, and left margins using margin-top, margin-right, margin-bottom and margin-left. Internet Explorer 4+ and Netscape Navigator 6 also

support the shorthand margin property that lets you define these values without listing all of the individual property names.

You can include the margin properties within a style rule associated with the body selector. List the specific margin properties and corresponding values, or use the shorthand margin property with the values you want to set. You can include a single value to

affect all four margins at once, such as margin: 0px, or include multiple values. If you include two values, such as margin: 10px 20px, the first value controls the top and bottom margins, while the second controls the left and right margins. A margin property with three values sets the top, side, and bottom margins, in that order. Include four values to set the top, right, bottom, and left margins.

SET PAGE MARGINS

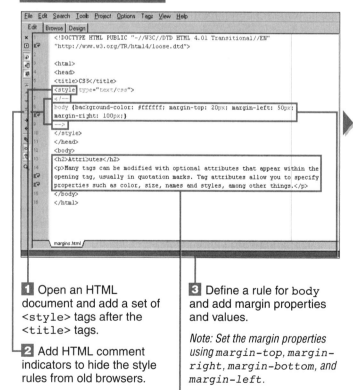

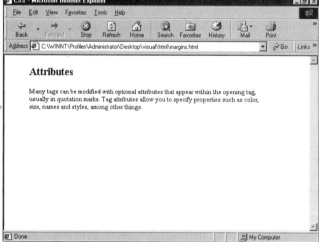

1 Open an HTML document and add a set of <style> tags after the <title> tags.

2 Add HTML comment indicators to hide the style rules from old browsers.

3 Define a rule for body and add margin properties and values.

Note: Set the margin properties using margin-top, margin-right, margin-bottom, and margin-left.

4 Add content to the body.

5 Save the document, and then view the page in a CSS-compliant Web browser.

■ The margins are rendered according to the values set in the style rule.

DEFINE FONT PROPERTIES

Y ou can use style sheets to define the appearance of fonts in your Web pages. Style sheet properties provide additional control not offered via HTML <font> tags, such as font size, font weight, and line height.

When defining font properties, you can use tag selector style rules to associate font styles with particular tags, or you can set up regular or generic classes and reference them

with the class attribute. Style sheets support a variety of font-related properties, including font-family, font-size, and font-weight. Use the font-family property to include a list of fonts the browser should use when rendering the document. Set the size of the font with the font-size property, which accepts sizes expressed as points, pixels, percentages, or keywords such as

x-small, small, medium, large, and x-large.

The font-weight property is the style equivalent of the <b> tag, which controls the boldness of a font. You can set the value to bold, or you can indicate a degree of lightness or boldness by setting the value to a multiple of 100, 100 being the lightest and 900 being the boldest.

DEFINE FONT PROPERTIES

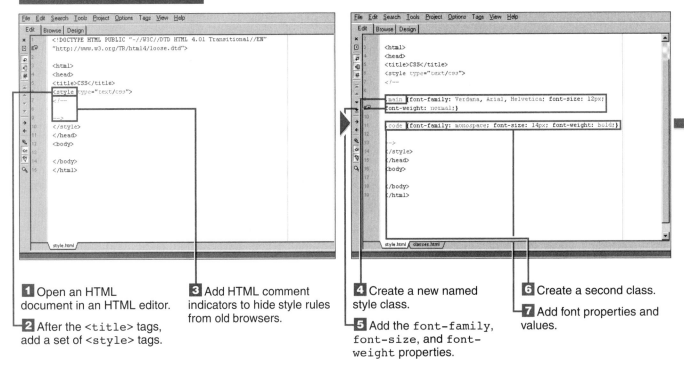

1 Open an HTML document in an HTML editor.

2 After the <title> tags, add a set of <style> tags.

3 Add HTML comment indicators to hide style rules from old browsers.

4 Create a new named style class.

5 Add the font-family, font-size, and font-weight properties.

6 Create a second class.

7 Add font properties and values.

Can I include any font name within the `font-family` property?

✔ Yes, your `font-family` list can include any font name. If the user does not have the font installed, the browser will attempt to use the next font in the font-family list. If a font name has multiple words, like "Times New Roman" for instance, enclose that name in quotation marks.

Can I indicate generic font types rather than specific fonts?

✔ Yes. The CSS standard supports five generic font types: serif, sans-serif, cursive, fantasy, and monospace. You can use these alone or combine them with font names in your font-family list.

How do I change the color of a font?

✔ Add the `color` attribute and value to the tag selector or class. The `color` attribute is not technically associated with font properties, but rather controls the foreground color of an element.

How do I italicize fonts?

✔ Use the `font-style` property. The default `font-style` is `normal`, but you can set the value to `italic` or `oblique`.

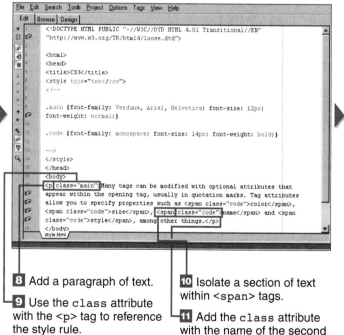

8 Add a paragraph of text.

9 Use the `class` attribute with the `<p>` tag to reference the style rule.

10 Isolate a section of text within `<span>` tags.

11 Add the `class` attribute with the name of the second class.

12 View the document in a Web browser.

■ The paragraph text is formatted according to the font properties.

■ The text within the `<span>` section is rendered with the font you specified in step 7.

DEFINE HYPERLINK PSEUDO-CLASSES

You can define the appearance of links using pseudo-classes. Unlike regular style classes, pseudo-classes are defined using a tag selector and a colon rather than a period. They also have predefined names, so you cannot create unique names for pseudo-classes as you would for regular style classes.

There are three principal pseudo-classes used to control the appearance of hyperlinks. a:link defines the general appearance of

links on a page. The a:active pseudo-class controls the appearance of a link when the user initially clicks a selection, and a:visited defines how the link looks if the user has already visited a page.

In addition, there is a fourth pseudo-class, a:hover, that lets you define the appearance of a link when the user moves the mouse over a hyperlink. Although a:hover is part of the CSS2

specification, it is currently supported only by Versions 4 and higher of Internet Explorer and Netscape Navigator 6.

Of course, you can always define link appearance using regular HTML attributes for the <body> tag, but with the a:hover pseudo-class, CSS offers an additional element of interactivity not available via HTML.

DEFINE HYPERLINK PSEUDO-CLASSES

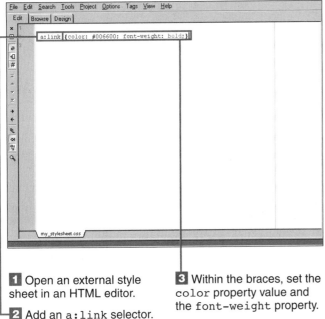

1 Open an external style sheet in an HTML editor.

2 Add an a:link selector.

3 Within the braces, set the color property value and the font-weight property.

4 Add an a:active selector and set the color property and the font-weight property.

5 Add an a:visited selector and set the color property.

6 Add an a:hover selector and set the color property and the font-weight property.

What happens if I indicate a font size or font weight for the hover pseudo-class that differs from the properties I set for the other link classes?

✔ If you change the size or weight of the font for one of the dynamic pseudo-classes (`active` or `hover`), any text surrounding the link shifts accordingly when the user moves the mouse over or clicks the link. This effect can be jarring on slower dial-up connections.

Are there certain colors that should not be used for hyperlinks?

✔ If you are coding for accessibility, avoid red and green for hyperlinks, since color-blind visitors have trouble distinguishing these hues. Lighter shades of gray are appropriate for the visited state, but generally not for the global link color.

How can I create links that are not underlined?

✔ To create hyperlinks without the underline effect, use the `text-decoration` property and set the value to `none`.

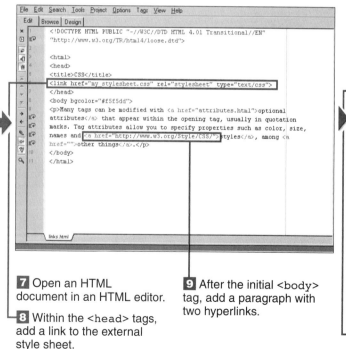

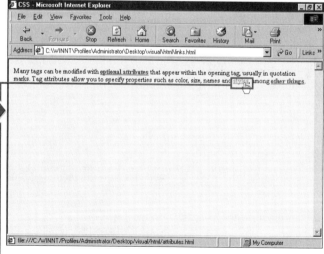

7 Open an HTML document in an HTML editor.

8 Within the `<head>` tags, add a link to the external style sheet.

9 After the initial `<body>` tag, add a paragraph with two hyperlinks.

10 Save the style sheet and the document, and then view the page in a Web browser.

11 Hover your mouse over the link.

■ In Versions 4 and higher of Internet Explorer and Version 6 of Netscape Navigator, the link's appearance is altered based on the `a:hover` style properties.

DEFINE MULTIPLE CLASSES FOR HYPERLINKS

You can combine pseudo-classes with regular classes to apply different styles to different sets of hyperlinks. By defining multiple classes for the a element, you could create one class for hyperlinks that appear on a dark background, such as a side navigation bar, and another class

for regular hyperlinks within the main content body. Or, you might have one class for external links and another for internal links.

Like any HTML element, you can set up multiple classes associated with the <a> tag by creating period-defined classes, such as a.navigation and a.external.

For each of these classes, you can create pseudo-class states by appending the pseudo-class to the end of the regular class. For example, the hover state for the a.navigation and a.external classes would be defined as a.navigation:hover and a.external:hover.

DEFINE MULTIPLE CLASSES FOR HYPERLINKS

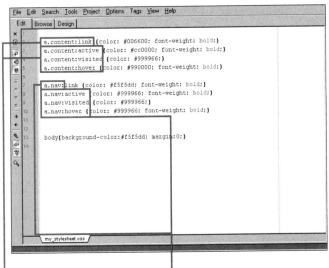

1 Create an external style sheet.

2 Define a named class for the a element.

3 For the named class, add pseudo-class properties and values.

Note: For more information, see "Define Hyperlink Pseudo-Classes."

4 Define a second class for the a element.

5 Add pseudo-class properties and values.

6 Within the body of the HTML page, create a table layout.

Note: For more information on tables, see Chapter 3.

7 Set the cellpadding, cellspacing, width, and border attributes.

8 Add different background colors to the table cells using bgcolor attributes.

Can pseudo-classes be used in contextual selectors?

✔ Yes. You can define a contextual selector, such as A IMG, where the `<a>` tag occurs with an image tag, and assign pseudo-class properties to it.

Is there any limit on the number of classes I can associate with the `<a>` tag?

✔ No, you can define as many classes for hyperlinks as you like. Keep in mind, though, that having too much variation in link color on a single page might confuse visitors.

Are pseudo-class names case sensitive?

✔ No, they are case insensitive, although the convention is to have pseudo-class names all lowercase.

Which HTML elements support pseudo-classes?

✔ CSS 1 defines pseudo-classes for the `<a>` tag as well as two pseudo-classes associated with the `<p>` tag: `:first-letter` and `:first-line`. For more information on these pseudo-classes, see the section "Define Paragraph Pseudo-Classes."

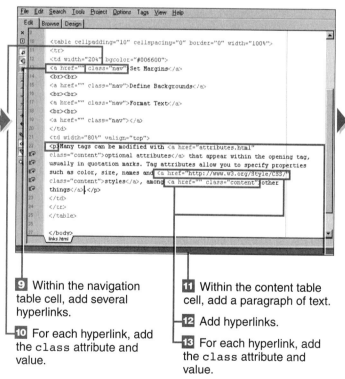

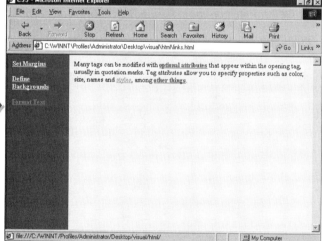

9 Within the navigation table cell, add several hyperlinks.

10 For each hyperlink, add the class attribute and value.

11 Within the content table cell, add a paragraph of text.

12 Add hyperlinks.

13 For each hyperlink, add the class attribute and value.

14 Save the document, and then view the page in a Web browser.

■ Different styles are applied to the two `<a>` tag classes.

DEFINE PARAGRAPH PSEUDO-CLASSES

S tyle sheets offer pseudo-classes that let you duplicate style conventions used in traditional print media. Two pseudo-classes associated with the paragraph element allow you to define style properties for the first line of text as well as the first letter. However, very few browsers accurately render these paragraph pseudo-classes, so you should test

your pages thoroughly when implementing these styles.

You can use the :first-line pseudo-class to apply distinct styles to the first line of a paragraph. You can use this pseudo-class to duplicate styles often seen in newspapers and magazines, where the first line of text might be in all uppercase or have different word-spacing.

You can use the :first-letter pseudo-class to create initial caps, or drop caps, at the beginning of each paragraph. When you define a drop cap, the first letter of the paragraph is formatted according to your style properties and docked to the left, with the remaining text flowing to the right.

DEFINE PARAGRAPH PSEUDO-CLASSES

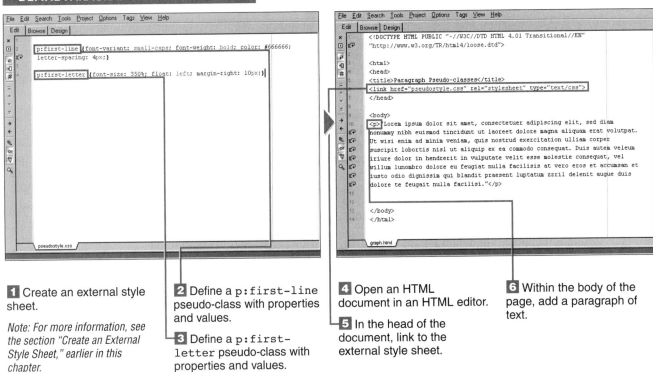

1 Create an external style sheet.

Note: For more information, see the section "Create an External Style Sheet," earlier in this chapter.

2 Define a p:first-line pseudo-class with properties and values.

3 Define a p:first-letter pseudo-class with properties and values.

4 Open an HTML document in an HTML editor.

5 In the head of the document, link to the external style sheet.

6 Within the body of the page, add a paragraph of text.

What style properties can be applied to the first-line pseudo-class?

✔ For the `first-line` pseudo-class, you can apply the following style properties: font properties, color and background properties, word-spacing, letter-spacing, text-decoration, vertical align, text-transform, line-height, and clear.

What style properties can be applied to the first-letter pseudo-class?

✔ For the `first-letter` pseudo-class, you can apply the following style properties: font properties, color and background properties, text-decoration, vertical-align, text-transform, line-height, margin properties, padding properties, border properties, float, and clear.

How does the browser define the first line of a paragraph?

✔ How the browser defines the first line of a paragraph depends on the current width of the browser window.

How does the first-letter pseudo-class handle paragraphs that begin with quotation marks?

✔ Normally if a paragraph begins with quotes, both the opening quotation mark and the first letter are rendered according to the styles defined in the `first-letter` pseudo-class.

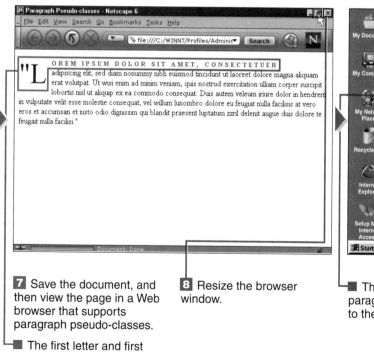

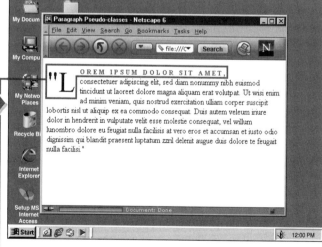

7 Save the document, and then view the page in a Web browser that supports paragraph pseudo-classes.

■ The first letter and first line of the paragraph are rendered according to the style properties set.

8 Resize the browser window.

■ The first line of the paragraph shifts according to the available space.

CREATE LISTS WITH STYLES

You can define the appearance of ordered and unordered lists using list properties available in CSS. Most of these list properties replace corresponding HTML list attributes and control items such as the type of bullet or ordering scheme.

Style sheets offer control over list appearances with the style

properties list-style-image and list-style-position, which do not have corresponding HTML attributes and can only be controlled via style sheets. The list-style-image property, supported by Internet Explorer and Netscape Navigator 6, allows you to use a custom image rather than a standard bullet in unordered lists.

You can use the list-style-position property with the value set to "**inside**" to have list item content flow around the list bullets. With the value set to "**outside**", the content indents to the left of the bullet or number item as it normally would in HTML-formatted lists.

CREATE LISTS WITH STYLES

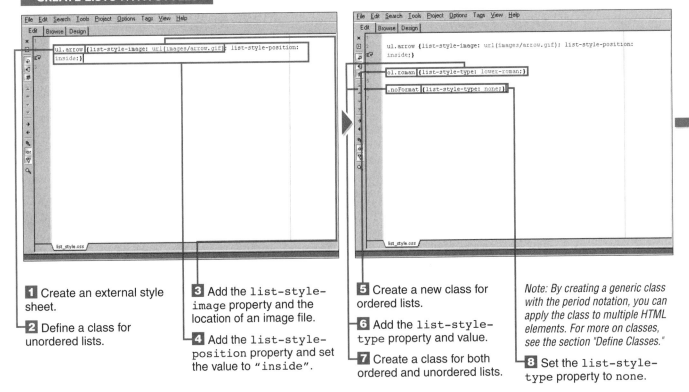

1 Create an external style sheet.

2 Define a class for unordered lists.

3 Add the list-style-image property and the location of an image file.

4 Add the list-style-position property and set the value to "inside".

5 Create a new class for ordered lists.

6 Add the list-style-type property and value.

7 Create a class for both ordered and unordered lists.

Note: By creating a generic class with the period notation, you can apply the class to multiple HTML elements. For more on classes, see the section "Define Classes."

8 Set the list-style-type property to none.

Can I create lists without any bullets or numbers?

✔ Yes. Set the list-style-type property to "**none**" to create lists without bullets or numbering sequences.

What are the possible values for the list-style-type property?

✔ For unordered lists, the list-style-type property can be set to disc, circle, square, or none. For ordered lists, possible values are decimal, lower-roman, upper-roman, lower-alpha, upper-alpha, or none.

Is there a shorthand for defining list properties?

✔ Yes. The shorthand version is the list-style property, which accepts values for the list-style-type, list-style-image, and list-style-position properties. These values can occur in any order within the curly braces.

How do browsers render lists if they do not support style sheets?

✔ Browsers that are not CSS-compliant simply ignore style properties and render default HTML lists. Unordered lists are rendered with the default disc bullet, and ordered lists are rendered using the decimal numbering scheme.

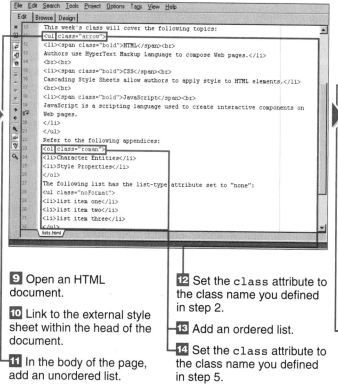

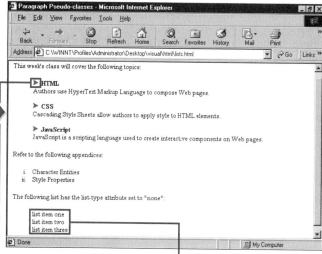

9 Open an HTML document.

10 Link to the external style sheet within the head of the document.

11 In the body of the page, add an unordered list.

12 Set the class attribute to the class name you defined in step 2.

13 Add an ordered list.

14 Set the class attribute to the class name you defined in step 5.

15 Save the style sheet and the document, and then view the page in a Web browser.

■ In browsers that support the list-style-image property, a custom image appears in the place of the bullet.

■ No bullet or numbering scheme is used when the list-style-type property is set to none.

ADD SCROLLING ELEMENTS

You can create boxes with scrollbars using the overflow style property. The overflow style property is used in conjunction with CSS boxes where the width and height values have been set to specific dimensions.

Setting the overflow property to scroll adds horizontal and

vertical scrollbars to the box so that users can read the content that overflows, or extends beyond, the set dimensions of the element.

Using the overflow property with CSS-defined boxes is a useful way to present content such as user agreements or terms of service. You could achieve the same result using a read-only <textarea> form field

or an inline frame, but CSS allows further control over the box presentation that you cannot achieve with form controls or inline frames, such as border styles, positioning, and visibility.

For more information on inline frames, see Chapter 5.

ADD SCROLLING ELEMENTS

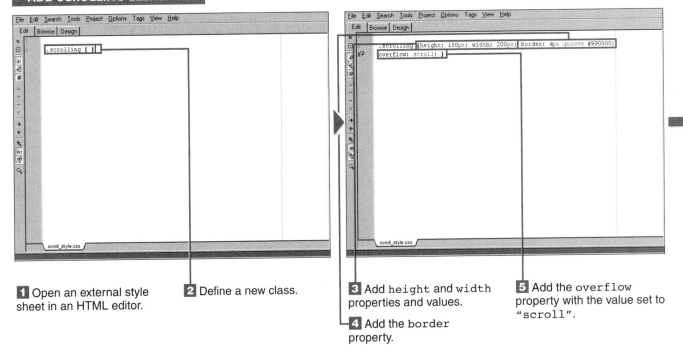

1 Open an external style sheet in an HTML editor.

2 Define a new class.

3 Add height and width properties and values.

4 Add the border property.

5 Add the overflow property with the value set to "scroll".

What happens when I set the overflow value to scroll but there is no excess content?

✔ The browser still implements the scrollbars, even when there is no overflow content to control.

Will the overflow property work on boxes without defined dimensions?

✔ No. If there are no defined height and width, the browser creates a box to fit the amount of content present.

What are the possible values for the overflow property?

✔ There are four possible values for overflow: visible, which is the default value, hidden, scroll, and auto. With overflow set to visible, the extra content is either rendered outside of the box or the box length expands to accommodate the overflow. With the property set to hidden, any overflow text is clipped and inaccessible to the user. A value of auto should supply scrollbars only when necessary.

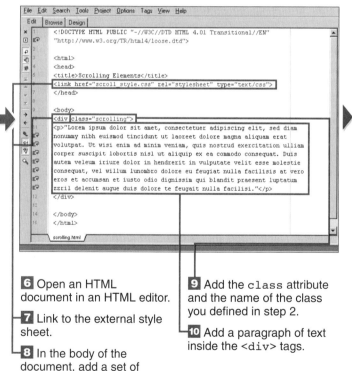

6 Open an HTML document in an HTML editor.

7 Link to the external style sheet.

8 In the body of the document, add a set of <div> tags.

9 Add the class attribute and the name of the class you defined in step 2.

10 Add a paragraph of text inside the <div> tags.

11 Save the style sheet and the document, and then view the page in a CSS-compliant Web browser.

■ With the overflow property set to scroll, the division box is rendered with both vertical and horizontal scroll bars.

POSITION PAGE ELEMENTS

Y ou can control the layout of elements on a page using the position property, part of the CSS2 specification. Before style sheets, Web authors had to develop creative ways to control page layout using HTML, a language that was never designed for complex visual layouts. CSS positioning replaces many of the HTML workarounds that authors have used to create pleasing visual layouts, including

complex tables and transparent spacing images. However, like all style sheet properties, the position property is only supported by the newest browser versions.

The position property is usually set to either relative or absolute and used in conjunction with offset properties, such as top, right, bottom, and left. These

offset properties dictate where the element should appear relative to the content box that contains it, such as a paragraph, table, or the document itself. Setting the value to relative causes the element to be moved from its initial position within the box containing it. Absolute positioning takes the element out of the normal flow and positions it relative to the top left corner of the document.

POSITION PAGE ELEMENTS

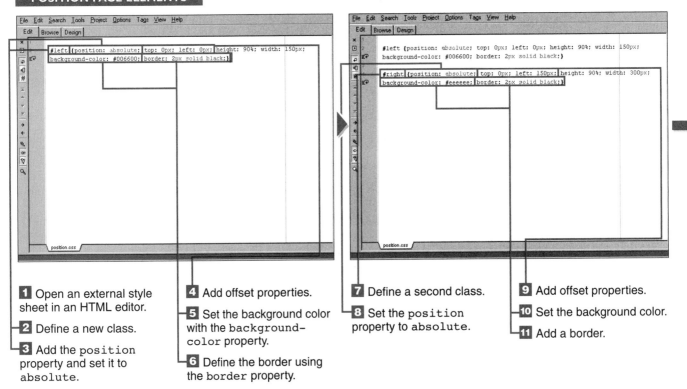

1 Open an external style sheet in an HTML editor.

2 Define a new class.

3 Add the position property and set it to absolute.

4 Add offset properties.

5 Set the background color with the background-color property.

6 Define the border using the border property.

7 Define a second class.

8 Set the position property to absolute.

9 Add offset properties.

10 Set the background color.

11 Add a border.

What values does the position property accept?

✔ The position property has four possible values: static, fixed, absolute, and relative. static is the default position property and cannot be used with offset properties. Fixed elements behave much like absolutely positioned elements. However, fixed elements are fixed with respect to the screen and should not scroll with the page contents.

How do I position one element to have other elements flow around it?

✔ The best way to have elements flow around others is to use the float property. For the element you want to position, set the float property to left or right. This causes other elements to flow around it, either to the right or the left of the floating box. For any element that you do not want to flow around the floating element, add the clear property and set the value to right, left, or both.

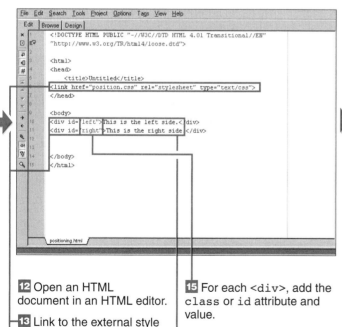

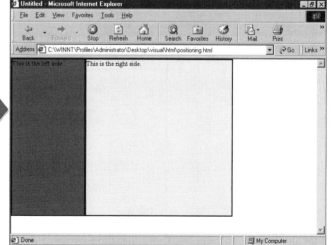

12 Open an HTML document in an HTML editor.

13 Link to the external style sheet.

14 In the body of the document, add two sets of <div> tags.

15 For each <div>, add the class or id attribute and value.

Note: Use the id attribute for id classes and the class attribute for generic classes.

16 Add text to each <div>.

17 Save the style sheet and the document, and then view the page in a CSS-compliant Web browser.

■ The divisions are relative to the top left corner because the position property is set to absolute.

Note: Setting the position property to relative rather than absolute offsets the div in relation to its normal placement in the page flow.

LAYER ELEMENTS WITH THE Z-INDEX PROPERTY

You can layer and overlap elements by using the z-index property to indicate three-dimensional position. The z-index refers to an element's position on the z-axis and is relative to the other elements occupying the same x and y coordinates on the page. Elements with higher z-index values are

placed "on top" of elements with lower z-index values. For example, on a page with two boxes occupying the same x and y positions, the box with a z-index of 2 is stacked on top of the box with a z-index value of 1.

To make two elements overlap, position the elements and offset them using the top, left,

bottom, and right values. Then, use the z-index property to indicate the stacking order. When overlapping two elements, you should set the background color of each element using the background-color property. Otherwise, content contained within one element bleeds into the other element.

LAYER ELEMENTS WITH THE Z-INDEX PROPERTY

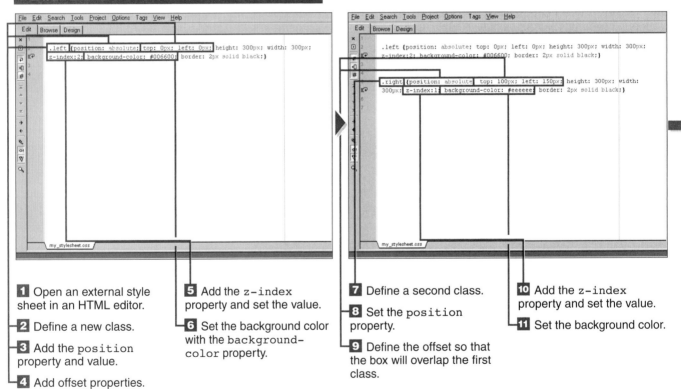

1 Open an external style sheet in an HTML editor.

2 Define a new class.

3 Add the position property and value.

4 Add offset properties.

5 Add the z-index property and set the value.

6 Set the background color with the background-color property.

7 Define a second class.

8 Set the position property.

9 Define the offset so that the box will overlap the first class.

10 Add the z-index property and set the value.

11 Set the background color.

What is the default stacking order if I do not specify the z-index value?

✔ If you do not specify the stacking order, elements are stacked one on top of the other in the order they appear within the HTML code.

What happens when I set z-index without adding any position or top left properties?

✔ The z-index property does not affect the formatting unless the elements are positioned and sharing the same two-dimensional space. Without any explicit positioning, the browser simply renders elements according to the normal flow of the page.

What happens if two elements share the same z-index value?

✔ In that case, the browser reverts back to the default stacking order as if no z-index values had been set. This means that the elements are stacked in the order in which they appear in the HTML document.

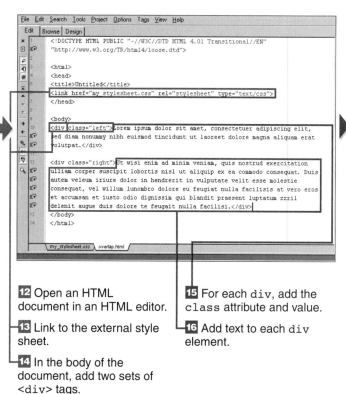

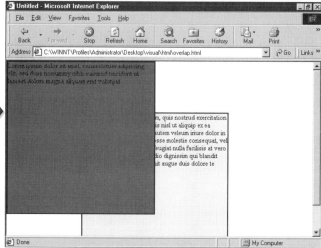

12 Open an HTML document in an HTML editor.

13 Link to the external style sheet.

14 In the body of the document, add two sets of `<div>` tags.

15 For each `div`, add the `class` attribute and value.

16 Add text to each `div` element.

17 Save the style sheet and the document, and then view the page in a CSS-compliant Web browser.

■ The division with the `z-index` set to 2 overlaps the other division.

CONTROL VISIBILITY

You can use the visibility property to control whether elements on a Web page are visible or hidden.

The visibility property is often used in conjunction with JavaScript to dynamically control content effects using DHTML techniques. For more information on JavaScript, see Chapter 14.

The visibility property accepts three values: visible, hidden, and collapse.

The visible value, as the name suggests, makes the element display on the page. When the value is set to hidden, the box is not visible, but it still affects layout and occupies space on the page.

The collapse value is used with table rows and columns to remove part of the table from the display. This technique might be used to dynamically replace table rows or columns with other content.

If the collapse value is used with elements other than table rows or cells, it creates the same effect as the hidden value.

CONTROL VISIBILITY

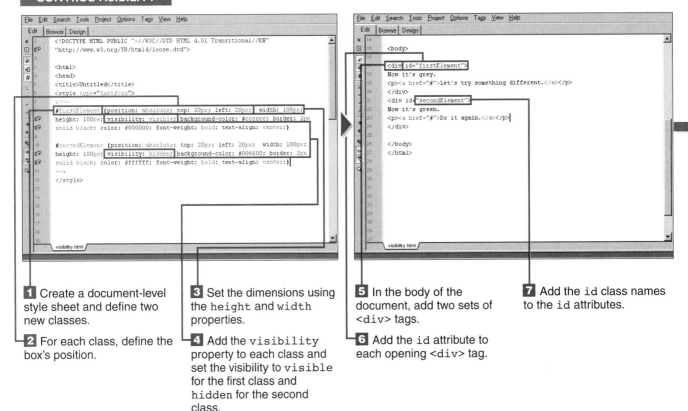

1 Create a document-level style sheet and define two new classes.

2 For each class, define the box's position.

3 Set the dimensions using the height and width properties.

4 Add the visibility property to each class and set the visibility to visible for the first class and hidden for the second class.

5 In the body of the document, add two sets of <div> tags.

6 Add the id attribute to each opening <div> tag.

7 Add the id class names to the id attributes.

How are hidden elements treated by browsers that do not support style sheets?

✔ Browsers that do not support style sheets simply ignore the style properties and render the hidden content.

What exactly is DHTML?

✔ DHTML stands for Dynamic HTML and is a way of combining scripting languages, cascading style sheets, and the browser Document Object Model (DOM) to create dynamic changes on a Web page. You can use DHTML to animate elements on a page and to create complex interactive elements such as expandable navigation menus where clicking on a navigation element offer additional buttons or links.

Does DHTML work on all browsers?

✔ No. DHTML works only on browsers that support style sheets. However, even among browsers that are CSS-compliant, implementing DHTML is a challenge because versions 4 of Netscape Navigator and Internet Explorer rely on different proprietary DOMs and Netscape 6 uses the new W3C-compliant DOM. For more information on the browser DOM, see Chapter 15.

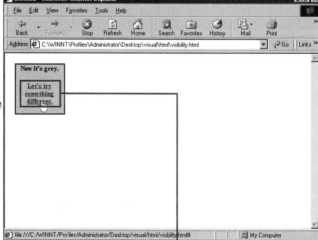

8 Add a script to change the `visibility` property.

Note: This script works with IE 5 and Netscape 6 and is compliant with the W3C's DOM specification. However, for fully cross-browser DHTML, it is necessary to adapt code to handle all browser versions.

9 Inside each `div` element, add a link to trigger the script event when the user clicks.

Note: For more on JavaScript, see Chapter 14.

10 Save the document, and then view the page in a CSS-compliant Web browser.

■ On load, the hidden division is transparent.

11 Click on the link.

■ The initial `div` is hidden while the second division becomes visible.

SECTION III

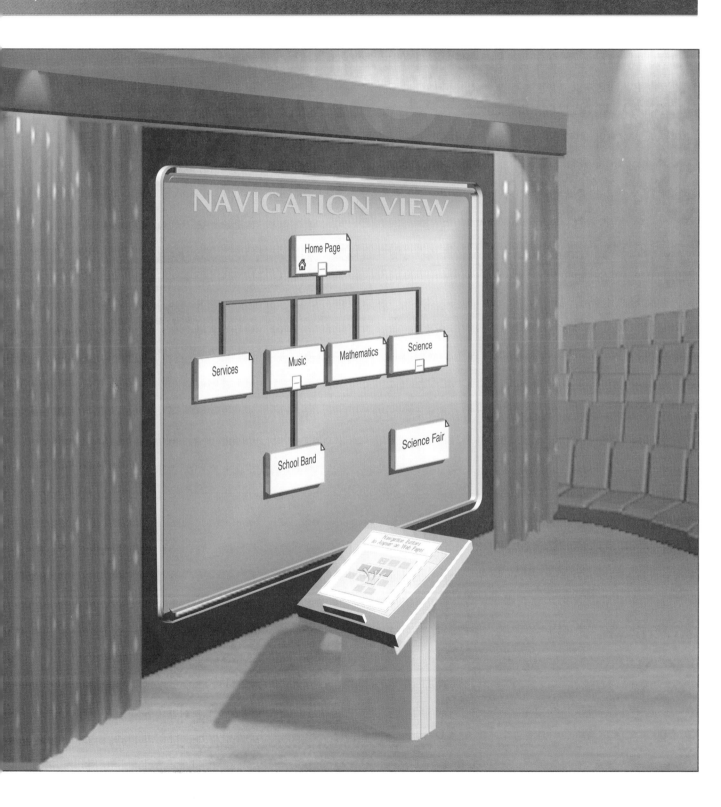

AN INTRODUCTION TO USABILITY ON THE WEB

Simply put, designing for usability means creating sites that are easy to use and accessible to everyone, regardless of what browser visitors may be using. Usability places the focus of design on how visitors use your site and on ways in which you can help visitors accomplish their goals quickly and easily.

Specific coding and design techniques can help make your site more usable for visitors, particularly those with disabilities. However, no matter how much time you invest in coding and designing for usability, the only way to truly gauge whether your site is effective and easy to use is to thoroughly test it with actual users.

Content Creation

Help users get what they want from your site by creating content that fits the medium. Some sites make the mistake of *repurposing*, or reusing, content they use offline, whether that content be articles from magazines and other publications or company marketing materials. What works well in print is rarely optimized for online media, and good usability requires that you craft content that best serves the needs of your Web audience.

For information on creating content that enhances usability, see the sections "Write Text for Scannability" and "Create Structured Text Bites," later in this chapter.

Accessibility

When you design Web sites, considering the needs of visitors with disabilities who may have difficulty accessing your site's content is important. In particular, visitors with visual impairments use special browsing clients that rely on alternative content and contextual meaning to properly render documents.

Learn how to code your pages for optimum accessibility in the sections "Code for Accessibility" and "Using Alt Attributes."

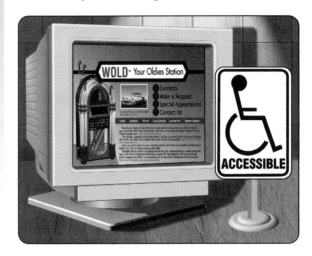

Degrade Gracefully

Although it is tempting to use cutting-edge technology to enhance your Web pages, it is important to "gracefully degrade" to support a variety of browser versions, including those that do not support new technologies. *Degrading gracefully* means that visitors are able to access your content and accomplish their goals, even if their browsers do not support all of the functionality your site has to offer.

To ensure that your Web pages degrade gracefully, consider the following:

• Include alternative content for any technology that requires a plug-in or is not fully supported by all browsers.

• Use browser or object detection to prevent errors on browsers that do not support scripting languages. Learn more about JavaScript detection techniques in Chapter 15.

• When implementing Cascading Style Sheets, test your pages on older browsers to ensure that users can read your content when formatting and layout styles are not applied.

Internationalization

As the number of Web users worldwide continues to grow, internationalization becomes an increasingly important concern for Web designers.

In order to serve visitors from every corner of the globe, take advantage of coding techniques such as indicating languages used in your pages, explored in the section "Specify Languages."

If your Web site serves a multilingual community, you might even consider offering content in various languages. Learn more about the advantages and disadvantages of creating alternative language sites in the section "Offer Alternative Language Versions."

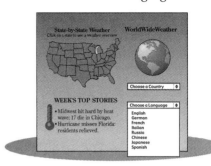

Test Your Site

Before you launch your online venture, make sure that you have actual visitors not involved with the design process test the site to verify that everything is functional and usable.

User testing does not have to involve a large group of people or a special environment with video cameras and one-way mirrors, although many companies offer these services for a fee. You can test the usability of your site by having a handful of people try to accomplish tasks on your site while you note which elements are effective and which are problematic. Functionality, structure, and navigation elements may seem intuitive to developers and designers, but if users struggle while trying to accomplish their goals, your site is not serving your visitors' needs.

CODE FOR ACCESSIBILITY

When you design your Web site, you should strive to build pages that are accessible to all visitors browsing the Web, including those who may use alternative browsing clients such as speech-enabled browsers or other browsers for the visually-impaired. The World Wide Web Consortium (W3C) maintains working drafts for Web Content Accessibility Guidelines that outline the fundamental elements of accessibility and provide additional resources on alternative user agents. The W3C's guidelines are available online at www.w3.org/WAI/.

Provide Alternatives

You can improve the accessibility of your site by always providing alternative content for any non-text materials, such as graphics, audio, and video. For multimedia presentations, always provide captions and transcripts, and include `alt` attributes to provide alternative text for all embedded images.

For more information on alternative text for images, see the section "Using Alt Attributes."

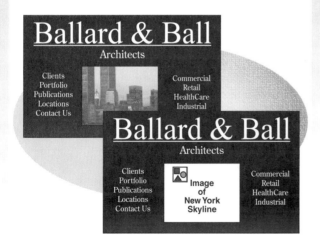

Using Contextual Markup Elements

HTML provides many elements to control the visual appearance of elements on a Web page, but this type of formatting has little meaning for visitors who are visually impaired. Rather than using `<font>` , `<b>`, and `<i>` tags to create headings and add emphasis to text, use content-based tags that transmit contextual meaning to the browser. While the `<b>` and `<i>` tags used to apply bold and italic styles change the visual appearance of text, the content-based equivalents, `<strong>` and `<em>`, can be interpreted by the browser depending on the user's needs. Speech-enabled browsers might render the enclosed text in a different inflection to transmit meaning, for example. For more information on using `<strong>` and `<em>` tags, see Chapter 3.

Create Accessible Forms

The HTML 4.0 specification includes several elements that you can use to make forms more accessible. The `<fieldset>`, `<legend>`, and `<label>` tags allow you to explicitly group related form elements together and provide descriptions that demonstrate the relationships between form elements. Grouping and labeling greatly improve the accessibility of online forms, which can be difficult for visually impaired users to navigate. In addition, the `<label>` tag enhances keyboard access by associating text labels with specific form controls. For more information on creating accessible forms, see Chapter 4.

Test Your Site's Compliance

There are a variety of online services that allow you to test your Web site against the W3C's accessibility guidelines. These services can help you recognize elements that might be problematic for users with disabilities, and they often offer tips and techniques for improving your site's compliance. One of the most popular of these services is Bobby, www.cast. org/bobby/, where you can enter your site's URL and generate a report outlining your site's level of accessibility.

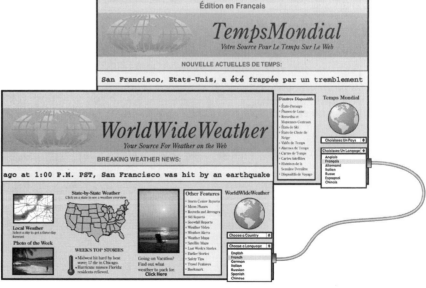

WRITE TEXT FOR SCANNABILITY

You can improve the usability of your site by ensuring that visitors can quickly scan your text content for meaning. Because reading text on a screen is more strenuous than reading print, you should format text so that your readers can easily identify the important elements on your pages.

In addition, readers on the Web are generally task-oriented. They want to get the information they need quickly without having to wade through extraneous material. Writing scannable documents helps users accomplish their goals more efficiently.

When writing text for scannability, remember the following:

- Break longer paragraphs into smaller, more concise chunks using <p> tags.

- Use HTML headings and subheadings such as <h2> and <h3> to isolate themes so users can jump to the portion of the page they want to read.

- Use formatting techniques such as bulleted lists to highlight key ideas and improve readability. For more information on creating HTML lists, see Chapter 3.

WRITE TEXT FOR SCANNABILITY

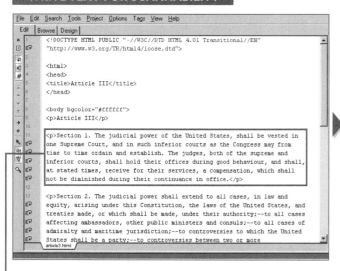

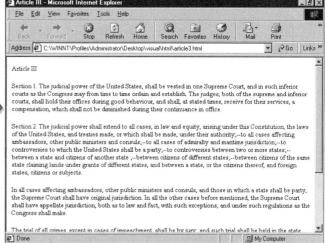

1 Open an HTML document.

2 After the initial <body> tag, add several paragraphs of text.

Note: For more on creating HTML paragraphs, see Chapter 3.

3 Save the HTML document.

4 View the page in a Web browser.

■ Without any formatting, the text is difficult to scan.

What other formatting techniques can I use?

✔ You can create pull quotes, or drop quotes, by using HTML and CSS formatting techniques. For more information on drop quotes, see Chapter 11.

What other elements can I use to help visitors scan pages?

✔ Simple page elements such as hyperlinks and bold or strong text can help users scan pages and isolate important elements. See Chapter 3 for more about hyperlinks and adding emphasis to text. However, overuse of bold text formatting can be distracting, so apply emphasis sparingly.

How can I use color to help visitors scan blocks of text?

✔ Applying color sparingly to key words can help visitors scan the document and absorb the important points of the text. You can use the `<font>` tag with the `color` attribute to apply color to specific words or phrases, or use CSS to apply styles to `<span>` tags. For more on CSS, see Chapter 6.

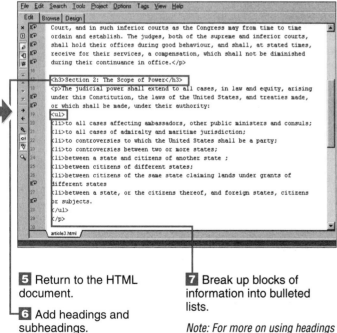

5 Return to the HTML document.

6 Add headings and subheadings.

7 Break up blocks of information into bulleted lists.

Note: For more on using headings and lists, see Chapter 3.

8 Save the HTML document.

9 View the page in a Web browser.

■ Formatting helps readers scan the page for the information they need.

CREATE STRUCTURED TEXT BITES

Y ou can make longer articles easier for visitors to digest by breaking them into structured text bites that span several pages. Rather than breaking long pieces of text at arbitrary points, create thematic subpages and link to each on a *wrapper*, or summary page.

This technique is often used on sites that feature longer articles, where the index.html page is the *wrapper* that provides a brief introduction along with links to each subpage in the article. This way visitors can go directly to the content they want and bookmark only the text that is relevant to them.

Your wrapper page should include a brief summary of the topics covered in each of the subpages as well as prominent links to each page. Providing descriptive link text for each page, rather than using text such as "next" or "page two," allows visitors to decide which portions they want to read and which pages they can skip.

CREATE STRUCTURED TEXT BITES

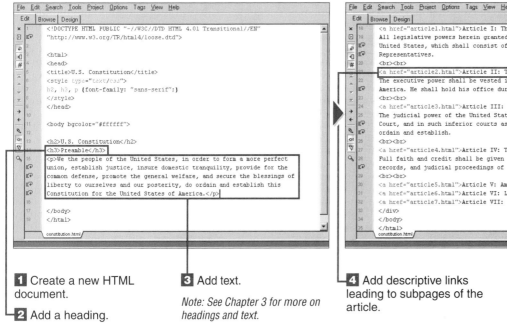

1 Create a new HTML document.

2 Add a heading.

3 Add text.

Note: See Chapter 3 for more on headings and text.

4 Add descriptive links leading to subpages of the article.

Note: For more information on using links, see Chapter 3.

5 Save the HTML document.

What techniques can I use to allow visitors to navigate between the wrapper page and subpages?

✔ A good way to provide navigation is to include an HTML table with links to all of the subpages. By integrating this table at the bottom of each subpage, visitors can jump around to any page. You can also provide links to the next page in the series as well as a link back to the previous page. This is referred to as *linear navigation* because it allows visitors to read the pages in order. For more on creating effective navigation schemes, see Chapter 9.

In general, how long should a page of text be?

✔ There is no hard and fast rule, but conventional wisdom dictates that you should try to keep content "above the fold" so that users do not have to scroll long pages to read text. To reduce the need to scroll down in order to read long passages, aim for pages with 400 words or less of text.

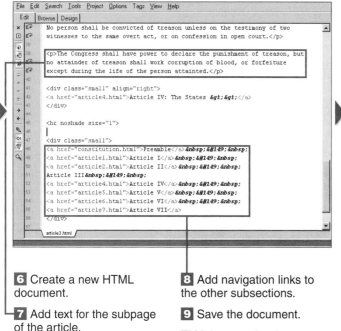

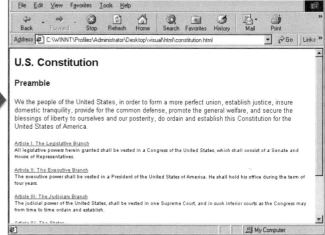

■ **6** Create a new HTML document.

■ **7** Add text for the subpage of the article.

■ **8** Add navigation links to the other subsections.

■ **9** Save the document.

■ Make sure the document name matches the wrapper page link reference.

■ **10** Open the wrapper page in a Web browser.

■ The wrapper page links allow visitors to jump directly to the content they want.

ELIMINATE DEAD ENDS

Avoid "dead-end" or orphaned pages by including hyperlinks to supplemental information or other related content on your site.

Visitors find themselves at *dead ends* when they arrive at pages that are completely isolated, without links or navigation. Without any way to proceed, the visitor must use the browser buttons to back out of the page or abandon the site entirely.

You can avoid dead ends by including persistent navigation links to other portions of your site, a link back to the front door in the form of a company logo, or links to other related materials on your site. You can place text links inside formatted HTML tables or enclose images within `<a href>` tags. For more information on formatting HTML links, tables, and images, see Chapter 3.

If you are not sure which of your pages might present dead ends, have a user test the site while you observe. Anytime the user is forced to click the browser's "Back" button or enter a new address into the address bar, the page is a dead end.

ELIMINATE DEAD ENDS

1 Open an HTML document.

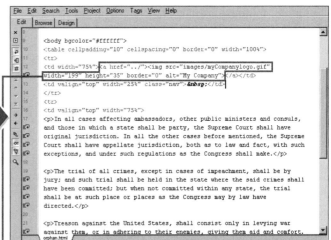

2 Add a link back to the front door of the site.

■ This link is attached to a graphic image. For specifics on using links, see Chapter 3; for more on graphics, see Chapter 12.

Can I provide links to external resources to eliminate dead ends?

✔ Yes, if you do not have additional related material on your site, provide links to external resources. Although the user leaves your site when loading external links, these external links still add value to your Web page and provide the user with paths to pursue.

What other strategies can I use to prevent dead-end pages?

✔ If your site features many contributors, link to other content written by the same author. You can elicit feedback or direct users to message boards and discussion forums.

Where should I be especially wary of dead ends?

✔ You often find dead-end pages at the conclusion of a multi-page article or at the completion of an online transaction such as a shopping cart page, where users find themselves at an impasse. Do not assume that because users have completed a particular task that they do not want to continue browsing your site. Be sure to provide links back to the category or product page last visited rather than returning them to the front door of the site.

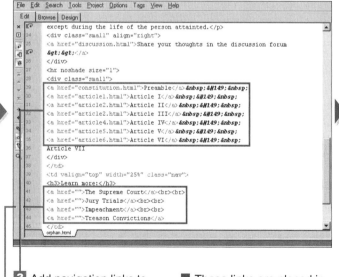

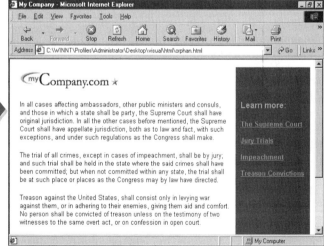

3 Add navigation links to other portions of the site.

4 Add links to additional related information.

■ These links are placed in a table cell. For more about tables, see Chapter 3.

5 Save the document.

6 Open the page in a Web browser.

■ Hyperlinks provide additional paths for the user to follow.

ELICIT FEEDBACK FROM VISITORS

I mprove the experience that visitors have on your site by providing ways for people to send you feedback.

Incorporating feedback mechanisms that are easy to locate is particularly important on e-commerce sites that rely on establishing trust with users, but even noncommercial sites should make it easy for visitors to send comments or questions.

The easiest way to elicit feedback from users is to provide an e-mail address in the form of an HTML mailto link. Make your e-mail link easy for visitors to locate by incorporating it into the site's front door, in article by-lines, and on technical support, help, and contact pages. You can read more about mailto links in Chapter 3.

You can also use HTML forms as feedback mechanisms. If you use an HTML form, you can include a

menu of possible subject lines, such as "Technical Support," "Sales and Sponsorships," and "Suggestions." Giving visitors a choice of subjects communicates to visitors that feedback is being routed to the appropriate person or department.

For more information on using forms for feedback, see Chapter 4.

ELICIT FEEDBACK FROM VISITORS

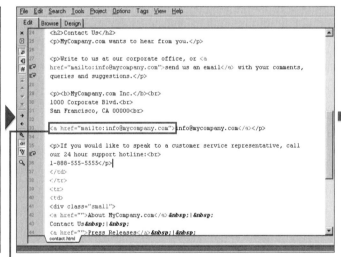

1 Open your HTML document.

2 After the opening <body> tag, add contact information for your site.

3 Add an <a> tag with an href attribute.

■ For the link text appearing between the <a> tags, you can include the e-mail address, or embed the link directly within a paragraph of text.

4 Add a mailto URL to the href attribute.

■ To add a mailto URL, type **"mailto:"** then the e-mail address.

Note: For more information on using mailto URLs, see Chapter 3.

5 Save the document.

If I use `<a href>` tags with `mailto` URLs, can I specify the subject line of the e-mail?

✔ Yes, you can prepopulate the subject line by adding a question mark and the words **"subject="** after the `mailto` URL. Then add the subject line you would like to appear in the e-mail message when the user clicks the mailto link. For example, for a "Comments" e-mail address that appears on a variety of pages, you could specify the title of the page in the subject line:
```
<a href="mailto:comments@
yoursite.com?article title
here">send us comments</a>
```

When prepopulating subject lines in `mailto` URLs, can I include text with spaces?

✔ Yes, in general, prepopulated subject lines can contain spaces. However, a few older browsers may not render the spaces in the URL correctly. To ensure that the spaces translate on all browsers, you can replace each space with `%20`, such as `"article%20title%20here."`

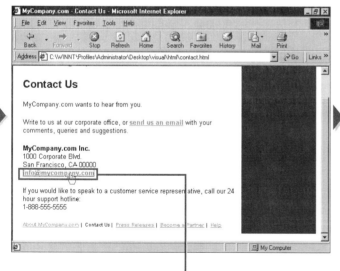

6 View the page in a Web browser.

7 Click the `mailto` link.

■ The browser opens an e-mail client and populates the "To" field with the `mailto` URL.

CREATE A PRINTER-FRIENDLY VERSION OF A WEB PAGE

You can give visitors the opportunity to take your Web content with them by offering a printer-friendly version of features and articles on your site. Because reading print on-screen can be straining, visitors often print copies so they can read them offline. Although most users are able to print pages using their Web browser, many Web site pages are

not optimized for print quality. Many Web sites have text formatted in fonts that are ideal for online reading but are not conducive to traditional print. Others use layout techniques such as frames that older browsers are unable to print.

You can create a simple, printer-friendly version of a Web page by

removing extraneous material, such as sidebar links and navigation, that is no longer necessary. For printer-friendly versions of pages, use serif fonts such as Times rather than sans-serif fonts commonly employed on the Web, because serif fonts are generally better for print media. Be sure to include items such as a logo, the name of your company, and a reference URL.

CREATE A PRINTER-FRIENDLY VERSION OF A WEB PAGE

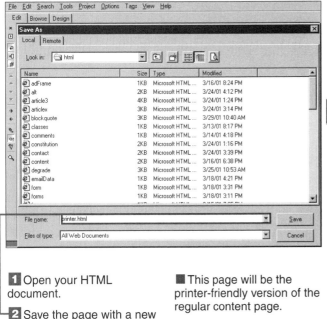

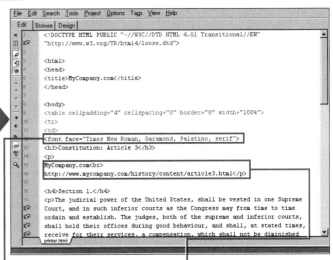

1 Open your HTML document.

2 Save the page with a new file name.

■ This page will be the printer-friendly version of the regular content page.

3 Use <font> tags to set the font type to serif fonts.

Note: You can also remove all <font> tags and font-formatting properties. In this case, the font is dictated by the user's browser preferences.

4 Add your Web site name and URL, in plain text, to the document.

5 Remove extraneous navigation links and images.

What is the difference between serif and sans-serif fonts?

✔ The term *serif* refers to the small lines found at the terminal ends of type characters. Some popular serif fonts include Times, Times New Roman, Palatino, and Garamond. The term *sans-serif* means "without serifs" and refers to the family of fonts that contains Arial, Helvetica, and Verdana, among others. For more about fonts and typography, see Chapter 11.

Why are serif fonts better to use in print?

✔ Studies show that the small accent lines used in serif characters are easier to read in longer portions of text. In print, sans-serif fonts are usually reserved for headings, captions, and shorter explanatory text. However, due to the lower resolution of computer screen monitors, sans-serif fonts are often a better choice on the Web. For more information on fonts and typography, see Chapter 11.

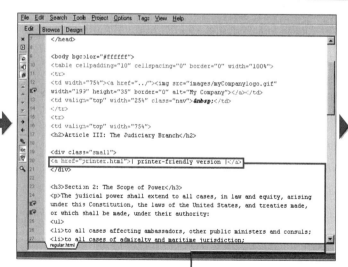

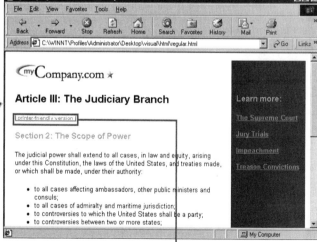

■6 Open the HTML page for the regular version of the printer-friendly document.

■7 Add a link to the printer-friendly version.

■8 View the page in a Web browser.

■9 Click the link for the printer-friendly version.

■ The printer-friendly version loads into the browser window.

USING ALT ATTRIBUTES

You can provide alternative text for images on your Web site by using `alt` attributes. `Alt` attributes allow alternative browsers and browsers that do not render images to provide users with a brief description of the image. Providing alternative text for any clickable images, such as images used for site navigation, is particularly important. If you do

not provide alternative text, non-graphical browsers simply tell the visitor that there is an image on the page.

Add the `alt` attribute with a text description to each `<img>` tag on your site. Text descriptions are enclosed within quotation marks, and should be brief and descriptive. For clickable images,

use alternative text to describe the purpose of the link. For example, navigation images might include text such as "About the Company" or "Contact Us."

In addition, always provide alternative text for each clickable region of an image map. For more information on creating image maps, see Chapter 12.

USING ALT ATTRIBUTES

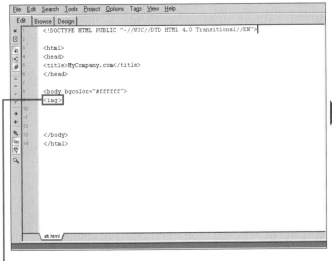

1 Open an HTML document.

2 If the document does not have an image, add an image to the page.

■ If the document already has an image, skip to step 5.

■ For more on adding images to pages, see Chapter 3. For more on adding transparent images to pages, see Chapter 12.

3 Indicate the source of the image.

■ Add the source, or file location, of the image using the `src` attribute.

4 Specify the width and height of the image.

Is there a character limit on alternative text?

✔ Yes, the character limit for alternative text is 1,024 characters.

A friend uses transparent graphics to control spacing on his Web page. If I use these transparent spacers, should I include alt attributes for them?

✔ The short answer is yes. The most popular format for transparent spacers is *GIF*, which stands for *graphics interchange format*, a widely used Web standard. If you use a transparent GIF, use the alt attribute but leave the value blank. This way, alternative browsers can skip over transparent images used for page layout.

Can I use HTML formatting in alternative text?

✔ No, text used with alt attributes should be plain text without any additional HTML formatting. However, you can use special characters. For more information on character entities, see Chapter 3.

Where can I read more about transparent GIFs?

✔ For more information about creating transparent spacer GIFs, see Chapter 12.

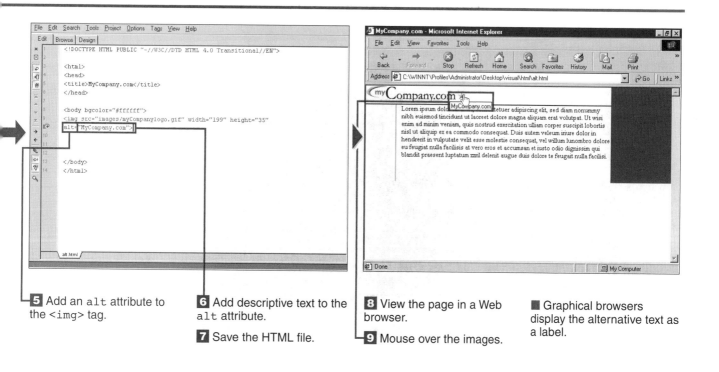

5 Add an alt attribute to the <img> tag.

6 Add descriptive text to the alt attribute.

7 Save the HTML file.

8 View the page in a Web browser.

9 Mouse over the images.

■ Graphical browsers display the alternative text as a label.

SPECIFY LANGUAGES

You can specify the languages used in your document and in individual page elements with the lang attribute. This attribute does not dictate the page language, but rather provides information to browsers about the language you are using. Search engines might use this information to filter results, or to offer a translation of the page. If you have elements that contain foreign language text, such as quotes, aural browsers might use the lang attribute to correctly "read" the text.

You can apply the lang attribute to almost any HTML element, including DIVs, SPANs, <font> tags, and the opening <html> tag itself. The value of the lang attribute is usually a two- or three-letter code, such as "en" for English. In addition, you can append some codes with dialect subcodes, such as "fr-CA" for Canadian French.

Specify the global language of your Web page by including the lang attribute in the opening <html> tag. If you have portions of text in languages other than the document's primary language, use the lang attribute with the specific tag to indicate the language.

SPECIFY LANGUAGES

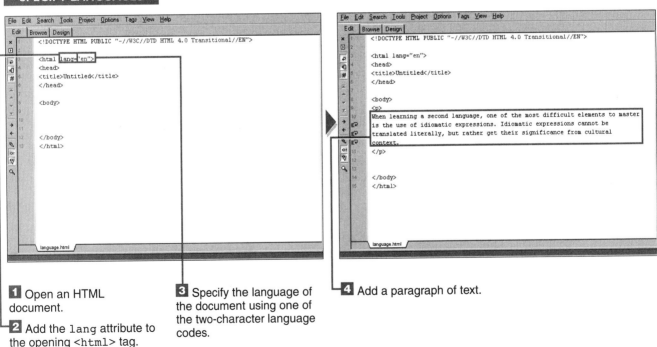

1 Open an HTML document.

2 Add the lang attribute to the opening <html> tag.

3 Specify the language of the document using one of the two-character language codes.

4 Add a paragraph of text.

What are some of the common codes for languages?

✔ Some common language codes include:

"zh" (Chinese)	"es" (Spanish)
"en" (English)	"hi" (Hindi)
"pt" (Portuguese)	"ru" (Russian)
"ja" (Japanese)	"de" (German)
"fr" (French)	

How do I specify languages in XHTML?

✔ The XHTML specification recommends that you use the `lang` attribute along with the `xml:lang` attribute. You can add both attributes to your opening `<html>` tag to be compliant with the W3C's XHTML specification. You can read more about XHTML in Chapter 21.

How can I specify the direction of the text?

✔ Use the `dir` attribute to tell the browser whether the page content should be rendered from left to right, or from right to left. The default value for the dir attribute is `"ltr"`, and renders the text from the left to the right. The other possible value is `"rtl"`, used to display text from the right to the left for languages such as Hebrew.

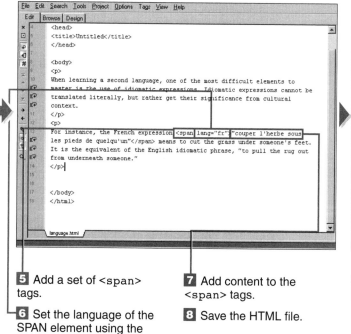

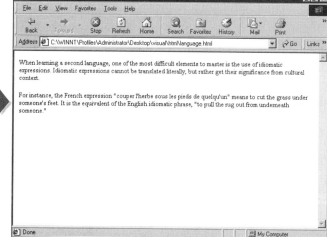

5 Add a set of `<span>` tags.

6 Set the language of the SPAN element using the `lang` attribute.

7 Add content to the `<span>` tags.

8 Save the HTML file.

9 View the page in a Web browser.

■ Setting the `lang` attribute does not effect visible formatting.

OFFER ALTERNATIVE LANGUAGE VERSIONS

I f many of your site's visitors do not speak English or if you have a multilingual audience, you can make your site's content more accessible by offering alternative language versions.

Sites that provide critical information such as public services and government institutions or sites that serve a multilingual geographic location should always provide alternative language content.

Alternative Language Sites

One common approach to offering alternative language versions is to build a mirror of your site and link to it from your front door using the language name. Large portals such as Yahoo! and AltaVista offer localized alternative language versions, and to preserve the strength of the site's brand identity, they usually feature consistent design elements, such as color and page layout.

Alternative Language Pages

The disadvantage to building an individual site for each language is that you then have multiple sites to maintain. Depending on the size of your multilingual audience segment, it might be sufficient to provide alternative versions of specific content pieces. For example, pages providing technical support, frequently asked questions and contact information are elements for which you might offer alternative language versions.

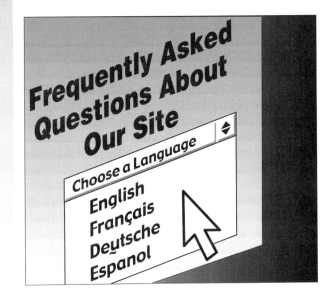

Link to Alternative Versions

Most sites that offer different language versions use one language as the default site, then offer links to other language versions. Using your primary audience language as the default version allows the majority of your visitors to begin browsing your site without having to load an additional page to proceed. When providing links to other language versions, use the name of the language as used in the native language itself. For example, a site that offers versions in French and Spanish would provide prominent links using the words "Français" and "Español." Using international flags to designate language versions can be confusing for

visitors, because flags do not always correspond to geographical boundaries. For example, using a Spanish flag would not be an effective way to communicate an alternative language version site to Spanish speakers in the Americas.

Explore Your Needs

If you are concerned that a significant portion of your site traffic is not being served by your primary language, refer to your Web server logs, which record user domains that are specific to particular countries, such as .fr (France) or .jp (Japan). However, geographic location is not always a useful indicator of language preferences.

AN INTRODUCTION TO INFORMATION ARCHITECTURE

Often when designers begin developing Web sites, they concentrate on aesthetic elements of visual design, or the functional and technical backbone of the site. However, in order to design effective, well-structured Web sites, it is necessary to first consider how content should be organized and labeled, and how visitors will navigate the site to find the information they are seeking. Together, these elements—organizational structures, labeling systems, and navigation and search interfaces—are referred to as *information architecture*.

Organization and Navigation

In everyday life, human beings interact with information architecture in a variety of different settings. Everything from a library to a department store or supermarket has its own structure and way of classifying, organizing, and labeling elements. A library is organized according to a thematic numbering system, while a department store uses an organizational structure based on types of clothing and customer segment.

The type of organizational structure implemented depends on the type of elements being classified, and choosing the wrong type of organization can make it difficult for customers or visitors to navigate a particular space and find what they are looking for. Imagine how difficult it would be to find a particular item if a department store were organized alphabetically, for example.

The section "Understanding Organizational Structure" in this chapter outlines the general ways in which you can organize information depending on the nature of your site. These structures include exact systems, such as alphabetical, chronological and geographical organizations, as well as more interpretative systems in which you create meaningful relationships between categories of information. After you decide on an appropriate organizational structure, you learn how to implement navigation systems in Chapter 9.

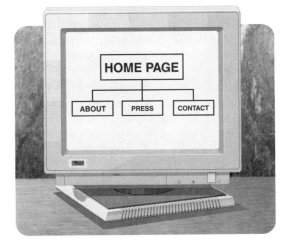

Metaphors

While you are devising your organizational scheme, it is often useful to think about your site in terms of metaphors.

A *metaphor* can be used to create a link between your site's organization and a concept that is familiar to your audience. For example, many online business sites rely on the metaphor of a traditional retail store, with contents organized into departments, shopping carts, checking out, and so on. Some sites extend the use of conceptual metaphors to closely fit the theme or content of the site, such as an entertainment Web site relying on the metaphor of a movie theatre, with ticket booth, screening room, and concession stand areas.

Thinking about metaphors can be a useful creative exercise, but be wary of forcing your site's organization to fit into a metaphor. If the link between your content and the metaphor is not clear, it might create more confusion on the part of the visitor.

Labeling Systems

Web designers use labels to communicate to visitors what type of information is contained within each organizational unit on a Web site. After you have developed your site's organization and navigation schemes, develop a labeling system that is consistent, efficient, and clear to users who may be unfamiliar with your Web site or company.

For more information, see the sections "Develop a Labeling System," "Using Scope Notes," and "Using Icon Labels."

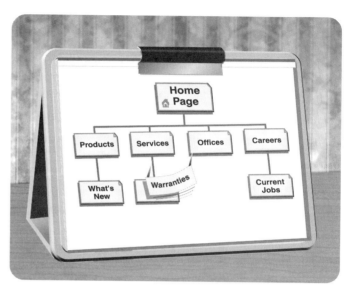

Search

Effective navigation schemes can help visitors find what they are looking for on your site, but if you have a medium- to large-scale site, you should offer users the ability to search for specific content. In fact, Web users are so accustomed to navigating by searching that they have come to expect it on sites of all sizes.

The most useful search interfaces take into account both the type of content being searched as well as the needs of the user. The sections "Design a Search Interface" and "Display Search Results" offer tips and guidelines to help you develop search functionality that best serves the needs of your users.

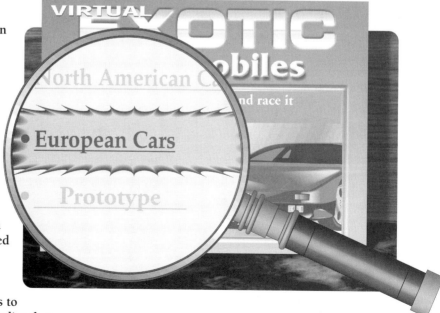

UNDERSTANDING ORGANIZATIONAL STRUCTURE

Organizational structures can be divided into two general groups: *exact structures* in which each piece of information fits into one category, and *interpretative structures,* which are more ambiguous and subjective. Alphabetical, chronological, and geographical schemes are all examples of exact organizational structures. These systems work best when users know precisely what they are looking for, and are appropriate for certain types of information. However, most Web sites rely on interpretative systems such as task-oriented or topic-oriented organizations. In these systems, you group information together according to relationships that you devise.

The following sections provide an overview of the five main organizational schemes. To fully implement any of them, you will need to be familiar with the HTML details in Part II; however, the overviews provide a listing of HTML Web skills that are especially important for each particular scheme.

Alphabetical Organization

One of the easiest ways to organize information is to use an alphabetical scheme. Although alphabetical organization is rarely used as the primary organization scheme, you can use it in subsections where appropriate. For example, you may use a topic-based organization in your higher-level content areas, but rely on alphabetical organization for the site index or member directory.

- **Typical uses:** Alphabetical organization is particularly useful for items such as dictionaries or indices where users know exactly what they are looking for.

- **Strengths:** Users are very familiar with alphabetical schemes. Relying on this type of organization does not require users to spend time learning a more interpretative structure such as topic-based organization.

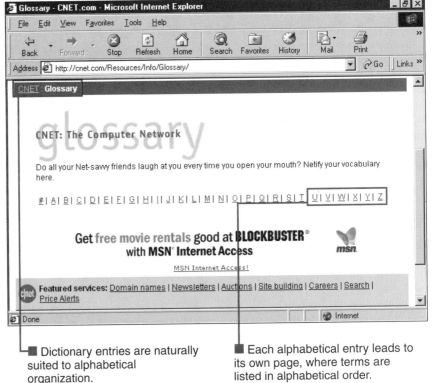

■ Dictionary entries are naturally suited to alphabetical organization.

■ Each alphabetical entry leads to its own page, where terms are listed in alphabetical order.

- **Special considerations:** When you use alphabetical organization, provide prominent navigation links to all the alphabetical categories. Depending on the amount of information in each alphabetical category, you might use alphabetical groupings such as A-C rather than a single letter for each subsection. If you have enough content for each alphabetical entry or group, create

individual subpages for each section. Otherwise, you can use anchors at the top of the page to allow users to jump directly to the letter group further down the page.

- **Skills needed:** To use an alphabetical organization, you should know how to add hyperlinks and mailtos, and how to create anchors. You can read more about both in Chapter 3.

Chronological Organization

Use a chronological organization scheme when you have content on your site that is easily categorized by dates. You can use chronological organization in conjunction with other forms of organization based on subject matter or topic areas.

- **Typical uses:** A news or magazine site might use a topical structure for its primary organization while having each topic's content or past archives arranged by date. Company press releases are also organized chronologically by month and year, with the most recent releases at the top of the page.

- **Strengths:** Chronological organization schemes highlight timely content such as breaking news or recent updates.

(Continued)

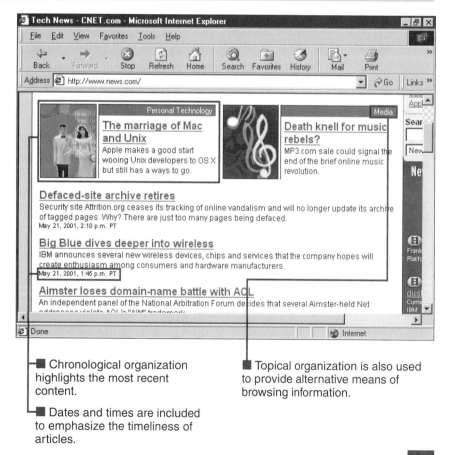

■ Chronological organization highlights the most recent content.

■ Dates and times are included to emphasize the timeliness of articles.

■ Topical organization is also used to provide alternative means of browsing information.

UNDERSTANDING ORGANIZATIONAL STRUCTURE (CONTINUED)

Chronological Organization (*Continued*)

- **Special considerations:** Although chronological organization is appropriate for archives, press releases, and regular columns, you should complement this structure with other types of information

organization, because users might prefer to search or browse content by category or subject rather than date.

- **Skills needed:** To use a chronological organization, you should know how to add hyperlinks and headings, and how to format text. Learn more in Chapter 3.

Geographical Organization

Use geographical organization when your content is easily divided into subsections based on geographical boundaries.

- **Typical uses:** News and information sites often take advantage of geographical organization to divide content into local, national, and international subcategories. Sites that focus on travel and leisure activities also rely on geographical organization to allow users to browse through content based on their destination.

- **Strengths:** When used on travel and leisure sites, geographical organization schemes can complement topic-based structures and offer users the means of exploring a topic without having a specific destination in mind. For example, city-specific leisure sites often allow users the option of browsing categories, such as restaurants or accommodations, based on neighborhood or district.

- **Special considerations:** Image maps present an ideal way to allow users to visually explore a geographical organization. However, image maps can require longer download times and are not effective on non-graphical browsers. Always provide other

means of navigation, such as text links, that do not rely on image support.

- **Skills needed:** To use a geographical scheme, you should know how to create an image map, which you can read about in Chapter 12.

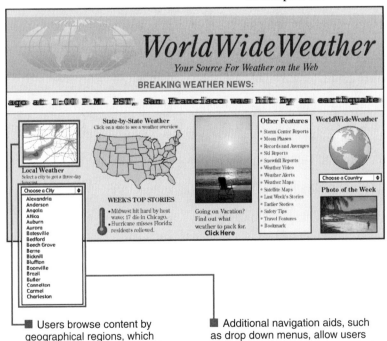

■ Users browse content by geographical regions, which become increasingly targeted as the user clicks through.

■ Additional navigation aids, such as drop down menus, allow users to jump directly to the geographical region of choice.

Task-Oriented Organization

Use task-oriented organization when you want to emphasize specific actions the user might undertake on your site. In this type of organization scheme, the structure and the navigational elements of the site are all geared towards actions rather than a presentation of information.

- **Typical uses:** Task-oriented organization works particularly well on sites that feature tools and online applications. For example, a Web site that features an online accounting application might have a task-oriented structure that includes elements such as "Pay Bills," "Write Checks," and "Send Invoices."

- **Strengths:** Task-oriented organization structures anticipate a set of primary tasks the user wants to accomplish.

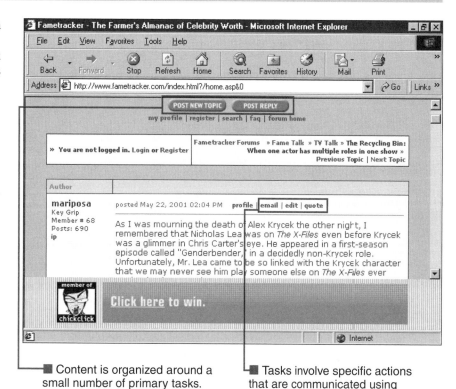

■ Content is organized around a small number of primary tasks.

■ Tasks involve specific actions that are communicated using verbs.

- **Special considerations:** These structures are rarely appropriate for sites that feature text content rather than functional applications.

- **Skills needed:** Task-oriented organizations usually focus on more advanced functionality and interactive tools. Learn about implementing interactive elements in Part V.

Topical Organization

When you use topical organization, content on your site is presented as a series of top-level subject areas, with each subject area then containing one or more sub-levels

that offer more specific information within the topic. For example, a bookstore organizes books by subject area, a non-fiction book organizes content by chapter, and

the yellow pages of a phone book organize entries by business category.

(Continued)

UNDERSTANDING ORGANIZATIONAL STRUCTURE (CONTINUED)

Topical Organization *(Continued)*

- **Typical uses:** Topical organization is used by e-commerce sites that divide products into categories, and by content sites that organize features and articles by subject matter.

- **Strengths:** When you organize information by topic, you create meaningful relationships between content pieces based on the subject areas in your structure. You might group content together based on the audience, such as clients, partners, and investors, or by subject area, such as film, television, and music. When you design your topical structure, you make conscious decisions about where each piece of content fits into the overall scheme based on these relationships you envision.

- **Special considerations:** Because they are inherently subjective, topical organizations can confuse users if they do not understand why content is in one topic area rather than another.

- **Skills needed:** For topical organizations, you should know how to implement HTML hyperlinks and Web graphics (Chapter 3), and how to add bread-crumb trails, site maps, and topical navigation elements (Chapter 9).

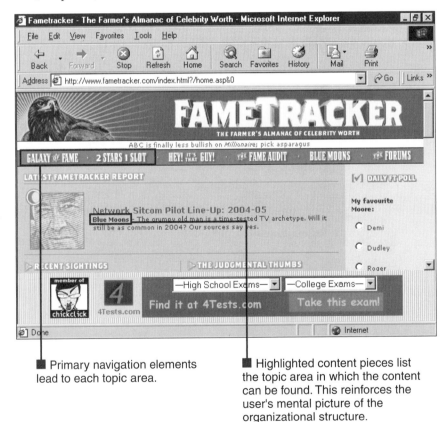

■ Primary navigation elements lead to each topic area.

■ Highlighted content pieces list the topic area in which the content can be found. This reinforces the user's mental picture of the organizational structure.

Choose Your Organization Structure

Use the following worksheet to decide which organizational structure is most appropriate for your site. While your primary organizational structure might be topic or task-based, most Web sites use schemes that combine various structures, depending on the content.

	ALPHABETICAL	CHRONOLOGICAL	GEOGRAPHICAL	TASK-ORIENTED	TOPICAL
Does your site include directories or index pages?	✔				✔
Is the timeliness of your content important?		✔			
Does your site feature historical content or archives?		✔			✔
Will users browse content based on geographical regions?			✔		✔
Does your site feature functional applications?				✔	
Does your site feature regular updates?		✔			
Does your content fit into a hierarchy of categories and subcategories?					✔
Is your site a resource library of features or articles?		✔			✔
Is your site a company marketing or communications tool?					✔
Is your site a personal portfolio or journal site?		✔			✔

MAP AN INFORMATION HIERARCHY

While developing the information architecture for your site, plotting out the information hierarchy of your site's content is often useful. Mapping out the information hierarchy of a site provides you with a blueprint for developing and refining organization and labeling systems. Additionally, clear hierarchies of site content also help users understand the underlying structure of your site.

When you map out an information hierarchy, note and label all of the top-level categories as well as the subclassifications within each category. Hierarchies should be flexible enough to grow with your site as you add new content. If you anticipate adding additional categories or subcategories in the near future, take these additions into account when you map your initial hierarchy to make sure they fit into the overall structure of the site.

Maps and Flowcharts

Web designers often create maps and flowcharts to visually represent the information hierarchy of a Web site. A *map* is a tree-like diagram that shows how top-level categories break down into secondary and tertiary categories. A *flowchart* is a map with paths and arrows that demonstrate how pages are linked together and the ways in which a visitor might move through the information hierarchy of a site.

For example, a map or flowchart for an e-commerce site would have a diagram of the front door—or home page—with arrows leading to the product areas offered. Each product area diagram leads to the individual product pages, which in turn lead to pages such as adding a product to a shopping cart and completing a transaction. In this way, maps and flowcharts can help you envision both the hierarchy of a site as well as how users might navigate through the structure. For more on navigation, see Chapter 9.

You can create maps and flowcharts using a graphics editor such as Fireworks or Photoshop; trial versions of both are available on the CD-ROM that accompanies this book. You can also purchase software specifically designed for creating maps, diagrams, and flowcharts. Popular software choices include Microsoft Visio (www.microsoft.com/office/visio/) for Windows users and Inspiration (www.inspiration.com/) for Macintosh users. To find other software solutions, visit www.download.com.

Exclusivity

When designing your information hierarchy, try to create categories that are mutually exclusive. This means that ideally one article or piece of content should fit clearly into only one category. In some cases it may be difficult to determine which category is the best fit for a piece of information.

For example, contact information might fit into a category that has information about your company, or it might be appropriate in a "Help" or "Frequently Asked Questions" section. At times it may be appropriate to have the same information in multiple categories, but if this happens too frequently, consider revising your hierarchy to create more exclusive content areas.

Breadth versus Depth

Developing an effective hierarchy also means striking a balance between breadth and depth of your classification categories. Shallow hierarchies with a lot of breadth present users with too many choices, and may be impractical in terms of providing navigation buttons or links.

On the other hand, very deep hierarchies force users to click through numerous pages to find the content piece they are looking for. This can be both frustrating and time consuming.

For a balance, consider using five to seven choices for the top level of the hierarchy. Keep content pieces within three to five clicks of the top-level page.

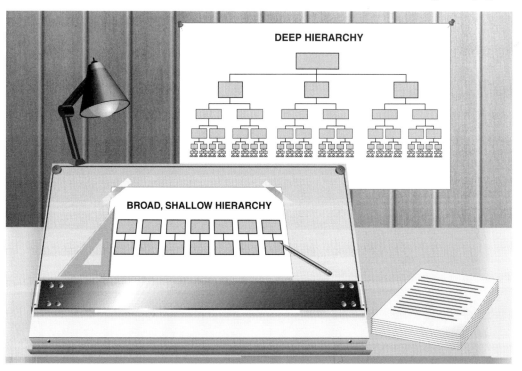

DEEP HIERARCHY

BROAD, SHALLOW HIERARCHY

DEVELOP A LABELING SYSTEM

You can help visitors understand the structure of your site by developing clear labeling systems.

A *labeling system* is the way you refer to each subsection of your site, such as "Contact," "Help," and "Home." Labels also serve as shortcuts that communicate the content contained within a given area of the site.

As you develop the organizational scheme for your site, you might employ a labeling system that makes sense to you but that does not have meaning for those unfamiliar with your site or company. For example, labels such as "Core Facilities Management" or "Business Solutions" may make sense to you but they do not adequately communicate meaning to the user. If your Web site sells specialty products, avoiding overly

technical jargon that some users may not understand is particularly important.

When you develop your final labeling system, ensure that the terms you use are clear to first-time users and do not rely on "insider" vocabulary. Consider using labels that are already familiar to users, so that they know what to expect in each organizational category.

What are some examples of commonly used labels?

✔ "Home," "Home Page," and "Main" are commonly used to refer to the front door of a site. Other common labels include "Contact," "Contact Us," "Help," "FAQ," "About," "About Us," and "About Company," where "Company" is your site's name.

Are there any commonly used labels that are problematic?

✔ Any label that might cause confusion for the user or visitor is problematic. For example, labels such as "Press" are ambiguous, and might refer to press releases or articles written in the press about the company. When implementing a labeling system, clarify any ambiguous terms so that they communicate the nature of your content to the user.

What techniques can I use to make sure that users understand technical or specialized labels?

✔ If you cannot avoid using technical or specialized terms, consider adding scope notes to offer more clarification on the meaning of the labels themselves. For more information, see the following section, "Using Scope Notes."

Develop A Labeling System

Follow these steps to develop a labeling system for your organizational structure. Labeling systems are most useful when developed in conjunction with a site's navigational structure. For more information on navigation, see Chapter 9.

1. Determine the site's organization system. See the section "Understanding Organizational Structure."

2. Assign each category or subcategory an initial label.

3. Make sure the labeling system is consistent.
    - Are all the labels topic-oriented or task-oriented?
    - For topic-oriented systems, are all of the labels nouns?
    - For task-oriented systems, are all of the labels verbs?

4. Ensure that the meaning of the labels is clear.
    - Will users unfamiliar with your company understand each label?
    - Are there any labels that have ambiguous meanings?

5. Apply the labeling system consistently across the entire site.
    - Are the labels the same from one page to another?
    - Do the headings on subpages correspond to the navigational labeling system?

USING SCOPE NOTES

Y ou can use scope notes to communicate the range of content covered in each area of your site. *Scope notes* specify exactly what content pieces each section includes, and often appear alongside navigation elements on the front door or home page of a Web site. For example, a navigational element labeled "About Us" might contain a brief scope list of the information contained in that section, including the history of the company, management biographies, press releases, and advertising information.

If your site uses a topical organizational scheme, create scope notes that highlight the subtopics of each directory. For task-oriented organizational schemes, you can use scope notes to further clarify how the user is going to accomplish the task on your site. For example, for a directory labeled "Find a Product," an appropriate scope note might indicate whether the task involves searching a database or exploring a subject directory of products.

Should I include scope notes on each page of a site?

✔ The purpose of these notes is to help the user understand the area covered by each of your organization labels. After you have established the scope on the front door, you do not need to include them on the subpages of your site.

How can I display scope notes when the user mouses over a navigation element?

✔ You can use Flash, DHTML, or simple JavaScript event handlers to display scope notes when a user mouses over a navigation button. For information on creating JavaScript mouseovers, see Chapter 15.

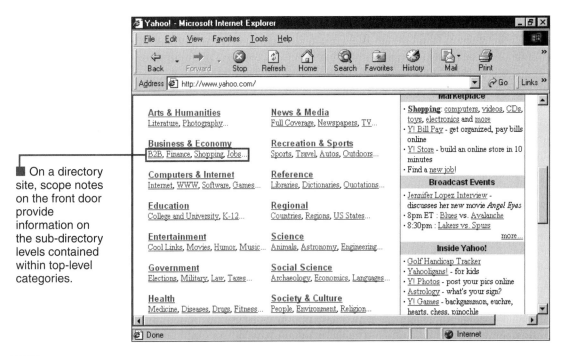

■ On a directory site, scope notes on the front door provide information on the sub-directory levels contained within top-level categories.

■ These scope notes also act as navigation links, allowing users to jump directly to lower-level categories.

USING ICON LABELS

You can use icon labels on your Web pages to visually represent informational organization. *Icon labels*, or small images used to represent each navigational element, can add to the visual impact of a page, but in order for icons to be effective, make sure that the meaning of each image is clear and understandable.

When using icon labels, developing icons that match exact content categories is sometimes difficult, and there are very few conventions in

use for icons on the Web that people easily recognize. Some Web sites use an icon of a house to represent the home page, a postal letter to represent the "Contact Us" section, and a question mark for frequently asked questions. Beyond these common content areas, you have to develop understandable icons to visually represent abstract concepts. For example, it might be difficult to come up with icons that represent categories such as "Clients," "Partners," or "Press Releases."

MASTER IT

If I use icon labels for navigation elements, should I also include text links?

✔ Including text links when you use images for navigation elements is always a good idea, because many alternative browsers are text-only and do not render images. In fact, including redundant text links helps a site meet the Web Content Accessibility Guidelines set forth by the W3C. For more information, visit www.w3.org/WAI/. At the very least, be sure to use descriptive *alternative text*—text that you add to images using the `alt` attribute—for any graphics that visitors use to navigate your site. For more on alternative text, see Chapter 7.

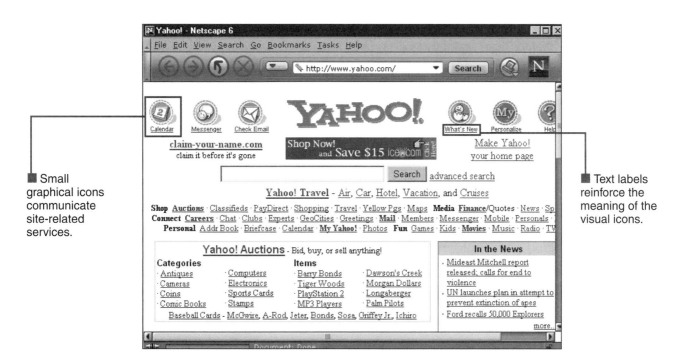

■ Small graphical icons communicate site-related services.

■ Text labels reinforce the meaning of the visual icons.

DESIGN A SEARCH INTERFACE

You can help users find the information they are looking for by designing an effective search interface. An effective search interface should be simple enough for users to understand, yet give them the ability to control the scope of the search.

When you design your search interface, decide whether you want to have a simple interface or whether you want to give users the ability to perform a power search, where they can select variables to limit or expand the scope of their search. You also need to decide whether your search interface

should use natural language or Boolean queries where the user includes words such as AND, OR, and NOT to define the scope of the search.

Most visitors browsing the Web have come to expect a simple search interface on the front door or home page of a site, usually in the side navigation bar or head of the page. If you offer visitors the option to limit or expand the scope of the search, you can include a link to a power search page near the primary search interface.

How do I determine if I need to add search capabilities to my site?

✔ The larger your site is, the more important search functionality becomes. If your site consists of just a few pages that users can easily navigate to find what they are looking for, you probably do not need to have search capabilities.

How do I integrate search functionality into my site?

✔ You can add search functionality to a site a variety of ways. You can use server-side scripting solutions such as Perl or CGI to search your site for keywords and phrases, or you can use a commercial software product or online search service. For a comprehensive list of software and online search options, visit www.searchtools.com.

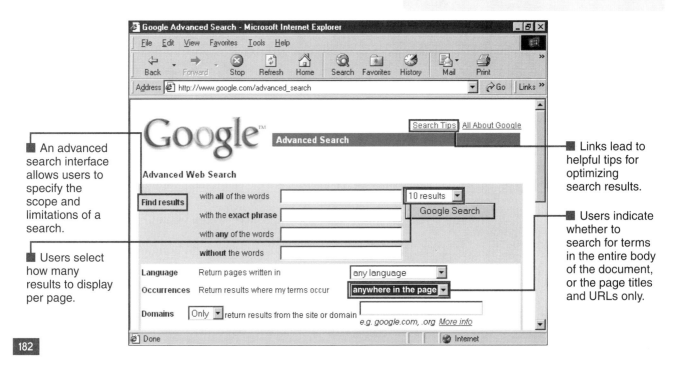

■ An advanced search interface allows users to specify the scope and limitations of a search.

■ Users select how many results to display per page.

■ Links lead to helpful tips for optimizing search results.

■ Users indicate whether to search for terms in the entire body of the document, or the page titles and URLs only.

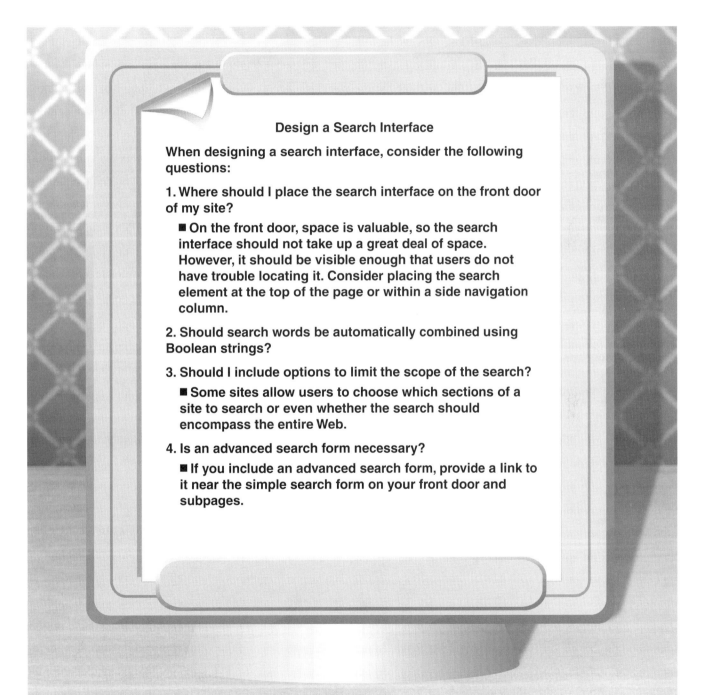

Design a Search Interface

When designing a search interface, consider the following questions:

1. Where should I place the search interface on the front door of my site?

  ■ On the front door, space is valuable, so the search interface should not take up a great deal of space. However, it should be visible enough that users do not have trouble locating it. Consider placing the search element at the top of the page or within a side navigation column.

2. Should search words be automatically combined using Boolean strings?

3. Should I include options to limit the scope of the search?

  ■ Some sites allow users to choose which sections of a site to search or even whether the search should encompass the entire Web.

4. Is an advanced search form necessary?

  ■ If you include an advanced search form, provide a link to it near the simple search form on your front door and subpages.

DISPLAY SEARCH RESULTS

When you design your search results templates, consider how much information to display, how many results you want per page, and how the results should be ordered.

How much information you display for each result returned depends on the type of information you have on your site and the information that is of most value to the user. Most search results should contain a hypertext title leading to the specific information page as well as a brief description. Any additional information you include with each result depends on your content. For example, if your site features news articles, search results might include the date of publication, because timeliness

may be a factor in how the user determines the relevance of each search result.

If you display a large amount of information for each result, only display a small number of results on each page. Display more results per page if your entries are very brief. Always let users know the total number of results returned for their query, and give them a way to easily navigate between result pages.

The way you order search results also depends on the type of content on your site. You can order results alphabetically, chronologically, or by relevance, based on how often the search terms occur on a page or the proximity of terms within the text.

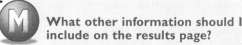

What other information should I include on the results page?

✔ Consider repeating the original search string, because searching is an iterative process. Most users perform multiple searches, refining the query each time to return better results. After a number of individual searches, users might not remember the string of keywords they are using. If you include an additional search box on the results page, pre-populate the form fields with the current keywords being searched.

How many search results should I display on each page?

✔ This depends on how much information you display for each individual result, but a good rule of thumb is to display 10 to 20 results per page. You can also give users the ability to decide for themselves how many results to display via a drop-down menu.

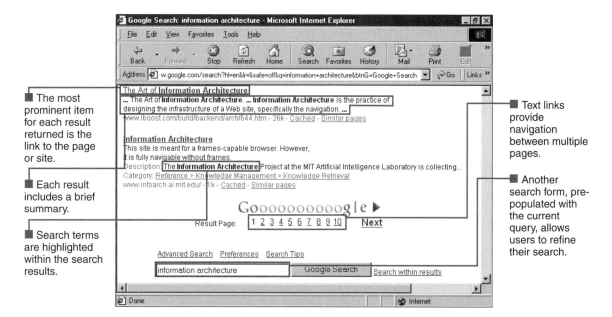

The most prominent item for each result returned is the link to the page or site.

Each result includes a brief summary.

Search terms are highlighted within the search results.

Text links provide navigation between multiple pages.

Another search form, pre-populated with the current query, allows users to refine their search.

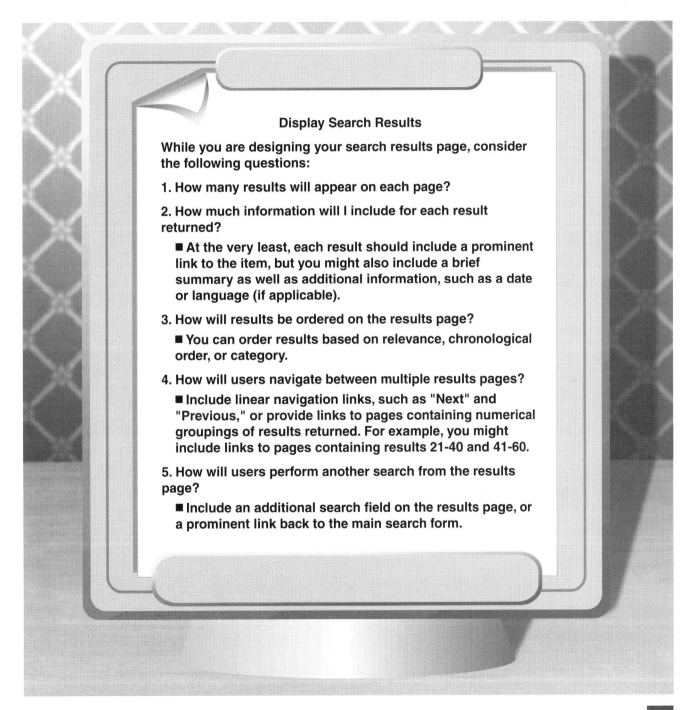

Display Search Results

While you are designing your search results page, consider the following questions:

1. How many results will appear on each page?

2. How much information will I include for each result returned?

■ At the very least, each result should include a prominent link to the item, but you might also include a brief summary as well as additional information, such as a date or language (if applicable).

3. How will results be ordered on the results page?

■ You can order results based on relevance, chronological order, or category.

4. How will users navigate between multiple results pages?

■ Include linear navigation links, such as "Next" and "Previous," or provide links to pages containing numerical groupings of results returned. For example, you might include links to pages containing results 21-40 and 41-60.

5. How will users perform another search from the results page?

■ Include an additional search field on the results page, or a prominent link back to the main search form.

AN INTRODUCTION TO WEB NAVIGATION

Although the Web is "virtual," users still think of the Web as a space to be navigated. Depending on what their goals are, users may navigate the Web or a particular site trying to get from point A to point B, or they might explore a space in a more non-linear way. Either way, Web designers must provide users with adequate means of finding their way around the space of a site.

Keys to Navigation

Being able to successfully navigate a space depends on having key pieces of information, such as your current location, where you can go, how you can reach your destination, and how you can find your way back. For example, when you travel to a new geographical location, you probably use a map to plot a path to and from your destination, but in order to do so, you have to be able to orient yourself and pinpoint your current location.

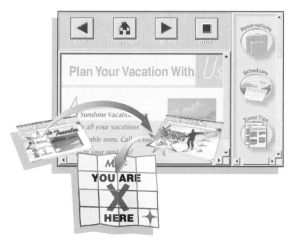

As you design your site's navigation system, stay focused on user actions and how visitors might go about accomplishing their goals. Whenever possible, take advantage of user personas and scenarios (see Chapter 1) to put yourself in the visitor's place. Remember that navigation systems should be clear and easy to use, and provide users with multiple means of reaching their destination. For more information, see the section "Incorporate Multiple Navigation Schemes."

Navigation and Structure

How we navigate information is related to how that information is structured and labeled. When you create navigation bars or tabs for your site, the navigational options that you offer correspond to the hierarchical structure of your site. Additionally, the text that you use for navigation links, buttons, page titles, and headings should be based on a consistent labeling system. Before you begin devising appropriate navigation schemes, you should first develop a coherent organizational structure and make sure that your section labels are consistent and clear. For more information, see Chapter 8.

Orientation

In order to navigate effectively, users need to know where they are in the context of the overall site structure. Web visitors are much like busy travelers, jumping quickly from one destination to the next until each town or city begins to resemble the last.

Similarly, as visitors explore a site, clicking on link after link, they can quickly become disoriented and lose sight of where they are in the overall structure. This makes it difficult for visitors to make their way to other parts of your site or to revisit previous pages.

One way to help users orient themselves is by reinforcing placement, or position. When you reinforce placement, you provide the visitor with a mental map of the site, complete with a metaphorical X that says, "You are Here."

Explore ways of letting users know exactly where they are on your site in the sections "Reinforce Position," "Using URLs to Reinforce Placement," and "Optimize Page Titles."

Providing Shortcuts

On the Web, movement does not have to be linear. A user-friendly navigation scheme gives users the ability to quickly jump directly to a destination page without having to click through numerous links or use the browser's back and forward buttons. This chapter details several ways you can provide users with shortcuts, including

- Site maps, which are similar to a book's table of contents. You can read more about site maps in "Implement a Site Map," later in this chapter.

- Bread-crumb trails, sometimes called *topic paths*, which ideally consist of clickable links that show how the current page fits into the overall hierarchy of the site. You can read more about bread-crumb trails in "Create a Bread-Crumb Trail or Topic Path."

- Homepage links, which can be either text or images. For more on the latter, see "Using a Logo as a Homepage Link."

CREATE A SIDE NAVIGATION BAR

One common way of presenting users with navigation options is to use a navigation bar in the left or right column of the site. When you use a side navigation bar, you can either present top-level navigation elements, or include links to content areas on the second level of the information hierarchy. This way you can provide users with shortcuts to the specific content pieces.

To add a side navigation bar to a Web page, you can use frames, CSS layout techniques, or HTML tables. When using a table layout, create one large table column for the main content and one smaller column for the navigation elements. To further control the layout of the navigation elements, place the links or buttons within an additional table.

Side navigation bars are often visually highlighted by using a different background color. When using different background colors for elements of a page layout, be sure to test your link colors to ensure that they are still legible. See Chapter 3 for more on link colors and Chapter 10 for an overall look at the visual interface.

CREATE A SIDE NAVIGATION BAR

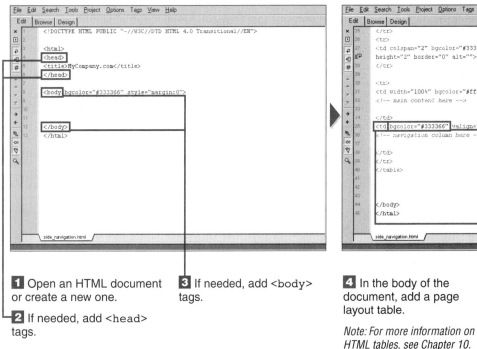

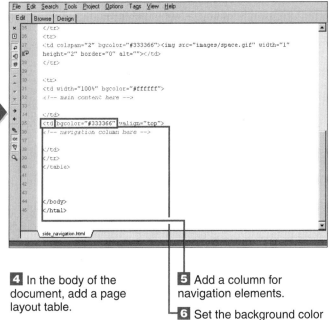

1 Open an HTML document or create a new one.

2 If needed, add <head> tags.

3 If needed, add <body> tags.

4 In the body of the document, add a page layout table.

Note: For more information on HTML tables, see Chapter 10.

5 Add a column for navigation elements.

6 Set the background color of the column.

MASTER IT

Can I use frames to implement a side navigation bar?

✔ Yes, you can use a frameset and have one frame devoted to navigation and the other to the site's main content. However, there are some disadvantages to using frames for this purpose. For more information, see Chapter 5.

Is it possible to have two different colors for links, one for the navigation bar and another for links within the main content area?

✔ Yes. You can use Cascading Style Sheets to define pseudo-classes for links. For more information, see Chapter 6.

How can I add an interactive element to navigation buttons?

✔ You can use JavaScript to change the image on mouseover. Then, use your "on" state image as the static navigation button on the destination page to reinforce placement. For more information on creating JavaScript rollovers, see Chapter 15.

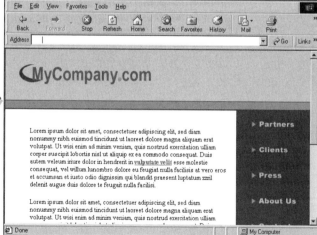

7 Add navigation images or links.

■ Use an embedded table to format navigation images.

8 Save the file.

9 View the page in a Web browser.

■ The main column is reserved for content, while the side column is used for site navigation.

CREATE A BASIC TABBED NAVIGATION BAR

You can provide users with an easy way of navigating between sections of your site by using a tabbed navigation bar. Tabbed navigation bars are usually located at the top of a Web page, below the main Company logo or header graphic. Clicking on one of the tabs loads the index page for a particular category. You can also use the navigation bar to reinforce position by having "on" state tabs

for each category (see the section "Reinforce Position").

When creating a tabbed navigation bar at the top of a Web page, you can use CSS or HTML tables to control the layout of the elements. See Chapter 10 for more on page layout options. If you use an HTML table, place all of the navigation "tabs" within the same table row. For even more control over the

placement of the navigation elements, use another HTML table inside the primary table row. Although you can create the individual tabs using regular HTML hyperlinks (see Chapter 3), it is more common to use Web images for the navigation elements. To learn more about creating and editing Web graphics, see Chapter 12.

CREATE A BASIC TABBED NAVIGATION BAR

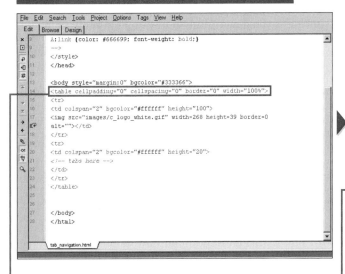

■ **1** Open an HTML document or create a new one.

■ **2** Use an HTML table or CSS box for page layout.

■ This example uses an HTML table.

Note: For more information on page layouts, see Chapter 10.

■ **3** Create a CSS box or table row to contain the navigation elements.

■ This example uses a table row.

■ **4** Inside the table row, add the navigation images using `<img>` tags.

■ **5** Enclose each navigation image within an `<a>` tag.

■ Each image is now a clickable link leading to the corresponding page.

■ **6** Save the file.

What should I keep in mind when considering topics for tabs?

✔ When using tabs, be consistent in the options you offer. If your navigation tabs represent a mix of topics, such as product categories, and tasks, such as "Contact Us" or "Check out," consider reorganizing your site's structure (see Chapter 8) to ensure that your hierarchy of information is consistent.

How can I add interactive elements to tabbed navigation bars?

✔ You can add an interactive element to navigation tabs by adding mouseover effects. If your navigation elements are regular hyperlinks, you can use style properties to add mouseover effects. If you use images in your navigation bar, use JavaScript to create mouseover image-swaps.

How many tabs should I include in a navigation bar?

✔ The navigation tabs should reflect the general hierarchy of your information architecture, and should neither be too shallow nor too broad, because too many choices overwhelm the user. Additionally, from the standpoint of page layout, including more than five to seven tab items takes up a great deal of horizontal space. To compensate, some Web sites that have a large number of topical categories use a multi-tiered navigation bar.

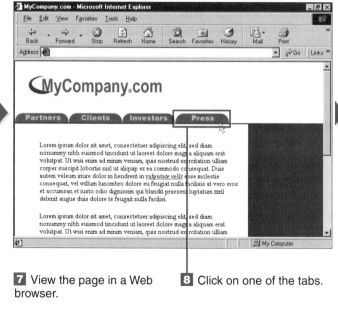

7 View the page in a Web browser.

8 Click on one of the tabs.

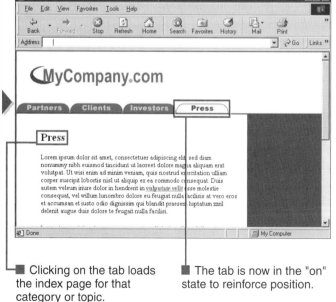

■ Clicking on the tab loads the index page for that category or topic.

■ The tab is now in the "on" state to reinforce position.

IMPLEMENT A SITE MAP

Give visitors a bird's eye view of your site structure and content by including a site map. A site map's purpose is two-fold: It provides direct links, or shortcuts, to all of the content pages on a site, and it illustrates how content relates to the overall site structure.

A site map is very similar to a book's table of contents, where a reader can see all of the sections of a book and the individual subsections contained within each chapter. For a Web-based site map, you can present this information in a table, listing the specific content pages contained within each area of your site's information hierarchy. If you use a table to format the site map, place each content section inside a new table data cell. You can then control alignment and other formatting elements by using `<td>` attributes such as `align` and `valign`. For more information on using tables for page layout, see Chapter 10.

In a site map, each content piece should be a hyperlink allowing users to jump directly to the desired page. In addition, each category or topic heading should link to the category's index page.

IMPLEMENT A SITE MAP

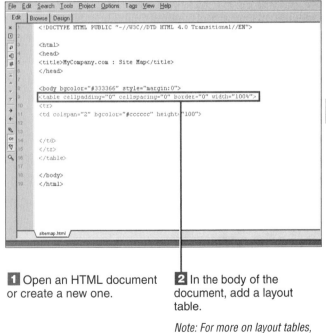

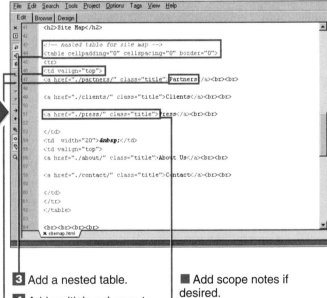

1 Open an HTML document or create a new one.

2 In the body of the document, add a layout table.

Note: For more on layout tables, see Chapter 10.

3 Add a nested table.

4 Add multiple columns to the table.

5 Add headings for each content area of your site.

■ Add scope notes if desired.

Note: For more information on scope notes, see Chapter 8.

6 Link each section heading to its index page.

How can I use different hyperlink colors in a site map?

✔ You can use CSS to create various *classes* of hyperlinks, each with a different color. For example, you might use CSS to create a different-colored link style for headings within your site map. When mixing hyperlink styles, keep in mind that visitors learn to associate a particular color with clickable text. If you alter the color, be sure that it is still clear that the text is a hyperlink. To learn how to create and apply classes, see Chapter 6.

Can I use a graphical site map rather than a text-based site map?

✔ You can, but there are a few disadvantages to using a graphical site map rather than a site map with text links. A graphical representation has a slower download time than an HTML table with text links. In addition, if you add or remove content, you will have to edit the image and map, rather than simply adding additional links where appropriate.

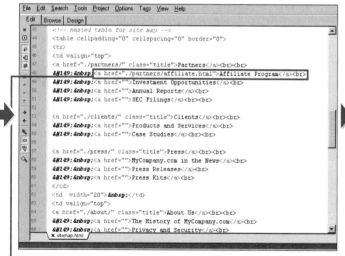

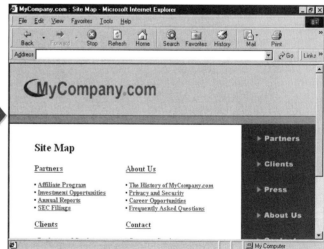

7 Add links to each piece of content.

Note: For more on links, see Chapter 3.

■ Linked text should be consistent with page titles.

8 Save the file.

9 View the page in a Web browser.

■ The site map or table of contents allows users to easily jump to specific content.

CREATE A BREAD-CRUMB TRAIL OR TOPIC PATH

You can reinforce position and allow users to navigate to higher category levels on your site by using a bread-crumb trail, also called a topic path.

Bread-crumb trails are usually placed at the top of a page, beneath the main header graphic, to demonstrate where the current page occurs within the overall hierarchy. For example, a Web site

that sells products might include a bread-crumb trail such as:

```
home > products >
accessories > product name
```

With the exception of the last element referring to the current page, the other elements in the bread-crumb trail should be clickable links and allow users to navigate back up to the front door of the site.

Bread-crumb trails begin with a link to the front door of the site, followed by links to the appropriate subdirectories. The last element is the name of the product or the title of the current page. You can separate each element using dashes, colons, ellipses, or greater-than signs.

CREATE A BREAD-CRUMB TRAIL OR TOPIC PATH

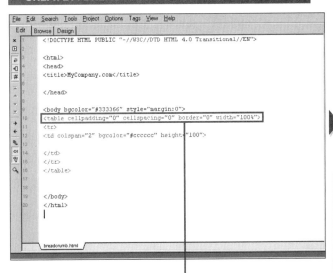

1 Open an HTML document in a text editor.

2 Add a page layout table.

Note: For more on layout tables, see Chapter 10.

3 Below the main page header, add a table row to house the topic path.

Note: For more on table rows, see Chapter 3.

4 Set the background color of the row.

5 Add links to higher level directories.

■ Separate each element with a colon or greater-than sign.

Is there a way to automate the creation of bread-crumb trails?

✔ Many content management tools are capable of automating the creation of bread-crumb trails or topic paths. In general, this requires server-side solutions and more advanced scripting techniques. However, you can use JavaScript to define the elements in the bread-crumb trail and then dynamically write them to the document. For more information on JavaScript, see Chapter 14.

How would a news or content Web site use a bread-crumb trail?

✔ On a news or content site, the bread-crumb trail should include a link to the front door of the site as well as links to the content directory and subdirectories in which the feature or article resides. For the final element in the bread-crumb trail, you can use the title of the article:

```
home > content area >
article title
```

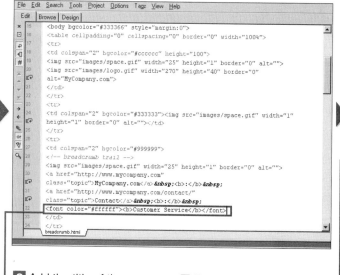

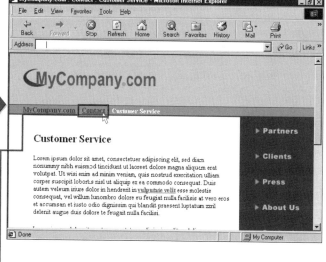

6 Add the title of the current page to the end of the topic path.

■ Format the text using HTML or style sheet properties. For more on HTML formatting, see Chapter 3; for style sheets, see Chapter 6.

7 Save the document.

8 View the page in a Web browser.

9 Click one of the links in the bread-crumb trail.

■ The links in the bread-crumb trail provide easy navigation to top level directories in the topic path.

REINFORCE POSITION

Help visitors orient themselves within your site by providing elements that reinforce position. Page titles, headings, graphic elements, and such act as markers to let the visitor know, "You are here." When users understand where they are within the site's hierarchy, they can then more easily navigate to other parts of the site.

The first step in reinforcing position is to make sure that your page headings and HTML titles communicate where the user is within the information hierarchy (see the section "Optimize Page Titles"). To avoid confusion, use consistent language in all text headings. For example, small variations between a page title and a heading—such as using both

"Customer Service" and "Support" to refer to the same page—can confuse visitors.

If you use graphic icon labels for each section of your site, use the appropriate icon at the top of the page or elsewhere within the body of the page as a repeating motif. For more information on icon labels, see Chapter 8.

REINFORCE POSITION

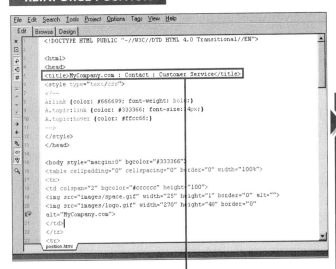

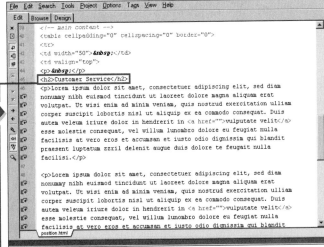

1 Open an HTML document in a text editor.

■ This example uses position.html.

2 Add a descriptive HTML title.

Note: For more information on effective page titles, see "Optimize Page Titles."

3 Add a page heading.

■ Headings should be consistent with your labeling system.

How can I reinforce position if my site uses frames?

✔ If your site uses frames for page layout—one frame for content and another for navigation—you have fewer opportunities to reinforce position for the site visitor. On a frame-based site, the HTML title and URL remain constant, and it is difficult to add "on" and "off" state images to framed navigation bars. To compensate, include elements such as bread-crumb trails, headings, and graphical icons in the main content pages. For more information on using frames, see Chapter 5.

How do I reinforce position within navigation bars?

✔ If your navigation bar uses text links, reinforce position by making the current page non-clickable. If you use images, you can implement rollover events with "on" state image swapping. On the current page, have the image set to the "on" state. For more information on scripting image mouseovers, see Chapter 15.

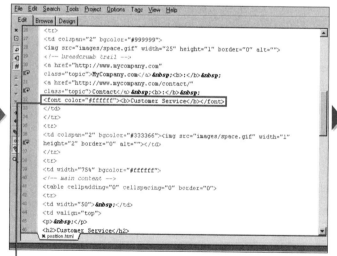

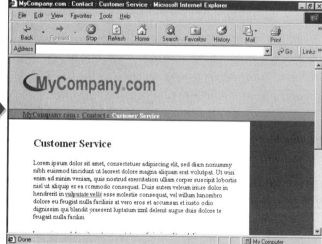

4 Within the bread-crumb trail, make the current page title non-clickable text.

Note: See "Create a Bread-Crumb Trail or Topic Path."

5 Save the document.

6 View the page in a Web browser.

■ Elements such as titles, headings, and navigation aids help orient the visitor.

USING URLS TO REINFORCE PLACEMENT

Web designers often forget that the URL of a Web page provides the user with information regarding the structure of the site and the placement of a particular page within the hierarchy. Optimize this information by ensuring that the names of your site directories and HTML pages are user-friendly and clearly communicate the content of the destination page.

When a user mouses over or selects a hypertext link, the URL of the destination page is displayed in the status line (see Chapter 15 for information on altering the status line). The information contained in this URL, including the directory names and the name of the HTML page, provides the user with valuable contextual information. This makes it easier for users to locate specific pages at a later date,

even if they do not remember the exact path.

For example, the URL "http://www.site.com/about/history. html" communicates information about the structure of the site and the content, whereas "/about/page1.html" does not.

USING URLS TO REINFORCE PLACEMENT

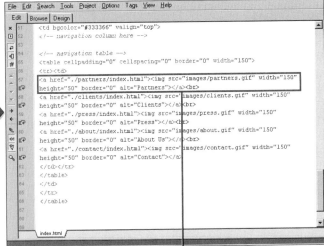

1 Create a local copy of your site.

2 If you have not already done so, organize your Web site into a directory and subdirectory structure.

Note: You can also create your directory structure from within an HTML application, an FTP utility, or via the command line.

3 Apply consistent labels that communicate the topic area of each directory.

4 Open a new or existing HTML document in an HTML or text editor.

5 Add links to content in subdirectories.

6 Save the document.

How can I optimize URLs if I am using a content management system that generates numbered pages?

✔ Unreadable URLs have become an increasingly widespread problem as more companies adopt sophisticated content management systems that dynamically serve Web pages. More often than not, these systems name pages using complex numbers, so that you might come across pages called "485143-3.html" or something similar. If your content system generates numbered pages, there is little you can do to optimize URLs. Compensate by reinforcing placement in other ways, through titles, headings, and graphic icons.

What techniques can I use if I am not able to optimize the URLs for my pages?

✔ If your pages are dynamically generated and you are unable to optimize the URLs, consider implementing link titles (see the section "Using Link Titles") or using JavaScript to provide users with information via the status line. With JavaScript, you can set the default status line for each individual page. While not as visible as the URL, the status line displays a message at the bottom of the browser window. For more information, see Chapter 15.

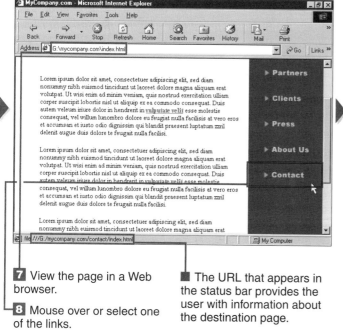

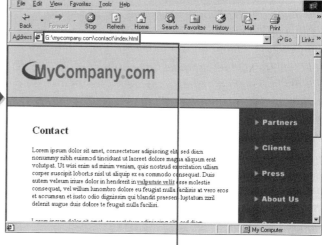

7 View the page in a Web browser.

8 Mouse over or select one of the links.

■ The URL that appears in the status bar provides the user with information about the destination page.

9 Click on the link.

■ The URL in the address bar reinforces position and helps users orient themselves within the site's structure.

OPTIMIZE PAGE TITLES

An easy way to reinforce position within the hierarchy of a site is through HTML page titles. Rather than simply including the title of the individual page, include the path leading from the front door of the site, down through the sub-directories, to the current page.

You can use colons, dashes, or other characters to clearly delineate each element within the title. For example, you might include titles such as "MyCompanyName : Press Releases : 2002 : January 5, 2002," where the last element refers to the current page.

Add titles to a Web page using the HTML <title> tags. Every HTML document must include a set of <title> tags within the head of the document. Only one title per document is allowed.

The text you include within this set of tags appears in the window bar of the browser itself, above the standard buttons (for more information on creating an HTML skeleton, see Chapter 3). The browser also uses the title text when adding a site to the user's bookmarks or favorites list.

OPTIMIZE PAGE TITLES

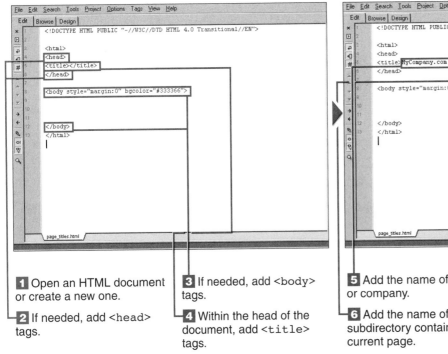

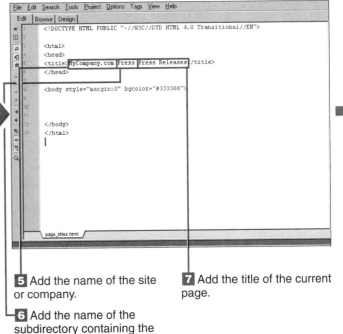

1 Open an HTML document or create a new one.

2 If needed, add <head> tags.

3 If needed, add <body> tags.

4 Within the head of the document, add <title> tags.

5 Add the name of the site or company.

6 Add the name of the subdirectory containing the current page.

7 Add the title of the current page.

Are there any optional attributes that can be used with the `<title>` tag?

✔ Two optional attributes, `dir` and `lang`, define the direction of the text in the document and the language in which the content is written. You can read more about the `lang` attribute in Chapter 7. For more information about using the `dir` attribute, consult the official HTML specification at www.w3.org/MarkUp/.

What is the difference between a page title and a page heading?

✔ A page title is the text displayed in the browser's own title bar. Headings are text elements that you add to the body of a document using special heading tags such as `<h1>`. For more information on heading tags, see Chapter 3.

Can I include HTML markup within the `<title>` tags?

✔ No. The browser only recognizes plain text within the `<title>` tags. Additional HTML tags do not cause errors, but they are rendered as text. For example, if you try to apply bold formatting using `<b></b>` tags, the browser treats those tags as regular text and prints the characters. You may, however, include character entities within the text of a title (see Chapter 3 for more on using special characters).

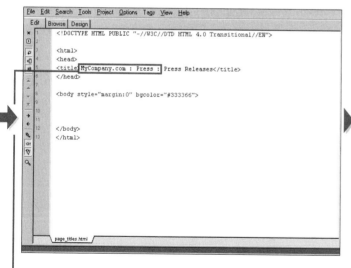

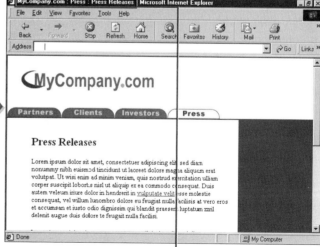

8 Separate each element of the title using colons or some other marker.

9 Add any desired additional content to the page.

10 Save the document.

11 View the page in a Web browser.

■ The title is displayed in the browser window, and provides contextual information about the page and site structure.

CLARIFY TEXT LINKS

Embedded text links provide users with an additional means of navigating content, this time based on editorial context. Within the paragraphs of text you have on a particular page, you might include embedded links to other content on your site or related content on external sites. For these links to be effective, be sure that the linked text provides enough context to communicate to the user exactly what information is being linked to.

When using embedded text links, make sure that the linked text provides the user with enough context. Sometimes linked text is too vague to be meaningful to the user or is not well integrated into the whole paragraph. For example, using text such as "Click here for more information" places the link out of the context of the text as a whole.

Providing adequate context is important because clicking a link means the user must abandon the current page. Users are less likely to follow links if they are unsure where the link will take them.

CLARIFY TEXT LINKS

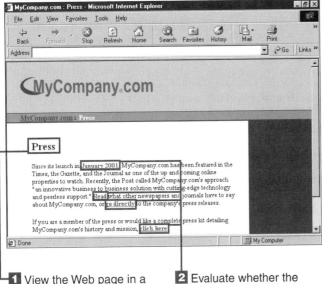

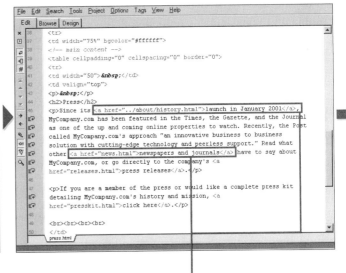

1 View the Web page in a Web browser.

■ This example uses the press.html document available on this book's CD-ROM.

2 Evaluate whether the existing embedded callout text provides the user with enough contextual information.

3 Open the document in a text or HTML editor.

4 Change the link text so that it better reflects the destination page.

How do I specify the color of embedded text links?

✔ You can specify link color through the `link`, `alink`, and `vlink` HTML attributes associated with the `<body>` tag. For more on setting link colors, see Chapter 3. Alternatively, you can use style sheets to specify link colors. See Chapter 6 for more on style sheets.

What other ways can I provide context for embedded links?

✔ You can provide additional context for links by using link titles with each `<a>` tag. For more information, see the section "Using Link Titles."

How else can I provide links to related information without embedding them into the main content?

✔ Rather than embedding links into your main content, you can include them at the bottom of the page in a list or table, or include them in a side navigation bar. These techniques allow you to provide additional information for each link, such as the source or specific location of the content, and prevent the links from distracting users from the main text.

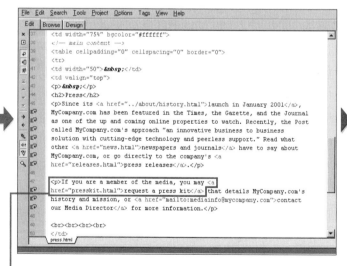

■ Remember to reword link text to avoid phrases such as "Click here."

5 Save the document.

6 Reload the page in a Web browser.

■ The embedded text is now more closely linked to the destination pages.

USING LINK TITLES

Provide additional context for hypertext links by using link titles. When the user mouses over or otherwise selects a link, the browser creates a small box containing the text you have indicated. Use this text to give the visitor additional information about the destination page.

The title attribute is one of the core attributes defined in the HTML 4.0 specification, and can be applied to almost any tag in the markup language. The title attribute is similar to the alt attribute that you use with images and embedded objects to provide a textual description. The title attribute allows you to add similar text descriptions to a wide variety of elements on a page. To add a title to a link, simply use the attribute within the opening <a> tag and specify the title within quotation marks.

```
<a href="URL" title="title
of destination page">
```

For consistency, you should include the title of the document as it appears on the destination page. For example, if the destination page is titled "Press Releases," use this title in the <a> tag:

```
<a href="press.html"
title="Press Releases">
```

USING LINK TITLES

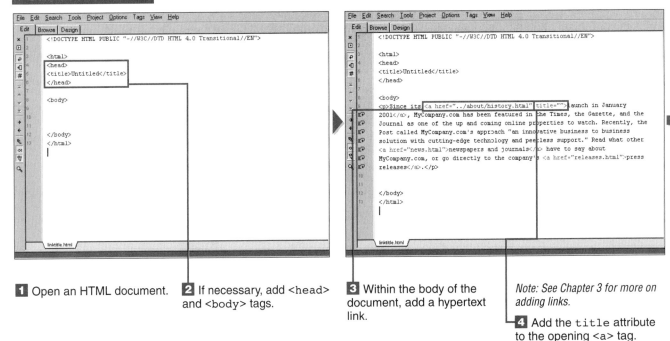

1 Open an HTML document.

2 If necessary, add <head> and <body> tags.

3 Within the body of the document, add a hypertext link.

Note: See Chapter 3 for more on adding links.

4 Add the title attribute to the opening <a> tag.

Is the title attribute supported by all browsers?

✔ The title attribute is not supported by older browsers, because the attribute is part of the more recent HTML 4.0 specification. However, browsers that do not support the attribute simply ignore it.

What other HTML tags support the title attribute?

✔ All HTML tags support the attribute except for a small number of document-level elements: HTML, HEAD, TITLE, META, SCRIPT, BASE, BASEFONT, and PARAM.

Do browsers that support the attribute render the title the same way?

✔ Depending on the browser and platform, the appearance of the title text may vary somewhat, much like the alternative text for images provided by the alt attribute (see Chapter 7 for more on using the alt attribute). In fact, the HTML specification notes that implementation of the title text may vary between browsing clients.

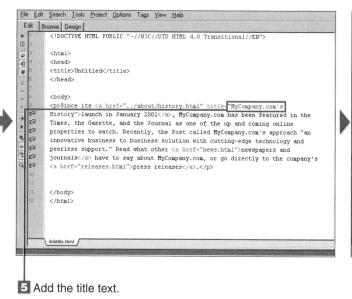

5 Add the title text.

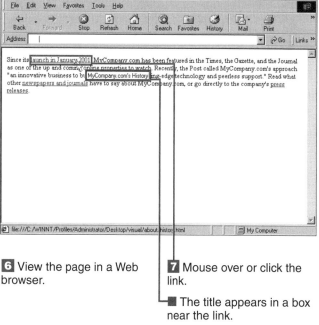

6 View the page in a Web browser.

7 Mouse over or click the link.

■ The title appears in a box near the link.

USING A LOGO AS A HOMEPAGE LINK

Every page on your site should include an easy way for visitors to return to the home page. One of the best ways to accomplish this is to incorporate a link into your main company or site logo.

Linking back to the home page through a company logo is standard practice on the Web today, which means that you can rely on learned behavior and incorporate the link without further explanatory text. Optionally, you can include instructive text using the <img> tag's alt attribute or the title attribute in the opening <a> tag. For example, you might provide alternative text such as "Click here to return to MyCompany's home page," or simply use the label "Home."

In addition to linking via the main logo, consider providing other links back to the home page. You can include a link in a text navigation bar at the bottom of the page, or include the link in your bread-crumb trail (see the section "Create a Bread-Crumb Trail or Topic Path").

USING A LOGO AS A HOMEPAGE LINK

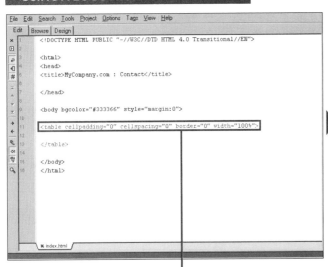

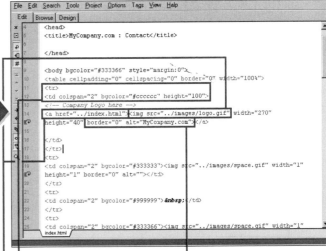

1 Open an HTML document or create a new one.

2 Add a table for layout purposes.

Note: see Chapter 10 for more information on page layout.

3 Create a row to contain your company logo.

4 Add the logo using an HTML <img> tag.

5 Add an <a> tag with the href attribute set to the home page of the site.

6 Set the border attribute and add alternative text or a link title.

■ Add additional content to the page.

7 Save the document.

How do I use a relative URL to link to a higher-level directory?

✔ Use relative URLs to point to directories higher up in the site structure by using the "../" notation. For example, if the current document is in a sub-directory, such as www.mysite.com/about/, you can include a link to the top-level directory by setting the `href` attribute to "../". Alternately, you can use the `<base>` tag within the head of the document to set the base URL. The browser then resolves all relative URLs in the document to absolute URLs.

How do I turn off the blue border around a clickable image?

✔ Any image that is enclosed with `<a>` tags includes a border in the link color you specify via the `link` attribute or `style` properties. If you do not specify a link color, the border is standard blue. To eliminate this border, add the `border` attribute to the `<img>` tag and set the value to 0 (zero).

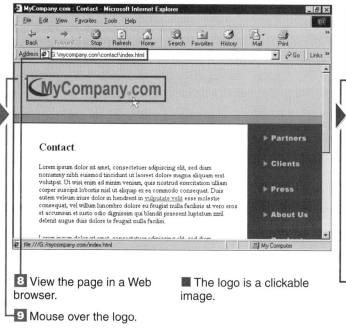

■ **8** View the page in a Web browser.

■ **9** Mouse over the logo.

■ The logo is a clickable image.

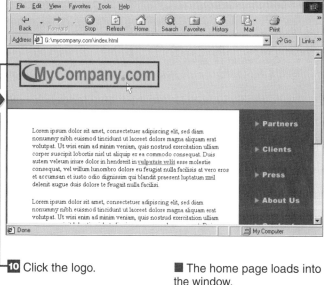

■ **10** Click the logo.

■ The home page loads into the window.

INCORPORATE MULTIPLE NAVIGATION SCHEMES

P rovide users with different ways of navigating your site by including multiple navigation elements, such as bread-crumb trails, navigation bars, text links, site maps, and search interfaces.

Including multiple schemes is important on the Web, because users navigate sites in a variety of different ways. Users who know what they are looking for navigate a site by searching for specific items, whereas users who want to explore tend to use elements such as navigation bars and tabs to drill down through a site's hierarchy. You should always accommodate both types of visitors by providing a search interface, a primary navigation bar, and a bread-crumb trail on each page of your site. At the foot of the page, provide links to other navigation aides, such as site maps, global directories or more advanced search options.

In addition, incorporating multiple and even redundant navigation elements helps ensure that if users do not immediately see the main site navigation, they can still move around the site and find what they are looking for. Remember that what may seem obvious to you may not be so apparent to a first-time visitor.

INCORPORATE MULTIPLE NAVIGATION SCHEMES

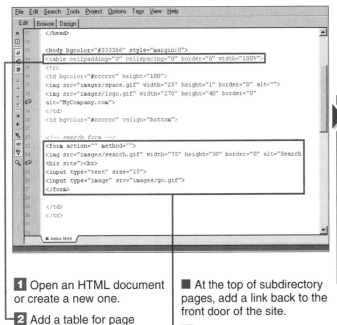

1 Open an HTML document or create a new one.

2 Add a table for page layout.

■ At the top of subdirectory pages, add a link back to the front door of the site.

3 Add a search interface.

4 Add a side navigation bar or tabbed navigation bar.

■ Add bread-crumb trail navigation to subdirectory pages.

Is it necessary to include search as a means of navigation?

✔ Most users expect to be able to search medium to large-scale sites. However, if your site consists of only a few pages, it probably is not necessary to include search functionality. For more information on incorporating search into your site, see Chapter 8.

What is the advantage of repeating the main site navigation at the top and the bottom of each page?

✔ If your pages contain a lot of content and require quite a bit of scrolling, it is useful to repeat the navigation at the bottom of the page so that users do not have to scroll back up to the top of the page.

How do I incorporate multiple navigation schemes without occupying too much space?

✔ Simple search interfaces can easily be added to the top of the page, and primary navigation can be placed in a small horizontal row beneath the masthead or in a side column. Remember to use the bottom of the page as well—particularly for redundant navigation links. For more on page layout techniques, see Chapter 10.

5 At the bottom of the page, repeat the primary navigation elements.

6 Add a link to a site map.

7 Save the document.

8 View the page in a Web browser.

■ Multiple navigation elements ensure that visitors can explore the site easily.

SECTION IV

12) CREATE WEB GRAPHICS

13) USING NEW WEB GRAPHICS STANDARDS

AN INTRODUCTION TO COLOR THEORY

One of the most important elements in a designer's toolbox is color. Designers use color to create impact, evoke a response, and guide the viewer through the visual flow of a document. In order to use color effectively on the Web, it is helpful to understand how colors are classified and created, depending on the medium at work.

This section briefly explores some of the common ways you can work with color, and provides an introduction to the RGB color model used on computer monitor displays.

Talking About Color

The following terms are commonly used to describe color properties:

- *Hue*: A particular color on the spectrum, such as "red" or "yellow."

- *Saturation*: The vividness or intensity of a hue.

- *Value*: The relative lightness or darkness of a color. Values can be either shades or tints.

- *Shade*: A gradation of a color produced by adding black.

- *Tint*: A gradation of a color produced by adding white.

- *Primary colors*: The three main colors of a color model or color wheel.

- *Secondary colors*: Colors produced when combining two primary colors.

- *Tertiary colors*: Colors produced by combining two secondary colors, or a primary color with an adjacent secondary color.

- *Complementary colors*: Colors across from one another on a color wheel.

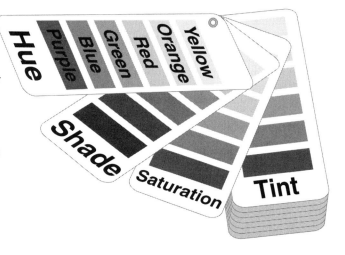

CMY(K) Color Model

CMY(K) is the color model used in traditional print and closely resembles the traditional artist's color wheel, where the primary colors are blue, red, and yellow. In the case of CMY(K), the primary colors are cyan, magenta, and yellow, and the secondary colors are red, green, and blue.

CMY(K) is a *subtractive* color model in which superimposed layers of the primary colors absorb certain wavelengths of light and reflect back the rest, producing the desired color.

In theory, setting the CMY values to one hundred percent should absorb all white light to create black. In practice, however, the three primary colors produce a dark brown, so designers add additional black (K) to complete the color model.

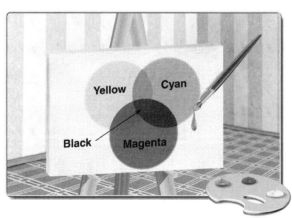

RGB Color Model

The *RGB* color model is essentially the inverse of CMY(K). Here the primary colors are red, green, and blue, while the secondary colors are cyan, yellow, and magenta.

Unlike its counterpart, RGB is an *additive* color system where colors are produced by combining certain wavelengths of light. When you combine red, green, and blue at full intensity, the product is white.

While CMY(K) is used in print media, RGB is the color system used on television screens and computer displays, because monitors produce color by firing red, green, and blue electrons. When you create graphics destined for the Web, you should always use the RGB color model.

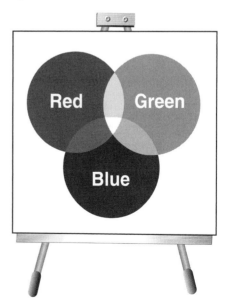

USING THE WEB-SAFE COLOR PALETTE

When you create graphics for the Web and set color properties using HTML or style sheets, you should select colors from the *Web-safe* color palette, otherwise known as the *Netscape* or *browser-safe* color palette. By using Web-safe colors, you can ensure that the colors you select appear correctly on a visitor's browser. Otherwise, Web browsers may substitute or dither colors, which can produce unattractive results.

Web-Safe = Not Sorry

The development of the Web-safe color palette dates to the emergence of the Web browser in 1994. At the time, computer monitors used 8-bit color depth, meaning that they could only display 256 colors at any time. However, 40 of those colors were different on Windows and Macintosh systems, leaving 216 colors that would be consistent across platforms.

Today, most users can set their computer monitors to either 8-bit, 16-bit (thousands of colors), or 24-bit color (millions of colors or *true color*). Although the number of users with 8-bit screens is relatively small, you should usually stick with the Web-safe color palette to avoid dithering and color substitution on these older monitors.

Dithering

Dithering occurs when users have their monitors set to 256 colors and you use colors unavailable on their palette. In this case the browser places pixels of colors next to one another to give the illusion of the unavailable color.

Unfortunately, the dithering process is rarely able to correctly simulate unavailable colors, and the effect on graphical elements is that the image appears with dots of visible color.

RGB Color Values

When you work with the Web-safe color palette, you specify color in terms of values for red, green, and blue components. In most image editors, you can express these values as decimals, with each of the three colors having a value between 0 and 255, or as hexadecimal code, where two letters or numbers represent each color channel.

When using the decimal system, Web-safe color values are always in multiples of 51: 0, 51, 102, 153, 204, and 255. For example, the decimal value for white is 255, 255, 255.

When you set color on a Web page using style sheets, you can indicate either the RGB decimal values or the hexadecimal notation used in HTML. Within the hexadecimal system, RGB decimal values are expressed in the following manner:

Decimal	Hexadecimal
0	00
51	33
102	66
153	99
204	cc
255	ff

Select Web-Safe Colors

Most graphics and image editors today include Web-safe palettes that you can use when creating graphics for the Web. If your image editor does not specify a Web-safe palette, look for options that allow you to "snap" to Web-safe colors or import Web-safe swatches to use.

There are also many online resources where you can download swatches, view Web-safe color tables, and convert RGB decimal values to hexadecimal codes. Some of the most popular online resources include Lynda Weinman's browser-safe color palette at www.lynda.com and Visibone's color lab at www.visibone.com.

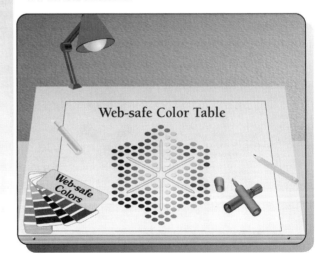

Web-safe Color Table

CONSIDER COLOR SIGNIFICANCE

When you develop the color palette to use on your Web site, be sure to consider the significance of each color you use. Colors have meaning depending on cultural background as well as psychological significance, so make sure that the colors you choose reflect the message that you are trying to convey on your site.

Color Connotations

Certain colors and combinations of colors are charged with meaning that you can use to your advantage when designing your site. For example, the color red can convey passion and excitement. However, red can also have a negative connotation if it is used in relation to financial matters, because it is the color used to express deficits. Green can represent nature, the environment, or money.

The following is a brief list of some common connotations for common colors. Note that colors often have both positive and negative meanings.

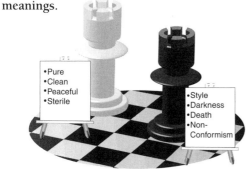

•Pure
•Clean
•Peaceful
•Sterile

•Style
•Darkness
•Death
•Non-Conformism

- Red: passion, violence
- Yellow: brightness, warmth, illness, cowardice
- Green: nature, growth, fertility, money, jealousy
- Blue: tranquility, stability, conservatism, coldness
- Violet: strength, power, royalty
- Black: style, non-conformism, darkness, death
- White: purity, cleanliness, peace, sterile environments

Color Psychology

Beyond the various meanings associated with colors, certain hues can also produce positive or negative psychological reactions. For example, the color yellow, when used extensively, causes excessive stimulation and aggravation. The color blue, on the other hand, is a relaxing color and produces feelings of peace and contemplation.

When you develop your color palette, make sure that the psychological reaction generated by your colors is consistent with the overall purpose of your site.

Cultural Significance

The significance of color is often culture-specific, so if you have a diverse audience for your site, make sure that the message conveyed by your color choice translates well across cultural borders. Colors that have precedence in nature — the color of the sky or the sun for example — have a more universal significance, while the meaning we derive from other color combinations is based on cultural elements such as politics, religion, and shared mythology. Consider the following examples of cultural-specific color significance:

- In many cultures, the colors red and green have come to mean "stop" and "go," respectively. However, these color connotations may not translate correctly in cultures that do not use these colors in traffic signals.

- Certain color combinations are associated with particular cultural holidays. In North America, the colors orange and black immediately bring to mind Halloween, but these colors would not carry the same meaning in cultures that do not celebrate this holiday.

- Many cultures associate a particular color with death and mourning. In some Western cultures, purple represents death. In Chinese culture, white is the color of death.

- The color red is considered a lucky color in Japan, but carries a negative connotation in other cultures.

If you are designing a site targeted to a multicultural audience, be sure to carefully research the cultural significance of each color in your palette. You can take a few moments to locate materials on the Internet, or consult your local library or bookstore for resources on color symbolism.

EXPLORE CONTRAST

You can use contrast between opposing elements to improve readability, add emphasis, and strengthen the impact of your visual design. Contrast comes in many forms, and can be based on size, shape, and typeface, but one of the easiest ways to create contrast is through the use of color.

When you have text against a colored or tiled image background,

make sure that there is sufficient contrast between the text color and the background color. If the hues or values are too similar, the text blends into the background and hinders readability.

Beyond simple legibility, you can juxtapose contrasting colors to create intense, powerful designs. Black and white and complementary colors—colors across from one another on the

color wheel—create the most contrast. However, too much contrast can be aggravating on the reader's eye.

Use colors that differ enough in value to enhance readability and impact without creating jarring visual effects.

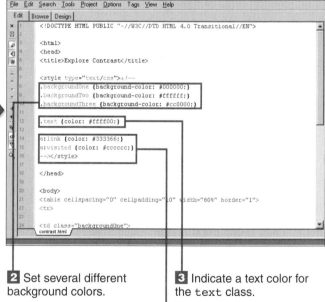

1 Create an HTML template to test contrasting colors.

■ This example uses the `contrast.html` file, available on the CD-ROM included with this book.

■ You can also test color contrast by using a graphics editor. See the appendix "What's on the CD-ROM" for more on graphics editors.

2 Set several different background colors.

Note: See Chapter 3 for more on adding color to HTML elements.

3 Indicate a text color for the `text` class.

4 Add color properties for regular and visited links.

What is simultaneous contrast?

✔ *Simultaneous contrast* is when the appearance of a color changes due to the colors that surround it. For example, when you place samples of the same color on varying backgrounds, the color appears darker on light backgrounds and brighter on dark backgrounds. In addition, two different hues placed on the same background color can appear to be the same color.

How does simultaneous contrast affect Web design?

✔ The effects of simultaneous contrast can be subtle, but they can affect the overall impact of your design. For example, light colored text placed on a dark background often appears thinner than dark text on light backgrounds.

Where can I find color wheels and information about color contrast online?

✔ There are many online resources that you can use to explore color relationships and test color contrast. One of the most popular is the Visibone Color Lab, located at www.visibone.com/colorlab. Mundi Design Studios offers a Flash-based color tool, located at www.mundidesign.com/webct/ webct.html, that you can also use to test various color combinations.

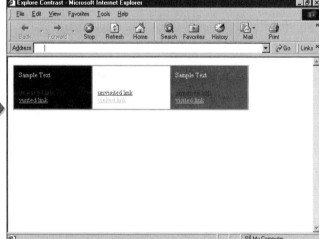

5 Within the body of the document, add links to a site you have recently visited.

■ If the link is still present in your Web browser's history, it appears as a visited link when you load the page.

6 Save the file.

7 Open the page in a browser to test the color contrast.

■ Colors with similar values can be difficult to read.

■ Colors with too much contrast "vibrate" and strain the reader's eye.

IDENTIFY AN ESSENTIAL COLOR PALETTE

For consistency across your site, identify an essential color palette before you start designing page layouts. When creating a palette to use, isolate colors that are unified and express the theme or message of your site. In addition, you should select the functional colors that will be used across your site and test them for legibility and visual impact.

Your essential color palette should include three or four colors that express the theme or message of your site. For example, a color palette composed of blue and grey hues conveys an idea of coolness, stability, and professionalism, appropriate colors for a bank or large corporation. In contrast, bright hues and primary colors would be better suited for a site geared towards children.

Besides the general design colors, your essential palette should include functional colors for elements such as headings, links, and other navigation elements. These colors help users understand the structure and function of your site, and should be applied consistently throughout all pages.

IDENTIFY AN ESSENTIAL COLOR PALETTE

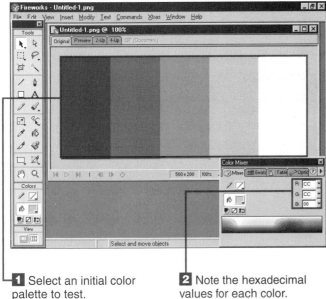

1 Select an initial color palette to test.

■ You can use a graphics editor as in this example, or test colors directly in an HTML document.

2 Note the hexadecimal values for each color.

3 In a text editor, open the page on which you want to test colors.

■ This example uses the `template.html` page from the book's CD-ROM. This page provides a simple page layout that you can use to test color combinations.

4 Set the background color.

5 Set the header and side panel colors.

Note: See Chapter 3 for more on adding color to HTML elements.

What is a good starting point for exploring color combinations?

✔ You can begin your exploration of color combinations, or schemes, by using a simple color wheel. Consider harmonies between secondary and tertiary colors, or analogous colors that occur next to one another on a color wheel. You can also begin by exploring monochromatic color combinations, consisting of one hue and various tones, shades, and tints.

Are there resources online that I can use to identify and test color combinations?

✔ Yes, there are many tools online that allow you to select colors and test combinations. One of the most popular online tools is the Visibone Color Lab, available at www.visibone.com/colorlab/. In addition, you can consult your local bookstore or book retailer for texts that provide color combinations that correspond to particular themes.

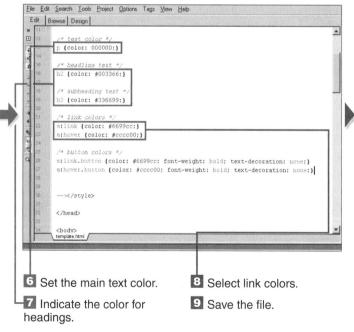

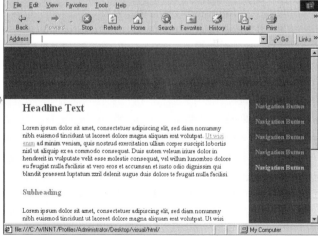

6 Set the main text color.

7 Indicate the color for headings.

8 Select link colors.

9 Save the file.

10 View the page in a CSS-compliant Web browser.

■ Test your essential color palette for readability and visual impact.

UNDERSTANDING AVAILABLE PAGE SPACE

Before you create your page layout and visual design, take into account the limited space available on a Web page when viewed on a browser. Designs that do not accommodate space limitations force many visitors to scroll vertically and horizontally to view content, creating a poor user experience.

Maximum Visible Space

Many Web designers make the mistake of assuming that the available page space is equal to the lowest common screen resolution, 640 x 480 pixels. However, these dimensions do not take into account the space occupied by elements such as the task bar on Windows systems or the browser window itself. Browser elements such as buttons, toolbars, address bars, and borders greatly reduce the visible page space, which might end up being as little as 600 pixels across and 300 pixels down.

If you are designing for lower screen resolutions, limit the width of your page to 600 pixels to prevent unsightly horizontal scrollbars, and keep pages short to prevent excessive vertical scrolling.

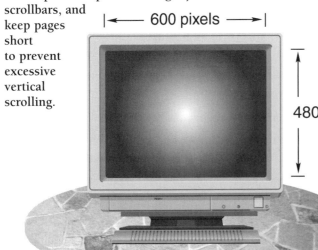

|◄— 600 pixels —►|

480 pixels

Using Prime Real Estate

When you create page layouts for the Web, always be aware of the prime real estate of a page. When you effectively utilize the prime real estate, you have a better chance of engaging users and having them explore your content. Ineffective use of page real estate may lead users to back out of the site, thinking that there is nothing of value to them.

The most valuable area of your page layout is the content that you have "above the fold." This phrase is used in the newspaper business to describe the portion of a front page that occurs above the fold of the paper. On the Web, it refers to content that is visible when users first load a page. Any content that visitors must scroll down to see is considered "below the fold."

What constitutes "above the fold" varies depending on the user's screen resolution. To maximize the effectiveness of your page, make sure that this space is filled with content that engages the visitor.

Many of the elements that are normally found above the fold—including company mastheads, navigation elements, and paid advertisements—do not offer the user any compelling reason to explore the site. Make sure that these elements do not overshadow the elements that will engage visitors, such as compelling link titles and content descriptions.

element of your Web site brand, but it can take up a large percentage of prime real estate. Many advertisers prefer that their banner advertisements appear above the fold. This placement can be vital for your Web business, but it does not present anything of value to your readers or customers, and pushes your primary content even further below the fold. One approach is to use a table layout with a large column for primary content and a second column for items such as advertisements, navigation, and additional resources. This type of layout allows you to maximize available page space while placing both primary content and secondary elements above the fold. To learn how to create page layouts with tables, refer to the section "Using Tables for Page Layout," later in this chapter.

Determine Content Placement

Determining what content pieces should go where on a page can be a challenge. In many cases you may have to strike a balance between content that supports your business—such as company logos and advertisements—and content that is of interest to your audience. Most sites include a company logo or masthead at the top of the page. This is an important

ESTABLISH VISUAL HIERARCHY

*V*isual hierarchy is a way of communicating structure and emphasis using visual clues. When you establish a visual hierarchy in your page layout, you convey structural information to the user, such as how the page is organized and the relative importance of elements on the page. A simple example of visual hierarchy is the set of HTML heading tags that range from H1, the largest, to H6, the smallest. In this case, the relative sizes of the heading levels establish the visual hierarchy of information. For more on typographical scale, see Chapter 11.

Direct Visual Flow

In many cases, visual hierarchy naturally conforms to the ways in which readers scan pages, usually from left to right and top to bottom, so that elements of greater importance appear at the top of the page. However, you can use elements such as white space, contrast, and color to direct the reader's eye to the most important elements on a page and establish a specific visual flow so that the reader is drawn from one element to another. For example, you can use highly saturated colors or contrasting colors to direct the viewer's attention to side navigation bars or particular graphic elements, but keep in mind that bold and highly contrasting colors can also repel the reader's eye if used in excess. For more information, see the section "Explore Contrast," earlier in this chapter.

Besides elements such as white space, contrast, and color, visual flow also applies to how you arrange text content on your Web pages. While readers usually read text from left to right and top to bottom, you can use layout columns to redirect the visual flow of text from top to bottom and from left to right. This corresponds to the visual flow often found in newspapers. Be careful about mixing this type of column layout with standard paragraph layout, because switching back and forth between two systems of visual flow can be confusing for readers.

Create Starting Points

At first glance, readers perceive a page in terms of overall layout, visual flow, and blocks of color and white space. As they begin focusing on page content, readers are drawn to headlines and graphic elements as main entry points, so make sure that the headings and subheadings you use are effectively written to entice the reader.

Since the advent of animated GIFs, designers have used motion to draw the reader's eye to specific elements in the page. This can be an effective way of creating a starting point in the visual hierarchy, but motion can also be distracting when overused. For more information on creating animated GIFs, see Chapter 12.

Apply a Consistent Hierarchy

Because readers rely on visual hierarchy to understand the structure of information, these elements should be applied consistently across your site. If the visual hierarchy changes from page to page, visitors are unable to learn the underlying organization of the site, leaving them frustrated and unable to easily navigate. To apply a consistent visual hierarchy throughout your site, design a master page layout—using either HTML tables or the CSS box model—and use this as a template for each page on your site. You can learn more about creating page layouts later in this chapter, in the sections "Using Tables for Page Layout" and "Using CSS for Page Layout."

USING WHITE SPACE

You can improve your visual design and page layout by effectively incorporating *white space*, also called negative space. White space refers to any open space between elements on a page. When used effectively, white space can help guide the visitor's eye from one element to another and create contrast.

You can incorporate white space into your page layout in many

ways. One way to utilize white space is to set appropriate margins on the right and left sides of the page so that the reader's eye is drawn to the text column. Without sufficient margins, pages appear crowded and without focus.

In addition, you can incorporate white space around headlines and between columns and paragraphs of text. However, be careful to avoid trapped white space, or large

chunks of space between design elements, that disrupt the visual flow of the document. Typographical styles can also produce trapped white space if you use too much word-spacing, letter-spacing, or leading. For more tips on using effective typography, see Chapter 11.

USING WHITE SPACE

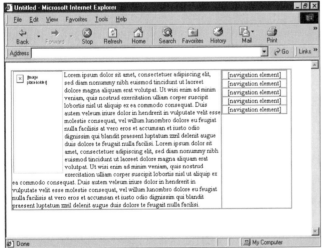

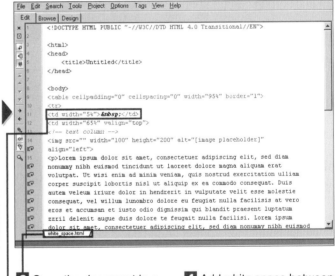

1 Open an HTML document in a Web browser.

■ This example uses `white_space.html`, available on this book's CD-ROM.

■ Lack of negative space produces a design without focus.

2 Open the document in a text editor.

3 Add an additional table data cell to the left of the text cell.

Note: For more on table columns and cells, see Chapter 3.

4 Add white space between the text and navigation cells.

■ Adequate margins and gutters help focus the readers' attention on the page content.

Are there any HTML tags used specifically to create white space?

✔ There is a Netscape-specific tag, `<spacer>`, that you can use to create blocks of white space. Within this standalone tag, set the `type` attribute to `horizontal`, `vertical`, or `block` to create white space. This tag is not part of the HTML specification.

What other techniques can I use to incorporate white space into my page layout?

✔ If you create your page layout using CSS, you can create blocks of white space using style properties. For more information, see the section "Using CSS for Page Layout."

What does the white-space style property do?

✔ The `white-space` style property specifies how the browser should handle white space within an element, such as a `<p>` or `<td>` tag. The default value is *normal*, which collapses white space and breaks lines as necessary to fill the box. Other values are *pre*, which does not collapse white space, and *nowrap*, which suppresses normal line breaks.

Does white space have to be white?

✔ Not at all. White space is really just a generic term for any open space between elements.

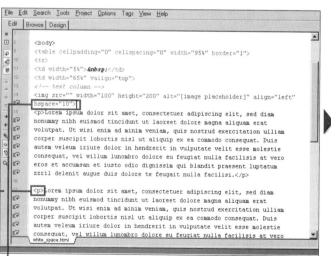

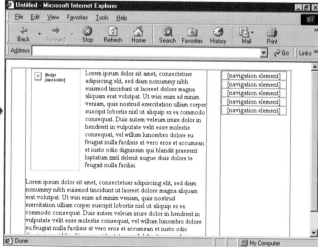

5 Add additional white space around inline images.

Note: See Chapter 3 for more information on <img> tags and attributes.

6 Format text into smaller, manageable chunks.

■ White space prevents the layout from appearing cramped and busy.

7 Save the HTML file.

8 Load the page into a Web browser.

■ The additional white space enhances readability and helps direct the visual flow.

USING TABLES FOR PAGE LAYOUT

HTML is not geared toward visual presentation, but there are ways you can use HTML tags to control the layout of Web documents. Specifically, you can use the HTML <table> tag to create a layout grid and place content within table data cells. Using the attributes available for tables, such as rowspan, colspan, and bgcolor, you can create

complex design layouts, control white space, and align elements.

To create a layout grid, insert a table directly after the opening <body> tag of your document. While you are developing your layout, turn the table border on to visualize the page divisions. Then, when you publish the page, set the table border to 0 so the grid is not visible to users.

HTML table data cells can contain any valid HTML content, including text, lists, media elements, and other tables. Incorrectly nested tables cause pages to render inproperly in some browsers, so if you place tables within other tables, be sure that each cell, row, and table is closed out in turn, according to correct nesting order.

USING TABLES FOR PAGE LAYOUT

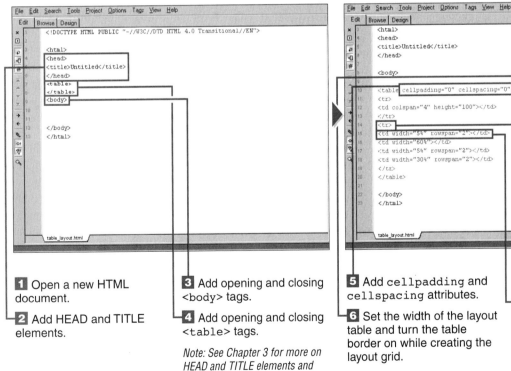

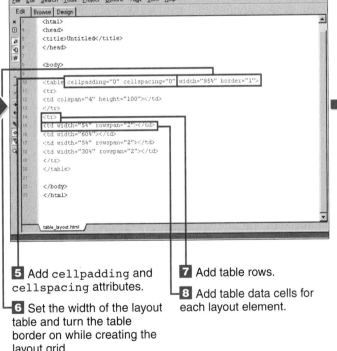

1 Open a new HTML document.

2 Add HEAD and TITLE elements.

3 Add opening and closing <body> tags.

4 Add opening and closing <table> tags.

Note: See Chapter 3 for more on HEAD and TITLE elements and <body> and <table> tags.

5 Add cellpadding and cellspacing attributes.

6 Set the width of the layout table and turn the table border on while creating the layout grid.

7 Add table rows.

8 Add table data cells for each layout element.

Can I set the height of an HTML table?

✔ There is a non-standard `height` attribute supported by Netscape and Internet Explorer that you can use to suggest a minimum height for a table. If additional space is needed to accommodate the table content, the browser adjusts the height accordingly.

How do I create complex tables by spanning rows and columns?

✔ Use the `rowspan` and `colspan` attributes with the TD element to create cells that stretch across multiple rows and columns. For more information, see Chapter 3.

Is it possible to have empty table data cells?

✔ According to the HTML specification, table cells may contain no data. However, in practice, many browsers have problems with empty cells, and they may collapse the entire table or render it improperly. To avoid these problems, always include some sort of data inside all table cells. You can use non-breaking spaces (` `) to fill otherwise empty cells without having any visible content.

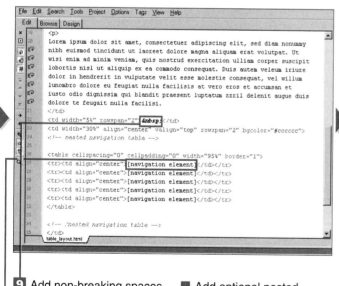

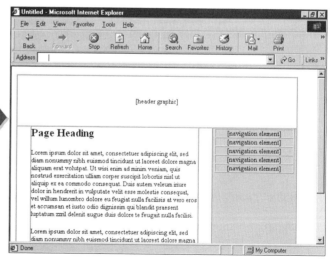

9 Add non-breaking spaces to empty data cells.

10 Add placeholder text to content areas.

■ Add optional nested tables.

11 Save the file.

12 View the page in a Web browser.

■ The table provides a basic layout template for all content elements.

USING CSS FOR PAGE LAYOUT

You can use the Cascading Style Sheet box model and positioning properties to create precise page layouts for your Web site. The advantage to using CSS for layout purposes is that it separates content from presentation, so you can easily apply differently styled layouts to the same content.

The CSS box model assumes that every element on a page is contained within a box. Each box can be positioned on a page using the

position property and the top and left offset properties, which dictate the location of the box element in relation to the top left corner of the page or the element containing it.

Each "box" that you define contains a content area surrounded by padding, a border, and margins. For each of these areas, you can specify independent values. For example, you can create a formatting box with 10 pixels of padding, a

2-pixel-wide border, and 10-pixel margins on each side. In addition, you can assign different values to each of the four sides of the box padding, border, and margin.

To lay out a page using these properties, create style rules to define the position, height, and width of each element and then reference these rules within the body of the HTML page. For more in-depth information on using style sheet properties, see Chapter 6.

USING CSS FOR PAGE LAYOUT

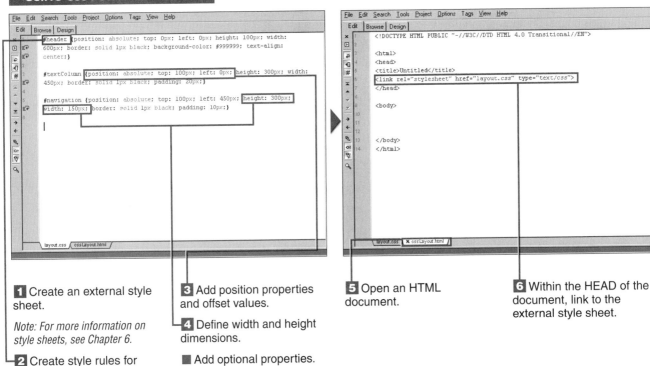

1 Create an external style sheet.

Note: For more information on style sheets, see Chapter 6.

2 Create style rules for each layout element.

3 Add position properties and offset values.

4 Define width and height dimensions.

■ Add optional properties.

5 Open an HTML document.

6 Within the HEAD of the document, link to the external style sheet.

Can I define box properties without setting the positioning to absolute?

✔ Yes. You can define properties such as padding, borders, and margins without explicitly setting the position of a box. In this case, the browser renders the elements vertically, one after the other, on the HTML page.

If I do not specify values for borders, padding, and margins, what are the default values?

✔ The default values for padding and margins are zero. If you do not indicate values for the `border` property, the border will have a medium width and will inherit any color that you have indicated using the `color` property. Consult the Cascading Style Sheet Reference in the appendix for more default CSS values.

Do all CSS-compliant browsers support positioning?

✔ No. The positioning properties are part of CSS2, and even browsers that support some style sheets properties do not yet support CSS positioning. Be aware that if you use positioning, older browsers—in many cases even version 4 browsers—disregard these CSS properties and render the page elements in the order in which they occur in the HTML document.

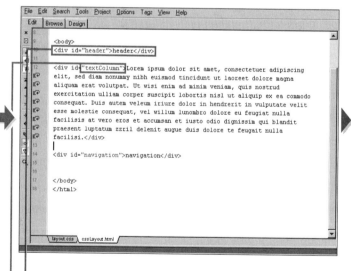

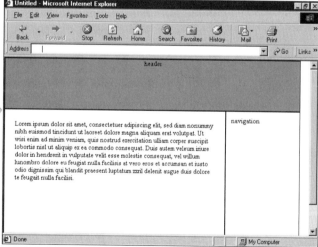

7 Within the BODY of the document, add divisions for each layout element.

8 Reference the style rule for each element.

9 Add content.

10 Save the document.

11 Open the page in a CSS-compliant Web browser.

■ CSS boxes provide a layout grid to contain content pieces.

AN INTRODUCTION TO TYPOGRAPHY ON THE WEB

Typography, the art of using type, characters, and symbols to communicate, has been an important element of print media since the invention of the printing press. Effective typography helps readers navigate through text, supports the structural hierarchy of a document, and directs the visual flow of a page. Poor use of typography, on the other hand, can confuse readers and actually hinder the communication process.

The Web Offers a World of Variety

Due to the lack of control inherent in Web design, typography is not highly developed on the Web.

In traditional print media, typographers can exert precise control over every character and symbol, because printers create a physical object—a book, magazine, or newspaper—and distribute replicas of that object. On the Web, there is no physical object created by the designer, and how a Web page looks depends entirely on the browsing environment.

With the variety of browsers on the market, dictating exactly how typographical elements appear on the page is impossible. In addition, the Web gives users the ability to control their browsing environment by applying their own font choices to override the typographical elements you set.

Rather than trying to impose rigid typographical styles such as specific font faces, consider using typographical elements to enhance the visual layout and highlight important elements on your Web page. If you do choose to specify fonts and font properties using HTML, Cascading Style Sheets, or embedded fonts, remember that you ultimately have no control over how your page appears on the user's browser. On the Web, your time might be better spent creating compelling, informative content rather than worrying about typographical details.

Font Families

A font family is a group of fonts that share certain characteristics, such as the width of the stroke or the presence or absence of a serif. HTML and CSS recognize five generic font families: serif, sans-serif, monospace, cursive, and fantasy. Serif fonts, such as Times and Times New Roman, have small lines, or *serifs*, at the top and bottom of character line strokes. *Sans-serif* fonts such as Arial and Helvetica do not have these small lines. The *monospace* font family defines a group of fonts where each character takes up the same amount of space, while *cursive* fonts mimic fluid handwriting styles. The *fantasy* font family is not widely supported by Web browsers, and there is no convention for how this font should appear, so you should probably avoid using it until it gains wider support.

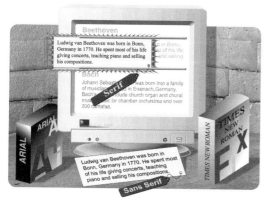

CSS Font Properties

Cascading Style Sheets (CSS) offer increased control over typographical elements, allowing you to define style elements such as line height and word-spacing. Because the HTML <font> tag is deprecated, CSS is the preferred method of handling type properties. However, support for

CSS is limited to versions 4 and higher of the major browsers, so be sure to test your pages on older browsers to ensure that the absence of style does not interfere with the readability of your text.

Typography and Graphics

In an attempt to control typographical elements, some Web designers use an overabundance of graphics to replace text elements on a page. Creating GIF images allows you to control the exact typeface, but this approach has a number of disadvantages. Graphic files add weight to a Web page and take longer to download, and graphics-heavy sites can cause problems for visitors using alternative or text-only browsers. In addition, text that is embedded within a graphic file is not indexable by search engines. If you do use graphics to replace regular HTML text, do so sparingly.

SPECIFY CROSS-PLATFORM FONTS

Increase the chances that users see text as you intended by using fonts that are common to most operating systems. When you specify a font via the <font> tag or style sheet rules using the CSS font-family property as in this example, the browser checks to see if the visitor has the font installed locally. If the font is not installed, the browser renders the text in the default font, usually a serif font such as Times or Times New Roman.

Although most systems have a large variety of fonts at their disposal, visitors using older operating systems may not have your preferred font installed. In particular, many versions of Windows and Macintosh operating systems have different serif and sans-serif fonts. You can cover your bases by providing a list of possible fonts from which the browser can choose. For sans-serif fonts, you can suggest Verdana, Arial, and Helvetica, for example. In addition, include a general font family, such as sans-serif, in your list so that browsers can use a substitute font within the same family.

SPECIFY CROSS-PLATFORM FONTS

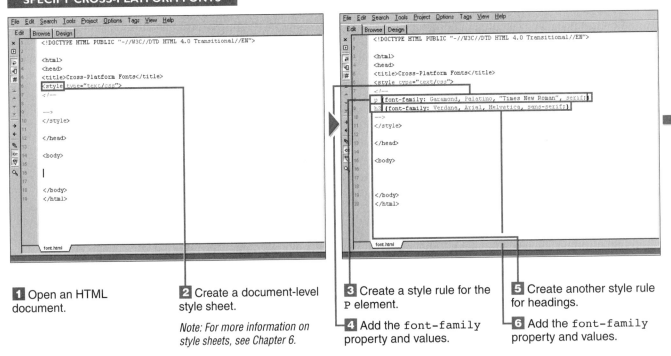

1 Open an HTML document.

2 Create a document-level style sheet.

Note: For more information on style sheets, see Chapter 6.

3 Create a style rule for the P element.

4 Add the font-family property and values.

5 Create another style rule for headings.

6 Add the font-family property and values.

Are there browsers that support only certain fonts?

✔ Yes. The WebTV browser supports only Helvetica and Monaco fonts.

Which fonts are common to Windows and Macintosh systems?

✔ For serif fonts, Windows has traditionally favored Times New Roman while Macintosh has used Times or Palatino. For sans-serif fonts, Arial is native to Windows, with Helvetica being the Macintosh equivalent.

Are there fonts designed specifically for screen use?

✔ Yes. Two fonts designed specifically for screens are Verdana, a sans-serif font, and Georgia, a serif. You can download both fonts from Microsoft's Web site, www.microsoft.com/truetype/.

What other generic font families can I specify?

✔ Besides serif and sans-serif, other font families are monospace, cursive, and fantasy.

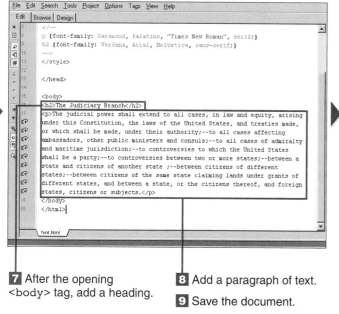

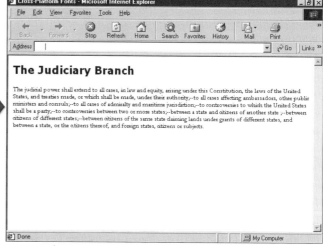

7 After the opening `<body>` tag, add a heading.

8 Add a paragraph of text.

9 Save the document.

10 View the page in a Web browser.

■ The heading and paragraphs are formatted according to the `font-family` properties.

Note: You can also use the `font-family` property with external style sheets. See Chapter 6 for more on external style sheets.

USING SCALE

Y ou can establish the information hierarchy and the visual flow on your page by using typographical scale. Effective scale helps visitors determine elements of primary and secondary importance and also serves to guide the reader's eye from one section to another.

To use scale for establishing information hierarchy on a page, use HTML heading tags for page titles and subheadings. For example, you might use a level 2 heading for initial page titles and a level 3 heading for each subsection on the page. In this way, scale communicates the structural hierarchy of the information on the page and helps the user isolate thematic subsections. For more information on using heading tags, see Chapter 3.

You can also use scale to dictate the visual flow of the page. When users visit a Web page, their eyes are drawn to the largest typographical element. Use scale to draw visitors to the point where they should start reading, and to trace the path they should follow through the text.

USING SCALE

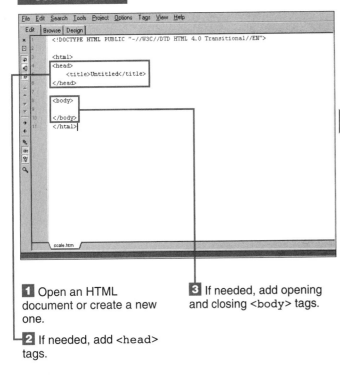

1 Open an HTML document or create a new one.

2 If needed, add <head> tags.

3 If needed, add opening and closing <body> tags.

4 After the opening <body> tag, add several different headings of various levels or change the levels of existing headings as desired.

Besides headings, how else can I create typographical scale?

✔ You can create scale by defining fonts of various sizes. Define font sizes using the `<font>` tag with the `size` attribute, or the `font size` style property. For more information on the `<font>` tag, see Chapter 3. To learn how to define font styles with CSS, see Chapter 6.

What other techniques can I use to establish visual flow?

✔ Color is another effective way of controlling the visual flow on a page. For more information on using color on your Web pages, see Chapter 10.

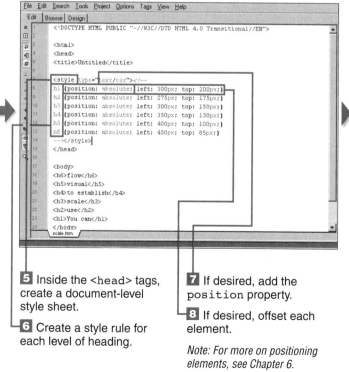

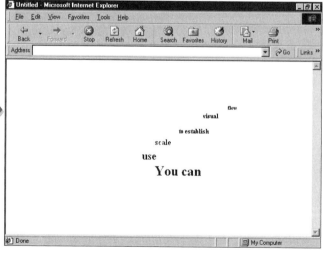

5 Inside the `<head>` tags, create a document-level style sheet.

6 Create a style rule for each level of heading.

7 If desired, add the `position` property.

8 If desired, offset each element.

Note: For more on positioning elements, see Chapter 6.

9 Save the document.

10 View the page in a CSS-compliant Web browser.

■ The visitor's eye is drawn to the largest element on the page.

USING PRE-FORMATTED TEXT

You can preserve spaces and carriage returns in your text by using the HTML <pre> tag.

The <pre> tag allows you to use pre-formatted text, which is particularly useful when displaying poetry or example programming code where you want to preserve indentations and line breaks. Keep in mind that

text contained with <pre> tags is formatted using a monospace font, such as Courier or Courier New.

When you use <pre> tags, normal word wrapping is disabled on the browser, and the lines continue unless you insert carriage returns— that is, press Enter/Return on your keyboard each time you want the line to break. This means that if a line

of text extends beyond the width of the window, the browser adds a horizontal scroll bar.

The width attribute, now deprecated, allows you to set the maximum number of characters in a line. When you use the width attribute, the browser may cut off any text that extends beyond the specified width.

USING PRE-FORMATTED TEXT

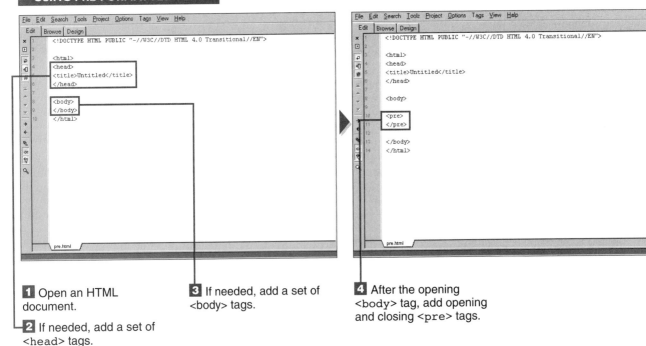

1 Open an HTML document.

2 If needed, add a set of <head> tags.

3 If needed, add a set of <body> tags.

4 After the opening <body> tag, add opening and closing <pre> tags.

Is additional HTML content allowed within `<pre>` tags?

✔ Yes, additional HTML tags may be used within `<pre>` tags with the exception of elements that cause paragraph breaks, such as `<p>` tags and headings. Because you can include HTML code within `<pre>` tags, you need to use character entities for reserved symbols, such as greater than (>) and less than (<) signs.

Can I use tabs within pre-formatted text?

✔ Yes, `<pre>` tags recognize tabs, although the actual length of a tab differs among browsers and operating systems. For more consistency, use multiple spaces rather than tabs.

Can you apply style properties to `<pre>` tags?

✔ Yes, you can apply style properties by using the `style` attribute or by creating rules and classes in a document-level or external style sheet. However, you should be careful when overriding the monospace type because this font is used specifically to keep the line-spacing and alignment constant. If you override this font type, you may get unexpected alignment results when you view the page in a browser.

```
<!DOCTYPE HTML PUBLIC "-//W3C//DTD HTML 4.0 Transitional//EN">

<html>
<head>
<title>Untitled</title>
</head>

<body>
Use the following code to turn images "on" on mouseover events:

<pre>
function imgOn(imgName) {
    if (document.images) {
        document[imgName].src = eval(imgName + "on.src");
        }
    }
</pre>

</body>
</html>
```

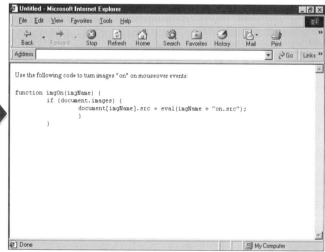

```
Use the following code to turn images "on" on mouseover events:

function imgOn(imgName) {
    if (document.images) {
        document[imgName].src = eval(imgName + "on.src");
        }
    }
```

5 Within the `<pre>` tags, add pre-formatted text.

6 Save the document.

7 View the page in a Web browser.

■ The spaces and carriage returns are preserved.

USING BLOCK QUOTES

Set off longer quotations as indented paragraphs by using HTML <blockquote> tags. Most browsers render a block quote with larger right and left margins so the enclosed text is offset. In addition, browsers treat block quotes as individual paragraphs, inserting white space above and below the quoted passage.

Some browsers may apply additional formatting styles to block quotes, but you can control the text formatting by applying style via the inline style attribute or tag selector rules. You can also create style classes and reference them using the class attribute. For more information on creating style rules, see Chapter 6.

Within the opening <blockquote> tag, use the cite attribute to include the URL of the original text that you are quoting. Although current browsers do not do anything with this attribute, future browser versions may allow users to click the block quote text to go to the original source document reference in the cite attribute.

USING BLOCK QUOTES

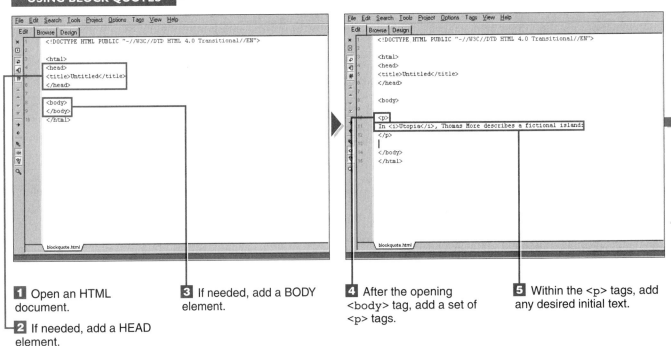

1 Open an HTML document.

2 If needed, add a HEAD element.

3 If needed, add a BODY element.

4 After the opening <body> tag, add a set of <p> tags.

5 Within the <p> tags, add any desired initial text.

Are there any other tags used to identify quotes?

✔ HTML 4.0 introduced the <q> tag for use with shorter, inline quotes. Unlike the BLOCKQUOTE element, text within opening and closing <q> tags is not offset or treated as a unique paragraph. The HTML 4.0 standard specifies that text enclosed within the <q> tags should begin and end with quote marks, so you should not explicitly add them to your quoted text.

Can I use additional HTML tags within the <blockquote> tags?

✔ Yes, you can use additional HTML tags inside <blockquote> tags.

Are there other ways to create block quotes?

✔ You can define block quotes using CSS by creating style rules and adding right and left margins. For more on controlling element margins, see Chapter 6.

Can <q> tags be nested?

✔ Yes, inline quotes can be nested within other inline quotes. Browsers are supposed to treat nested quotes differently, using single quote marks rather than double quotes.

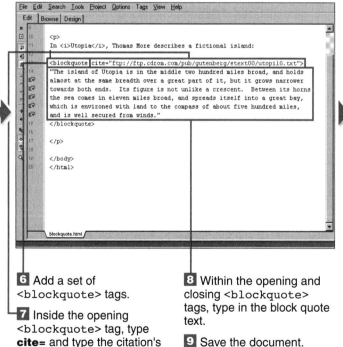

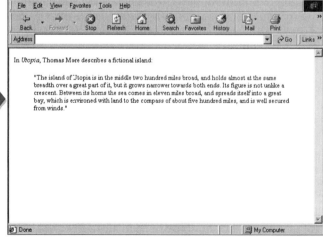

6 Add a set of <blockquote> tags.

7 Inside the opening <blockquote> tag, type **cite=** and type the citation's source URL in quotes.

8 Within the opening and closing <blockquote> tags, type in the block quote text.

9 Save the document.

10 View the page in a Web browser.

■ The blockquote is offset and treated as a new paragraph.

USING ANTI-ALIAS GRAPHIC TEXT

Y ou can improve the look of text embedded within graphics by making sure the text is anti-aliased. *Anti-aliasing* smoothes the pixel edges around fonts. If you do not use anti-aliasing when you create images with a graphics editor, graphical text appears jagged on a computer monitor.

Pixels on a screen can be only one color, which is fine for straight lines, but on curves this causes a jagged-edge effect. Anti-aliasing softens the jagged edges by adding pixels of intermediary colors to create a blend effect. Most graphics editors give you the option of turning anti-aliasing on or off, and some applications allow you to select the degree of anti-aliasing you want, from strong, which

applies more intermediary pixels colors, to crisp.

You should also take into consideration that anti-aliasing adds additional weight to the image file because it requires additional colors. Choose the degree of anti-aliasing that produces the best result without adding too much additional weight to the image.

USING ANTI-ALIAS GRAPHIC TEXT

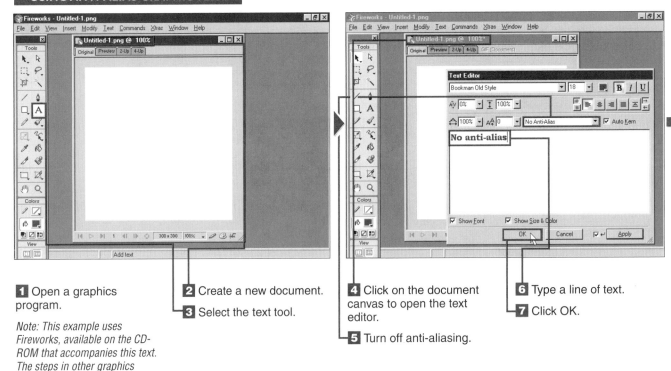

1 Open a graphics program.

Note: This example uses Fireworks, available on the CD-ROM that accompanies this text. The steps in other graphics programs will be similar, but check your manual.

2 Create a new document.

3 Select the text tool.

4 Click on the document canvas to open the text editor.

5 Turn off anti-aliasing.

6 Type a line of text.

7 Click OK.

Does anti-aliasing have any other disadvantages?

✔ In addition to adding weight to the image file, anti-aliasing also increases the number of colors used in the color palette. For example, your original text may only contain 2 colors, but when anti-aliasing is turned on, the application adds additional intermediate colors to soften the edges. Graphics with anti-aliasing are also more difficult to resize later on, because the blurry edges become even more pronounced as the graphic is enlarged. For more on resizing images, see Chapter 12.

Is anti-aliasing graphic text always better?

✔ If the text in your GIF is particularly small, you should probably not anti-alias, as the anti-aliased edges appear blurry on very small font sizes. When deciding whether you should apply anti-aliasing, be sure to view your graphics on a Web browser to test the readability and appearance of the text.

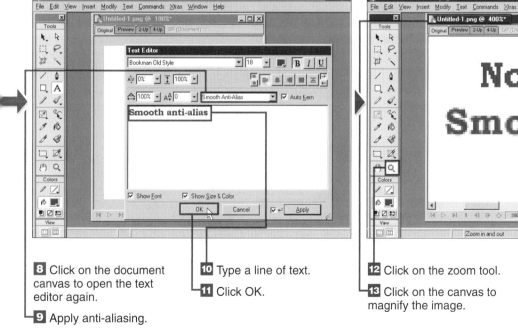

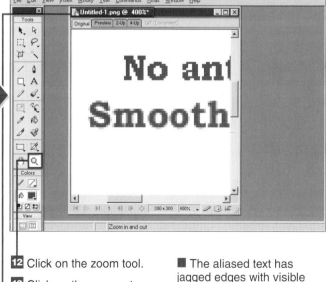

8 Click on the document canvas to open the text editor again.

9 Apply anti-aliasing.

10 Type a line of text.

11 Click OK.

12 Click on the zoom tool.

13 Click on the canvas to magnify the image.

■ The aliased text has jagged edges with visible square pixels, while the anti-aliased text has smoother, blended edges.

CREATE A DROP CAP WITH CSS

You can create a drop cap using the CSS first-letter pseudo-class. A *drop cap* is a special way of formatting the first letter of a paragraph so that the letter is significantly larger than the surrounding text and drops down to span several lines. The first letter of this paragraph is an example of a drop cap. This

technique is often used in novels and traditional print to accentuate the beginning of text.

Use the first-letter pseudo-class to create a style rule for the first letter of a paragraph. You can specify style properties to control the color, font and size of the first letter. Then, use the float property to anchor the

first letter to the left and have the remaining text flow around it, creating a drop cap effect. Because CSS treats each element as a box on the page, you can also control the padding, borders, and dimensions of the box containing the drop cap. For more on using style sheet classes and paragraph pseudo-classes, see Chapter 6.

CREATE A DROP CAP WITH CSS

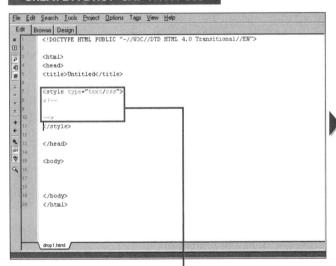

1 Open an HTML document.

2 Create a document-level style sheet.

Note: For more information on style sheets, see Chapter 6.

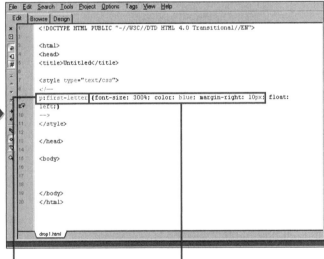

3 Type **p:first-letter {}**.

■ This creates a first-letter pseudo-class.

4 Inside the brackets, add any desired style properties and values.

Note: See Chapter 6 for more on style properties.

Which browsers support the first-letter pseudo-class style element?

✔ In general, versions 4 and higher of Netscape and Internet Explorer and versions 3.5 and higher of Opera have some level of support for Cascading Style Sheets. Be sure to test your pages thoroughly to verify that individual browser versions support the first-letter pseudo-class.

Are punctuation elements included in the first-letter drop cap?

✔ Yes, browsers that support the first-letter pseudo-class render initial punctuation, such as opening quotation marks, as part of the first-letter element.

What other ways are there to create drop caps?

✔ You can use HTML tables to create a contained drop cap by aligning the table to the left and having the paragraph text flow around it. For more information on creating HTML tables, see Chapter 3. In addition, you can create an image to use as a drop cap. For more on this technique, see the section "Create a GIF Drop Cap."

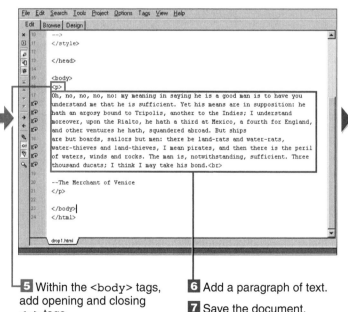

5 Within the <body> tags, add opening and closing <p> tags.

6 Add a paragraph of text.

7 Save the document.

8 View the page in a CSS-Compliant Web browser.

■ The browser renders the first letter of the paragraph according to the defined pseudo-class.

CREATE A GIF DROP CAP

You can create an image of a single character in a graphics editor and add it to your page in the form of a drop cap. You can also create drop caps using CSS style rules or HTML formatting tricks, but image drop caps allow you to use a wider variety of fonts and visual effects that are not available via HTML or CSS. In addition, image drop caps work on all browsers that support images, while support for CSS is limited.

Add your drop cap image to your Web page using the HTML <img> tag. By adding the align attribute and setting the value to "**left**", any text that immediately follows the image flows to the right of the drop cap. In addition, you can use the vspace and hspace attributes with the <img> tag to add additional padding around the image so it does not crowd the accompanying text.

When you create an image drop cap, remember to keep the file size as small as possible so the image does not add too much additional weight to the page. For tips on optimizing graphics, see Chapter 12.

CREATE A GIF DROP CAP

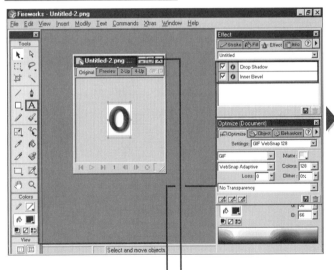

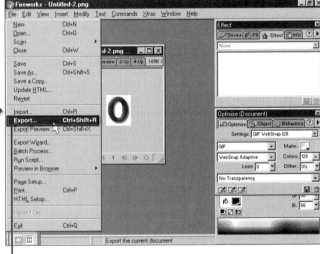

1 Open a graphics program.

Note: This example uses Fireworks, available on the CD-ROM that accompanies this book. The steps in other graphics programs will be similar, but check your manual.

2 Create a new document.

3 Using the text tool, add a single character for the drop cap.

4 Add any additional desired effects.

5 Export the image as a GIF.

What other values can I use with the align attribute?

✔ The align attribute for the `<img>` tag accepts the following values: `right`, `left`, `top`, `middle`, and `bottom`. The `top`, `middle`, and `bottom` attributes align the image vertically, but you must use the `right` or `left` values to have text flow around the image. If you do not explicitly specify the alignment, the image is aligned vertically with the text baseline. For more information on using the `<img>` tag and its attributes, see Chapter 3.

Should I include the alt attribute with drop cap images?

✔ Yes, you should add `alt` attributes to all images on your Web page, including drop caps. For the `alt` value, simply indicate the letter represented by the drop cap. That way, non-graphical browsers can render the `alt` text so the first line of your text is still comprehensible. For more on using `alt` attributes with images, see Chapter 7.

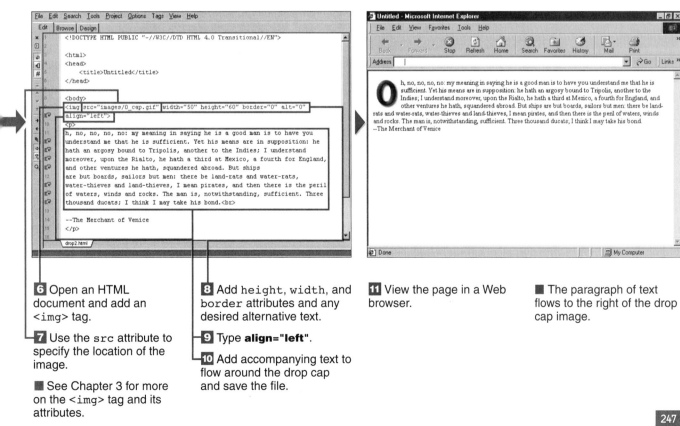

6 Open an HTML document and add an `<img>` tag.

7 Use the `src` attribute to specify the location of the image.

■ See Chapter 3 for more on the `<img>` tag and its attributes.

8 Add `height`, `width`, and `border` attributes and any desired alternative text.

9 Type **align="left"**.

10 Add accompanying text to flow around the drop cap and save the file.

11 View the page in a Web browser.

■ The paragraph of text flows to the right of the drop cap image.

CREATE PULL QUOTES

Y ou can highlight interesting and provocative sections of your text by adding pull quotes to your Web page. *Pull quotes* are frequently found in newspapers and magazines, and help attract the reader's attention and draw them into the text.

Create pull quotes by isolating teaser text within an HTML table. By using

the align attribute with the <table> tag, you can anchor the table to the left or right side of the page to have the regular content flow around the pull quote. For more information on formatting HTML tables, see Chapter 3. Within the table, you can enclose the pull quote and citation within <p>, <div>, or <span> tags, then format the text by using either HTML

text formatting techniques or CSS style rules outlined in Chapter 6. You can apply formatting styles (such as color, typeface, bold, or italics) to distinguish the quote from surrounding text. Whichever formatting style you use for your pull quotes, be consistent with this style throughout your pages.

CREATE PULL QUOTES

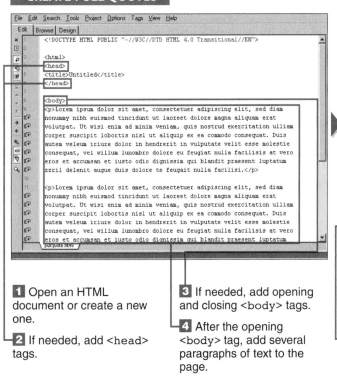

1 Open an HTML document or create a new one.

2 If needed, add <head> tags.

3 If needed, add opening and closing <body> tags.

4 After the opening <body> tag, add several paragraphs of text to the page.

5 Add an HTML table where you want to place the pull quote.

6 Set the table width.

■ Add the optional align attribute and value to anchor the table to the right or left.

Note: For more on HTML tables, see Chapter 3.

7 Create a style class for the pull quote text.

Note: For more on CSS font properties, see Chapter 6.

8 Repeat step 7 to create another style class for the pull quote citation.

Can I use CSS rather than HTML to create pull quotes?

✔ Yes. Besides using CSS to format the pull quote text, you can use the CSS box model rather than traditional HTML tables to format the pull quote container. By using CSS, you can set the position, dimensions, margins, and borders of the pull quote container. To learn about these and other CSS box properties, see Chapter 6. However, if you implement pull quotes using CSS, take the necessary steps to make sure your style elements degrade gracefully on browsers that do not support style properties and positioning.

Some Web sites I visit have pull quotes with unusual fonts or precise formatting. How can I create more elaborate pull quotes?

✔ If you want absolute control over the formatting of text or want to use unusual, stylized fonts, you can create image pull quotes using a graphics program. This allows for increased control over the visual layout and formatting of the pull quote, but also adds weight to your HTML page. For more information on creating and editing graphics for the Web, see Chapter 12.

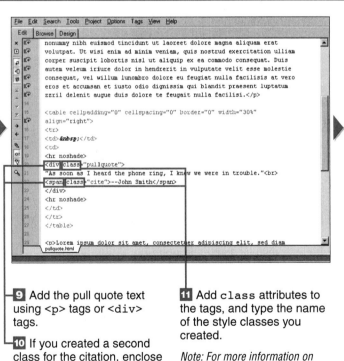

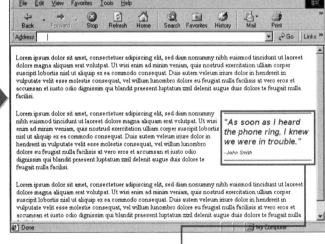

9 Add the pull quote text using <p> tags or <div> tags.

10 If you created a second class for the citation, enclose that text in <span> tags.

11 Add class attributes to the tags, and type the name of the style classes you created.

Note: For more information on using style classes, see Chapter 6.

12 View the page in a Web browser.

■ The pull quote helps draw the reader into the text.

USING SMALL CAPS

You can format text in small caps by using the CSS font variant property. Small caps are often used for acronyms and abbreviations, and sometimes in the first line of text.

With true small caps, lowercase letters look similar to the uppercase version but are smaller and have slight variations in the internal proportions and weight of the font strokes. For inline text elements such as acronyms, small caps are less jarring than text in regular uppercase letters and help improve the readability of your document.

To format inline text elements in small caps, create style classes with the font variant property:

```
.classname {font-variant:
small-caps}
```

After you have created your classes in a document-level or external style sheet, you can reference them using <span> tags. To learn how to implement <span> tags, see Chapter 6. Alternatively, you can create a style rule associated with a particular HTML tag, and assign the font variant property. In this case, all of the occurrences of this tag are formatted in small caps.

USING SMALL CAPS

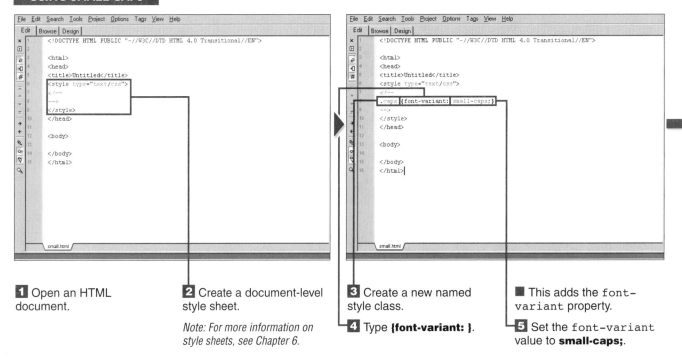

1 Open an HTML document.

2 Create a document-level style sheet.

Note: For more information on style sheets, see Chapter 6.

3 Create a new named style class.

4 Type **{font-variant: }**.

■ This adds the font-variant property.

5 Set the font-variant value to **small-caps;**.

Can I set the letter-spacing when using small caps?

✔ Yes, you can use the letter-spacing style property in conjunction with the `font variant` property to add additional space. For more information, see the section "Define Letter Spacing."

What other values are possible with the `font-variant` property?

✔ Other than `small-caps`, the only other value that the `font-variant` property accepts is `normal`, which is the default value.

Do browsers use true small caps?

✔ It depends on the browser. Many simply render the text in all uppercase letters rather than true small caps. According to the CSS specification, if the browser does not use a true small caps font, it may create a small caps version by taking a regular font and creating a scaled version based on the font's uppercase letters. As a last resort, browsers that support the property may simply replace the contained text with all uppercase characters.

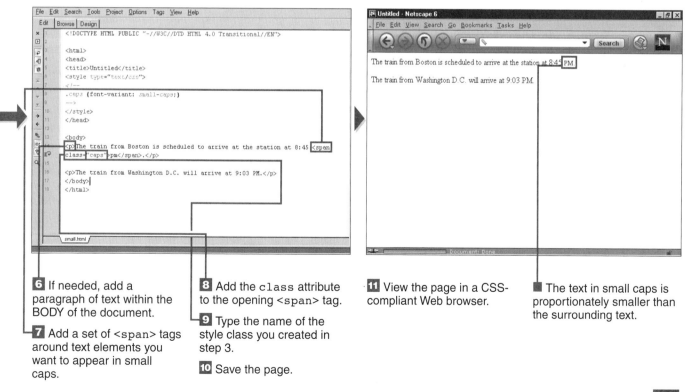

6 If needed, add a paragraph of text within the BODY of the document.

7 Add a set of `<span>` tags around text elements you want to appear in small caps.

8 Add the `class` attribute to the opening `<span>` tag.

9 Type the name of the style class you created in step 3.

10 Save the page.

11 View the page in a CSS-compliant Web browser.

■ The text in small caps is proportionately smaller than the surrounding text.

DEFINE LETTER-SPACING

You can set the spacing between letters by using the letter-spacing style property. You can increase letter-spacing to create distinct typographical effects or to make text elements more readable, particularly text in uppercase characters or small caps where additional letter spacing can improve the clarity of text.

The syntax for the letter-spacing style property is:

```
.classname {letter-spacing: value}
```

You can also combine the letter-spacing property with other text and font-related properties, such as font-family and font-property. Simply separate each property with a semicolon.

The letter-spacing style property has a default value of normal, but you can give it a specific length to either increase or decrease the normal amount of space between letters.

When setting the letter-spacing value, you can use one of several different length units, such as pixels, points, or the *em* unit, used to set the length relative to the height of the font. For example, for a 12 point font, a letter spacing of .5em is equal to half the height of the font being used, or 6 points.

DEFINE LETTER-SPACING

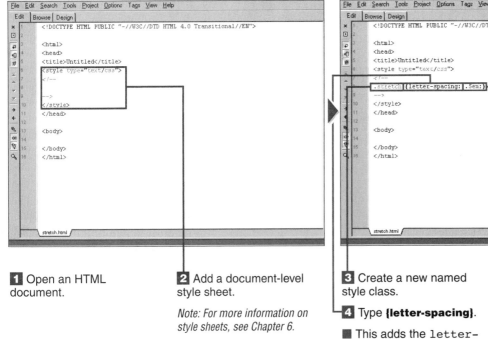

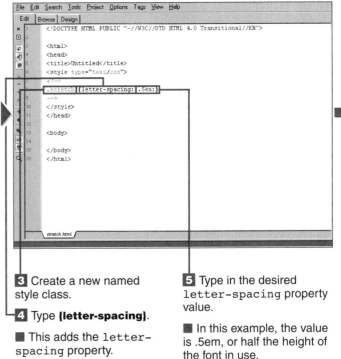

1 Open an HTML document.

2 Add a document-level style sheet.

Note: For more information on style sheets, see Chapter 6.

3 Create a new named style class.

4 Type **{letter-spacing}**.

■ This adds the letter-spacing property.

5 Type in the desired letter-spacing property value.

■ In this example, the value is .5em, or half the height of the font in use.

What other units can I use when setting the length of letter-spacing?

✔ For all style properties that accept a length as a value, you can use the em unit; the *ex* unit, equal to the width of the letter "x"; or *px* for pixels. To set absolute lengths, you can use pt (points), pc (picas), in (inches), cm (centimeters), and mm (millimeters).

Can I specify negative values for letter-spacing?

✔ Yes, you can set negative values to reduce the amount of space between letters.

If I use the `text-align` property to justify text, how does that effect letter-spacing?

✔ If you set the letter spacing to a specific length, the browser should not alter the space between letters when the text is justified, or is set so that both the left and right margins are even. If there is no specific length set for the letter-spacing, the browser may adjust it to accommodate the justified text.

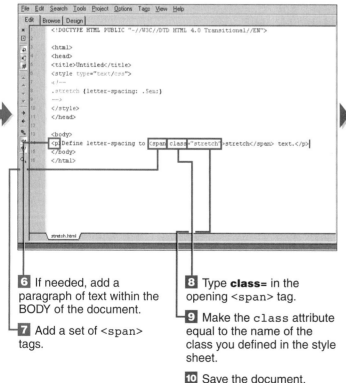

6 If needed, add a paragraph of text within the BODY of the document.

7 Add a set of `<span>` tags.

8 Type **class=** in the opening `<span>` tag.

9 Make the `class` attribute equal to the name of the class you defined in the style sheet.

10 Save the document.

11 View the page in a CSS-compliant Web browser.

■ The browser defines the letter-spacing as instructed, in this case adding additional space between the letters of the text.

DEFINE WORD-SPACING

Define the space between words in your text by using the word-spacing style property.

Word-spacing, or tracking, is an important typographical element that can either help or hinder the readability of text. If there is too little word-spacing, readers find it difficult to distinguish individual words. Loose tracking between words

can produce vertical columns of white space that disrupt the flow of text. If you adjust the word-spacing using style sheets, be sure that it does not adversely effect the overall readability of the document.

The syntax for the word-spacing style property is:

`.classname {word-spacing: value}`

You can set the word-spacing property to normal, the default value, or set it to a specific length. Lengths can be expressed in relative terms, using pixels, the em unit, or the ex unit. *Em* refers to the height of the font in use, while *ex* is the width of the letter "x." You can also set the width using absolute values and units such as inches (in), centimeters (cm), or millimeters (mm).

DEFINE WORD-SPACING

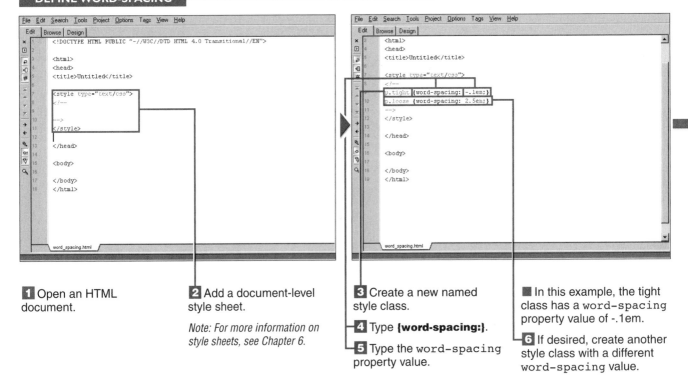

1 Open an HTML document.

2 Add a document-level style sheet.

Note: For more information on style sheets, see Chapter 6.

3 Create a new named style class.

4 Type **{word-spacing:}**.

5 Type the word-spacing property value.

■ In this example, the tight class has a word-spacing property value of -.1em.

6 If desired, create another style class with a different word-spacing value.

If I have one text element nested within another, does the word-spacing apply to both elements?

✔ If you define the word-spacing of the *parent*, or higher level, element, then the *child*, or nested, element inherits the word-spacing applied to the parent element. You can override this inheritance by setting the child element's word-spacing to `normal`.

How do I control the amount of space between lines of text?

✔ To control the spaces between lines of text, use the `line-height` property. For more information, see the section "Define Line-Height."

Is the word-spacing affected if I set the `text-align` property to justify?

✔ Yes, if the text-align property is set to `justify`, this may influence the word-spacing, depending on the browser.

Is there any way to define word-spacing using HTML?

✔ No. HTML is designed as a document layout language and focuses on content elements rather than style. The only way to define word-spacing is by using Cascading Style Sheets, explored in-depth in Chapter 6.

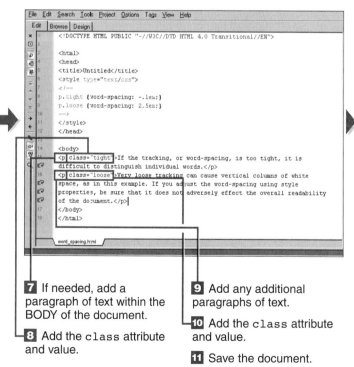

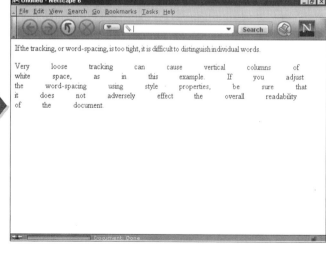

7 If needed, add a paragraph of text within the BODY of the document.

8 Add the `class` attribute and value.

9 Add any additional paragraphs of text.

10 Add the `class` attribute and value.

11 Save the document.

12 View the page in a browser that supports the `word-spacing` property.

■ The browser defines `word-spacing` as directed. Note that too much space between words makes it difficult to read the text.

DEFINE LINE-HEIGHT

You can define the line-height of an element by using the CSS line-height property. *Line-height* is equal to the height of the font plus the space above and below the text, also known as the *leading*. For example, if your font is set to 12 pixels and you assign a line-height of 16 px (16 pixels), the leading is 4 pixels total, with 2 pixels above and 2 pixels below the text.

The syntax for the line-height style property is

`.classname {line-height: value}`

The line-height property can also appear in conjunction with other text and font-related properties, such as font-family and font-property. Simply separate each property using a semicolon:

`.classname {line-height: value; font-size: value;}`

When you define the line-height using the line-height property, you can use values expressed as lengths (such as pixels or points), percentages, or numerical values without units. If you use percentages as line-height values, the browser sets the line-height as a percentage of the font size. Alternatively, if you use numerical values without units, the browser multiplies the font size by the number specified to derive the line-height value.

DEFINE LINE-HEIGHT

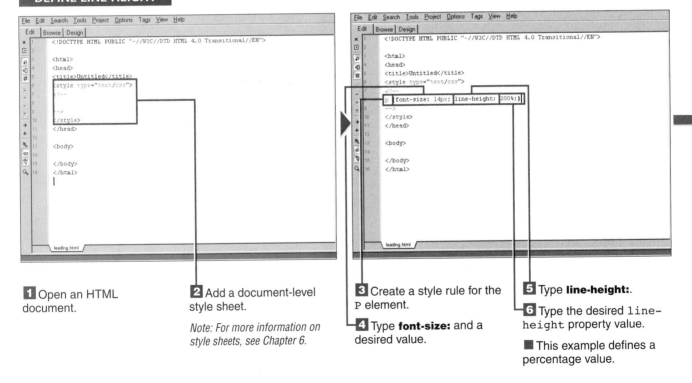

1 Open an HTML document.

2 Add a document-level style sheet.

Note: For more information on style sheets, see Chapter 6.

3 Create a style rule for the P element.

4 Type **font-size:** and a desired value.

5 Type **line-height:**.

6 Type the desired line-height property value.

■ This example defines a percentage value.

What is the difference between using percentages and numbers when setting the line-height?

✔ For the element that you are defining, percentages and numbers without units produce the same value. For example, for a font sized at 12 pixels, values of 150% and 1.5 both produce a line-height value of 18. The only difference is how child elements inherit the line-height property. When you use percentages, child elements inherit the calculated value, in this case 18 pixels, rather than the original percentage. When you use a numerical value, the number is passed to the child element rather than the calculated value.

What is the default value of normal line-height?

✔ The default line-height may vary from browser to browser, but the CSS specification suggests that browsers set normal line-height to between 100 and 120% of the font size in use.

Can I use negative values with the line-height property?

✔ No, negative values are not allowed.

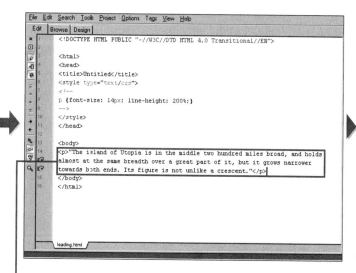

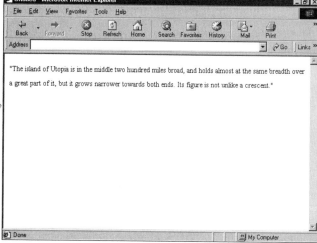

7 If needed, add a paragraph of text within the `<body>` of the document.

8 Save the document.

9 View the page in a CSS-compliant Web browser.

■ The line-height is calculated as directed, in this case a percentage of the font size.

OVERLAP TEXT

You can create blocks of overlapping text by using Cascading Style Sheets (CSS). With CSS, you can use overlapping text to create shadow effects or other visual design elements.

In order to create blocks of overlapping text, you need to use four style properties—position, top, left, and z-index—when creating your style classes. Set the position property to *absolute*, and use the top and left properties to offset the overlap elements. The syntax for the style rules is as follows:

.classname {position: *absolute*; left: *Xpx*; top: *Ypx*; z-index: *1*;}

.classname {position: *absolute*; left: *Xpx*; top: *Ypx*; z-index: *2*;}

To create overlapping shadow effects, create two or more style classes and offset the elements using the top and left properties so that their positions differ by only a few pixels. Then use the z-index property to set the stacking order. Elements with higher z-index values appear on top of elements with lower values. For more information on using z-index and other Cascading Style Sheet properties, see Chapter 6.

OVERLAP TEXT

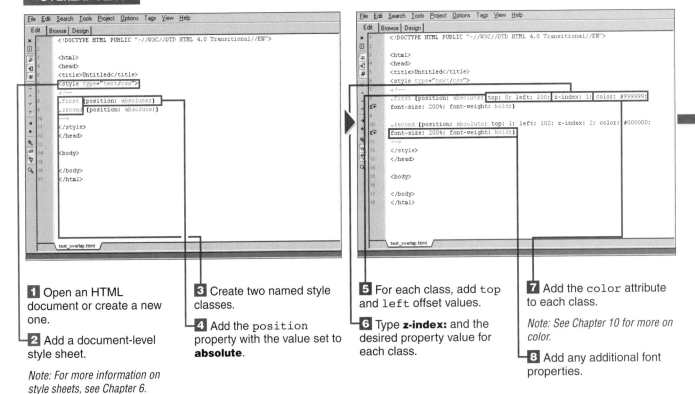

1 Open an HTML document or create a new one.

2 Add a document-level style sheet.

Note: For more information on style sheets, see Chapter 6.

3 Create two named style classes.

4 Add the position property with the value set to **absolute**.

5 For each class, add top and left offset values.

6 Type **z-index:** and the desired property value for each class.

7 Add the color attribute to each class.

Note: See Chapter 10 for more on color.

8 Add any additional font properties.

How does overlapped text appear on browsers that do not support CSS?

✔ On non-CSS browsers, the text is simply rendered as regular text according to the document flow.

Can I set the background color when I create overlapping text effects?

✔ You can set the background color using the background-color style property, but only on the lowest element in the stacking order. If you set the background color for the top element, the browser creates a filled box that obscures the elements beneath it. For more information on defining boxes and background colors, see Chapter 6.

Is there any other way to create shadow effects using CSS?

✔ The CSS2 specification includes a text-shadow property that allows you to create shadow effects. The text-shadow property accepts values for the color of the shadow, the amount the shadow is offset from the element, and an optional blur radius. Unfortunately, this property is not widely supported by current browsers.

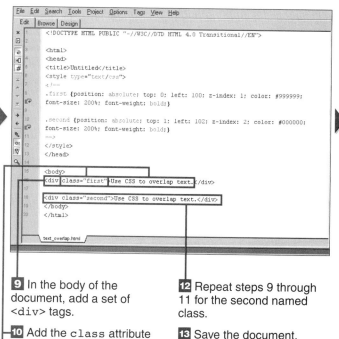

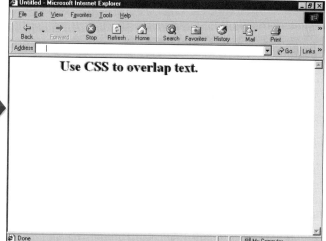

9 In the body of the document, add a set of <div> tags.

10 Add the class attribute and value.

11 Insert text between the opening and closing <div> tags.

12 Repeat steps 9 through 11 for the second named class.

13 Save the document.

14 View the page in a CSS-compliant browser.

■ The overlapping text creates a shadow effect.

EMBED A FONT

One approach to overcoming the typographical limitations of Web design is to use *embedded fonts*. Although the use of embedded fonts is not widespread, the technology gives you the power to use custom fonts to add visual accent to your pages. Before attempting to implement embedded fonts, be sure to review the competing technologies, available tools, and permission considerations.

How Embedded Fonts Work

When you embed fonts, you convert your font of choice into a file, and then link to that font file in the head of your HTML document. When the user accesses your site, the browser loads the embedded font and is able to use it to render the text on your page. Browsers are also able to cache embedded fonts so that users have to download the font file only once.

Why Adaptation Has Been Slow

Embedded fonts have been slow to take hold among Web developers. Like many technologies, competing implementations of font embedding are supported by Netscape and Internet Explorer, and most developers prefer to use solutions that are cross-browser compatible.

In addition, one of the fundamental principles of Web design is the variability of the browsing environment. Imposing specific typefaces, either through HTML elements, style sheets, or embedded fonts, is an attempt to regulate an environment that is fundamentally beyond the designer's control.

TrueDoc vs. OpenType

You can embed fonts in a Web page two different ways. Netscape versions 4.x support a dynamic font technology called *Bitstream TrueDoc*, while Internet Explorer versions 4 and higher support *OpenType* embedded fonts. To use TrueDoc dynamic fonts, you create a font file with the extension PFR, which stands for *Portable Font Resource*. To embed fonts with OpenType, you convert fonts into EOT, or *Embedded OpenType*, files.

Both TrueDoc and OpenType technologies have advantages and disadvantages. TrueDoc PFR files can contain characters for multiple typefaces, meaning that you can use several dynamic fonts while creating only one PFR file. For OpenType embedded fonts, you must create a separate EOT document for each font you want to embed.

However, the biggest stumbling block for both technologies is limited browser support. TrueDoc is supported by Netscape 4 but not Netscape 6, and visitors using Internet Explorer must download and install a font player to view the dynamic fonts. OpenType is supported by Internet Explorer versions 4 and higher, but is not supported by Netscape browsers. Browsers that do not support embedded fonts simply see the text in a font they do support or in the browser's default font.

Tools For Converting Fonts

Bitstream, the company that developed TrueDoc technology, offers commercial tools to create PFR files. You can purchase WebFont Maker at Bitstream's Web site, www.bitstream. com.

For OpenType embedded fonts, the only tool currently available for creating font files is Microsoft's WEFT (Web Embedding Fonts Tool). WEFT is available as a free download from Microsoft's Web site.

Font Permissions

Whether you use TrueDoc dynamic fonts or OpenType embedded fonts, make sure the fonts that you want to use do not have any restrictions. Some font designers protect their fonts and only allow them to be installed or embedded if you first get written permission. Other fonts are freely available for you to use.

You can check the permissions on individual fonts by using a utility program such as Microsoft's Font Properties Extension, available as a free download from Microsoft's Web site, www.microsoft.com.

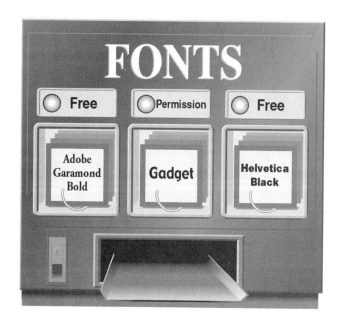

CONVERT A FONT TO USE ON THE WEB

You can convert a font to use on your Web page by using Microsoft's WEFT tool. WEFT analyzes your Web page; then it converts the referenced fonts into Embedded OpenType, or EOT, files that you can then upload to your server.

When you convert a font with WEFT, the first step is to reference the font in your HTML document as you normally would, using HTML <font> tags or style sheet font properties. When you run WEFT, it analyzes what font you are using and creates the embedded font files. WEFT also generates the style sheet code to reference the font files and automatically updates your Web pages, although you can make these alterations yourself if you prefer.

You can use WEFT to view the available fonts on your local system by clicking View, then Available Fonts. Be sure that the fonts you use are installable and that they do not have any usage restrictions.

CONVERT A FONT TO USE ON THE WEB

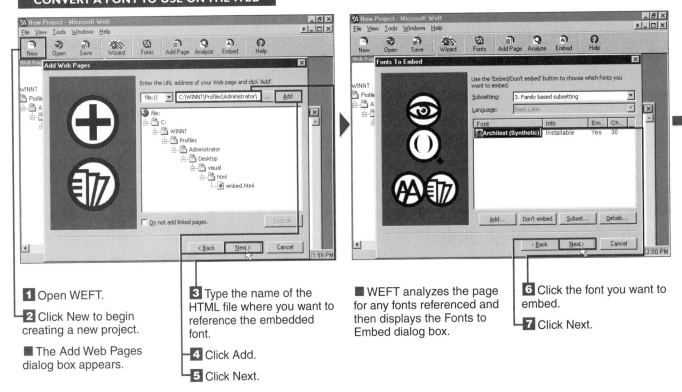

■1 Open WEFT.

■2 Click New to begin creating a new project.

■ The Add Web Pages dialog box appears.

■3 Type the name of the HTML file where you want to reference the embedded font.

■4 Click Add.

■5 Click Next.

■ WEFT analyzes the page for any fonts referenced and then displays the Fonts to Embed dialog box.

■6 Click the font you want to embed.

■7 Click Next.

How do I test to see whether the embedded font works?

✔ Testing embedded fonts is a bit tricky because you have the fonts installed on your local drive. One way to work around this is to change the font-family name in the `font-face` declaration to some fictitious font name. Then change your `<font>` tag or font style property to match this word. This way, when you test the page, you can be sure the font is loading from the EOT file rather than your local font repository

When visitors access sites with embedded fonts, are the fonts downloaded to their local system?

✔ No, the embedded fonts are used by the browser to render the page, but they are not added to the user's local collection of available fonts.

Can I embed more than one font?

✔ Yes, you can have multiple embedded fonts on your Web page, but for each font you embed you must create an individual EOT file.

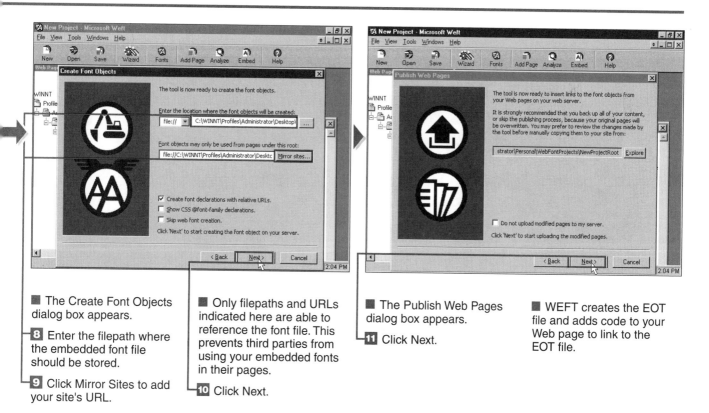

■ The Create Font Objects dialog box appears.

8 Enter the filepath where the embedded font file should be stored.

9 Click Mirror Sites to add your site's URL.

■ Only filepaths and URLs indicated here are able to reference the font file. This prevents third parties from using your embedded fonts in their pages.

10 Click Next.

■ The Publish Web Pages dialog box appears.

11 Click Next.

■ WEFT creates the EOT file and adds code to your Web page to link to the EOT file.

AN INTRODUCTION TO WEB GRAPHICS

You can use graphics such as logos, animations, screenshots, and image maps to enhance the visual appeal of your Web site. However, before you add images to a Web page, you need to understand the fundamental concepts behind designing graphics for the Web.

When you create and edit graphics destined for the Web, the medium itself imposes certain limitations in terms of the color, resolution, and file format. All of the tasks outlined in this chapter, from optimizing graphics to creating multi-frame animations, require a basic understanding of the concepts detailed below.

Image Resolution

If you are accustomed to creating graphics for print, you probably use high-resolution images where there are 300 dots per inch (dpi) or pixels per inch (ppi). However, most computer monitors are low-resolution, so there is no point in creating high-resolution Web graphics. Instead, set the resolution in your image editor to 72 dpi.

Color Space

When you create graphics using an image editor, you can represent colors numerically in several ways. These techniques for representing color are called *color spaces*.

Computer monitors use a color space called RGB, which uses degrees of red, green, and blue to create color combinations. For each of the three colors, you can set the intensity from 0 to 255, and the combination of these three values produces the desired color. Alternatively, you can set RGB values by using hexadecimal code, which uses two alphanumeric characters to represent each color. You can learn more about Web color theory and using RGB color values in Chapter 10.

GIF and JPEG File Formats

Although most graphics programs and image editors support a large number of file formats, most browsers have native support for only two image formats: GIF and JPEG. Each format has advantages and disadvantages, depending on the type of image you are encoding.

The Graphics Interchange Format (GIF) can contain a maximum of 256 colors, and so is usually the best choice for images with a small color palette. The GIF format, or more specifically the GIF89a version, also supports multi-frame animation and transparency. The section "Add Transparency to a GIF" outlines techniques for using this special transparency support in the GIF format.

The Joint Photographic Experts Group (JPEG) format supports tens of thousands of colors and is particularly suited to detailed, photographic images. However, the JPEG format is a *lossy* format, meaning that information is lost when compressed. In addition, compressing JPEGs often creates artifacts, or imperfections, in large blocks of solid color. To learn how to optimize JPEGs while reducing artifacts, see the section "Optimize a JPEG."

File Size

Because visitors must dowload the images that you add to your Web page, giving special consideration to file size is important. Heavy images with large file sizes take longer to download, so you should always optimize graphics to reduce the number of bytes or kilobytes (K).

Depending on the file format you choose, there are a variety of techniques you can use to reduce the overall file size without sacrificing too much image quality. The sections "Optimize a JPEG" and "Optimize a GIF" demonstrate how to optimize images to strike a balance between quick download times and image integrity.

TAKE A SCREENSHOT

You can use screenshots or screen captures to create illustrated examples of computer-related tasks or to create images of other Web sites to use on your own site. For example, if you have a portfolio site, you can include screenshots of sites you have built to illustrate your work.

Screenshots are among the easiest pieces of artwork to acquire, as you can use either Windows or the Mac

OS to capture them. When you take a screenshot, you can either capture the entire contents of your monitor or only the active window.

The Windows method captures the screen image and stores it temporarily. After you capture the screen image, you can paste the screenshot into a new document in a graphics editor and save it in the image format of your choice. The Mac method creates a PICT file;

however, you can use an image editor to make any desired changes.

When you capture screenshots, keep in mind that what you see is what you get, so do not leave anything on screen that you do not want viewers to see. If you have extra windows or folders open when you capture the shot, for example, you either have to reshoot, edit the unwanted items out, or live with the result.

TAKE A SCREENSHOT

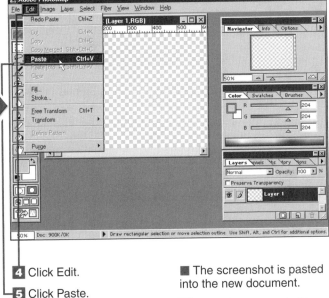

**TAKING SCREENSHOTS
IN WINDOWS**

1 With the desired view on your screen, press Print Screen on your keyboard.

2 Open an image editing program, such as Photoshop.

3 Create a new document.

4 Click Edit.

5 Click Paste.

■ The screenshot is pasted into the new document.

6 Save the screenshot in your preferred file format.

Is there software available to automate the process of taking screenshots?

✓ Yes, many free and inexpensive utilities are available that automate the screenshot process. Many of these programs include functionality to automatically save screenshots, print image catalogs, and set a custom hot key on your keyboard. For a listing of available utilities, visit www. download.com. One of the most popular image editors is Adobe Photoshop, a trial version of which is available on this book's CD-ROM. See Chapter 25 for more about Photoshop.

What file format should I save screenshots in?

✓ Any screenshot that you plan on adding to a Web page should be in either the GIF or the JPEG format. Try optimizing in both formats to gauge which one gives you the best quality at the smallest file size. For more on optimizing images, see the sections "Optimize a JPEG" and "Optimize a GIF." Saving the original screenshot in a true image format, such as BMP, PICT, TIFF, or PNG, is also a good idea. That way you can edit the original rather than work with a compressed GIF or JPEG image.

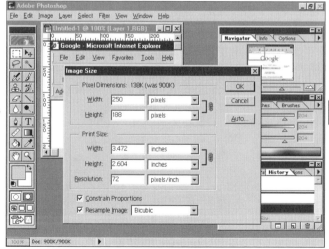

■ Adjust the dimensions of the screenshot if necessary.

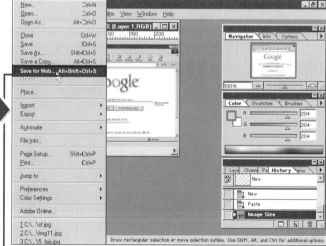

7 Click File.

8 Click Save as, or the equivalent.

9 Save the screenshot in your preferred file format.

TAKING SCREENSHOTS ON A MACINTOSH

■ To capture the entire screen on a Macintosh with OS 9.1 or below, press Ctrl+⌘+Shift+3.

CROP AN IMAGE

You can crop an image if you want to remove unnecessary elements or use only one section of an image. Crop images to create a thumbnail of a larger image if you prefer to highlight one section rather than reducing the size of the entire image.

Most image-editing programs, including Macromedia Fireworks 4 and Adobe Photoshop 6, both

available in trial versions on the CD-ROM included with this book, offer you the ability to crop images using a crop tool available on a tool palette or toolbox. To crop an image using the Crop tool, highlight the area you want to retain. Anything beyond this area is removed when you crop the image. Cropping techniques are fairly consistent across most image-editing tools, so

the Photoshop techniques described here can be applied to other programs.

In addition, you can crop paths from overlapping objects when you create new images. For example, if you have two overlapping elements, you can create a new shape by removing portions of the elements that do not overlap.

CROP AN IMAGE

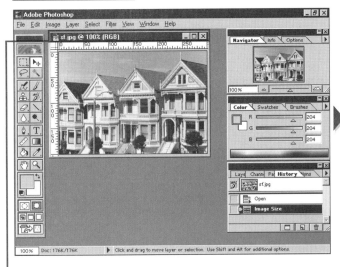

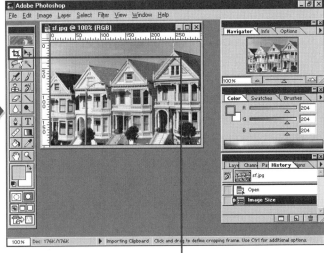

1 Open an image in a graphics editor.

■ This example uses Photoshop. A trial version of Photoshop is available on this book's CD-ROM.

2 Click and hold the Marquee tool (▣) until other options are visible.

3 Click the Crop tool (▣).

Is there a way to crop while retaining specific proportions?

✔ Yes. In Photoshop or Fireworks, press Shift while clicking and dragging the corner handle. This allows you to define the crop area while retaining the proportions of the original marquee.

How do I cancel cropping?

✔ In Photoshop and Fireworks, you can right-click to get a pop-up menu with the option to cancel the cropping action. You can also cancel a cropping action by clicking the Crop tool again or by selecting another tool from the toolbox.

Can I crop an image to specific dimensions?

✔ Yes, most image editors allow you to specify dimensions when cropping. In Photoshop, for example, you can enter a target size, with specific width and height dimensions, and crop the image accordingly. To set a target size, open the Crop Options palette by either double-clicking the Crop tool or by clicking Window, Show Options.

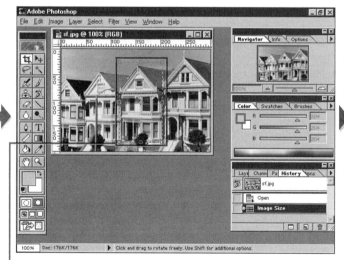

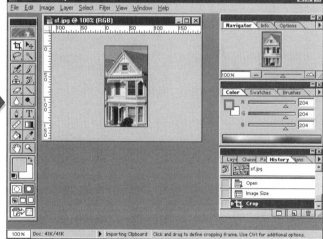

4 Create a marquee around the area of the image you want to retain.

■ Click and drag the sizing boxes at the corners and edges of the marquee to resize the crop area.

5 Double-click inside the marquee, or press Enter/Return.

■ The image is cropped along the marquee lines.

OPTIMIZE A JPEG

You can reduce the time it takes for your Web page to load by optimizing your JPEG images.

Optimizing your images means finding the right balance between image quality and file size so that the download time is manageable.

When you optimize an image using a graphics editor such as Photoshop or Fireworks, you select a quality level from a range of 0 to 100, 100 being the highest quality and file size and 0 being the lowest quality and file size. For the best results, experiment with quality levels between 50 and 80. This range reduces the file size while minimizing the *artifacts*, or

imperfections, that result from the optimization process.

Many editing programs also allow you to select certain areas to which you can then apply a different quality level. For example, you may have background areas or areas of less detail where you can reduce the quality level without effecting the overall quality of the image.

OPTIMIZE A JPEG

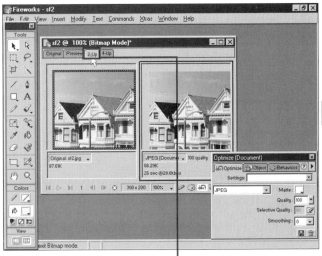

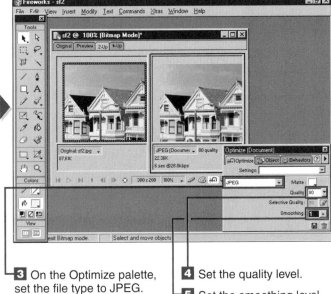

1 Open an image in a graphics editor.

■ This example uses Fireworks 4, a trial version of which is available on this book's CD-ROM.

2 Click the 2-Up View.

■ This view compares the original image to the optimized image.

3 On the Optimize palette, set the file type to JPEG.

4 Set the quality level.

5 Set the smoothing level.

Can I save the optimization settings I use in Fireworks?

✔ Yes, you can save the settings to reuse later. Click the disk icon in the optimization panel to assign a name to the settings. The settings then appear as an option with the other preset choices.

What preset optimization options are available for JPEGs?

✔ In Fireworks, there are two preset options for JPEGS, "better quality" and "smaller file." Better quality sets the quality level to 80 and the smoothing to 0. "Smaller file" sets the quality level to 60 and the smoothing to 2.

How does the Smoothing or Blur option help reduce file size?

✔ These options blur the hard lines around edges, which do not compress very well in JPEG format.

What are progressive JPEGs?

✔ Progressive JPEGs are similar to interlaced GIFs (see the section "Optimize a GIF"). *Progressive* JPEGs display at low resolution, then transition to a high-resolution version. Create progressive JPEGs in Fireworks by selecting Progressive from the Optimize options menu.

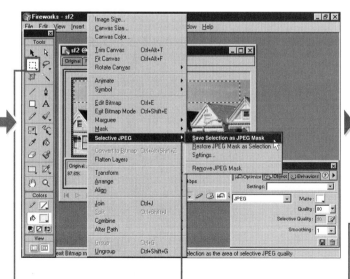

6 Click the Marquee tool (▦) in the toolbox.

7 Highlight an area where you want to set a selective quality level.

8 Click Modify.

9 Click Selective JPEG.

10 Click Save Selection as JPEG Mask.

■ The selection is overlayed with a different color during editing.

11 On the Optimize palette, indicate the selective quality value.

■ The optimized version has a smaller file size and quicker download time.

OPTIMIZE A GIF

You can optimize GIFs by reducing the color palette used in images and manipulating the amount of dithering that occurs when the image is compressed.

As with optimized JPEGs (see the section "Optimize a JPEG"), the key is to reduce the file size and download time of the image while still retaining image quality.

The GIF file format uses a maximum of 256 colors. By reducing the total number of colors in the palette, you can shrink the file size of the compressed image.

You can reduce the number of colors until you find the right balance between file size and image quality. Some graphics editors allow you to manually remove individual colors from the palette to reduce the color depth.

The amount of dithering you select when optimizing your GIFs can also affect the overall file size. Dithering occurs when a color is not available in the palette, so pixels of similar colors are arranged side by side to simulate the missing color. Higher dithering levels can slightly increase the overall file size.

OPTIMIZE A GIF

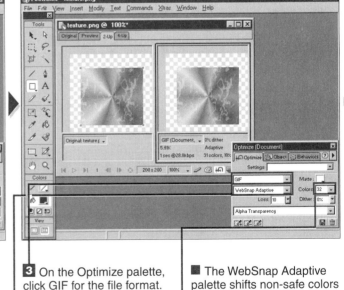

1 Open a file in a graphics editor.

■ This example uses Fireworks 4, a trial version of which is available on this book's CD-ROM.

2 Click the 2-Up view.

■ This view compares the original image to the optimized image.

3 On the Optimize palette, click GIF for the file format.

4 Select a color palette.

■ The WebSnap Adaptive palette shifts non-safe colors to their closest Web-safe approximations.

5 Select the number of colors to use.

Are there any other ways to optimize images in Fireworks besides using the Optimize palette?

✔ Yes, you can optimize the image when you export by clicking File, Export Preview.

What are interlaced GIFs?

✔ Interlaced images initially download as a low-resolution version, then transition to the higher-resolution version. This does not actually speed the download process, but it gives the illusion of quicker downloads because the user has something to see on the page. You can create interlaced GIFs in Fireworks by selecting Interlaced from the Options menu on the Optimize palette.

What preset optimization options are available for GIFs?

✔ Fireworks has several preset options for GIFs. The GIF Web 216 option uses only the Web-safe palette with a maximum of 216 colors. For more information on Web-safe colors, see Chapter 10. The two GIF Websnap options convert non Web-safe colors to similar Web-safe colors with a maximum of either 128 or 256 colors. The GIF adaptive palette contains only colors actually used in the image.

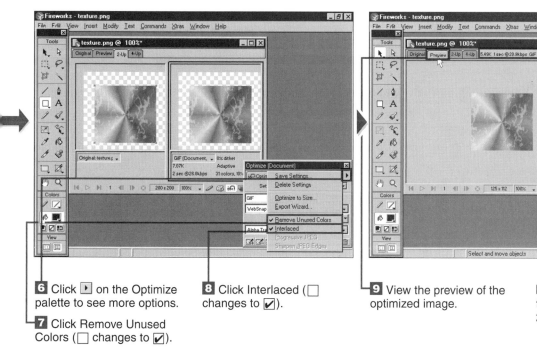

6 Click ▶ on the Optimize palette to see more options.

7 Click Remove Unused Colors (☐ changes to ✔).

8 Click Interlaced (☐ changes to ✔).

9 View the preview of the optimized image.

■ The size of the file and the download time on a 28.8 modem is shown.

RESIZE A GIF

When resizing images, working with vector images or images that have not yet been compressed is always best. For this reason, it is always useful to save original artwork in a true image format, such as BMP, PICT, TIFF, or PNG.

However, sometimes you must resize, or scale, a compressed GIF. Generally,

you can scale the image down, but increasing the size of a GIF leads to poor image quality. The exception to this rule is if your images are aliased and composed entirely of rectangles. In this case you can increase the size of the GIF without losing image quality, because aliased images do not have the additional pixels used to "blur" the jagged appearance of curved lines.

When you scale down a GIF, you can use various filters to sharpen and blur the image. This can improve the clarity of the resized version.

Experiment with sharpen and blur effects both before and after scaling the image to arrive at an optimal quality level.

RESIZE A GIF

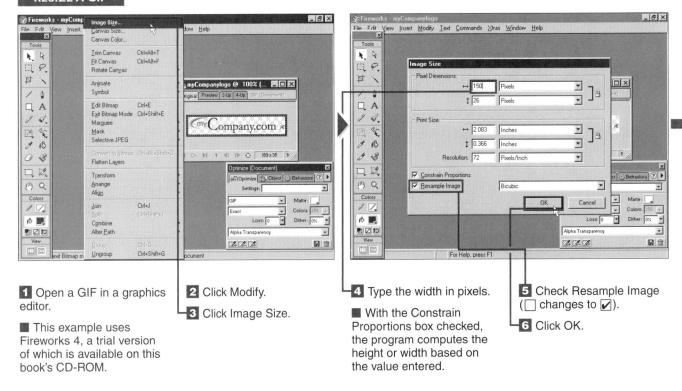

1 Open a GIF in a graphics editor.

■ This example uses Fireworks 4, a trial version of which is available on this book's CD-ROM.

2 Click Modify.

3 Click Image Size.

4 Type the width in pixels.

■ With the Constrain Proportions box checked, the program computes the height or width based on the value entered.

5 Check Resample Image (☐ changes to ☑).

6 Click OK.

Can JPEGs be scaled?

✔ You can increase the size of a JPEG slightly and retain fairly high quality. You can scale down a JPEG without losing any quality.

Are there other ways to resize an image?

✔ Yes. In most image-editing programs, you can use a Scale tool to resize an image. To use this tool, click on the Scale icon in the toolbox and resize the image by clicking and dragging one of the corner handles.

Why can I increase the size of aliased images but not anti-aliased images?

✔ Anti-aliased images have additional pixels around curved edges to create a blend effect. When you increase the size of anti-aliased images, these intermediate pixels are more visible and create blurred lines. Aliased images and images with rectangles and straight lines do not have these intermediary pixels, so you can scale them up and they do not appear blurry.

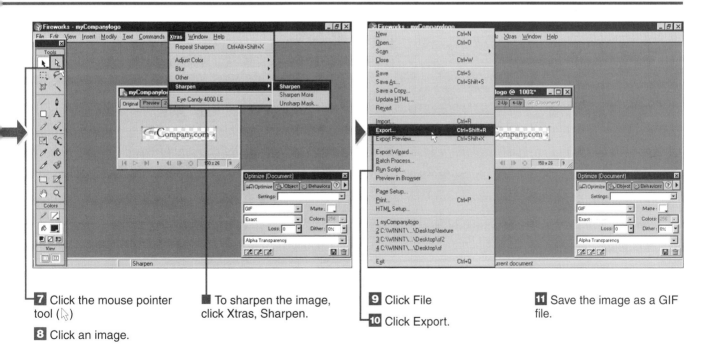

■ **7** Click the mouse pointer tool (⬉)

■ **8** Click an image.

■ To sharpen the image, click Xtras, Sharpen.

■ **9** Click File

■ **10** Click Export.

■ **11** Save the image as a GIF file.

ADD TRANSPARENCY TO A GIF

You can add transparency to a GIF image so that the background of your Web page is visible. This is particularly useful if you have an image placed on top of a tiled or textured background.

The GIF file format supports index transparency, meaning that you can

select one color to be completely transparent. You can either choose to have the background transparent when you create a new document, or select the specific color to render transparent when you optimize and export the image.

If your image is anti-aliased and you make the background transparent,

make sure that this is the same background color of the Web page where the image will be located. With anti-aliased edges, there are additional pixels in an intermediary range between the object color and the background color. If the background is rendered transparent, this creates a halo effect around the object.

ADD TRANSPARENCY TO A GIF

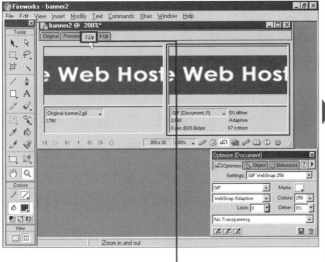

1 Open a GIF image in a graphics editor.

■ This example uses Fireworks 4, a trial version of which is available on this book's CD-ROM.

2 Click the 2-Up view.

3 On the Optimize palette, click ▾ and click Index Transparency.

Is there any way to select the degree of transparency?

✔ With the GIF file format, transparency is either on or off. There are no intermediary values. The PNG file format supports alpha channel transparency, meaning that you can select the degree of transparency. For more information on PNG images, see Chapter 13.

Does JPEG support transparency?

✔ No, the JPEG file format does not support transparency.

If I select one color to be transparent, are all occurrences of that color rendered transparent?

✔ Yes. For example, if your background color is white and you choose to make that background transparent, any white pixels in your image will also be transparent. To work around this, choose a background color that is not used anywhere else in your image.

■4 Click the Add Transparency button (⊞) to add color to transparency.

■ The cursor changes to an eyedropper.

■5 Click the color you want to be transparent.

■ The selected color is rendered transparent.

■6 Save or export the image as a GIF file.

CREATE A TRANSPARENT SPACER GIF

You can create complex page layouts by using transparent spacer GIFs. A *transparent spacer GIF*, also referred to as a *pixel shim*, is simply a 1 pixel by 1 pixel GIF that has no visible color. You can use these transparent GIFs to force the browser to maintain specific table dimensions, or to create blocks of white space or vertical lines of color.

You can create a transparent spacer GIF using any graphics program or image editor that supports index transparency and GIF exports. Create an image as you normally do, but set the dimensions to 1 pixel by 1 pixel and the background color to Transparent. When you reference the spacer GIF in your HTML document, you can set the dimensions using the width and height attributes with the

`<img>` tag. Be sure to add `alt` attributes to spacer images, but always leave the value as an empty string. This way alternate browsers do not try to read the text associated with the spacer GIF. For more information on using spacer GIFs for page layout purposes, see Chapter 10.

CREATE A TRANSPARENT SPACER GIF

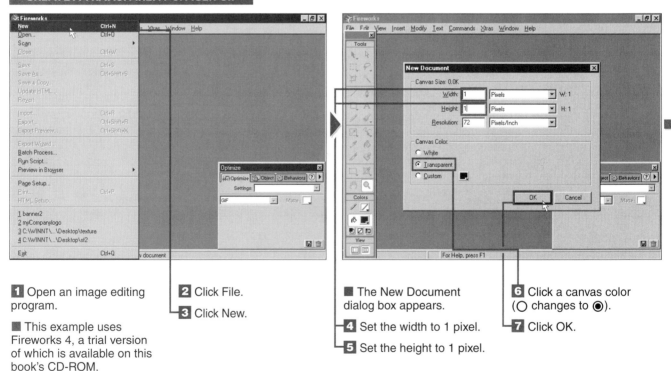

1 Open an image editing program.

■ This example uses Fireworks 4, a trial version of which is available on this book's CD-ROM.

2 Click File.

3 Click New.

■ The New Document dialog box appears.

4 Set the width to 1 pixel.

5 Set the height to 1 pixel.

6 Click a canvas color (○ changes to ●).

7 Click OK.

Is there any other way to control layout space besides using spacer GIFs?

✓ Yes, you can use Cascading Style Sheets, rather than HTML tables, to control the layout of a page. For more information on this technique, see Chapter 10.

What is the difference between alpha transparency and index transparency?

✓ With index transparency, pixels are either visible or transparent. With alpha channel transparency, you can select a degree of transparency, usually as a percentage value. GIFs only support index transparency.

Why is the spacer GIF not transparent on my Macintosh browser?

✓ Some Macintosh browser versions display the transparent GIF unless you explicitly set the background color of the table cell containing it. For more information on using color with table cells, see Chapter 3.

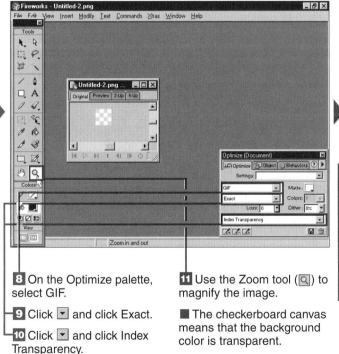

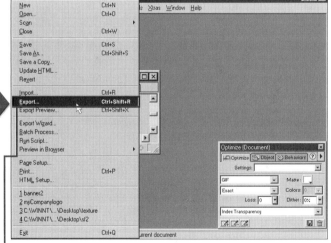

8 On the Optimize palette, select GIF.

9 Click ▾ and click Exact.

10 Click ▾ and click Index Transparency.

11 Use the Zoom tool (🔍) to magnify the image.

■ The checkerboard canvas means that the background color is transparent.

12 Click File.

13 Click Export.

14 Save the spacer GIF to your images directory.

CREATE AN ANIMATED GIF

Make your Web page more dynamic by using animated GIF images.

Animated GIFs are single image files composed of several other individual images. By quickly rotating through the individual images, you can create the illusion of motion. You can also use animated GIFs to create messages that transition from one frame to another. This technique is often used in banner advertisements and promotional images.

There are many commercial programs and inexpensive shareware products that you can use to create animated GIFs. In addition, all-purpose graphics editors such as Fireworks and Adobe ImageReady include functionality that allows you to build animated GIFs.

You control the speed and smoothness of an animation by setting the tweening and time delay. *Tweening* refers to the transition frames between each individual

image in the animation. More frames between each image causes a smoother animation but also increases the file size. For each frame in the animation, you can set the time delay, usually in seconds or tenths of a second. For smoother transitions, set the delay for transition frames to one or two tenths of a second.

CREATE AN ANIMATED GIF

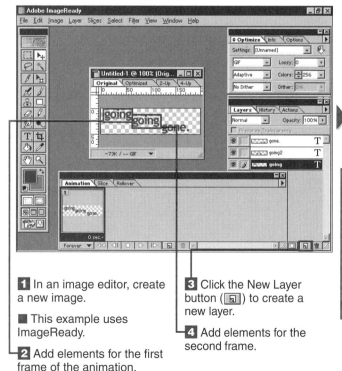

1 In an image editor, create a new image.

■ This example uses ImageReady.

2 Add elements for the first frame of the animation.

3 Click the New Layer button (⊡) to create a new layer.

4 Add elements for the second frame.

5 Add additional frames to the animation.

6 Use the Layers palette to indicate which layer should be visible on each frame.

■ See Chapter 25 for more on how to work with layers in ImageReady and Photoshop.

Can JPEGs be animated?

✔ No, the JPEG file format does not support animation. You can, however, use JPEGs in individual frames, but the final animation must be exported as a GIF file.

How do I add animated GIFs to a Web page?

✔ Because animated GIFs are a single image file, you can add them to a Web page using the standard HTML `<img>` tag. For more information on the `<img>` tag, see Chapter 3.

How does animation effect file size?

✔ Animation GIFs are much larger in file size than static GIF images. This increase in weight is due to the multiple frames that compose the animation, and each frame that you add to an animation adds additional weight.

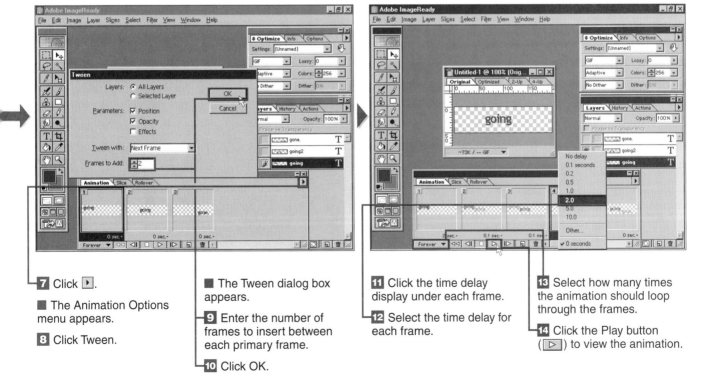

7 Click ▶.

■ The Animation Options menu appears.

8 Click Tween.

■ The Tween dialog box appears.

9 Enter the number of frames to insert between each primary frame.

10 Click OK.

11 Click the time delay display under each frame.

12 Select the time delay for each frame.

13 Select how many times the animation should loop through the frames.

14 Click the Play button (▷) to view the animation.

CREATE AN IMAGE MAP

Y ou can have one image link to several different Web pages or sites by creating a client-side image map.

An *image map* is a standard graphic, such as a GIF or JPEG, for which you define multiple hot spots where the user can click to load a new page. Sites that feature geographical organization schemes often use image maps for navigation. For example, a

travel site might have an image of a particular continent with each country as a hot spot that the user can click.

Adding an image map to an HTML page involves using a standard **<img>** tag and referencing the name of a map you define using **<map>** tags. Within the opening and closing **<map>** tags, use **<area>** tags to define the shape, coordinates, and

URL for each hot spot on the image map. See Part II for more about HTML tags.

Most image-editing programs, including Fireworks 4, allow you to define hot spots and export images as maps. This example uses Fireworks 4; the steps with other graphics programs involve similar issues.

CREATE AN IMAGE MAP

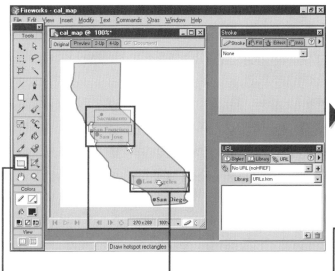

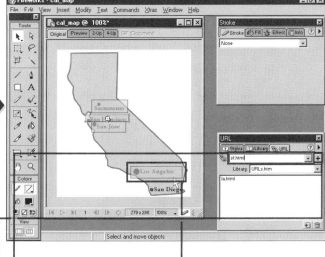

1 Open an image file in a graphics program or image editor. This example uses Fireworks 4.

2 Click the Hot Spot tool (▢) on the Tools palette.

■ You can create rectangle, circle, or polygon hot spots.

3 Drag the cursor across the image and release to define a hot spot for the image map.

4 Define additional hot spots.

5 In the URL palette, type the URL for the Hot Spot.

■ You can click the Add URL icon to add the URL to your library.

6 Use the Pointer tool to select a different hot spot.

7 Add the URL in the URL palette.

In the HTML generated for the image map, what do the coordinates represent?

✔ For rectangle-shaped hot spots, the x and y coordinates you indicate refer to the top left and bottom right corners of the hot spot. For circular areas, include x and y values for the center of the circle as well as a value for the radius. For polygons, define x and y coordinates for each point of the shape. For more information on HTML, see Chapter 3.

Do I have to place the <map> tags near the image map in my HTML page?

✔ No, the <map> tags can occur anywhere inside the opening and closing <body> tags of the HTML document.

Can I attach events to image maps?

✔ Yes, you can use event-related attributes such as onMouseOver and onMouseOut with the <area> tag to reference JavaScript methods and functions. For more information on scripting techniques, see Chapter 14.

Can I use alt attributes with image maps?

✔ Yes. Rather than adding the alt attribute to the <img> tag, include individual alt attributes for each area of the image map that you define.

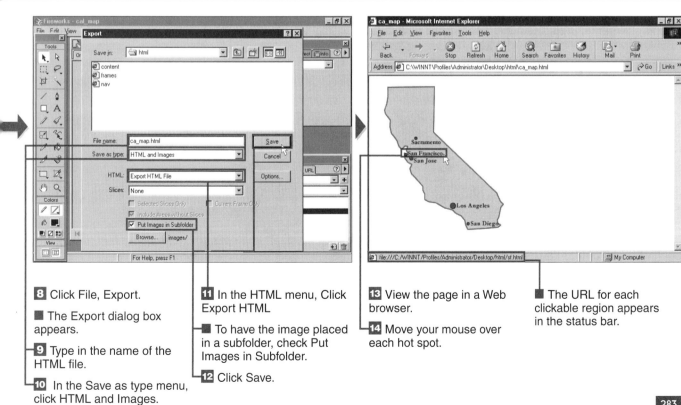

■8 Click File, Export.

■ The Export dialog box appears.

■9 Type in the name of the HTML file.

■10 In the Save as type menu, click HTML and Images.

■11 In the HTML menu, Click Export HTML

■ To have the image placed in a subfolder, check Put Images in Subfolder.

■12 Click Save.

■13 View the page in a Web browser.

■14 Move your mouse over each hot spot.

■ The URL for each clickable region appears in the status bar.

CREATE A THUMBNAIL IMAGE

You can create thumbnail images by scaling larger images down to a fraction of the original size. Thumbnail images are particularly useful if you have limited space on a page and want to keep download times manageable. Thumbnails can also be used to link to larger size or higher-resolution versions of images that only a portion of your audience wants. By using thumbnails, you can make the larger versions available without slowing down the load time of your main Web page.

To create a thumbnail of a larger image, use a graphics program or image editor to scale down the original. If your original image is a JPEG, you can scale down without losing any image quality. If the original image is a GIF, you may need to use additional filtering techniques to sharpen the thumbnail for optimal clarity. After you have created your thumbnail image, add it to your Web page using the `<img>` tag. For more information on adding images with the `<img>` tag, see Chapter 3.

CREATE A THUMBNAIL IMAGE

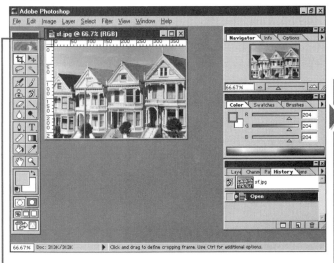

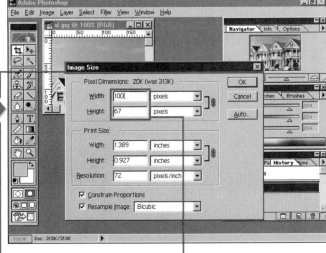

1 Open an image in an image editor.

■ This example uses Photoshop.

2 Click Image.

3 Click Image Size.

■ The Image Size dialog box appears.

4 Enter width and height values.

5 Export or save the image to the appropriate directory.

What other techniques can I use to create thumbnails?

✔ Rather than scaling down the entire image, you can create thumbnails by cropping out one portion of the image. This is a good alternative if you want to convey more detailed information in the thumbnail itself. To crop images, see the section "Crop an Image."

Can I use the height and width attributes with the `<img>` tag to create a thumbnail image?

✔ Yes, but keep in mind that if width and height values you assign are not exactly proportional to the actual dimensions of the image, the image appears distorted.

How do I alert users they can click on the thumbnail to get a larger version?

✔ You can use a number of techniques to convey that the thumbnail is clickable. You can include caption text telling the user to click the image for a larger version, include instructional text using `alt` attributes, or add a link-colored border by using the `<img>` tag's border attribute. Another technique is to integrate a small icon, such as a magnifying glass, into the thumbnail image itself.

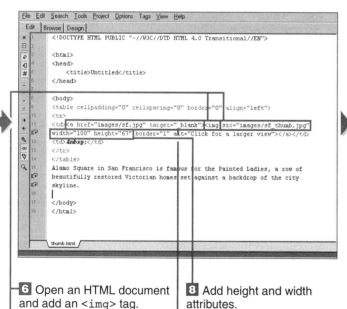

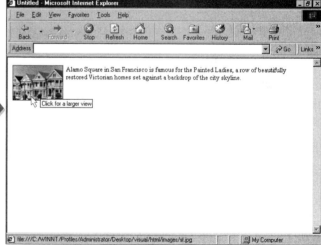

-6 Open an HTML document and add an `<img>` tag.

-7 Add an `src` attribute and value.

8 Add height and width attributes.

-9 Add a set of `<a>` tags and indicate the location of the original image file.

10 View the page in a Web browser.

■ Click the thumbnail to load the larger version of the image.

INTRODUCING THE NEW WEB GRAPHICS STANDARDS

Since the Web's inception, designers have used the GIF and JPEG formats to add images to Web pages. You can learn how to create and edit these popular formats in Chapter 12. More recently, groups such as the World Wide Web Consortium (W3C) have encouraged the development of other types of graphics, such as PNG and SVG, that more closely fit the needs of the Web. Specifically, these standards developed out of the need to support open-source formats that are not owned by one particular entity. In addition, both PNG and SVG offer Web-specific enhancements, such as improved file compression in the case of PNG and scalability in the case of SVG. However, as is the case with most new technologies, the major browser makers have been slow to embrace these emerging standards.

Introducing PNG

PNG, pronounced "ping," stands for Portable Network Graphics, and was designed as an open-source alternative to the GIF format. The GIF format uses a proprietary compression method patented by the Unisys Corporation, so any software company that develops a tool that uses the GIF format must pay a license fee. PNG, on the other hand, is open source and non-proprietary, meaning PNG is not owned by anyone.

The PNG format offers several improvements over GIF. It supports alpha channel transparency, meaning that you can set the amount of transparency for colors, rather than simply having transparency on or off. It

also features gamma correction so the brightness of the image is consistent across platforms. In addition, PNG is a lossless file format that compresses better than GIF. To learn how to export an image in the PNG format, see section "Create a PNG Image."

Introducing SVG

Scalable Vector Graphics, or SVG, marks an attempt to bring vector graphics to the Web using XML (see Chapter 22). File formats such as GIF and JPEG are *raster graphics*, which means that they record information for each individual pixel. *Vector graphics*, on the other hand, store information for the lines and curves that make up the image. This may seem like a small distinction, but it becomes important when you try to edit

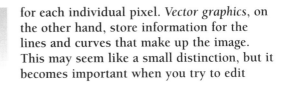

graphics or scale them to different sizes. For example, with SVG images, users can increase or decrease the size of an image without losing any image quality.

SVG offers several distinct advantages over other image formats. SVG can be used independently to display graphics and animations, or can work in conjunction with HTML, XML, and SMIL to create complex interactive Web applications. SVG files can interact with style sheets, incorporate scripted events, and be dynamically generated. In addition, any text contained within an SVG file is fully indexable by search engines. However, the most

notable aspect of SVG is that you can code graphics using a simple text editor. The section "Create an SVG File" demonstrates how to begin coding SVG files using XML.

Browser Support

The biggest obstacle facing designers who want to use PNG and SVG formats is the lack of full support in the two most popular browsers, Netscape and Internet Explorer. Newer versions of Internet Explorer support the PNG format, but do not correctly handle alpha transparency, while only the latest version of Netscape (6 at the time of this writing) correctly renders PNGs with transparency.

As for scalable Vector Graphics, neither browser type has native support for SVG, so

users and developers must download a plug-in or viewer to be able to view SVG files.

Currently, only a small number of SVG viewers are available, the most popular and widespread being the Adobe SVG viewer. See "Download the Adobe SVG Viewer," later in this chapter, for instructions on downloading and installing the plug-in.

For the time being, this lack of browser support for SVG may prevent Web developers and designers from fully embracing the scalable graphics format, because it may be years before the majority of Web visitors are using compliant browser versions.

CREATE A PNG IMAGE

You can create images and export them as PNGs by using one of the many graphics programs on the market, such as Adobe Illustrator, Deneba Canvas, CorelDRAW, and Macromedia Freehand. Because the PNG format supports alpha transparency rather than the single color transparency common to GIFs, PNG is an ideal format when you want to have semi-transparent

overlap images or have a partially visible background.

This example uses Macromedia Fireworks 4.0, which uses PNG as its native file format. A trial version of Fireworks 4.0 is included on this book's CD-ROM. Although the steps in this example are specific to Fireworks, steps in other programs should be similar.

When you optimize and export PNG images in Fireworks, you can select from 8-bit, 24-bit, or 32-bit color depth. 8-bit PNG images can contain up to 256 colors, like the GIF file format. If you are exporting photographic images or images with more than 256 colors, you can increase the color depth. However, this significantly increases the file size of the image.

CREATE A PNG IMAGE

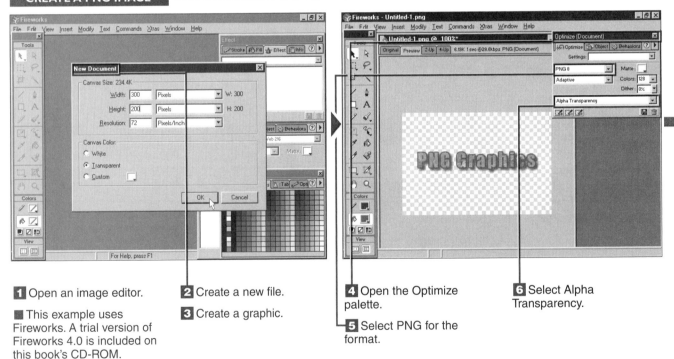

1 Open an image editor.

■ This example uses Fireworks. A trial version of Fireworks 4.0 is included on this book's CD-ROM.

2 Create a new file.

3 Create a graphic.

4 Open the Optimize palette.

5 Select PNG for the format.

6 Select Alpha Transparency.

Does PNG support multi-frame animation?

✔ No, the PNG format does not support multi-frame animation, although there is a subset of PNG called *Multiple-image Network Graphics* (MNG) designed to handle animation. In addition, you can still use the GIF format to create animated graphics. To learn more about creating animated GIFs, see Chapter 12.

Can I create interlaced PNGs?

✔ Yes, you can create interlaced PNGs just as you would create interlaced GIFs. See Chapter 12 for more information on interlaced GIFs. Technically, PNGs feature two-dimensional interlacing while GIFs have only one-dimensional interlacing. This means that the user is able to see the low resolution version of the PNG image much quicker. To create interlaced PNG images in Fireworks, click the options arrow on the Optimize palette and select Interlaced.

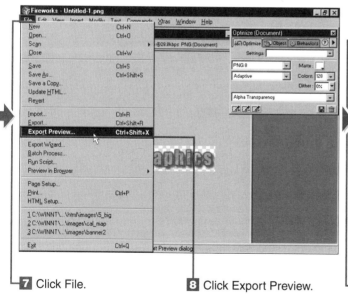

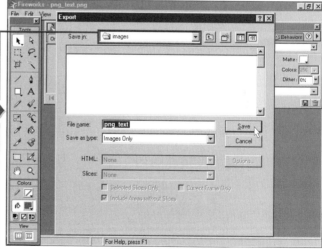

7 Click File.

8 Click Export Preview.

9 Export the image to your images directory.

■ The image is exported with the .png extension.

ADD A PNG IMAGE TO AN HTML PAGE

The easiest way to add a PNG image to an HTML page is to use the <img> tag. When you use the <img> tag on your page, indicate the file location of the PNG image using the src attribute as you would with GIFs or JPEGs. For more information on the <img> tag and its optional attributes, see Chapter 3.

When you add a PNG using the <img> tag, newer browsers that support the PNG format render the image properly. However, older browsers do not recognize the .png extension. In theory, you can use the <object> tag to reference a PNG and have a GIF or JPEG version enclosed within the OBJECT element. This way, newer browsers should be able to render

the PNG while older browsers that do not support the <object> tag can display the substitute. Unfortunately, even the newest browser versions do not fully support the <object> tag. Until they do, there is no ideal way to implement PNG images while degrading gracefully. For more on degrading gracefully, see Chapter 7.

ADD A PNG IMAGE TO AN HTML PAGE

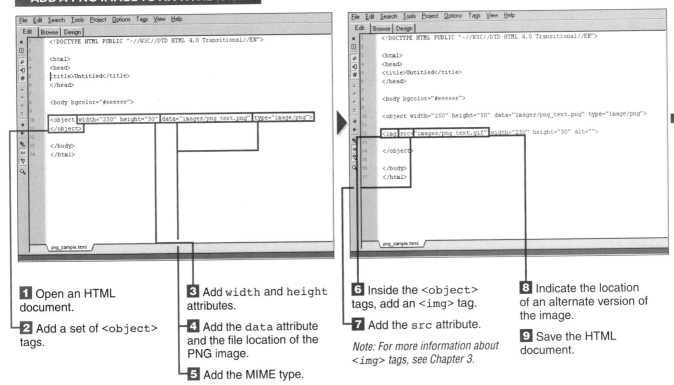

1 Open an HTML document.

2 Add a set of <object> tags.

3 Add width and height attributes.

4 Add the data attribute and the file location of the PNG image.

5 Add the MIME type.

6 Inside the <object> tags, add an <img> tag.

7 Add the src attribute.

Note: For more information about <img> tags, see Chapter 3.

8 Indicate the location of an alternate version of the image.

9 Save the HTML document.

Can I add a PNG image using the <embed> tag?

✔ You can use the <embed> tag to add a PNG image to a page. In this case, older browsers that do not have native support for the format issue a prompt to the user, letting them know that they need a plug-in to view the embedded content. However, the <embed> tag is non-standard HTML and is not part of the official specification.

What happens when a browser does not support the PNG format?

✔ Browsers that do not support the PNG format render a placeholder for the image.

What exactly is the <object> tag?

✔ The <object> tag, part of the HTML 4.0 specification, is used to embed content such as applets or other objects that may need a plug-in to be displayed. Between the opening and closing <object> tags, you can include alternative content for browsers that do not support the tag.

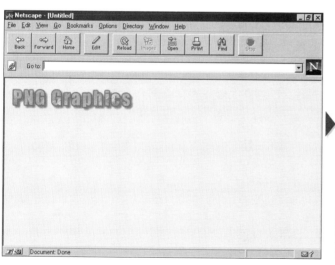

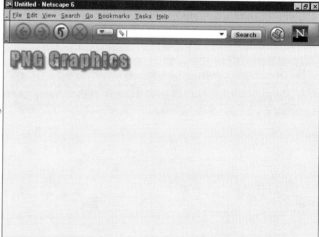

🔟 Open the page in an older Web browser.

■ This example uses Netscape 3.

■ The alternate version of the image is displayed.

1️⃣1️⃣ Open the page in a browser that supports the <object> tag.

■ This example uses Netscape 6.

■ The browser renders the PNG version of the image.

DOWNLOAD THE ADOBE SVG VIEWER

Because most browsers do not natively support the SVG file format, you need a special application or plug-in to view SVG files via a Web browser. While you can create SVG files in a plain text editor, you need an SVG application to view the files you create, so you should download a viewer before you begin working on your files. With the viewer installed, you can then test how the SVG graphic appears as you add tags, attributes, and styling elements. For more information on authoring SVG graphics, see "Create an SVG File."

Currently, the best way to view SVG files is to use the Adobe SVG Viewer, which you can download and install for free from the Adobe Web site.

Besides the Adobe SVG Viewer, you can view SVG files using a handful of other products, including the Batik SVG Viewer, a Java-based toolkit that allows you to generate SVG content from Java code and view SVG files stored locally or on a Web page. For more information on using the toolkit, visit the Batik Web site at http://xml.apache.org/batik/.

DOWNLOAD THE ADOBE SVG VIEWER

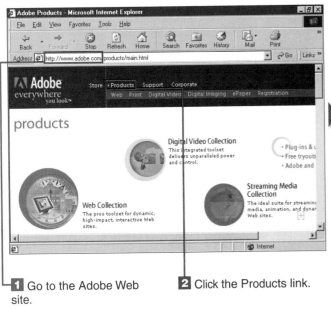

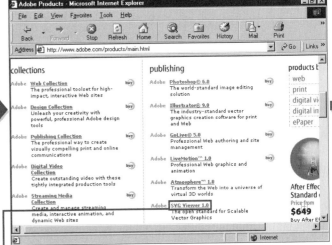

■1 Go to the Adobe Web site.

■2 Click the Products link.

■3 Click the link for SVG Viewer.

Does the Adobe viewer correspond exactly to the SVG specification?

✔ The viewer, in its current form, supports most of the features listed in the W3C's specification, however some elements have not yet been implemented. You can find a complete list of the features supported on the Adobe Web site.

For which platforms is the Adobe SVG Viewer available?

✔ The Adobe SVG Viewer is available for both Netscape and Internet Explorer browsers for the Windows and Macintosh platforms.

Which browser version do I need to use the Adobe SVG Viewer?

✔ The viewer works on versions 4 and higher of Netscape and Internet Explorer. However, on the Macintosh platform, the viewer does not support SVG files with scripting functionality.

Does the Adobe Viewer work with other browsers, such as Opera?

✔ According to the Adobe Web site, the viewer does not work with Opera browsers. For more information on requirements and limitations, visit the Adobe Web site at www.adobe.com.

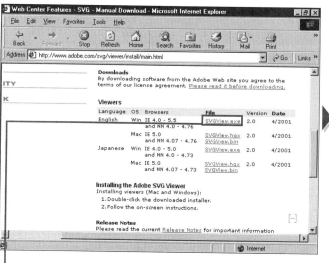

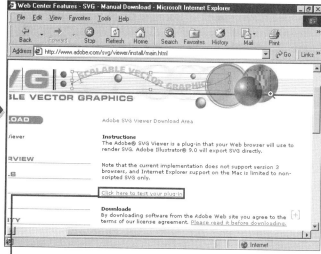

4 Click the appropriate link to initiate the download.

■ After you have downloaded the software, double-click the installer and follow the instructions provided.

5 Click the link to test your plug-in.

■ If the plug-in has been successfully installed, you should see the SVG graphic.

CREATE AN SVG FILE

You can create an SVG image using a regular text editor because the entire image is written in XML. You create graphic and text elements by using XML markup code, such as <text></text> tags.

An SVG file should begin with the XML document-type declaration so the viewing client knows that the page is an SVG file, rather than another file format such as HTML.

After the initial XML declaration, add a set of opening and closing <svg> tags. All the code you use to create graphics and text should be contained within these tags. For more on XML, see Chapter 22.

SVG includes code for basic shapes, such as rectangles, circles, and polygons, that you can easily add to pages. SVG also has many of the same style properties found in CSS, so you can use these

properties within your SVG images. For more information on CSS, see Chapter 6.

Beyond the pre-set shapes, SVG gives you the ability to create extremely complex designs, apply effects, and implement animation and interactivity. To learn more about creating SVG files, consult the W3C's specification at www.w3.org/Graphics/SVG.

CREATE AN SVG FILE

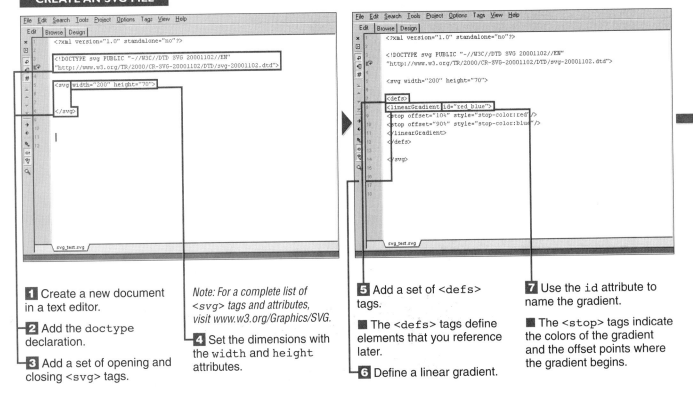

1 Create a new document in a text editor.

2 Add the doctype declaration.

3 Add a set of opening and closing <svg> tags.

Note: For a complete list of <svg> tags and attributes, visit www.w3.org/Graphics/SVG.

4 Set the dimensions with the width and height attributes.

5 Add a set of <defs> tags.

■ The <defs> tags define elements that you reference later.

6 Define a linear gradient.

7 Use the id attribute to name the gradient.

■ The <stop> tags indicate the colors of the gradient and the offset points where the gradient begins.

Are there commercial authoring products that I can use to create SVG graphics?

✔ Currently there are very few applications available to create SVG graphics. Adobe Illustrator 9 supports the SVG file format, and there are products such as WebDraw by Jasc that allow you to create SVG graphics using a standard image editor interface. You can download WebDraw from Jasc's Web site at www.jasc.com.

Where can I find a complete list of elements and attributes?

✔ The SVG specification has a complete list of all features. The specification is available online at www.w3.org/Graphics/SVG.

Can I embed SVG files into regular HTML pages?

✔ Yes, you can embed SVG files by using the <object> tag. Within the opening <object> tag, indicate the location of the SVG file with the data attribute and the MIME type with the type attribute. The MIME type for SVG files is either image/svg or image/svg+xml.

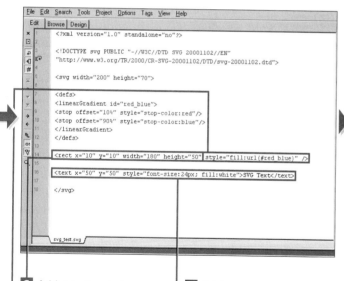

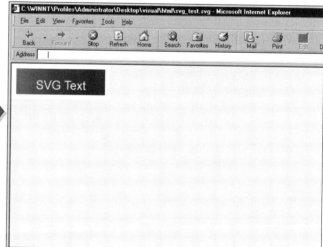

8 Add a rectangle tag, defining the width and height.

9 Using the style attribute, reference the gradient id.

Note: For more information on style properties, see Chapter 6.

10 Add <text> tags with optional style properties.

■ Use x and y attributes to offset the elements.

11 Save the document as an .svg file.

12 View the file in a Web browser.

■ If you have installed the SVG Viewer, the file is displayed.

SECTION V

16) ADD MULTIMEDIA

17) USING SYNCHRONIZED MULTIMEDIA

AN INTRODUCTION TO CLIENT-SIDE JAVASCRIPT

The Web is an interactive medium that can respond to user events such as mouseovers, clicks, and keystrokes. You can add interactive elements to a Web site many ways, but one of the best ways is to use JavaScript, an object-based scripting language that allows you to create and execute programs within a Web page. Unlike other technologies used to add interactivity, JavaScript does not require additional plug-ins and is widely supported by most browsers.

This chapter provides a brief introduction to the lexical structure of JavaScript, while Chapter 15 outlines common ways in which you can implement functionality on your Web site. While these chapters should provide you with the skills necessary to create and edit simple JavaScript programs, they by no means represent a full exploration of the power and complexity of the JavaScript language. For more in-depth information, pick up a copy of *JavaScript: Your visual blueprint for building dynamic Web pages*, by Kelly Murdock (also published by Hungry Minds, Inc.).

JavaScript vs. Java

If you are completely new to programming languages, you may be surprised to learn that JavaScript and Java are two completely different languages. In fact, despite the obvious similarities in name, Java and JavaScript are unrelated.

Java is a compiled programming language, meaning that after you write a program, the Java code is run through a compiler and compressed. For more information on Java applications for the Web, see Chapter 16.

JavaScript, like Perl, is an interpreted language, meaning that it is not compiled and is only checked for errors at run-time, when the program is executed.

Versions of JavaScript

Netscape released the first version of JavaScript, now known as JavaScript 1.0, back in 1995, and the Netscape 2 browser was the first to support the language. Since then, Netscape has released several subsequent versions of the language, with the most recent browser supporting JavaScript version 1.5. At the same time, Microsoft has developed its own JavaScript-compatible scripting language, called JScript. JavaScript and JScript are very similar, but each has its own proprietary extensions to support their DOMs.

In an effort to standardize the core language, the European Computer Manufacturers Association (ECMA) has developed a platform-independent known as ECMAScript. Both JavaScript 1.3 and higher and recent versions of JScript comply with the ECMAScript standard.

Client-Side JavaScript

This chapter focuses primarily on core JavaScript, meaning the structure of the language itself. Chapter 15 deals more directly with client-side JavaScript, the core language as it applies specifically to the Web browsing environment. Netscape, Internet Explorer, Opera, and other browsers come with a built in JavaScript interpreter so that they can understand and process JavaScript statements. This means that you can add JavaScript to HTML pages by using <script> tags, external JavaScript files, or adding JavaScript commands into <a href> tags and event handlers such as onclick. In addition, client-side JavaScript allows you to use the scripting language to interact with the browser's Document Object Model (DOM) to respond to user events and dynamically alter Web page content.

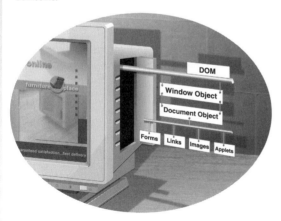

The DOM is a tree-like organization structure that represents every element on a Web page, from windows and frames to form field values. Because each browser has its own DOM, the ways in which you implement JavaScript applications can vary quite a bit depending on the browser make and version number. For more information, see Chapter 15.

Core Language Features

JavaScript has a number of core features, such as variables, arrays, and objects, that allow you to manipulate data within your scripts. A *variable* is a symbolic name that you assign to a particular value, such as $x = 3$, where x is the variable name and 3 is the value. While a variable is a single value, an *array* is a collection of values stored within a single name. Within an array, each value is referenced using an index number, such as car_model[0] = "Toyota." *Objects* are similar to arrays, but they allow you to reference values via named properties rather than numbers. For more on variables, arrays, and objects, see "Declare JavaScript Variables," "Create a JavaScript Array," and "Create a JavaScript Object."

JavaScript also has a number of *statements* that you can use to execute code. Some JavaScript statements, such as for, while, and do while, are loop statements, meaning they repeatedly execute code until a condition is no longer true. For example, a loop statement might be used to validate all of the fields in a form until it reaches the end of the form. For more on loop statements, consult *JavaScript: Your visual blueprint for building dynamic Web pages.* Another statement that is common to JavaScript applications is the conditional if statement, which executes code only if a condition is true. For more information on conditional statements, see "Create an if Statement."

ADD SCRIPTS TO A WEB PAGE

You can add JavaScript programs to a Web page by using <script> tags. You can include these tags within the head or body of the document, and the Web browser executes the JavaScript statements in the order that they appear.

Within the opening <script> tag, specify the scripting language by either using the language attribute or the type attribute.

Always specifying the scripting language as *JavaScript* is important, because there are other possible scripting languages, such as VBScript, that can be used on the Web. Many Web designers continue to use the language=JavaScript attribute, although this attribute is deprecated in favor of the type attribute. If you use the type attribute, set the value to *text/javascript*.

Inside the opening and closing <script> tags, you can include all of your JavaScript statements as well as JavaScript comments. Add single-line comments using the // sequence used in C++ programming. For multiple-line comments, use C-style comments that begin with a forward slash and asterisk (/*) and end with another asterisk and forward slash (*/).

ADD SCRIPTS TO A WEB PAGE

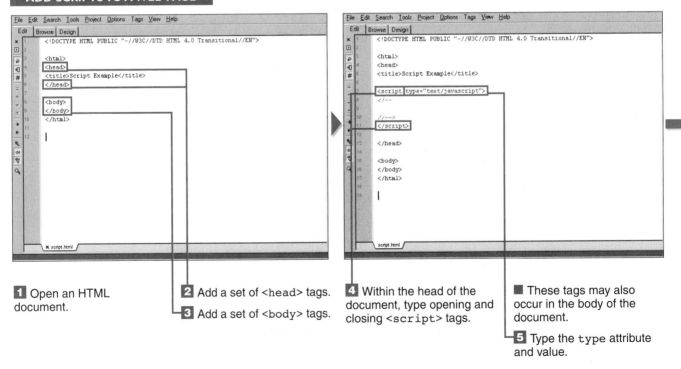

1 Open an HTML document.

2 Add a set of <head> tags.

3 Add a set of <body> tags.

4 Within the head of the document, type opening and closing <script> tags.

■ These tags may also occur in the body of the document.

5 Type the type attribute and value.

Can I use regular HTML comments within scripts?

✔ No. JavaScript recognizes the opening HTML comment sequence (`<!--`) and treats this as a single line comment like `//`. However it does not recognize the closing comment sequence used in HTML. This opening HTML comment should only be used in order to hide scripts from old browsers. For more information, see "Hide JavaScript from Old Browsers."

What other ways can I add JavaScript to HTML pages?

✔ In addition to the `<script>` tags, you can add JavaScript to URLs by using the javascript: protocol or as an event-handler with an HTML attribute, such as onMouseOver. For more information on these techniques, see *JavaScript: Your visual blueprint for building dynamic Web pages* (Hungry Minds, Inc.).

Can statements in one set of `<script>` tags reference statements in another set of `<script>` tags?

✔ Yes. For example, you could define a variable in one section of an HTML page and then reference it elsewhere in the page by using another set of `<script>` tags.

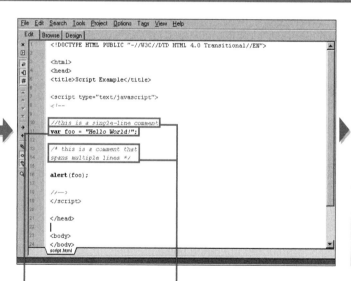

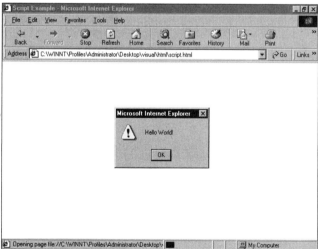

6 Add JavaScript statements.

■ This statement causes a simple dialog box to appear on-screen. For more on statements, see *JavaScript: Your visual blueprint for building dynamic Web pages* (Hungry Minds, Inc.).

7 Type any comments.

■ This is a single-line comment.

■ This a multi-line comment.

8 Save the file.

9 View the page in a Web browser.

■ The browser executes JavaScript statements contained within the `<script>` tags.

USING ESCAPE SEQUENCES

JavaScript uses certain characters, such as apostrophes and quote marks, as signals. If you want to use those characters in your JavaScript code, you must use *escape sequences*, snippets of code that indicate the signal characters are to be interpreted as themselves, not as signals. You must also use escape sequences to create special characters, such as ampersands.

For example, you cannot use apostrophes with text enclosed inside single quotes because the apostrophe signals the end of the text string and causes an error. Instead, you need to use an escape sequence, in this case a backslash and then an apostrophe (\ '). All JavaScript escape sequences are composed in this way, with an initial backslash and a character or alphanumeric sequence.

Other escape sequences include backspace (\b), form feed (\f), new line (\n), carriage return (\r), tab (\t), quote (\"), and backslash (\\). Note that if you want to render a

backslash character, you need to include two backslashes.

Another instance in which you need to use escape sequences is when you want to insert line breaks into text strings. Because JavaScript does not recognize breaks that you add by using a text editor, you can specify explicit line breaks by using the new line sequence (\n). This escape sequence might be used if you have an alert dialog box and you want to format the text in a specific way.

USING ESCAPE SEQUENCES

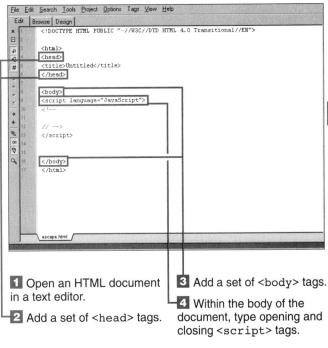

1 Open an HTML document in a text editor.

2 Add a set of <head> tags.

3 Add a set of <body> tags.

4 Within the body of the document, type opening and closing <script> tags.

5 If desired, add an alert dialog box with a text message.

Note: For more on alert boxes, see the section "Script an Alert Dialog Box."

6 Insert new line escape sequences.

■ Use multiple \n sequences to create additional line breaks.

What are some other characters for which I need to use special coding?

✔ In addition to common punctuation marks, you can use Latin-1 codes to add special characters. For example, the escape sequence \46 produces the ampersand character. You can find a listing of these special characters and their escape sequences in Appendix A.

What happens if I use a backslash with a character that is not a recognized escape sequence?

✔ If the character is not recognized as an escape sequence, the browser simply ignores the backslash and prints the character as it normally would.

Do HTML and JavaScript use the same numbers for special characters?

✔ No. Both HTML and JavaScript use the Latin-1 character list, but HTML expresses these characters using the *decimal* (base 10) numbering system. JavaScript uses the *octal* (base 8) equivalents. Appendix A provides both decimal and octal numbers for the Latin-1 character list.

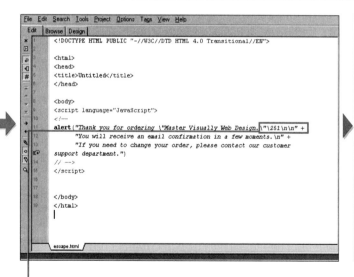

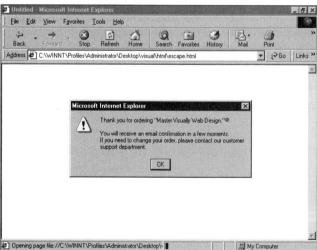

7 Add additional escape sequences for quotation marks and special characters.

8 Save the file.

9 View the page in a Web browser.

■ Escape sequences allow you to format plain text alert messages.

SCRIPT AN ALERT DIALOG BOX

Communicate event-related messages to site visitors by using an alert dialog box. You create these simple dialog boxes with the `alert()` method associated with the Window object, the top-level object in the browser's Document Object Model. See Chapter 15 for more Window-related methods. The `alert()` method causes the browser to pop up a small box containing the

message you have indicated along with an OK button. The syntax for the `alert()` method is:

```
alert("This is the alert
message.");
```

When scripting alert boxes, remember that the text contained within the box can only be plain text, so you cannot include any HTML formatting in the message. In addition, you must use

JavaScript escape sequences to add formatting elements such as new lines. For more information on escape sequences, see the section "Using Escape Sequences."

Keep in mind that while you can format the text message using spaces, underscores, and line breaks, you cannot control the color or visual appearance of the dialog box itself.

SCRIPT AN ALERT DIALOG BOX

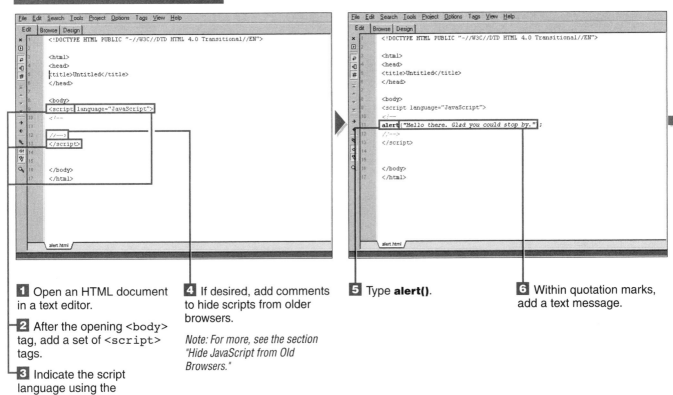

1 Open an HTML document in a text editor.

2 After the opening `<body>` tag, add a set of `<script>` tags.

3 Indicate the script language using the `language` attribute.

4 If desired, add comments to hide scripts from older browsers.

Note: For more, see the section "Hide JavaScript from Old Browsers."

5 Type **alert()**.

6 Within quotation marks, add a text message.

What other types of dialog boxes are possible in client-side JavaScript?

✔ Besides the alert dialog box, the Window object in client-side JavaScript supports the prompt() and confirm() methods, both of which create dialog boxes that allow for additional user response. Both methods are outlined in Chapter 15.

Can I create an alert box with an option to cancel?

✔ The alert box only offers the user the opportunity to click OK in order to continue. If you want to offer the choice of canceling an action, use the confirm() dialog box. See Chapter 15.

Do I have to reference the Window object when using the alert() method?

✔ No. It is not necessary to type **window.alert()** when calling this method, because the Window object— the top-level object in the browser's window—is assumed. However, including the reference to the Window object will not cause any errors, so you may do so if you wish.

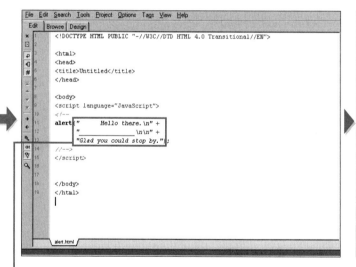

7 Format the message.

Note: To add new lines, you must use JavaScript escape sequences. For more information, see the section "Using Escape Sequences."

8 Save the file.

9 View the page in a Web browser.

■ The browser launches an alert box with the message you created.

WRITE TO A DOCUMENT

You can use JavaScript to dynamically write HTML code to a Web page by using the document.write() method. Include the document.write() method within <script> tags in the body of your document, and the browser generates the HTML code as it renders the document. You can use this method to output variables or generate different content based on user responses.

Although you can use the document.write() method by itself when writing to the current document, if you use it to write content to another window or frame, the document.write() method should be used in conjunction with two other methods: document.open() and document.close().

The document.open() method tells the browser to open a new HTML document to write to, while the document.close() method signals that the output process is complete. The document.open() method is optional. If you omit it, the browser automatically opens a new HTML document. However, the close() method is required.

WRITE TO A DOCUMENT

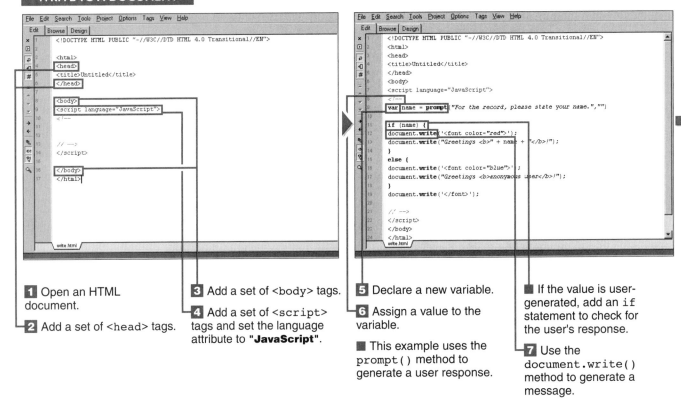

■1 Open an HTML document.

■2 Add a set of <head> tags.

■3 Add a set of <body> tags.

■4 Add a set of <script> tags and set the language attribute to **"JavaScript"**.

■5 Declare a new variable.

■6 Assign a value to the variable.

■ This example uses the prompt() method to generate a user response.

■ If the value is user-generated, add an if statement to check for the user's response.

■7 Use the document.write() method to generate a message.

Can I call the document.write() method from an event handler?

✔ Generally, this is not a good idea. If you invoke the method from an event handler, such as onClick, the method overwrites whatever is in the current document.

Is there any other way to write to a document?

✔ Another method associated with the Document object, document.writeln(), also allows you to write to a page. This method is identical to document.write() except that it adds a new line character at the end.

Can the document.write() method take more than one argument?

✔ Yes it can. Rather than using plus (+) signs to *concatenate*, or link together, the various elements you want to write, you can simply separate each element with a comma. The output is exactly the same.

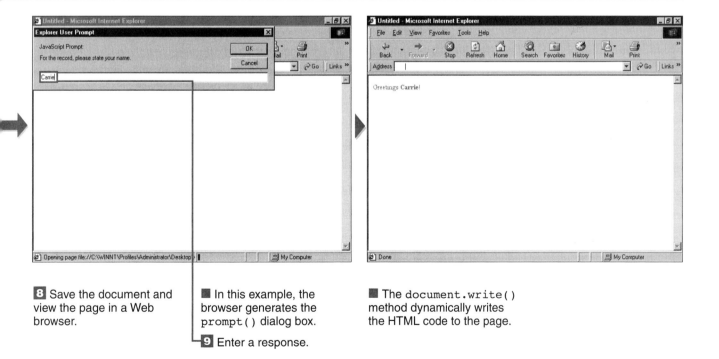

8 Save the document and view the page in a Web browser.

■ In this example, the browser generates the prompt() dialog box.

9 Enter a response.

■ The document.write() method dynamically writes the HTML code to the page.

DECLARE JAVASCRIPT VARIABLES

You can store and manipulate information in your scripts by declaring variables. To declare variables, you create a variable name and assign a value to it. After you declare the variable, you can reference and use it throughout your scripts.

To declare a variable, use the var keyword with the name of the variable:

var x;

The var keyword is optional, so you can declare a variable without it. If you omit the var keyword, JavaScript creates a global variable for you. You can also initialize the variable—that is, assign it an initial value—at the same time you declare it:

var x = 3;

If you declare a variable without giving it an initial value, the variable itself is defined, but the value is undefined.

Variables you define can either be globally accessible to your entire JavaScript program or local to a specific function. To define a local variable, declare it within the body of a function.

For more information on functions, see "Create a JavaScript Function," later in this chapter.

DECLARE JAVASCRIPT VARIABLES

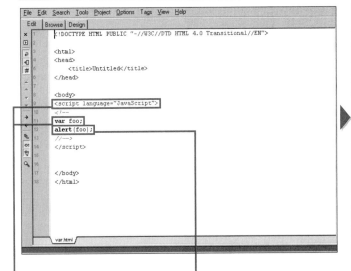

1 Open an HTML document.

2 In the body of the document, add a set of <script> tags.

3 Declare a new variable by typing **var** and the name of the variable.

4 Use the alert() method to check for the value of the variable.

Note: For more on alert dialog boxes, see the section "Script an Alert Dialog Box."

5 Save the HTML file, then view the page in a Web browser.

■ The value of the variable is undefined.

Are there any words that cannot be used as variable names?

✔ Certain reserved words cannot be used to name variables or functions because they are part of the JavaScript language itself and carry special meaning. Reserved JavaScript words include `break, case, continue, default, delete, do, else, export, for, function, if, import, in, new, return, switch, this, typeof, var, void, while,` and `with`. In addition, you should never name variables with words that are the names of properties or methods, such as "alert" or "confirm."

If I assign a number value to a variable, can I later assign a text value to it?

✔ Yes, you can. In JavaScript, variables are untyped, meaning that the value is not limited to one data type when you declare it.

Can I define and assign values to multiple variables at once?

✔ Yes, you can declare and initialize multiple variables at once by using the var keyword. Simply separate each variable with a comma.

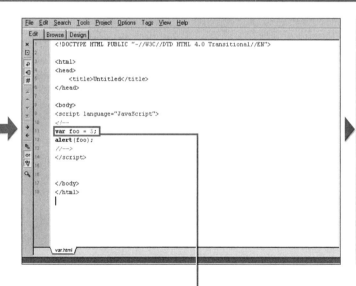

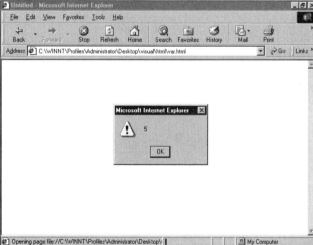

6 Return to the HTML page in your text editor.

7 Initialize the variable by assigning it a value.

8 Save the HTML file again.

9 Reload the page in a Web browser.

■ The variable now has an initial value.

CREATE A JAVASCRIPT OBJECT

With JavaScript, you can not only work with pre-existing objects, such as elements of the browser's document object model, but you can also create new objects. By creating new objects, you can store and manipulate values by referencing the properties associated with an object.

Create a new JavaScript object by defining a variable with the new

Object() operator. You can then create and set properties for the object by using the object's name and adding a period (.) and the name of the property. The syntax for creating a new object is as follows:

var *objectname* = new Object();

The optional var keyword stores a reference of the object to a new variable. After you create the

object, you can assign properties and values with the (.) operator:

objectname.property = *value*;

Using objects creates better organized code, because data is packaged according to a tree-like structure of properties, and using objects also allows for code that is easier to reuse.

CREATE A JAVASCRIPT OBJECT

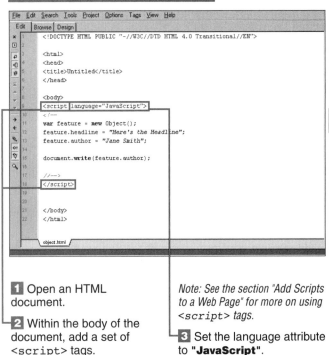

1 Open an HTML document.

2 Within the body of the document, add a set of <script> tags.

Note: See the section "Add Scripts to a Web Page" for more on using <script> tags.

3 Set the language attribute to **"JavaScript"**.

4 Type **var feature = new Object();**.

■ This creates an object called **feature**.

5 Add properties for the object.

■ This example has two properties, feature.headline and feature.author, with their assigned values in quotes.

Is there a way to create objects without using the `new Object()` operator?

✔ You can also create objects by using a constructor function. In this approach, you define a function, include properties as the parameters, and use the "this" keyword to initialize the object. The advantage to the constructor function is that it allows you to create a *class* of similar objects. For more information on this and other object-oriented programming techniques, see *JavaScript: Your visual blueprint for building dynamic Web pages.*

How can I delete a property of an object?

✔ You can delete a specific property of an object by using the delete operator, as in `delete objectName.propertyName`. However, this technique is not supported in JavaScript versions 1.0 and 1.1.

How are methods related to objects?

✔ A method is essentially the same as a function (see the section "Create a JavaScript Function"), but it applies specifically to a given object. For example, the `alert()` method is invoked through the browser's Window object, and the `write()` method is invoked through the Document object. With custom objects, you can define methods by assigning a function to an object in the following way:

```
objectName.methodName =
functionName;
```

Then you can invoke the method with the code `objectName.methodName()`.

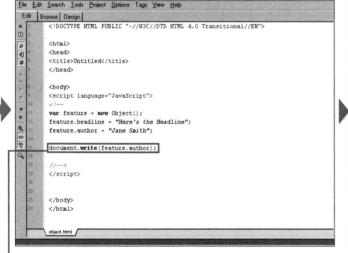

6 If desired, type **document.write()** and the name of a property you want to print.

Note: For more information about the document.write() method, see the section "Write to a Document."

7 Save the file.

8 View the page in a Web browser.

■ The value of the object property is written to the page.

CREATE A JAVASCRIPT ARRAY

Create a JavaScript array by using the Array() constructor. An *array* is very similar to an object (see the section "Create a JavaScript Object") and is nothing more than a way of storing pieces of data. After you create an array, you can reference specific pieces of data by using its assigned number, called its index.

The syntax for creating an array is:

```
var arrayname = new
Array("arrayvalue1",
("arrayvalue2", ...)
```

The optional var keyword stores a reference of the array to a variable.

When you first create an array, you can create an empty array with no data by leaving the parentheses empty, or you can set the values of the contained data within the parentheses. In some programming languages, you must specify the number of elements contained in an array, also known as the length of the array. However, in JavaScript it is not necessary to specify an array's length.

When you reference elements in an array, remember that, in JavaScript, the first element has an index of 0 (zero). For example, the fourth element in an array would have an index of 3.

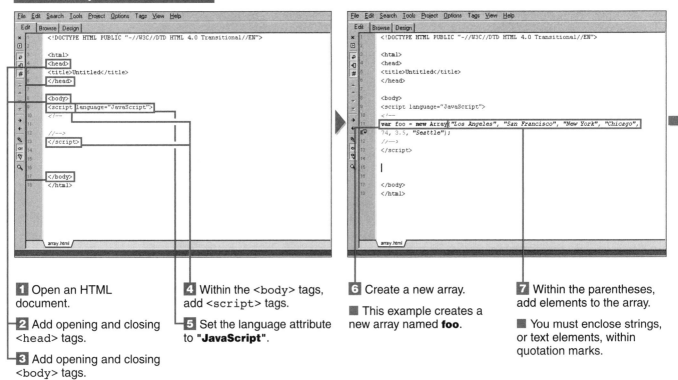

1 Open an HTML document.

2 Add opening and closing <head> tags.

3 Add opening and closing <body> tags.

4 Within the <body> tags, add <script> tags.

5 Set the language attribute to **"JavaScript"**.

6 Create a new array.

■ This example creates a new array named **foo**.

7 Within the parentheses, add elements to the array.

■ You must enclose strings, or text elements, within quotation marks.

How do I add a new element to an array?

✔ To add an additional element to an array, simply use the [ ] operator with an index number to assign a value to the element. For example, for an array called cities, add an element with the following line of code:

`cities[15] = "Houston";`

How do I change the length of an array?

✔ The length of an array changes when you add new elements to it. In addition, you can change the length using the read/write length property. If the value you assign the length property is smaller than the actual number of elements in an array, JavaScript deletes any element beyond the new length.

Can I create two-dimensional arrays in JavaScript?

✔ Yes. You can create two-dimensional arrays—arrays that contain other arrays—by assigning a new array to an existing array element:

```
arrayname[0] =
("arrayvalue1",
"arrayvalue2");
```

You could then reference these elements using the [ ] notation, such as `arrayname[0][1]`.

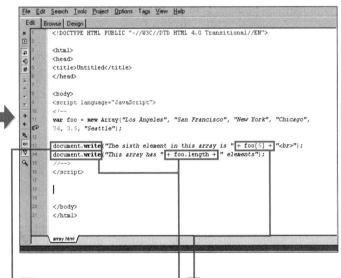

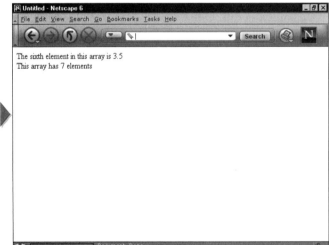

■ 8 If desired, add a `document.write()` method.

■ You can use this method to test and view the output of JavaScript statements. For more information, see the section "Write to a Document."

9 Reference an element in the array by using the [ ] operator.

10 Add another `document.write()` method.

11 Use the `length` property to return the number of elements in the array.

12 Save the document; then view the page in a Web browser.

■ The script writes the value for the specified array element as well as the length of the array.

CREATE AN IF STATEMENT

You can create programs that respond differently, depending on conditions, by using if statements. For example, you can use if statements to direct users to particular pages or issue different alert messages, depending on the actions the user takes.

The if statement is made up of three parts: the *if* keyword, the *condition* enclosed in parentheses, and the *action statement*. When the conditional statement is evaluated and the result is true, then the action statement is executed. You can include action statements to use if the conditional value is false by using the else clause. In this case, the program's syntax is:

```
if (condition) {
action statement;
action statement;
}
else {
action statement;
}
```

When only one statement is executed for a condition, the statements do not have to be placed in curly braces. However, many programmers always include the curly braces around statements, making scripts easier to read and debug.

For more on the action statements you can use in if statements, consult *JavaScript: Your visual blueprint for building dynamic Web pages* (Hungry Minds, Inc.).

CREATE AN IF STATEMENT

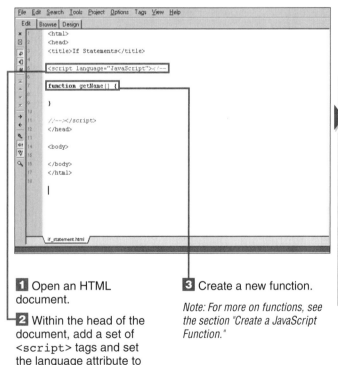

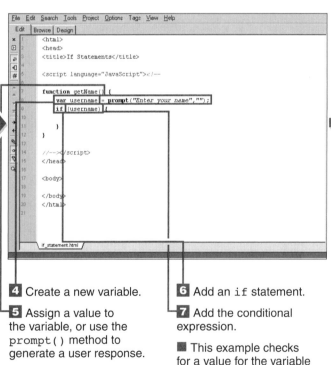

1 Open an HTML document.

2 Within the head of the document, add a set of `<script>` tags and set the language attribute to **"JavaScript"**.

3 Create a new function.

Note: For more on functions, see the section "Create a JavaScript Function."

4 Create a new variable.

5 Assign a value to the variable, or use the `prompt()` method to generate a user response.

Note: See Chapter 15 for more on the `prompt()` method.

6 Add an if statement.

7 Add the conditional expression.

■ This example checks for a value for the variable created.

How can I use `if` statements when I have more than two outcomes possible?

✔ Use the `else if` statement. In this case the condition is still defined within the `if` clause, but the subsequent outcomes are defined using `else if`. The statement syntax is:

```
if (condition) {
action statement;
}
else if (condition) {
action statement;
}
else {
action statement;
}
```

For more information on these statements, refer to *JavaScript: Your visual blueprint for building dynamic Web pages*.

What other ways are there to evaluate conditions and perform operations in JavaScript?

✔ In addition to the `if` statement, JavaScript supports several other statements, including `while`, `do/while`, and `for`. For more information on these JavaScript statements, consult *JavaScript: Your visual blueprint for building dynamic Web pages*.

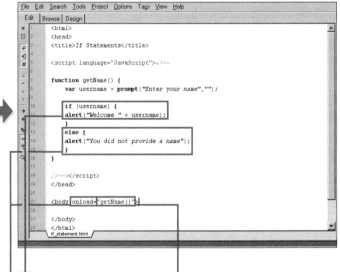

8 Add statements to be executed if the expression is true.

9 Add statements to be executed if the expression is false.

10 Include an event handler to trigger the function.

■ This example uses the `onload` attribute with the `<body>` tag.

11 Add the name of the function.

■ This causes the browser to run the script when the page is loaded.

12 Save the document; then open the page in a Web browser.

■ In this example, the browser generates the prompt dialog box. When you enter your name and click OK, the script evaluates the expression and executes the appropriate statement.

CREATE A JAVASCRIPT FUNCTION

Functions are collections of JavaScript statements that are defined by using a single name, so that you can invoke the function at any time by referring to its identifier. You can create functions to respond to specific user actions and invoke the functions through HTML event attributes, such as onClick.

To create a function, use the function statement to give the function a unique name and optional set of arguments, set off in parentheses. After the arguments, include the function's statements

within curly braces. Within the curly braces, you can define local variables, set up conditional tests using if statements, and include any other statements that should be executed.

The syntax for creating a function is as follows:

```
function
functionName(argument1,
argument2) {

// JavaScript statements
here;

}
```

When you invoke the function later in your HTML document, refer to the function's name, including the parentheses.

For example, to invoke a function named foo when the user clicks a link, add a javascript: URL to the href attribute and indicate the name of the function.

Alternatively, you can add the onClick="foo()" attribute to the <a> tag.

CREATE A JAVASCRIPT FUNCTION

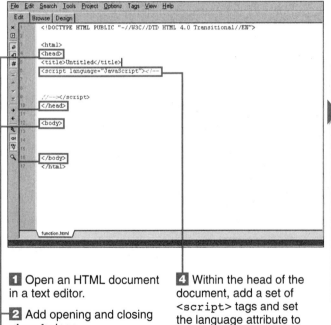

1 Open an HTML document in a text editor.

2 Add opening and closing <head> tags.

3 Add opening and closing <body> tags.

4 Within the head of the document, add a set of <script> tags and set the language attribute to **"JavaScript"**.

5 Create a new function.

6 Add opening and closing curly braces.

7 Add JavaScript statements inside the curly braces.

Note: For more information on conditional statements, see "Create an If Statement."

If a function contains only one statement, can I omit the curly braces?

✔ No, unlike `if` statements where you might omit curly braces in some cases, functions must always include them. For more on `if` statements, see the section "Create an If Statement."

Can I nest functions within functions?

✔ JavaScript versions 1.0 and 1.1 do not allow nested functions. If you are using JavaScript 1.2 or higher, you can define functions within other functions. Because JavaScript 1.2 is only supported on versions 4 and higher of the popular browsers, you should only use nested functions if you are certain that your visitors are not using older browsers.

How do I get a function to execute when the HTML page loads?

✔ To have a script execute after the HTML page has loaded, add the `onload` event handler to the HTML `<body>` tag and reference the name of the function to be invoked. For more information on event handlers, consult *JavaScript: Your visual blueprint for building dynamic Web pages* (Hungry Minds, Inc.).

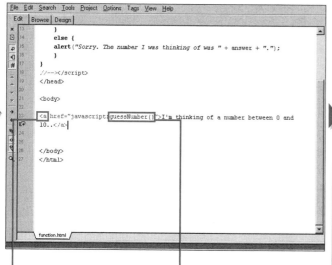

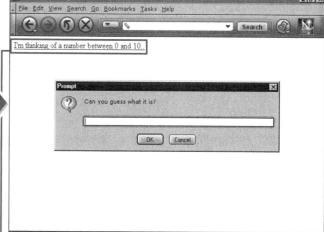

8 Within the body of the document, add code to invoke the function.

■ This example uses a `javascript:` URL with the `href` attribute.

9 Within the event handler or `javascript:` URL, reference the function by its name.

10 View the page in a Web browser.

11 Invoke the JavaScript function.

■ In this example, clicking the link invokes the defined function.

Note: For more in-depth coverage of JavaScript functions, refer to JavaScript: Your visual blueprint for building dynamic Web pages (Hungry Minds, Inc.).

TEST JAVASCRIPT CODE

Before you launch any new JavaScript features on your site, you should always thoroughly test your code to insure that it works correctly. Small errors in syntax or logic can cause errors and prevent the script from running correctly. In addition, because the client-side JavaScript engine varies from browser to browser, code that works on one make and version of a browser may not work on others.

You can use several techniques to test and isolate errors, or bugs, in

your JavaScript code. This process is called *debugging* and is a necessary step in developing programming applications. One way to debug code is to use alert boxes to print out variables to make sure that they are correctly defined and have the expected value. For more information on using alert boxes, see the section "Script an Alert Dialog Box." For additional tips on debugging JavaScript, see Chapter 15 of

JavaScript: Your visual blueprint for building dynamic Web pages (Hungry Minds, Inc.).

In addition, some versions of Netscape Navigator allow you to evaluate expressions and display errors by using a JavaScript console. To activate the JavaScript console in Navigator, type **"javascript:"** into the address bar. The last two diagrams of this task demonstrate how to use this feature.

TEST CODE USING ALERT BOXES

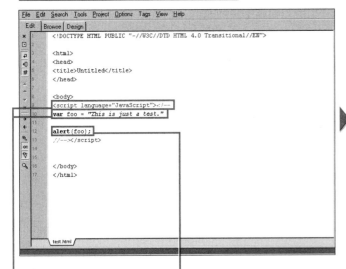

1 Open an HTML document in a text editor.

2 If necessary, add `<script>` tags within the body of the document.

3 If needed, declare a new variable and assign a value to the variable.

Note: For more on variables, see the section "Declare JavaScript Variables."

4 Add an `alert()` method to check for the value of a variable.

5 Save the file.

6 Open the page in a Web browser.

7 The alert dialog box verifies the value of the variable.

■ If the value does not appear, repeat steps 3 and 4 to verify that you have declared the variable and assigned it a value.

What types of errors occur in JavaScript?

✔ Some errors, called *load-time errors,* occur as the browser initially loads the JavaScript code and usually result from a syntactical error, such as a missing curly brace in a function. Other errors occur when the program is executed. These are called *run-time errors.*

Is the JavaScript console available in all versions of Netscape?

✔ The console is available in versions 4 and higher of Netscape. The console is not available in Internet Explorer. However, you can enter JavaScript directly into the address bar on Internet Explorer to have the browser execute statements.

Are there products available to help debug JavaScript?

✔ Both Netscape and Microsoft offer debugging programs that you can download and use to debug your scripts. The Netscape debugger is available at developer.netscape.com/tech/javascript/ index.html. Download the Internet Explorer debugger at msdn.microsoft. com/scripting/default.htm.

TEST CODE USING A NETSCAPE CONSOLE

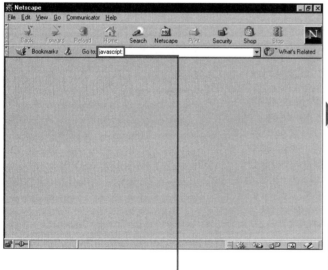

1 Follow steps 1 through 5 of the previous section.

2 Open Netscape Navigator.

3 In the address bar, type **javascript:**.

■ Versions 4.x have the two-frame JavaScript console with the input field.

4 In the input field, declare a variable.

5 Add an `alert()` method to check for the value.

■ The browser creates the alert dialog box and prints the variable value.

CREATE AN EXTERNAL JAVASCRIPT FILE

You can write scripts and reference them in multiple HTML pages by creating external JavaScript files. This technique is similar to using external style sheets—see Chapter 6 for more on style sheets—and allows you to more easily maintain your scripts, because you only need to edit one JavaScript file rather than several HTML files. In addition, keeping scripts in one file allows the browser to store them in the cache so they load more quickly when used on subsequent pages.

To create an external JavaScript file, save a text file with the extension .js. Within this file, you can include all your JavaScript statements and comments. To reference the external file in your HTML document, use the <script> tags with the optional src attribute. The value of the src attribute is the location of the .js file on your Web server, so if the .js file is located in the same directory as the current page, the tag would be <script src="NameofFile. js"></script>. Even if you do not include any JavaScript statements within the <script> tags, you must still include the closing </script> tag.

CREATE AN EXTERNAL JAVASCRIPT FILE

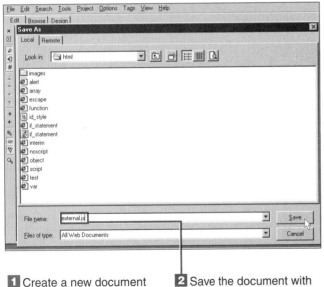

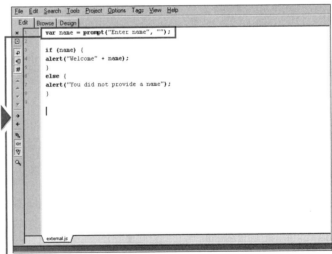

1 Create a new document in a text editor.

2 Save the document with the .js file extension.

3 Enter your JavaScript statements.

Do I need to use `<script>` tags within the external JavaScript file?

✔ No. Only use the opening and closing `<script>` tags when embedding scripts into the head or body of an HTML document.

Can external JavaScript files contain HTML code?

✔ No. External script files can only contain JavaScript code and JavaScript comments.

Do I need to configure my Web server to handle external JavaScript files?

✔ You should make sure that your Web server is able to handle .js files by configuring the MIME type as `application/x-javascript`. If your site is running on an Apache server, you can add a MIME type by including the following code in the .htaccess file:

`AddType application/x-javascript js`

However, if you are unsure about the configuration of your Web server, you should contact the system administrator for assistance with MIME type settings.

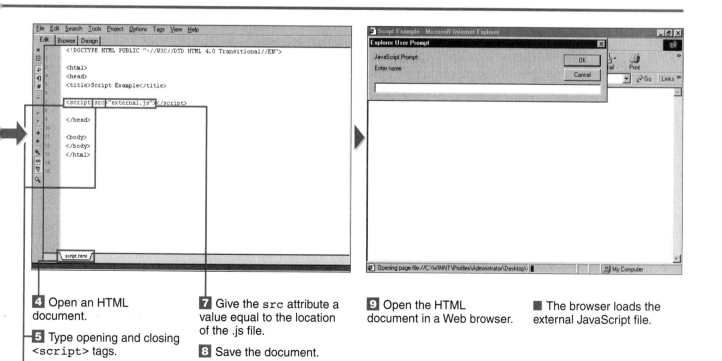

4 Open an HTML document.

5 Type opening and closing `<script>` tags.

6 Add the `src` attribute to the opening `<script>` tag.

7 Give the `src` attribute a value equal to the location of the .js file.

8 Save the document.

9 Open the HTML document in a Web browser.

■ The browser loads the external JavaScript file.

HIDE JAVASCRIPT FROM OLD BROWSERS

JavaScript code is usually added to HTML pages by using opening and closing `<script>` tags, but not all browsers support the `<script>` tag. Because browsers that do not recognize these tags try to render the JavaScript code as HTML text, you sometimes must "hide" JavaScript elements from older browsers by using a combination of HTML and JavaScript comments.

After the initial `<script>` tag, add an opening HTML comment sequence (`<!--`); then before the closing `</script>` tag, add a JavaScript comment (`//`) marker followed by the closing HTML comment (`-->`). Older browsers disregard everything contained within the HTML comments, while browsers that support the `<script>` tag are able to process the JavaScript statements.

Note that because JavaScript does not recognize the closing HTML comment sequence (`-->`), you must include the JavaScript comment marker (`//`) before the HTML comment sequence so the browser does not try to interpret it as a JavaScript statement.

HIDE JAVASCRIPT FROM OLD BROWSERS

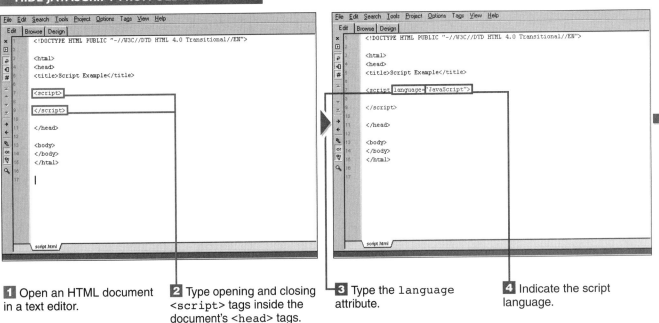

1 Open an HTML document in a text editor.

2 Type opening and closing `<script>` tags inside the document's `<head>` tags.

3 Type the `language` attribute.

4 Indicate the script language.

What happens if a browser recognizes the <script> tag but does not support JavaScript?

✔ These browsers simply ignore all the statements occurring between the opening and closing <script> tags. This is also the case for visitors that have JavaScript disabled in their browser.

If I use a language other than JavaScript, do I use the same comment sequences?

✔ The closing comment sequence depends on the scripting language in use. If you use VBScript, for example, the closing comment would be ' -->, because the single quote (') is the comment used in this language.

If I use newer versions of JavaScript, do I need to hide my scripts from browsers that only support older versions?

✔ Yes. Indicate the JavaScript version number by using the language attribute of the <script> tag. For example, if your script uses JavaScript version 1.3, set the language attribute to *JavaScript1.3*. Browsers that do not support this version of JavaScript ignore any code contained within the <script> tags.

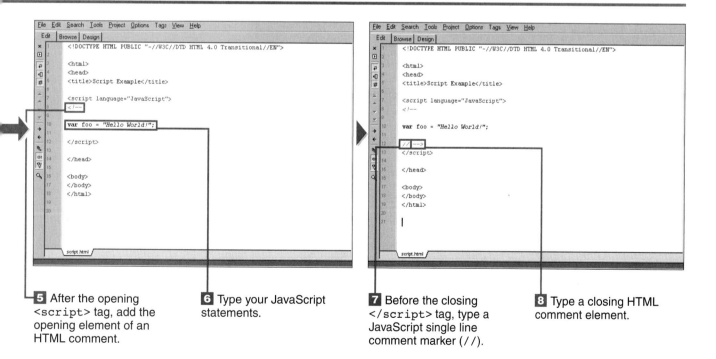

5 After the opening <script> tag, add the opening element of an HTML comment.

6 Type your JavaScript statements.

7 Before the closing </script> tag, type a JavaScript single line comment marker (//).

8 Type a closing HTML comment element.

USING <NOSCRIPT> TAGS

Y ou can use the <noscript> tags to provide a message or alternate content for browsers that do not support JavaScript. Wherever you have scripts in your page, include the opening and closing <noscript> tags directly after the closing </script> tag. Browsers that support scripting ignore anything contained within the <noscript> tags, while browsers that do not

support scripting render the alternative content.

According to the HTML specification, browsers that support scripting can render the <noscript> content if the browser does not support the scripting language in use, or if the browser is configured with scripting turned "off." Remember that some users have script-capable browsers but choose to disable

JavaScript for a variety of reasons. If the functionality on your site requires JavaScript, include this information in your <noscript> tags and repeat it in the body of your HTML document. For example, if you use JavaScript extensively on your site, consider including a warning that visitors should enable JavaScript to experience the full functionality your site has to offer.

USING <NOSCRIPT> TAGS

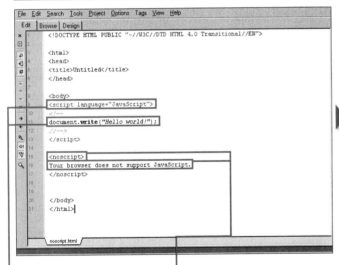

1 Open an HTML document.

2 After the opening <body> tag, add <script> tags.

3 Add JavaScript statements.

■ This example uses the document.write() method. For more information on this method, see the section "Write to a Document."

4 Add a set of <noscript> tags.

5 Add any alternative content and save the file.

6 View the page in a script-aware browser.

■ The browser executes the JavaScript code but does not render the alternative content.

Do the \<noscript> tags work on all browsers?

✔ There are some older browsers that do not recognize the \<noscript> tag, although they represent a very small portion of the total browser market. In particular, Netscape 2 does not support the \<noscript> tag, although it does support scripting. As a result, Netscape 2 browsers render the \<noscript> content even though they support JavaScript.

Are there any optional or required attributes for the \<noscript> tag?

✔ There are no attributes associated with the \<noscript> tag.

What sort of alternative content can I include within \<noscript> tags?

✔ Within \<noscript> tags, you can include any HTML tags and content. You can take advantage of this to offer alternative functionality that mirrors your JavaScript functionality. For example, if you use JavaScript to implement a scrolling navigation list or to redirect to a new page, use the \<noscript> tags to include a regular HTML drop-down menu or a \<meta> refresh tag. For more on implementing HTML functionality, see Chapter 3.

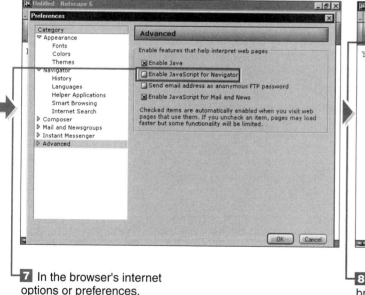

7 In the browser's internet options or preferences, disable JavaScript.

8 Reload the page in the browser.

■ With JavaScript disabled, the browser renders the \<noscript> content.

ADD TEXT TO THE STATUS WINDOW

At the bottom of the browser window is a status line. Normally, when a Web visitor mouses over a link or image map hot spot, the status line displays the URL of the hyperlink. However, you can change this behavior and have the status line display a text message by setting the value of the Window object's status property.

To set the value of the status property, use the onMouseOver event handler with the <a> tag. For more on event handlers, consult *JavaScript: Your visual blueprint for building dynamic Web pages* (Hungry Minds, Inc.). After the status line text message, add the "return true" statement. This tells the browser that it should not perform the usual action of displaying the hyperlink URL but

should instead display your status line text.

Most browsers erase the status line message when the user moves the mouse off of a link, but some continue to display the custom text. You can explicitly clear the status message by adding the onMouseOut event handler and setting the status property to an empty string.

ADD TEXT TO THE STATUS WINDOW

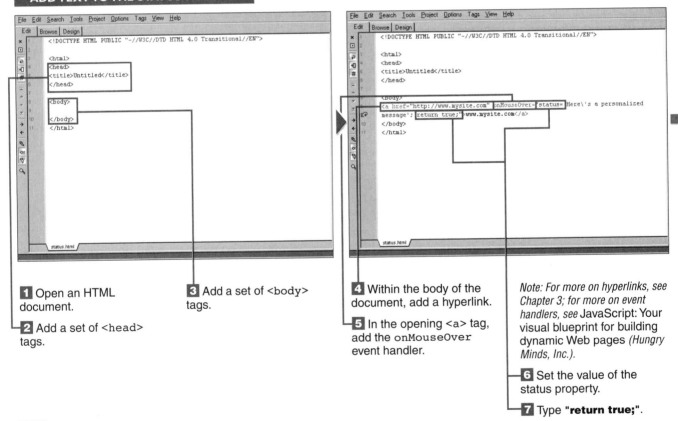

1 Open an HTML document.

2 Add a set of <head> tags.

3 Add a set of <body> tags.

4 Within the body of the document, add a hyperlink.

5 In the opening <a> tag, add the onMouseOver event handler.

Note: For more on hyperlinks, see Chapter 3; for more on event handlers, see JavaScript: Your visual blueprint for building dynamic Web pages *(Hungry Minds, Inc.).*

6 Set the value of the status property.

7 Type **"return true;"**.

How can I set the status property to display a constant message?

✔ Use the `defaultStatus` property to display a continuous message in the status line. To set the `defaultStatus` message, add the following code to your page:

```
<script
language="JavaScript">
defaultStatus = "message
here.";
</script>
```

Any link-specific status line messages or URLs temporarily override the default status line that you set with this property.

Do I have to use escape sequences when setting status line text?

✔ If you want to include quotation marks or apostrophes within the status line text, you need to use JavaScript escape sequences. For example, to include an apostrophe in a status line message of an `<a>` tag, add a backslash before the apostrophe:

```
<a href="#"
onmouseover="status='Here\'s
a status message.';">click
here</a>
```

If you do not, the browser interprets the apostrophe or quotation mark as the end of the string, which generates an error. For more information on using escape sequences, see Chapter 14.

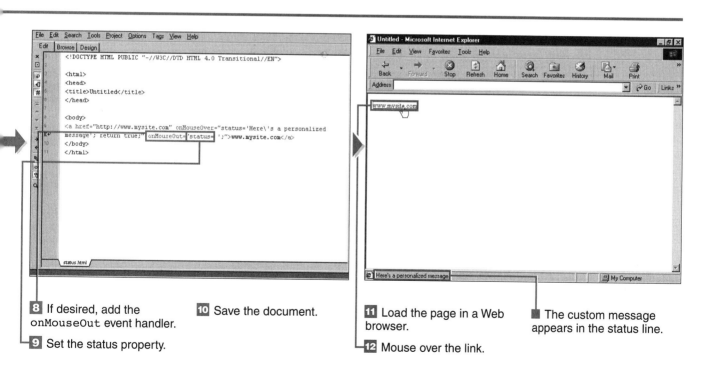

8 If desired, add the onMouseOut event handler.

9 Set the status property.

10 Save the document.

11 Load the page in a Web browser.

12 Mouse over the link.

■ The custom message appears in the status line.

PROMPT THE USER FOR A RESPONSE

You can use the prompt() method to obtain a response from users and then issue personalized messages based on the response. Like the alert() and confirm() methods also associated with the Window object, the prompt() method generates a simple dialog box in which you can display a text message. The prompt dialog box also includes a text entry field along with two buttons, "OK" and "Cancel." For more on

the alert() method, see Chapter 14; for more information on using the confirm() method, see the section "Get Confirmation."

This method takes two arguments—the message printed in the dialog box and the default value for the response. The syntax for the prompt() method is:

```
prompt("Message appearing
in the dialog box", "");
```

If you include a default value when calling the prompt() method, this value is displayed in the text entry field. If you do not specify a value, the browser displays "undefined" in the field. To avoid this, include an empty string ("") as the default value.

PROMPT THE USER FOR A RESPONSE

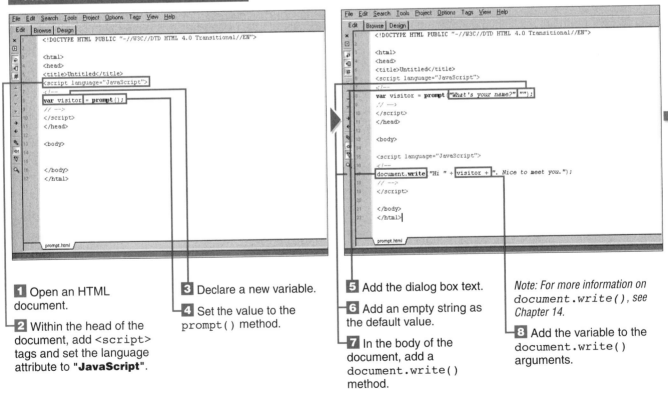

1 Open an HTML document.

2 Within the head of the document, add <script> tags and set the language attribute to "**JavaScript**".

3 Declare a new variable.

4 Set the value to the prompt() method.

5 Add the dialog box text.

6 Add an empty string as the default value.

7 In the body of the document, add a document.write() method.

Note: For more information on document.write(), *see Chapter 14.*

8 Add the variable to the document.write() arguments.

Is there any way to alter the appearance of the dialog box itself?

✔ No, there is no way to change the appearance of the dialog box.

Can I include special characters in the text message?

✔ Yes. To include special characters, use JavaScript escape sequences with appropriate Latin-1 codes. For more information about escape sequences and Latin-1 codes, see Chapter 14.

Can I use HTML to format the text message used in the prompt dialog?

✔ No. As with the other window dialog methods, the prompt() message cannot contain any HTML formatting and must be plain text. You can use spaces, underscore characters, and newline sequences to add minimal formatting to the text message.

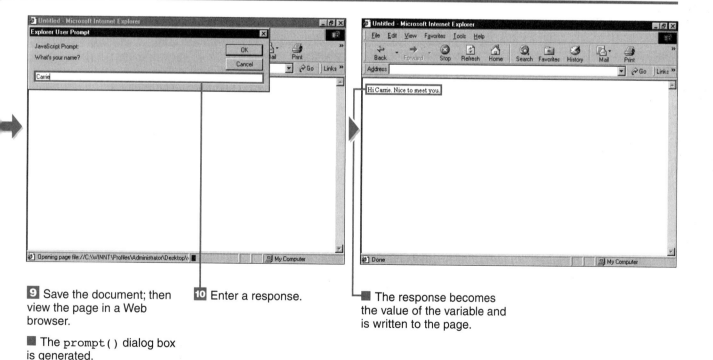

9 Save the document; then view the page in a Web browser.

■ The prompt() dialog box is generated.

10 Enter a response.

■ The response becomes the value of the variable and is written to the page.

GET CONFIRMATION

Give visitors the ability to confirm or cancel an action by using the confirm() method.

This method, associated with the Window object, is similar to the alert() method discussed in Chapter 14 in that it generates a dialog box to which the user must respond before proceeding. However, while the alert() method only has the option of affirming the action, the confirm()

method gives the user the choice of continuing or canceling.

The syntax for a confirm() method is:

```
confirm("dialog box
message.");
```

In addition, you can assign the dialog box message to a variable and then reference that variable inside the parentheses of the confirm() method:

```
var msg = "dialog box
message.";
```

```
confirm(msg);
```

Because the confirm() method allows for two possible responses, "OK" or "Cancel," the method is most often used in conjunction with a conditional if statement (see Chapter 14). One common application is to direct users to different destination pages based on their response.

GET CONFIRMATION

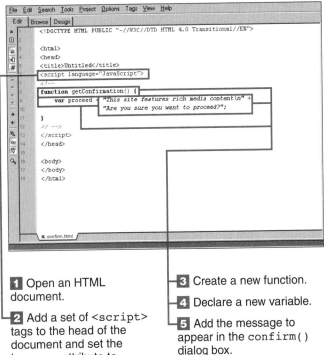

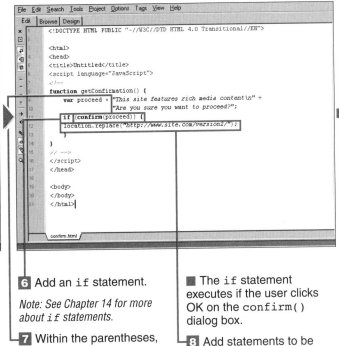

1 Open an HTML document.

2 Add a set of <script> tags to the head of the document and set the language attribute to **"JavaScript"**.

3 Create a new function.

4 Declare a new variable.

5 Add the message to appear in the confirm() dialog box.

6 Add an if statement.

Note: See Chapter 14 for more about if statements.

7 Within the parentheses, type **(confirm())** and the name of the message variable you created.

■ The if statement executes if the user clicks OK on the confirm() dialog box.

8 Add statements to be executed if the message is confirmed.

330

Is it necessary to create a new custom function in order to use the `confirm()` method?

✔ No, it is not necessary to create a new function that contains the `confirm()` method. You can also include the `confirm()` method and related statements on their own with `<script>` tags. In this instance, the browser executes the `confirm()` method as the HTML page loads.

Can I alter the value of the confirmation buttons so they read something other than "OK" and "Cancel"?

✔ No, you cannot customize the buttons in a `confirm()` dialog box.

What value does JavaScript return when a user clicks "OK" or "Cancel" on a confirm dialog box?

✔ If the user clicks "OK," JavaScript returns a value of true. If the user clicks "Cancel" or closes the dialog box, the value returned is false.

Can I have scripts running in the background while the user is responding to the `confirm()` prompt?

✔ No, all three of the dialog prompts associated with the Window object—`alert()`, `prompt()`, and `confirm()`—are modal, meaning that they block the continuation of the script until the user responds to the dialog.

9 In the body of the document, add a hypertext link or event handler to trigger the confirmation function.

■ This example uses a hypertext link with a `javascript:` URL.

10 View the page in a Web browser.

11 Click the link or event handler.

■ In this example, clicking the link generates the dialog box.

ADD A LAST MODIFIED DATE

You can use JavaScript to indicate to your visitors when your site was last updated. The document.lastModified property, available since JavaScript version 1.0, allows you to automatically generate a timestamp, rather than altering your HTML code each time you update a page.

The document.lastModified property is a read-only string sent by the Web server that records the date and time of the last modification made to the file.

To read the document.lastModified property, use the following JavaScript code:

document.lastModified;

You can write the value of this property to your page by using document.write(), discussed in Chapter 14:

document.write(document.lastModified);

When using the document.lastModified property, be aware that not all Web servers provide this last-modified date. If there is

no string sent for this date, JavaScript assigns a value of 0 (zero) and records the date as midnight, January 1, 1970 (GMT). Therefore, include code to verify that the value of the lastModified string is not equal to zero. You can use the Date.parse() method, which converts a date string to milliseconds, to check for a zero value. For more on Date() methods, see *JavaScript: Your visual blueprint for building dynamic Web pages* (Hungry Minds, Inc.).

ADD A LAST MODIFIED DATE

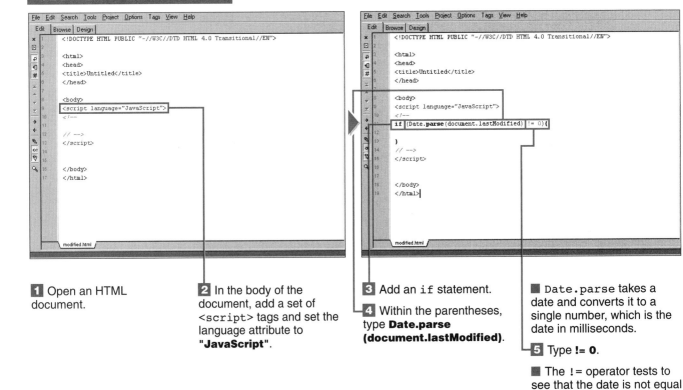

1 Open an HTML document.

2 In the body of the document, add a set of <script> tags and set the language attribute to **"JavaScript"**.

3 Add an if statement.

4 Within the parentheses, type **Date.parse (document.lastModified)**.

■ Date.parse takes a date and converts it to a single number, which is the date in milliseconds.

5 Type **!= 0**.

■ The != operator tests to see that the date is not equal to zero.

What is the format of the document.lastModified date?

✔ The date for the **document. lastModified** property is expressed in MM/DD/YEAR format, while the time is expressed using the 24-hour clock and includes the hour, minutes, and milliseconds. The time zone is GMT (Greenwich Mean Time).

How do I change the time zone when printing the last-modified date?

✔ If you convert the **document. lastModified** value to a **Date** object, you can use the **toLocaleString()** method to set the date to the local time zone. For more information on working with **Date** objects, see *JavaScript: Your visual blueprint for building dynamic Web pages.*

Can I change the formatting of the date?

✔ You can use the **Date** object, the **Date()** constructor, and the associated methods to have the date print in a variety of formats. For more information on using the **Date** object, see Chapter 10 of *JavaScript: Your visual blueprint for building dynamic Web pages.*

Can I use the document. lastModified property on dynamically generated pages?

✔ You can use the property on both static and dynamic pages. However, on dynamic pages that use templates, such as a template for a product page, the date will only indicate the last change to the template.

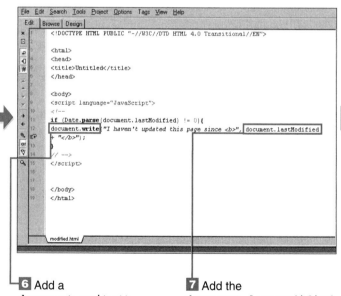

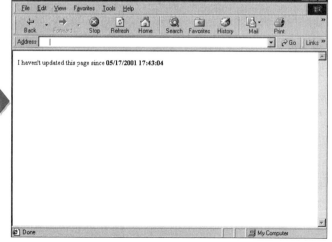

6 Add a document.write() method.

7 Add the document.lastModified property to the method's arguments.

8 View the page in a Web browser.

■ The browser displays the date and time of the last update made to the page.

SCRIPT A SCROLLING LIST

You can use JavaScript to create a scrollable options list that automatically loads the page or site when the visitor makes a selection. By using JavaScript, you can avoid using "Go" buttons with your `<select>` fields and create a more seamless user experience.

In the Document Object Model, the Select object represents the HTML `<select>` tag and includes a property called `selectedIndex`. This property indicates the index

number of a selected `<option>` within a drop-down or scrollable `<select>` list. (See Chapter 4 for more information on the `<select>` tag.)

If you set the value of each option to the destination URL, you can use the `selectedIndex` property to determine the value of the selected option and redirect the user to that URL using `window.location.href`:

```
window.location.href =
document.formName.options
[selectedIndex].value;
```

To initiate the code when the user selects an option, use the `onChange` event handler in the opening `<select>` tag. If you include the JavaScript code directly in the `onChange` handler—rather than referring to a custom function in the head of the document—you do not have to reference the `document.formName`.

SCRIPT A SCROLLING LIST

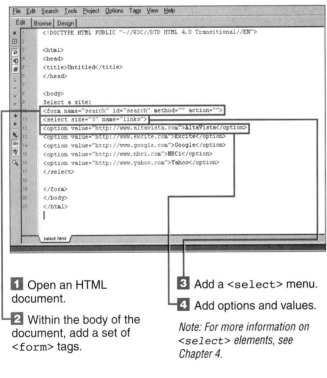

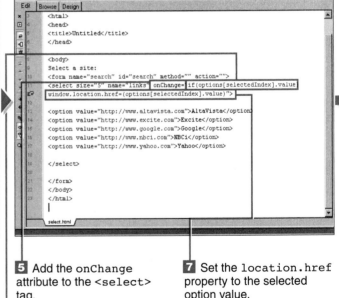

1 Open an HTML document.

2 Within the body of the document, add a set of `<form>` tags.

3 Add a `<select>` menu.

4 Add options and values.

Note: For more information on `<select>` elements, see Chapter 4.

5 Add the `onChange` attribute to the `<select>` tag.

6 Use a JavaScript `if` statement to check for the `selectedIndex` value.

Note: For more on `if` statements, see Chapter 14.

7 Set the `location.href` property to the selected option value.

Note: For more on the `location` property, see the section "Redirect to a New Page."

Is the selectedIndex property available in all versions of JavaScript?

✔ The property is supported by all versions of JavaScript, including JavaScript 1.0. Additionally, in JavaScript 1.1, `selectedIndex` is a writable property. This means that you can use the property to indicate which option should be selected. To deselect all options, set the `selectedIndex` property to -1.

How do I degrade gracefully with browsers that do not support scripting?

✔ Because browsers that do not support scripting simply ignore the script elements, the code will not cause errors. However, it is a good idea to add a "Go" button inside of `<noscript>` tags so that non-script browsers can still use the menu to navigate. For more information on `<noscript>` tags, see Chapter 14.

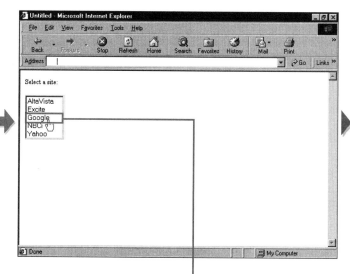

8 Save the document and view the page in a Web browser.

9 Select one of the options.

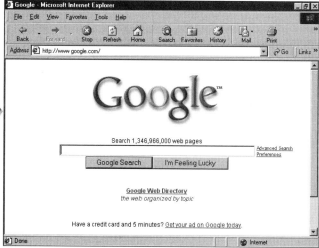

■ The browser replaces the window's location property with the value of the selected option.

SCRIPT BETWEEN FRAMES

You can use JavaScript to provide interaction between different frames in a window's frameset.

Each browser window has a frames[] property that represents each frame in a frameset, so variables and functions defined in one frame are accessible from the other frames as well as the parent frame. Because frames can communicate with each other and

with the parent frameset, you can use frames to *maintain state,* meaning that the browser remembers data from one page to another.

When you reference frames contained within a frameset, you can either use the array index number or the name of the frame, which you assign within the <frame> tag by using the name attribute. If you reference a frame

by using its index number, remember that the first element in an array has an index of 0 (zero).

If a window contains frames, the top-level window containing the frames is called the *parent.* Subframes can refer to other subframes by referencing the parent. For example, the first frame would access variables and objects in a second frame by referencing the parent.frames[1] property.

SCRIPT BETWEEN FRAMES

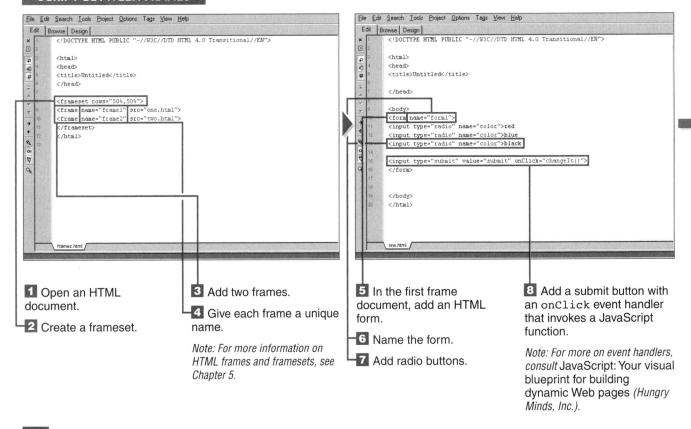

1 Open an HTML document.

2 Create a frameset.

3 Add two frames.

4 Give each frame a unique name.

Note: For more information on HTML frames and framesets, see Chapter 5.

5 In the first frame document, add an HTML form.

6 Name the form.

7 Add radio buttons.

8 Add a submit button with an onClick event handler that invokes a JavaScript function.

Note: For more on event handlers, consult JavaScript: Your visual blueprint for building dynamic Web pages *(Hungry Minds, Inc.).*

**Can I use the window.close()
method to close frames?**

✔ No, the window.close() method
can only be used to close top-level
windows, not individual frames.
However, you can use the
window.close() method from
within a frame to close the top-level
window. Rather than using
window.close() or self.close()
in this case, you would use
parent.close().

**What other properties are
associated with the frames[] array?**

✔ Another property associated with this
array is the window.frames.length
property, which indicates how many
frames are in a frameset.

**How else can I use JavaScript to
maintain state?**

✔ Normally in order to maintain state,
you would need to use cookies (see
the section "Set a Cookie"). Unlike
frame scripting techniques, which only
store the values for variables while the
window is open, you can set the
expiration dates for cookies so that
you can retrieve data the next time the
user visits the site.

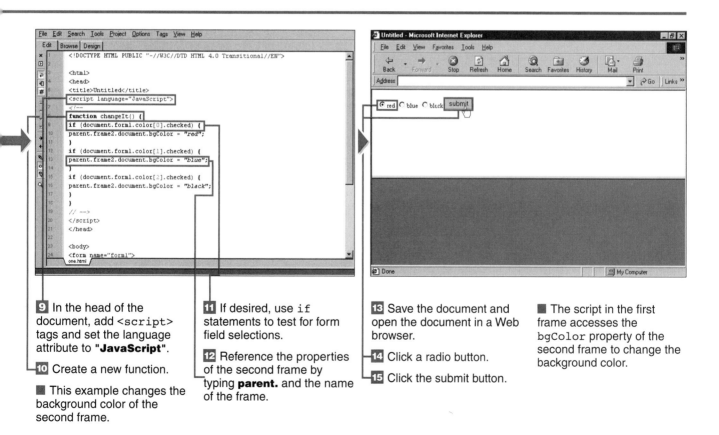

9 In the head of the
document, add <script>
tags and set the language
attribute to **"JavaScript"**.

10 Create a new function.

■ This example changes the
background color of the
second frame.

11 If desired, use if
statements to test for form
field selections.

12 Reference the properties
of the second frame by
typing **parent.** and the name
of the frame.

13 Save the document and
open the document in a Web
browser.

14 Click a radio button.

15 Click the submit button.

■ The script in the first
frame accesses the
bgColor property of the
second frame to change the
background color.

SCRIPT AROUND FRAMES

By using the length property of the Window object's frames[] array, you can prevent other Web sites from placing your own page in a frameset. Although having your site appear within someone else's frameset is little more than a nuisance, it can disrupt the design and presentation of your site. To prevent your site from being "framed," use JavaScript code to read the length of the frames[] array and then force the browser to reload your site into the top window.

Every window has a frames[] array that references all of the frames that are contained within a frameset. In the object hierarchy, the window containing the frameset is the *parent*, and the frames are the *children* (see the section "Script Between Frames"). The length property indicates how many child frames are present. For example, if

the parent.frames.length property is equal to 2, two frames are contained within the frameset. You can use this property to see if your site is contained within a parent window frameset by verifying that the parent.frames.length property is greater than zero. If it is greater than zero, you can then replace the location property of the parent window with the location property of your own site.

SCRIPT AROUND FRAMES

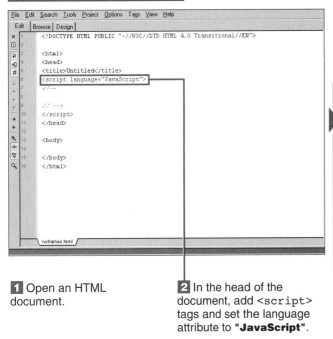

1 Open an HTML document.

2 In the head of the document, add <script> tags and set the language attribute to **"JavaScript"**.

3 Type **if**. **(parent.frames.length > 0)**.

■ This uses the parent.frames.length property to see if the top window contains frames. If it does not contain frames, the length property is equal to zero.

4 Type **{parent.location.href = location.href;}** to set the location.href property of the top window to the location.href property of the document.

5 Save the document.

Can I use JavaScript to force my site to load into a new window rather than the top browser window of the frameset?

✔ Yes. Rather than setting the `parent.location.href` property, you can use the `window.open()` method to launch the site into a new browser window:

```
if (parent.frames.length
> 0) {
window.open(location.href);
}
```

For more information on using the `window.open()` method, see the section "Open a New Window."

In JavaScript, I sometimes see a reference to a `top` property. Is the top frame the same as the parent frame?

✔ Not exactly. The parent is the document containing the current frame, while `top` refers to the top-level window. In most cases, parent and top are the same window and can be used interchangeably. However, if the document contains nested framesets—frames within frames—then the parent may not represent the top-level window.

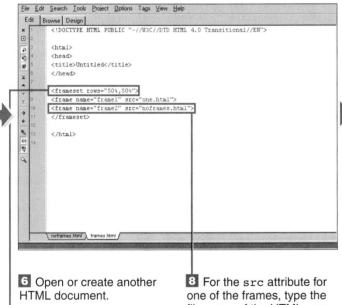

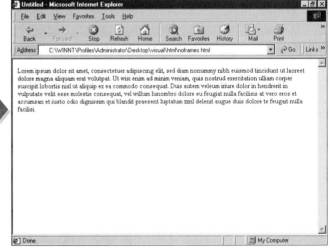

6 Open or create another HTML document.

7 Add a frameset.

8 For the `src` attribute for one of the frames, type the file name of the HTML page you created.

Note: To learn about creating HTML frames, see Chapter 5.

9 Save the document.

10 View the frameset document created in step 7 in a Web browser.

■ The script overrides the frameset to load the frame page into the top window.

CAPTURE KEYSTROKES

JavaScript includes several event handlers that can capture keyboard events, such as a user depressing a key. You can use this to determine which key a user pressed and have the code respond accordingly. However, versions of Netscape and Internet Explorer support keystoke events differently. In order to achieve cross-browser compatibility, you must use object or browser detection. For more information, see the section "Check for Browser Versions."

In order to capture keystrokes, use the HTML onKeyPress event handler and create a custom function to print the code that corresponds to the key:

onkeypress="*functionName* (event)"

Within your function, add JavaScript code for both Internet Explorer and Netscape to translate keystroke events. Internet Explorer browsers allow you to determine

which key a user pressed by referencing the event.keyCode property. This property returns the character code generated by pressing a particular keyboard key. Netscape browsers have a similar property, event.which, that also returns the Unicode character code for the key. If you want to convert the code back into the keyboard character, use the String.fromCharCode() method.

CAPTURE KEYSTROKES

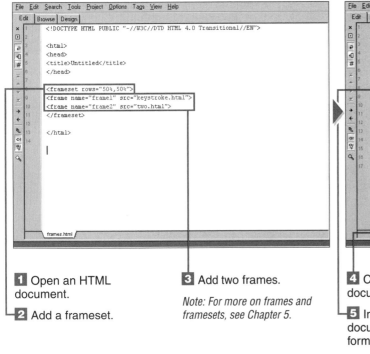

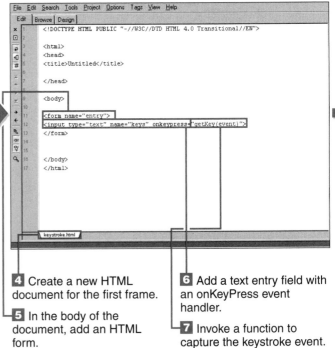

1 Open an HTML document.

2 Add a frameset.

3 Add two frames.

Note: For more on frames and framesets, see Chapter 5.

4 Create a new HTML document for the first frame.

5 In the body of the document, add an HTML form.

Note: See Chapter 4 for more on HTML forms.

6 Add a text entry field with an onKeyPress event handler.

7 Invoke a function to capture the keystroke event.

■ This function captures the code that corresponds to the keystroke.

Is it necessary to pass the "event" argument from the event handler to the function?

✔ For Netscape browsers, it is necessary to pass this argument when using HTML event handlers. If you omit the "event" argument, Netscape browsers will not register the keystroke. Because Internet Explorer stores events differently, it still processes the event if you omit this argument.

What other event handlers are associated with keystroke events?

✔ In addition to onKeyPress, there are also event handlers for when the user presses down on a key (onKeyDown) and when the user releases a key (onKeyUp). The onKeyPress handler is really a combination of these two more-specific events. Note that when you use event handlers as HTML attributes, the name of the event handler is case insensitive, so that onkeypress is synonymous with onKeyPress. For more information on event handlers, consult *JavaScript: Your visual blueprint for building dynamic Web pages* (Hungry Minds, Inc.).

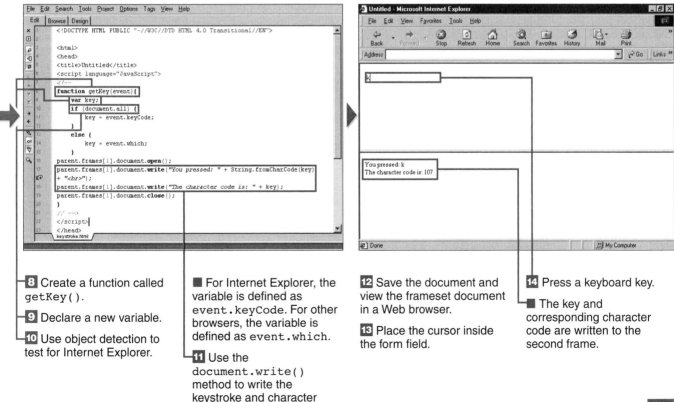

8 Create a function called getKey().

9 Declare a new variable.

10 Use object detection to test for Internet Explorer.

■ For Internet Explorer, the variable is defined as event.keyCode. For other browsers, the variable is defined as event.which.

11 Use the document.write() method to write the keystroke and character code to the second frame.

12 Save the document and view the frameset document in a Web browser.

13 Place the cursor inside the form field.

14 Press a keyboard key.

■ The key and corresponding character code are written to the second frame.

OPEN A NEW WINDOW

You can have links on your page load into new windows by using the window.open() method associated with the Window object. HTML gives you the ability to do this as well, by setting the target attribute of the <a> tag, but the JavaScript method provides additional control over the presentation of the new window. For example, the open() method allows you to set the size of the window

and disable certain elements, such as toolbars and resizing.

The window.open() method can take several optional arguments, including the link URL, the name of the new window, and a list of features. For the window's features, you can specify the width and height of the window in pixels, include or remove scrollbars and the browser toolbar, and indicate whether or not the user can resize

the window by dragging the border. The syntax for using the window.open() method is as follows:

```
window.open("URL",
"windowName","width=x,
height=y,scrollbars,
toolbar,resizable");
```

Any features not included in the method's arguments are omitted in the new window.

OPEN A NEW WINDOW

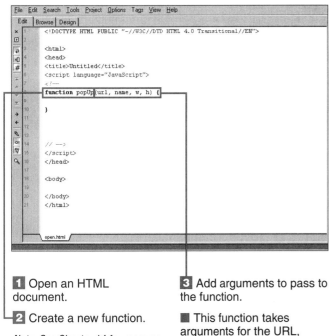

1 Open an HTML document.

2 Create a new function.

Note: See Chapter 14 for more on functions.

3 Add arguments to pass to the function.

■ This function takes arguments for the URL, window name, height, and width.

4 Type **win = window.open**.

5 Add the arguments.

■ The arguments allow you to pass values for the URL, window name, width, and height.

6 Add optional features.

■ **Scrollbars** indicates that scrollbars should be included if necessary; **resizable** allows the user to resize the window. **Menubar** and **toolbar** are the browser buttons.

Can I leave out the reference to the Window object and just use the open() method as a shortcut?

✔ No, you must include the Window object when you invoke the method because there is another open() method associated with the Document object. For more information on the document.open() method, see Chapter 14.

What happens if I assign a window a name that is already in use with another window?

✔ If there already exists a window with the assigned name, the browser loads the URL into that window. It creates a new window only if there are no pre-existing windows with that name or if a name is not specified.

What are the features available for the window.open() method?

✔ In addition to the standard features, such as menubar, toolbar, and scrollbars, you can set the status line with the status attribute (see the section "Add Text to the Status Window"). You can also set the position of the window by using top and left for Internet Explorer browsers and screenX and screenY for Netscape.

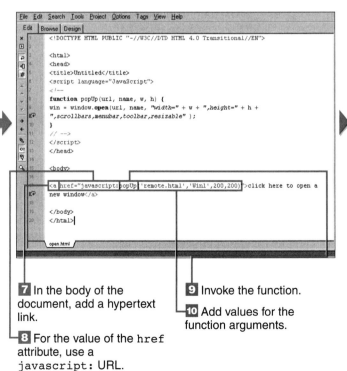

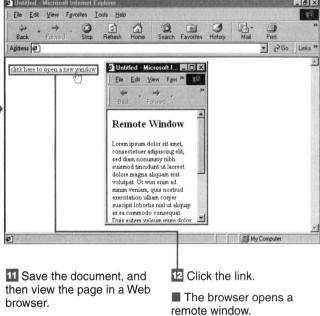

7 In the body of the document, add a hypertext link.

8 For the value of the href attribute, use a javascript: URL.

9 Invoke the function.

10 Add values for the function arguments.

11 Save the document, and then view the page in a Web browser.

12 Click the link.

■ The browser opens a remote window.

CLOSE A WINDOW

Whenever you open a remote or *pop-up* window, always provide the user with a link or button to close the window and return to the primary page. Of course, the user can always close the window by using the browser's own closing mechanism, but providing the user with the means to do this from within the Web page itself is always better.

To provide a link to close a remote window, use the window.close()

method. You can reference this method using a javascript: URL in the href attribute of an <a> tag:

```
<a href="javascript:window.
close()">close this
window</a>
```

You can also include this method with an event handler, such as onclick, with both hyperlinks and form buttons:

```
<input type="button"
onclick="window.close()">
```

For more information on using form fields, see Chapter 4.

Alternatively, you can also use the self.close() method, which is synonymous with window.close() and simply tells the current window to close itself. Unlike the window.open() method, the window.close() method does not take any optional arguments and does not have any features associated with it.

CLOSE A WINDOW

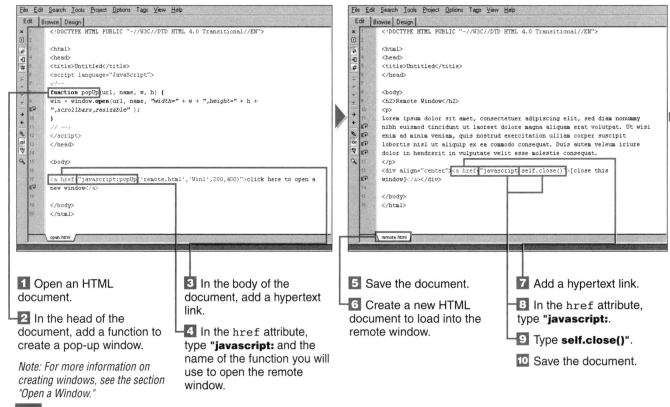

1 Open an HTML document.

2 In the head of the document, add a function to create a pop-up window.

Note: For more information on creating windows, see the section "Open a Window."

3 In the body of the document, add a hypertext link.

4 In the href attribute, type **"javascript:** and the name of the function you will use to open the remote window.

5 Save the document.

6 Create a new HTML document to load into the remote window.

7 Add a hypertext link.

8 In the href attribute, type **"javascript:**.

9 Type **self.close()"**.

10 Save the document.

Can I close other windows that I did not create by using JavaScript?

✔ Usually, if you try to close a window that you did not create with JavaScript, the browser presents the user with a confirmation dialog box. This is a security measure to prevent you from being able to close the user's browser window without permission.

Is there a way to check to see if the user has closed one of the remote windows?

✔ Yes. Use the `window.closed` property to verify whether a window is open or closed. If you assigned the window a name when you created it (see the section "Open a Window"), you can use this name to read the `closed` property, which returns a value of "true" if the window is closed or "false" if it is open. For example, you could execute JavaScript code, such as writing to a remote window, if the remote window were still open, or create a new window if the remote window had been closed.

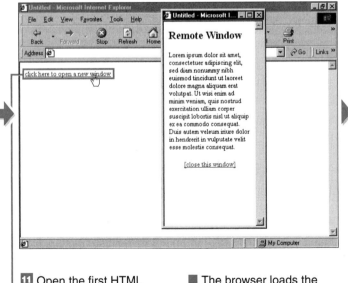

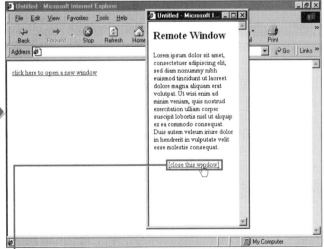

11 Open the first HTML document in a Web browser.

12 Click the link to launch a remote window.

■ The browser loads the second page into a remote window.

13 In the remote window, click the link.

■ The browser closes the window.

REDIRECT TO A NEW PAGE

You can use the location property in the browser's Document Object Model to redirect users to a new page. The location property stores the URL of the current page displayed in the user's Web browser. When you assign a new value to this property, the URL changes, and the user is redirected to the new page.

The location property is often used to redirect users to new pages

when content is moved. To use the location property to direct the user to a new page, add the following code to your script:

```
location = "newPage.html";
```

or:

```
location.href="newPage.html";
```

In addition, you can also use the location property to direct users to different pages based on elements such as browser version, plug-ins

present, or user responses to form fields or dialog boxes. When you set the value of the location property, the previous value still remains part of the browser's history. As a result, using the browser "Back" button to navigate returns the user to the original page. To have the browser overwrite the original URL with a new URL, use the location. replace() method.

REDIRECT TO A NEW PAGE

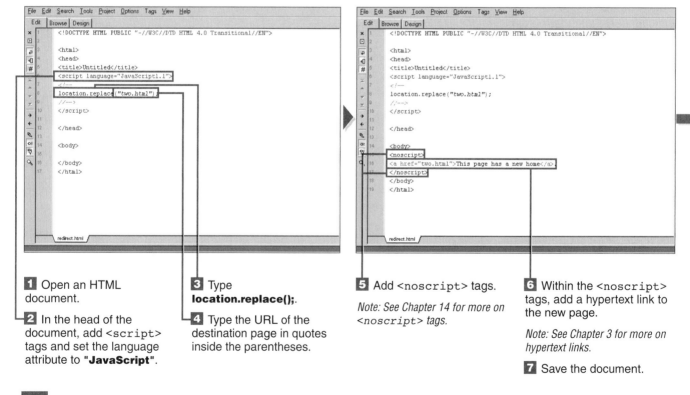

1 Open an HTML document.

2 In the head of the document, add <script> tags and set the language attribute to **"JavaScript"**.

3 Type **location.replace();**.

4 Type the URL of the destination page in quotes inside the parentheses.

5 Add <noscript> tags.

Note: See Chapter 14 for more on <noscript> tags.

6 Within the <noscript> tags, add a hypertext link to the new page.

Note: See Chapter 3 for more on hypertext links.

7 Save the document.

Is the `location.replace()` method supported in all versions of JavaScript?

✔ This method is not supported in JavaScript 1.0 but is supported in all subsequent versions. You can enclose the `location.replace()` code in script tags with the language set to "JavaScript1.1" to ensure that it is not executed on JavaScript 1.0 browsers. For those browsers, add another set of `<script>` tags and use the `location.href` property.

Is there a way to redirect pages using HTML?

✔ Yes. You can use the `<meta>` tag with the `http-equiv` attribute set to "refresh" and the content attribute set to the URL. For more information on using `<meta>` tags, see Chapter 3.

What is the difference between using `location` and `location.href`?

✔ Functionally, they are the same and contain the same value—the URL for the current Web page. You can use either location or location.href when redirecting users to different pages.

Besides location.href, what other properties are associated with location?

✔ The Location object contains four additional properties that store references to different parts of the complete URL: `protocol` (such as ftp or http), `host` (the domain name), `pathname`, and `search` (the query string, or any information after a question mark).

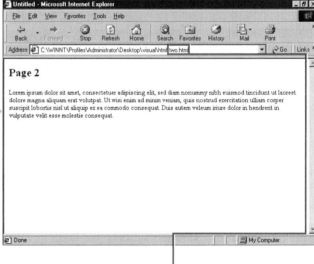

8 Create another HTML document.

9 Save it with the same name as you indicated in the `location.replace()` method.

10 View the first page in a Web browser.

■ The browser redirects the user to the destination page.

REFERENCE THE DOM

You can access and dynamically manipulate elements on a Web page by using JavaScript to reference the *Document Object Model* (DOM). While the Window object refers to the top-level browser window or frame, the document object contains references to both properties of the HTML document, such as the background color, and all of the objects contained within the document, such as forms, images, and links.

In the Document Object Model, all of the elements on a Web page are grouped as arrays (see Chapter 14). Each specific element is one object within the array. For example, on a Web page containing two <form> tags, the document.forms[] array contains two Form objects.

Because array index numbers always begin with 0 (zero), you can access the first form by using the expression document.forms[0] or document.formName if you have assigned the form a name. Moving down the Document Object Model, you can access individual form elements and their values in the same way:

document.*formName*.*inputName*.value;

Or, you can reference one of the form's *elements* via the elements[] array:

document.*formName*.elements[*x*].value;

Similarly, you would access the third image in an HTML document with the expression document.images[2]. For more information on manipulating images, see the section "Script Image Mouseovers."

REFERENCE THE DOM

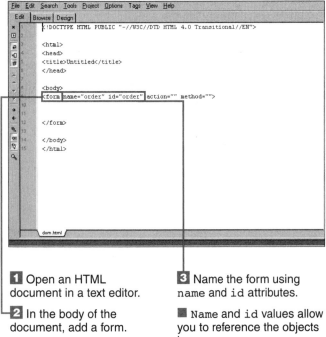

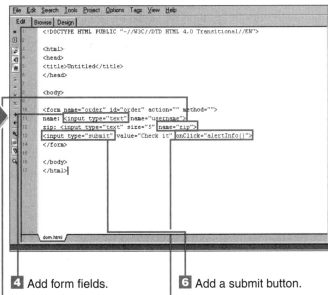

1 Open an HTML document in a text editor.

2 In the body of the document, add a form.

Note: For more on HTML forms, see Chapter 4.

3 Name the form using name and id attributes.

■ Name and id values allow you to reference the objects by name.

4 Add form fields.

■ This example uses text entry fields. For more information, see Chapter 4.

5 Indicate the name of each INPUT element.

6 Add a submit button.

7 Invoke a new function that will read the value of the form elements.

■ This example uses the onClick attribute to invoke the function.

Are there different version numbers for the Document Object Model?

✔ Yes. The original DOM implemented by browser makers, containing the standard references to windows, documents, forms, and other HTML elements, is referred to as DOM level 0. The new standardized DOM is known as DOM level 1.

Is the Document Object Model consistent across browser make and versions?

✔ No, each browser make implements its own version of the Document Object Model, and even among Netscape and Internet Explorer browsers, there are significant differences in the DOM, depending on the browser version number.

What other properties of the Document object are accessible?

✔ In addition to color properties, such as `bgColor` (background color), `fgColor` (text color), `linkColor`, `alinkColor`, and `vlinkColor`, you can access the title of the document, the URL, and the referrer. The `document.referrer` property indicates the URL of the document that contained the link to the current document. The Document object also contains several different arrays of objects that you can reference. These arrays include `anchors[]`, `applets[]`, `embeds[]`, `forms[]`, `image[]`, `links[]`, and `plugins[]`.

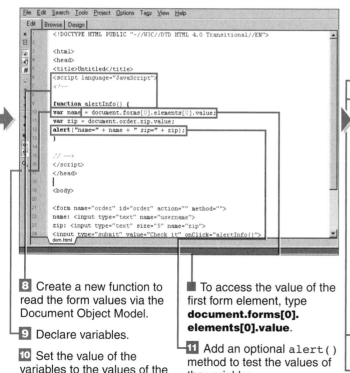

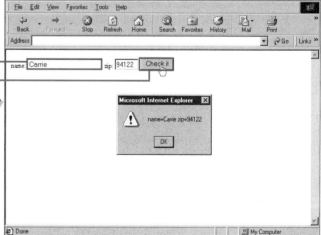

8 Create a new function to read the form values via the Document Object Model.

9 Declare variables.

10 Set the value of the variables to the values of the form fields.

■ To access the value of the first form element, type **document.forms[0]. elements[0].value**.

11 Add an optional `alert()` method to test the values of the variables.

12 Save the document and view the page in a Web browser.

13 Enter text into the form fields.

14 Click the submit button.

■ The Document Object Model allows you to read the values of the form fields.

■ In this example, the alert box prints the values of the form fields.

VALIDATE A FORM

You can use JavaScript to validate your HTML forms and make sure that visitors fill out required fields. You can use form validation to check for responses in text input fields, checked boxes and radio buttons, and any other type of form entry field. You can also use JavaScript to ensure that responses, such as postal codes, telephone numbers, and e-mail addresses, are formatted

correctly. You can accomplish this type of form validation through an application on the server, such as a CGI, but JavaScript validation is more efficient because the processing occurs on the client-side and does not require data to be sent to the server.

To validate a form by using JavaScript, define a function in the head of your document that checks for required fields. Use

`if-else` statements to return error messages for missing fields. For more information on `if-else` statements, see Chapter 14. After you have defined your validation function, invoke it by using an HTML event handler, such as `onSubmit`. For more on HTML event handlers, consult *JavaScript: Your visual blueprint for building dynamic Web pages* (Hungry Minds, Inc.).

VALIDATE A FORM

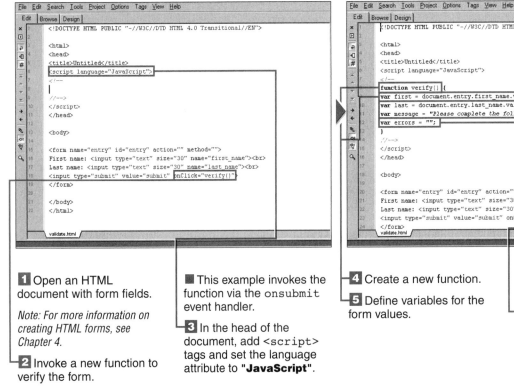

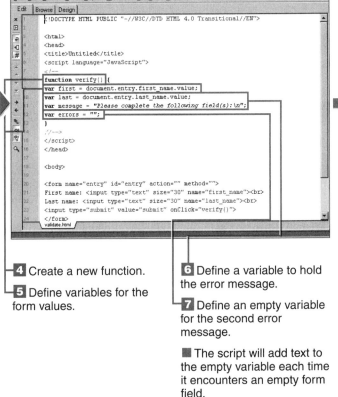

1 Open an HTML document with form fields.

Note: For more information on creating HTML forms, see Chapter 4.

2 Invoke a new function to verify the form.

■ This example invokes the function via the `onsubmit` event handler.

3 In the head of the document, add `<script>` tags and set the language attribute to **"JavaScript"**.

4 Create a new function.

5 Define variables for the form values.

6 Define a variable to hold the error message.

7 Define an empty variable for the second error message.

■ The script will add text to the empty variable each time it encounters an empty form field.

How do I use JavaScript to verify that form responses are formatted correctly?

✔ You can verify that responses are formatted correctly several ways. You can use methods associated with the `String` object, such as `String.indexOf()` and `String.length()`, to search for particular characters and to make sure that responses contain a certain number of characters.

How do I submit the form if there were no errors?

✔ Use the "return true" statement to process the form if there were no errors. Use the "return false" statement to prevent the form from being submitted if there were errors on validation.

How do I validate form fields, such as radio buttons and check boxes?

✔ To validate radio buttons and check boxes, use the `checked` property. Each radio button or check box is stored in an array and has a `checked` property that returns "true" if the element is selected and "false" if it is not selected. To verify that the first radio button is selected for example, use the following code:

```
if
(document.formName.radioName
[0].checked)
```

For more information, consult *JavaScript: Your visual blueprint for building dynamic Web pages* (Hungry Minds, Inc.).

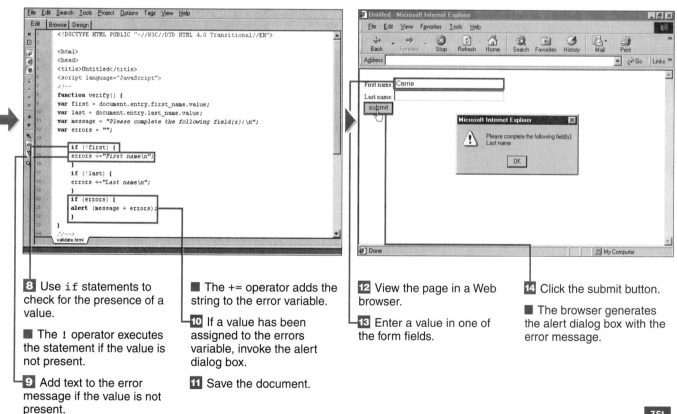

■ **8** Use `if` statements to check for the presence of a value.

■ The `!` operator executes the statement if the value is not present.

■ **9** Add text to the error message if the value is not present.

■ The `+=` operator adds the string to the error variable.

■ **10** If a value has been assigned to the errors variable, invoke the alert dialog box.

■ **11** Save the document.

■ **12** View the page in a Web browser.

■ **13** Enter a value in one of the form fields.

■ **14** Click the submit button.

■ The browser generates the alert dialog box with the error message.

PRELOAD IMAGES

You can use JavaScript to load images into the browser cache and then reference them later when swapping images with mouseover events.

Preloading images into the browser's cache allows for instantaneous image-swapping. If you fail to preload your images, there will be a slight delay on the mouseover event, because the browser must retrieve the image from the server.

To preload images for later use, use the Image() constructor to create a new Image object and assign its URL to the image's src property. This creates an off-screen image that can be referenced later when you create image mouseovers (see "Script Image Mouseovers," later in this chapter).

The following example uses a technique called *object detection* to prevent errors from occurring on browsers that do not support the document.images property,

which is a reference to the array of images contained within the HTML page. Because the Image() constructors are contained within an if statement, the JavaScript is executed only if the browser's Document Object Model contains the document.images property. Object detection is a useful way to prevent errors without resorting to browser detection techniques (see the section "Check for Browser Versions").

PRELOAD IMAGES

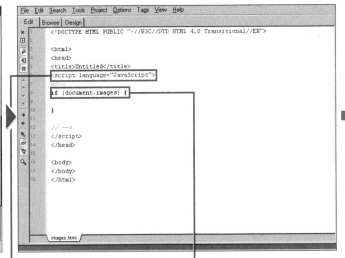

1 Open a graphics editor.

■ This example uses Fireworks.

2 Create two navigation graphics for the "on" and "off" states of a rollover.

Note: For more information on Web graphics, see Chapter 12.

3 Open an HTML document.

4 In the head of the document, add a set of <script> tags and set the language attribute to **"JavaScript"**.

5 Add a JavaScript if statement to test for the document.images object.

■ The if statement will contain all of the code to preload images.

Note: For more information on if statements, see Chapter 14.

Is the document.images property supported in all versions of JavaScript?

✔ The document.images property, used to test for the presence of the images[] array, is supported in JavaScript versions 1.1 and higher. This means that versions 3 and higher of Netscape and Internet Explorer support document.images.

When I preload images, can the src property be a relative or absolute URL?

✔ You can use either relative or absolute URLs when setting the src property for images. To use relative URLs, indicate the location of the image file relative to the current document:

```
imageName.src =
"../directoryName/
imageName.gif";
```

Can the new Image() constructor take any arguments?

✔ There are two optional arguments, width and height, that you can use to specify the dimensions of the image. To specify the dimensions of an image with the new Image() constructor, use the following syntax:

```
imageName = new Image(width,
height);
```

However, because image dimensions are usually specified within the HTML <img> tag itself, it is not necessary to define the width and height by using the new Image() constructor.

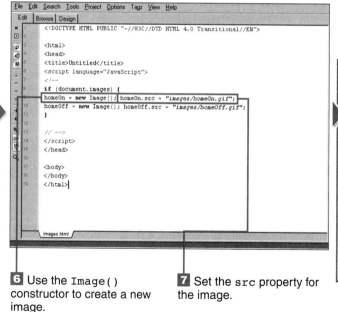

6 Use the Image() constructor to create a new image.

7 Set the src property for the image.

8 View the page in a Web browser.

■ The Image() constructor does not render the image visible on a page, but rather loads it into the browser's cache.

SCRIPT IMAGE MOUSEOVERS

One way to add an interactive element to your Web page is through *image mouseovers*, or rollovers. Within the browser's Document Object Model, every image has a read/write src property, meaning that you can use JavaScript to change the source of any image on the page.

The first step when scripting image mouseovers is to make sure all the images are preloaded in the browser's cache (see the section

"Preload Images"). After the images are preloaded, use the onMouseOver and onMouseOut event handlers to invoke a function to swap in the new image. Within the <img> tag, add the following code to invoke a mouseover function:

```
onMouseOver="functionName()"
```

Inside the parentheses, specify the *name* of the image—as set using the name attribute—and use it in the

image-swapping functions to point to a different image. Simply make sure that the images you are swapping share the same name but have "on" and "off" suffixes:

```
document[imageName].src =
eval(imageName +
"On.src");
```

The eval() function takes the name of the image, adds the "On.src" suffix, and matches it to the preloaded image.

SCRIPT IMAGE MOUSEOVERS

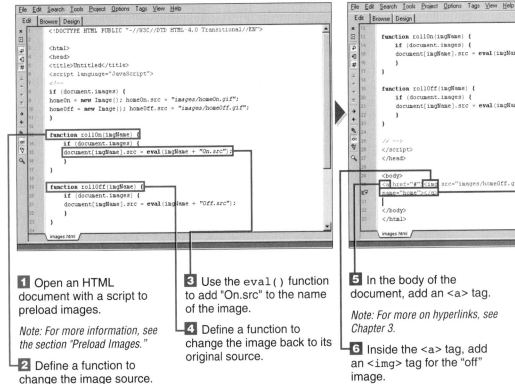

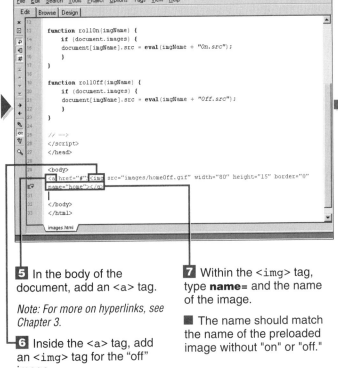

1 Open an HTML document with a script to preload images.

Note: For more information, see the section "Preload Images."

2 Define a function to change the image source.

3 Use the eval() function to add "On.src" to the name of the image.

4 Define a function to change the image back to its original source.

5 In the body of the document, add an <a> tag.

Note: For more on hyperlinks, see Chapter 3.

6 Inside the <a> tag, add an <img> tag for the "off" image.

7 Within the <img> tag, type **name=** and the name of the image.

■ The name should match the name of the preloaded image without "on" or "off."

Can the images I use for the "on" and "off" states be different sizes?

✔ For a seamless rollover effect, the "on" and "off" state images should be the same size.

What other ways are there to code mouseovers?

✔ You can change the source property for individual images by adding JavaScript code to the onMouseOver and onMouseOut attributes. Reference the image by its array index number, such as document.images[0].src, or by its name. Then set the src property to reference the image you want to swap in or out.

What happens if I use only the onMouseOver attribute and do not include the onMouseOut attribute?

✔ If you do not use the onMouseOut attribute to switch the src property back to the original image, the image remains in the "on" state, even after the user mouses away from the image.

Can I use this technique with other event handlers, such as onClick?

✔ Yes, you can use the onClick event handler to swap in another image when the user clicks a hypertext link.

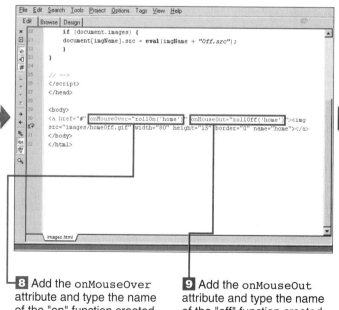

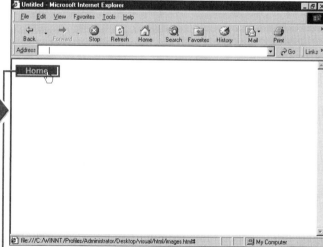

8 Add the onMouseOver attribute and type the name of the "on" function created in step 2.

■ Inside the parentheses, type the name of the image.

9 Add the onMouseOut attribute and type the name of the "off" function created in step 4.

10 Save the document.

11 View the page in a Web browser.

12 Mouse over the image.

■ The function alters the src property of the image to create an image-swap effect.

CHECK FOR BROWSER VERSIONS

You can use JavaScript to check for browser make, version number, and other information, such as Java or plug-in support. By using browser detection techniques, you can write different versions of code, depending on the user's particular browser.

The Navigator object contains several properties that store information about the user's browser. You can check the browser

make by reading the navigation.appName property, which returns "Netscape" for Netscape browsers and "Microsoft Internet Explorer" for IE browsers. The navigator.appVersion property contains the browser version number in addition to other information, such as platform and encryption data. In order to extract the version number from this string, you can use the parse.Int() or parse.Float() methods. For example:

```
parse.Int(navigator.
appVersion);
```

These methods evaluate a string and return only the integer or floating point number. Be aware that the browser version number stored in the appVersion property is sometimes the version with which the browser is compatible, rather than the actual version number. For example, Internet Explorer 5 returns a value of "4.0 compatible."

CHECK FOR BROWSER VERSIONS

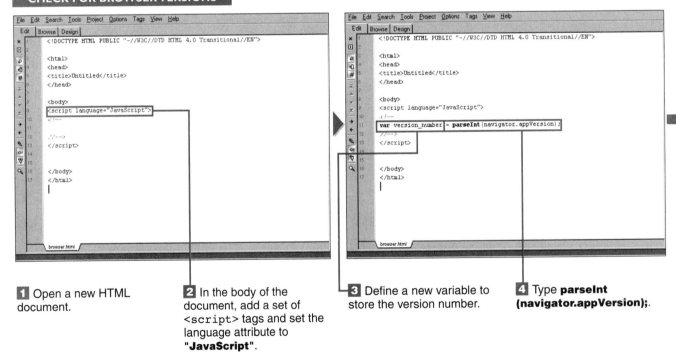

1 Open a new HTML document.

2 In the body of the document, add a set of `<script>` tags and set the language attribute to **"JavaScript"**.

3 Define a new variable to store the version number.

4 Type **parseInt (navigator.appVersion);**.

What other properties are associated with the Navigator object?

✔ In addition to `navigator.appName` and `navigator.appVersion`, other properties include `navigator.platform`, which returns the operating system, and `navigator.language`, which returns a two letter language code such as "en" (English).

How can I use the Navigator object to test for plug-ins?

✔ The Navigator object includes the `plugins[]` array that includes all of the plug-ins installed in the browser. However, in Internet Explorer 4, this array exists but is always empty.

Are there other ways to handle browser incompatibilities?

✔ Rather than using browser detection, you can use object detection to determine whether a user's browser supports a particular object you are using in your script. This is sometimes a more efficient way to handle incompatibilities, because you only have to check for the object in question rather than writing different code for numerous browser versions. To check for a particular object, use a conditional `if` statement and include the object, such as `document. images`, in the parentheses. If the object exists, the browser executes the code. For an example of object detection, see the section "Preload Images."

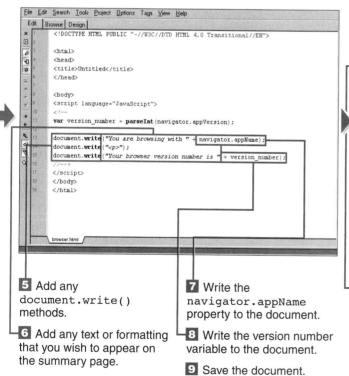

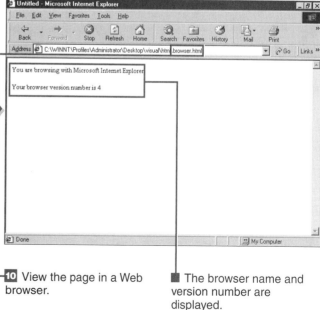

5 Add any `document.write()` methods.

6 Add any text or formatting that you wish to appear on the summary page.

7 Write the `navigator.appName` property to the document.

8 Write the version number variable to the document.

9 Save the document.

10 View the page in a Web browser.

■ The browser name and version number are displayed.

SET A COOKIE

You can use client-side JavaScript to set cookie values that you can later retrieve to personalize a visitor's experience on your Web site or pass information from one page to another. *Cookies* are small pieces of data that are stored by the Web browser and associated with particular Web pages or sites.

By storing data directly to the user's browser, cookies allow you to *maintain state*, meaning that the

browser can remember specific data that would normally be only temporarily stored while the user is visiting a particular page.

Set a cookie by using the document.cookie object to assign name/value pairs. The *name* is the name you assign to the cookie, and the *value* is the value of the named cookie. For example, in a cookie called login the value is the visitor's login name:

```
login=visitorLoginName;
```

Because values cannot contain commas, semicolons, or spaces, you may have to use the escape() function to properly encode the cookie value before setting it.

For more information on encoding special characters, see *JavaScript: Your visual blueprint for building dynamic Web pages.*

SET A COOKIE

```
<!DOCTYPE HTML PUBLIC "-//W3C//DTD HTML 4.0 Transitional//EN">

<html>
<head>
<title>Untitled</title>
<script language="JavaScript">
<!--
function setCookie() {
login = prompt("Please choose a member login","");

document.cookie = "Login=" + escape(login);

var myExpire = new Date();
}
//-->
</script>
</head>

<body>

</body>
</html>
```

```
<!DOCTYPE HTML PUBLIC "-//W3C//DTD HTML 4.0 Transitional//EN">

<html>
<head>
<title>Untitled</title>
<script language="JavaScript">
<!--
function setCookie() {
login = prompt("Please choose a member login","");

document.cookie = "Login=" + escape(login);

var myExpire = new Date();
myExpire.setMonth(myExpire.getMonth() + 6);
}
//-->
</script>
</head>

<body>

</body>
</html>
```

1 Open an HTML document.

2 In the head of the document, add a set of <script> tags and set the language attribute to **"JavaScript"**.

3 Define a new function.

Note: For more on JavaScript functions, see Chapter 14.

4 Define a new variable.

5 For the value, type **prompt()**.

■ This method generates a user response. For more information on using the prompt() method, see the section "Prompt the User for a Response."

When is it necessary to use the escape() and unescape() methods when reading and writing cookies?

✔ When you set a cookie, the value stored in a name/value pair cannot contain commas, semicolons, or spaces. If the user-generated value is a piece of data such as a member name or other string, using the escape() method to encode the value is a good idea because the value may contain spaces. If you retrieve the value without using the unescape() method, any spaces are represented with the code %20. Using the unescape() method converts the string back to regular characters, replacing %20 with a space.

Is there a limit on the number of cookies I can set?

✔ Yes. A Web browser is only required to store a maximum of twenty cookies per Web server. This is a particularly important restriction if there is more than one site on your Web server.

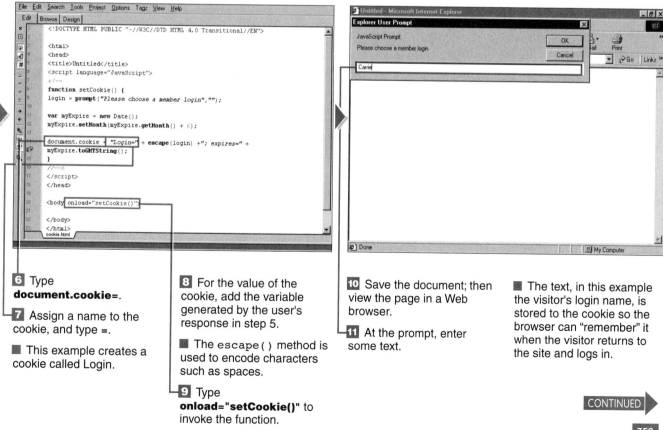

6 Type **document.cookie=**.

7 Assign a name to the cookie, and type =.

■ This example creates a cookie called Login.

8 For the value of the cookie, add the variable generated by the user's response in step 5.

■ The escape() method is used to encode characters such as spaces.

9 Type **onload="setCookie()"** to invoke the function.

10 Save the document; then view the page in a Web browser.

11 At the prompt, enter some text.

■ The text, in this example the visitor's login name, is stored to the cookie so the browser can "remember" it when the visitor returns to the site and logs in.

CONTINUED

SET A COOKIE (CONTINUED)

When you set cookies for your site, you can include several optional attributes to extend the capabilities of the cookie.

Use the expires attribute to set an expiration date for information you are storing with the cookie. This allows the browser to "remember" a login name for a specified amount of time, for example. Add the expiration date after the name/value pair in the cookie:

```
document.cookie="cookieName
=value;expires=expiration
Date";
```

To set the cookie to expire in a certain number of months, you can use the new Date() constructor to create a reference to the current date; then add a specific number of months and set the new date:

```
var expirationDate = new
Date();

expirationDate.setMonth =
(expirationDate.getMonth +
x);
```

Expiration dates for cookies must be set in the GMT format. For more on using JavaScript dates, consult *JavaScript: Your visual blueprint for building dynamic Web pages.*

The path attribute allows cookies to be accessible to directories other than the one in which it was created. By setting the path to "/", a cookie is accessible from any page on the Web site. The domain attribute allows you to use the same cookie across multiple Web sites using the same domain name.

SET A COOKIE EXPIRATION DATE

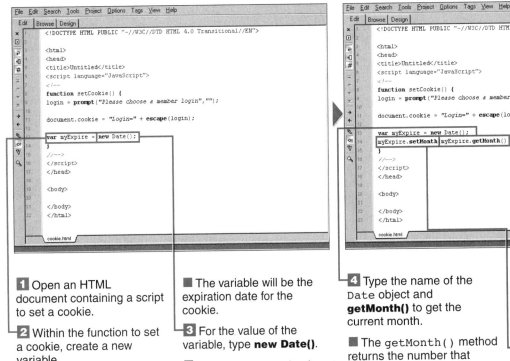

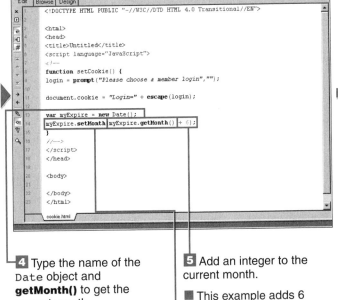

1 Open an HTML document containing a script to set a cookie.

2 Within the function to set a cookie, create a new variable.

■ The variable will be the expiration date for the cookie.

3 For the value of the variable, type **new Date()**.

■ The Date() constructor creates a Date object set to the current date and time.

4 Type the name of the Date object and **getMonth()** to get the current month.

■ The getMonth() method returns the number that corresponds to the current month.

5 Add an integer to the current month.

■ This example adds 6 months to the current date.

6 Type the name of the Date object and **setMonth()** to set the new month value.

How can I be sure that an expiration date is in the correct format?

✔ JavaScript provides several methods to convert dates to specific formats. One of these methods is `toGMTString()`, which converts a date to the correct GMT format. You can use this method by referencing your date object by name:

`dateObjectName.toGMTString();`

For more on JavaScript dates, see *JavaScript: Your visual blueprint for building dynamic Web pages.*

Is the data transmitted in cookies secure?

✔ No, cookies are passed via a regular HTTP connection, so they are insecure. To ensure that your cookie is transmitted only when there is a secure connection between the browser and the server, use the `secure` attribute:

`cookieName=value; secure`

The `secure` attribute can be added to the cookie along with any other optional attributes, such as `expires`, `path`, or `domain`. Simply separate each attribute with a semicolon.

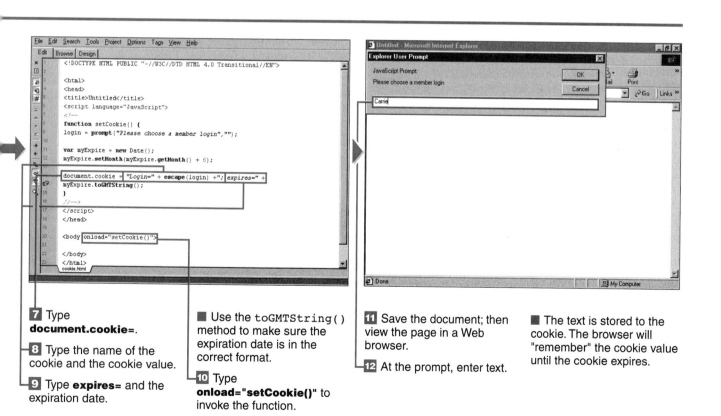

7 Type **document.cookie=**.

8 Type the name of the cookie and the cookie value.

9 Type **expires=** and the expiration date.

■ Use the `toGMTString()` method to make sure the expiration date is in the correct format.

10 Type **onload="setCookie()"** to invoke the function.

11 Save the document; then view the page in a Web browser.

12 At the prompt, enter text.

■ The text is stored to the cookie. The browser will "remember" the cookie value until the cookie expires.

READ A COOKIE

After you have stored user data to a cookie, you can retrieve the values stored by using JavaScript. Use stored data to pre-populate form fields or remember purchase information as the visitor completes an e-commerce transaction.

In order to read and retrieve data from a cookie, you must search the document.cookie property for the specific name/value pair of your cookie data (see the section "Set a

Cookie") and then extract the appropriate value. To search the cookie to find the beginning and the end of the value, use the String.indexOf() method:

```
document.cookie.indexOf
("cookieName=");
```

After you have found the value, extract it by using the String.substring() method. The substring() method extracts a part of a string according to two

values: *start* and *end*. Within a cookie, the start position is the character after *cookieName=*, and the end position is the semicolon that separates each individual cookie. If there is only one cookie present, the end is simply the end of the cookie string, represented by document.cookie.length. If you used the escape() method when setting the cookie, use the unescape() method to decode the cookie data's value.

READ A COOKIE

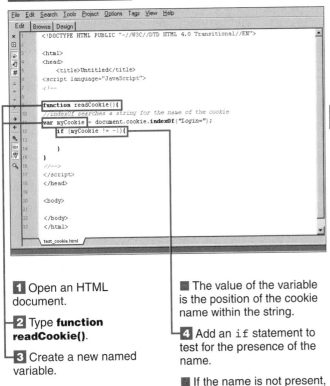

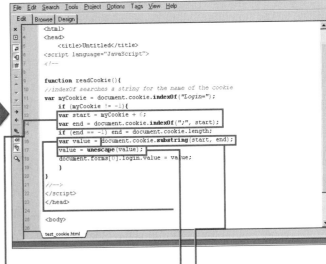

1 Open an HTML document.

2 Type **function readCookie()**.

3 Create a new named variable.

■ The value of the variable is the position of the cookie name within the string.

4 Add an if statement to test for the presence of the name.

■ If the name is not present, the value returned is "-1."

5 Search the string for the start and end points of the value.

■ The start value is equal to the position of the name plus the number of characters in the name. The end value is the semicolon.

6 Create a new variable to store the cookie value.

7 Extract the value using the substring() method and the start and end variables, and use the unescape() method to decode Latin-1 characters.

Why are string methods, such as indexOf() and substring(), used when reading cookies?

✔ When you retrieve a cookie by using the document.cookie property, JavaScript returns a string value containing all of the cookies for that page. This string is a collection of name/value pairs separated by semicolons. That means that if you read the entire document.cookie property, JavaScript returns a string in the following form:

cookieName=value;
cookieName2=value

You can use any of the methods associated with strings to search and extract only the part of the string that you need.

What other methods can I use to extract the cookie value?

✔ Rather than using String.indexOf() and String.substring(), you can use the String.split() method to break the string into discrete pieces based on the delimiter used to separate each element, such as a semicolon. For more information, see *JavaScript: Your visual blueprint for building dynamic Web pages.*

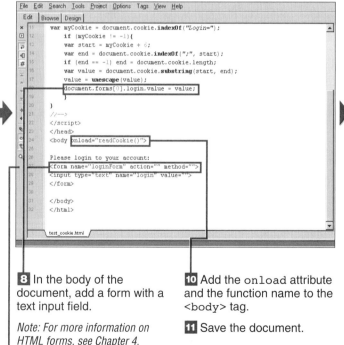

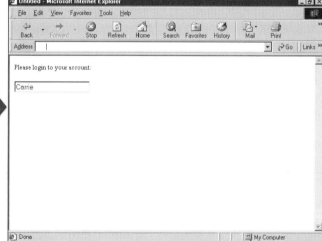

8 In the body of the document, add a form with a text input field.

Note: For more information on HTML forms, see Chapter 4.

9 Within the script, set the value of the text input field to the value of the cookie data.

10 Add the onload attribute and the function name to the <body> tag.

11 Save the document.

12 View the page in a Web browser.

■ The form field is populated with the cookie value.

INTRODUCTION TO SOUND

Adding sound to your Web page can be very helpful. Ambient music playing softly in the background can set the mood for your site. Including simple clicks and audio clues to actions, such as clicking buttons, provides valuable feedback to the user.

However, including sound on your Web page can be very expensive, not in terms of cost but in terms of the file size and download time.

Big Sound = Big File

Sound files can be some of the largest elements of a Web page; therefore, use them with care.

The reason sound files are so large is that quality sound requires a high sampling rate. *Sampling rate* is the number of times per second the sound is recorded, or sampled. This means that data for every audible frequency needs to be stored in the file many times each second.

You can also specify the size of the data to be 8-bit or 16-bit. Audio files recorded at 16-bit use 16 bits of memory to store the recorded sound. This is twice the size of 8-bit sound resulting in more detail and higher quality sound. Selecting 16-bit sound doubles the size of the file. Also, if the sound is recorded in stereo, the file size doubles.

Sound files with a lower sampling rate are of lower quality, but they have smaller file sizes. For example, an 8-bit, mono sound recorded with an 11,025 Hz sampling rate requires 22 kilobytes (K) for each second. This quality level is comparable to sound heard through a telephone. On the other hand, CD-quality sound is 16-bit stereo with a 44,100 Hz sampling rate, which requires 172K for each second.

When a sound file is added to a Web page, the browser cannot play the sound, but it can pass the file off to a separate application that can play it. The information that enables the browser to identify the file type and pass it off to a separate program is the *MIME* type, which stands for Multipurpose Internet Mail Extensions. When the browser encounters a file with a known MIME type, it looks for the appropriate helper application that can handle the file.

If the browser encounters a file with an unknown MIME type, it displays a "File Not Found" error page. The ability of a user to hear the sound file on your Web page depends on the capabilities of the user's system.

Luckily, many different audio formats are available. Each of these formats has different advantages and disadvantages.

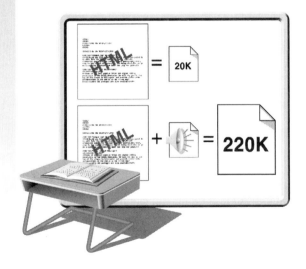

AU Format

The *AU* audio format is the default audio format used by the UNIX and Linux systems. The AU format is common on the Internet because of the low sound quality, thereby resulting in small file sizes. The MIME type for AU files is audio/basic.

AIFF Format

The *AIFF* audio format is used with Macintosh computers and offers a high-quality audio option, but the file sizes can be very large. The MIME type for AIFF files is audio/aiff.

WAV Format

The *WAV* audio format is another high-quality audio option with large file sizes that is commonly found on Windows machines. The MIME type for WAV files is audio/wav.

motorcycle.wav

MIDI Format

The *MIDI* format is different than the other audio formats. Instead of storing sound frequencies, this format stores the notes that are played. The main advantage of this format is that it produces relatively tiny files, but the disadvantage is that they can be used only for music and not for speech or sounds.

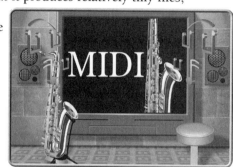

MP3 Format

The MP3 format is a digital compression format that is quite popular for recording entire songs or audio tracks. MP3 is not used much for Web page audio clips but is heavily in use for exchanging audio files across the Internet.

UNDERSTANDING MULTIMEDIA PLUG-INS

*P*lug-ins are external programs or helper applications that you can add to the browser to enhance its capabilities. They enable browsers to be much more powerful and to support many more file types than they would otherwise.

Several plug-ins have become very popular and are continually being updated and supported. These plug-ins allow the browser to view specialized content, such as animation, published content, virtual reality worlds, and streaming audio and video.

This section highlights some of these popular plug-ins and explains how to use them.

Adobe Acrobat Reader

The Adobe Acrobat program lets you take existing documents produced with a word processor or desktop publishing program and save them as *PDF* files. The advantage of PDF files is that the exact look and layout of the original document is maintained. You do not need the full Adobe Acrobat product to view these documents; you only need to download the Acrobat Reader plug-in and install it on your computer.

You can find this plug-in and information about PDF files on Adobe's Web site at www.adobe.com.

RealAudio and RealVideo

RealAudio and *RealVideo* are popular streaming formats that enable you to see and hear large audio and video files even over a dialup modem connection. A streaming format is one that plays the content as it is downloaded. RealAudio is a very popular format for listening to live radio broadcasts over the Internet, sporting events, or multimedia training presentations.

Information about RealAudio and the RealPlayer plug-in are available at www.real.com.

QuickTime

Apple's *QuickTime* streaming video format is the default standard for Macintosh systems. QuickTime is a popular multimedia format for movie trailers, music videos, and short films that are viewable over the Internet. QuickTime is not just for Macintosh computers; it is also available for Windows computers and can be installed quickly on a Windows system. The plug-in and information can be found at www.apple.com/quicktime.

Shockwave and Flash

Macromedia has several plug-ins that enable files generated with their commercial products, such as Director and Flash, to be displayed on the Web. Using these formats, you can create interactive multimedia presentations that include sound and animation. Flash applications and the Web are also discussed later in this chapter.

Information on these formats can be found at Macromedia's Web site at www.macromedia.com.

VRML

VRML stands for the Virtual Reality Modeling Language. This language is similar to HTML and can create three-dimensional virtual worlds. Using a VRML plug-in, you can load and navigate around these three-dimensional worlds inside a browser. For example, you could enter a VRML world and move around as if you were in the world. You can choose from several different VRML plug-ins.

To find more information about this format and download a VRML plug-in, visit the Web 3D Consortium at www.vrml.org.

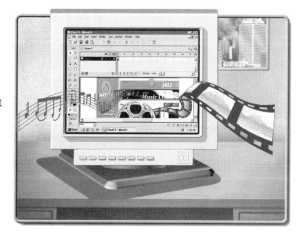

RECORD AND SAVE SOUND FILES

Before you can add a sound file to a Web page, you need to obtain the sound file. You can find repositories of sound files throughout the Web, but perhaps the best source for obtaining sound files is to record them yourself by using your computer's sound card, recording software, and perhaps a microphone.

Most operating systems, such as

Windows and the Mac OS, include utilities that can record sound files. These utilities are simple, easy-to-use applications that resemble a tape recorder. You can also use audio grabbing software to grab sounds from CDs that you own.

To record sound, you need to plug a microphone into the sound card. Then, click the Record button and speak into the microphone. When

you are done recording, click the Stop button and save the sound file.

While these are specific to the application that ships with Windows, other multimedia recording and editing programs (such as those on a Macintosh) use similar steps to record sound. Check your sound application's help file for detailed information.

RECORD AND SAVE SOUND FILES

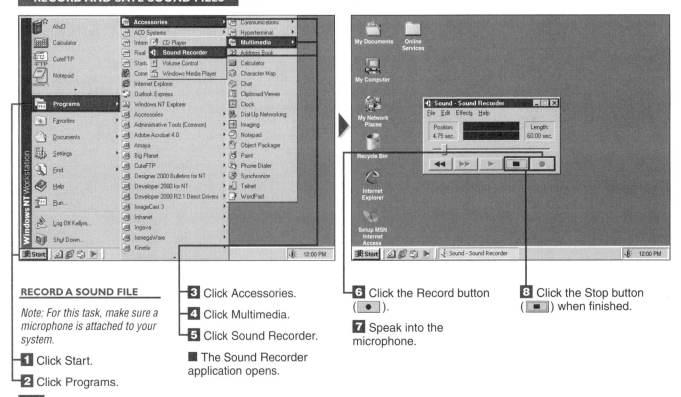

RECORD A SOUND FILE

Note: For this task, make sure a microphone is attached to your system.

1 Click Start.

2 Click Programs.

3 Click Accessories.

4 Click Multimedia.

5 Click Sound Recorder.

■ The Sound Recorder application opens.

6 Click the Record button (●).

7 Speak into the microphone.

8 Click the Stop button (■) when finished.

Can I use Sound Recorder to save the sound file as other formats, such as AU and AIFF?

✔ Sound Recorder is a program that works only with WAV files, but plenty of other programs can convert between the various audio formats. These programs include CoolEdit, Sonic Forge, and Goldwave.

I noticed the Effects menu option. What effects are possible?

✔ The effects are fairly simple. They include increasing or decreasing the volume, increasing or decreasing the playback speed, adding an echo, and reversing the sound.

Should I have multiple copies of audio files on my Web pages?

✔ Sometimes it is a good idea to have more than one version available for your users. If bandwidth is tight, such as over a dialup account, use a smaller bit rate or lesser sound quality. If different plug-ins will be used, save your file in a complementary format.

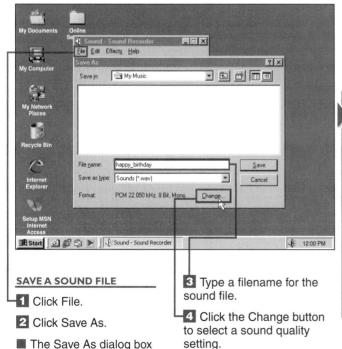

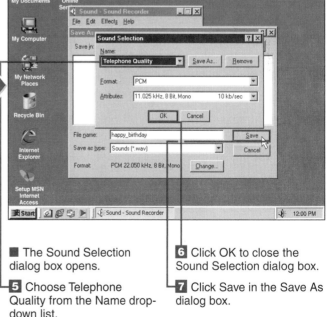

SAVE A SOUND FILE

1 Click File.

2 Click Save As.

■ The Save As dialog box opens.

3 Type a filename for the sound file.

4 Click the Change button to select a sound quality setting.

■ The Sound Selection dialog box opens.

5 Choose Telephone Quality from the Name drop-down list.

6 Click OK to close the Sound Selection dialog box.

7 Click Save in the Save As dialog box.

ADD SOUND FILES AS LINKS ON WEB PAGES

Sound files are easy ways to add another dimension to your Web pages. They are a quick way to add audio greetings to your visitors, such as a recording of your cat or dog yelling for attention. Sound files can run the gamut, and your file is limited only by your imagination.

After you have a sound file, you can add it to a Web page in one of several ways. The easiest way to add a sound file to your Web page is by using the <a> tag. This way works just like linking to another Web page, except the sound filename replaces the Web page filename as the value for the href attribute.

For example, if you add the <a> tag and set the href attribute equal to a file called mysound.wav and the user's system recognizes the sound file, then when the user clicks the link, the required audio player application loads and automatically plays the mysound.wav file. If the user's system does not recognize this audio file type, the browser generates a "File Not Found" error.

ADD SOUND FILES AS LINKS ON WEB PAGES

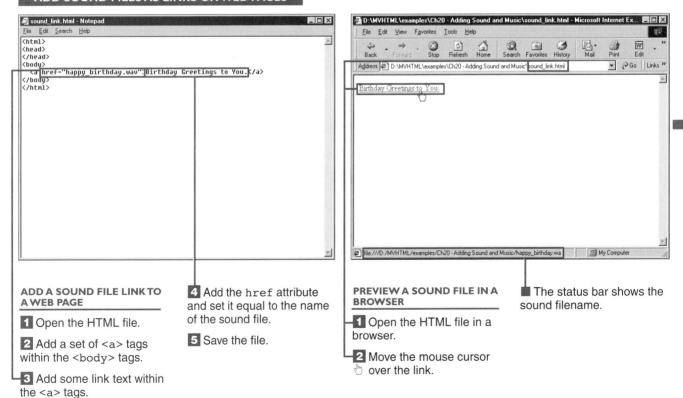

ADD A SOUND FILE LINK TO A WEB PAGE

1 Open the HTML file.

2 Add a set of <a> tags within the <body> tags.

3 Add some link text within the <a> tags.

4 Add the href attribute and set it equal to the name of the sound file.

5 Save the file.

PREVIEW A SOUND FILE IN A BROWSER

1 Open the HTML file in a browser.

2 Move the mouse cursor over the link.

■ The status bar shows the sound filename.

Why does my audio player look different from the one in the figure?

✔ On a default Windows system, the associated audio player for WAV files is the Windows Media Player, but you may have a different application set to play audio files. Many computers ship with complete audio recording, mixing, and editing applications already installed on the hard drive. Common ones include Sonic Forge, Cakewalk Gold, and CoolEdit. Check your Programs folder and see if another audio application is installed.

What happens when a Macintosh user clicks a link to a WAV file?

✔ The default audio application for the Mac OS is QuickTime. This application can play WAV files as well as many other audio formats, including MP3. If the system does not recognize the file type, then the click is ignored or a "File Not Found" error page loads. To prevent this, you can convert the sound file into several different formats and include a link for each format.

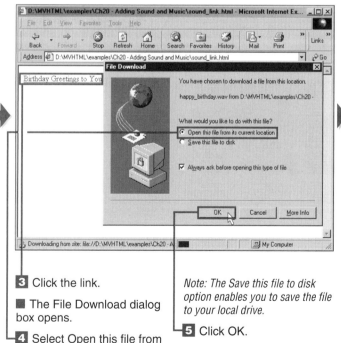

3 Click the link.

■ The File Download dialog box opens.

4 Select Open this file from its current location.

Note: The Save this file to disk option enables you to save the file to your local drive.

5 Click OK.

■ The default audio player loads and automatically plays the sound file.

ADD SOUND FILES AS OBJECTS ON WEB PAGES

A more robust way to add sound files to your Web page than adding links to sound files is to use the <object> tag. This tag includes many more attributes that enable you to control the behavior of the sound file.

The <object> tag loads the sound file immediately without waiting for a user to click a link for the sound file to play. Alternative text

for the object can be placed between the <object> tags. This text displays if the object cannot load.

You can also include nested <object> tags as a way to provide multiple possible solutions. If several nested <object> tags are included, the browser looks at each successive <object> tag and loads the first one that it recognizes.

When using an <object> tag, you can also include <param> tags within the <object> tags. These <param> tags let you specify additional parameter values to the object. See the section "Add Video Files as Objects on Web Pages" for an example of using the <param> tag.

ADD SOUND FILES AS OBJECTS ON WEB PAGES

1 Open the HTML file and add <object> tags.

2 Type **data=** and set the data attribute equal to the sound filename.

3 Type **type=** and set the type attribute equal to the MIME type for the sound format.

4 Add descriptive text between the inner <object> tags.

5 Save the file.

6 Open the file in a browser.

■ The browser displays an area reserved for the object, but because the object is a sound file, the Windows logo is displayed.

Can I resize the sound application icon in the Web page?

✔ When a sound file is loaded on a Windows system using the `<object>` tag, the Media Player icon, shown as the Windows logo on a black background, in the browser is displayed as a 240 x 180 pixel icon. Other audio players may include different sized icons. You can resize this icon by using the width and height attributes. You can also make this icon disappear by setting the width and height attributes to 0.

When is the text inside the innermost `<object>` tag visible?

✔ The alternate text that is placed within the innermost `<object>` tag is displayed in the browser only if none of the specified sound files can be opened. Alternate text is also useful for vision-impaired people over the Internet, or for people running a text-only browser such as Lynx. That way some information is conveyed to all surfers.

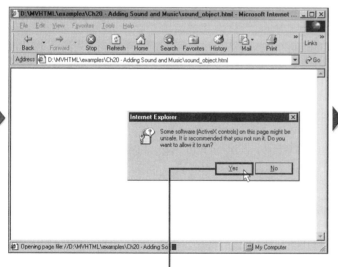

■ The browser then displays a warning message stating that it received a request to load the external application.

Note: This warning is displayed in case the call to load an external application was generated by a virus. If you have any doubts, click No or Cancel.

7 Click Yes.

■ The default audio application loads and automatically plays the sound file.

ADD VIDEO FILES AS LINKS ON WEB PAGES

You can add a link to a video file by using an <a> tag. Including videos on a Web page can add some spice and flare to the site. Videos can also help the user see motion that would not be possible with normal images. Video files, however, can be very large because they include images and audio.

To link to a video file by using the <a> tag, you simply need to set the href attribute to the video filename. Which video format to use depends on the capabilities of the user's computer. When the user clicks the link, the video player associated with the file type loads, if available, and plays the video

file. If the file type is not recognized, the link is ignored or the user sees a "File Not Found" error page.

Common file formats include .ram for RealAudio streaming files, .mov for QuickTime movies, and .asf for Windows Media Player files.

ADD VIDEO FILES AS LINKS ON WEB PAGES

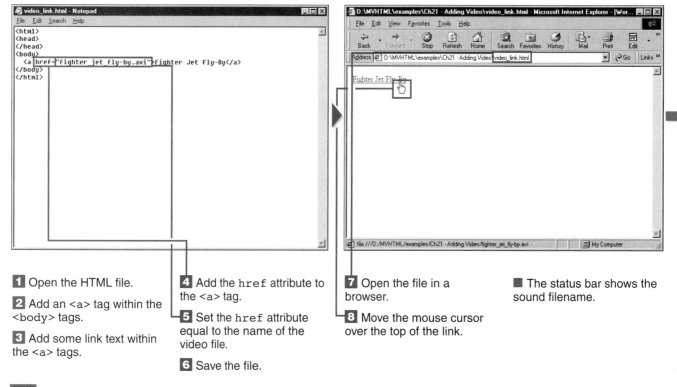

1 Open the HTML file.

2 Add an <a> tag within the <body> tags.

3 Add some link text within the <a> tags.

4 Add the href attribute to the <a> tag.

5 Set the href attribute equal to the name of the video file.

6 Save the file.

7 Open the file in a browser.

8 Move the mouse cursor over the top of the link.

■ The status bar shows the sound filename.

What happens if a Macintosh user clicks a link to an AVI file?

✓ When a browser on a Macintosh computer accesses a link to an AVI file, it tries to load the AVI if the default video player can play this format. If no such video player exists, the browser opens a "File Not Found" error page. Luckily, QuickTime is the default video player, and more-recent versions of the QuickTime Player can load and play AVI files.

What happens if a Windows user clicks a link to a QuickTime file?

✓ If the default Windows video player can play the QuickTime file, the file loads into the player and plays. If the default Windows video player cannot play the QuickTime file, the "File Not Found" error page loads. Recent versions of Windows Media Player can play QuickTime videos.

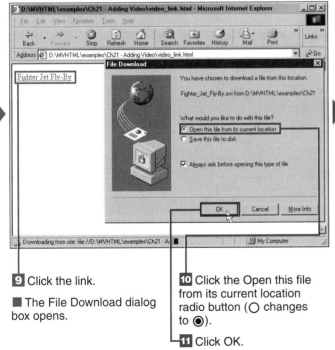

9 Click the link.

■ The File Download dialog box opens.

10 Click the Open this file from its current location radio button (○ changes to ◉).

11 Click OK.

■ The Windows Media Player application loads and automatically plays the video file.

ADD VIDEO FILES AS OBJECTS ON WEB PAGES

In addition to adding video files as links on your Web page, you can also add video files with a set of <object> tags. Using the <object> tag gives Web page designers greater control over the file's appearance and behavior.

The content included within the <object> tags is displayed if the video format is not recognized. This content can be descriptive text or another video format within an <object> tag for the system to try.

The <object> tag includes many attributes that offer control over the video file, such as the width and height attributes for setting video dimensions. The <object> tag can also include align, border, vspace, and hspace attributes. These attributes work the same as those attributes for the <img> tag, discussed in Chapter 3.

The <object> tags can also contain <param> tags that are used to load parameters. One such parameter is the hidden parameter, which hides the video player controls.

To view the video player controls, set the name attribute of the <param> tag to "hidden" and the value attribute to "false." This displays the controls, allowing the user to play, stop, and pause the video.

ADD VIDEO FILES AS OBJECTS ON WEB PAGES

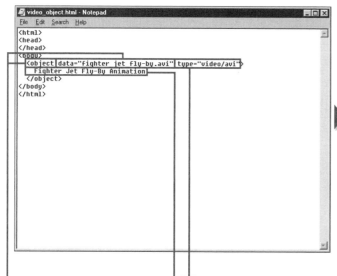

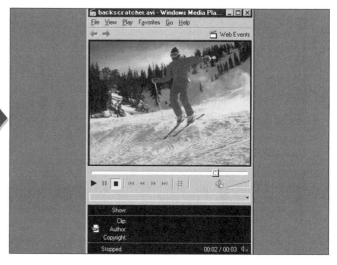

ADD A VIDEO OBJECT TO A WEB PAGE

1 Open the HTML file and add a set of <object> tags.

2 Add a data attribute equal to the video filename.

3 Add a type attribute equal to the MIME type for the video format.

4 Add some descriptive alternate text between the <object> tags.

5 Save the file.

6 Open the file in a browser.

■ The Windows Media Player application loads and automatically plays the video file.

Can I load several different formats of a video file using several <object> tag sets?

✔ In order to support a wide range of systems, you can include several <object> tags within one another. Each <object> tag can specify different video files in different formats. The browser then looks at each <object> tag in order from top to bottom and displays the first format that it recognizes.

Can I include an <img/> tag inside of the <object> tags instead of just plain text?

✔ Any HTML code that is included within the <object> tags is displayed if the specified video file cannot load and play. This code can be descriptive formatted text, an image file, or any other HTML element.

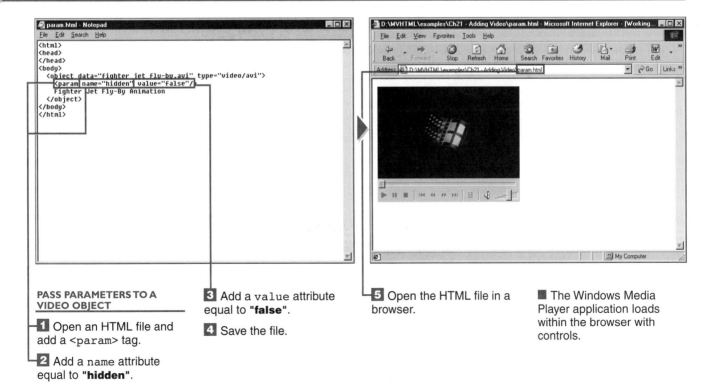

PASS PARAMETERS TO A VIDEO OBJECT

1 Open an HTML file and add a <param> tag.

2 Add a name attribute equal to **"hidden"**.

3 Add a value attribute equal to **"false"**.

4 Save the file.

5 Open the HTML file in a browser.

■ The Windows Media Player application loads within the browser with controls.

INTRODUCTION TO FLASH ANIMATIONS

Flash is an innovative program that enables users to create all kinds of animation effects and interactive features for the Web. Flash 5 is a compilation of tools for drawing and animating graphics, designing interactive elements, and generating the HTML code needed to display such creations on Web pages.

This chapter can give you only an idea of the potential of Flash. For more information on the program, check out *Teach Yourself VISUALLY Flash 5*, by Sherry Kinkoph, or *Teach Yourself VISUALLY Macromedia Web Collection*, both published by Hungry Minds, Inc.

Raster Graphics on the Web

Most graphics on the Web are raster graphics, such as BMPs, JPEGs, and GIFs. A *raster graphic* image contains a mapping of each pixel or picture element. Changing or editing raster graphics without losing some image information is difficult. Raster graphics, due to their size, take longer to display on a Web page.

Vector-Based Graphics

Vector-based graphics, such as those you can create in Flash, are much smaller in file size. They use mathematical equations to describe an image, so only the mathematical information is sent to the client. The information is converted to a raster image on the client's computer and then displayed.

Vector graphics display much faster on a downloading Web page and are a more efficient method of delivering images over the Internet.

Drawing Graphics with Flash

The ability to draw vector-based graphics is one of the reasons Flash is such a popular program. Flash comes with numerous tools you can use to quickly draw scalable artwork ranging from simple objects to complex graphics.

Animate Graphics

Another reason Flash is so widely used is its animation tools. Flash frames let you animate graphics you create with Flash or any other graphic-editing program. You can easily animate graphic objects, buttons, and even text.

Add Sounds

Flash also has controls for adding and manipulating sound files. You can include sound effects or music files with an animation for added pizzazz and interest. You can make your sounds as simple as short sound effect clips or as complex as coordinating background music.

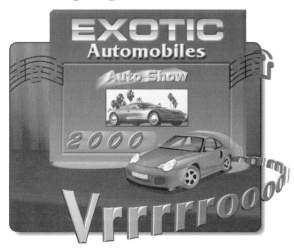

Create Interactive Elements

You can create interactive Web page features by using Flash, such as a button that performs an action as soon as the user moves the mouse pointer over it. You can also use Flash to create interactive elements, such as forms or search engines, or to create complex interactive elements, such as games.

In Flash, anything that causes an action is called an *event.* Flash recognizes three types of events: *mouse events,* or button actions, which occur when a user interacts with a button; *keyboard events,* which occur when a user presses a keyboard key to which an action is assigned; and *frame events,* which are placed in movies to trigger actions at certain points.

Play Movies

Flash has features for playing back movies you create and fine-tuning how the animations display. Flash movies can be played inside Flash itself, or through the Flash Player plug-in program, included with most browsers today.

UNDERSTANDING FLASH DISTRIBUTION METHODS

You can distribute your Flash projects to an audience in several ways, depending on what resources you think may be available to them. For example, you might publish a Flash movie to a Web page. Most computers on the Web have some version of the Flash plug-in installed, so you can be fairly sure your viewers will be able to see your Flash animations.

If you do not want to make the animation public to everyone, you can save it as a QuickTime movie and then send it to another user via e-mail. This is a fairly common tactic when you have training materials or department-specific information and you use Apple's QuickTime player for your audio-video platform.

Lastly, you can deliver the movie as a self-playing file. This is useful for people who may not have Flash on their computer or have a locked-down hardware and software configuration. When you save an animation as a self-playing file, Flash includes a standalone player so no other applications are required.

Start with an Authoring File

When you create content in Flash, you start by creating an *authoring file*. The authoring file is where you draw and animate your movie's content. This file contains all the elements that make up your movie, such as bitmap objects, sounds, symbols, buttons, text, and so on. The authoring file can be quite large in file size. Authoring files use the .fla file extension.

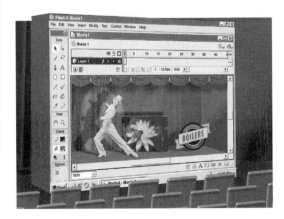

Create an Export File

After you create the authoring file and get it working just the way you want, you can turn it into an export file, an actual Flash movie. The process of exporting or publishing compresses the file contents, making it easier for others to view the file. The resulting file is uneditable, so you cannot change its contents. Flash movie files use the .swf file extension.

Distribute as a Flash Movie

When you distribute a movie as a movie file, Flash assigns it a .swf file format, which requires the Flash Player plug-in to view.

Distribute to a Flash Projector

Another way to distribute your movie is to turn it into a *projector*. A projector is a stand-alone player that runs the movie without the need of another application.

Publish Flash Movies on Web Pages

The Flash Publish feature can help you publish your movies on the Web. It exports your movie as a Flash Player (.swf) file and creates an HTML file that displays the movie in a Web browser. The HTML file includes the tags needed to view the page in both Microsoft Internet Explorer and Netscape Navigator. These tags utilize the browser's built-in Flash Player, meaning the HTML document sets up the browser settings and activates the movie.

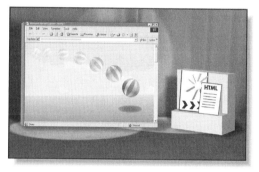

Distribute to Other File Formats

You can export your movies into other file formats, such as QuickTime or Windows AVI. You can even export your movie as a series of GIF or PNG images. Flash can export over a dozen different file formats in both Windows and Mac platforms. When exporting to other file formats, you can choose to export the entire Flash movie as an animated sequence or as still images.

START AND SAVE A FLASH FILE

You can start a new Flash file at any time, even if you are currently working on another file.

As you create movies in Flash, you need to save them in order to work on them again. FLA is the default file format for Flash movies.

Before you begin an animation project, you should draft some type of screenplay or storyboard. A

screenplay is a scene-by-scene description of your animation, while a *storyboard* is a set of hand sketches that tell the story visually. These will give you an idea of how long your animation will run and give you a rough framework of how the animation elements will tie together.

After you have an animation outline, take time to set up the size of your movie and the speed at

which you want it to play. A movie's dimensions refer to its vertical and horizontal size on the Flash Stage. The movie's play speed determines the number of frames per second, or fps, that the animation occurs. Planning out your project in advance saves you time and headaches later.

START A NEW FLASH FILE

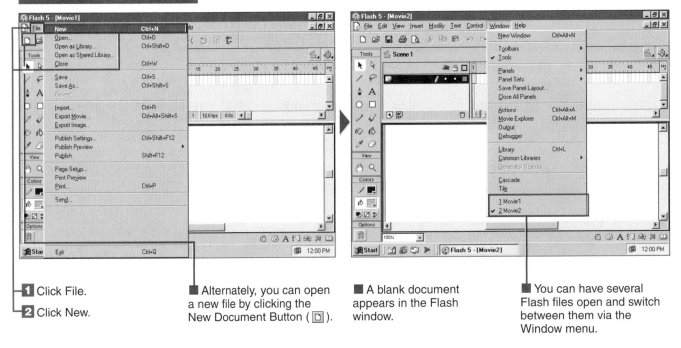

■ Click File.

■ Click New.

■ Alternately, you can open a new file by clicking the New Document Button ( ).

■ A blank document appears in the Flash window.

■ You can have several Flash files open and switch between them via the Window menu.

What is a good frame rate for my movie?

✔ The default frame rate of 12 fps works well for most projects. The maximum rate you should set is 24 fps, unless you are exporting your movie as a QuickTime or Windows AVI video file (which can handle higher rates without consuming computer processor power). If you set a higher frame rate, slower computers struggle to play at such speeds. Most simply cannot, and a very high fps rate slows all but a supercomputer down.

How do I set my frame rate and screen size?

✔ You can easily set your frame rate and screen size. With your animation open in Flash, click Modify, then Movie. The Movie Properties dialog box opens and has text boxes where you can set the frame rate, animation width, and animation height. After you have done this, click OK. The Flash stage adjusts to the new dimensions you assigned.

SAVE A FLASH FILE

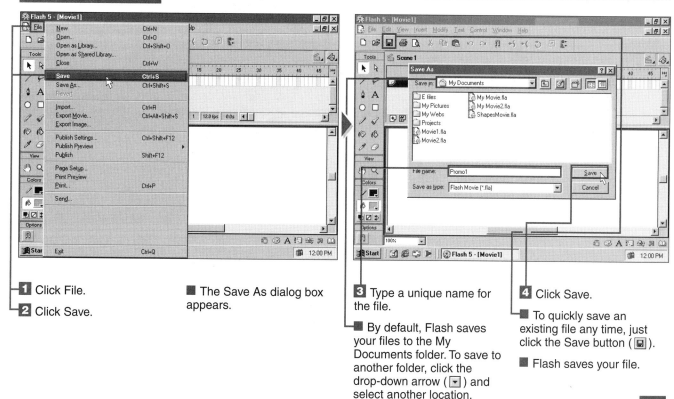

1 Click File.

2 Click Save.

■ The Save As dialog box appears.

3 Type a unique name for the file.

■ By default, Flash saves your files to the My Documents folder. To save to another folder, click the drop-down arrow (▼) and select another location.

4 Click Save.

■ To quickly save an existing file any time, just click the Save button (▣).

■ Flash saves your file.

PUBLISH A FLASH MOVIE

I n order to create a Flash movie, you need to generate the movie by publishing it. Flash generates the necessary files that produce a Flash movie for use in a Flash player, in a Web browser, or as a multimedia object for a Web page. The end result is an export file that is uneditable but is viewable by end users.

If you need to make any changes to your movie, you can not change the published file; you need to go back and edit the Flash file directly, then re-publish the file. This can get repetitive, so it is to your advantage to test your movie first before publishing it.

You use two phases to publish your Flash movie. First you prepare the

files for publishing by using the Publish Settings dialog box, and then you publish the movie by using the Flash Publish command. By default, Flash is set up to publish your movie as an SWF file for the Web, but you can choose to publish in other formats.

PUBLISH A FLASH MOVIE

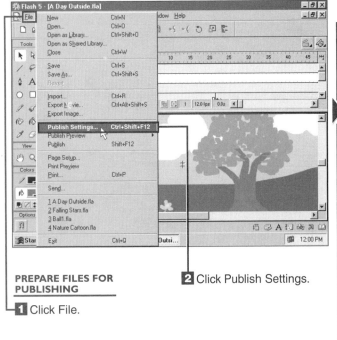

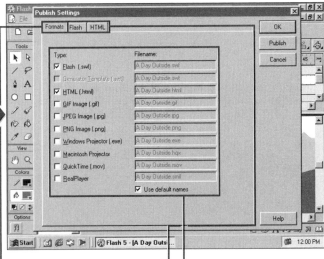

PREPARE FILES FOR PUBLISHING

1 Click File.

2 Click Publish Settings.

■ Flash opens the Publish Settings dialog box.

Note: If you have previously published your file, tabs from your last changes appear in the dialog box.

3 Click Formats.

4 Click the Format option you want to use (☐ changes to ☑).

■ Depending on which format you select, additional tabs appear in the dialog box with options related to that format.

How many other formats should I use when I save my Flash animation?

✓ It depends on the circumstances. Sometimes you need to strike a balance between supporting all possible media formats and conserving space on your file server or bandwidth on your network. For example, you can save your animation in Flash format (.swf) for your initial "rough cuts" or for testing purposes. Then, when you are ready to roll out the final animation, you can save it in other formats, such as QuickTime (.mov) format.

Can I preview a Flash movie before I publish it?

✓ Testing your movie often is a good idea, especially in a browser, to check how it plays. Flash has a feature that lets you preview a movie in a browser window before you publish the movie. To preview a movie, click File, then Publish Preview, and then click Default. Flash opens the movie in your default Web browser.

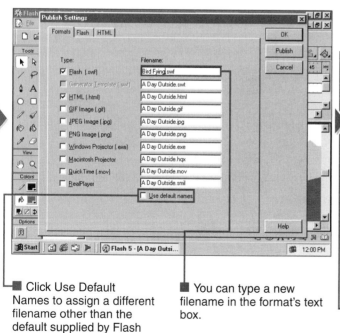

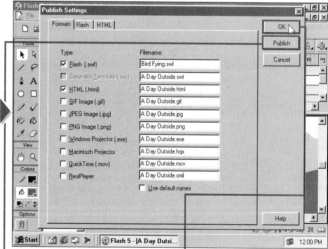

■ Click Use Default Names to assign a different filename other than the default supplied by Flash (☑ changes to ☐).

■ You can type a new filename in the format's text box.

PUBLISH A FLASH MOVIE

5 When you are ready to publish the movie by using the settings you selected, click Publish.

■ Flash generates the necessary files for the movie.

6 Click OK to save the settings and close the Publish Settings dialog box.

Note: If you click Cancel to close the Publish Settings dialog box, Flash will not save the settings you selected.

PUBLISH A FLASH MOVIE IN HTML FORMAT

Y ou can save a Flash movie in HTML format. In response, Flash creates an HTML page that displays your movie along with the SWF movie file. Flash generates all the necessary HTML code for you, including the tags needed to view your page in both Microsoft Internet Explorer and Netscape Navigator. You can then upload the HTML document, along with the Flash movie, to your Web server.

See Chapter 23 for information on editing HTML.

After the page is generated, you can either edit the Web page with another program to add buttons, graphics, and other interactive goodies, or you can copy the Flash-generated HTML and paste it into an existing Web page. The choice is purely up to you. See Chapter 24 for information on using

Dreamweaver to create multimedia Web pages.

No matter which method you use, remember to copy the Flash movie along with your HTML page to the new directory. That way, you can test your Web page's links and test your animations before deploying the final product to a Web server.

PUBLISH A FLASH MOVIE IN HTML FORMAT

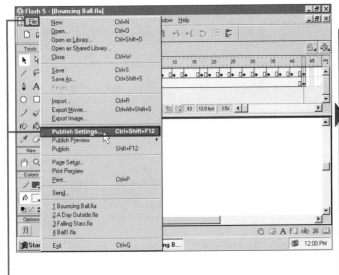

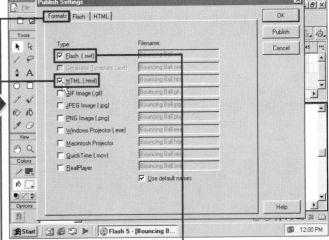

■ 1 Click File.

■ 2 Click Publish Settings.

■ Flash opens the Publish Settings dialog box.

Note: If you have previously published your file, tabs from your last changes appear in the dialog box.

■ 3 Click Formats.

■ 4 Click HTML.

■ Flash automatically selects the Flash format (.swf) for you.

Note: The Flash and HTML formats are selected by default the first time you use the Publish Settings dialog box. See "Publish a Flash Movie" to find out more about publishing Flash movies.

What HTML tags does Flash insert into the HTML document?

✔ The Publish feature inserts the tags necessary for playing a Flash movie file in the browser window, including the <object> tag needed for Microsoft's Internet Explorer browser and the <embed> tag needed for Netscape's Navigator browser. Flash also inserts the <img> tag for displaying the movie file in another format, such as animated GIF or JPEG. The <object>, <embed>, and <img> tags create the movie display window used to play the Flash movie.

Can I just build an HTML page with the <img>, <embed>, and <object> tags myself?

✔ You can, but that is useful only for a quick Web page mock-up. When you publish a file as HTML, Flash also generates the necessary JavaScript that checks to see if the Flash plug-in is installed. You can go into the page and fine-tune the HTML yourself, but for many people, all the necessary code is neatly created for them by using this option.

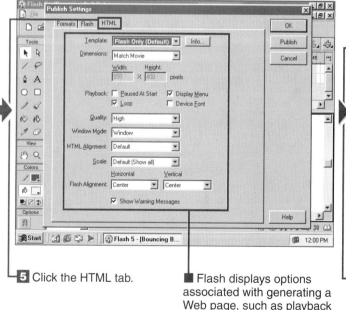

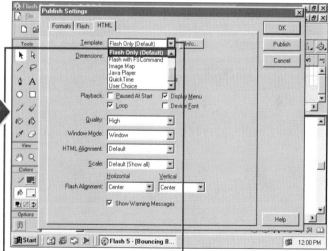

5 Click the HTML tab.

■ Flash displays options associated with generating a Web page, such as playback options and movie dimensions.

6 Select any options you want to apply.

■ The default Flash Only template allows other Flash users to view your movie. Those without the Flash plug-in cannot view the movie.

■ Click the Template box drop-down arrow (▼) and select another template from the list.

CONTINUED

PUBLISH A FLASH MOVIE IN HTML FORMAT (CONTINUED)

Y ou can use the options in the Publish Settings dialog box to specify exactly how you want your movie to appear in the browser window. You can set alignment, dimensions, and even playback options. You can set the movie to play immediately on loading or to pause first, to loop indefinitely, to change the

background color, or even show the Flash playback controls. Any changes you make to the settings override any previous settings for the file.

If you make any changes to these settings, preview your Flash movie first before publishing it and deploying it to a Web server. You need to strike a balance between

download size and movie quality, and the best way to do this is by previewing your movie first.

To learn how to preview a Flash movie, see the tip in the section "Publish a Flash Movie."

PUBLISH A FLASH MOVIE IN HTML FORMAT (CONTINUED)

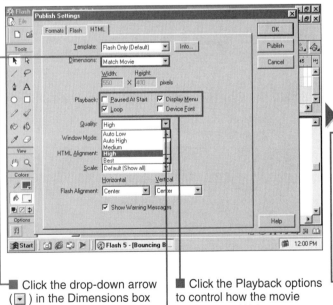

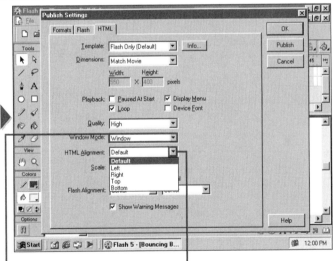

■ Click the drop-down arrow (▼) in the Dimensions box to set width and height attribute values for the movie-display window—the area where the Flash plug-in plays the movie.

■ Click the Playback options to control how the movie plays on the Web page (☐ changes to ☑).

■ Click the Quality box drop-down arrow to view options for controlling the image quality during playback.

■ Click the Window Mode box drop-down arrow and select options for playing your movie on a regular, opaque, or transparent background (Windows browsers only).

■ Click the HTML Alignment box drop-down arrow and change the alignment of your movie as it relates to other Web page elements.

How do I make my movie full-size in the browser window?

✔ To make your Flash movie appear full-screen size in the browser window, click the Dimensions box drop-down arrow (see the first figure on this two-page spread) and select Percent. All you have to do then is type 100 as the values in the Width and Height text boxes.

My users say they cannot see the movie. What happened?

✔ Flash defaults the Publish Settings dialog box to "Flash Only (default)." Try changing the setting to another template type, and then republish your movie. You can also try publishing the file in a different format, such as QuickTime. See the next section for details.

They still cannot see the movie!

✔ You may need to add the correct MIME type to your Web server so it knows how to handle requests for Flash movies. See your Flash online help for more information about MIME types, or talk to your Web server administrator about adding the Flash MIME type to the server.

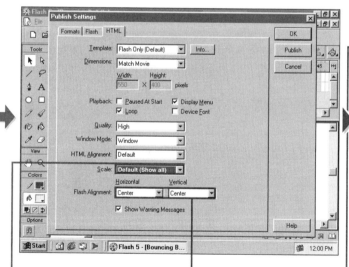

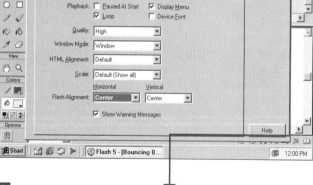

■ If you choose to set new dimensions for the movie, you can click the Scale box drop-down arrow to rescale movie elements to fit the new size.

■ Click the drop-down arrow in the Flash Alignment control boxes and designate how the movie aligns in the movie window area.

-7 When you are ready to publish the movie by using the settings you selected, click the Publish button.

■ Flash generates the necessary files for the HTML document.

8 Click OK to save the settings and close the Publish Settings dialog box.

Note: If you click Cancel to close the Publish Settings dialog box, Flash will not save the settings you selected.

EXPORT A FLASH MOVIE TO ANOTHER FORMAT

You can easily export a Flash movie into another file format for use with other applications.

For example, you might save your movie as a Windows AVI file or as a QuickTime file. These are commonly available multimedia viewers that your users may have installed instead of the Flash plug-in.

This is an incredibly helpful option that you can take full advantage of when creating multimedia for your Web pages. By providing multiple playback formats you make it easier for users to see your animations without requiring them to download a plug-in or helper application from another Web site.

The downside to providing these other formats is that you will take

up much more Web space with the multiple versions, and you will need to regenerate all the download formats if you ever update or change your animation. In addition, you will need to think about bandwidth concerns as multiple requests for multiple file types hit your Web server.

EXPORT A FLASH MOVIE TO ANOTHER FORMAT

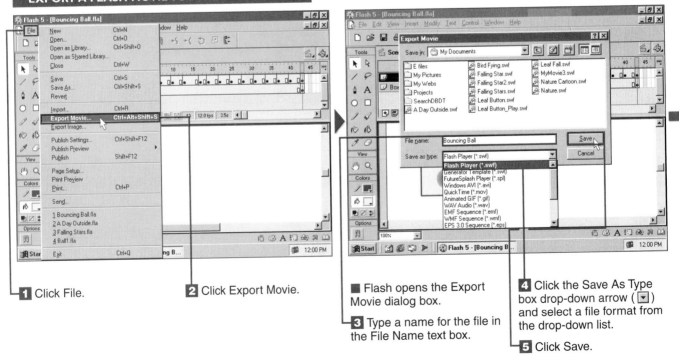

1 Click File.

2 Click Export Movie.

■ Flash opens the Export Movie dialog box.

3 Type a name for the file in the File Name text box.

4 Click the Save As Type box drop-down arrow (▼) and select a file format from the drop-down list.

5 Click Save.

What is the difference between publishing a movie and exporting a movie?

✔ When you publish a movie, you can publish to Flash (SWF), QuickTime, and RealPlayer formats, as well as some static formats, such as GIF. When you export a movie, you can save the file in over a dozen different file formats, such as Windows AVI or animated GIF.

Are there any reasons to prefer publishing a movie to exporting it?

✔ Some of the formats and options are the same between publishing a movie and exporting it, but when you publish a movie as opposed to exporting it, Flash saves information about the movie's Publish settings along with the movie file. When you export a movie, you are saving it to a single format. It is quicker to publish a movie in several formats at once than to export a movie to a single format several times.

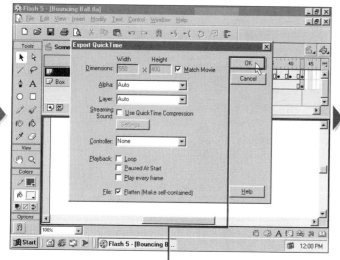

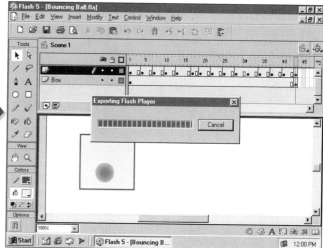

■ Depending on the file type you selected, an additional Export dialog box opens with options for size, sound, and video format.

■ You can make any selections necessary.

6 Click OK.

■ Flash exports the movie to the designated file type.

Note: Interactive elements you include in your Flash movies might not export to other file formats properly.

■ Depending on the file type, another dialog box, such as the Video Compression dialog box, may open first. Make any selections necessary, and click OK to continue exporting the file.

INTRODUCTION TO JAVA APPLETS

*J*ava applets are small programs that can run within a browser. These small programs are written by using the Java programming language, which is a robust language similar in many ways to C++, but Java includes many unique capabilities that make it ideal for writing programs that run on the Web.

This chapter can give you only an idea of the potential of Java. For more information on the language, check out *Java: Your visual blueprint for building portable Java programs,* by Dr. Ernest Friedman-Hill (published by Hungry Minds, Inc.).

Understanding Java's Benefits

One of the traits that makes Java suitable for the Web is its portability. Java programs can be written once and run on multiple different platforms. On the Web, where many different computers are all networked together, Java enables a computer to run the program whether it is a Windows, Macintosh, or UNIX machine.

Java is also *object-oriented,* a programming paradigm that enables a single program to be broken up into smaller pieces. The pieces that are common between multiple programs can be reused rather than being rewritten, which saves programmers time because they can build and use standard libraries of functions that can be reused in a variety of ways.

The way Java is designed it can be used on the Web without causing any problems to a user's system. If a user accesses a Web applet that is designed to destroy the user's computer, the Java system does not permit the program access to the user's system files. This security lets users execute Java programs without fearing that they can destroy their system.

Compiling Java Applets

Just like writing HTML, you can write Java code by using Notepad. Java files have the .java extension. However, you cannot view or run Java files in a browser until you compile them.

Compiling is the process of converting Java files into a class file. *Class files* are streamlined files that only can be interpreted by a system program called the *Java Virtual Machine* (JVM). Class files are identified with the .class extension.

The program that is used to compile Java files can be found within the Java Development Kit (JDK). The latest JDK can be downloaded from the Sun Microsystems Java site at www.javasoft.com. After you download the JDK, you must install it to your computer. After the installation finishes, you can compile your Java programs.

The compiler examines the Java file for errors before producing a class file. If any errors exist in the Java file, an error is reported. When all errors are eliminated from the Java file, a class file is generated.

Embedding Java Applets

Java applets can be embedded within a Web page by using the `<object>` tag. This tag points to a Java class file. When the browser encounters an embedded Java applet, the Java Virtual Machine is loaded into memory, and the applet is run within the browser.

The `<object>` tag includes several attributes that can be used to change the dimensions and alignment of the applet.

Running Java Applets

You do not need to install the Java Development Kit on every computer in order to run Java applets. Instead, end users need only a Java Virtual Machine installed on their system. Sun distributes a runtime version of the JVM, called the Java Runtime Engine (JRE), that users can install on their machines and run Java applets. In addition, most recent versions of Microsoft Windows have Microsoft's version of a JRE called the Microsoft Virtual Machine (VM). The VM allows Windows users to run Java applets without requiring them to download and install a JVM.

CREATE A JAVA APPLET

Java is a complex programming language that can generate small applets for Web pages as well as full-blown commercial applications. You can write Java programs using a standard text editor, such as Notepad. All you need are the Java development kit and a text editor, and you are ready to start writing code.

Java code begins with import statements at the top of the code that allow access to specific Java libraries. These libraries include functions that are used within the code. For example, the AWT library includes functions like drawString, which is used to display text to the applet.

The simplest Java programs consist of the definition of a single *class*, the smallest independent unit of Java source code, consisting of the class keyword and a pair of curly braces. Preceding the class keyword with public declares the class to be public.

After you enter the code, save the file with the .java extension. This helps you to identify the file as Java code to the compiler.

CREATE A JAVA APPLET

```
import java.awt.*;
import java.util.*;
```

```
import java.awt.*;
import java.util.*;

public class test extends java.applet.Applet {

}
```

1 Open a new file in Notepad and enter two import keywords.

2 Type the import library to import after each import keyword.

3 Add a semicolon (;) to the end of each import statement.

4 Save the file.

5 Open the file in Notepad.

6 Add a public class name that extends the java.applet.Applet class.

7 After the class name definition, add opening and closing brackets.

8 Save the file.

Which Java development environments are available?

✔ Many Java-based development environments are available. Sun Microsystems makes Forte for Java, Microsoft makes Visual J++, Borland has a product called JBuilder, and Symantec's product is called Visual Café. You can find demo versions of these products at the respective company Web sites. All of them provide you with tools to manage projects, compile, and debug applets and applications, and have extensive online help and Java language references. If you want to get serious about Java, you should look into getting one of these environments.

Is there a good reference available that can help get me started with Java?

✔ Java is an exciting, powerful language, and you can do a lot with it for nearly any application you can imagine. For more information on the language, check out *Java: Your visual blueprint for building portable Java programs*, by Dr. Ernest Friedman-Hill (published by Hungry Minds, Inc.).

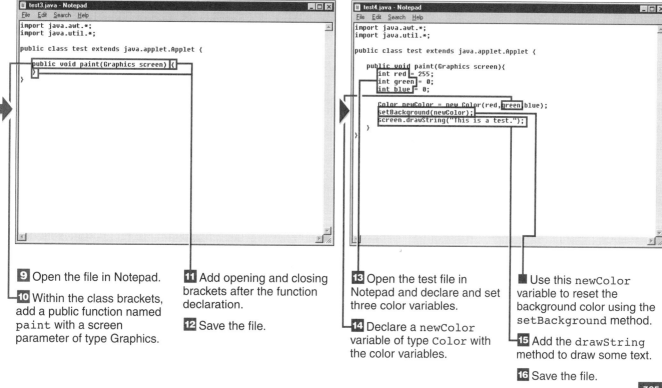

9 Open the file in Notepad.

10 Within the class brackets, add a public function named `paint` with a screen parameter of type Graphics.

11 Add opening and closing brackets after the function declaration.

12 Save the file.

13 Open the test file in Notepad and declare and set three color variables.

14 Declare a `newColor` variable of type `Color` with the color variables.

■ Use this `newColor` variable to reset the background color using the `setBackground` method.

15 Add the `drawString` method to draw some text.

16 Save the file.

COMPILE JAVA CODE

After you write some Java code, you need to compile the code into a class file. Compiling the code produces a small portable class file that can be executed within a browser.

A JDK program called javac.exe compiles the Java code. You can find it in the \bin directory under the main directory where you installed the JDK.

The compiler command can be run from a command line like the DOS window. To compile, you need to type the javac.exe command followed by the name of the Java file you want to compile.

If the Java file has any errors, the compiler recognizes them and displays an error message. If the Java file does not have any errors, the compiled class file is created with the same name as the Java file. You can then distribute the compiled class file to anyone with a Java virtual machine, and they can run your program.

COMPILE JAVA CODE

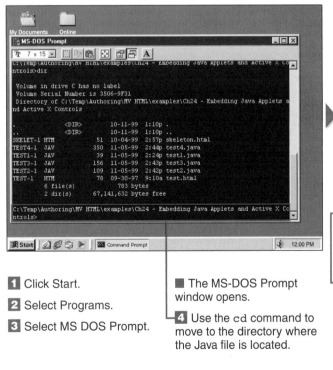

1 Click Start.

2 Select Programs.

3 Select MS DOS Prompt.

■ The MS-DOS Prompt window opens.

4 Use the cd command to move to the directory where the Java file is located.

5 Type the compile directive, **javac.exe**, starting with its path, which is typically something like c:\jdk1.2.2\bin\ javac.exe.

6 Type the name of the Java file.

How can I fix a Java program that has errors?

✔ If an error message appears while you compile a Java file, you see the line and place where the error occurred. It also gives you a brief error message that helps you identify the problem. From this information, you can return to the Java file, correct the error, resave the file, and then try to compile it again. The class file cannot be created until you remove all errors.

If the Java file compiles without any errors, does a message appear stating that the compile was successful?

✔ If a Java file is successfully compiled by using the JDK, no message is displayed, which can be confusing. If you view the directory, however, you may notice that the class file has been created and does actually exist.

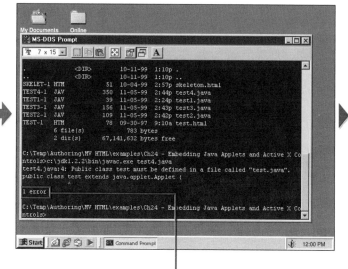

7 Press Enter.

■ The compiler generates a class file. If an error exists in the Java file, the error will be displayed.

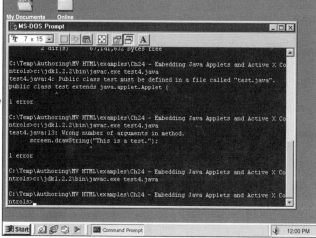

■ If the file successfully compiles, the compiler creates the class file in the same directory as the Java file.

EMBED AN APPLET IN A WEB PAGE

C lass files can be embedded in a Web page and executed within a browser. To do this, you need to use <object> tags in your Web page.

Within the opening <object> tag, include the classid and codetype attributes. The classid is set to the keyword java: followed by the class file name. The codetype defines the MIME type to the browser. For Java

files, the MIME type is set to application/octet-stream.

The <object> tags can also include other attributes like width and height to set the applet dimensions and the align attribute to align the applet to the left or right margin.

If the applet class file exists in a subdirectory, you can use the codebase attribute to indicate the

name of the subdirectory. For example, <object codebase= "classes/myJava.class" would embed the class file name myJava.class in the classes subdirectory.

In this example, you add the necessary <object> attributes to an HTML file so your applet will run, and you set the applet's alignment attributes.

EMBED AN APPLET IN A WEB PAGE

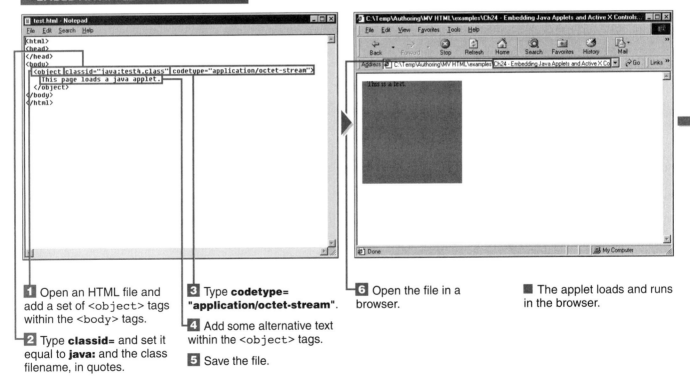

1 Open an HTML file and add a set of <object> tags within the <body> tags.

2 Type **classid=** and set it equal to **java:** and the class filename, in quotes.

3 Type **codetype= "application/octet-stream"**.

4 Add some alternative text within the <object> tags.

5 Save the file.

6 Open the file in a browser.

■ The applet loads and runs in the browser.

Can I use applets without writing the Java code?

✔ You need the .java files only to compile the .class files. If you have the class file, you do not need the source files unless you want to make changes to the applet. Many Java applet repositories on the Web let you use precompiled Java applets. To embed files obtained from these repositories, you do not need to download the JDK and compile the code; simply embed the applet, as shown in this task.

Can I determine if an object in the browser is an applet?

✔ If you move the mouse pointer over the top of an applet in the browser, the Status Bar at the bottom of the browser displays the message "Applet Started." This message can be used to help identify applets embedded within the Web page.

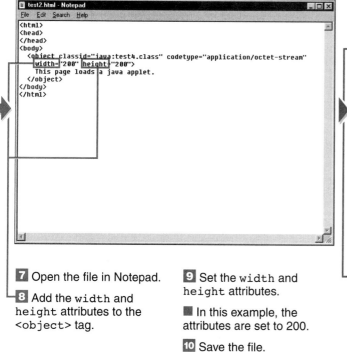

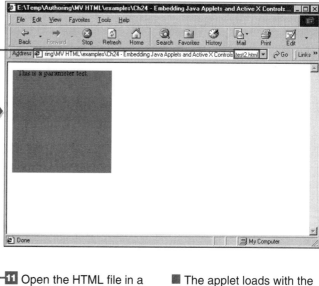

7 Open the file in Notepad.

8 Add the `width` and `height` attributes to the `<object>` tag.

9 Set the `width` and `height` attributes.

■ In this example, the attributes are set to 200.

10 Save the file.

11 Open the HTML file in a browser.

■ The applet loads with the new dimensions.

CHANGE APPLET PARAMETERS

You can make Java applets that include variables and that can be modified within the Web page file by using applet parameters. If a Java applet is coded correctly, you can specify applet parameter values within the Web page file that can affect the output of the applet.

These parameter values are sent to the applet from the HTML file by

using the <param> tag. The <param> tag includes two attributes—name and value. The name attribute is the name of the parameter, and the value is the value that is sent to the applet.

The name attribute needs to match the name of the variable included in the Java code. All parameters sent to the applet as part of the <param> tag are received by the

applet as a string. These strings need to be converted to a number type if you intend to do calculations with them.

In this example, you add parameters to a Web page, and the applet uses those parameters when it runs to modify its output.

CHANGE APPLET PARAMETERS

1 Open the java file.

2 Modify the code to accept a parameter using the getParameter function.

3 Save the file.

4 Enter the command in the DOS window to compile the class file for this code.

Note: See the section "Compile Java Code."

I saw a great applet that rotates banner ads on a Web site. Do I have to code that type of applet myself?

✔ You do not have to spend your time reinventing the wheel. Because there are a lot of Java developers out there, and a lot of Web sites, you can find applet repositories that contain pre-written applets (both source code and compiled form) that you can use or modify for your Web site. One handy site is http://java.sun.com/openstudio/; another is www.javafile.com/; a third is www.thefreesite.com/Free_Java_JavaScript/.

What is the benefit of using the <param> tag?

✔ Using the <param> tag, you can control the applet using parameters that are sent from the Web page. This functionality does not require the Java class to be recompiled for a subtle change. For example, if you send a color as a parameter, the applet can be programmed to use the color parameter as the background color. If you want to change the background color, you need only to change the value in the <param> tag instead of the entire Java class file.

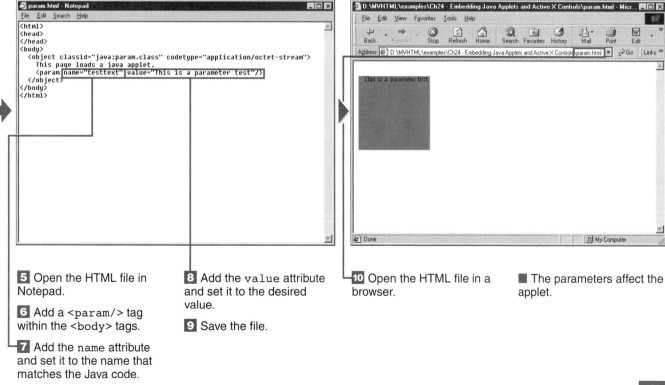

5 Open the HTML file in Notepad.

6 Add a <param/> tag within the <body> tags.

7 Add the name attribute and set it to the name that matches the Java code.

8 Add the value attribute and set it to the desired value.

9 Save the file.

10 Open the HTML file in a browser.

■ The parameters affect the applet.

AN INTRODUCTION TO SMIL

Synchronized Multimedia Integration Language (SMIL), pronounced "smile," is a standard for streaming multimedia across the Internet in a coordinated fashion. It enables multiple data streams to be broadcast and then coordinated at the desktop, and it can define the presentation space for images, text, multimedia players, animations, and interactive components.

The advantages of SMIL are numerous. You can have multimedia clips reside anywhere in the world, not just on a single server or at a single site. You can have different streaming language tracks available, whether for audio, text, or video, and can automatically provide the correct one based on a user's local language settings. You can automatically select a bandwidth for a presentation, rather than force users to choose one by guessing. You can control the layout so that information is presented cleanly, not with overlapping windows or confusing relationships between components.

SMIL revolves around the concept of a timeline. SMIL uses a timeline to determine which resources become available during a presentation and coordinates the requests to the appropriate entities.

This enables the creation of "rich media," much like a television broadcast, but can include links to external sources, the ability to pause some or all of the presentation or to click links to get additional information in real time, and so on.

Although SMIL is relatively new, there has not been an explosion in the area of rich media applications. But with the rapid growth of broadband connections to homes and businesses, the demand for multimedia presentations, long-distance education, and "Internet TV" applications are expected to grow dramatically.

W3C

The World Wide Web Consortium (W3C) is the formal approving body for the SMIL specification and for all things related to the Internet. You can find the SMIL 1 and 2 specifications at the W3C's Web site, along with links to people active in the SMIL organization, industry news, product links, and tutorials. Visit www.w3.org/AudioVideo/ for more information.

Real.com

Real.com is one of the first industry giants to get fully behind the SMIL specification. You can view the RealSystem Production Guide, which discusses SMIL and how it is used with Real products, at http://service.real.com/help/library/guides/production/realpgd.htm. The Web site also has a RealSystem authoring kit that contains documentation and utilities for creating SMIL applications that can be streamed using the RealSystem.

CWI

CWI (Centrum voor Wiskunde en Informatica) is a Netherlands-based site that has plenty of links to other SMIL sites, including the GRiNS client. Visit www.cwi.nl/~media/SMIL/ for more information.

THE ANATOMY OF A SMIL DOCUMENT

A SMIL document is a text document in an XML format, complete with its own tags and sets of DTDs (document type definition) that are used to validate the document and its elements. If you are familiar with XHTML or XML, you will quickly notice similarities between the formats.

As a standard, SMIL has some support on the Internet: Real.com's RealPlayer 8 and Apple's QuickTime 4.1 clients support Version 1, Microsoft Internet Explorer 5.5 supports several parts of Version 2, and GRiNS from Oratrix is a third-party client and development platform for both the Version 1 and 2 specifications.

More client support is expected as it becomes easier to both create rich media presentations and to stream them over broadband to a client. Some clients already provide Version 2–compatible support.

This example shows a basic SMIL document that could be used for a multimedia presentation over the Internet.

Prolog

Every SMIL document should have a prolog that describes which XML specification and DTD that it adheres to. A prolog is not officially required, but it is considered good form to include one.

DTD and Root Element

The DTD identifies which document provides the validating parameters for the SMIL document and identifies the root element in your document. In all SMIL documents, the root element must be <smil>.

Head

The <head> section and its contents are optional, but are typically present in most SMIL applications.

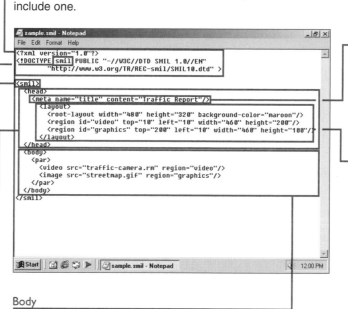

Meta

The meta section behaves similarly to <meta> tags in HTML: It provides identifying information that may be useful outside the application.

Layout

The layout section describes how media can be laid out within a client.

Body

The body section is required and contains information and descriptors for media sources.

CREATE A SMIL DOCUMENT

A pplication designers who want to deliver rich media content to a client create SMIL documents. The SMIL document is sent to the client, which then parses the document and coordinates the various rich media that will be displayed to the end user. Like an HTML page, a SMIL document contains presentation information, URIs (uniform resource identifiers, a

superset of URLs), timing information, and other useful details.

In the example in this section, Microsoft Notepad is used to write the SMIL file. However, you can use more sophisticated tools such as Allaire's HomeSite, which is included on the book's CD-ROM. The Allaire program is a text editor that lets you edit SMIL documents,

tab and untab indented text, and validate your documents against a DTD.

The text format makes it very easy to understand what the elements are and how they are related; and making changes or edits to the SMIL presentation is very simple. The ASCII text is also portable across platforms so you can deploy SMIL applications from any server that supports SMIL.

CREATE A SMIL DOCUMENT

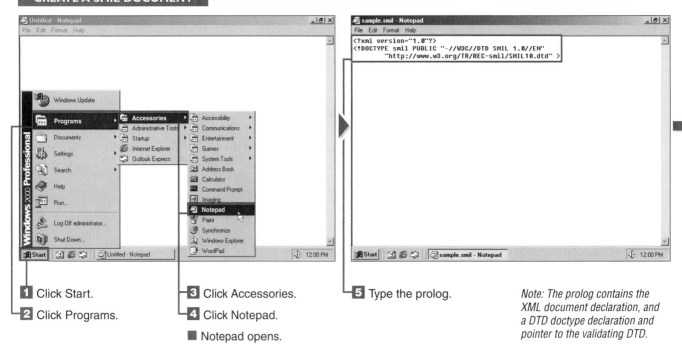

1 Click Start.

2 Click Programs.

3 Click Accessories.

4 Click Notepad.

■ Notepad opens.

5 Type the prolog.

Note: The prolog contains the XML document declaration, and a DTD doctype declaration and pointer to the validating DTD.

Are there any syntax rules that I should follow when creating SMIL documents?

✔ Because SMIL is an XML-based language, you should follow the same rules that you would for any other XML document:

• Use all lowercase in your XML tags.

• XML is case-sensitive, so make sure that your tags agree—mainecoon is not the same as MaineCoon.

• White space is ignored, so indent your elements to make your document more readable.

• Most tags use opening and closing pairs. In some cases, a tag may terminate with a forward slash and not require a closing pair, such as <audio src="rush-hour.rm"/>.

Where can I read more about XML?

✔ Chapter 21 gives an overview of XML. For additional information, pick up a copy of *XML: Your visual blueprint for building expert Web pages* by Emily Vander Veer and Rev Mengle (published by Hungry Minds, Inc.).

Is there a way to add comments to my document?

✔ You can add comments by using a <!-- and --> pair. You can extend the comment over multiple lines if you need to.

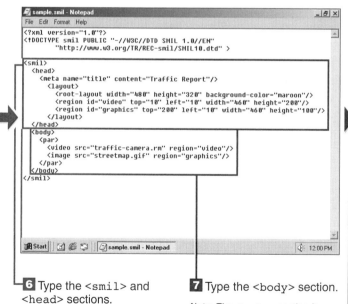

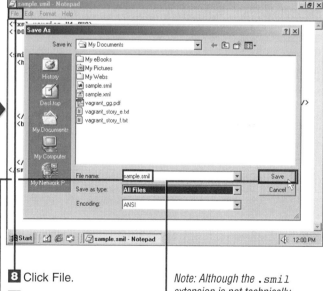

━ **6** Type the <smil> and <head> sections.

Note: The <smil> *section identifies the start of your root element and is required; the* <head> *section identifies layout features and is not required but recommended for most applications.*

7 Type the <body> section.

Note: The <body> *section is required and contains media descriptors for your SMIL components.*

8 Click File.

9 Click Save.

■ If you have not saved your document yet, the Save As dialog box appears.

━ **10** Name your file, including a **.smil** extension.

Note: Although the .smil *extension is not technically required, you should always include it in your filenames to avoid confusion with other document types.*

━ **11** Click Save.

VIEW A SMIL DOCUMENT

A SMIL document can be viewed in just about any editor, whether a text editor or SMIL authoring program. But because SMIL is in itself an XML document, it must meet two criteria:

• **It must be well**-formed. An XML document is well-formed when it meets XML syntax rules, such as using the proper nesting of

elements or having all tags in lowercase.

• **It must be valid.** An XML document is valid if it meets the descriptors found in a DTD document or an XML schema. The descriptors identify what the valid elements are in the document, what the valid attributes are, and in some cases what the valid data types are for an element.

Before deploying your SMIL document, you should run it through an XML parser and validator to ensure that it is well-formed and valid. Microsoft Internet Explorer 5.x ships with an XML parser that checks for the proper form. This parser can also validate a document if a DTD is included.

VIEW A SMIL DOCUMENT

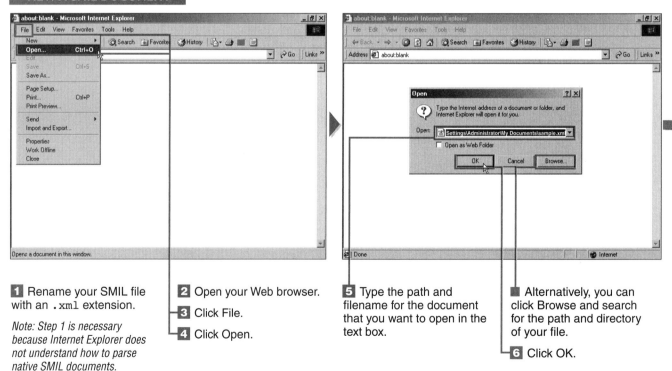

1 Rename your SMIL file with an `.xml` extension.

Note: Step 1 is necessary because Internet Explorer does not understand how to parse native SMIL documents.

2 Open your Web browser.

3 Click File.

4 Click Open.

5 Type the path and filename for the document that you want to open in the text box.

■ Alternatively, you can click Browse and search for the path and directory of your file.

6 Click OK.

Why do I get an error message when I try to view my document?

✔ You can get error messages for a number of reasons:

- The document is not well-formed: Open your document in a text editor (or click View and then Source) and correct the problem. Then try again.

- You do not have the correct DTD specified (such as if you have a typo or just specified the incorrect DTD). Make sure that you have access to the DTD, that it is spelled properly, and that the path is correct.

- You did not rename the file with an .xml extension. Rename the file and try again.

Where can I read more about DTDs?

✔ Chapter 21 gives an overview of XML. For additional information, pick up a copy of XML: *Your visual blueprint for building expert Web pages.*

How do I coordinate several different media types?

✔ You need a client that understands SMIL; plus you need a server and authoring program that lets you generate the appropriate documents, streams, and applications. Check with a SMIL vendor for specifics on how a SMIL server can be set up for your application.

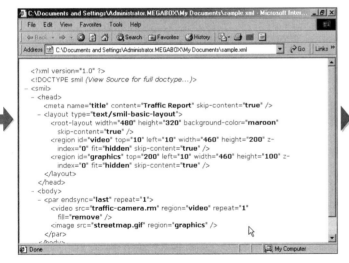

■ The XML file appears in your Web browser.

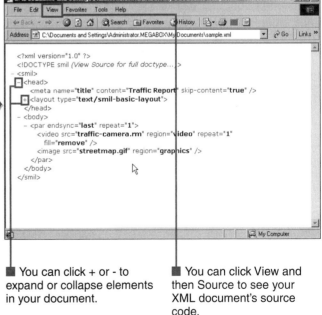

■ You can click + or - to expand or collapse elements in your document.

■ You can click View and then Source to see your XML document's source code.

SECTION VI

AN INTRODUCTION TO WEB SERVERS

Web servers are the workhorses of the Internet. They are the first point of contact between people and information of all kinds. Web servers can be portals to Web applications, database front ends, message boards, e-commerce sites, or just a list of personal pictures and links that you find interesting. Behind the scenes, Web servers are doing all the heavy lifting, making the user experience a positive one.

Web servers at the core are computers that deliver Web pages with varying types of content. But they are not just for static HTML delivery; nearly all Web servers also deliver some type of dynamic content through the use of server-side scripting languages. This powerful capability is what delivers customized stock quotes to investors, shows you the favorites in your sports page, or keeps a list of your past purchases at an online merchant.

A number of server-side scripting languages are available. The choice of which one to use depends on your server, your operating system,

the type of task that you are looking to automate, and your familiarity with the scripting language itself.

Automation runs in two main flavors: one that is interpreted on the server and primarily controls content and another that is interpreted on the client and primarily controls presentation. There are overlaps, of course, and you can frequently use a single language for both purposes.

A perfect example is the difference between Java and JavaScript. Java is a cross-platform, object-oriented language that can run either on a client or on a server and, in today's programming environment, is used primarily to develop Java servlets (applets that run on a server).

Servlets are used to extract and compile data and then present it to another application, such as a Web server, for further processing.

JavaScript is not Java, despite its name. It is a scripting language that is similar to Java but is focused more on presenting data and information or controlling presentation aspects within a browser. DHTML (Dynamic HTML) is one example of how JavaScript is used to control presentation within a browser, as you can use it to change the text color when a mouse cursor moves over the text. JavaScript can also be used to script Java applications; so in a sense, it can be used to control server-side applications as well.

When using a server-side scripting language (or programming language, for that matter), you need to have an engine installed that knows how to parse your script and hand the results off to the server. Java servlets require that a Java Virtual Machine be installed and a servlet engine run within the virtual machine; Perl requires a Perl interpreter; and Microsoft's Active Server Pages requires that the ISAPI (Internet Services API) engine be installed.

STRUCTURE YOUR WEB SITE DIRECTORIES

When you go to set up your Web site directories, you need to keep in mind some general principles:

- Your site structure should mimic your data.
- The site should use names that are easy to figure out.
- You should design your directories with an eye toward breaking it all apart and redoing it within a year.

What this means is that, when you sit down to design what your site will look like on a Web server, you should plan on making it as simple to understand and work with as possible—because you will be reworking it again when some VP announces a merger with another company.

For example, if you work for a news organization with rapidly changing content, it makes sense to have a chronological directory structure, but there are several ways to implement such a structure. The home directory may have subdirectories called News, Sports, Weather, and

Entertainment; each of those may have a year/month/day tree underneath it. Or you may have a year/month/day tree descending from your directory root, with each of the four article categories repeated inside it.

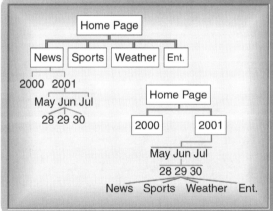

Within these categories, it is generally considered a good idea to have your HTML pages in one directory, graphics and images in another directory, scripts in a third, and miscellaneous Web files (such as style sheets) in a fourth. This makes it easy to assign execute permissions for scripts without extending those permissions to other potentially harmful files. It also makes it easy for you and

other developers to figure out how the site is structured when it comes time to do maintenance. It can be tough to know that `/A239xxA/xyzzy.gif` is a randomly generated picture of the day, whereas `/pic-o-day/jun13.gif` is more sensible and simpler to figure out.

One good way to get ideas on Web site structure is to visit other Web sites and save their Web pages onto your local computer. This way you can sometimes get an idea of how they structure their information storage and retrieval methods.

As your site expands in size, try to think modularly. If you have a company that rapidly grows to have corporate divisions, each with their own Web site needs and styles, consider creating virtual directories for each division. Ideally, you would maintain a similar directory structure across all the divisions, but if this is not realistic, try to make the components for each division as modular and discrete as possible so that they can be reorganized in the future.

CREATE AN FTP VIRTUAL DIRECTORY

N early all Web sites use the File Transfer Protocol (FTP) to transfer project files and HTML pages to Web servers. This may not always be the case; for example, your development team may have direct access to a Web server's file system across your internal network and can simply drag and drop files by using Windows Explorer. But

because this can present its own set of security and stability issues, most development teams use FTP to publish Web pages to a server.

To upload files to your Web server, you need to create an FTP virtual directory for your site that points to your Web site's root directory. A virtual directory is a name that points to a physical directory on

the same server; for example, the virtual directory sailing may actually reside at inetpub\ wwwroot\sailing. This gives you flexibility in being able to point to a directory anywhere on your server, to improve security by requiring a valid username and password, and to hide the physical directory structure from the Internet.

CREATE AN FTP VIRTUAL DIRECTORY

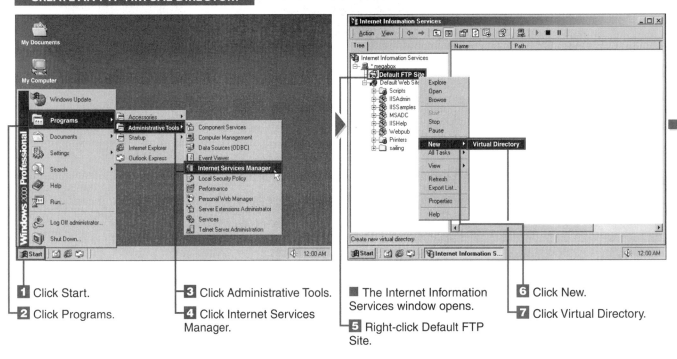

1 Click Start.

2 Click Programs.

3 Click Administrative Tools.

4 Click Internet Services Manager.

■ The Internet Information Services window opens.

5 Right-click Default FTP Site.

6 Click New.

7 Click Virtual Directory.

How do I create an FTP virtual directory on UNIX?

✔ UNIX, Linux, and other variants are systems that were designed from the ground up to be Internet-based machines. They are highly configurable and modifiable, but there are variances between the versions in how they are configured: Some use graphical interfaces; some use command-line editing tools. You should read the online documentation, the HOWTOs, and the man pages for a particular operating system before using it. One very useful Linux HOWTO that covers operating a Web server and FTP daemon is "ISP-Setup-RedHat-HOWTO." You can find it at www.linux.org/docs/ldp/howto/HOWTO-INDEX/howtos.html.

What does the Read permission do?

✔ The Read permission allows file downloads and directory listings. If you are operating behind a firewall and only your development team will have access, the Read permission is probably okay. There are legitimate concerns about having an FTP directory allow both reads and writes open to the public; if you have doubts, turn off the Read permission.

■ The Virtual Directory Creation Wizard appears.

8 Click Next.

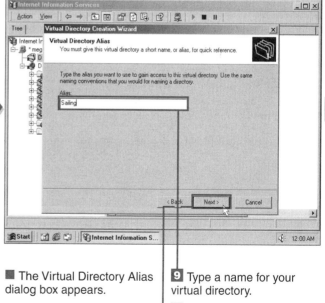

■ The Virtual Directory Alias dialog box appears.

9 Type a name for your virtual directory.

10 Click Next.

CONTINUED

CREATE AN FTP VIRTUAL DIRECTORY (CONTINUED)

You can point different virtual directories to the same directory and set different user access rights or directory permissions as a way of providing security.

For example, you can create a virtual directory with read-only rights. Another virtual directory can point to the same physical directory and

can allow read-write access. You then control access by limiting who can log in to each FTP virtual directory.

Access is a function of two factors: which user belongs to a group and what permissions are set for that group or user. The combination creates an access control list. The Web server and the file system both check to see if the user or group is

permitted access, and if not, access is denied.

Usually, when compiling access control lists, the most restrictive one applies. Troubleshooting often involves detective work to find out whether a user is a member of a group that is denied access.

CREATE AN FTP VIRTUAL DIRECTORY (CONTINUED)

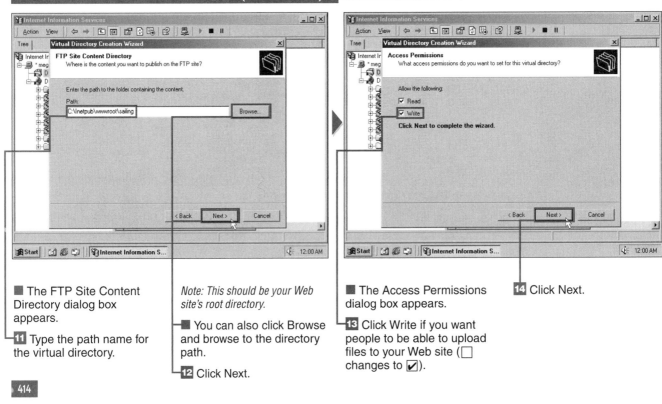

■ The FTP Site Content Directory dialog box appears.

11 Type the path name for the virtual directory.

Note: This should be your Web site's root directory.

■ You can also click Browse and browse to the directory path.

12 Click Next.

■ The Access Permissions dialog box appears.

13 Click Write if you want people to be able to upload files to your Web site (□ changes to ☑).

14 Click Next.

Is deploying all my documents directly to the production server a good idea?

✔ You may want to consider designating a "staging server" for your Web site. This is a server that duplicates the OS, applications, and Web pages that you intend to make public but exists behind the firewall or elsewhere in your network and has developer-only access. After you design a Web site, you can publish it to the staging server for testing instead of publishing it to the production server. This gives you and your team the opportunity to shake out any last-minute bugs, conduct usability tests with end users, and make sure that the site can stand up to load and scalability testing. Then, after you and your team are satisfied that the new Web site meets your requirements for functionality, usability, and performance, you can publish the new Web site from the staging server to the production server.

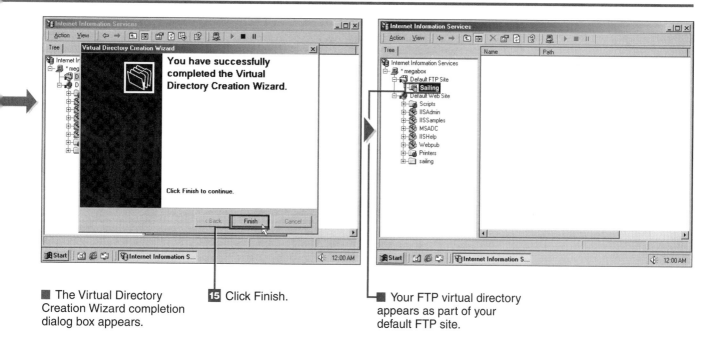

■ The Virtual Directory Creation Wizard completion dialog box appears.

15 Click Finish.

■ Your FTP virtual directory appears as part of your default FTP site.

USING TELNET FOR SERVER ACCESS

Telnet is almost as old as the Internet. Telnet is a program that mimics a dumb terminal across an Internet connection and is a commonly used administration tool for all kinds of network devices, such as Web servers, routers, or other computers. Telnet is most commonly used in the UNIX world but can also be used with Windows NT (with a separate

product installed) and Windows 2000.

Telnet enables users to log on to a server and be presented with a command-line prompt, just as if they were sitting at the machine itself staring at a DOS box or bash shell. Many administrators prefer this method because they have numerous shell scripts that automate administrative tasks, and

they can run these scripts remotely through the Telnet client. Telnet is a very quick, very easy way to gain instant access to a server.

Another great benefit of using Telnet is its low bandwidth. Telnet does not require much bandwidth to send a text stream across the Internet, so Telnet makes an ideal remote client.

USING TELNET FOR SERVER ACCESS

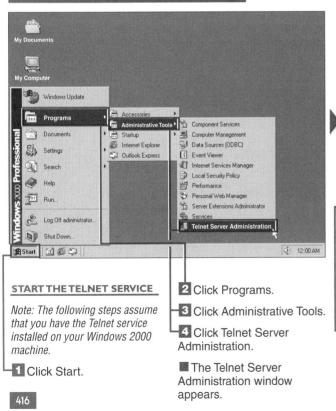

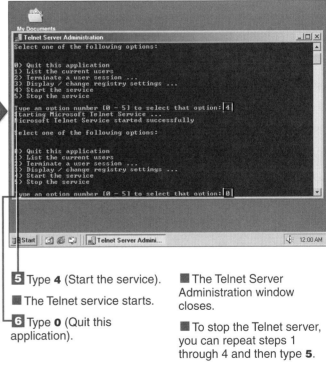

START THE TELNET SERVICE

Note: The following steps assume that you have the Telnet service installed on your Windows 2000 machine.

-1 Click Start.

-2 Click Programs.

-3 Click Administrative Tools.

-4 Click Telnet Server Administration.

■ The Telnet Server Administration window appears.

-5 Type **4** (Start the service).

■ The Telnet service starts.

-6 Type **0** (Quit this application).

■ The Telnet Server Administration window closes.

■ To stop the Telnet server, you can repeat steps 1 through 4 and then type **5**.

Are there alternatives to using Telnet to administer servers?

✔ Nearly all Web servers have native management applications that can be used to control a server. Many of these also work across a network, connecting to a special administration port that you set up. Other Web servers have browser-based interfaces that can work over a regular HTTP connection or over another port that you set up. These can add a layer of protection by encrypting data traffic across a network. See your Web server's help files for more information on these options.

Can I keep the Telnet server running full time?

✔ This presents an interesting dilemma. Telnet is a fast and easy way to get access into a system, which also makes it a huge security risk. Many network attacks begin with Telnet probes of well-known ports as a way of gathering information about a remote system. If you do not have a firewall to filter out Telnet packets to your network, you should not run a Telnet service more than absolutely necessary.

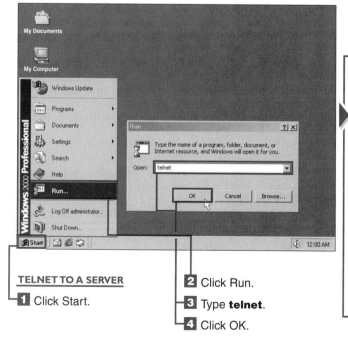

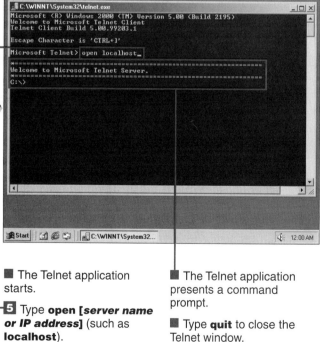

TELNET TO A SERVER

1 Click Start.

2 Click Run.

3 Type **telnet**.

4 Click OK.

■ The Telnet application starts.

5 Type **open [*server name or IP address*]** (such as **localhost**).

■ The Telnet application presents a command prompt.

■ Type **quit** to close the Telnet window.

NAVIGATE DIRECTORIES ON A WEB SERVER

A fter you have Telnetted into a server, you can navigate around the server by using directory commands.

These commands are similar for UNIX and Windows 2000. If you are familiar with navigating in DOS or Windows, you can navigate in UNIX.

However, if you are Telnetting into a server, be aware that default directory structures are very different on UNIX and Windows boxes. If you get lost, take a deep breath and get your bearings. You can always quit and log back in again.

In Windows, the shell prompt, by default, echoes the full directory

path. If it does not, type **cd** and press Enter, and the shell echoes the full path to your location. In UNIX or Linux, the prompt may or may not show you the full directory path. You can type the **pwd** (print working directory) command, and you will get a full directory path to your current location.

NAVIGATE DIRECTORIES ON A WEB SERVER

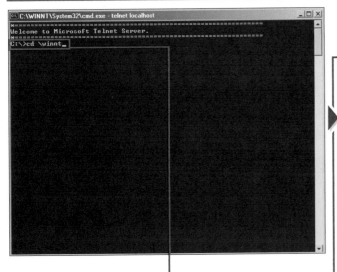

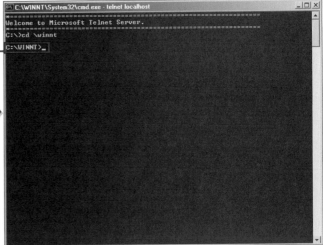

CHANGE DIRECTORIES IN WINDOWS

1 Start the Telnet service as shown in the section "Using Telnet for Server Access."

2 Open a Telnet connection to the server and log in.

3 At the shell prompt, type **cd \winnt** and press Enter.

■ The working directory changes to winnt.

Why do I start off in a directory that has my account name in it?

✔ In UNIX, when you first log in, you start off in your home directory. It is a space uniquely yours, one that you can store files in and return to when you get lost. Because it is so important, UNIX provides a quick way to return to your home directory: Type **cd ~**, and you will jump straight to your home directory. Windows (or DOS, for that matter) does not have this feature.

Do you have a list of the change directory commands?

✔ The list is similar for both Windows and UNIX systems:

cd [directory]	Change to the named child directory.
cd /[path]	Change to the fully named directory, starting from the root.
cd /	Change to the root directory.
cd ..	Change to the parent directory.

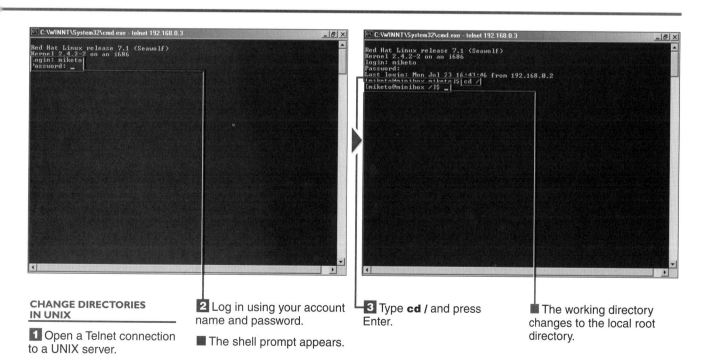

CHANGE DIRECTORIES IN UNIX

1 Open a Telnet connection to a UNIX server.

2 Log in using your account name and password.

■ The shell prompt appears.

3 Type **cd /** and press Enter.

■ The working directory changes to the local root directory.

USING UNIX COMMANDS

For many system administrators, making the jump from Windows-based systems to UNIX is a bit of a shock. Everything that was learned one way has to be relearned another. If you are one of these administrators, do not panic. You only need to learn a few things to be able to move around and work with files as you do in a DOS or Windows shell.

Most UNIX commands are close enough in name to be vaguely familiar, and you should be able to pick up the UNIX commands easily. Perhaps the single biggest difference is that UNIX is case-sensitive, whereas Windows is not. `Mainecoon` is different from `mainecoon`; if you find that a command will not execute or you cannot change a directory, make sure that you have used the correct upper- and lowercase.

If you will be working with UNIX machines on a daily basis, you will want to pick up a reference guide to help you with the command-line options and syntax.

USING UNIX COMMANDS

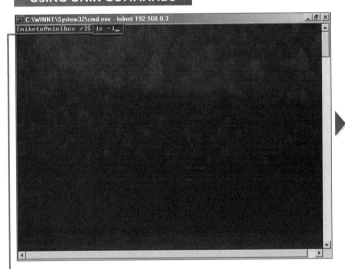

LIST FILES IN A DIRECTORY

1 From a shell prompt, type **ls -l** and press Enter.

■ A file and directory listing appears.

Do you have a list of similar commands between Windows and UNIX?

✔ This is by no means a complete list. For now, this will get you started:

Function	UNIX Command	Windows Command
Copy a file	cp	copy
List files	ls	dir
Remove (delete) files	rm	del
Create a directory	mkdir	md
Remove a directory	rmdir	rd

What does all the information mean in an ls -l listing?

✔ Here is a typical file listing:

```
drwxr-xr-x  3    root    root
    4096 Jun 12 14:55 Private
```

The d signifies a directory; otherwise it is a file. The next nine letters indicate permissions for the owner, group, and other, in that order. Permissions can be read, write, and execute. In this case, the directory can be read and executed by everyone, but only the owner can write to it. The two root indicators are for the owner and the owner's group, respectively. This is followed by file size, last modified date, and, in this case, a directory name.

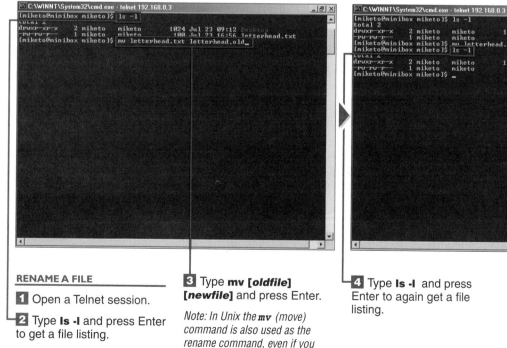

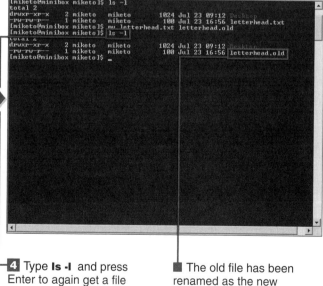

RENAME A FILE

1 Open a Telnet session.

2 Type **ls -l** and press Enter to get a file listing.

3 Type **mv [oldfile] [newfile]** and press Enter.

Note: In Unix the mv (move) command is also used as the rename command, even if you don't change directories.

4 Type **ls -l** and press Enter to again get a file listing.

■ The old file has been renamed as the new filename.

STOP AND START A WEB SERVER

Most Web servers run as automated processes. They start up when a computer is booted, load up the necessary files, and start churning out Web pages.

But the time will come when you need to take down a server for maintenance or need to do some emergency repairs. You need a way to stop and start a server without a hard reboot, which kills every other process running on your server.

In Windows NT and Windows 2000, you have two different ways of remotely controlling the stopping and starting of a service. One way is through the graphical Internet Services Manager. It provides a clear, simple, CD player–like interface for stopping, starting, and pausing a server. You can use it to manage local or remote servers so that you do not have to be at the server to manage it.

The other way is through a command-line interface. The simplest way is to manage the server through a Telnet connection. The only trick is knowing what the service name is.

STOP AND START A WEB SERVER

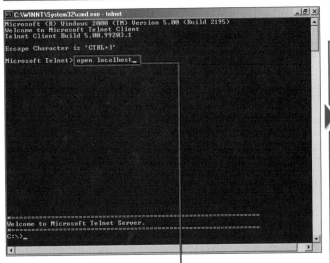

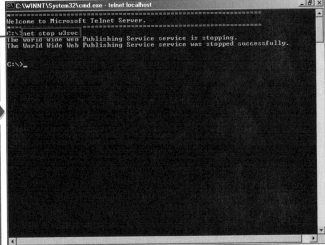

STOP A WINDOWS WEB SERVER

Note: These steps assume that you have the Telnet service running on the local machine.

1 Open a Telnet session.

2 Type **open [servername or IP address]** (such as **localhost**).

■ A Telnet session starts, and you are at the shell command prompt.

3 Type **net stop w3svc** and press Enter.

■ The server stops successfully.

How do I stop and start the Apache service on Linux?

✔ In Apache Version 1.3, a Perl script has been included to make starting and stopping the Apache server simple. If you have `perl_mod` installed, change your directory to `usr/local/apache/bin` and type **apachectrl stop** or **apachectrl start**. This stops or starts your Apache server on Linux. If you have an earlier version of Apache, see the online documentation for using the `kill httpd.pid` command and its options.

How do I stop and start the FTP service on Windows?

✔ Use the same process as for the Web server. At the command prompt, issue the command `net start "ftp publishing service"` including the quotes. For a list of other services that you can start and stop using command-line statements, see the online help topic "Windows 2000 Command Reference Main Page," select N, and browse to the `net start` section.

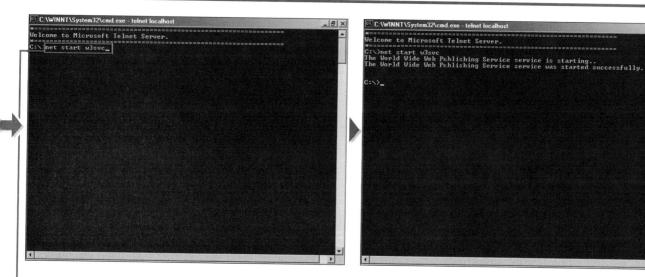

START A WINDOWS WEB SERVER

4 Type **net start w3svc** and press Enter.

■ The server starts successfully.

CREATE A SERVER-SIDE INCLUDE

Server-side includes (SSIs) are instructions to a Web server to automatically generate a Web page and include some text in that page at the time it is requested by a client. Using SSIs is a way of dynamically generating information on a Web page without requiring the server to dynamically generate the entire contents of the page.

Server-side includes are great for placing small, relatively static

amounts of content in a Web page, such as a copyright notice, a Webmaster e-mail address, or a corporate slogan. You need to evaluate how much of your page is static, the nature of the dynamically inserted content, and the traffic volume at your Web site before deciding that SSI will be helpful. For example, if you are generating a large amount of content at the request time, such as

stock quotes, SSI probably will not be an ideal method to use.

A server-side include Web page contains the include directive and ends in .shtml, .shtm, or .stm. Check with your Web server administrator to confirm which file extension is preferred for your server.

CREATE A SERVER-SIDE INCLUDE

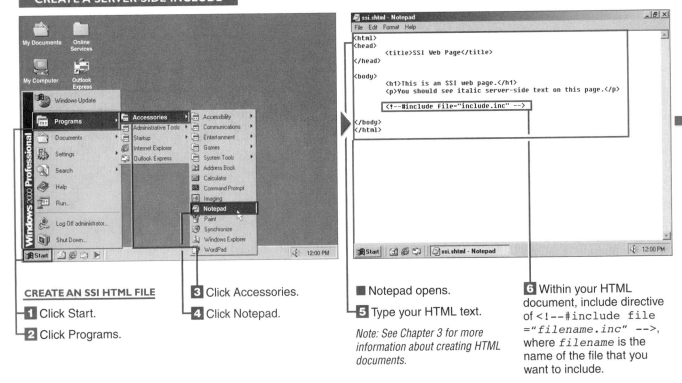

CREATE AN SSI HTML FILE

1 Click Start.

2 Click Programs.

3 Click Accessories.

4 Click Notepad.

■ Notepad opens.

5 Type your HTML text.

Note: See Chapter 3 for more information about creating HTML documents.

6 Within your HTML document, include directive of <!--#include file ="filename.inc" -->, where filename is the name of the file that you want to include.

What is the difference between a specific path and a virtual path to an included file?

✔ A specific path is an actual directory and filename, usually one that is relative to the directory with the include directive document, such as `file="include.inc"`. A virtual path is relative to the Web site. For example, `virtual="/includes/include.inc"`. You can use a URL for the virtual directory, but it should be on the same server as the `.shtml` file.

What should I name my include files?

✔ You can name an include file anything you want to. For clarity's sake, though, you may want to use an `.inc` extension for your included files. This helps you get an idea of the type of content the file contains and how it is used. For example, there is nothing to indicate that "copyright.html" is used elsewhere on your site; but "copyright.inc" indicates the include file may be used on multiple pages and should not be moved or deleted.

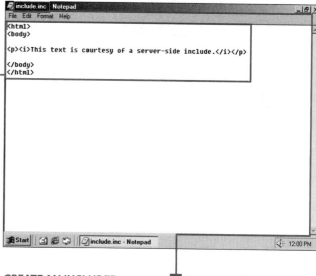

7 Save your file, naming it with an `.shtml`, `.shtm`, or `.stm` extension.

Note: Your server may require that you use specific file extensions. Check with your Web server administrator to see which ones are preferred.

CREATE AN INCLUDED HTML FILE

1 Open Notepad.

2 Type the text that you want in the included file.

3 Save your file with an `.inc` extension, giving it the filename that you specified in step 6.

Note: You do not have to use the .inc extension, but it is common practice to use it for include files.

ADD SSI MIME TYPES TO YOUR SERVER

Before your Web server can begin handing out SHTML pages to a requesting wireless device or browser, you need to edit the server's MIME types. MIME stands for Multipurpose Internet Mail Extensions and is used to identify the different types of information and documents that can be requested over the Internet. Your Web server does not natively know about SHTML documents or how they might be used; you need

to tell it to expect a request for a SHTML document and what extensions are used to identify such a document.

Three MIME types may be used by your application:

The example in this section uses Microsoft Windows 2000 and Internet Information Server (IIS) 5. If you are using other Web servers, consult your server's help files for information on configuring MIME types.

SSI File	MIME Type	Extension
SHTML file	text/html	.shtml
SHTML file	text/html	.shtm
SHTML file	text/html	.stm

ADD SSI MIME TYPES TO YOUR SERVER

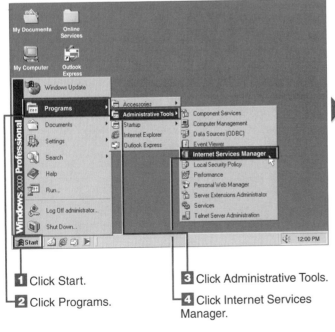

1 Click Start.

2 Click Programs.

3 Click Administrative Tools.

4 Click Internet Services Manager.

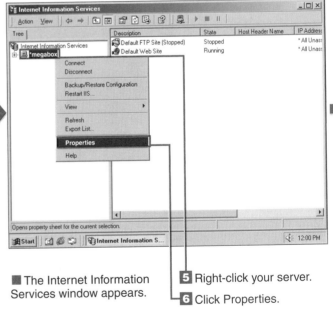

■ The Internet Information Services window appears.

5 Right-click your server.

6 Click Properties.

How do I configure an Apache Web server for SSI MIME Types?

✔ Recent versions of Apache already have a default configuration that supports SHTML MIME types. You can check to see if your server is configured for SHTML:

1. Go to your `/etc/httpd/conf` directory and open your `httpd.conf` file.

2. Check for the following line inside the "Section 1: Global Settings" section for your Web server's root configuration directory (or the directory where you will be serving `.shtml` pages):
   `Options +Includes`. If this line does not appear in the file, add it to the Global Settings ""section.

3. Check for the following lines inside the "Section 2: 'Main' Server Configuration" section, and if they are not present, add them:
   ```
   AddType        text/html      .shtml
   AddHandler     server-parsed  .shtm.
   ```

   You need to add the particular SSI file extension you will be using; if you will be using `.stm` as your file extension, then you would edit the AddType line appropriately. You can have more than SSI extension; make sure you add the appropriate handler for your file type—in this case, .shtm.z

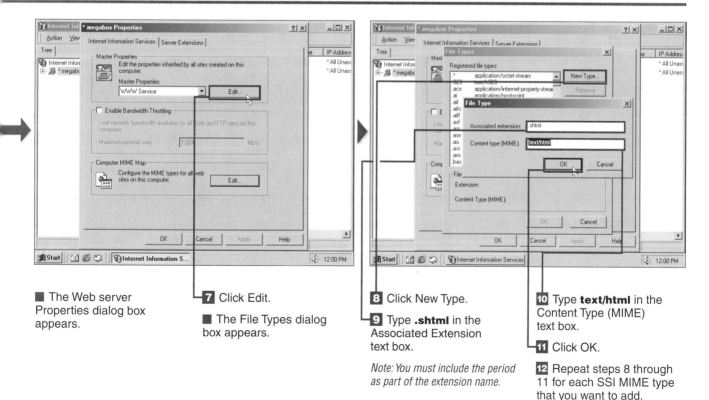

■ The Web server Properties dialog box appears.

7 Click Edit.

■ The File Types dialog box appears.

8 Click New Type.

9 Type **.shtml** in the Associated Extension text box.

Note: You must include the period as part of the extension name.

10 Type **text/html** in the Content Type (MIME) text box.

11 Click OK.

12 Repeat steps 8 through 11 for each SSI MIME type that you want to add.

SET EXECUTE PERMISSIONS

Because server-side includes are processor directives, an SHTML page must either have execute permissions set for it, or it must reside in a directory that has execute permissions set for it. *Execute permissions* allow an application to "run" the code on the server in order to perform a task; in this case, parsing an HTML file and inserting text from an include file. Without these permissions, you will receive an error message when you attempt to view the Web page.

If you are using Microsoft IIS as a Web server, you need to make sure that the virtual directory has scripting permissions set and that the file itself has the appropriate permissions set. When accessing a file through the Web server, the most restrictive permissions go into effect; if you have execute permissions set for a directory but a file is set to read-only, you will receive an error or be presented with an authentication dialog box.

SET EXECUTE PERMISSIONS

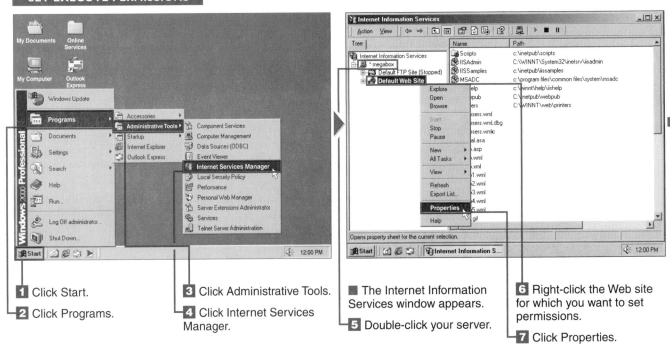

1 Click Start.

2 Click Programs.

3 Click Administrative Tools.

4 Click Internet Services Manager.

■ The Internet Information Services window appears.

5 Double-click your server.

6 Right-click the Web site for which you want to set permissions.

7 Click Properties.

How do I set execute permissions on an Apache Web server?

✔ If you want to control which pages are parsed for server-side includes, you can set the XBitHack option and then individually set execute permissions for specific Web pages. You do this by using the following syntax:

- Add **XBitHack on** to your **httpd.conf** file. For convenience, you should place it in the same section as your root directory (or whichever directory is serving your **.shtml** files).

- To set execute permissions on a file, use **chmod +x ssi.shtml**.

When you set the XBitHack option, you should set permissions on individual HTML files with the include statement and not on an entire Web site or Web directory. That would force Apache to parse all the HTML files on your site or in a directory for include directives. This will slow down your Web site's performance and is not a good idea for high-volume Web sites.

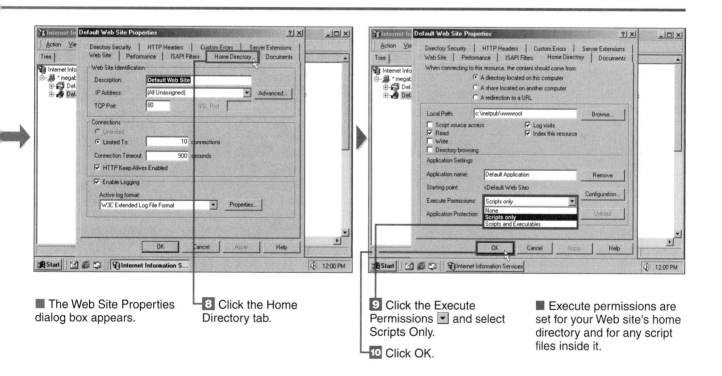

■ The Web Site Properties dialog box appears.

8 Click the Home Directory tab.

9 Click the Execute Permissions ▾ and select Scripts Only.

10 Click OK.

■ Execute permissions are set for your Web site's home directory and for any script files inside it.

VIEW AN SSI WEB PAGE

A Web page with included text is viewed the same way as any other Web page: An HTTP request is sent to the server; the server parses the request, assembles the HTML, and returns it to a browser.

With SSI, the server parses through an HTML document to determine whether any includes are listed. If so, the server dynamically

generates some of the page's content based on the includes, assembles it into the HTML, and returns the modified HTML document to the browser.

It is possible to have fairly complex documents parsed and built using the SSI directives. You can generate custom error pages for applications, execute shell scripts that return values to be displayed, and so on.

But probably the most common use is to have a standard footer on Web pages from a company or to have standardized contact information available (such as a Webmaster's e-mail address). It is up to you how much reliance you want to put on SSI and how much should be developed by using a full-featured server scripting language.

VIEW AN SSI WEB PAGE

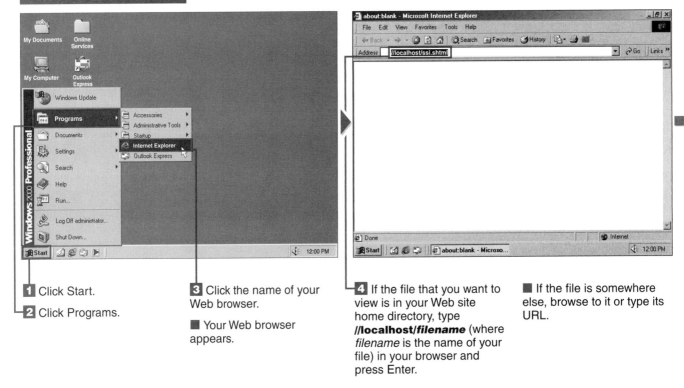

■ Click Start.

■ Click Programs.

■ Click the name of your Web browser.

■ Your Web browser appears.

■ If the file that you want to view is in your Web site home directory, type **//localhost/filename** (where *filename* is the name of your file) in your browser and press Enter.

■ If the file is somewhere else, browse to it or type its URL.

What other types of SSI directives are there?

✔ You can use several basic types of include directives on Web pages:

`#include`	Includes a file in a Web page.
`#exec`	Executes a script or shell program. (`#exec` can pose a security risk.)
`#echo`	Inserts an environment variable into a Web page.
`#flastmod`	Inserts the date and time that a file was last modified.
`#fsize`	Inserts a file size into a Web page.
`#config`	Configures the format of dates, file sizes, and so on.

On Apache servers, you can use more-advanced includes, such as setting variables and conditional logic (`if`/`elif`/`else` statements). This allows you to create complex scripting, such as presenting different text to users depending on what type and version of a Web browser they are using. For more complex dynamically generated pages, you should consider using a server-side scripting language, such as Java, Perl, PHP, Python, or VBScript.

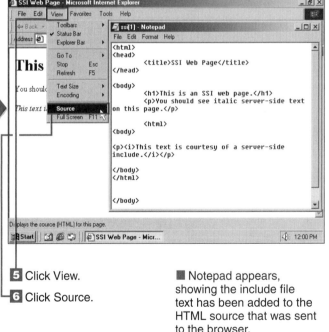

■ The SSI Web page appears, with the included text.

5 Click View.

6 Click Source.

■ Notepad appears, showing the include file text has been added to the HTML source that was sent to the browser.

SECTION VII

22) CODE PAGES IN XHTML

```
<weather>
  <city>Seattle</city>
<state>Washington</state>
  <temp>65</temp>
  <wind>
    <speed>5</speed>
    <dir>SSW</dir>
  </wind>
  <sky>Partly Cloudy</sky>
</weather>
```

AN INTRODUCTION TO WAP AND WML

The hottest new Web access method is wireless access. All across the world, especially in Europe and Japan, people are buying and using Web-enabled cell phones to send messages, read news stories, view train schedules, and order merchandise. The wireless explosion is just now taking off in the United States as it figures out what the rest of the world knows— that wireless is the wave of the future.

But this is not limited to just cell phones; other wireless devices (such as PDAs, inventory bar code readers, and medical diagnosis panels) are using wireless to bring information closer to where it is needed. Some of these systems use proprietary hardware and software; yet today's powerful systems are switching to more flexible, programmable, and interoperable systems.

Enter the wireless access protocol (WAP) and wireless markup language (WML). *WAP* is a set of

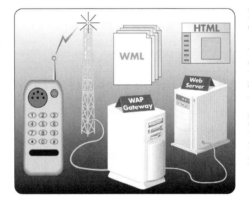

standards that defines how wireless devices interoperate, from transmission methods and frequencies to high-level languages and application integration. *WML* is a subset of WAP and is a specific implementation of XML (Extensible Markup Language) written especially for low-bandwidth, low-processing-power devices such as cell phones.

These wireless devices typically have a software or firmware application called a *microbrowser* that is used to display WAP applications. The microbrowser handles all rendering and navigation tasks, much like a regular browser does.

A Wireless Device (Cell Phone)

You need a WAP-enabled device to receive WML-formatted data and to converse with a WAP gateway. This is typically a cell phone but can be any wireless device, as long as the gateway and the device can set up and tear down a mutually understandable connection.

WAP cell phone vendors include Nokia, Motorola, and Ericsson.

A WAP Gateway

A WAP gateway is used to handle the connections between the cell phone and the Internet or intranet and makes the WML page requests for the wireless device. You must have a WAP gateway to make these types of connections. The good news is that most cell phone providers have a WAP gateway in place; contact them when you roll out a WAP application to the Internet.

If you work for a large institution or have a private intranet that does not use a provider's gateway, you will need to set up a WAP gateway. Contact your cell phone provider about purchasing and installing a gateway.

A Web Server

The Web server is the easiest part of the equation. The Web server handles HTTP requests from the gateway and returns WML documents to the gateway for handoff to a wireless device. WAP applications can be deployed to a Web server with only slight modifications to the server.

A BASIC WML DOCUMENT

A WML document resembles an HTML document that uses XML syntax. A WML document will probably look familiar to anyone who has worked with HTML or XHTML. See Chapters 21 and 22 to find out more about these formats.

Each WML document must follow an XML-based syntax to be considered "well-formed:" All tags must be lowercase because XML is case-sensitive; you must use opening and closing tags, not just start a new tag without closing out the previous one; you cannot list nested tags out of order; and you cannot contain any superfluous tags that are not defined in the specification.

Most WML is devoted to presentation-like tags or functional tags, as opposed to content descriptor tags. WML does have some limited ability to work with variables, and a language called WMLScript exists for dynamic data handling, decision trees, or if-then flow control. WMLScript is not covered in this book because it is a language of its own; if you decide that you want to build more complex applications, you should pick up a book on WMLScript.

Prolog

Every WML document must have a prolog that describes which XML specification it adheres to and identifies its document type definition (DTD).

Deck

Each document contains a deck within the document. In most cases, <wml> is the root element, and a WML document contains only one deck.

DTD

The DTD identifies which document provides the validating parameters for the WML document and identifies the root element in your document. You can use either an internal or external DTD as a reference; if you use more than one WML document, an external DTD is recommended.

```
hello.wml - Notepad
File  Edit  Format  Help
<?xml version="1.0"?>
<!DOCTYPE wml PUBLIC "-//WAPFORUM//DTD WML 1.3//EN"
          "http://www.wapforum.org/DTD/wml13.dtd" >
<wml>
    <card>
        <p>Hello, World!</p>
    </card>
</wml>
```

Card

Each deck is made up of one or more cards. A card contains a single block of information or instructions that is displayed or processed by a microbrowser.

Content

The content is what is displayed or processed within a microbrowser. This area may contain formatting instructions, browser or navigation instructions, or even image tags or browser links.

435

A QUICK LOOK AT INTEROPERABILITY AND USABILITY

Wireless device manufacturers face a real challenge: They need to display WAP applications and conform to the WAP and WML specifications, even though wireless devices vary widely in shape, size, and functionality. There is no uniform screen size, character height, or keypad layout that would make specification compliance easier.

So while all manufacturers likely will continue to make displays in different sizes, the manufacturers are making it easier to determine how a particular application will work on a wireless device. This is done by providing software development kits (SDKs) that include cell phone simulators to emulate what a display may look like and how it may function. A developer's work becomes much easier with such a kit because now she does not need to have one of every type of cell phone available for testing—she can just use a simulator.

What this means for you is that you must check your application for interoperability against as many simulators and real WAP devices as possible. For example, if you are expecting table data to align on the right of a column but the simulator shows it on the left and the actual phone shows it not displayed as a table at all, you need to rethink how you display data to the end user.

Next, you should consider usability testing to bring out all the application bugs and interface design flaws. If your end users cannot figure out your application, you should redesign how you present data and options to them.

Where can I obtain WAP toolkits and phone simulators?

✔ Most phone vendors have simulators, design kits, design documents, and help files that show you how to configure phone software or provide development tips. Some vendors even include sample applications and tutorials for you to use as a reference. If you know which vendor's device you will use, then download that one; otherwise, get a number of simulators so that you can see how your application looks on each simulator.

• Openwave (formerly Phone.com) has a free software development kit. Version 4.1 is approximately 7MB; you can find it at www.openwave.com/products/sdk/.

• Nokia has its WAP Toolkit Version 2.1 available at www.nokia.com/corporate/wap/ sdk.html; registration is required. The kit can also be found on the CD-ROM at the back of this book. It is approximately 16.6MB and contains a copy of the Java JRE (Java Runtime Engine) for use with the toolkit.

• Motorola has its development solutions at http://developers.motorola.com/developers/ wireless/; registration is required. The development environment is 13.7MB, and the 2.0 Beta wireless kit is 21.4MB. You should have a broadband connection if you plan on downloading this kit.

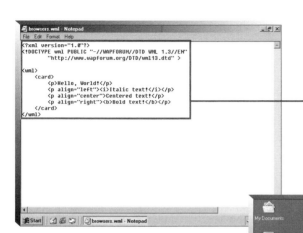

Note: In this section, you take a look at a WML document and three different interpretations of that document by three different simulators.

The Original WML Document

The original WML document has a block of text with bold and italic tags applied to several words within the text. Each word has the text aligned differently.

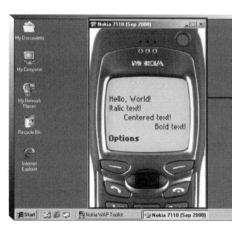

The Openwave Simulator

The Openwave simulator aligns the text and makes the proper words bold and italic.

The Nokia Simulator

The Nokia simulator aligns the text correctly but does not have any text formatting available.

The Motorola Simulator

The Motorola simulator is the inverse of the Nokia: It properly applies text formatting but does not support aligned text.

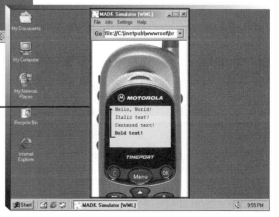

ADD WML MIME TYPES TO YOUR SERVER

Before your Web server can begin handing out WML pages to a requesting wireless device or browser, you need to edit the server's MIME types. MIME stands for Multipurpose Internet Mail Extensions and is used to identify the different types of information and documents that can be requested over the Internet. Your Web server does not natively know about WML documents or how they can be used; you need to tell it to expect a request for a WML document and what extensions are used to identify such a document.

WML File	MIME Type	Extension
Plain WML file	text/vnd.wap.wml	.wml
Wireless bitmap image	image/vnd.wap.wbmp	.wbmp
Compiled WML file	application/vnd.wap.wml	.wmlc
WMLScript file	text/vnd.wap.wmlscript	.wmls
Compiled WMLScript file	application/vnd.wap.wmlscript	.wmlsc

There are five MIME types that may be used by your application.

For the examples in this book you will only need the first three MIME types; the WMLScript files are not needed in this book but may be used by your application and are listed here for reference.

ADD WML MIME TYPES TO YOUR SERVER

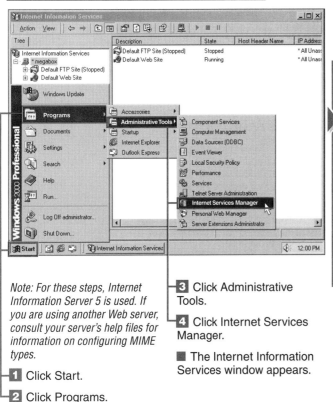

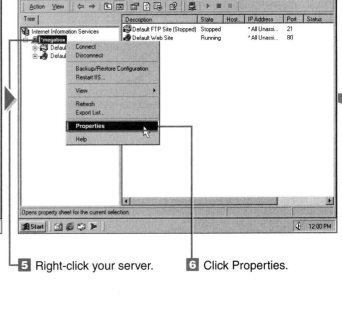

Note: For these steps, Internet Information Server 5 is used. If you are using another Web server, consult your server's help files for information on configuring MIME types.

-1 Click Start.

-2 Click Programs.

3 Click Administrative Tools.

4 Click Internet Services Manager.

■ The Internet Information Services window appears.

5 Right-click your server.

6 Click Properties.

Why do I not see the File Types dialog box in my version of IIS?

✔ Different versions of IIS—such as IIS Version 5 (which runs on Windows 2000), IIS Version 4 (which runs on Windows NT Server), and the Personal Web Server (which runs on Windows NT Workstation)—have different dialog boxes. For the Personal Web Server, you need to edit the Registry to add MIME types. Consult the Microsoft Web site for information on how to edit the Registry. *Warning*: Editing the Registry can leave your computer unstable or even unbootable. Do not edit the Registry unless you have made a Registry backup and know exactly what you are changing and why.

Do I have to set the MIME type for my entire server?

✔ You do not have to have your entire Web server configured to work with MIME types. Most Web servers let you configure MIME types for the whole server, specific Web sites, or even specific application directories.

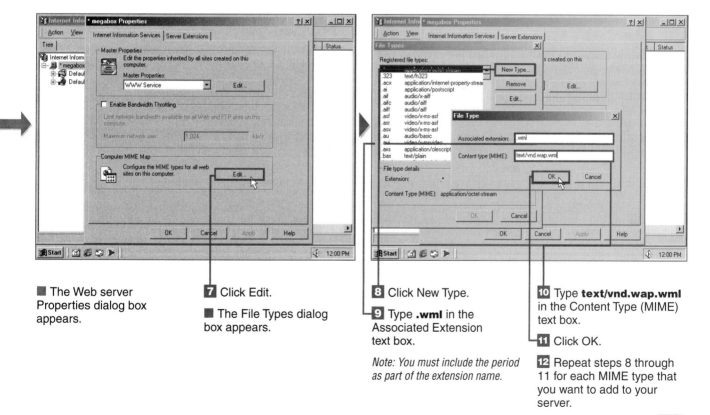

■ The Web server Properties dialog box appears.

7 Click Edit.

■ The File Types dialog box appears.

8 Click New Type.

9 Type **.wml** in the Associated Extension text box.

Note: You must include the period as part of the extension name.

10 Type **text/vnd.wap.wml** in the Content Type (MIME) text box.

11 Click OK.

12 Repeat steps 8 through 11 for each MIME type that you want to add to your server.

CREATE A BASIC WML DOCUMENT

A Web server sends WML document text to a WAP gateway as part of an HTTP request. The gateway compiles the text into a binary format and then sends the binary code to a microbrowser, where it is parsed and shown on the display.

A WML document is much like an HTML document: It contains elements that provide display information or information about how to navigate around other HTML documents (or even itself). When you write a WML document, it consists of a deck that in turn consists of cards. For now, think of a document as equaling one deck.

Within that deck, you build a set of cards. The cards contain information that is displayed in one go on a wireless device, much like you would show a card one at a time from a deck of playing cards. The cards are where most of your hard work takes place, as you work with display and formatting issues, insert links to other cards or other decks, and build fields that execute a task when a phone button is pressed.

CREATE A BASIC WML DOCUMENT

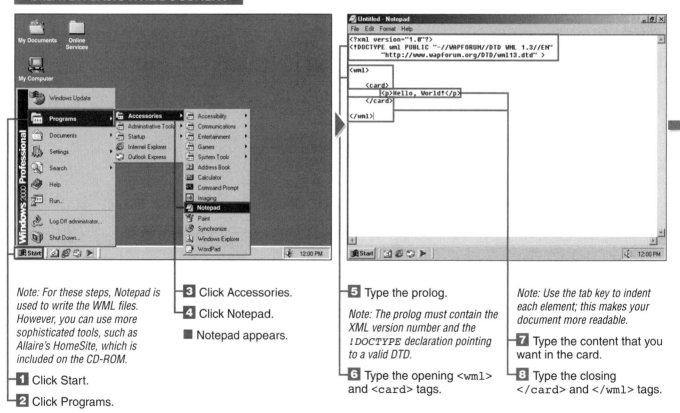

Note: For these steps, Notepad is used to write the WML files. However, you can use more sophisticated tools, such as Allaire's HomeSite, which is included on the CD-ROM.

1 Click Start.

2 Click Programs.

3 Click Accessories.

4 Click Notepad.

■ Notepad appears.

5 Type the prolog.

Note: The prolog must contain the XML version number and the !DOCTYPE declaration pointing to a valid DTD.

6 Type the opening <wml> and <card> tags.

Note: Use the tab key to indent each element; this makes your document more readable.

7 Type the content that you want in the card.

8 Type the closing </card> and </wml> tags.

How large can I make my WML documents?

✔ WML documents can theoretically be as large as you want. However, wireless devices operate over low bandwidth connections and have low processing power and memory available, so there are practical limits to document size. Compiled WML has a limit of 1,400 bytes. If your development environment provides a tool to check compiled size you should use it.

Where can I find more information about the WAP and WML specifications?

✔ You can find the WAP and WML specifications at the World Wide Web Consortium Web site, www.w3c.org, which has information and specifications on anything having to do with the Internet. For information specific to WAP and WML, check out the WAP Forum Web site at www.wapforum.org. You will find specifications, news, white papers, and more. For marketing information, reviews, and a page with links to mobile phone apps, games, tones, and more, see the site www.wap.com.

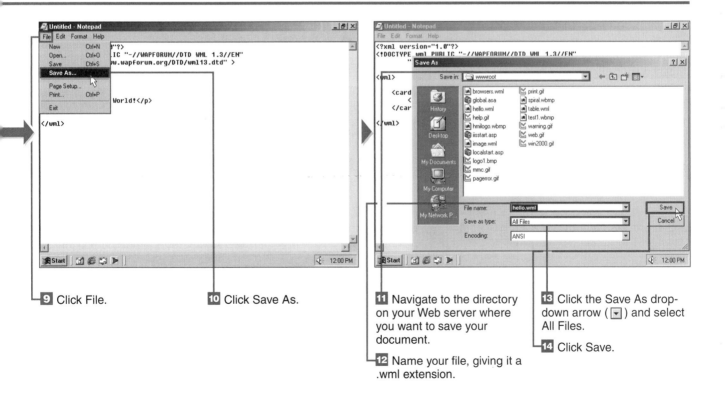

−9 Click File.

10 Click Save As.

11 Navigate to the directory on your Web server where you want to save your document.

12 Name your file, giving it a .wml extension.

13 Click the Save As drop-down arrow (▼) and select All Files.

14 Click Save.

VIEW A WML DOCUMENT

After you have written a WML document, you will want to see whether the document is well-formed, or valid, or whether it appears the way you think it should on a wireless device. You can view a WML document two ways.

The first way is to view the file by using a Web browser that supports XML documents. Microsoft Internet Explorer 5.x and Netscape Navigator 6 have built-in XML parsers that display a well-formed XML document. You can use them to check your WML document's syntax. In order to use a browser to view your document, you need to rename your file with an .xml extension, or you can make a copy of your WML file as an XML file.

The second way to view a WML document is in a wireless simulator. A simulator shows you how your document appears on a particular device and may give you additional information about the compiled file's size, HTTP error messages, and other troubleshooting or debugging information.

VIEW A WML DOCUMENT IN A BROWSER

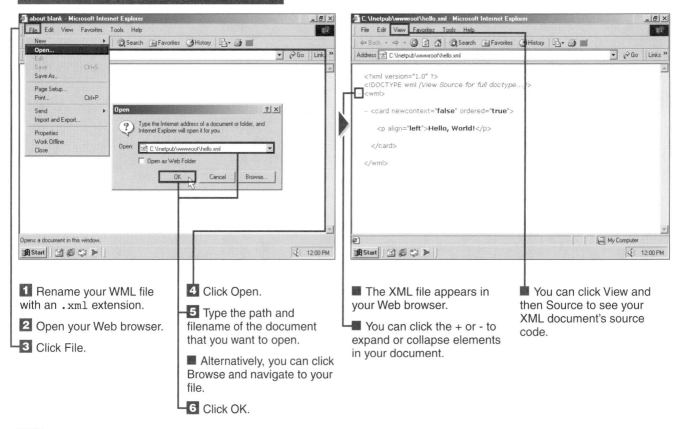

1 Rename your WML file with an .xml extension.

2 Open your Web browser.

3 Click File.

4 Click Open.

5 Type the path and filename of the document that you want to open.

■ Alternatively, you can click Browse and navigate to your file.

6 Click OK.

■ The XML file appears in your Web browser.

■ You can click the + or - to expand or collapse elements in your document.

■ You can click View and then Source to see your XML document's source code.

Why is my simulator not working?

✓ Check to see that you have done the following:

- Add the WML MIME types to your Web server. If you do not, the server will return a 406 error (object not found). See the section "Add WML MIME Types to Your Server" to find out how to do this.

- Copy your WML files to a directory with appropriate privileges. You may need to set up a virtual directory and assign read privileges before the document can be seen.

- Make sure that the HTTP service is started.

- Check to see if you are going through a proxy server or a personal firewall. You may need to set up special settings or filtering rules to make the system work.

- Make sure that you followed the instructions in the README file.

- If all else fails, visit the Web site where you got the simulator to see if there are any known bugs, workarounds, or FAQs that can help you get connected.

VIEW A WML DOCUMENT IN A SIMULATOR

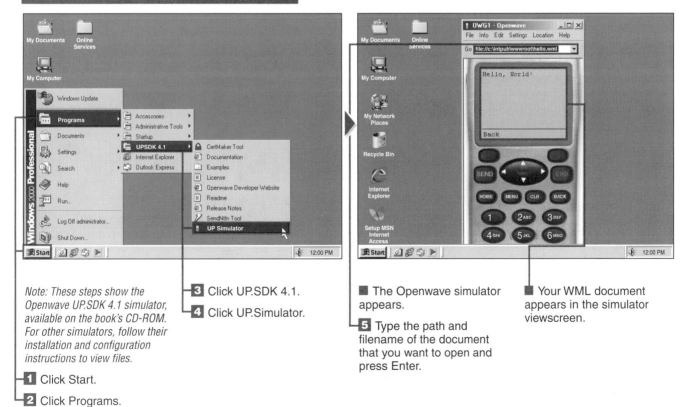

Note: These steps show the Openwave UP.SDK 4.1 simulator, available on the book's CD-ROM. For other simulators, follow their installation and configuration instructions to view files.

1 Click Start.

2 Click Programs.

3 Click UP.SDK 4.1.

4 Click UP.Simulator.

■ The Openwave simulator appears.

5 Type the path and filename of the document that you want to open and press Enter.

■ Your WML document appears in the simulator viewscreen.

ALIGN AND FORMAT TEXT

WAP-enabled devices have limited ability to display text. Because of these limitations, it is up to the coder to observe a simple rule: Use formatting sparingly, and only to increase usability or readability.

The basic element in any card is the paragraph element, `<p>`. You control text alignment by using an attribute within the paragraph tag: `<p align="right">`. By default,

the paragraph tag left-aligns text, but its possible values are `left`, `center`, and `right`.

The wrapping attribute is less likely to be used; you can set `<p mode="wrap" | "nowrap">` to determine whether text is wrapped to fit the display. Some wireless devices do not support horizontal scrolling, so setting the display mode to `nowrap` means otherwise-viewable data will be lost.

You can control bold and italic formatting by using `bold` and `italic` tags around any text within a paragraph tag, like this: `<p><b>bold text</b></p>`. Notice that the tags are properly nested; it would break the well-formed document rule to reverse the closing tag order, like this: `</p></b>`, which would return an error.

ALIGN TEXT

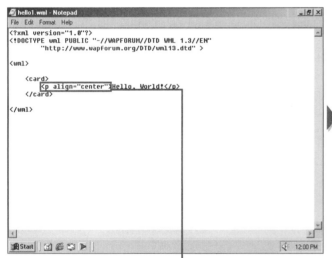

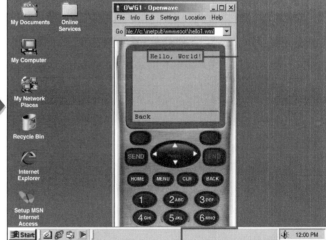

1 Open Notepad.

2 Open your WML document.

3 Within the text that you want to align, edit the opening paragraph tag to read `<p align="left">`, `<p align="center">`, or `<p align="right">`.

4 Save your file.

5 View your file in a simulator.

■ The text is aligned according to your specifications.

Can I add comments to my documents?

✔ Yes, you can (and should) add comments to your WML documents to describe what is happening in your code. You can add comments to document variables, explain actions that are taken, or provide other information that will be useful when you come back to your code in a few months, especially if you forget what you were trying to do. Ideally, you will have an as-built document that can be referred to later, but code comments should be considered a bare minimum.

How do I add comments?

✔ Add comments by using the following syntax: `<!-- This is a comment. -->`. (This format is similar to that used in Active Server Pages.) A comment can span multiple lines. Comments are not included in the compiled document, so they do not take up any additional room. Be liberal with your comments; you should document your application structure, its functions, and any notes needed for its operation on a Web server.

FORMAT TEXT

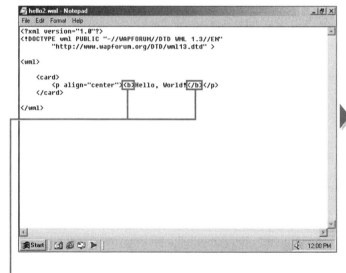

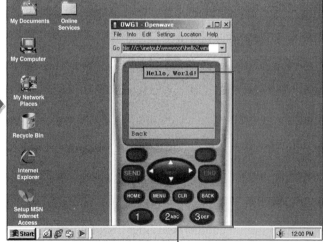

1 Open Notepad.

2 Open your WML document.

3 Add tags to format the text.

Note: For example, you can add the <b></b> tags to make the text bold and/or the <i></i> tags to make it italic.

4 Save your file.

5 View your file in a simulator.

■ The text is formatted according to your specifications.

MOVE AROUND DOCUMENTS BY USING ANCHORS AND LINKS

You can help your WML users move between cards within a deck or to cards in other decks by using anchors and links. *Anchors* are tags that contain links to other documents and link descriptions that can be read by a user. *Links* are simply hyperlinks to other documents, whether within a WML application or on another Web site.

You may be familiar with anchors in HTML. The WML syntax is very similar: `<a href="document. wml#card-id" title= "button-id">User Text</a>`. The anchor begins with an absolute or relative link reference to another document or card, contains a button title to be displayed, and ends with text that is displayed inline to the user.

For links to work, there has to be a way of identifying which card in a deck is being pointed to. In the preceding sample link, there is a reference to `#card-id`; this is an attribute for a card element within a deck and is where the link will jump to when the link is activated. The syntax for a card attribute is `<card id="name" title="Title">`.

MOVE AROUND DOCUMENTS BY USING ANCHORS AND LINKS

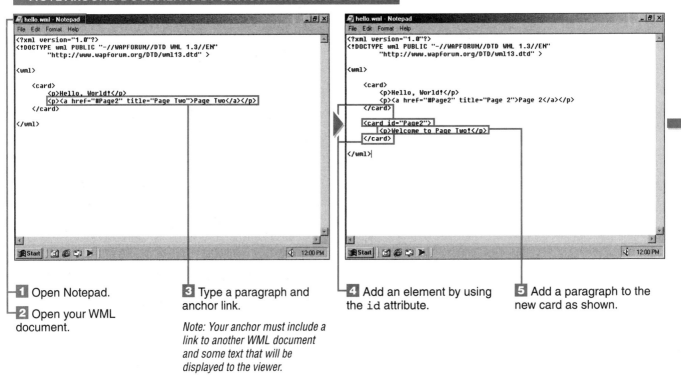

1 Open Notepad.

2 Open your WML document.

3 Type a paragraph and anchor link.

Note: Your anchor must include a link to another WML document and some text that will be displayed to the viewer.

4 Add an element by using the `id` attribute.

5 Add a paragraph to the new card as shown.

What is the difference between relative and absolute links?

✔ *Relative links* assume that the document you are looking for is located in the same directory; *absolute links* contain the fully qualified URL or path to the document. Relative links are preferred because they are shorter than absolute links and thus compile to smaller file sizes; they are simpler to edit and troubleshoot; and if you move your application to another directory, your relative links do not break.

Absolute links are used for external site links or references to resources elsewhere on the Internet. If you are referring to decks and cards within your application, relative links are the way to go.

Why do I not see the card titles in the simulator window?

✔ The WAP specification does not require microbrowsers to handle card titles or display them. Some simulators and cell phones do show them, whereas others ignore them. Depending on the devices that you expect to use, you can choose to implement or ignore the card titles when you code your application.

6 Save the file.

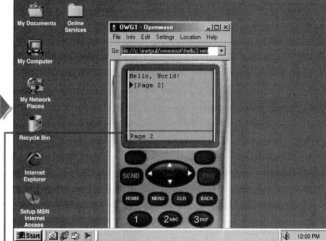

7 View your WML document in a simulator and select the link to verify that it jumps to the new card.

ASSIGN LINKS TO ACCESS KEYS

The anchor tag <a> has another useful attribute for navigation but one that is not implemented in all microbrowsers: accesskey. The accesskey attribute provides a way of generating a numeric list of links so that an end user only has to press the numeric button on the

keypad in order to activate the link. The accesskey attribute can be helpful for providing quick and easy shortcuts that do not require scrolling and selecting links.

The accesskey attribute typically consists of the keypad numbers 0 through 9, the star key (*), and the

pound sign (#), depending on the wireless device. Other keys can be assigned—so this is one instance where, if you use this attribute, you are strongly recommended to test your code in both a simulator and on actual devices that will access your decks.

ASSIGN LINKS TO ACCESS KEYS

1 Open Notepad.

2 Open your WML document.

3 Add a paragraph and accesskey tag.

4 Edit the new paragraph and add the accesskey tag.

Note: For readability, in this example, word wrap is turned on, and the paragraph formatting adjusted.

5 Save your file.

What is the difference between the `<a>` and `<anchor>` tags in WML?

✔ The `<a>` tag is a useful and easily abbreviated form of an anchor. It provides the most common functionality for linking between cards in a deck and between decks. The `<anchor>` tag enables more advanced navigation between cards and decks, such as the ability to use `<go>`, `<prev>`, and `<do>` tags. These tags are detailed thoroughly in the WML specification.

Why are there so many ways to link to different WML pages?

✔ WAP-enabled devices vary widely in their displays and keypads. You cannot count on a device having a specific button to press or even offering the ability to scroll through text and activate a link. Thus, there are a number of ways to work around these limitations. It is up to you as the developer to test your WML applications on as many simulators and devices as possible and to conduct usability studies with your end users to find out which linking method is easiest to use.

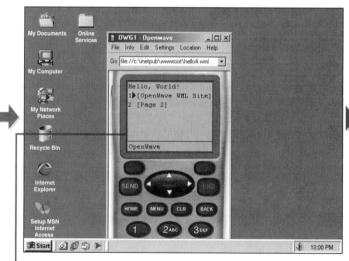

6 View your WML document in a simulator and verify that the first selection button works.

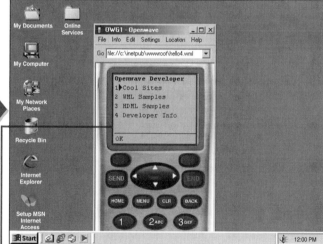

7 Verify that any other selection buttons you added work.

USING A WIRELESS BITMAP CONVERTER

Some wireless devices are capable of displaying inline images. These images are neither complex nor large because of screen-size limitations. Further, because there are no rendering capabilities inherent in a microbrowser, an image must be rendered elsewhere and then downloaded, which means that vector graphic images or JPEG images are not allowed.

There is a unique bitmap format for wireless devices. Wireless bitmap format images have the extension .wbmp and must be created by using a software program specifically for wireless bitmaps, or you must use a program that converts regular bitmap images into wireless bitmap format.

Adobe Photoshop and other image editing programs have plug-ins

available for free download that handle wireless bitmaps; alternatively, you can use the Java freeware program pic2wbmp that is available at www.gingco.de/wap. You will need to have a Java runtime engine installed to use the converter—see the pic2wbmp readme file that is included in the zip archive.

USING A WIRELESS BITMAP CONVERTER

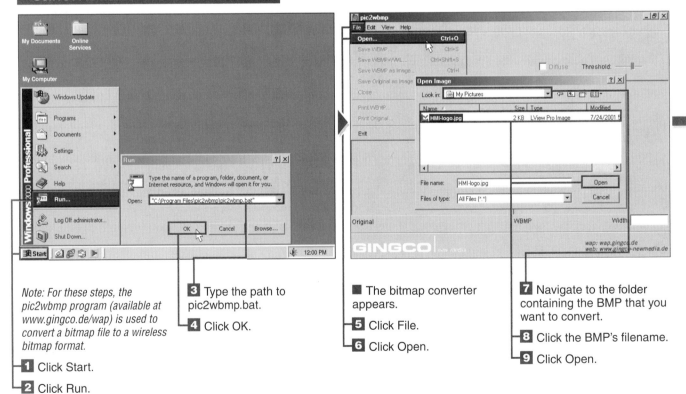

Note: For these steps, the pic2wbmp program (available at www.gingco.de/wap) is used to convert a bitmap file to a wireless bitmap format.

1 Click Start.

2 Click Run.

3 Type the path to pic2wbmp.bat.

4 Click OK.

■ The bitmap converter appears.

5 Click File.

6 Click Open.

7 Navigate to the folder containing the BMP that you want to convert.

8 Click the BMP's filename.

9 Click Open.

How do I create bitmap images in the first place?

✔ Many programs are available that create .bmp images. Microsoft Paint is a program that ships with Windows and can create files in the .bmp format. You can also download a freeware program called CoffeeCup Wireless Web Builder from http://coffeecup.com/software or from www.tucows.com, which includes a WBMP image-editing program. It also includes a WAP application builder that helps automatically generate WAP applications using a WYSIWYG designer. Although Wireless Web Builder does not eliminate hand-editing your WML files, it can help generate prototypes or usability demos for you.

Can I use bitmap images on all my WML pages?

✔ Bitmap images can be drawn on some wireless devices. Whether they *ought* to be is another question. You and your end users may decide that images only slow down a wireless connection, or together you may decide that properly used images add to the application's appearance and are desirable despite the additional download time. Make sure that you work with your end users if you are planning to use bitmap images in your application.

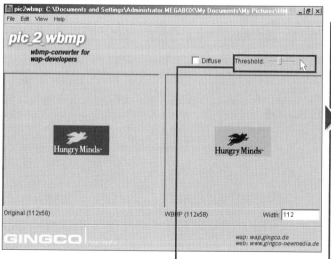

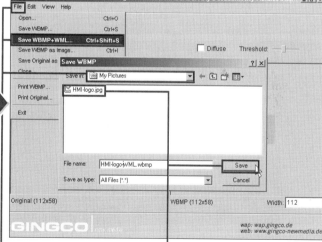

■ Your bitmap image appears, along with a .wbmp image for comparison.

⑩ Make any adjustments that you need to image diffusion by adjusting the Threshold slider bar.

⑪ Click File.

⑫ Click Save WBMP.

⑬ Navigate to the folder where you want to save the WBMP file.

Note: You should probably save the image in the same directory where your .wml files reside.

⑭ Type a filename for your wireless image.

⑮ Click Save.

ADD AN IMAGE TO A DOCUMENT

You can use the `<img>` tag to place an image in a WML document and specify its vertical alignment and alternative text that can be used. The `<img>` tag syntax is `<img align="top | middle | bottom" localsrc="browser-dependent" src="href" alt="alt-text">`.

The `src` attribute is required and is a hyperlink to an image file on your server; the `alt` attribute is also required and specifies the text to be displayed if the image is unavailable or cannot be rendered.

The `align` attribute is not required but provides vertical placement within a line. Horizontal placement within a line is done by using the `<p align>` attribute. The `localsrc` attribute is not required and specifies a local, predefined image on the wireless device, if one is available. Your wireless developer kit will list which images are available with `localsrc`.

Other attributes are available, such as vertical and horizontal spacing around the image, but these are not required to be supported by a wireless device and should not be relied on unless you have tested them thoroughly on the actual device.

ADD AN IMAGE TO A DOCUMENT

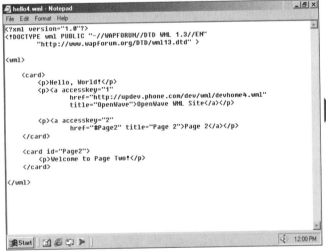

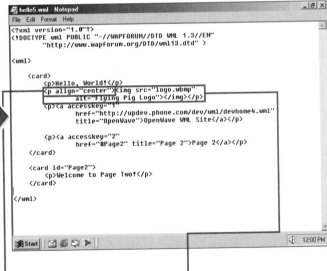

1 Open Notepad.

2 Open your WML document.

3 Type a new paragraph tag.

4 Within the paragraph tag, type the image element with the attributes that you want to include.

Note: Make sure that you have copied the `.wbmp` *file to your WML directory.*

Why can I not see my image in the simulator?

✔ There can be several reasons why you are not seeing an image in your simulator:

• You may not have added the .wbmp MIME type to your server. Without the MIME type, the server does not know what file to give when a .wbmp get request arrives.

• The simulator does not support images. You should still see the alternative text, however.

• You may not have copied or saved your image file to the same directory as your WML documents.

• You are trying to view an unconverted .bmp image. You need to convert a .bmp image to a .wbmp image by using an image converter. You should still see the alternative text.

What size images can I display on my wireless device?

✔ You can sometimes find pixel size information on a manufacturer's Web site or in the SDK that comes with a simulator. Be aware that some devices scroll vertically but not horizontally, so any image information that extends off the right side of the display is lost.

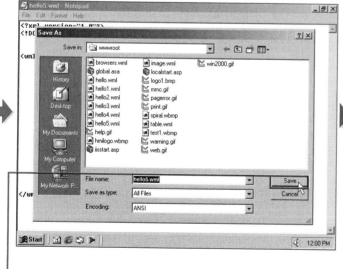

5 Save your file.

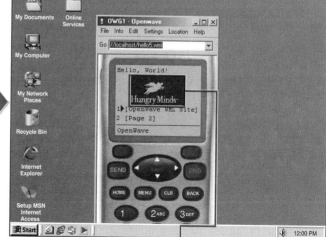

6 View your WML document using a simulator.

Note: You cannot view the file directly using your browser; you must connect to the Web server so it can properly compile the WML page.

■ Your image appears in the simulator.

ADD A TABLE TO A DOCUMENT

There is something both simple and compelling about well-ordered, easy-to-find information presented in a table. When designed properly, a table is unobtrusive yet provides the necessary structure to lend weight to the data.

But with wireless devices, space is at a premium, and there is not a lot of room for table borders, pretty formatting, or other things that are taken for granted. This presents an interesting dilemma for the developer: Should tables be used at all for wireless applications, or should they be used knowing that some devices will not display them properly?

The best answer for this will come from your end users. If you can present them card options that show table-formatted data, tableless data, and a variety of display devices to view the cards, you can enlist them to help you make that choice.

The syntax for a table is `<table columns="n" align="table-align" title="table-title">`, with table rows using the `<tr>` tag and table data elements using the `<td>` tag. The `columns` attribute is required; all others are optional.

ADD A TABLE TO A DOCUMENT

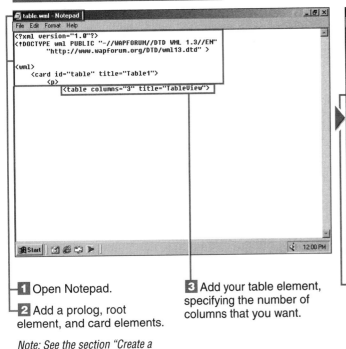

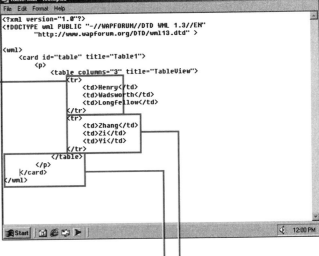

1 Open Notepad.

2 Add a prolog, root element, and card elements.

Note: See the section "Create a Basic WML Document" for help with step 2.

3 Add your table element, specifying the number of columns that you want.

4 Type the first table row's elements, including the same number of elements (`<td>`s) that you specified for the number of columns.

Note: For example, if you specified three columns in step 3, include three `<td>` elements.

5 Repeat step 4 for all the table rows that you need.

6 Remember to close the table, card, and root element tags.

What do I do if my table is not displaying properly?

✔ If you are trying to list more than three columns of data, you may want to come up with a better way to display your data. For example, train schedules are easy to display—you can place the track in one column and the depart time in another. Invoices, on the other hand, are difficult to display, as there may be part numbers, quantities, per-unit cost, total cost, shipping charges, and so on, most of which will not fit on a wireless display.

Can I use images in my tables?

✔ Yes, you can insert an `<img>` as a table data element. This is an easy way to provide bullets, dingbats, or other small symbols in a table.

Can I put anchors in tables?

✔ Yes, you can place an anchor in a table as a table data element, just like an image. This provides an alternative to access keys as a way of listing active links to other decks and cards.

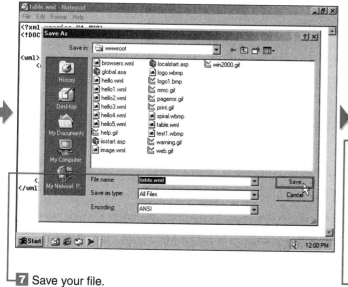

7 Save your file.

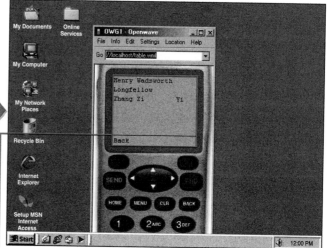

8 View your file in a simulator.

USING ASP TO GENERATE WML TEXT

Most of this chapter discusses techniques used for generating static WML pages, which are pages whose content never or rarely changes. But for sites whose content changes frequently, you need different methods to generate WML.

One method is to use some form of scripting language on the server that generates content at the time an HTTP request is made. This allows the server to do all the work, wrapping up the content in the appropriate WML tags and sending the information to a WAP gateway and then to the wireless device.

Several scripting languages are available for server-side content generation. These include JavaServer Pages, Perl, Python, PHP, CGI, and JavaScript. This chapter is not intended to show you all you need to know about these languages; instead, the examples used here will be Active Server Pages, a server-side scripting technology from Microsoft that can generate pages for you. You can adapt the procedure in the steps below to one of the other scripting languages or write your own script-based solution.

USING ASP TO GENERATE WML TEXT

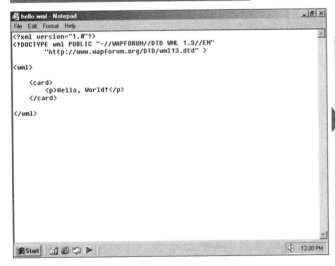

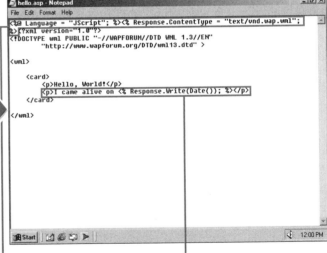

1 Open Notepad.

2 Open your WML document.

3 Type your ASP handler code before the WML prolog.

Note: Your ASP code requires you to identify the script handler and the response content type declaration.

4 Type the new paragraph line as shown.

Note: You can use the `response.write` *method to insert values such as the* `date()` *string.*

Why does my ASP file not work?

✔ There may be several reasons why you cannot view your WML page:

- You may have saved your file to a directory that does not have execute permissions set. Check with your Web administrator to see if there is a particular directory you need to put your WML files in.

- Your file must be in a directory that allows the server to run scripts. For security purposes, many administrators limit Web site directories to read only. You may need to set up a Web site directory with permission to run scripts in that directory.

Can I view an ASP file in the simulator by just typing in the filename?

✔ You need to use an HTTP request to view an ASP page. Because generating ASP pages requires Internet Information Server (on Windows NT Server and Windows 2000 Professional and Server) or the Personal Web Server (on Windows NT Workstation) to process the code directives, your simulator will not recognize the ASP code and will generate an error.

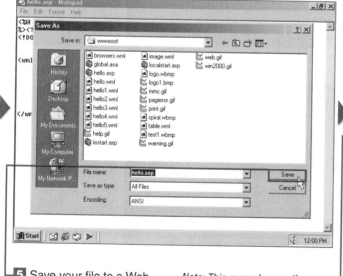

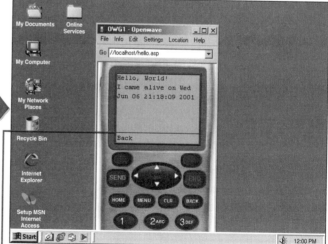

5 Save your file to a Web server directory, naming it with an .asp extension.

Note: This example uses the default c:\inetpub\ wwwroot directory.

6 View your file in a simulator.

■ Your dynamically generated text appears on your WML page.

INTRODUCTION TO XML

In many ways, HTML is a "quick-and-dirty" way to publish Web pages. For example, HTML has no way to distinguish any document content from other elements on the Web page, and thus more sophisticated Web applications cannot parse or use the data without extensive custom programming. For this and other reasons, serious Web-page developers demanded a more robust language that overcomes the limitations of HTML.

Enter XML, which stands for *Extensible Markup Language*. XML can be used to extend HTML to meet specific needs. Many Web page creators need support for tags that tell more about the text they mark. XML is the answer to these demands.

XML will not supplant HTML overnight, but you should be aware of the potential of XML. This chapter gives you a brief overview of the language. For more on XML, check out *XML: Your visual blueprint for building expert Web pages*, by Emily Vander Veer and Rev Mengle (published by Hungry Minds, Inc.).

XML traits

XML documents share the following traits:

- They define data in a precise, structured format that follows a simple repeating pattern: <TAG>someData</TAG>.

- They can include arbitrary amounts of white space for readability, as long as that white space does not appear between tags.

- They are saved as simple text files with the .xml suffix.

- They can be created with a text editor or an XML-supporting editor.

- They are transferred from Web server to Web client via HTTP (HyperText Transfer Protocol), just like HTML files.

- They are an essential component of an XML-based application, which, in addition to an XML file, also includes an optional DTD or schema, an XML parser, and presentation/processing logic.

How XML works

XML separates content and presentation by eliminating presentation-related tags from the document. Instead, tags in an XML document are used to describe the data itself—what is commonly referred to as *metadata*, or "data about data."

Here is an example of XML code. Suppose you want to have a document that contains weather information in it. An XML fragment within that document might look like this:

```
<weather>
      <city>Seattle</city>
      <state>Washington</state>
      <temp>65</temp>
      <wind>
            <speed>5</speed>
            <dir>SSW</dir>
      </wind>
      <sky>Partly Cloudy</sky>
</weather>
```

You can see that the tags are human-readable and define what the data is. There is no guesswork needed to understand what the particular elements are. In addition, no presentation information is included anywhere in the fragment.

XML as an exchange agent

XML can also help with information interchange. If you are building a commerce site that moves information between databases, you have already run across problems with data being in different formats in the different databases. Using the "weather" example above, one database has the location in two fields: one for city, one for state. Another database has the location in a single field: city, state. With XML you can write a simple routine to concatenate the two fields into one and put the single field into the second database. XML is admirably suited to data normalization tasks such as this.

XML, DTDs, and Schemas

The tags, attributes, and their meanings are defined in a separate document called a *Document Type Definition*, or DTD. Current Web browsers compare HTML documents by default against the HTML 4 DTD. Using the <!doctype> tag, you can specify which DTD to use.

If the specified DTD for a Web page is an XML DTD, then the Web page will be able to use the additional tags and attributes that are defined in that DTD.

An alternative to a DTD is a *schema*, or a collection of semantic validation rules designed to constrain XML data values. Unfortunately, the rules governing schemas are far from mature, and few schema-supporting tools are available. As such, an in-depth discussion of schemas is beyond this chapter.

XML, XHTML, and HTML

XHTML is a bridge or link between the XML data-driven model and the HTML presentation-driven model. XHTML takes HTML and makes it follow the more rigorous and consistent XML syntax, such as opening and closing all paragraphs with <p></p> tags. For more on XHTML, see Chapter 22.

CREATE AN XML DOCUMENT

Creating an XML document is the first step in creating an XML-based application. The directive you use to create an XML document is

```
<?xml version="version"?>
```

Because XML documents are simple text files, you can create the file by using any text editor. The editor used in this chapter is Microsoft Notepad, a simple text editor that comes bundled with Windows 95/98/NT/2000.

However, if you are creating more sophisticated documents, you may wish to use an editor designed especially for writing XML documents. One popular editor for serious document writers is XML Spy (www.xmlspy.com/), which lets you edit XML documents, schema, and stylesheets. A less complex but perfectly suitable one is XML Notepad from Microsoft (http://msdn.microsoft.com/xml/ NOTEPAD/download.asp),

a free XML editor for basic XML documents.

Lastly, you can use Macromedia's HomeSite that is included on the book's CD. HomeSite generates text documents and has the benefit of an XML syntax checker built in. HomeSite—covered more thoroughly in Chapter 23—is highly recommended if you want to get started quickly with XML.

CREATE AN XML DOCUMENT

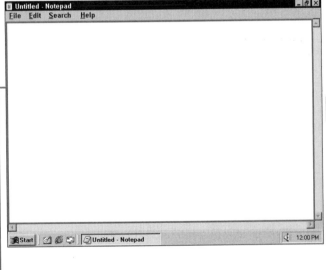

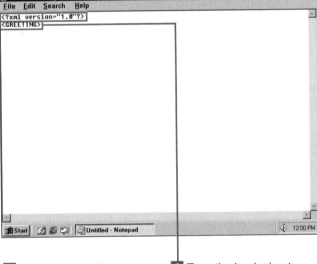

1 Create a new text file in the text editor of your choice.

■ This example shows a Notepad document.

2 Type the XML directive.

■ The version="1.0" attribute/value pair specifies that this document conforms to the XML 1.0 specification.

3 Type the beginning tag for an XML element.

Do I have to use an .xml extension for my documents?

✔ XML parsers identify a file as an XML document as long as the XML declaration tag appears at the top of the file. However, saving XML files by using the .xml extension is good programming practice.

Should I worry about how many spaces or tab stops are used?

✔ XML imposes relatively few syntax rules, and formatting your documents properly is easy. The hardest part is figuring out how your data should be organized for your Web application; after that, the syntax will take care of itself. The "Verify an XML Document" section shows you how to check your XML syntax by using a parser.

Where should I save my XML files?

✔ XML applications typically include multiple documents, such as XML, HTML, CSS, and schemas or DTD documents. Organizing these documents in a single directory is a good idea so that all related documents are kept in the same place. It is also a good idea to keep a project plan or functional specification in the same directory, describing how the documents interrelate.

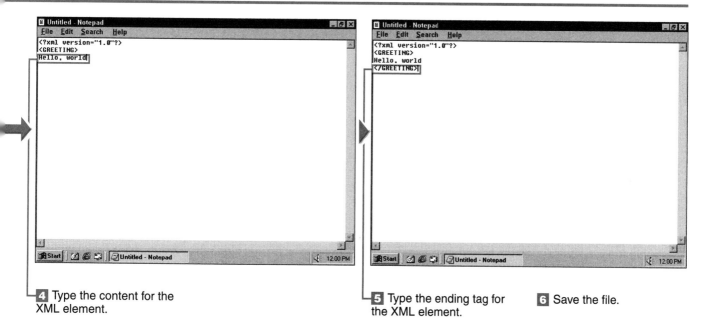

4 Type the content for the XML element.

5 Type the ending tag for the XML element.

6 Save the file.

VERIFY AN XML DOCUMENT

You can verify if your first XML document is well-formed (free of syntax errors) by running it through an XML parser. Two types of XML parsers exist—validating and nonvalidating.

Validating parsers check XML document syntax. They also confirm that XML data matches predefined validation rules, if any, by comparing XML documents to DTDs (document type definitions) and schemas. Validating parsers currently available include:

- The Scholarly Technology Group at Brown University's online XML Validation Form at www.stg.brown.edu/service/xmlvalid/.

- Apache's open-source parser Xerces, available at xml.apache.org.

- Microstar's Aelfred at www.opentext.com/services/content_management_services/xml_sgml_solutions.html#aelfred_and_sax.

- Textuality's Larval at www.textuality.com/Lark/.

- IBM's XML Parser for Java at www.alphaworks.ibm.com/tech/xml4j.

Nonvalidating parsers check XML document syntax to see if the document is well-formed, but they do not match XML documents against DTDs or schemas. Nonvalidating parsers currently available include:

- XML.com's RUWF, which is based on the Lark parser; go to www.xml.com/pub/a/tools/ruwf/check.html.

- James Clark's expat at www.jclark.com/xml/expat.html.

In this section, you test your XML document against MSXML, the validating parser built into Internet Explorer 5.0.

VERIFY AN XML DOCUMENT

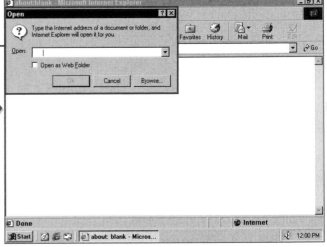

1 Run Internet Explorer.

■ Be sure that you have established an Internet connection.

2 Invoke Internet Explorer's Open dialog box.

Why do I not see my document, only an error message?

✔ The MSXML parser only displays your XML document if the document is well formed. If you attempt to parse a document that is not *well formed*—in other words, a document containing XML syntax errors—you see an error instead of the XML document data.

How do I view my document without the data tags?

✔ To display the data intelligently— without the XML tags and in an attractive, easy-to-read format—you must create an XML processor that describes how you want the data to appear. Find out how to create a simple XML processor later in "Create a Simple XML Processor."

What if I do not have Internet Explorer 5.0 on my PC?

✔ A stand-alone version of the MSXML parser was provided for use with Internet Explorer 4.x, but it has been upgraded significantly for use with Internet Explorer 5. Internet Explorer 5 recognizes the .xml extension, and its built-in MSXML parser understands how to interpret and display a well-formed XML document. Navigator 4.0x does not support XML, although the beta release of Navigator 6.0 does. Some independent browsers, such as Jumbo, support XML. MSXML is available separately from www.msdn. microsoft.com/downloads/tools/ xmlparser/xmlparser.asp.

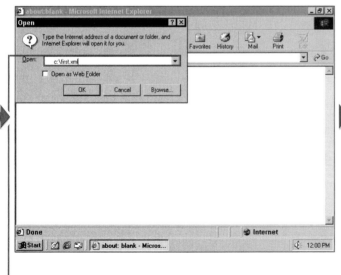

3 Type the name of the XML document you want to parse into the Open dialog box.

4 Examine the results.

■ If the XML document is well formed, it appears in the browser window, as shown in this example.

DECLARE A ROOT ELEMENT

Every valid XML document contains one and only one root element. A *root element* is an element that contains all the other elements in a document; in other words, the root element is at the top of the XML data hierarchy, both conceptually and syntactically. Defining a root element enables you to encapsulate all data in an XML document for easy access and manipulation.

Root elements are declared the same way as any other element,

with one difference: Root elements must appear at the top of the XML document, after the XML declaration but before any other element declarations.

The syntax for declaring a root element is

```
<rootElementName>
</rootElementName>
```

rootElementName is the name of the root element you want to declare.

One thing to keep in mind is that XML is case-sensitive and that opening and closing tags must match exactly. For example, <veryHairyCat> is not the same as <VERYHAIRYCAT>. If your element tags do not match in the case used, your document will not be well formed and will not pass through a parser.

DECLARE A ROOT ELEMENT

1 Open the XML file in which you want to create the root element.

2 Position your cursor directly after the XML declaration.

What should be my root element in a Web page?

✔ Ordinary Web pages written in HTML do not have root elements; because those kinds of pages contain presentation information only, they do not adhere to any kind of structured, data-driven content. Including a `!DOCTYPE html` statement at the top of your Web page to help you transition your HTML pages to XHTML cannot hurt, though. See Chapter 22 for more information on XHTML and how Web pages can take advantage of XML syntax.

How do I determine which element should be the root element?

✔ Deciding which XML element should be a root element is a two-step process. First, understand your data before you begin the implementation phase. XML files should correspond to data requirements; in other words, model your data first and select as your XML root element the element that lies conceptually at the top of your data hierarchy. Second, choose a naming convention and stick with it.

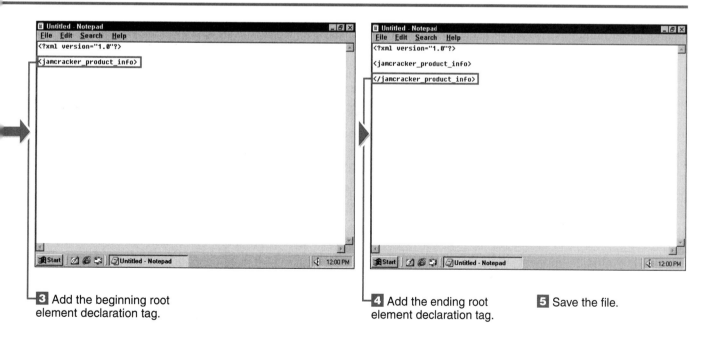

3 Add the beginning root element declaration tag.

4 Add the ending root element declaration tag.

5 Save the file.

DECLARE NON-ROOT DATA ELEMENTS

I n XML, you describe the structure of data elements by nesting elements within other elements. All non-root data elements are contained inside the document's root element. Non-root data elements, which you use to define the bulk of your XML data, are the "meat" of your XML document.

Here is the syntax for declaring non-root data elements:

```
<containerElement
[attributeInfo]>
[<containedElement
[attributeInfo]>
</containedElement>]
</containerElement>
```

containerElement is the name of a data element that contains one or more additional data elements.

containedElement (optional) is the name of a data element that is contained by another data element.

attributeInfo (optional) is a string of attribute-value pairs that specify the attributes associated with a given data element.

No white space can appear inside tags. For example, <price per unit> is an illegal tag declaration.

DECLARE NON-ROOT DATA ELEMENTS

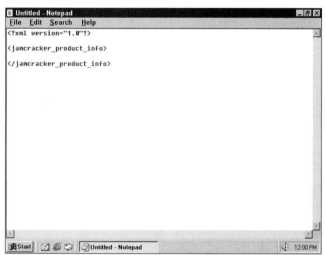

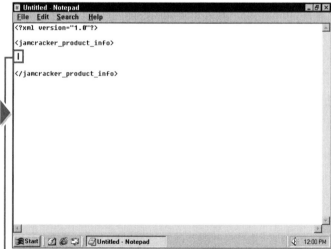

1 Open the XML file in which you want to create non-root data elements.

2 Position your cursor between the beginning and ending root element tags.

MASTER IT

What is the best way to handle having redundant elements and data in different documents?

✔ If you had three instances of a user's name and address on three different documents—such as a purchase order, invoice, and bill of lading—you could have a single XML document with the name and address on it rather than repeat that information in each of the three documents. You would then have a pointer from the three documents to the single document that would be referenced when the documents were processed.

Is there a limit to how many non-root data elements I can have in a document?

✔ Theoretically, you can have as many elements in an XML document as you want, up to practical limits of computer hardware and software. Realistically, most XML documents are short, not exceeding a few pages in length. This is because keeping your data separated into discrete modules is much easier than putting it into one large blob.

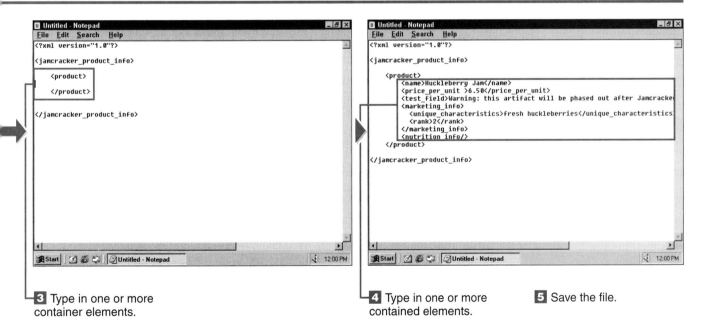

3 Type in one or more container elements.

4 Type in one or more contained elements.

5 Save the file.

DESCRIBE DATA ELEMENTS WITH ATTRIBUTES

You can declare attributes and associate them with individual XML elements to model sophisticated data groupings.

You must declare an attribute inside the beginning tag of an element. Here is the syntax required to declare attributes in XML:

```
<elementName
[attributeName1="attribute1
Value"]
[attributeName2="attribute2
Value"]
[attributeNameN="attributeN
Value"]
```

`>elementValue</elementName>`

elementName is the name of the element to which you want to associate an attribute.

attributeName1 is the name of an attribute. Attribute names must begin with a letter or an underscore and may only contain letters, digits, underscores, hyphens, and periods. For example, `currency`, `product_code`, and `deptCode` are both examples of valid attribute names.

attributeValue is the value to associate with that attribute. Attribute values, which must be

surrounded by either single or double quotes, can contain any character data, including white space.

elementValue is the value associated with the XML element.

You cannot associate two identically named attributes with the same element. For example, the following XML declaration causes a parse error:

```
<nutrition_info
calories="123"
calories="456">
```

DESCRIBE DATA ELEMENTS WITH ATTRIBUTES

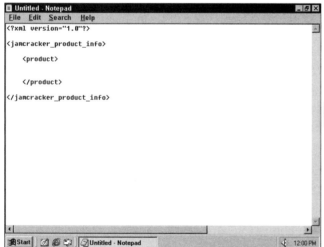

1 Open the XML file in which you want to declare an attribute.

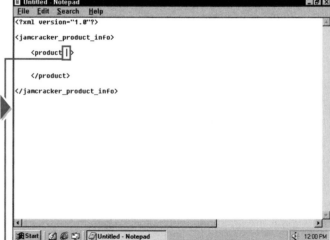

2 Position your cursor directly before the closing angle bracket (>) of the element to which you want to associate the attribute.

When should I use data as an element and when should I use data as an element attribute?

✔ A good design rule to follow is to model data that is essential to your application as an element. That is, any data you expect to manipulate directly should be cast as an element. This makes it easier to parse the document and refer directly to the data. You should model data that is only meaningful in the context of some other element or is relatively static over time as an attribute.

What type of data would be static over time?

✔ It all depends on your data model and business model, but an example might help here. An inventory item could use an attribute to provide static information about it, like this: `<invItem name="left-handed widget">`. You would use child elements to contain the part number, price per unit, quantity in stock, and so forth, because those values are likely to change over time. The `name` attribute probably will not change, so it is well-suited for use as an attribute.

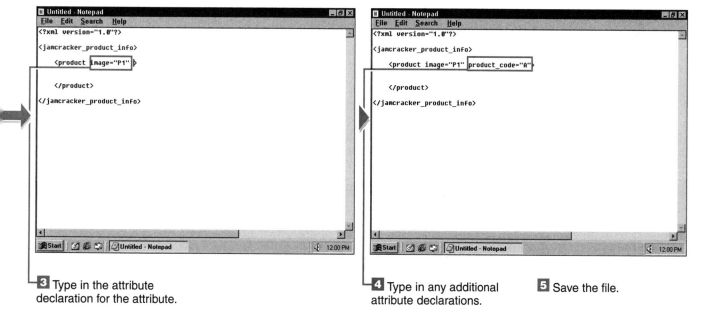

3 Type in the attribute declaration for the attribute.

4 Type in any additional attribute declarations.

5 Save the file.

CREATE CDATA FOR SPECIAL CHARACTERS

I f you need to incorporate a large number of special characters in your XML documents, you can use a construct designed specifically for that use: the CDATA section.

The CDATA section enables you to incorporate large blocks of text containing special characters into an XML document without replacing each special character with an entity reference.

Here is the syntax:

`<![CDATA[text]]>`

text is a string of text containing special characters. The XML parser will not check this text; instead, the text is "passed through." The XML processor application has the responsibility to parse or otherwise use this text in a meaningful way.

For example, you can embed characters of Unicode—a 16-bit character set that is capable of representing all of the world's languages—in your document so

they can be displayed on a Web page. This gives you a way of displaying Japanese, or line-drawing characters, or other characters on a page. If you embed Unicode characters, however, your users will still need to have the appropriate character sets installed on their computers to view the characters. The characters do not just magically appear simply because they are embedded in an XML document.

CREATE A CDATA SECTION

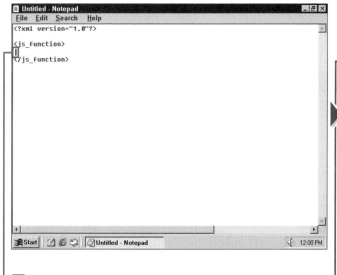

1 Open the XML document in which you want to declare a CDATA section.

2 Position your cursor where you want to declare the CDATA section.

■ In this example, the CDATA section will be declared directly below the `<js_function>` opening element tag.

3 Type in the beginning CDATA tag (`<![CDATA[`).

Are there any CDATA syntax rules I should be aware of?

✔ Because the purpose of the CDATA section is to hold unrestricted character data, few syntax rules apply to CDATA contents. These rules are that CDATA sections must be represented as element values, and only one string—]]—cannot occur between the beginning and ending CDATA tags.

When would I include a block of scripting code as CDATA?

✔ You can embed scripting code as CDATA any time you need an application to work with the data in your XML document. For example: You have an XML document you want to display as a Web page, such as a listing of items in a shopping cart. Your XML document would include the item name, item number, price, and a section of CDATA scripting code that calculates the total cost of items in the basket and displays the result. This collection of data and scripting would be parsed and processed, have an XML transform applied to it to change it into HTML, and sent to a user as a Web page.

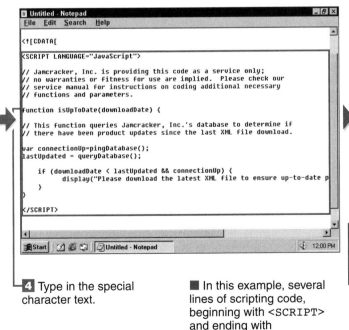

4 Type in the special character text.

■ In this example, several lines of scripting code, beginning with <SCRIPT> and ending with </SCRIPT>, form the text of the CDATA section.

5 Add the ending CDATA tag (]]>).

CREATE A SIMPLE XML PROCESSOR

To process XML data, you must create an *XML processor* (code that accesses, manipulates, or displays XML data intelligently). You can choose from four general categories of XML processors:

- Cascading style sheets. Cascading style sheets (CSS) provide a simple form of XML data display. They are presentation-focused, not data-driven, and so cannot flexibly adapt to changes in data.

See Chapter 6 for more information on CSS.

- XSL style sheets. eXtensible Stylesheet Language (XSL) is a dynamic XML data display language that provides data-driven presentation capabilities. XSL is the most flexible display option but is also the most complicated.

- Data island plus script. Incorporates XML data into an HTML presentation and performs some processing (such

as error checking or data manipulation) in addition to display. This is similar to server-side includes and is a hybrid of static style sheets and XSL.

- Data object model plus script or client-side program. Create a full-blown XML application. This format uses XML at nearly all layers of your application and is the most complex to code.

This example uses CSS to create a simple processor.

CREATE A SIMPLE XML PROCESSOR

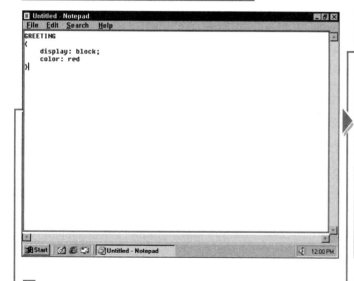

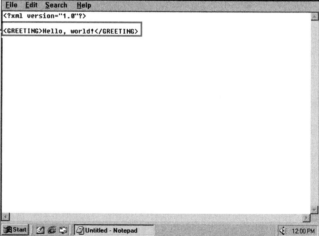

1 Create a cascading style sheet.

Note: See Chapter 6 for more on creating cascading style sheets.

2 Save the cascading style sheet using a .css extension.

■ In the example, the styles surrounded by curly braces ({ }) are applied to an XML element named GREETING.

3 Create the XML element you want to display using cascading style sheet rules.

■ This example creates a single XML element named GREETING.

Is there an easy way to handle formatting for XML documents?

✔ Because both XML and HTML were derived from *Standard Generalized Markup Language*, or SGML, you can use cascading style sheets to format both HTML and XML documents. Cascading style sheets enable you to control the color, font, and placement of all the elements in an XML document, either individually or in groups. CSS are simpler to use than XSL and are a quick way to get your Web pages using XML data.

Is there an easier way to generate CSS? The syntax looks like it can be kind of tricky.

✔ If you would like a tool to help you create CSS, check out an evaluation copy of StyleMaker. You can find it on the Internet; a free download is available at www.zdnetcom/devhead/filters10,,2133212,00.html. Many other freeware and shareware utilities are available to help you generate anything Web page-related.

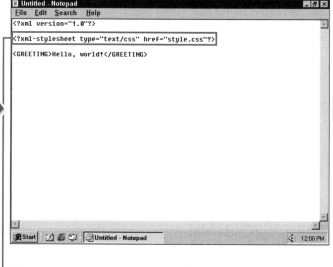

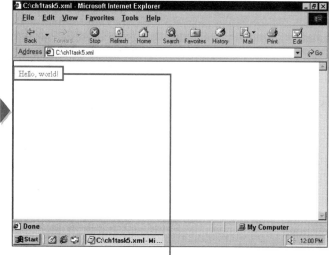

■**4** Add a cascading style sheet directive to the XML document, specifying the cascading style sheet you want to apply.

■**5** Save the file.

■ In this example, the cascading style sheet document named `style.css` is applied to the XML data.

■**6** Launch the Internet Explorer browser.

■**7** Click File.

■**8** Click Open.

■ The Open dialog box appears.

■**9** Type the name of the XML file you want to load into the Open field.

■ The XML data displays based on the specified cascading style sheet rules.

CREATE A SIMPLE XSL STYLE SHEET

Y ou can create a simple XML style sheet (XSS) using the Extensible Style Language (XSL) to load XML data into a client-side object model, manipulate that data, format, and display it.

Here is the syntax:

```
<?xml:stylesheet
xmlns:xsl="http://www.w3.
org/tR/WD-xsl">
</xsl:stylesheet>
```

You can create cascading style sheets (CSS) to format and display XML data. However, XSS offers several advantages over CSS:

- XSS enables you to "plug" XML data into a display template, much as you "plug" addresses into a form letter. Using CSS, you can only display information declared in the XML document.

- XSS enables you to format and display XML attributes and

elements. CSS enables you to format and display XML elements only.

- XSS enables you to manipulate, reorder, and display data dynamically. CSS enables you to display static XML data only.

Because scant support for this emerging standard is currently available, XSS is currently appropriate for prototyping efforts only.

CREATE A SIMPLE XSL STYLE SHEET

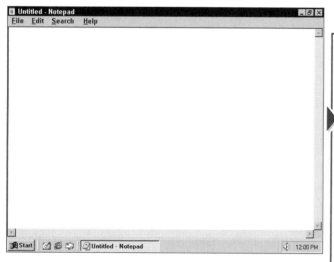

1 Create a new text file in the text editor of your choice.

■ This example shows a blank Notepad document.

2 Type the XML directive.

■ Because XSL is implemented as an XML application, you implement an XSS as an XML document.

What is XSL?

✔ XSL performs two separate roles. First, XSL provides sophisticated formatting rules that are then applied to XML data, such as font size and style, columns, spacing, footnotes, and so forth. Second, XSL transforms XML data into another format, such as changing the text string "July 15, 1970" into the numeric string "07/15/2001." These two roles give XSL the ability to parse and convert data, and to format data for display on any device.

Where can I find more information on XSL?

✔ Many tools, online tutorials, and newsgroups are dedicated to this hot topic. For current information on XSL, visit the World Wide Web Consortium at www.w3.org/TR/xsl/. For a well-written FAQ on XSL, XSLT and XML, see www.dpawson.co.uk/ xsl/xslfaq. html. For details on XSL support in Internet Explorer, visit the XSL Developers Guide at http://msdn. microsoft.com/isapi/msdnlib.idc? theURL=/library/psdk/xmlsdk/ xslp8tlx.htm.

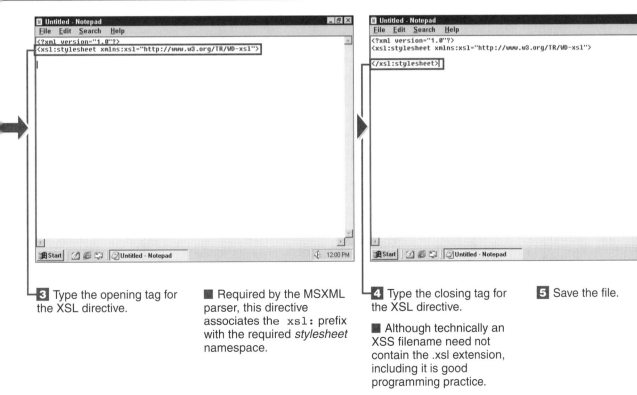

3 Type the opening tag for the XSL directive.

■ Required by the MSXML parser, this directive associates the `xsl:` prefix with the required *stylesheet* namespace.

4 Type the closing tag for the XSL directive.

■ Although technically an XSS filename need not contain the .xsl extension, including it is good programming practice.

5 Save the file.

ADD A COMMENT TO AN XML STYLE SHEET

Y ou can add a comment to an XML style sheet (XSS) to aid in code debugging and maintenance.

Here is the syntax:

`<!-- comment -->`

Although the length of a style sheet varies according to its complexity, an XSS for a typical XML application is quite lengthy.

As with any application development effort, thorough and appropriate documentation is crucial. Documenting your style sheets enables you to describe display rules so that human readers can easily understand the intent and purpose of each rule, including browser-specific workarounds. Because XSS are implemented as XML files, you document an XSS by using an XML comment line, so

XSS comments follow the standard XML comment guidelines:

- Comments can appear anywhere in a style sheet except before the XML declaration.
- You also may *not* use comments inside tags.
- The string "--" cannot appear in an XSS comment.
- Comments can span lines.

ADD A COMMENT TO AN XML STYLE SHEET

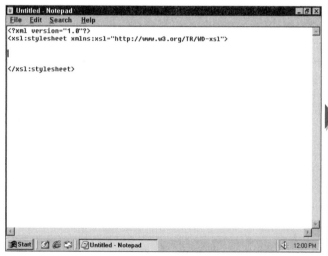

1 Open the XSL file in which you want to create the comment.

2 Type the opening comment tag (<!--).

■ Put the tag between the opening and closing XSL declaration statements.

How important are comments in XSS documents?

✔ Tool support for XSS is maturing apace with the XSS and XML specifications. At the time of this writing, however, support for XML style sheets is relatively immature. In addition, XSS syntax is complex, incorporating elements from XML, Microsoft's style sheet vocabulary, HTML, JavaScript, and the client-side object model. Because the syntax for XSS is non-intuitive, and because gaps in Microsoft's implementation may require workarounds in the near future, commenting your XSS documents thoroughly is very important.

Where can I find out more information on XML style sheets and tools for style sheets?

✔ Many resources are available on XML style sheets, including tools and tutorials available for evaluation or download. You can visit www.xslt.com/ if you need an overview of what is available. You can also check out www.w3c.org for the latest status on specifications, new software, and other announcements for the XML community.

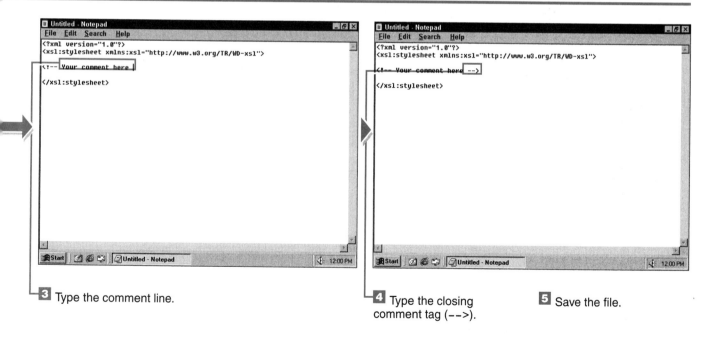

3 Type the comment line.

4 Type the closing comment tag (-->).

5 Save the file.

WORK WITH CHILD ELEMENTS USING XSL

lements that are contained inside other elements are called contained, or *child*, elements. Elements that contain other elements are called container, or *parent*, elements. Using XSL, you can identify the child elements associated with a given parent element, if any, iterate over them one by one, and display them as you want.

This parent/child structure, which you define by the structure of your XML document, can be traversed at runtime by using a combination of:

• Conditional elements. You use the XSL if element to identify a specific parent element.

• Context-sensitive patterns. Using the built-in context() method, you can loop through all the child elements associated with a specified parent element.

Here is the syntax:

```
<xsl:for-each
select="elementName">
<xsl:value-of />
<xsl:if
test="context()[not(end())]
">
</xsl:for-each>
```

elementName is the name of the parent element over which you want to iterate.

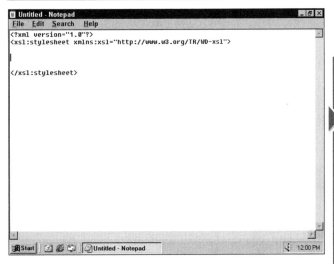

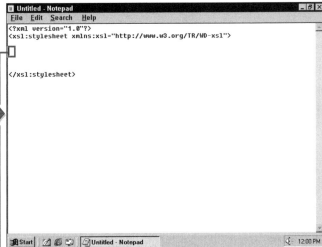

1 Open the XSL file to which you want to add the iterative XSL statement.

2 Position your cursor between the XSL opening and closing directive tags.

Does the Internet Explorer XSL parser support pattern methods and operators?

✔ Internet Explorer's XSL parser supports dozens of pattern methods and operators, including the ones used earlier:

context():	A method that returns the first element in the previously defined context.
end():	A method that returns true for the last element in a collection and false for all other elements.
not():	The negation operator.
[ ]:	An operator that applies a filter pattern; translates to "where."

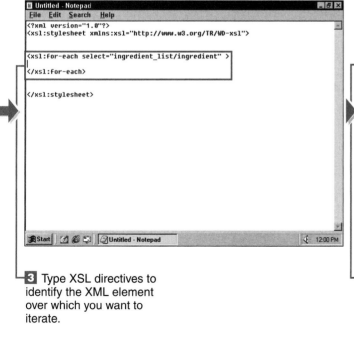

3 Type XSL directives to identify the XML element over which you want to iterate.

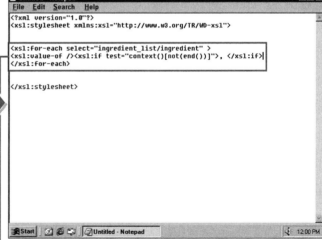

4 Type XSL directives to iterate over contained elements.

■ In this example, you see how to loop through each `ingredient` element contained in the `ingredient_list` element.

5 Save the file.

DEFINE A NAMESPACE

Y ou can create a namespace to uniquely identify elements within an XML document.

Consider an element called name, for example. Many XML application developers could reasonably incorporate a name element into their documents, representing everything from the name of a product to the name of a customer, magazine, or airplane. Without a method for uniquely identifying which XML document defines which name, an application would be unable to make use of any

name-related data. Namespaces enable XML developers to resolve these potential conflicts.

Here is the syntax required to create a namespace:

```
<namespace:elementName
xmlns:namespace="globallyUn
iqueURI">
[<namespace:containedElement
[namespace:attributeName=
"attributeValue"]>
</namespace:containedElemen
t>]
</namespace:elementName>
```

namespace is a unique name for the namespace. elementName is the name of an XML element to which the namespace will apply.

globallyUniqueURI is a globally unique uniform resource identifier. containedElement is the name of an element contained within elementName.

attributeName and attributeValue are the name and associated value, respectively, of an attribute associated with containedElement.

DEFINE A NAMESPACE

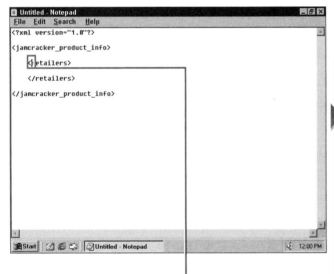

1 Open the XML file in which you want to define the namespace.

2 Put your cursor directly before the name of the element for which you want to define the namespace.

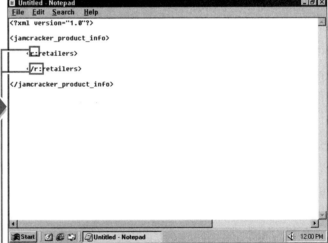

3 Append the element name in both the beginning and ending declaration tag with the name of the namespace, followed by a colon.

■ In this example, the name of the namespace is r.

Are there any rules for namespace names?

✔ Two. Namespace names begin with a letter or underscore and contain only letters, underscores, digits, hyphens, and periods, and cannot be named *xml* or *xmlns*, which are reserved names.

What is a URI?

✔ URI, which stands for *uniform resource identifier*, is a generic term meaning "any unique identifier." URL, or *uniform resource locator*, is one common type of URI, but the World Wide Web Consortium is considering other types. A URI can be represented by any unique string of characters, underscores, hyphens, and numbers.

Do I have to point my namespace URI to an actual resource out on the Internet?

✔ Because the sole purpose of a namespace value is to identify an element, or a group of elements and attributes, uniquely, the value of the namespace does not have to "point" to a resource—although it certainly may. The XML parser's job is to generate an error in the event that two namespaces referenced in an XML application bear the same name.

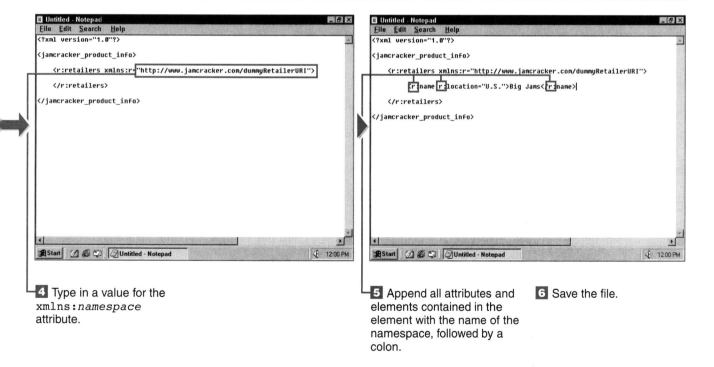

◄ 4 Type in a value for the `xmlns:namespace` attribute.

◄ 5 Append all attributes and elements contained in the element with the name of the namespace, followed by a colon.

6 Save the file.

DEFINE AN ENTITY DATA TYPE

You can define a validation rule to constrain the value of an XML attribute to a developer-defined external data source. Doing so enables you to organize XML code in multiple files and pull the XML code together at runtime.

You use the ENTITY keyword to declare an attribute of *external* type. At runtime, the only data types allowed for an element declared as type ENTITY are those data types defined in the DTD file using the <!ENTITY> declaration.

Here is the syntax:

```
<!ATTLIST elementName
attributeName ENTITY
#REQUIRED/#IMPLIED >
```

<!ATTLIST is the opening tag to define an attribute list. elementName is the name of an XML element.

attributeName is the name of an attribute associated with elementName.

ENTITY is an XML keyword denoting a developer-defined external data source.

#REQUIRED specifies that data for this XML attribute be present at runtime.

#IMPLIED specifies that data for this XML attribute may not be present at runtime.

For example, the steps in this section show you how to ensure that an attribute contains values representing GIF files at runtime. You could constrain an attribute or element to any other type of external file—whatever type makes sense for your application.

DEFINE AN ENTITY DATA TYPE

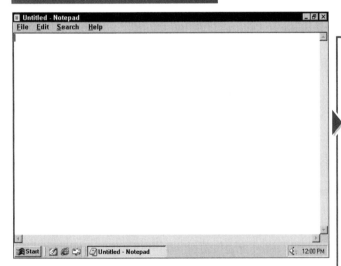

1 Open the DTD file in which you want to create the entity constraint.

■ This file can be an existing DTD document or a new Notepad file.

2 Type (or, in the case of an existing file, position your cursor beneath) the appropriate attribute list tag.

■ In this example, the <!ATTLIST> tag defines an attribute list for an XML element called product.

When would I use an entity data type within my DTD?

✔ An `<!ENTITY>` tag allows you to declare an entity data type in a DTD file but have the reference contained in another file. You could define P1 as an image associated with a product element in your DTD like this: `<!ENTITY P1="image.gif">`. A related XML file might include this element: `<product image="P1">`. This declares P1 as the image attribute for `product`, but you can easily change P1 in the appropriate XML file without having to edit your DTD.

What is the difference between a DTD and a schema?

✔ DTDs and schemas describe XML document content. Rather than include that information within the data itself, separate out that information so it can be easily changed in the future. The two main differences are that each uses a different descriptor syntax within its document, and that a schema is itself a well-formed and valid XML document with its own schema. As of mid-2001, schemas are inching closer to being an approved part of the XML specification; for now, DTD's are the only official descriptor language.

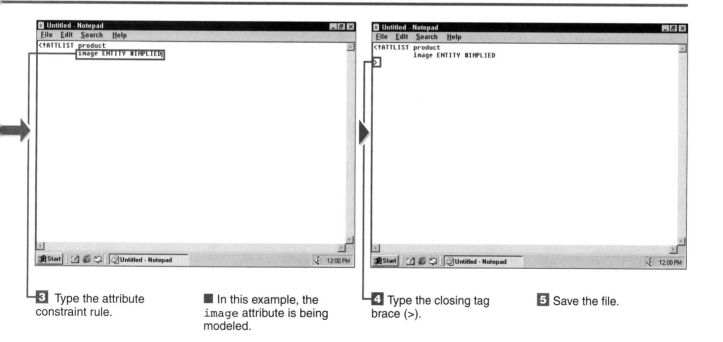

3 Type the attribute constraint rule.

■ In this example, the image attribute is being modeled.

4 Type the closing tag brace (>).

5 Save the file.

DECLARE AN INLINE DTD

You can define specific data types for each of the components of an XML document by using a *document type definition*, or DTD. DTDs are sometimes referred to as *vocabularies* because they define a common set of structured elements and attributes, much like human vocabularies establish common words and syntax rules. For example, you can use a DTD to restrict the value of an XML element to contain only character data.

You can implement DTDs two ways:

- You can include the text for a DTD inside your XML document, as shown on this page. So-called *inline DTDs* are most appropriate for short XML documents and all XML documents during the development process, and if you do not intend your DTD to be applied to other XML documents.

- You can save the text for a DTD as a separate file and refer to this file inside your XML

document. This *external DTD* approach is covered in "Declare and Save an External DTD File," next in this chapter.

The syntax required to create an inline DTD is

```
<!DOCTYPE rootElement [
dtdRules
]>
```

rootElement is the root element of the XML document in which this DTD is included. *dtdRules* is one or more XML statements that define DTD rules for individual elements within *rootElement*.

DECLARE AN INLINE DTD

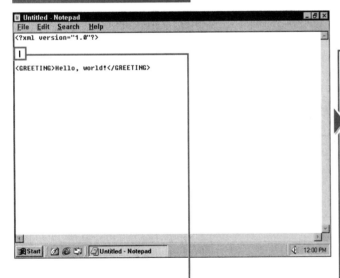

1 Open the XML file to which you want to add an inline DTD.

2 Put the cursor directly below the XML declaration and above the root element declaration.

3 Type **<!DOCTYPE** and the root element of the XML document.

What do I do when I want to exchange information with someone else but I don't have a DTD?

✔ In an ideal world, you would have a DTD for every application so that you can easily figure out what changes are needed to work with application data. In actuality, you need to sit down with the application to figure out the data formatting. Because this can be arduous for large applications, industries have started publishing their DTDs for commonly used applications. You can check the DTD repository at www.xml.org to see if your industry has one published.

Where can I learn more about DTD's?

✔ You can consult a number of resources to get more information about DTDs. The XML Consortium at www.xml.org is the best starting place for hard-core information on anything XML, including DTD and schema repositories. You can also check out www.xml101.com for useful, easy-to-read descriptions of DTDs and other XML documents. You can also pick up a copy of *XML: Your visual blueprint for building expert Web pages* (Hungry Minds, Inc.).

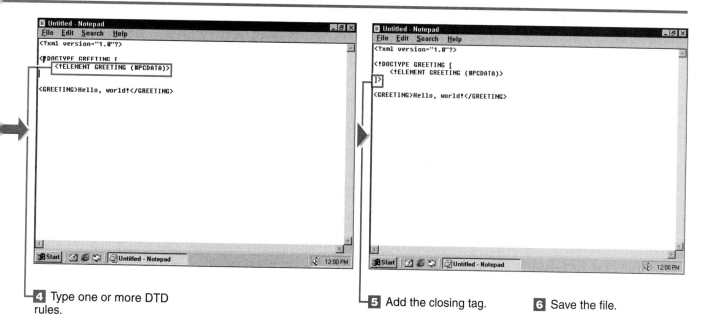

4 Type one or more DTD rules.

5 Add the closing tag.

6 Save the file.

DECLARE AND SAVE AN EXTERNAL DTD FILE

I f you intend your DTD to be applied to other XML documents, you can save the text for a DTD as a separate, external file and refer to the DTD file inside your XML document by using the DOCTYPE declaration in conjunction with the SYSTEM keyword.

Because it separates validation rules from XML data, this external DTD approach promotes document reusability. Multiple XML documents can refer to the same DTD file without having to replicate validation rules physically.

The syntax required to create an external DTD file is

```
<!DOCTYPE rootElement
SYSTEM "dtdFile">
```

rootElement is the root XML element to which the DTD file is to be applied. *dtdFile* is the name of the external DTD file.

The name of any existing DTD file is valid for the DTD filename parameter of the DOCTYPE declaration. By convention, all DTD files end in the .dtd suffix.

DECLARE AND SAVE AN EXTERNAL DTD FILE

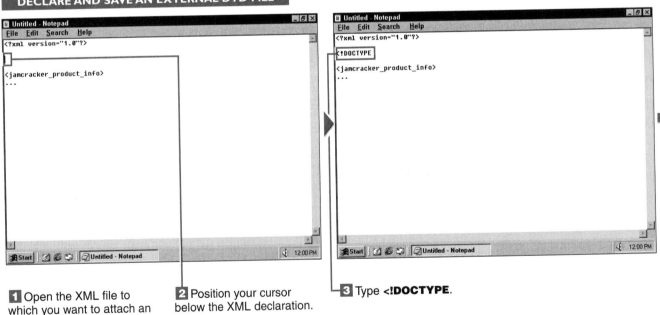

1 Open the XML file to which you want to attach an external DTD file.

2 Position your cursor below the XML declaration.

3 Type **<!DOCTYPE**.

When should I use an external DTD?

✔ External DTDs are useful not only for your own internal Web applications, but they are useful when you want to exchange data with external trading partners. With a DTD, independent groups of people can agree to use a common DTD for interchanging data. Your application can use a standard DTD to verify that data that you receive from the outside world is valid. You can also use a DTD to verify your own data from internal applications.

Do I need to publish my external DTD to a location on the Internet for it to be used?

✔ Not necessarily. Many companies do not want their internal data structures made public, so they keep their DTDs and schemas on private servers on an intranet or on an internal Web server. If you are validating your documents as part of the process, you need to have the DTD available somewhere; if you are not validating your data, then consider using an internal DTD instead.

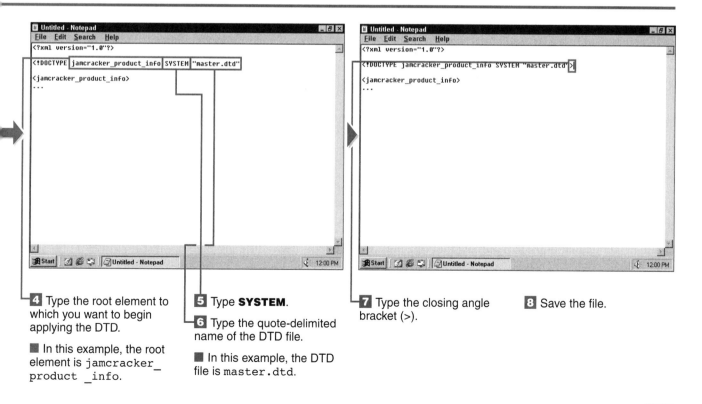

4 Type the root element to which you want to begin applying the DTD.

■ In this example, the root element is `jamcracker_ product _info`.

5 Type **SYSTEM**.

6 Type the quote-delimited name of the DTD file.

■ In this example, the DTD file is `master.dtd`.

7 Type the closing angle bracket (>).

8 Save the file.

EXPLORING DIFFERENCES BETWEEN HTML AND XHTML

XHTML documents must follow several rules to be considered valid. These rules are not necessarily required for standard HTML documents.

The first rule is that all tag sets must have a closing tag: They must include a slash symbol (/) before the last greater than symbol (>) if they are a single HTML tag. Tag sets must also not overlap one another.

Another rule is that all tags and attributes must be lowercase. Standard HTML did not care if a tag was uppercase, lowercase, or a combination, but XHTML documents are case-sensitive.

In XHTML documents, all attribute values must be in quotes. This even includes attributes that do not require a value, such as the nowrap attribute. These attributes must be set as the value, such as nowrap="nowrap".

Sections of an XHTML document can be ignored by the browser. These sections include the CDATA keyword. This keyword needs to include comments and brackets on either end, beginning with <![CDATA[and ending with]]>. These markings should surround all <script> and <style> tags included in the document.

EXPLORING DIFFERENCES BETWEEN HTML AND XHTML

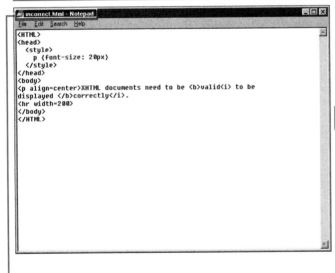

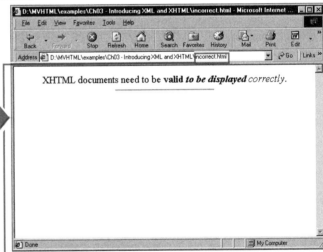

1 Open the incorrect.html file in a word processor.

■ This example uses Notepad.

■ Notice how this standard HTML file is not valid.

2 Open the incorrect.html file in a browser.

■ The document is displayed without errors in the browser.

Why do `<script>` and `<style>` tag sets need to be commented out with the `<![CDATA[` tag?

✔ The `<script>` tags are used to contain JavaScript statements, and `<style>` tags are used to contain style sheet definitions. Both JavaScript and style sheets are extensions to the original HTML specification. The XHTML specification needs a way to identify such sections that are not included in the specification. Even though these sections are commented out, the browser still recognizes and uses them.

Is there a way to see an error with an XHTML document?

✔ If you were to check an invalid XHTML document in an XML browser, you would see some errors generated, but the current HTML browsers are still forgiving to invalid XHTML documents. Until XML browsers are available, you can use HTML Tidy to check your documents for validity. This utility is covered in the next section.

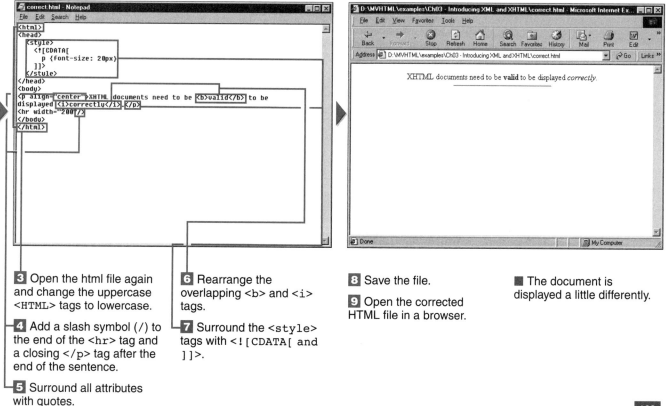

3 Open the html file again and change the uppercase `<HTML>` tags to lowercase.

4 Add a slash symbol (/) to the end of the `<hr>` tag and a closing `</p>` tag after the end of the sentence.

5 Surround all attributes with quotes.

6 Rearrange the overlapping `<b>` and `<i>` tags.

7 Surround the `<style>` tags with `<![CDATA[` and `]]>`.

8 Save the file.

9 Open the corrected HTML file in a browser.

■ The document is displayed a little differently.

CONVERT HTML DOCUMENTS TO XHTML

Y ou can check for validity problems that exist with a Web page by using a utility called *HTML Tidy*, created by Dave Raggett, a member of the World Wide Web Consortium. This utility can be used to help you convert standard HTML documents into XHTML documents. It can check for common errors, such as open-ended tags, syntax goofs, and lack of attribute quotes, and correct them.

HTML Tidy is run from the command line, such as a DOS window. To check a document using this utility, type **tidy.exe** and the name of the file to check. If you include the errors option, Tidy displays a report of errors.

HTML Tidy can also indent the entire document by using the indent flag, to make it easier to read and maintain. Using the asxml option, you can convert an HTML document to an XHTML document.

This example has you convert an incorrect file on the CD-ROM accompanying this book. Make sure you have the CD-ROM available before trying this step.

CONVERT HTML DOCUMENTS TO XHTML

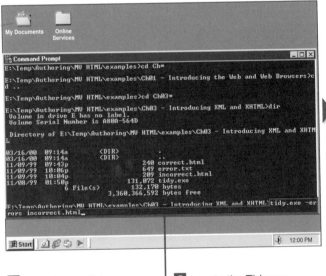

1 Click Start, click Programs, then click MS-DOS Prompt.

■ The DOS Prompt window opens.

2 Locate the Tidy.exe program on this book's CD-ROM along with the content for this chapter.

3 Type **Tidy.exe -errors incorrect.html** at the DOS prompt.

4 Press Enter.

■ The error report is generated and displayed.

What other options are available for HTML Tidy?

✔ HTML Tidy includes several additional options. All available commands can be viewed using the tidy.exe `help` option. The most common options used are `indent`, which formats the file by indenting the text to make it more readable; `modify`, which enables the original file to be modified; `errors`, which lists only errors in the output without modifying the file; and `asxml`, which converts the HTML file to a well formed XML document.

Is there a version of HTML Tidy available for the Macintosh?

✔ HTML Tidy is in Windows format only on the CD-ROM included with this book, but there are numerous other versions available including one for the Macintosh. There is also a Java version, and if you are ambitious, the source code is available for those who want to see how Tidy works its magic. All of these versions are available for download at www.w3.org/People/Raggett/tidy.

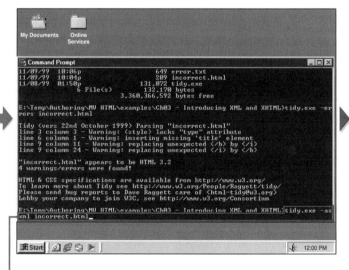

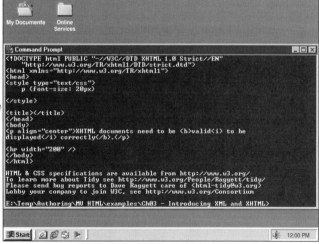

5 Type **Tidy.exe -asxml incorrect.html** after the DOS prompt in the DOS window.

6 Press Enter.

■ The changes needed by the file are displayed.

UNDERSTANDING XHTML DTDS

XHTML provides for essentially three different DTDs. These are *Strict, Transitional,* and *Frameset.* The same three types also exist for HTML 4.

The *Strict* DTD is a stickler, requiring clean tag markup and use of the latest tags throughout the document. The *Transitional* DTD is the most widely used DTD because it includes support for many older tags, such as the

bgcolor attribute to the <body> tag, that are still being used. The *Frameset* DTD is used when you want to break your Web pages up into frames.

You can see all of these DTDs online at www.w3.org/TR/ xhtml1/#dtds.

Within each of these DTD documents is a public line of text that shows the correct syntax that

should be used to include the DTD in the <!doctype> tag.

If you need information on adding a DTD to an XHTML document, see Chapter 21. The following example shows you some sample DTDs you can use in your document.

UNDERSTANDING XHTML DTDS

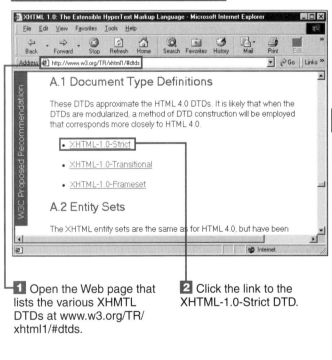

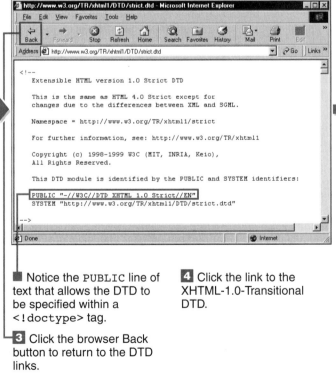

1 Open the Web page that lists the various XHMTL DTDs at www.w3.org/TR/ xhtml1/#dtds.

2 Click the link to the XHTML-1.0-Strict DTD.

■ Notice the PUBLIC line of text that allows the DTD to be specified within a <!doctype> tag.

3 Click the browser Back button to return to the DTD links.

4 Click the link to the XHTML-1.0-Transitional DTD.

What other DTDs can I use?

✔ Besides the HTML 4.01 and XHTML 1.0 DTDs, you can select to use older DTDs for HTML version 2.0 and 3.2. A number of XML DTDs are beginning to appear, especially for industries that have already set up trading exchanges or business-to-business exchanges. These DTDs are published so that developers do not have to reinvent the wheel—they can download an existing DTD to see what format their data should be in.

Why would I want to use the XHTML specification instead of the HTML specification?

✔ The DTD that you use depends on your future plans. If the HTML files that you are creating will someday be used alongside XML content, it is in your best interest to make your code adhere to the XHTML specification. However, if you can be sure that your HTML files will never be used on an XML browser, the HTML specification will suffice.

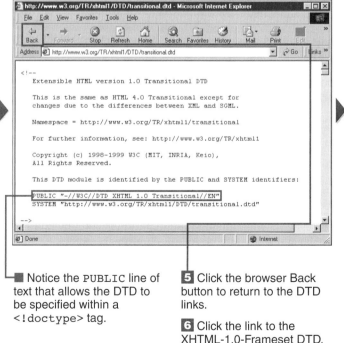

■ Notice the PUBLIC line of text that allows the DTD to be specified within a `<!doctype>` tag.

5 Click the browser Back button to return to the DTD links.

6 Click the link to the XHTML-1.0-Frameset DTD.

■ Notice the PUBLIC line of text that allows the DTD to be specified within a `<!doctype>` tag.

VALIDATING XHTML WEB PAGES

After you have completed your Web page and checked it in a browser, another way to check the page is to use a validating utility. These utilities are found on the Web and can be downloaded from a repository such as www.download.com.

Validating utilities compare the Web page syntax in your Web page file

with the accepted specification and show you if there are any syntax errors in your HTML code.

For example, the HTML 4.0 specification requires closing tags for certain tags. If a closing tag is missing, the validation utility lists this as an error.

These validation utilities also make suggestions for better

enabling your Web pages to be viewed in a browser.

One such validating service can be found on the W3C's Web site at http://validator.w3.org. This example uses the W3C's validating service. Steps for using other validation utilities may vary but follow roughly the same procedures.

VALIDATING XHTML WEB PAGES

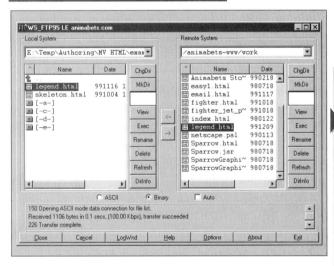

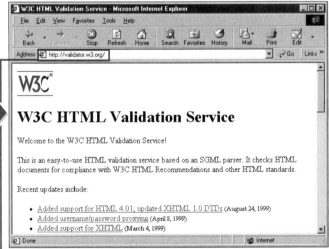

1 Use an FTP program to copy the Web page file to a Web server.

■ See Chapter 18 for more on transferring files.

2 Enter the URL for the W3C HTML Validation Service in a browser.

What other validation utilities are available?

✔ Many such validation utilities are available. Another good validation Web site can be found at www.Weblint. org. Other validation utilities can be downloaded, such as CSE HTML Validator, which can be downloaded at www.htmlvalidator.com.

Can validation utilities automatically correct your Web page files?

✔ The functionality of the various validation utilities is different. Some utilities can be configured to automatically correct certain errors. You need to give the utility access to your files in order for it to make the needed changes.

Can validation utilities be used to check spelling and links?

✔ Many utilities can be used to perform multiple functions, such as spell and link checking, in addition to HTML validation. If you will be working extensively with HTML and Web site management, you should invest in an IDE (integrated development environment) specifically built for Web sites. Microsoft FrontPage is one; Allaire's HomeSite is another. HomeSite is covered in Chapter 23.

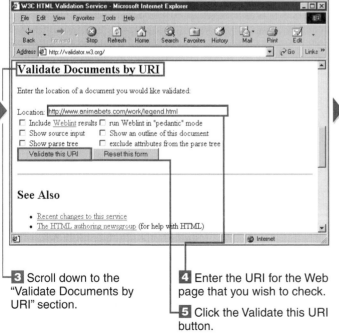

3 Scroll down to the "Validate Documents by URI" section.

4 Enter the URI for the Web page that you wish to check.

5 Click the Validate this URI button.

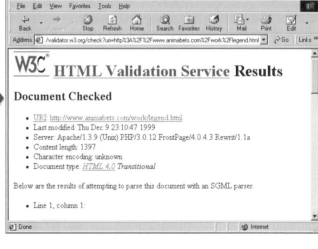

■ The results are displayed on a Web page.

25) EDIT GRAPHICS WITH PHOTOSHOP

AN INTRODUCTION TO HOMESITE

Macromedia's HomeSite 4 is an excellent Web page editor that you can use to create, edit, and publish Web pages. It has all the power and flexibility of a full-featured word processor but with the highly desirable capability to work directly with HTML. This enables Web page designers to fine-tune Web pages, work with HTML without fussing with WYSIWYG (what you see is what you get) environments, and directly

test and view Web pages without having to save and exit the editor (in order to view the pages with a Web browser).

HomeSite is more properly known as a Web page editor, rather than a Web page authoring program (like Microsoft FrontPage). Although authoring programs are popular for working more with visual elements or Microsoft-specific Web servers, HomeSite and other Web page editors enable you to get into the

fine details of HTML, something that Web authoring programs lack. Notepad can do this, as can any text editor, such as vi, or a more powerful environment, such as emacs. But most Web page developers prefer a development environment that gives them powerful tools to manipulate HTML directly. HomeSite has these tools, and it has a powerful and highly customizable interface to enable you to set up an editing environment that meets your specific needs.

W3C Documents

You can use HomeSite for all of your document editing needs, for any document standard defined by the World Wide Web Consortium (W3C). You can create, edit, and maintain any of several different document types: HTML 2, 3.2, and 4; WML 1 and 2; SMIL 1; and any XML-based document type. The environment is extensible, so you can add to or define your own document types for any projects that you are working on. HomeSite even includes extension support specific to Netscape Navigator and Internet Explorer, so you can write code for a specific browser if you are certain that it will be the only one used to view your pages.

Server-Side Environments

HomeSite has built-in support for the three most popular server-side environments: JSP (JavaServer Pages), ASP (Active Server Pages), and CFML (ColdFusion Markup Language). You can generate script for these

environments and include them in your Web pages. Or you can generate a server-side solution that does not have any user interface. The possibilities are almost unlimited.

Online Help

There is an enormous amount of online help and assistance within HomeSite, from wizards to validators to reference materials. Macromedia also maintains a developer Web site where you can download free add-ons or plug-ins for your projects—www.allaire.com/support/index.cfm as of the time of this writing, although with the recent merger between Macromedia and Allaire, the location of the site may change. And the editor's help files are extensible, so you can create your own help materials for projects that you and your team are working on.

The HomeSite Interface

HomeSite is a multiple document interface (MDI) program, which means that you can have multiple documents open within the same frame. HomeSite also has the most commonly used features and functions available within different panes, toolbars, and tabs, so you can quickly move between your files and make your edits as needed.

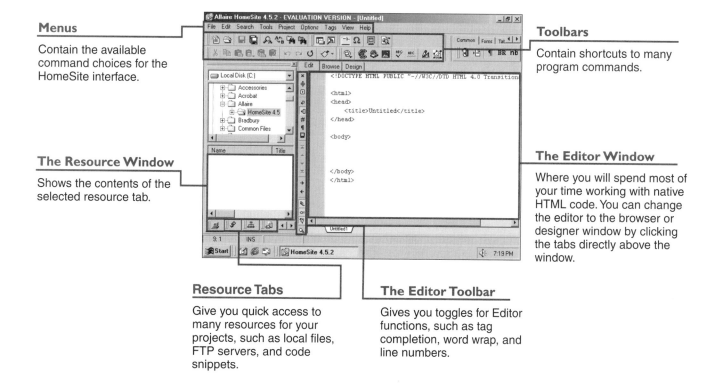

Menus

Contain the available command choices for the HomeSite interface.

The Resource Window

Shows the contents of the selected resource tab.

Toolbars

Contain shortcuts to many program commands.

The Editor Window

Where you will spend most of your time working with native HTML code. You can change the editor to the browser or designer window by clicking the tabs directly above the window.

Resource Tabs

Give you quick access to many resources for your projects, such as local files, FTP servers, and code snippets.

The Editor Toolbar

Gives you toggles for Editor functions, such as tag completion, word wrap, and line numbers.

CUSTOMIZE YOUR WORKSPACE

Developers insist on two features in any editor or development environment: that it be both easy and powerful to get the task done and that it be highly customizable. Developers are notoriously finicky about having absolute control over an application and its options, and if the application will not behave the

way that they think it ought to, they will not use it.

HomeSite has become a developer favorite because it meets both conditions. It has easy, powerful features in abundance (as covered in other sections in this chapter). In this section, you will see the many configuration options that can make HomeSite your editor of choice. The

goal of these options is to let you get your job done, unobtrusively, without forcing you to use a particular way of writing your code.

As you go through some of these options, you will see others that are not explained. Feel free to read the online help for more information, or just change some settings and see what they do.

CUSTOMIZE YOUR WORKSPACE

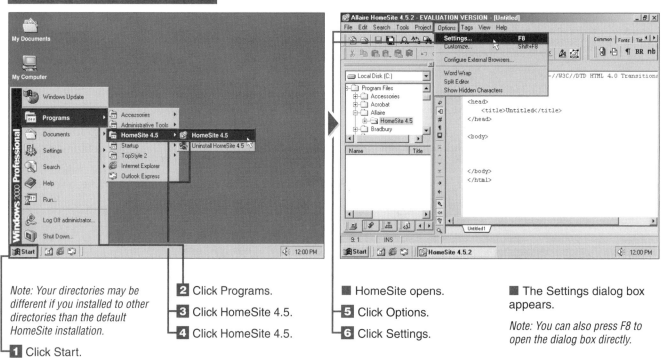

Note: Your directories may be different if you installed to other directories than the default HomeSite installation.

■1 Click Start.

■2 Click Programs.

■3 Click HomeSite 4.5.

■4 Click HomeSite 4.5.

■ HomeSite opens.

■5 Click Options.

■6 Click Settings.

■ The Settings dialog box appears.

Note: You can also press F8 to open the dialog box directly.

Why should I use lowercase tags? I thought that the specification calls for uppercase tags.

✔ In the early days of HTML, browsers were not case-sensitive. Developers used uppercase tags to distinguish the tags from page content. However, XHTML- and XML-based documents are case-sensitive and have begun requiring lowercase tags. Although the choice is yours to implement whichever style you want, you may want to use lowercase tags in your documents for easier maintenance in the future.

Can I have HomeSite start in a folder rather than start with a particular project or document?

✔ HomeSite can start in just about any combination of files, folders, and projects that you want. To have HomeSite start in a home folder rather than with a particular project, click Options, Settings, and then Startup and, under the Startup Folder section, type a drive and directory name in the text box. You can also browse for a folder if the path is particularly long or complex.

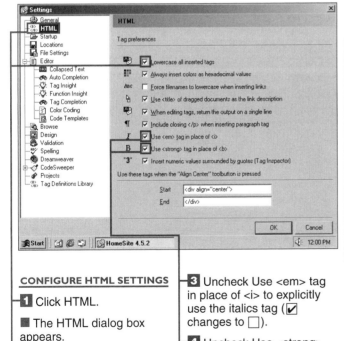

CONFIGURE HTML SETTINGS

■1 Click HTML.

■ The HTML dialog box appears.

■2 Click Lowercase all inserted tags to use lowercase instead of uppercase (☐ changes to ☑).

■3 Uncheck Use <em> tag in place of <i> to explicitly use the italics tag (☑ changes to ☐).

■4 Uncheck Use <strong> tag in place of <b> to explicitly use the bold tag (☑ changes to ☐).

CONFIGURE STARTUP SETTINGS

■1 Click Startup.

■ The Startup dialog box appears.

■2 Click Restore last opened documents at startup to automatically restore your last opened document.

■3 Click Restore last opened project at startup to automatically reload all the files in your project.

Note: These settings save you time when you close and reopen HomeSite to work on projects.

CONTINUED ▶

CUSTOMIZE YOUR WORKSPACE (CONTINUED)

One of the more useful functions that HomeSite provides is the Tag Completion function. Tag Completion automatically inserts the closing tag after you finish typing the opening tag. This way, you can avoid having any open tags or improperly closed tags in your HTML documents.

At first, this may seem annoying; many HTML documents do not use closing tags for common elements such as paragraphs, instead starting another paragraph with a new <p> opening tag. Although this is sometimes considered sloppy coding, it is also very convenient, and most browsers are very forgiving of pages lacking proper closing tags.

However, new, more rigorous standards are on the horizon. XHTML is a hybrid of XML and HTML, in essence applying XML formatting standards to HTML documents. XHTML creates a more readily editable and portable document for future use and can be parsed for correctness and validity. Tag Completion can help take the work out of following the standard, automatically.

CUSTOMIZE YOUR WORKSPACE (CONTINUED)

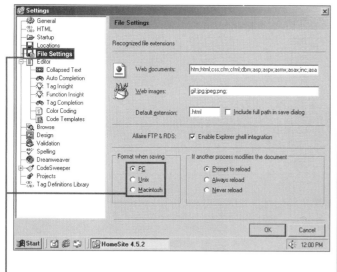

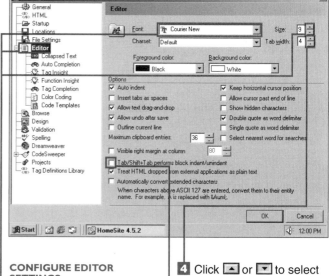

CONFIGURE FILE SETTINGS

1 Click File Settings.

■ The File Settings dialog box appears.

2 Click the file format to use when you save files (○ changes to ●).

Note: PC, UNIX, and Macintosh text files use different file formats. If you know which platform your file will be hosted on, save your files in that format.

CONFIGURE EDITOR SETTINGS

1 Click Editor.

2 Click ▾ and select your font style.

3 Click ▲ or ▾ to select your font size.

4 Click ▲ or ▾ to select the number of spaces a tab moves.

5 Click Tab/Shift+Tab performs block indent/unindent to have selected text indent and "unindent" as a group (☐ changes to ☑).

Why should I use the Auto Indent and block Indent/Undent features?

✔ White space is ignored by compilers and browsers, which means that it costs you nothing to make a document easily readable. Nearly all developers indent text and remove indention from text to indicate which blocks of text belong together; in addition, hierarchical document languages, such as XML, use indenting and "unindenting" to indicate parent-child relationships. Unless you have a good reason not to, it is strongly suggested that you indent and unindent your text as needed to improve readability.

Can I use any font I want to in the editor window?

✔ You can use any font that is installed on your machine. However, most developers use a monospaced font, such as Courier or Fixedsys, when working in development environments; these fonts are easy to read and are installed on nearly every machine.

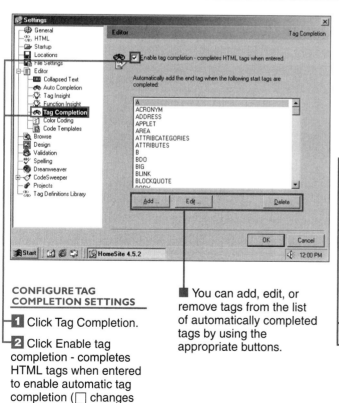

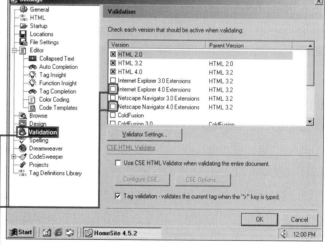

CONFIGURE TAG COMPLETION SETTINGS

1 Click Tag Completion.

2 Click Enable tag completion - completes HTML tags when entered to enable automatic tag completion (☐ changes to ☑).

■ You can add, edit, or remove tags from the list of automatically completed tags by using the appropriate buttons.

CONFIGURE VALIDATION SETTINGS

1 Click Validation.

2 Click the HTML definitions or Web browser extensions to be included when validating your documents (☐ changes to ☒).

Note: It is recommended that you do not change any validator settings unless you are working with advanced document types or sophisticated applications.

WORK WITH TOOLBARS

Toolbars are a developer's best friend. With toolbars, you can group together commonly used functions for a particular type of code or environment, move them around your desktop, dock them inside the HomeSite window, and in general, configure them to your exact, most helpful standards.

Most of the toolbars can be dragged and dropped to float or dock anywhere within HomeSite. Some toolbars are strictly associated with their windows and cannot be moved or edited, such as the Edit and Browse windows. Together, they provide a wealth of tools for just about any possible configuration of technologies, scripting languages, and Web site features.

You can also drag a toolbar onto the Quick bar, which provides a "master index" of open toolbars that you can switch between by clicking a Quick bar tab. The Quick bar provides another way of maximizing easy availability while minimizing the screen real estate used by all the tools. If you are working on a project that involves multiple technologies or scripting languages, you will find yourself using the Quick bar extensively.

WORK WITH TOOLBARS

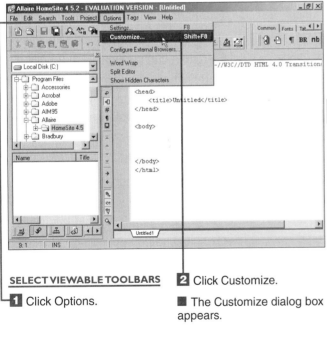

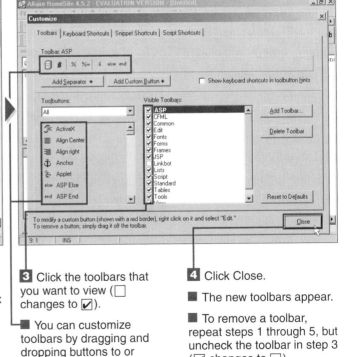

SELECT VIEWABLE TOOLBARS

■1 Click Options.

■2 Click Customize.

■ The Customize dialog box appears.

■3 Click the toolbars that you want to view (□ changes to ☑).

■ You can customize toolbars by dragging and dropping buttons to or removing buttons from any of the toolbars.

■4 Click Close.

■ The new toolbars appear.

■ To remove a toolbar, repeat steps 1 through 5, but uncheck the toolbar in step 3 (☑ changes to □).

How can I tell what a toolbar button does?

✔ Hover your mouse cursor over a button, and after a few seconds, a ToolTip appears, telling you what the button's function is.

Is there really a secret game hidden in HomeSite?

✔ The "secret game" is not actually hidden, but it is a bit of fun for when you need a break from coding. In the Customize dialog box, at the bottom of the Toolbuttons list is a button called Easter Egg. Drag it onto a toolbar, close the Customize dialog box, and then click your new toolbar button. The game will start. Have fun!

I want to create a custom toolbar. How do I do it?

✔ Creating a toolbar is a great way to customize HomeSite, especially if you want to have your most frequently used functions available but do not want all the screen clutter. In the Customize dialog box, click Add Toolbar, type in a new name, click OK, and then drag the buttons that you want from the Toolbuttons list on the left onto your new toolbar. You can add buttons from any of the other toolbars to create your new one.

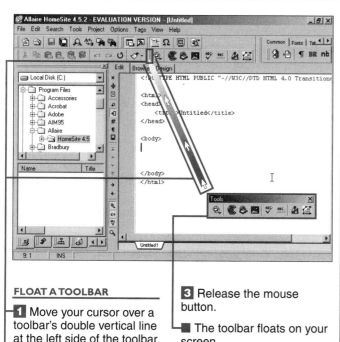

FLOAT A TOOLBAR

1 Move your cursor over a toolbar's double vertical line at the left side of the toolbar.

2 Click and drag your mouse cursor to a new point on the screen.

3 Release the mouse button.

■ The toolbar floats on your screen.

DOCK A TOOLBAR

1 Move your mouse cursor over the toolbar's title bar.

2 Click and drag your mouse cursor to the side of a window.

3 Release the mouse button.

■ The toolbar is docked at the side of the window.

Note: You can dock a toolbar on any side of a window.

CONFIGURE AND USE EXTERNAL BROWSERS

One of the more difficult aspects of coding a Web site is knowing how your Web pages will appear in different browsers. Some browsers have proprietary HTML extensions that are incompatible with other browsers. To make matters worse, there are no specifications for basic things, such as font styles or sizes for headings, paragraphs, and so on; thus, each browser

manufacturer can make its "best efforts" to have a common look and feel with other browsers, but you are not guaranteed that the Web pages will appear the same.

Enter HomeSite and its ability to configure external browsers. HomeSite has a rudimentary internal browser that you can use to view static Web pages, and if you are running a system that has

Microsoft Internet Explorer 4.x or higher, HomeSite can use that browser as the default internal browser. But you can install other browsers on your computer and use those as external browsers to view your Web pages during development. This lets you switch between browsers to see how your Web pages and applications will look to your end users.

CONFIGURE AND USE EXTERNAL BROWSERS

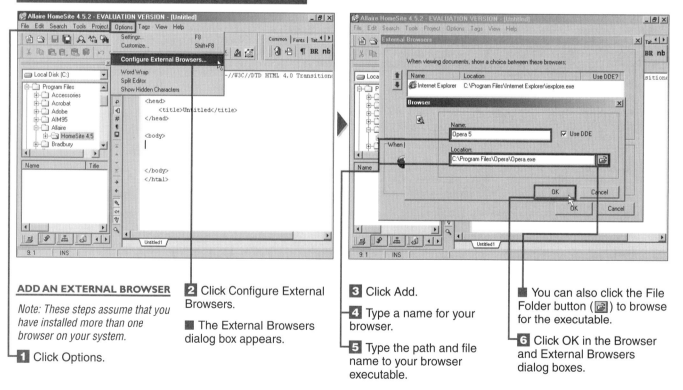

ADD AN EXTERNAL BROWSER

Note: These steps assume that you have installed more than one browser on your system.

1 Click Options.

2 Click Configure External Browsers.

■ The External Browsers dialog box appears.

3 Click Add.

4 Type a name for your browser.

5 Type the path and file name to your browser executable.

■ You can also click the File Folder button (📁) to browse for the executable.

6 Click OK in the Browser and External Browsers dialog boxes.

Do I have to use Internet Explorer as my internal browser?

✔ You can set up almost any browser to be your default internal browser. However, some browsers require you to download and install some additional software to build in hooks for that browser. Netscape Navigator, for example, requires that you download and install the Mozilla NGLayout control before you can run it as your internal browser. If you have questions, check the online help and the Macromedia or Allaire Web sites for FAQs or instructions on other browsers.

Can I use HomeSite's built-in browser instead of Internet Explorer to view my Web pages?

✔ You can certainly use the built-in HomeSite browser, with a very big caveat: It works for static pages only. If you are using any kind of server-side scripting, the built-in browser will not work. You need to upload your pages to an actual server and view them with a full-featured browser. See the next section, "Configure an Internal Browser," to find out how to do this.

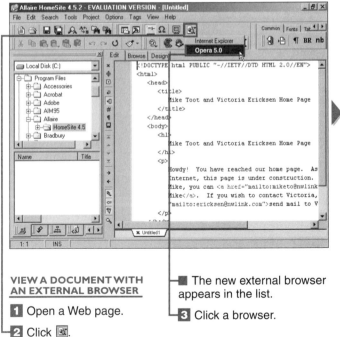

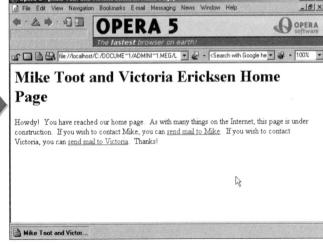

VIEW A DOCUMENT WITH AN EXTERNAL BROWSER

1 Open a Web page.

2 Click 🖳.

■ The new external browser appears in the list.

3 Click a browser.

■ The document appears in the external browser.

CONFIGURE AN INTERNAL BROWSER

Y ou can use either internal or external browsers to view static Web pages—that is, ones that do not have any server-side scripting in them. The HomeSite built-in browser is useful for viewing these kinds of pages; in addition, if you have Microsoft Internet Explorer 3.01 or later installed, HomeSite will use it as the default browser for viewing your pages.

However, there is still the issue of how to handle server-side scripting. HomeSite typically reads a file directly from a disk into memory and then displays the contents of that file in a browser window. It does not do any script processing as a Web server would do.

There is a way, though, that you can preview pages with server-side scripting with HomeSite's internal

browser. You can configure HomeSite to map file directories to a Web server's virtual directory. This means that an HTTP request is sent to the Web server, and the page is returned to the browser. This way, you can see the effect that your script has on a page.

CONFIGURE AN INTERNAL BROWSER

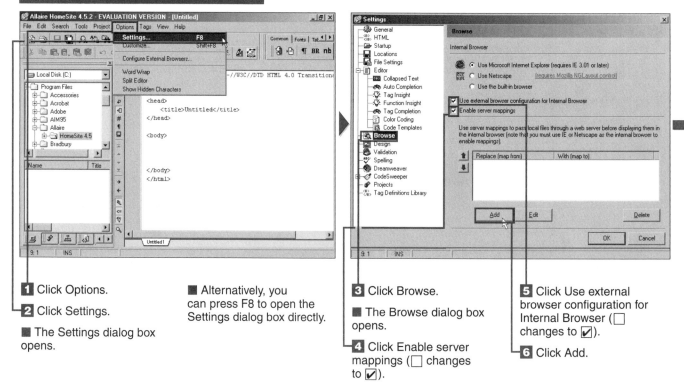

1 Click Options.

2 Click Settings.

■ The Settings dialog box opens.

■ Alternatively, you can press F8 to open the Settings dialog box directly.

3 Click Browse.

■ The Browse dialog box opens.

4 Click Enable server mappings (□ changes to ☑).

5 Click Use external browser configuration for Internal Browser (□ changes to ☑).

6 Click Add.

How do I check to see if I have mapped everything correctly?

✔ Open the File Resources window and double-click a file from the newly mapped Web site root directory. You can now view the document using the internal browser with all the scripting being processed by the Web server.

Can I have more than one mapping available?

✔ You can have any number of mappings. Add them in the normal way and then use the up and down arrows to move a mapping to the top of the list to serve as the default.

Should I use an external browser to view pages with script or configure the internal browser to do so?

✔ The choice is up to you. Sometimes it is handy to switch between Edit and Browse mode, and an internal viewer helps keep the mouse clicks to a minimum. Other times, you may want to compare multiple views of the same Web page, and external browsers are best for that. Either way, HomeSite lets you configure your environment to work the way that you want to.

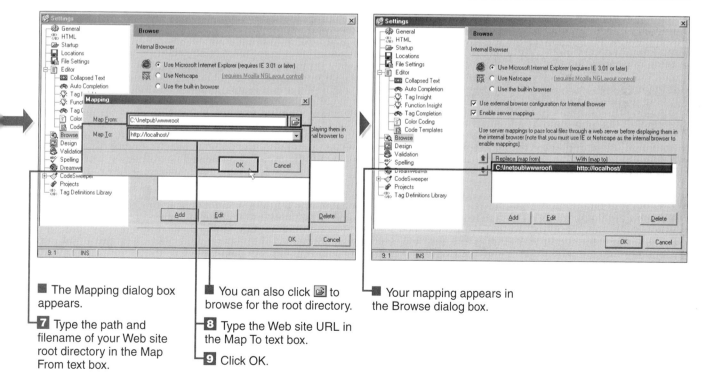

■ The Mapping dialog box appears.

7 Type the path and filename of your Web site root directory in the Map From text box.

■ You can also click 🖼 to browse for the root directory.

8 Type the Web site URL in the Map To text box.

9 Click OK.

■ Your mapping appears in the Browse dialog box.

INSERT SPECIAL CHARACTERS

Web pages can have a variety of characters on them. These include characters from non-English character sets, dingbats, and special images or codes for programs. There are also characters that are used to describe Web page content itself, such as <, that can be displayed on a Web page. But how do you tell a browser not to parse a < as an opening bracket of a tag?

The answer lies in special characters. These are characters that can be displayed in a browser but require some additional text to keep them from being treated improperly. Special characters use the ampersand character (&) followed by other "shorthand" characters. For example, the less-than sign (<) is represented in a Web page as < and the greater-than sign (>) as >. Each

character set terminates with a semicolon, so the browser knows the special character description section has ended.

HomeSite gives you a quick and easy way to insert special characters without having to remember the abbreviated special character names.

INSERT SPECIAL CHARACTERS

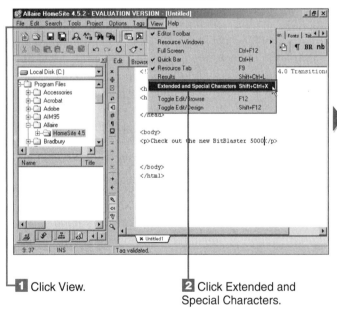

1 Click View.

2 Click Extended and Special Characters.

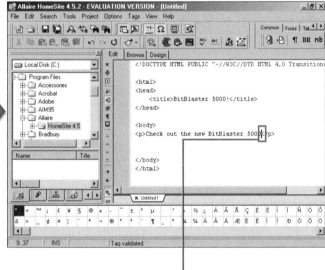

■ The Special Characters pane appears.

Note: You can also press Shift+Ctrl+X to open the Special Characters pane.

3 Place your cursor in the document where you want to insert the special character.

Can I insert characters that are not in the Special Characters pane?

✔ All characters are represented by a Unicode double-byte character sequence that you can plug into a browser. If you want to display a certain Greek character, you can insert an ampersand followed by a pound sign, the Unicode string, and a semicolon, like this: &#03B6; (lowercase zeta). There are over 16,000 Unicode characters; if you want to use Unicode but don't know the double-byte sequence, you can find Unicode charts in PDF or GIF format at www.unicode.org/charts/.

Can I insert non-English characters into a Web page?

✔ You can insert nearly any character into a Web page, with the caveat that many browsers may not be able to display them. For example, you can insert the character codes for Mandarin Chinese characters, but unless a browser is set up to display double-byte character sets, the end user will not see the characters at all.

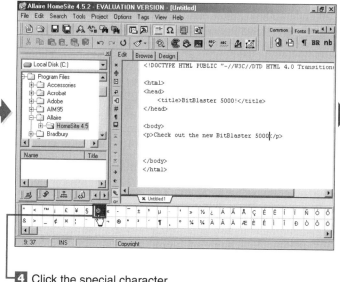

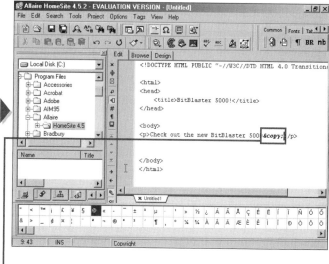

4 Click the special character that you want to insert in the Special Characters pane.

■ The special character appears in the document.

■ You can hide the Special Characters pane by repeating steps 1 and 2 or by pressing Shift+Ctrl+X.

USING EXTENDED SEARCH AND REPLACE

Nearly every program on the market, from spreadsheets to text editors, offers the capability to find and replace text. But what do you do when you are asked to make wholesale changes to some element in your Web page? The changes are usually nontrivial, such as a product name, a company name, or other wide-ranging term.

Even in the best of circumstances, the thought of opening documents one by one and doing a search and replace through each of those is daunting.

Well, you are not alone. Other developers have had the same task to perform. The HomeSite developers recognized the problem

and provided a solution. HomeSite offers a number of powerful, fast ways to search for and replace terms or expressions, not just in a single document, but within multiple documents and folders— or throughout an entire project. You can search for large blocks of text or regular expressions.

USING EXTENDED SEARCH AND REPLACE

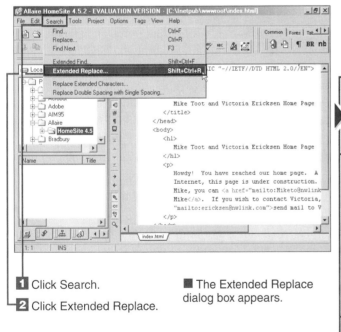

■ **1** Click Search.

■ **2** Click Extended Replace.

■ The Extended Replace dialog box appears.

■ **3** Type the text that you want to search for.

■ **4** Type the replacement text for your search term.

■ **5** Select the path and filename of the folder or click 🖻 to browse to it.

■ You can click ▼ and select particular file types to search for.

■ **6** Click Replace.

Can I view the search results in a browser?

✔ You can right-click a file that is returned as a search result and then click Open in Browser. The default external browser opens and displays your file.

Can I save search strings, such as long blocks of text?

✔ Yes. You can save and re-search text by using the large arrow button at the left side of the search term window.

What are regular expressions?

✔ Think of *regular expressions* (often abbreviated *regex* or *regexp*) as pattern-matching expressions that use special characters to define combinations of letters, numbers, or other characters. A wildcard filename search of `*.*` is a regular expression. A search for `[Mm]ike` searches for all instances of upper- or lowercase Ms that make up the word `Mike`. For more information on regular expressions in HomeSite, see the online help.

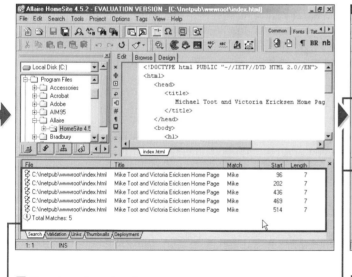

■ Your search and replace results are returned in the Results window.

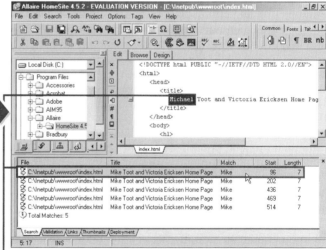

7 Double-click a filename in the Results pane to open the replaced text in HomeSite.

CREATE AND ADD CODE SNIPPETS

C ode snippets are blocks of code that you keep handy for reuse elsewhere in your projects. Instead of typing and retyping the same information or section of code, you can keep a minilibrary of code snippets that can be quickly pasted into a project.

The blocks of code can contain just about any kind of text information: trademark names with symbols, company slogans, footer text, phone numbers, e-mail addresses, specially formatted text, such as comment blocks, and so on. All of this can be kept in folders off your project's root directory for easy access.

Adding, editing, and maintaining snippets is easy. Snippets are stored in the Snippets resource tab and can be deleted, reorganized, or edited quickly. You can even set up keyboard shortcuts to paste a snippet without using the mouse.

CREATE AND ADD CODE SNIPPETS

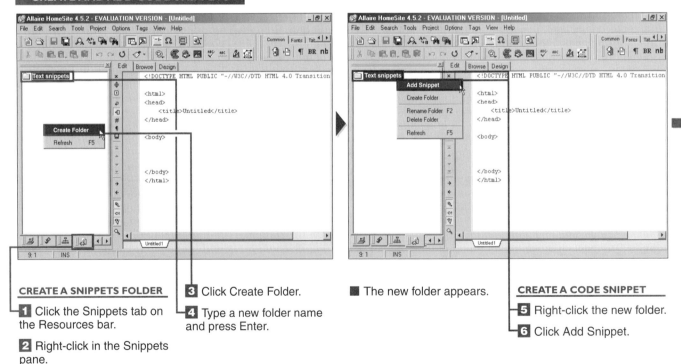

CREATE A SNIPPETS FOLDER

1 Click the Snippets tab on the Resources bar.

2 Right-click in the Snippets pane.

3 Click Create Folder.

4 Type a new folder name and press Enter.

■ The new folder appears.

CREATE A CODE SNIPPET

5 Right-click the new folder.

6 Click Add Snippet.

MASTER VISUALLY WEB DESIGN

Using Web Design Applications

Why can I specify both starting and ending text for a snippet?

✔ You do not need to specify both; you can have just the starting text as your snippet. But if you have a lengthy section of tags for text formatting, you can set up your snippet as the formatting start tags and the ending text as the closing tags. When you paste your snippet into a document, both blocks will be pasted, and your cursor will be between the blocks, ready for typing.

Is there a way to set up a macro to paste snippets into my Web page?

✔ You can set up a keyboard shortcut to quickly paste a snippet without using the mouse. Click Options and then Customize; then select the Snippet Shortcuts tab. Select a snippet and then press the keystroke sequence that you want to use. Click Apply. Then you can use your keyboard shortcut any time that you choose.

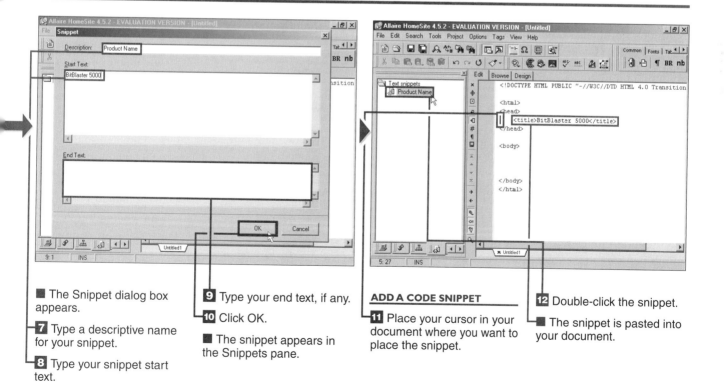

■ The Snippet dialog box appears.

7 Type a descriptive name for your snippet.

8 Type your snippet start text.

9 Type your end text, if any.

10 Click OK.

■ The snippet appears in the Snippets pane.

ADD A CODE SNIPPET

11 Place your cursor in your document where you want to place the snippet.

12 Double-click the snippet.

■ The snippet is pasted into your document.

VALIDATE A DOCUMENT

Because Web projects are highly syntactical, HomeSite provides two different methods of validation: tag validation and document validation.

Tag validation occurs automatically when you are in design mode, notifying you if you generated a typo or used an improper attribute in a tag. Tag validation takes a second or two when you are in design mode, but you can turn it

off and validate a document after you have finished designing the document.

With document validation, the entire document is run through a parser and compared with valid tags and attributes. Any errors or warning messages that are generated appear in the Results pane, along with line numbers for easy reference.

You can validate numerous document types against various W3C standards, including HTML 2 through 4, SMIL, WML, and CFML. Browser-specific extensions are also available so that you can compare browser versions to see whether your code will pass muster for the different versions.

VALIDATE A DOCUMENT

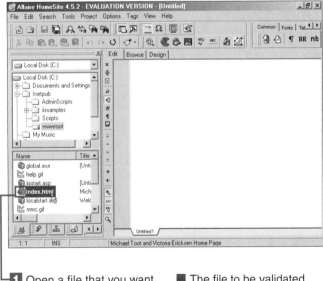

1 Open a file that you want to validate by double-clicking it in the File Resource pane.

■ The file to be validated appears.

2 Click Tools.

3 Click Validate Document.

■ You can also press Shift+F6 to validate the document.

Can I choose which standards to validate against?

✔ The validation settings are located in the Settings dialog box. Click Options, Settings, and then Validation. You can select and unselect the various standards and customize the level of error warnings when you press the Validator Settings button, but it is recommended that you do not change the configuration unless you have specific advanced validation needs. If you are writing for Internet Explorer or Netscape Navigator specifically, add its extension to the validation process. This is an easy way to see if your tags will cause any problems in these browsers.

I find tag validation annoying; is there an easy way to turn it off?

✔ You can postpone validation until you do a full document validation. This will allow you to type text, edit it, and cut and paste snippets without having HomeSite pause for a second or two each time you create a tag. To turn off tag validation, click the Tag Validation button on the Editor toolbar.

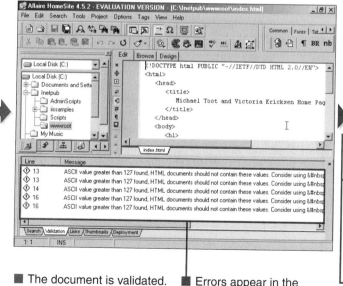

■ The document is validated.

■ Errors appear in the Results pane.

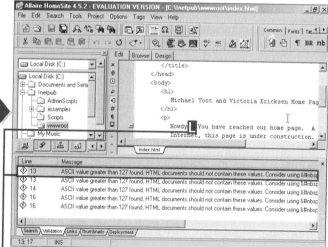

4 Double-click an error message to be taken to the document error.

CREATE A PROJECT

HomeSite provides a robust framework for managing your work on Web sites. It does this by enabling you to manage projects as a whole. A project can contain files, graphics, script widgets, or anything else that you need to make a Web site work.

When you update a project, you can make sure that you update all the affected files in a project at once without having to search through them individually.

The Project tab is where you maintain your projects. You can add

files to a project, add or remove folders, or open existing files. The project folders are shown in the upper pane, and individual files are shown in the lower pane. You can double-click any file to load it, or you can right-click a folder and open all files in that folder.

CREATE A PROJECT

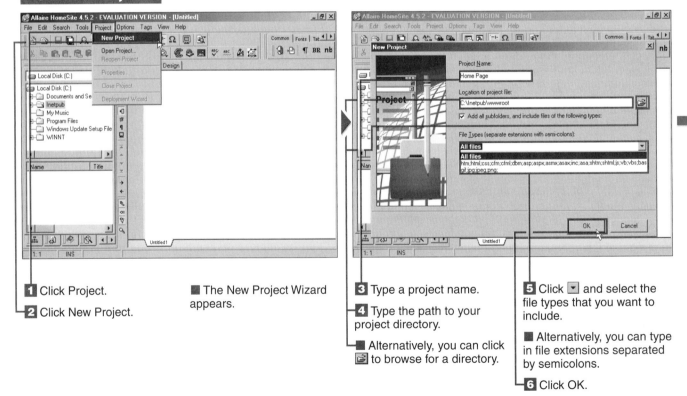

1 Click Project.

2 Click New Project.

■ The New Project Wizard appears.

3 Type a project name.

4 Type the path to your project directory.

■ Alternatively, you can click 📁 to browse for a directory.

5 Click ▾ and select the file types that you want to include.

■ Alternatively, you can type in file extensions separated by semicolons.

6 Click OK.

Can my entire team work on a project?

✔ One way is to store all your files in a central location, such as a file server or an FTP server, and create your new project on that file server. A project file with an `.apj` extension will be created, and everyone on your team will be able to open the project to work on it. However, you will not have any file locking protection, so team members can overwrite each other's changes during project updates.

Is there a method that a team can use to work on a project with less danger of overwriting?

✔ You can use a version control system, which gives you check-in and check-out privileges for files and prevents others from overwriting your changes. If Microsoft's Visual SourceSafe or Merant's PVCS is installed on your computer, HomeSite will let you manage projects using one of those systems. See the online help for more information.

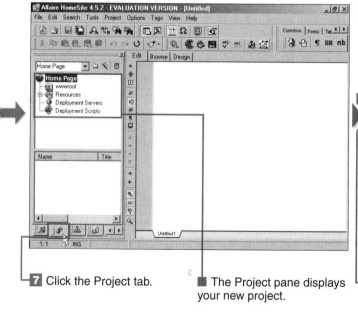

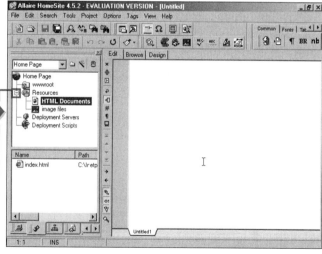

7 Click the Project tab.

■ The Project pane displays your new project.

■ You can expand the tree to show your project files in detail.

CONFIGURE AN FTP CONNECTION

When you are finished working on a project and want to deploy it to a Web server, you probably will not have direct access to the server that it is sitting on. Instead, you will probably use FTP—*file transfer protocol*—to publish your Web site to a Web server. FTP has been around since the early days of the Internet and was created for the

express purpose of moving files between computers.

HomeSite provides the ability to use FTP to move your Web site onto a Web server, re-creating your directory structure so that your links will not break. This way, you can edit the local copy on your own machine and then upload the final copy to the Web server and publish your site to the world. HomeSite

does this automatically, keeping the drudgery of hand-creating directories and subdirectories hidden from you.

Before you can publish a Web site, you need to configure a remote FTP server in HomeSite. The easiest way to do this is by adding an FTP server as a resource to an existing project.

CONFIGURE AN FTP CONNECTION

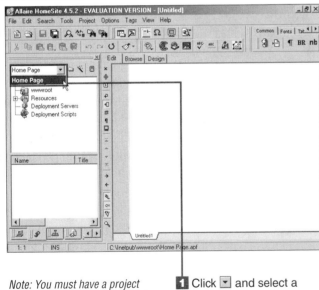

Note: You must have a project configured before performing the steps in this section.

1 Click ▾ and select a project.

■ The project with its folders and resources appears.

2 Right-click Deployment Servers in the folder pane.

3 Click Add FTP Server.

Where will I get the FTP server information for my Web site?

✔ Talk to your Internet service provider and find out what server name, username, and password you have been assigned, along with any directory information for your Web site files. You need this information before you can log in and upload files.

How many FTP resources can I have listed for my project?

✔ You can have as many servers as you want. When it comes time to publish your site, you can choose which servers you want to publish to.

What if I work for a company that uses only one server for its Web pages?

✔ If you have only one server that you publish to, it would be a waste of time to keep adding the same resource to each project that you develop. You can configure a global server resource for all your projects by right-clicking the Allaire FTP and RDS icon under My Computer and configuring your FTP server there. Your FTP server will appear in the list of servers when you go to publish your Web site.

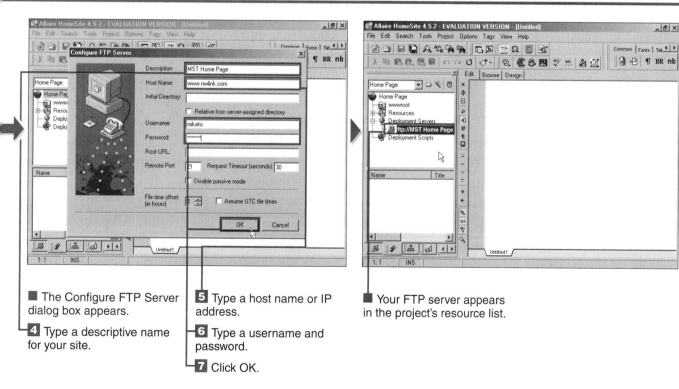

■ The Configure FTP Server dialog box appears.

4 Type a descriptive name for your site.

5 Type a host name or IP address.

6 Type a username and password.

7 Click OK.

■ Your FTP server appears in the project's resource list.

UPLOAD A PROJECT

HomeSite has a fairly powerful and complex set of tools to handle uploading and maintaining Web sites on remote servers. Depending on the project complexity, you can upload an entire project, selected folders or directories, or individual files. You can also upload files to multiple servers and create upload scripts so

that you can schedule Web page updates automatically.

This flexibility comes at a slight price: You must spend some time experimenting with all the publishing and folder options to see how they interrelate. You need to understand the difference between virtual directories and physical ones, how you can upload

some folders but not others, and how to configure scripting options for your Web site.

Most of these abilities are beyond the scope of this section, but you should be aware of them when you go to create and maintain a large Web site. You can always find more information by checking the online help.

UPLOAD A PROJECT

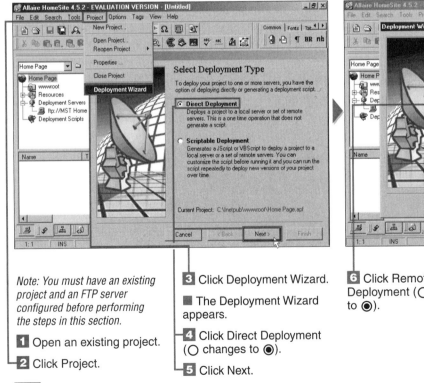

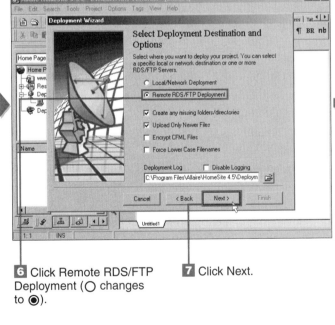

Note: You must have an existing project and an FTP server configured before performing the steps in this section.

1 Open an existing project.

2 Click Project.

3 Click Deployment Wizard.

■ The Deployment Wizard appears.

4 Click Direct Deployment (○ changes to ◉).

5 Click Next.

6 Click Remote RDS/FTP Deployment (○ changes to ◉).

7 Click Next.

Would it be better just to edit the Web pages directly on the server?

✔ You can edit pages "live" on a Web server, but you may make the pages unreadable to visitors during your edits. You are better off editing your Web site pages locally; that way, you can upload the pages when you are ready to publish them. In addition, if you need to share your Web pages with a team, you can configure HomeSite to create a remote project, where the source files are stored on a remote file or Web server. The difference between publishing a site and creating a remote project is that, with the former, your Web pages are accessible to anyone on the Internet; with the latter, only your team will see the pages until you are ready to publish them.

Why do I not see an FTP deployment server in my project?

✔ If you configured a global server resource under the Allaire FTP and RDS icon, you will see that server listed as an available server when you go to publish your site.

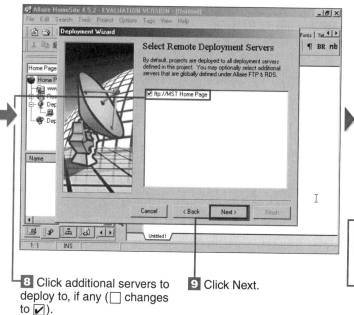

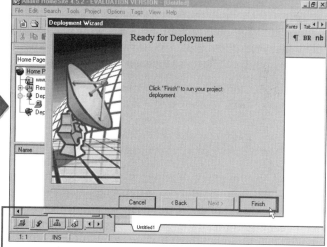

▶ **8** Click additional servers to deploy to, if any (☐ changes to ☑).

▶ **9** Click Next.

▶ **10** Click Finish.

■ Your Web site is published to the FTP servers.

■ The transmission results and error messages, if any, appear in the Results pane.

INTRODUCTION TO DREAMWEAVER

Dreamweaver is a program that enables you to create Web pages that feature text, images, and multimedia. You can use Dreamweaver to create Web pages without knowing HTML because Dreamweaver writes the HTML for you behind the scenes. It also helps you link your pages together and includes tools that let you transfer the finished files to a Web server where others can then view them. When you are ready to publish your pages on the Web, Dreamweaver can connect to a Web server and transfer your files to it.

Why Use Dreamweaver?

Dreamweaver is unique among software development programs for the Internet. Unlike other Web page building programs, Dreamweaver's focus is producing Web-enabled applications, of which Web pages are just the beginning. Dreamweaver can build multimedia pages containing Flash and Shockwave animations, work with JavaScript, participate in collaborative development, and track group assets.

But all that power comes with a price. Dreamweaver is one of the more expensive programs available, and unless you are working for a company or require Dreamweaver for your projects, you may be forced to look elsewhere. Nonetheless, you should strongly consider Dreamweaver for any Web application development scenario, whether simple Web pages or complex multimedia application development.

Using Dreamweaver Effectively

Programs like Dreamweaver work best when you

- Organize your ideas. Build your site on paper before you start building it in Dreamweaver. Sketching out a site map, with rectangles representing Web pages and arrows representing hyperlinks, can help you visualize the size and scope of your project.

- Define your audience. Carefully defining your audience can help you decide what kind of content to offer on your Web site. Knowing how technologically advanced your audience is can help you decide whether to include more advanced features on your pages.

You can read more about these topics in Part I.

WINDOWS

Menu

Contains the available command choices for the Document window.

Objects Panel

Allows you to add images, tables, and multimedia to your Web pages.

Dialog Box

Allows you to enter specific information when executing a Dreamweaver command.

Property Inspector

A window where you can view and modify properties of an object that is selected in the Document window.

Toolbar

Contains shortcuts to many Document window commands, and a text field where you can specify a title for a page.

Panel

An accessory window that enables you to manage the features of your Web page, or apply commands.

Document Window

Provides you with a work area to insert and arrange the text, images, and other elements of your Web page.

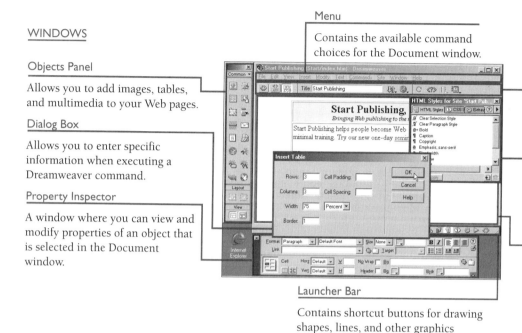

Launcher Bar

Contains shortcut buttons for drawing shapes, lines, and other graphics

MACINTOSH

Menu

Contains the available command choices for the Document window.

Objects Panel

Allows you to add images, tables, and multimedia to your Web pages.

Dialog Box

Allows you to enter specific information when executing a Dreamweaver command.

Property Inspector

A window where you can view and modify properties of an object that is selected in the Document window.

Toolbar

Contains shortcuts to many Document window commands, and a text field where you can specify a title for a page.

Panel

An accessory window that enables you to manage the features of your Web page, or apply commands.

Document Window

Provides you with a work area to insert and arrange the text, images, and other elements of your Web page.

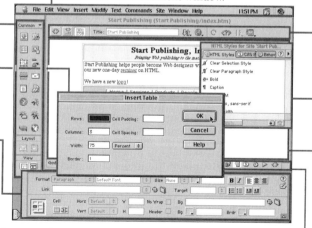

Launcher Bar

Contains shortcut buttons for drawing shapes, lines, and other graphics elements.

Note: The screen shots you see in this section were taken on a PC. Except for minor differences, the icons, menu, and commands are the same on a Macintosh. When PC and Macintosh commands are different, the Macintosh commands are in parentheses. For instance: Press Enter (Return).

SET UP A LOCAL SITE

Site design frequently happens on an as-needed basis: As needs change, new pages and content are haphazardly added without much thought given to content organization. Dreamweaver contains tools to help you get organized and to maintain your site in an optimal fashion. After you have defined your site, you need to think about how your site will be organized. You can read more

about defining your site in Chapter 1 and organizing your site in Chapter 8.

You can build a Web site one of two ways:

- Build the site directly on the Web server
- Build the site on a local computer, which then uploads the Web site to a remote server

Before creating your site's Web pages in Dreamweaver, you need to define a local site for storing the information in your site, such as your HTML documents and image files. Defining a local site allows you to manage your Web-page files in the Site window and then upload those files to a remote Web server.

SET UP A LOCAL SITE

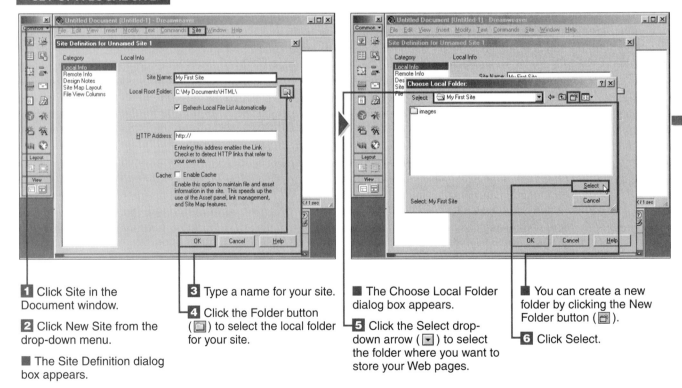

1 Click Site in the Document window.

2 Click New Site from the drop-down menu.

■ The Site Definition dialog box appears.

3 Type a name for your site.

4 Click the Folder button (🗀) to select the local folder for your site.

■ The Choose Local Folder dialog box appears.

5 Click the Select drop-down arrow (▾) to select the folder where you want to store your Web pages.

■ You can create a new folder by clicking the New Folder button (🗁).

6 Click Select.

Can I open Web pages created in HTML editors other than Dreamweaver?

✔ Yes. You can open any HTML file in Dreamweaver, no matter where it was created. You can also open non-HTML text files; however, the layout of such Web pages may look haphazard in Dreamweaver because they do not include HTML formatting.

How should I store the files for my Web site on my computer?

✔ You should save all the files for your Web site in the folder that you defined as the local root folder. This makes it easier to hyperlink between local files and transfer files to a remote Web server.

Why is it important to keep all my Web site files in a single folder on my computer?

✔ Keeping everything in the same folder enables you to easily transfer your site files without changing the organization of the files. If you do not organize your site files on the Web server the same as they are organized on your local computer, hyperlinks will not work, and images will not display properly.

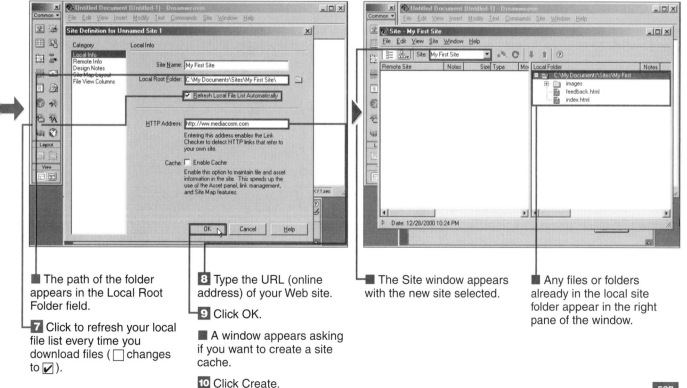

■ The path of the folder appears in the Local Root Folder field.

7 Click to refresh your local file list every time you download files (☐ changes to ☑).

8 Type the URL (online address) of your Web site.

9 Click OK.

■ A window appears asking if you want to create a site cache.

10 Click Create.

■ The Site window appears with the new site selected.

■ Any files or folders already in the local site folder appear in the right pane of the window.

CREATE A NEW WEB PAGE

Because HTML documents are plain text files, you can open and edit them with any text editor. In fact, in the early days of the Web, most people created their pages with simple editors, such as Notepad (Windows) and SimpleText (Macintosh). But writing HTML by hand can be a slow, tedious process, especially when creating advanced HTML elements, such as tables, forms, and frames.

Dreamweaver streamlines the process of creating Web pages by giving you an easy-to-use, visual interface with which to generate HTML. You specify formatting with menu commands and button clicks, and Dreamweaver takes care of writing the HTML code behind the scenes. When you build a Web page in the Document window, you see your page as it will eventually appear in a Web browser, instead of as HTML. This makes spotting mistakes when they occur easy and gives you immediate feedback on the look and feel of your site.

CREATE A NEW WEB PAGE

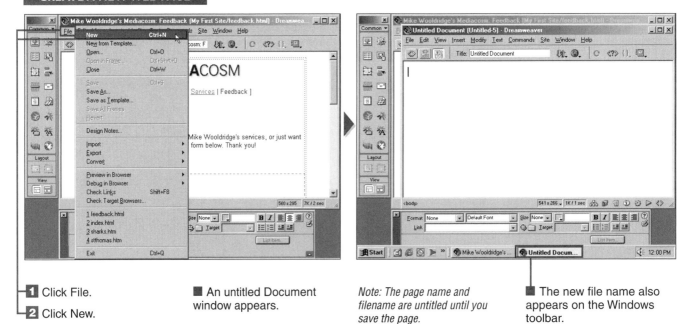

1 Click File.

2 Click New.

■ An untitled Document window appears.

Note: The page name and filename are untitled until you save the page.

■ The new file name also appears on the Windows toolbar.

Do I have to use the document view to edit my Web pages?

✔ Dreamweaver gives you direct access to the raw HTML code if you want it. This can be an advantage for people who know HTML and want to do some formatting of their page by typing tags. The Code View mode, Code inspector, and Quick Tag Editor in Dreamweaver enable you to edit your page by adding HTML information manually. Access to the code also means you can add HTML features that Dreamweaver does not yet support.

Why does my Web page need a title?

✔ A Web page title appears in the title bar when the page opens in a Web browser. Adding a title to a Web page makes the page identifiable by viewers and search engines. A title also helps with site navigation, especially when it may not be clear which frame has the focus or is being used to navigate the rest of your site.

ADD A TITLE TO A WEB PAGE

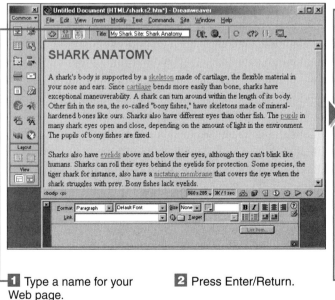

1 Type a name for your Web page.

2 Press Enter/Return.

■ The title appears in the title bar of the Document window.

SAVE A WEB PAGE OR REVERT TO A PREVIOUS SAVE

You should save all of your Web pages and images in your local site before you upload them to your remote Web server. Having several Web pages open at the same time for editing, copying and pasting, and comparing look and feel is fairly common. If you do not save your files, you will not have the most

recent version available for uploading. Dreamweaver makes saving files easy.

Saving all your files frequently to prevent work from being lost due to power outages or system failures is also a good idea. Although you can help prevent losing data by investing in an uninterruptable power supply (UPS), you should

save your files frequently while you work.

Dreamweaver also has a feature whereby you can revert your Web page to the last saved version. This lets you "rewind" your changes to the last saved state, in case you mix things up too much and want to start over.

SAVE A WEB PAGE OR REVERT TO A PREVIOUS SAVE

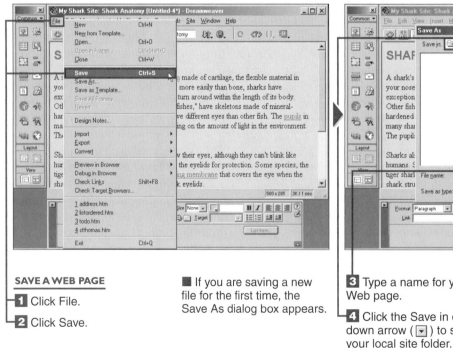

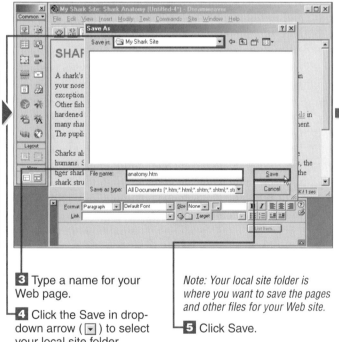

SAVE A WEB PAGE

■1 Click File.

■2 Click Save.

■ If you are saving a new file for the first time, the Save As dialog box appears.

■3 Type a name for your Web page.

■4 Click the Save in drop-down arrow (▾) to select your local site folder.

Note: Your local site folder is where you want to save the pages and other files for your Web site.

■5 Click Save.

What file formats are Web pages saved in?

✔ Static Web pages—ones that do not have any changing content or no scripting in them—are HTML files and must be saved with an `.htm` or `.html` filename extension. Dynamic Web pages may have an `.asp` or `.jsp` filename extension; ASP is for Active Server Pages while JSP is for JavaServer Pages. These pages typically have scripted server-side commands or changing content. Your filename extension should reflect the type of page you are creating.

Can I undo a revert file command and recover the changes I made?

✔ No. After you go back to a previously saved version, all your changes are lost. You will need to re-create them in your previous version. Clicking File, then Save As and saving your file with a temporary name before using the Revert command is a good idea. That way you can have both versions available if you need them.

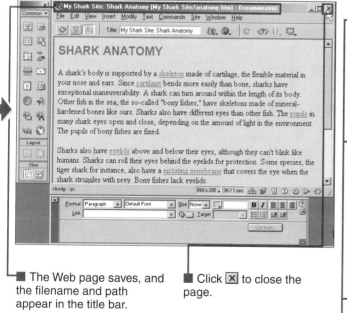

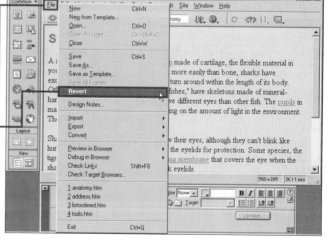

■ The Web page saves, and the filename and path appear in the title bar.

■ Click ☒ to close the page.

REVERT TO A PREVIOUS SAVE

1 Click File.

2 Click Revert.

■ The page reverts to the previously saved version. All the changes made since saving will be lost.

VIEW AND EDIT SOURCE CODE

Y ou can switch to Code View in the Document window. Code View lets you inspect and edit your HTML and other code in your Web pages directly, without having Dreamweaver generate the code for you. This allows you to tweak your code or put in custom information that may be useful to others, such as source

code comments or site structure information.

Code View is handy if you are already familiar with HTML syntax and want to enter it directly. Or, if you found some HTML source code you like from another Web site, you can copy the source code and paste it directly into the Code View area.

Most of the time, you will probably do your Web page building using the Document View. This lets you generate Web pages much like a word processing program: What you see is what you get. For most people, this is the easiest way to generate headings, bold text, italics, tables, and other Web page effects.

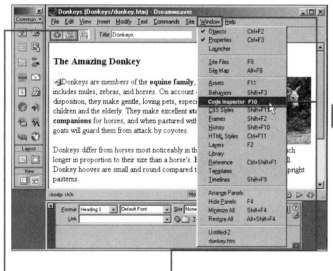

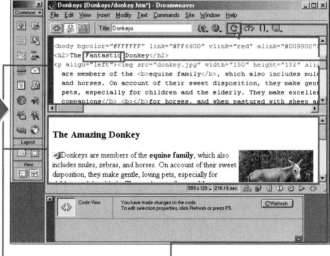

-1 Click a code-viewing option.

■ The Code View button (🔲) displays the Web page source code in the Document window.

■ The Split Views button (🔲) splits the window and displays both your source code and the design in the Document window.

━ Selecting Code Inspector under the Window menu displays the code in a separate window.

■ The split view appears in the Document window.

━ The HTML and other code appear in one pane.

━ The design view appears in the other pane.

-2 Click in the code to edit the text or add to or modify the HTML.

-3 Click the Refresh button (🔲).

What is the Head Tag Editor?

✔ The Head Tag Editor is a specialized editor that allows you to quickly view or edit head content, where keywords or descriptive information is stored. To activate the editor, go into Document View; then click Head Content on the View menu.

Is there an easy way to clean up my HTML so it loads faster?

✔ You can optimize HTML in your Web page by deleting extraneous or nonfunctional tags. This can decrease a page's file size and make the source code easier to read in Code View. You can access this option by clicking the Code View button, then clicking Commands, and then Clean up HTML.

I need to edit some custom HTML tags for an applet we built in-house; do I need to go into Code View to do this?

✔ The Quick Tag Editor gives you easy access to HTML without having to switch to Code View. You use the Editor to add or modify HTML tags when you are working inside the Document window. To use the Quick Tag Editor, go into Document View, select an object by highlighting it or dragging to select it, and then click the Quick Tag button.

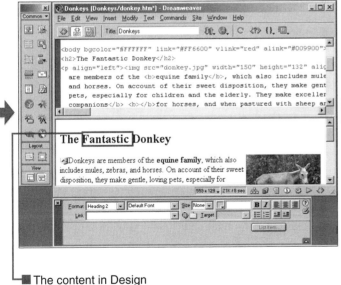

■ The content in Design View updates to reflect the code changes.

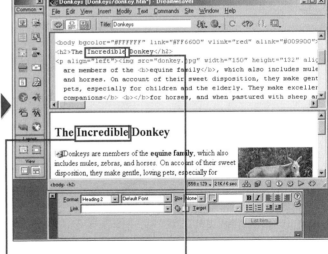

■4 Click anywhere in the Design View code and type to make changes.

■ The content in Code View updates dynamically as you make your changes.

INSERT AN IMAGE INTO A WEB PAGE

The most common way to spice up a Web page is to add pictures or artwork to it. Most Web pages today have some kind of imagery to complement the text. You can insert images into your Web page easily by using Dreamweaver.

Dreamweaver provides quick, seamless image integration into your Web pages. Dreamweaver can link in Flash or Fireworks elements such as buttons, graphics bars, animated GIFs, image maps, movies, or nearly any other sort of image you can find on the Web. If you are familiar with Flash, you will appreciate how easily you can add your Flash movies to a Web page by using Dreamweaver.

Nearly all these components (and many other features) are accessible by using the Objects panel. You will find yourself using it more than the menus, thanks to the panel's convenience and ease of use.

INSERT AN IMAGE INTO A WEB PAGE

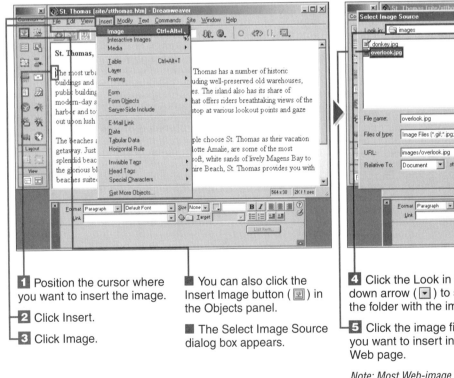

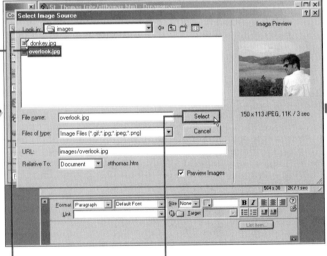

1 Position the cursor where you want to insert the image.

2 Click Insert.

3 Click Image.

■ You can also click the Insert Image button (🖼) in the Objects panel.

■ The Select Image Source dialog box appears.

4 Click the Look in drop-down arrow (▾) to select the folder with the image.

5 Click the image file that you want to insert into your Web page.

Note: Most Web-image files will end in .gif (for GIF files) or .jpg (for JPEG files).

■ A preview of the image appears.

Note: If you want to insert an image that exists at an external Web address, you can type the address into the URL field.

6 Click Select.

What are the file formats for Web images?

✔ The majority of the images you see on Web pages are GIF or JPEG files. Both GIF and JPEG are compressed file formats, which means they excel at storing image information in a small amount of file space. GIF is best for flat-color illustrations and other images that contain a limited number of colors (it only supports a maximum of 256 colors in an image). JPEG excels at storing photographic information (it supports millions of colors in an image). You insert GIF and JPEG files into your Web page by using the steps described below.

How can I tell how much file space my images and text are taking up on my Web page?

✔ The total size of your page appears in kilobytes (K) on the status bar. The total size includes the size of your HTML file, the size of your images, and the size of anything else on the page. Next to the size is the estimated download time for the page. You can determine the estimate with the connection speed in your Preferences.

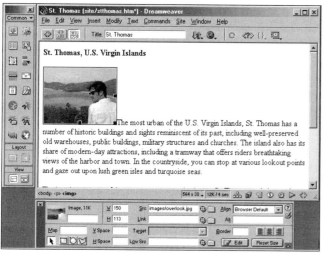

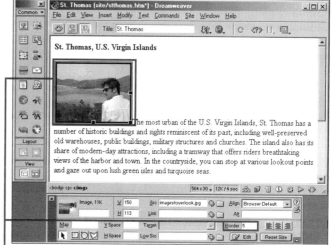

■ The image appears where you positioned your cursor in the Web page.

■ To delete an image, click the image and press the Delete key.

ADD A BORDER TO AN IMAGE

1 Click the image to select.

2 Type the width (in pixels) into the Border field.

3 Press Enter/Return.

■ A border appears around the image in the same color as the text.

CREATE HYPERLINKS TO OTHER PAGES

You can quickly create hyperlinks to content by using Dreamweaver. You can link to other file types, such as image files, word-processing documents, or multimedia files. You can give viewers access to additional information or topics by linking to pages in other Web sites. Dreamweaver makes this process easy to do by putting its hyperlink creation tools close at hand.

Because hyperlinks are one of the most common insertions into Web pages, you can add links quickly by using the steps outlined below.

One note of interest to developers: Blue is the default link color in the Dreamweaver Document window. What color the viewers see when the page opens in a browser depends on the user's browser settings. By default, most browsers display unvisited links as blue, visited links as purple, and active links as red.

CREATE HYPERLINKS TO OTHER PAGES

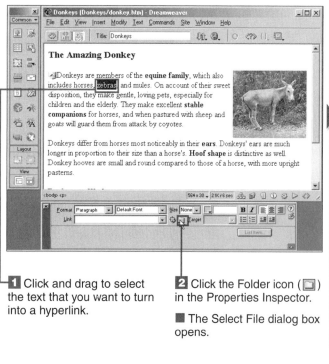

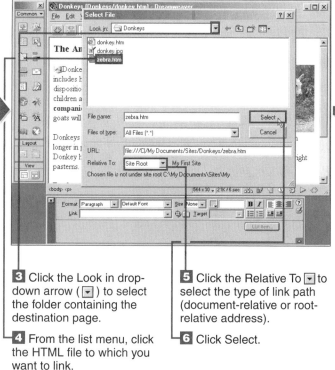

1 Click and drag to select the text that you want to turn into a hyperlink.

2 Click the Folder icon (🗀) in the Properties Inspector.

■ The Select File dialog box opens.

3 Click the Look in drop-down arrow (▼) to select the folder containing the destination page.

4 From the list menu, click the HTML file to which you want to link.

5 Click the Relative To ▼ to select the type of link path (document-relative or root-relative address).

6 Click Select.

How do users see files that are not HTML documents?

✔ What users see when they click links to other types of files depends on how their Web browser is configured and what applications they have on their computer. For example, if you link to a QuickTime movie, users need to have QuickTime software installed on their computer to see the movie. If a user does not have the software installed, the browser typically asks if the user wants to download the file and save it so they can view it later (after they have installed the correct software).

How do I make sure my links always work?

✔ You can automatically verify a Web page's links and get a report listing any that are broken by opening a Web page, then clicking Check Links on the File menu. You cannot verify links to other Web sites, only links within your site. If you have linked to a Web page that is later renamed or taken offline, your viewer will receive an error message when they click the link. Maintain your site by periodically testing your links.

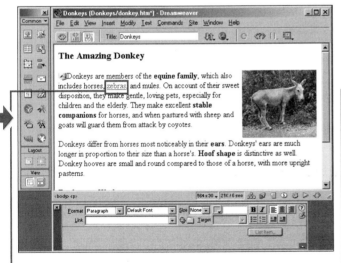

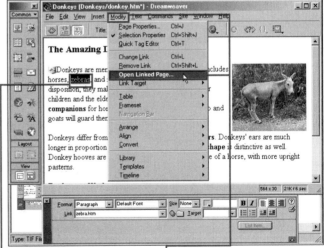

■ The new hyperlink appears in color and underlined.

■ Hyperlinks are not clickable in the Document window, but you can access the linked page via the Modify menu.

■ You can also test the link by previewing the file in a Web browser.

OPEN THE LINKED PAGE

1️⃣ Click and drag to select the text of the hyperlink whose destination you want to open.

2️⃣ Click Modify.

3️⃣ Click Open Linked Page.

■ The link destination opens in a Document window.

INSERT A TABLE INTO A WEB PAGE

You can insert a table into a Web page by using only a few clicks of the mouse in Dreamweaver. Tables provide a simple way to organize content on your Web pages. When information is placed into columns and rows, cross-referencing that information in useful or meaningful ways is easy.

Creating tables with HTML is covered in Chapter 3. However, setting up tables in HTML can be a long, thankless task. Dreamweaver takes care of the drudgery and generates table elements quickly and easily.

By default, a Dreamweaver Web page table has table borders that outline the rows and columns, but you can turn these off, making them transparent to users. You can also customize all other aspects of your tables, such as border size, background color and image, and cell padding and spacing.

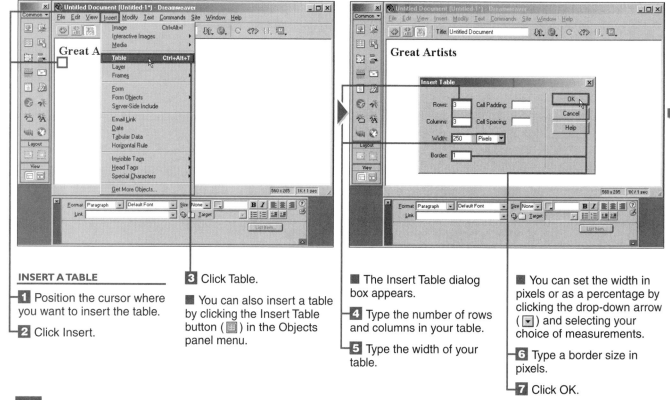

INSERT A TABLE

1 Position the cursor where you want to insert the table.

2 Click Insert.

3 Click Table.

■ You can also insert a table by clicking the Insert Table button ( ) in the Objects panel menu.

■ The Insert Table dialog box appears.

4 Type the number of rows and columns in your table.

5 Type the width of your table.

■ You can set the width in pixels or as a percentage by clicking the drop-down arrow ( ) and selecting your choice of measurements.

6 Type a border size in pixels.

7 Click OK.

What happens to the content of a deleted table?

✔ The content is deleted along with the table. Dreamweaver does not warn you if the cells you are deleting in a table contain content. If you accidentally remove content when deleting rows or columns, you can select Undo from the Edit menu to undo the last command. If you want to compare different table layouts, save the original under one filename and the new layout under a different filename. Re-creating a table from memory is never fun.

How can I add captions to images on my Web page?

✔ The best way to add a caption to the top, bottom, or side of an image is by creating a two-celled table. Place the image in one cell and the caption in the other. You can then adjust the table's size and alignment to fit the captioned image in with the rest of your page's content.

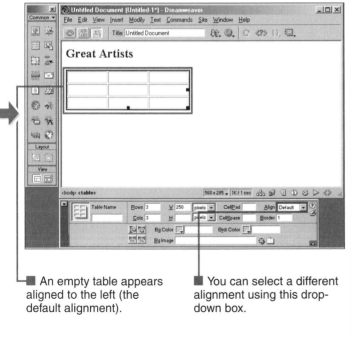

■ An empty table appears aligned to the left (the default alignment).

■ You can select a different alignment using this drop-down box.

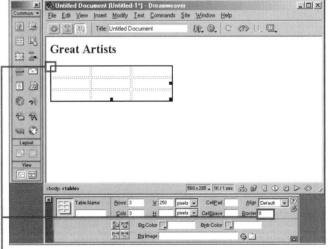

TURN OFF TABLE BORDERS

1 Click the upper-left corner of the table to select.

2 Type **0** in the Border field.

3 Press Enter/Return.

■ Dashed lines define the turned-off borders.

■ The dashed lines do not display when you open the page in a Web browser.

SET TABLE PROPERTIES

You can use Dreamweaver to change the dimensions of your table to better fit it into your Web page. Some designers make the mistake of not setting the dimensions, so the text runs off the screen and scrolling is needed to see the text. Other designers try to fit all of their information into the table, which can lead to a table that is cramped and hard to read. Table dimensions can easily be changed to help you format your table for readability.

Using Dreamweaver, you can also change the alignment of a table to center it or to wrap text and other content around it. This helps your Web page avoid looking like blocky chunks of text and images and more like a newspaper or magazine spread. Most designers start out using simple block style, but as they get more sophisticated, they begin flowing text around tables.

CHANGE TABLE DIMENSIONS

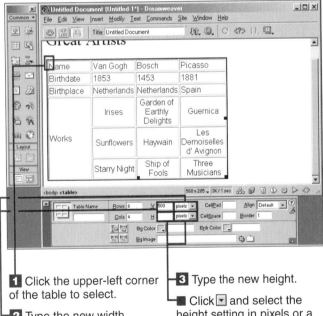

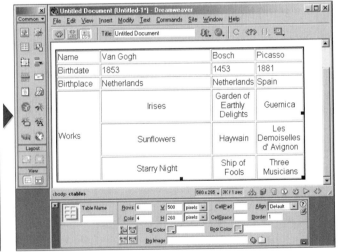

1 Click the upper-left corner of the table to select.

2 Type the new width.

■ Click ▼ to select the width setting in pixels or a percentage.

3 Type the new height.

■ Click ▼ and select the height setting in pixels or a percentage.

4 Press Enter/Return.

■ The table readjusts to its new dimensions.

Note: Table dimensions may be constrained by content. Dreamweaver cannot shrink a table smaller than the size of the content it contains.

How do I change cell content properties in my table?

✔ You can adjust the content alignment much the same way as you would with Web page text. Highlight the content you want to adjust; then use any of the text alignment or text formatting tools to change the cell content properties.

Can I add a background color to my table?

✔ Background colors can be easily added to tables. Click on the upper-left corner of a table, click the Bg Color swatch from the Color palette, and then click a color. Your table will fill with a background color.

Can I add a background image to my table?

✔ Images can also be added to tables. Click the upper-left corner of a table, click on the Folder button to open the Select Image Source dialog box, click an image file, and then click Select. The image will fill in as a background to your table.

CHANGE TABLE ALIGNMENT

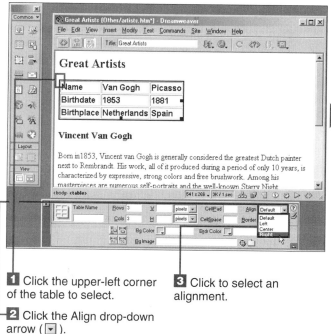

1 Click the upper-left corner of the table to select.

2 Click the Align drop-down arrow (▾).

3 Click to select an alignment.

■ The table aligns in the page.

CREATE AN HTML TEMPLATE

Y ou can save time by using Dreamweaver to create generic HTML pages for use as starting points for new pages. In Dreamweaver, these commonly used Web page layouts are called *templates*.

Templates not only save you time; they can also help you maintain a consistent page design throughout a site. After you make changes to a

template, Dreamweaver automatically updates all the pages of your site that are based on that template. If you use just a few page layouts across all the pages in your site, consider defining those layouts as templates.

In this example, you will create a generic Web page with optional data placeholders and then save the page as a template on your local

site. You can then use the template in your site and have a consistent look and feel across your Web pages.

After you create a Web-page template, you must define which regions of the template are editable. These regions are changeable in a page according to the template design.

CREATE AN HTML TEMPLATE

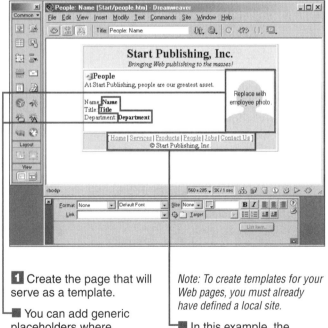

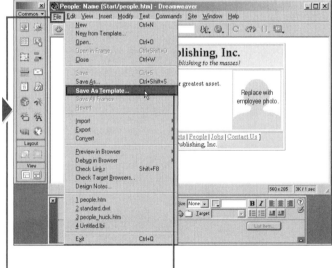

1 Create the page that will serve as a template.

■ You can add generic placeholders where information will change from page to page.

Note: To create templates for your Web pages, you must already have defined a local site.

■ In this example, the template includes a library item.

2 Click File.

3 Click Save As Template.

What are the different types of content in a template?

✔ A template contains two types of content: editable and locked. After you create a new Web page based on a template, you can only change the parts of the new page that are defined as editable. To change locked content, you must edit the original template.

What parts of a template should be defined as editable?

✔ You should define any part that needs to be changed from page to page as editable. Generally, variable areas in the page body are defined as editable, while site navigation, disclaimers, and copyright information are kept locked.

How does Dreamweaver store page templates?

✔ Dreamweaver stores page templates in a folder called *Templates* inside the local site folder. You can open templates by clicking Open on the File menu and then clicking the down arrow to select the Template folder. After opening the Template folder, click to select a template file. You can also open templates from inside the Assets panel.

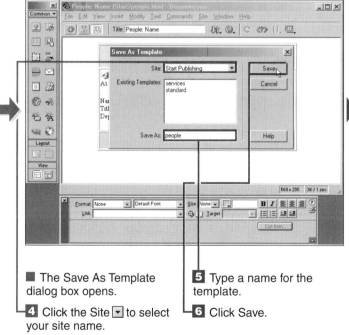

■ The Save As Template dialog box opens.

4 Click the Site ▼ to select your site name.

5 Type a name for the template.

6 Click Save.

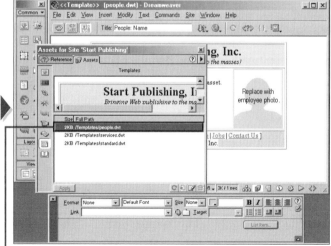

■ Dreamweaver saves the page with a .dwt extension within the Templates folder.

Note: To make the template functional, you must define the editable regions where you want to be able to modify content.

CREATE A ROLLOVER IMAGE

Y ou can add interactivity to your Web pages with a behavior. A *behavior* is a cause-and-effect feature that you set up in your Web page. You specify a user event, such as a mouse click, and the resulting action, such as a pop-up window appearing, that should take place when that event occurs.

Dreamweaver offers several standard behaviors, including:

• A *rollover*, in which the cursor passing over an object causes an action. Rollover effects are often applied to navigation buttons, where passing your cursor over the button causes it to light up or appear depressed, like a real button.

• A *status bar message*, in which the cursor passing over a hyperlink causes a pop-up message to be displayed. Status bar messages are used to describe where the hyperlink will take the user.

• You can *check a user's browser version* and then forward the user to a page built specifically for that browser. This lets you present advanced features only to the users that can experience them.

Dreamweaver's standard behaviors all work in Version 4 or later of Microsoft Internet Explorer and Netscape Navigator. Some behaviors also work in earlier browsers.

CREATE A ROLLOVER IMAGE

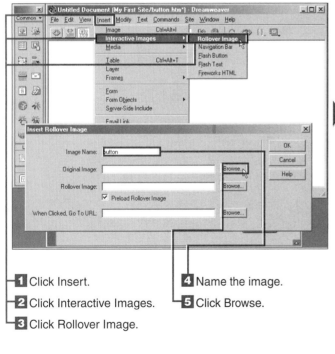

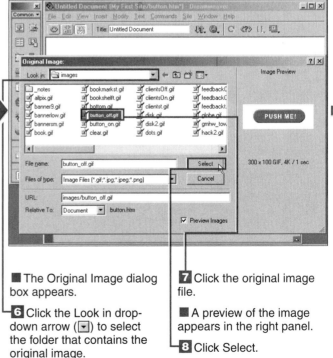

█1 Click Insert.

█2 Click Interactive Images.

█3 Click Rollover Image.

█4 Name the image.

█5 Click Browse.

■ The Original Image dialog box appears.

█6 Click the Look in drop-down arrow (▼) to select the folder that contains the original image.

█7 Click the original image file.

■ A preview of the image appears in the right panel.

█8 Click Select.

MASTER IT

How do I create interesting rollover buttons for my page navigation?

✔ You can create interesting buttons to use for navigation in an image editor, such as Adobe Photoshop or Macromedia Fireworks. Both programs include commands that let you easily create contoured or interestingly colored shapes or buttons that you can then label with text. Some common ways to create the swapped version of a rollover button are to reverse its colors, add a border, or shift the art slightly so it looks like the graphic has been pressed down. See Chapter 12 for more on creating graphics and Chapter 25 for more on Photoshop.

What features might I want to hide from users with older browsers?

✔ Dynamic HTML (DHTML) can only be viewed in Version 4 or later browsers. Some JavaScript and style-sheet features also do not work in older browsers. There are also incompatibilities between Netscape and Internet Explorer browsers, so instead of having your users encounter a "broken" Web page, you can redirect them to one that displays normally without the incompatible feature.

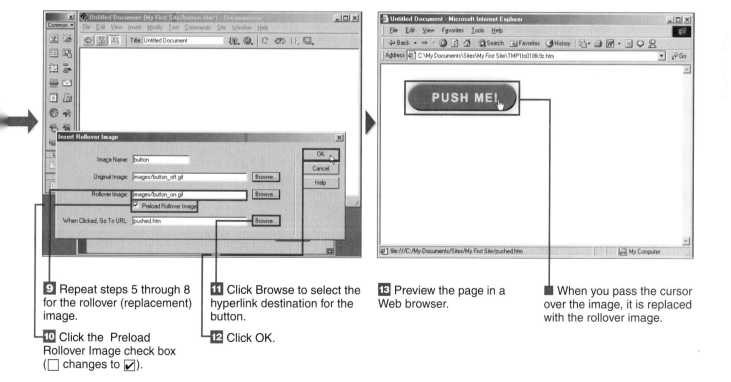

9 Repeat steps 5 through 8 for the rollover (replacement) image.

10 Click the Preload Rollover Image check box (☐ changes to ☑).

11 Click Browse to select the hyperlink destination for the button.

12 Click OK.

13 Preview the page in a Web browser.

■ When you pass the cursor over the image, it is replaced with the rollover image.

USING THE SITE MAP VIEW

Y ou can help gain control of your site's maintenance chores by creating a site map in Dreamweaver. The Site Map View enables you to see your site in a flowchart form with link lines connecting document icons. This view highlights pages that have broken internal links, which can help you maintain your site.

A site map can also help you when you need to complete a massive overhaul of your site. Most companies redo parts or all of their Web sites every six to nine months, and keeping track of what to keep and what to revamp can be arduous. With a site map, you can help designers determine

which parts are intertwined and which can be removed with relative ease. A site map can also help you present new ideas and new site layouts to your designers, which helps with development and interdepartment coordination.

USING THE SITE MAP VIEW

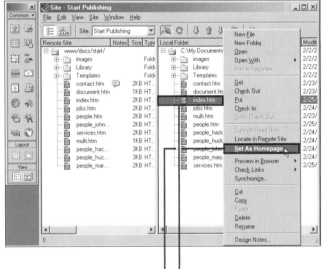

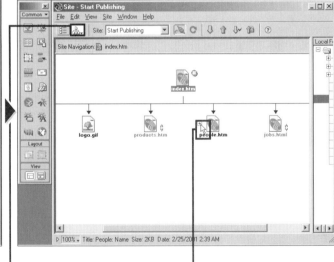

1 Open the Site window.

■ To create a site map in Dreamweaver, you must first define the home page of your site. It serves as the root file of your Site Map.

2 Right-click the file you want to use as your home page in the local site pane.

3 Click Set As Homepage.

4 Click the Site Map button ( ).

■ A site map appears in the left pane. By default, the Site Map displays the site structure two levels deep beginning from the home page.

5 Click + to view files below the second level.

■ To save the Site Map as a BMP image, click File and then Save Site Map.

How do I fix a broken link in the Site Map?

✔ A broken chain icon in the Site Map means the link to a page is broken. You can fix a broken link by right-clicking the destination page and clicking Change Link. Links can break because a destination page is renamed or deleted.

How do I remove an item from the Assets panel entirely?

✔ You need to delete the item from your local site folder. You can right-click (Option-click) the item in Site window and click Delete from the menu that appears. When you return to the Assets panel and click the Refresh button, the asset is gone.

How do I add additional content to my site?

✔ You can add frequently used content to your site directly from the Assets panel. This technique can be more efficient than using a menu command or the Objects panel. Click one or more items in the Assets panel, click Copy to Site in the Assets panel drop-down menu, and click a site to copy. The assets appear in the Favorites list under the same category in the other site.

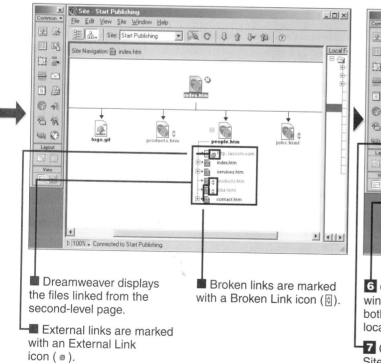

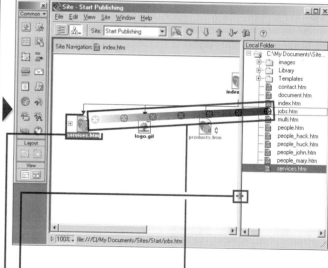

■ Dreamweaver displays the files linked from the second-level page.

■ External links are marked with an External Link icon (⊘).

■ Broken links are marked with a Broken Link icon (🔗).

6 Click and drag the Site window border to display both the Site Map and the local site.

7 Click a file in the Site Map.

8 Click and drag ⊕ to the file of your choice in the local site.

■ A new link appears at the top of the page selected in the Site Map.

■ You can double-click the page to open it.

MAKE DESIGN NOTES

You can attach accessory information, such as editing history and an author name, to your Web pages with Design Notes. Such notes can be useful if you are working on a site collaboratively because they let you add information about the development status of a file.

If you are not using a version control system to check your source files in and out, then design notes become even more useful. You can use the notes to keep more global or strategic information about your project's architecture or functionality. For example, if you have two different home pages for two different groups within your

company, you can place detailed information about the group or the type of information in the design note. The note can then help you make better design decisions later on for those groups, such as text-centric pages for dialup users and graphics-heavy pages for LAN users.

MAKE DESIGN NOTES

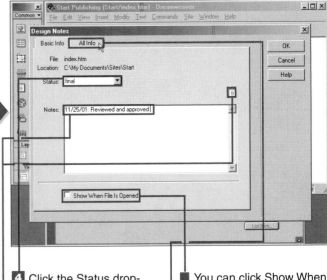

■ Design Notes are on by default when you create a site. You can turn them off in your site definition settings by clicking Site and then Define Sites.

1 Open the page that you want to attach to Design Notes.

2 Click File.

3 Click Design Notes.

4 Click the Status drop-down arrow (▼) to select a status for the page.

5 Type any notes that are relevant to the development of the page.

■ You can click 📅 to enter the current date in the Notes field.

■ You can click Show When File Is Opened to automatically show any Design Notes when a file is opened.

6 Click the All Info tab.

When should I use Design Notes, and when should I use HTML Comments?

✔ Because Design Notes are secured within Dreamweaver, Design Notes are a good place to store information that is relevant to your development team. This would include questions or notes to each other or design alternatives or operational information. HTML Comments are a good place to document tags used within the Web page or describe how a set of pages work together or any information that would be useful to a team responsible for maintaining the Web site in the future.

What are HTML comments?

✔ Similar to Design Notes, HTML comments let you attach text information to your page, information that does not show up in the browser. HTML comments are bracketed by `<!--` and `-->` characters and are stored in a page's HTML. Design Notes offer more security than HTML comments because they are stored separately from the HTML file. Design Notes are stored in a "_notes" folder inside the local site folder.

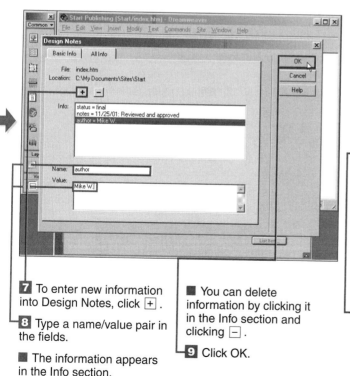

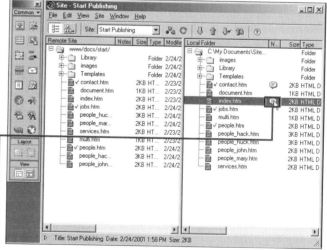

7 To enter new information into Design Notes, click ⊞.

8 Type a name/value pair in the fields.

■ The information appears in the Info section.

■ You can delete information by clicking it in the Info section and clicking ⊟.

9 Click OK.

VIEW DESIGN NOTES

1 From the Site window, double-click the Notes icon 🗐 next to a file.

■ The Design Notes for that file open.

■ You can view the notes of a page by clicking File and then Design Notes when the page is open in the Document window.

INTRODUCTION TO PHOTOSHOP

Photoshop is the leading photographic editing program on the market. Photoshop lets you create, modify, combine, and optimize digital images for the Web and print media. You can use the program to make subtle changes, such as to adjust the color in a scanned photo, or you can use its elaborate filters to make your snapshots look like abstract art.

An evaluation version of Photoshop is included on the CD-ROM that accompanies this book. Appendix C tells you how to install the software from the CD. The evaluation version of Photoshop and this chapter give you just an idea of Photoshop's potential. If you decide to buy Photoshop, you might also want to pick up a copy of *Teach Yourself VISUALLY Photoshop 6*, by Mike Wooldridge, or *Master VISUALLY Photoshop 6*, by Ken Milburn (both published by Hungry

Create within a Digital Darkroom

Before desktop computing, photographic professionals spent years learning how to crop negatives, work with filters, and painstakingly splice negatives together to achieve visual effects. With computers and high-resolution photographic and scanning equipment, those techniques are almost obsolete. You can achieve all those effects and combine different image elements quickly and easily in Photoshop. Your compositions can include photos, scanned art, text, and anything else you can save on your computer as a digital image. By putting elements in Photoshop onto separate layers, you can move, transform, and customize them independently of one another.

After you edit your work, you can use your images in a variety of ways. Photoshop lets you print your images, save them in a format suitable for use on a Web page, or prepare them for use in a page-layout program.

Edit Pixels

Digital images in Photoshop are made up of solid-color squares called *pixels*. Photoshop works on images by rearranging and recoloring these squares. You can zoom in close and see the pixels that make up a digital image.

To edit specific pixels in your image, you first have to select them by using one of Photoshop's selection tools. Photoshop also has a number of commands that help you select specific parts of your image, including commands that expand or contract your existing selection or select pixels of a specific color.

Paint With Color

After you have selected your pixels, you can apply color to them by using Photoshop's paintbrush, airbrush, and pencil tools. Photoshop's painting features make it a formidable illustration tool as well as a photo editor. You can apply colors or patterns to your images with a variety of brush styles. You can also fill your selections with solid or semitransparent colors.

You can brighten, darken, and change the hue of colors in parts of your image. Other commands display interactive dialog boxes that let you make wholesale color adjustments, giving you the ability to precisely correct overly dark or light digital photographs.

Apply Effects and Filters

Photoshop's effects let you easily add drop shadows, 3D shading, and other styles to your images. You can also perform complex color manipulations or distortions by using filters. Filters can make your image look like an impressionist painting, can apply sharpening or blurring, or can distort your image in various ways.

Add Type

You can use Photoshop's typographic tools to integrate stylized letters and words into your images. Photoshop's type tools enable you to easily apply titles and labels to your images. You can combine these tools with Photoshop's special effects commands to create warped, 3D, or wildly colored type.

SET PREFERENCES

Y ou can use the Photoshop Preferences dialog box to change default settings and customize how the program looks. The Preferences dialog box also lets you adjust preferences to match the way you work.

This ability to preconfigure your software is not unique to Photoshop. But because Photoshop is a specialized and powerful tool, you

will want to take some time and explore the Preferences to see how you can take advantage of them.

For example, you can use the Photoshop Preferences dialog box to set the file save location and format for your projects and files, set default cursors, choose your measurement units such as inches or pixels, and set scratch disk size.

You can configure Photoshop's look and feel in other ways. If you always have certain palettes open and certain brushes selected, you can choose which palettes will load and be available for use when Photoshop starts. You select palette preferences in the Windows menu and choose whether to Show or Hide palettes at startup.

SET PREFERENCES

-1 Click Edit.

-2 Click Preferences.

3 Click General to bring up the General options.

-4 Click the Color Picker drop-down arrow (▾) and select an interface.

■ This determines the dialog box that appears when you select a color.

5 Click the Interpolation ▾ and select an interpolation type.

-6 Click the interface options you want to use (☐ changes to ☑).

-7 Click the preferences type ▾ and select Display & Cursors.

What type of measurement units should I use in Photoshop?

✔ Typically, you should use the units most applicable to the type of output you are interested in. Pixels are useful for Web imaging because screen dimensions are measured in pixels. Inches or picas are useful for print because those are standards for working on paper.

Where should I save my files?

✔ You can change your file save locations, depending on your project. If you are working collaboratively, you should save files on a server where your team members have access. If you are working on your own, you can save files on your own computer.

What are scratch disks?

✔ Scratch disks are areas on your hard drives where Photoshop can store the information it is working with. Photoshop will use these areas when it runs out of RAM on your computer. You can configure your scratch disks by clicking Preferences on the Edit menu and then clicking Plug-Ins & Scratch Disks, or, if you have the Preferences dialog box already up, by selecting Plug-ins and Scratch Disks from the preferences type drop-down list.

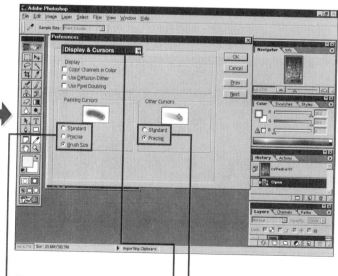

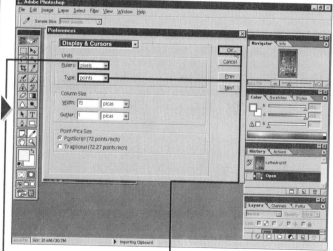

■ The Display & Cursors Preferences options appear.

8 Click a cursor type to use for the painting tools, such as the paintbrush, eraser, and others (○ changes to ⊙).

9 Click a cursor type to use for the other tools (○ changes to ⊙).

10 Click the preferences type ▾ and select Units & Rulers.

■ The Units & Rulers Preferences options appear.

11 Click the Rulers ▾ and select the units to be displayed on the window rulers.

■ These units will also be the default units selected when you resize an image.

12 Click the Type ▾ and select the default units for type.

13 Click OK to close the Preferences dialog box.

UNDO A COMMAND OR REVERT TO LAST SAVED FILE

You can undo multiple commands or revert to a previously saved state by using the Photoshop History palette. The History palette maintains a record of your previous commands and actions as you perform them, and it provides a way for you to back out of any changes you have made. You can

also revert to the last saved state on your image. All changes you made since you last saved will be undone, providing you with a quick way to return to a baseline image after you've altered it.

The History palette can be a lifesaving feature, especially when you commit a drastic change, such

as merging layers or applying a filter to an entire image. The History palette also gives you the freedom to try new things: Because you can undo your commands or actions, you can try out different filters or effects to see how they look and then undo them in an instant if the changes don't quite look like what you want.

UNDO A COMMAND

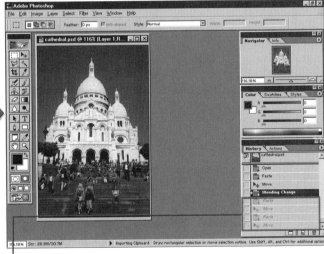

1 Click Window and then Show History to display the History palette.

■ The History palette lists recently executed commands with the most recent command at the bottom.

2 Click and drag the History slider upward (or click a previous command in the History palette).

■ Photoshop undoes the previous commands.

How can I keep from overwriting any source images or files?

✔ You can keep from accidentally overwriting your original materials by either copying the files to a working directory and working on those images or by setting Read Only permissions for source files and saving your edited ones to a different name or location.

Can I use document management systems with Photoshop images?

✔ Many document management systems will let you check in or check out a file no matter what type it is. If you want to use document management with your Web projects, check to see that it can accept binary files in its database.

How does the History palette affect my computer's memory use?

✔ Photoshop has to store image information for each command it remembers in the History palette. The accumulation of such saved commands can sometimes cause Photoshop to run out of memory. You can limit the number of commands Photoshop saves in the History palette in the Preferences settings. You can also free up memory by clicking Purge on the Edit menu and then clicking Histories, which deletes the content of the History palette.

REVERT TO LAST SAVED FILE

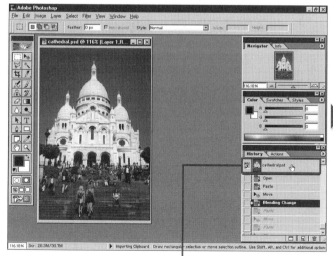

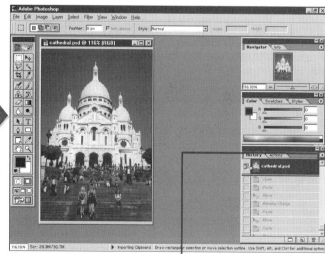

Note: Photoshop stores the last saved state as a snapshot at the top of the History palette.

■1 Click the snapshot image.

■ The image reverts to the last saved state.

■ You can add additional snapshots to the history palette as you work by clicking the history menu and then New Snapshot. You can then return to the previous image state by clicking the snapshot.

USE RULERS AND GUIDES

You can turn on rulers and create guides, which help you accurately place elements in your Photoshop image. These rulers and guides are helpful when you need your text to align perfectly or image elements must be exactly a certain distance apart. Rulers and guides are also helpful when you are placing repeating images on a background or need

to ensure that a corporate logo is accurately placed.

In most cases, Web-based images do not need to be precision-aligned. If you are working with print media, you will need to use as much precision as possible. High-end printers have extremely fine resolution, and they require fine-grained control over image

placement. But even on the Web, cleanly aligned images and text show a sense of professionalism and attention to detail that will serve your Web site well.

Guides are not visible in your final image, so you can use them as needed when editing images.

USE RULERS AND GUIDES

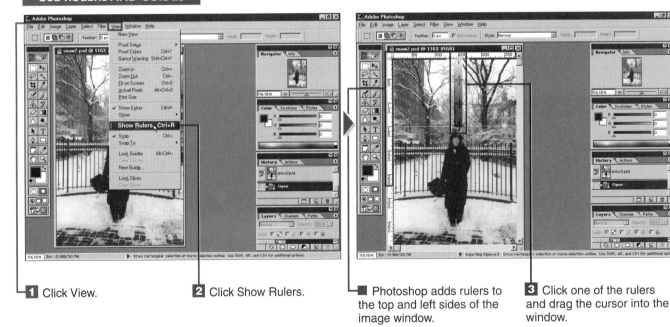

1 Click View.

2 Click Show Rulers.

■ Photoshop adds rulers to the top and left sides of the image window.

3 Click one of the rulers and drag the cursor into the window.

How do I change my ruler units?

✔ Click Preferences on the Edit menu, and then click Units & Rulers. A dialog box appears that lets you change the units to pixels, inches, centimeters, points, picas, or percent. Pixels are useful for Web-based images, while inches or picas are useful for print-based images.

How do I snap image elements to a grid?

✔ Your elements can be aligned to a grid by using the same method as for guides. Click View, then Snap To, and then click Grid, and your elements will snap to the nearest grid lines.

Can I use multiple guides on my images?

✔ You can either set up and use multiple guides for your images, or you can use a grid. The grid is similar to a set of guides that overlays your image and helps you organize elements within your image. You can turn on grids by clicking Show and then Grid on the View menu.

■ A thin colored line called a *guide* appears.

Note: Guides help you position the different elements that make up your Photoshop image. These lines do not appear on the printed image.

4 Click the Move tool (⊞) to adjust the placement of a guide.

5 Place the cursor over a guide and click and drag.

Note: To align elements moved into an image with the guides, click View and then Snap To Guides from the drop-down menu.

CREATE A NEW IMAGE

Most new Photoshop projects start with a blank image. If you are creating a new image from scratch, you can open up a new image without worrying too much about the type of image, its resolution, or its size. But if you have some ideas or size requirements for your image, you can set those parameters up when you create a new image.

For instance, if you are working on a Web image that cannot be larger than a standard VGA screen, you can define your new image to be 640 x 480 pixels in size. If you are working with an image that needs to be saved at different resolutions, you can set up the largest image size, create your image, then save it in progressively smaller resolutions.

This ability to define new image parameters is very helpful but requires that you plan out your Web page designs ahead of time so you can avoid wasting time with image editing and resizing later. For more on designing page layouts, see Chapter 10.

CREATE A NEW IMAGE

1 Click File.

2 Click New.

3 Type a name for the new image.

4 Type in the desired dimensions and resolution.

5 Click the type of pixels the new image will be initially made up of (○ changes to ◉).

6 Click OK.

What types of existing files can Photoshop work with?

✔ Photoshop can work with most of the image file formats in common use today. A few of the more popular ones include: BMP (Bitmap), the standard Windows image format; PICT, the standard Macintosh image format; TIFF (Tagged Image File Format), a popular format for print on Windows and Macintosh; EPS (Encapsulated PostScript), another print-oriented format; JPEG (Joint Photographic Experts Group), a format for Web images; GIF (Graphics Interchange Format), another format for Web images; and PSD (Photoshop Document), Photoshop's native file format. You can read more about many of these file types in Section IV.

How do I choose a resolution for a new image?

✔ The appropriate resolution depends on how the image will eventually be used. For Web or multimedia images, select 72 pixels/inch (the standard resolution for on-screen images). For black-and-white images to be printed on regular paper on a laser printer, 150 pixels/inch probably suffices. For full-color magazine or brochure images, you should use a higher resolution—at least 250 pixels/inch.

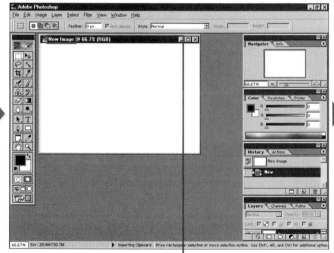

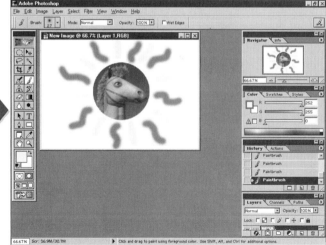

■ Photoshop creates a new image window at the specified dimensions.

■ The filename appears in the title bar.

7 Use Photoshop's tools and commands to create your image.

■ In this example, part of another image has been cut and pasted into the window, and color streaks were added with the paintbrush tool.

CREATE AND ADD TO A LAYER

A Photoshop image can be made up of multiple layers, with each layer containing different elements of the image. You can easily create new layers and add new material to layers.

Layered Photoshop files act like several images combined into one. Each layer has its own set of pixels that can be moved and transformed independently of the pixels in other layers. This gives you the ability to change one element without disturbing others in your image.

The layers of an image are listed in the Layers palette in descending order, with the bottom layer at the bottom. You select a layer by clicking on the layer's name in the Layers palette.

You can merge, duplicate, and hide layers in an image. You can also shuffle the order in which layers are stacked. Layers can have transparency areas, where the elements on the layers below can show through. When you perform a cut or erase command on a layer, the affected pixels become transparent.

CREATE A LAYER

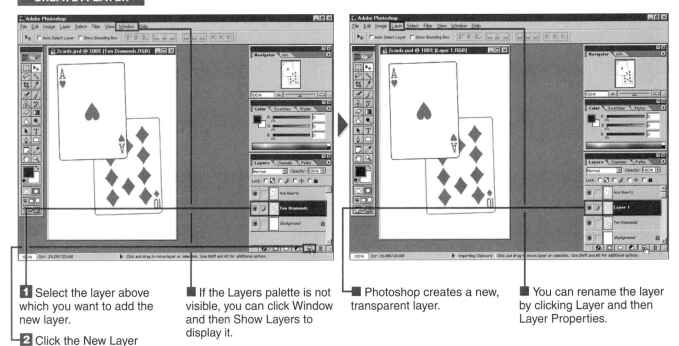

1 Select the layer above which you want to add the new layer.

2 Click the New Layer button (▢) (or click Layer, New, and then Layer) in the Layers palette.

■ If the Layers palette is not visible, you can click Window and then Show Layers to display it.

■ Photoshop creates a new, transparent layer.

■ You can rename the layer by clicking Layer and then Layer Properties.

What is the Background layer?

✔ The Background layer is the default bottom layer that appears when you create a new image or when you import an image from a scanner. You can create new layers on top of a Background layer (but not below). Unlike other layers, a Background layer cannot contain transparent pixels.

How do I change the order of layers?

✔ Select the layer in the Layers palette. To shift the layer forward in the stack, press Ctrl/⌘+]. To shift the layer backward, press Ctrl/⌘+[.

Why would I want to merge layers?

✔ Merging layers lets you permanently combine elements of your image when you are happy with how they are arranged relative to one another. To merge layers, arrange the two layers you wish to merge next to each other, select the topmost layer, click Layer, then click Merge Down. The two layers are now merged. If you want to be able to rearrange all the original layers in the future, save a copy of your image before you merge layers.

ADD TO A LAYER

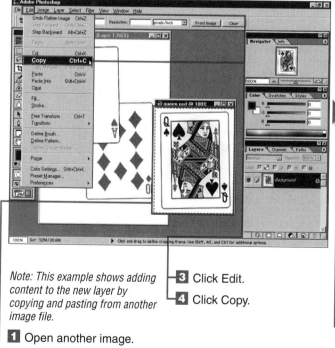

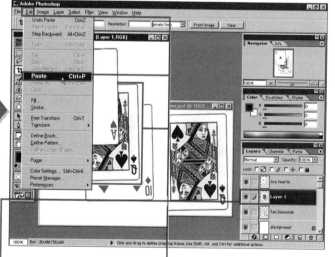

Note: This example shows adding content to the new layer by copying and pasting from another image file.

1 Open another image.

2 Select the content you want to copy in the other image by using a selection tool.

3 Click Edit.

4 Click Copy.

5 Click the image window where you created the new layer to select it.

6 Select the new layer in the Layers palette.

7 Click Edit.

8 Click Paste.

■ The content from the other image is pasted into the new layer.

APPLY BLUR AND SHARPEN FILTERS

With Photoshop's image filters, you can quickly and easily apply enhancements to your image.

Artistic filters make your image look as though it was created by using traditional artistic techniques. Filters can also help you correct defects in your images, such as fuzzy outlines or loss of detail from enlarging original images. Image filters are some of the most powerful and creative effects you can apply to images.

One example of an image filter is a blur filter. Blur filters reduce the amount of detail in your image. The Gaussian Blur filter has advantages over the other Blur filters in that you can control the amount of blur added.

Another example is the Sharpen filter, which intensifies detail and reduces blurring in your image. The Unsharp Mask filter has an advantage over the other Sharpen filters in that it lets you control the amount of sharpening applied.

APPLY THE GAUSSIAN BLUR FILTER

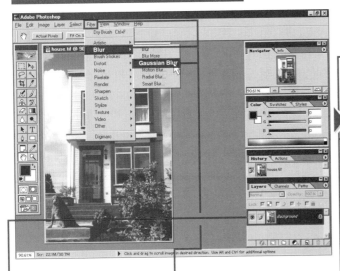

1 Select the layer to which you want to apply the filter. If you want to apply the filter to just part of your image, make the selection with a selection tool.

Note: In this example, the image has a single background layer.

2 Click Filter.

3 Click Blur.

4 Click Gaussian Blur.

■ A small window displays a preview of the filter's effect.

5 Click the – or + button to zoom out or in.

6 Click Preview to preview the effect in the main window (☐ changes to ☑).

7 Click and drag the Radius slider to control the amount of blur added.

8 Click OK.

■ Photoshop applies the filter.

How do I add directional blurring to an image?

✔ You can add directional blur to your image with the Motion Blur filter. This can add a sense of motion to your image. For example, you can make a snail appear as if it is reaching Mach 1 by using the Motion Blur filter. Apply the filter by selecting Filter, Blur, and then Motion Blur.

When should sharpening be applied?

✔ Sharpening an image after you have changed its size is a good idea because changing an image's size will add blurring. This is especially noticeable when going from a smaller size to a larger one. Applying the Unsharp Mask filter can also help clarify scanned images.

Am I limited to the filters that come with Photoshop?

✔ No. You can obtain Photoshop plug-ins that apply different filters or styles to your images. If you need an exotic effect and can't quite get the right combination by using the built-in effects, then you can go shopping for a new effect to add to your repertoire. Many plug-ins can be downloaded for free from Adobe's Web site; others are available for purchase from third-party vendors.

APPLY THE UNSHARP MASK FILTER

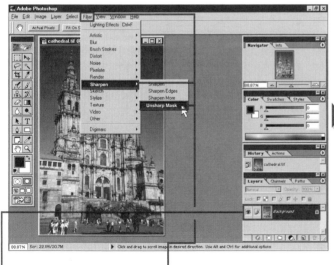

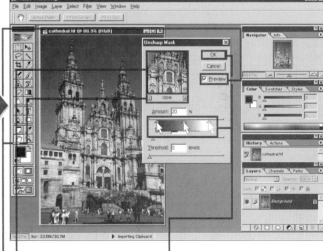

1 Select the layer to which you want to apply the filter. If you want to apply the filter to just part of your image, make the selection with a selection tool.

Note: In this example, the image has a single background layer.

2 Click Filter.

3 Click Sharpen.

4 Click Unsharp Mask.

■ A small window displays a preview of the filter's effect.

5 Click the – or + button to zoom out or in.

6 Click Preview to preview the effect in the main window (☐ changes to ☑).

7 Click and drag the sliders to control the amount of sharpening applied to the image.

8 Click OK.

■ Photoshop applies the filter.

APPLY DRY BRUSH AND DISTORTION FILTERS

Photoshop contains numerous artistic filters that you can use to modify your image in interesting and unique ways. You can change that old boring picture into something thoughtful, artistic, or just plain wild.

Brush stroke filters make your image look as though it was painted,

not photographed. You can have a crosshatched effect, or ink outlines, spattering, or spray-can-like strokes, whichever matches the mood you are creating. The Dry Brush filter applies a painted effect by converting similarly colored areas in your image to solid colors, as if a dry paintbrush had been dragged across still-damp paint.

Distort filters take your image and warp, stretch, and squeeze areas of your image to achieve a real (or surreal) look to your image. Distort filters include ocean ripples, glass-like warping, waves, and zig-zag patterns. For example, the Spherize filter makes your image look as though it is being reflected off a mirrored sphere.

APPLY THE DRY BRUSH FILTER

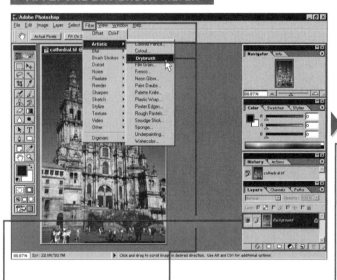

1 Select the layer to which you want to apply the filter. If you want to apply the filter to just part of your image, make the selection with a selection tool.

Note: In this example, the image has a single background layer.

2 Click Filter.

3 Click Artistic.

4 Click Drybrush.

■ A small window displays a preview of the filter's effect.

5 Click the – or + button to zoom out or in.

6 Fine-tune the filter effect by adjusting the Brush Size, Brush Detail, and Texture values.

7 Click OK.

■ Photoshop applies the filter.

What does the Sponge filter do?

✔ The Sponge filter reduces detail and modifies the shapes in an image to create the effect you get when applying a damp sponge to a wet painting. Color blotches appear, with areas of greater and lesser saturation. Apply it by clicking Filter, Artistic, and then Sponge.

What does the Charcoal filter do?

✔ The Charcoal filter makes an image look as if it was sketched by using charcoal on paper. You can get dramatic monochrome images by applying this filter to an original image, and you can change the size of your charcoal brush to add fine or bold strokes. Apply it by clicking Filter, Sketch, and then Charcoal.

What happens when I type a negative value in the Amount field of the Spherize dialog box?

✔ A negative value "squeezes" the shapes in your image instead of expanding them. The Pinch filter (also under the Filter and Distort menu selections) produces a similar effect. Think of these effects as configurable black holes—that's the type of effect you can generate.

APPLY THE SPHERIZE FILTER

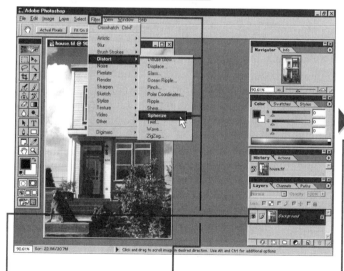

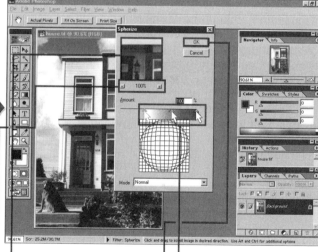

1 Select the layer to which you want to apply the filter. If you want to apply the filter to just part of your image, make the selection with a selection tool.

Note: In this example, the image has a single background layer.

2 Click Filter.

3 Click Distort.

4 Click Spherize.

■ A small window displays a preview of the filter's effect.

5 Click the – or + button to zoom out or in.

6 Click and drag the Amount slider to control the amount of distortion added.

7 Click OK.

■ Photoshop applies the filter.

ADD TYPE TO AN IMAGE

Adding type lets you label elements in your images or use letters and words in artistic ways. You can select from different typefaces and can download or purchase new typefaces to add to your font library. Just as with a word processor, you can make your fonts bold, italic, and sometimes use other effects if the font supports them.

Fonts come in two basic types: serif and sans serif. Serif fonts—such as Times Roman—have decorative flourishes at the letter tips, while sans serif fonts—such as Ariel—do not.

When you design your images, consider which other fonts will be on your Web page. Try not to have more than three different types of fonts on your page: One for corporate logo, one for headings and labels, and one for text. Chapter 11 offers more tips on using effective typography.

ADD TYPE TO AN IMAGE

1 Click the Type tool (T).

2 Click where you want the new type to appear.

3 Click the respective drop-down arrows (▾) and select a font, style, and size for your type.

4 Click the color swatch to select a color for your type.

Note: The foreground color is applied by default.

How do I reposition my type?

✔ Added type is placed in its own layer. You can move the layer with the Move tool. Select the layer of type, click the Move tool, and then click and drag to reposition your type.

How do I rotate type?

✔ You can rotate type in your image by rotating the layer that contains the type. Choose the layer in the Layers palette and click Edit and Free Transform. A bounding box appears. You can click and drag outside the box to rotate the layer. Press Enter/Return to apply the rotation.

What is antialiasing?

✔ *Antialiasing* is the process of adding semitransparent pixels to curved edges in digital images to make the edges appear more smooth. You can apply antialiasing to type in Photoshop to improve its appearance. (Text that is not antialiased often looks jagged.) You can control the presence and style of your type's antialiasing with the Options bar.

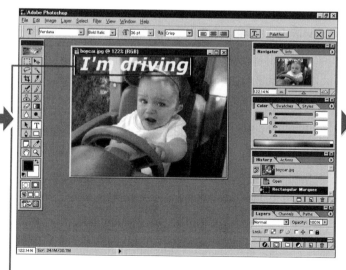

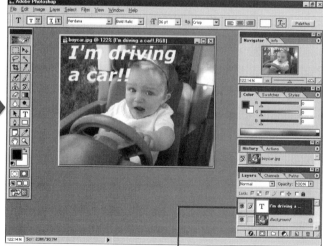

5 Type your text. To create a line break, press Enter/Return.

6 When you finish typing your text, press Enter on your keyboard's number pad or click a different tool in the toolbox.

■ The type is placed in its own layer.

CROP AN IMAGE

Cropping refers to the method of trimming off areas around an image's borders. You can use Photoshop to do in minutes what used to take hours in the darkroom, adjusting image borders and subject alignment until the photo's composition is just right.

Cropping helps image composition by centering the image's subject in a more pleasing manner, or eliminating extraneous objects around the edges that only serve to defocus attention. This has the added benefit of reducing your image size, making it faster to download over slower Internet connections.

When you crop a digital image, you have the freedom to crop an image as often as you like before saving your changes as a new image. Photoshop also allows you to rotate your cropping window to add artistic touches to your image, such as a "keyhole" effect or to reinforce a regular geometric pattern with the shape of the photograph.

CROP AN IMAGE

1 Click the Crop tool (⊡) in the toolbox.

2 Click and drag to select the area of the image you want to keep.

Note: You can also crop an image by changing its canvas size.

3 Click and drag the side and corner handles to adjust the size of the cropping boundary.

■ Click and drag inside the cropping boundary to move it without adjusting its size.

4 Double-click inside the cropping boundary or press Enter.

Note: To exit the cropping process, you can press Esc/⌘ +period.

Can I crop individual layers?

✔ Yes. You can also choose to hide the cropped area rather than delete it. The Hide option retains the pixels but does not delete them, so you can restore them later if you don't like the cropping effect.

How do I change the canvas size?

✔ The canvas is the area on which your image sits. You can change the canvas size as an alternative to cropping. To change the canvas size, click Image, Canvas Size, type the new canvas dimensions, and then click OK.

How do I increase the area of an image by using the Crop tool?

✔ Enlarge the image window to add extra space around the image. Then apply the Crop tool so that the cropping boundary extends beyond the borders of the image. When you apply cropping, the image canvas enlarges.

How does changing the canvas size affect the image size and resolution?

✔ Changing the canvas size affects on-screen and print sizes but not image resolution.

■ Photoshop crops the image, deleting the pixels outside of the cropping boundary.

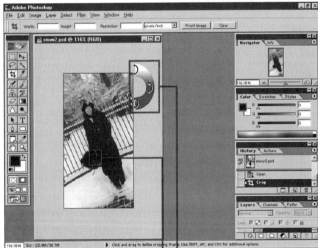

ROTATE THE CROPPING AREA

1 Perform steps 1 through 3 earlier in this section.

2 Click and drag outside of the boundary lines. Photoshop rotates the cropping boundary.

3 Double-click inside the cropping boundary.

CREATE AND SAVE SLICED IMAGES

You can use Photoshop to divide a large image that you want to display on the Web into smaller rectangular sections called *slices*. The different slices of an image can then be optimized independently of one another for faster download. You can save an image that has been partitioned by using the Slice tool. Photoshop

saves the slices as different images and also saves an HTML file that organizes the slices on a Web page. Slices enable you to save some parts of an image as GIF and others as JPEG. One way to slice an image is to divide it by areas of color, so one slice is a solid block of red, another green, a third has logo lettering, and so forth. This can

result in an overall image that has a smaller file size.

Slices can also be used to create special Web effects, such as animations and rollovers, in ImageReady. ImageReady is a Web imaging application that comes with Photoshop.

CREATE AND SAVE SLICED IMAGES

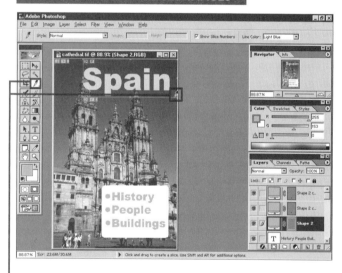

CREATE SLICED IMAGES

1 Click the Slice tool ( ).

2 Click and drag inside the image to create a slice.

■ Photoshop creates a slice where you clicked and dragged.

Note: Slices you define are called user-slices. User-slices *remain fixed when you add more slices to your image, whereas auto-slices can change size.*

SAVE SLICED IMAGES

1 Open your sliced image.

2 Click File.

3 Click Save for Web.

How do I resize or delete slices in my image?

✔ First, click the Slice Select tool. To resize a user-slice, click inside it and then click and drag a border handle. To delete a user-slice, click inside it and then press the Delete key.

Where can I learn more about ImageReady?

✔ You can read more about ImageReady in *Master VISUALLY Photoshop 6* by Ken Milburn (published by Hungry Minds, Inc.). You can also learn more about how to use slices in ImageReady in Photoshop's online Help information.

What types of images work best with slices?

✔ The best images for slices are ones that either have large amounts of solid color in them or ones that have distinct regions that can be used for image maps or hyperlink bars. The solid color images optimize well for download times, while the image maps work best for sets of links that can be easily tied to distinctive images.

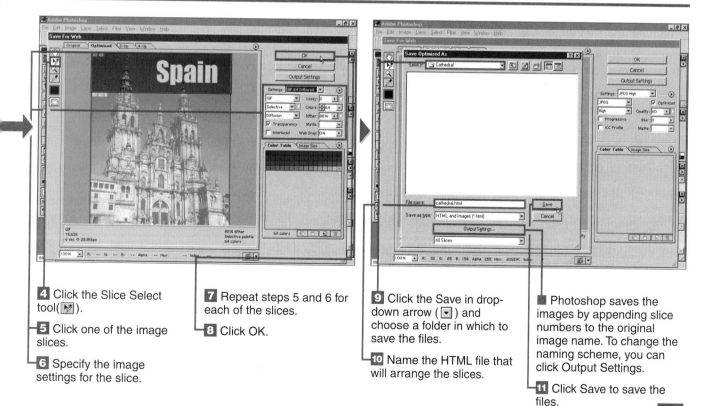

4 Click the Slice Select tool(▶).

5 Click one of the image slices.

6 Specify the image settings for the slice.

7 Repeat steps 5 and 6 for each of the slices.

8 Click OK.

9 Click the Save in drop-down arrow (▼) and choose a folder in which to save the files.

10 Name the HTML file that will arrange the slices.

■ Photoshop saves the images by appending slice numbers to the original image name. To change the naming scheme, you can click Output Settings.

11 Click Save to save the files.

OPTIMIZE FILE SIZES FOR THE WEB

One of the most frequent complaints about Web sites is the time it takes to load images or graphics-intensive Web pages. Photoshop not only allows you to optimize your Web graphics; you can compare the results of different compression schemes on your Web images. This helps you choose which scheme is most efficient and generates the best-looking image. You can then save

the image by using that scheme and use the optimized image in your Web page.

Optimization is the process of striking a balance between quick download times and image integrity. Web designers search for the optimal combination of small file size and best image quality. See Chapter 12 for more on incorporating graphics in your site.

Photoshop can save files in several formats, but it can only optimize files using GIF or JPEG files. *GIF files* are bitmap files that are best used for solid-color areas, while *JPEGs* use lossy compression algorithms and are best for true-color or near-true-color picture resolutions.

OPTIMIZE FILE SIZES FOR THE WEB

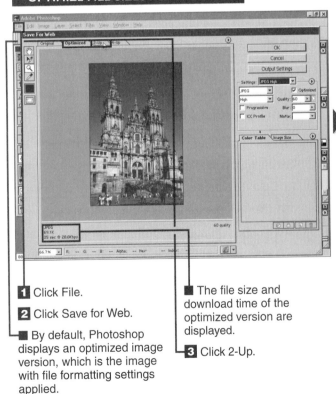

1 Click File.

2 Click Save for Web.

■ By default, Photoshop displays an optimized image version, which is the image with file formatting settings applied.

■ The file size and download time of the optimized version are displayed.

3 Click 2-Up.

■ Photoshop displays the original image on the left side.

■ Photoshop displays the image with the file formatting settings applied on the right side.

4 To select different settings, click either image and change the settings in the right side of the dialog box.

What determines file size?

✔ An image's file size depends on the number of pixels and colors it contains. For a given image, a monochrome version (which has just two colors) takes up less file space than a grayscale version (which has up to 256 shades of gray), and a grayscale version takes up less space than a color version (which can have millions of colors). File size also varies with the file format. An image saved in an uncompressed format, such as TIFF or BMP, takes up more space than one saved in a compressed format, such as JPEG or GIF.

What is "lossy compression"?

✔ When crunching down files to decrease size, there are two types of compression: lossless and lossy. *Lossless compression* preserves all the image information but at the expense of file size, which tends not to reduce very much. *Lossy compression* loses some information but results in much better file size compression. As information is lost, picture quality degrades; so when optimizing JPEGs (which use lossy compression), you should strike a balance between file size and viewable image quality.

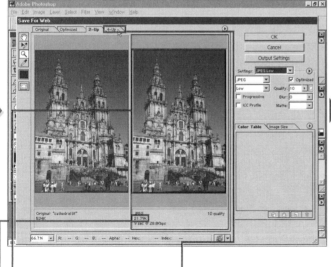

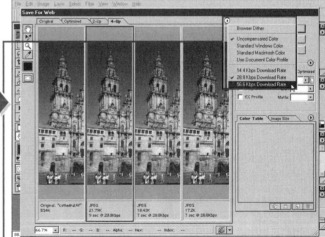

■ Photoshop displays the image with the new settings applied.

■ The new file size is displayed.

5 Click 4-Up to compare four versions of the image at a time.

■ You can change the modem speed that Photoshop uses to estimate download time by clicking the top menu ⊙ and selecting different options.

SPECIAL CHARACTERS

Use the following named or numeric entities to add special characters to HTML code. The numeric entities from 160 to 255 all have name equivalents, while most of the entities from 32 to 126 do not. For these, you must use the numeric notation. In addition, characters ranging from 127 to 159 are not part of the HTML standard, and the output may vary among operating systems. These entities are marked with an asterisk (*).

To include character entities in JavaScript code, use a JavaScript escape sequence (\) with the octal number.

Character Entities				
HTML Numeric Entity	**HTML Name**	**Octal Number**	**Symbol**	**Description**
&#032;		40		Space
&#033;		41	!	Exclamation point
&#034;	&quot;	42	"	Quotation mark
&#035;		43	#	Hash mark
&#036;		44	$	Dollar sign
&#037;		45	%	Percent sign
&#038;	&amp;	46	&	Ampersand
&#039;		47	'	Apostrophe
&#040;		50	(	Left parenthesis
&#041;		51	)	Right parenthesis
&#042;		52	*	Asterisk
&#043;		53	+	Plus sign
&#044;		54	,	Comma
&#045;		55	-	Hyphen
&#046;		56	.	Period
&#047;		57	/	Forward slash
0–9		60–67, 70, 71	0–9	Numbers 0–9
&#058;		72	:	Colon
&#059;		73	;	Semicolon

HTML Numeric Entity	HTML Name	Octal Number	Symbol	Description
&#060;	&lt;	74	<	Less than sign
&#061;		75	=	Equals sign
&#062;	&gt;	76	>	Greater than sign
&#063;		77	?	Question mark
&#064;		100	@	At sign
A–Z			A–Z	Uppercase letters A–Z
&#091;		133	[	Left bracket
&#092;		134	\	Back slash
&#093;		135	]	Right bracket
&#094;		136	^	Caret
&#095;		137	_	Underscore
&#096;		140	`	Grave accent
a–z		a–z	Lowercase letters	a–z
&#123;		173	{	Left curly brace
|		174	|	Vertical bar
&#125;		175	}	Right curly brace
&#126;		176	~	Tilde
&#133;			…	*Ellipsis
&#134;			†	*Dagger
&#135;			‡	*Double dagger
&#136;			^	*Circumflex
&#137;			‰	*Permil
&#145;			'	*Left single quote
&#146;			'	*Right single quote
&#147;			"	*Left double quote
&#148;			"	*Right double quote
&#149;			•	*Bullet
&#150;			–	*En dash
&#151;			—	*Em dash

Continued

HTML Numeric Entity	HTML Name	Octal Number	Symbol	Description
&#153;			™	*Trademark sign
&#159;			Ÿ	*Capital Y, umlaut
		240		Nonbreaking space
&#161;	&iexcl;	241	¡	Inverted exclamation point
&#162;	&cent;	242	¢	Cent sign
&#163;	&pound;	243	£	Pound sign
&#164;	&curren;	244	¤	Currency sign
&#165;	&yen;	245	¥	Yen sign
&#166;	&brvbar;	246	¦	Broken vertical bar
&#167;	&sect;	247	§	Section sign
&#168;	&uml;	250	¨	Umlaut
&#169;	&copy;	251	©	Copyright sign
&#170;	&ordf;	252	ª	Feminine ordinal sign
&#171;	&laquo;	253	«	Left angle quote
&#172;	&not;	254	¬	Not sign
&#173;	&shy;	255	-	Soft hyphen
&#174;	&reg;	256	®	Registered trademark sign
&#175;	&macr;	257	¯	Macron accent
&#176;	&deg;	260	°	Degree sign
&#177;	&plusmn;	261	±	Plus or minus sign
&#178;	&sup2;	262	²	Superscript 2
&#179;	&sup3;	263	³	Superscript 3
&#180;	&acute;	264	´	Acute accent
&#181;	&micro;	265	µ	Micro sign
&#182;	&para;	266	¶	Paragraph sign
&#183;	&middot;	267	·	Middle dot
&#184;	&cedil;	270	¸	Cedilla
&#185;	&sup1;	271	¹	Superscript 1

HTML Numeric Entity	HTML Name	Octal Number	Symbol	Description
&#186;	&ordm;	272	º	Masculine ordinal
&#187;	&raquo;	273	»	Right angle quote
&#188;	&frac14;	274	¼	One-fourth fraction
&#189;	&frac12;	275	½	One-half fraction
&#190;	&frac34;	276	¾	Three-fourths fraction
&#191;	&iquest;	277	¿	Inverted question mark
&#192;	&Agrave;	300	À	Capital A, grave accent
&#193;	&Aacute;	301	Á	Capital A, acute accent
&#194;	&Acirc;	302	Â	Capital A, circumflex
&#195;	&Atilde;	303	Ã	Capital A, tilde
&#196;	&Auml;	304	Ä	Capital A, umlaut
&#197;	&Aring;	305	Å	Capital A, ring
&#198;	&AElig;	306	Æ	Capital AE ligature
&#199;	&Ccedil;	307	Ç	Capital C, cedilla
&#200;	&Egrave;	310	È	Capital E, grave accent
&#201;	&Eacute;	311	É	Capital E, acute accent
&#202;	&Ecirc;	312	Ê	Capital E, circumflex
&#203;	&Euml;	313	Ë	Capital E, umlaut
&#204;	&Igrave;	314	Ì	Capital I, grave accent
&#205;	&Iacute;	315	Í	Capital I, acute accent
&#206;	&Icirc;	316	Î	Capital I, circumflex
&#207;	&Iuml;	317	Ï	Capital I, umlaut
&#208;	&ETH;	320	Ð	Capital eth, Icelandic
&#209;	&Ntilde;	321	Ñ	Capital N, tilde
&#210;	&Ograve;	322	Ò	Capital O, grave accent
&#211;	&Oacute;	323	Ó	Capital O, acute accent
&#212;	&Ocirc;	324	Ô	Capital O, circumflex
&#213;	&Otilde;	325	Õ	Capital O, tilde
&#214;	&Ouml;	326	Ö	Capital O, umlaut

Continued

HTML Numeric Entity	HTML Name	Octal Number	Symbol	Description
&#215;	&times;	327	×	Multiply sign
&#216;	&Oslash;	330	Ø	Capital O, slash
&#217;	&Ugrave;	331	Ù	Capital U, grave accent
&#218;	&Uacute;	332	Ú	Capital U, acute accent
&#219;	&Ucirc;	333	Û	Capital U, circumflex
&#220;	&Uuml;	334	Ü	Capital U, umlaut
&#221;	&Yacute;	335	Ý	Capital Y, acute accent
&#222;	&THORN;	336	Þ	Capital thorn, Icelandic
&#223;	&szlig;	337	ß	SZ ligature
&#224;	&agrave;	340	à	Small a, grave accent
&#225;	&aacute;	341	á	Small a, acute accent
&#226;	&acirc;	342	â	Small a, circumflex
&#227;	&atilde;	343	ã	Small a, tilde
&#228;	&auml;	344	ä	Small a, umlaut
&#229;	&aring;	345	å	Small a, ring
&#230;	&aelig;	346	æ	Small ae ligature
&#231;	&ccedil;	347	ç	Small c, cedilla
&#232;	&egrave;	350	è	Small e, grave accent
&#233;	&eacute;	351	é	Small e, acute accent
&#234;	&ecirc;	352	ê	Small e, circumflex
&#235;	&euml;	353	ë	Small e, umlaut
&#236;	&igrave;	354	ì	Small i, grave accent
&#237;	&iacute;	355	í	Small i, acute accent
&#238;	&icirc;	356	î	Small i, circumflex
&#239;	&iuml;	357	ï	Small i, umlaut
&#240;	&eth;	360	ð	Small eth, Icelandic
&#241;	&ntilde;	361	ñ	Small n, tilde
&#242;	&ograve;	362	ò	Small o, grave accent
&#243;	&oacute;	363	ó	Small o, acute accent

HTML Numeric Entity	HTML Name	Octal Number	Symbol	Description
&#244;	&ocirc;	364	ô	Small o, circumflex
&#245;	&otilde;	365	õ	Small o, tilde
&#246;	&ouml;	366	ö	Small o, umlaut
&#247;	&divide;	367	÷	Divide sign
&#248;	&oslash;	370	ø	Small o, slash
&#249;	&ugrave;	371	ù	Small u, grave accent
&#250;	&uacute;	372	ú	Small u, acute accent
&#251;	&ucirc;	373	û	Small u, circumflex
&#252;	&uuml;	374	ü	Small u, umlaut
&#253;	&yacute;	375	ý	Small y, grave accent
&#254;	&thorn;	376	þ	Small thorn, Icelandic
&#255;	&yuml;	377	ÿ	Small y, umlaut

CASCADING STYLE SHEET REFERENCE

The CSS Properties table lists the Cascading Style Sheet properties defined in the Level 1 specification as well as key Level 2 positioning properties. Support for Level 1 and Level 2 style properties varies from browser to browser, so be sure to adequately test CSS style sheets on a variety of browser versions. Some online resources also provide CSS compatibility charts that you can use as a reference. The W3C's CSS home page at www.w3.org/Style/CSS/ provides a list of online resources.

Although some CSS properties only accept certain keyword values, others can take values such as colors, lengths, and percentages. The CSS Values table defines the correct formatting for these values.

CSS Values

Value	Format
COLOR	Colors may be expressed in the form of a color name or a hexadecimal value. You may also specify colors in RGB form, $rgb(r, g, b)$, where r, g, and b are either numbers or percentages.
LENGTH	Lengths may contain an optional plus or minus sign followed by a numeric entity and a unit identifier. Unit identifiers include em (height of the font), ex (height of the letter x), px (pixels), in (inches), cm (centimeters), mm (millimeters), pt (point), and pc (picas). If the value of the length is zero, you may omit the unit identifier.
NUMBER	A number may contain an optional plus or minus sign followed by the number.
PERCENT	Percent values may contain an optional plus or minus sign, followed by a number and the percent sign.
URL	For properties that accept URL values, use the keyword url, followed by the URL enclosed within single or double quotes and parentheses: url("http://www.mysite.com")

CSS Properties

Property	Possible Values	Default Value	Description
background			Shorthand property for defining values for the other background properties, listed in any order.
background-attachment	scroll | fixed	scroll	Fixes the background image to the window, or allows it to scroll with the document.
background-color	COLOR | transparent	transparent	Sets the background color of an element.
background-image	URL | none	none	Sets an image for the background of an element.
background-position	PERCENT | LENGTH | top | center | bottom | left | right	0% 0%	Defines initial position of the background image. Paired values correspond to x and y coordinates.

Property	Possible Values	Default Value	Description
background-repeat	repeat | repeat-x | repeat-y | no-repeat	repeat	Specifies how the background image should be tiled.
border			Shorthand property to set all four borders of an element. May include one or more COLOR values, a value for border-width and a value for border-style.
border-bottom			Defines the bottom border of an element. May include COLOR, a value for border-bottom-width, and a value for border-style.
border-bottom-width	LENGTH | thin | medium | thick	medium	Defines the width of the bottom border.
border-color	COLOR		Defines the color of all four borders.
border-left			Defines the left border of an element. May include COLOR, a value for border-left-width, and a value for border-style.
border-left-width	LENGTH | thin | medium | thick	medium	Defines the width of the left border.
border-right			Defines the right border of an element. May include COLOR, a value for border-right-width, and a value for border-style.
border-right-width	LENGTH | thin | medium | thick	medium	Defines the width of the right border.
border-style	dashed | dotted | double | groove | inset| none | outset | ridge | solid	none	Define the style of all four borders.
border-top			Defines the top border of an element. May include COLOR, a value for border-top-width, and a value for border-style.
border-top-width	LENGTH | thin | medium | thick	medium	Defines the width of the top border.
border-width	LENGTH | thin | medium | thick	medium	Defines the width of all four borders.
bottom	LENGTH | PERCENT | auto	auto	Defines the bottom offset for positioned elements where position is other than static.
clear	both | left | none | right	none	Moves an element down until it is clear of the specified margin.
clip	SHAPE | auto	auto	Defines what portion of an element's content should be visible. The only SHAPE currently available is rect where the top, bottom, left, and right offsets are defined as either LENGTH or auto.
color	COLOR		Defines the color of an element.

Continued

CSS Properties (continued)

Property	Possible Values	Default Value	Description
display	block | inline | list-item | none	block	Sets the display type of an element.
float	left | none | right	none	Sets whether an element should float to either the left or right.
font			Shorthand property that defines all of the font-related properties in the following order: font-style, font-variant, font-weight, font-size, line-height, font-family.
font-family		list of fonts	Defines the fonts for a particular element.
font-size	xx-small | x-small | small | medium | large | x-large | xx-large| larger | smaller | LENGTH | PERCENT	medium	Sets the font size.
font-style	normal | italic | oblique	normal	Sets the font style.
font-variant	normal | small-caps	normal	Sets the font to small caps.
font-weight	normal | bold | bolder | lighter | NUMBER	normal	Defines the weight of the font. When numbers are used, they must be in multiples of 100 and may range from 100 to 900.
height	LENGTH | auto	auto	Defines the height of an element.
left	LENGTH | PERCENT | auto	auto	Defines the left offset for positioned elements where position is other than static.
letter-spacing	LENGTH | normal	normal	Defines the amount of space between letters.
line-height	LENGTH | NUMBER | PERCENT | normal	normal	Sets the height of a line of text.
list-style			Shorthand property to define the style of a list. May include values for list-style-image, list-style-position, and list-style-type.
list-style-image	URL | none	none	Sets an image to use as a list's bullet.
list-style-position	inside | outside	outside	Sets the indentation of list items.
list-style-type	circle | disc | square | decimal | lower-alpha | lower-roman | upper-alpha | upper-roman	disc	Defines a list's marker for ordered or unordered lists.
margin	LENGTH | PERCENT | auto		Sets all four margins of an element.
margin-bottom	LENGTH | PERCENT | auto	0	Sets the bottom margin.

Property	Possible Values	Default Value	Description
margin-left	LENGTH | PERCENT | auto	0	Sets the left margin.
margin-right	LENGTH | PERCENT | auto	0	Sets the right margin.
margin-top	LENGTH | PERCENT | auto	0	Sets the top margin.
overflow	visible | hidden | scroll | auto	visible	Determines how overflow content should be handled.
padding			Sets the padding on all four sides of an element.
padding-bottom	LENGTH | PERCENT	0	Sets the bottom padding.
padding-left	LENGTH | PERCENT	0	Sets the left padding.
padding-right	LENGTH | PERCENT	0	Sets the right padding.
padding-top	LENGTH | PERCENT	0	Sets the top padding.
position	static | absolute | relative | fixed	static	Defines the type of positioning of an element.
right	LENGTH | PERCENT | auto	auto	Defines the right offset for positioned elements where position is other than static.
text-align	center | justify | left | right		Defines how text should be aligned.
text-decoration	blink | line-through | none | overline | underline	none	Defines any special text decorations.
text-indent	LENGTH | PERCENT	0	Defines the amount of indentation for the first line of text.
text-transform	capitalize | lowercase | none | upper-case	none	Transforms the text contained within the element.
top	LENGTH | PERCENT | auto	auto	Defines the top offset for positioned elements where position is other than static.
vertical-align	PERCENT | baseline | bottom | middle | sub | super | text-bottom | text-top | top		Controls the vertical positioning of an element.
visibility	visible | hidden | inherit	inherit	Determines whether positioned elements are visible or transparent.
word-spacing	LENGTH | normal	normal	Sets the amount of space between words.
white-space	normal | nowrap | pre	normal	Defines how white space within an element should be handled.
width	LENGTH | PERCENT | auto	auto	Defines the width of an element.
z-index	auto | INTEGER	auto	Sets the stacking index of an element.

WHAT'S ON THE CD-ROM

The CD-ROM included in this book contains many useful files and programs. Before installing any of the programs on the disc, make sure that a newer version of the program is not already installed on your computer. For information on installing different versions of the same program, contact the program's manufacturer.

SYSTEM REQUIREMENTS

To use the contents of the CD-ROM, your computer must be equipped with the following hardware and software:

- A PC with a Pentium 133 MHz or faster processor, or a Mac OS computer with a 68040 or faster processor. A Pentium 200 MHz is recommended for working with Photoshop, an evaluation version of which is included on the CD-ROM.

- Microsoft Windows 95 or later, Windows NT 4 or later, or Mac OS system software 7.5.5 or later. Windows 98 or later and Mac OS 8.5, 8.6, or 9.0 are recommended for Photoshop.

- At least 16MB of total RAM, with 64MB recommended for working with Photoshop.

- A ten-speed (10x) or faster CD-ROM drive.

- A sound card for PCs.

- A monitor capable of displaying at least 800 x 600 resolution in 256 colors.

- A modem with a speed of at least 28.8 Kbps.

INSTALLING AND USING THE SOFTWARE

For your convenience, the software titles appearing on the CD-ROM are listed alphabetically.

Author's sample files

For Mac and Windows 95/98/NT. This folder contains two types of files. The Word files are worksheets for contemplating the important issues you should consider when planning your Web site. The worksheets were based on material in Chapter 1. We have also included sample HTML files for exercises in other parts of the book.

BBEdit, from BareBones Software

For Macintosh. Demo version. BBEdit is the premier HTML text editor for Macintosh users. The demo has all of the features of the full version but expires after 24 launches.

BBEdit Lite, from BareBones Software

For Macintosh. Freeware. BBEdit Lite is the premier freeware text editor for Mac OS. BBEdit Lite now runs natively on Mac OS X.

CuteFTP, from GlobalSCAPE

For Windows. Shareware version. CuteFTP features an easy-to-use interface that enables you to quickly transfer files to remote servers. This version expires after 30 days.

Dreamweaver, from Macromedia

For Macintosh and Windows. Trial version. Dreamweaver is a professional Web design application that combines a code-editing environment with a visual layout interface. Dreamweaver enables you to easily add advanced scripts, dynamic HTML, and multimedia elements. This trial version expires after 30 days.

Fetch, from Fetch Softworks

For Macintosh. Trial version. Fetch is a full-featured FTP client for the Macintosh platform. This trial version expires after 15 days.

Fireworks, from Macromedia

For Macintosh and Windows. Trial version. Fireworks is a robust yet easy-to-use graphics application that allows you to create, edit, and optimize images for the Web. This trial version expires after 30 days.

Flash, from Macromedia

For Macintosh and Windows. Trial version. Create animations and interactive Web site interfaces with this powerful multimedia application. This trial version expires after 30 days.

GIF Animator, from Ulead Systems

For Windows. Trial version. GIF Animator is a powerful application for creating and optimizing Web animations. This fully-functional trial version expires after 15 days.

GoLive, from Adobe

For Macintosh and Windows. Trial version. GoLive is a professional Web design application that incorporates a coding environment, visual design interface, and site management tools. This trial version expires in 30 days.

HomeSite, from Macromedia

For Windows. Evaluation version. HomeSite is a professional HTML text editor designed for hand-coders. HomeSite supports a variety of advanced technologies, including Cascading Style Sheets, JavaScript, Perl, and many others.

HTML Tidy, from Dave Raggett

For Windows on the CD; available for Macintosh, Unix, and other operating systems from the Web site. Open Source. HTML Tidy is a utility that helps clean up your Web page documents and point out common coding errors, and has some ability to work with XML documents. The utility is fully functional. You can find other versions and updates at www.w3.org/People/Raggett/tidy/ - download

Paint Shop Pro, from Jasc Software

For Windows. Evaluation version. Paint Shop Pro is a robust yet affordable image-editing program. This fully functional trial version expires after 30 days.

Nokia WAP Toolkit

For Windows 98/2000 with SP4. Evaluation version. Use the Nokia WAP Toolkit to create WML-based applications and then test them on a Nokia wireless simulator to see how the applications will look. You must have the Java Runtime Environment (JRE) 1.3 installed to use the product.

Photoshop, from Adobe

For Macintosh and Windows. Evaluation version. Photoshop, the industry-leading image editor from Adobe, enables you to edit, retouch, and optimize images for the Web and other media. This evaluation does not allow you to save, export, or print artwork.

SmartSaver Pro, from Ulead

For Windows. Trial version. SmartSaver Pro is a versatile application for optimizing Web-based graphics and creating interactive images. This fully functional trial version expires after 15 days.

TROUBLESHOOTING

We tried our best to compile programs that work on most computers with the minimum system requirements. Your computer, however, may differ, and some programs may not work properly for some reason.

The two most likely problems are that you do not have enough memory (RAM) for the programs you want to use, or you have other programs running that are affecting installation or running of a program. If you get error messages like Not enough memory or Setup cannot continue, try one or more of these methods and then try using the software again:

- Turn off any antivirus software.

- Close all running programs.

- In Windows, close the CD-ROM interface and run demos or installations directly from Windows Explorer.

- Have your local computer store add more RAM to your computer.

If you still have trouble installing the items from the CD-ROM, please call the Customer Service phone number: 800-762-2974 (outside the U.S.: 317-572-3994).

MASTER VISUALLY WEB DESIGN ON THE CD-ROM

You can view *Master VISUALLY Web Design* on your screen by using the CD-ROM included at the back of this book. The CD-ROM allows you to search the contents of the book for a specific word or phrase. The CD-ROM also provides a convenient way of keeping the book handy while traveling.

You must install Acrobat Reader on your computer before you can view the book on the CD-ROM. This program is provided on the disc. Acrobat Reader allows you to view Portable Document Format, or PDF, files. These files can display books and magazines on your screen exactly as they appear in printed form.

To view the contents of the book by using Acrobat Reader, display the contents of the disc. Open the PDF folder. Then double-click the chapter you want to view.

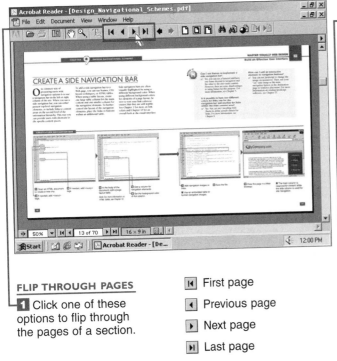

FLIP THROUGH PAGES

1 Click one of these options to flip through the pages of a section.

|◄| First page

|◄ Previous page

►| Next page

►| Last page

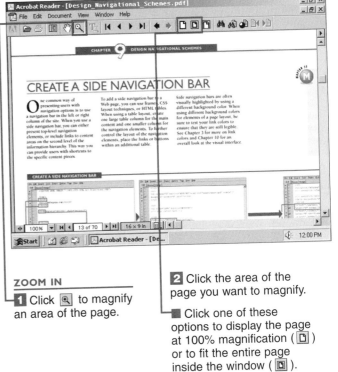

ZOOM IN

1 Click 🔍 to magnify an area of the page.

2 Click the area of the page you want to magnify.

■ Click one of these options to display the page at 100% magnification (🔲) or to fit the entire page inside the window (🔲).

How do I install Acrobat Reader?

✓ Open the `Software\Reader` folder on the CD-ROM disc. Double-click the `rp500enu.exe` file and then follow the instructions on your screen. Or, you can use the visual interface to install Acrobat Reader. (Begin by clicking the idg.exe icon.)

How do I search all the sections of the book at once?

✓ You must first locate the index. While viewing the contents of the book, click 🔍 in the Acrobat Reader window. Click Indexes and then click Add. Locate and click the index.pdx file, click Open, and then click OK. You need to locate the index only once. After locating the index, you can click 🔍 to search all the sections.

How can I make searching the book more convenient?

✓ Copy the Acrobat Files folder from the CD-ROM disc to your hard drive. This enables you to easily access the contents of the book at any time.

Can I use Acrobat Reader for anything else?

✓ Acrobat Reader is a popular and useful program. There are many files available on the Web that are designed to be viewed using Acrobat Reader. Look for files with the `.pdf` extension.

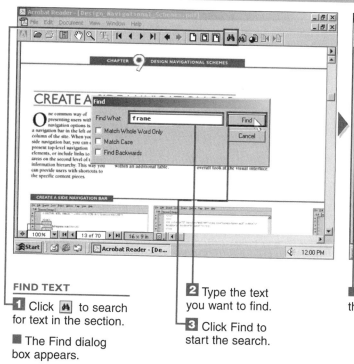

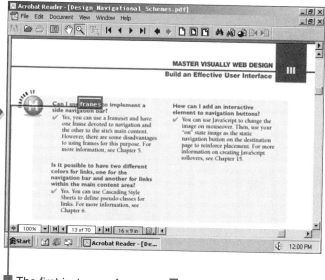

FIND TEXT

1 Click 🔍 to search for text in the section.

■ The Find dialog box appears.

2 Type the text you want to find.

3 Click Find to start the search.

■ The first instance of the text is highlighted.

■ Repeat steps 1 and 3 to find the next instance of the text.

TECHNIQUES DESCRIBED IN THIS BOOK. HMI DOES NOT WARRANT THAT THE FUNCTIONS CONTAINED IN THE SOFTWARE WILL MEET YOUR REQUIREMENTS OR THAT THE OPERATION OF THE SOFTWARE WILL BE ERROR FREE.

(c) This limited warranty gives you specific legal rights, and you may have other rights that vary from jurisdiction to jurisdiction.

6. Remedies.

(a) HMI's entire liability and your exclusive remedy for defects in materials and workmanship shall be limited to replacement of the Software Media, which may be returned to HMI with a copy of your receipt at the following address: Software Media Fulfillment Department, Attn.: *Master VISUALLY Web Design*, Hungry Minds, Inc., 10475 Crosspoint Blvd., Indianapolis, IN 46256, or call 1-800-762-2974. Please allow four to six weeks for delivery. This Limited Warranty is void if failure of the Software Media has resulted from accident, abuse, or misapplication. Any replacement Software Media will be warranted for the remainder of the original warranty period or thirty (30) days, whichever is longer.

(b) In no event shall HMI or the author be liable for any damages whatsoever (including without limitation damages for loss of business profits, business interruption, loss of business information, or any other pecuniary loss) arising from the use of or inability to use the Book or the Software, even if HMI has been advised of the possibility of such damages.

(c) Because some jurisdictions do not allow the exclusion or limitation of liability for consequential or incidental damages, the above limitation or exclusion may not apply to you.

7. U.S. Government Restricted Rights.

Use, duplication, or disclosure of the Software for or on behalf of the United States of America, its agencies and/or instrumentalities (the "U.S. Government") is subject to restrictions as stated in paragraph (c)(1)(ii) of the Rights in Technical Data and Computer Software clause of DFARS 252.227-7013, or subparagraphs (c) (1) and (2) of the Commercial Computer Software - Restricted Rights clause at FAR 52.227-19, and in similar clauses in the NASA FAR supplement, as applicable.

8. General.

This Agreement constitutes the entire understanding of the parties and revokes and supersedes all prior agreements, oral or written, between them and may not be modified or amended except in a writing signed by both parties hereto that specifically refers to this Agreement. This Agreement shall take precedence over any other documents that may be in conflict herewith. If any one or more provisions contained in this Agreement are held by any court or tribunal to be invalid, illegal, or otherwise unenforceable, each and every other provision shall remain in full force and effect.

INDEX

INDEX

INDEX

INDEX

INDEX

with these two-color Visual™ guides

 "Master It" tips provide additional topic coverage.

Title	ISBN	Price
Master Active Directory VISUALLY	0-7645-3425-4	$39.99
Master Microsoft Access 2000 VISUALLY	0-7645-6048-4	$39.99
Master Microsoft Office 2000 VISUALLY	0-7645-6050-6	$39.99
Master Microsoft Word 2000 VISUALLY	0-7645-6046-8	$39.99
Master Office 97 VISUALLY	0-7645-6036-0	$39.99
Master Photoshop 5.5 VISUALLY	0-7645-6045-X	$39.99
Master Red Hat Linux VISUALLY	0-7645-3436-X	$39.99
Master VISUALLY Adobe Photoshop, Illustrator, Premiere, and After Effects	0-7645-3668-0	$39.99
Master VISUALLY Dreamweaver 4 and Flash 5	0-7645-0855-5	$39.99
Master VISUALLY Dreamweaver MX and Flash MX	0-7645-3696-6	$39.99
Master VISUALLY FrontPage 2002	0-7645-3580-3	$39.99
Master VISUALLY HTML 4 and XHTML 1	0-7645-3454-8	$39.99
Master VISUALLY Office XP	0-7645-3599-4	$39.99
Master VISUALLY Photoshop 6	0-7645-3541-2	$39.99
Master VISUALLY Web Design	0-7645-3610-9	$39.99
Master VISUALLY Windows 2000 Server	0-7645-3426-2	$39.99
Master VISUALLY Windows Me Millennium Edition	0-7645-3496-3	$39.99
Master VISUALLY Windows XP	0-7645-3621-4	$39.99
Master Windows 95 VISUALLY	0-7645-6024-7	$39.99
Master Windows 98 VISUALLY	0-7645-6034-4	$39.99
Master Windows 2000 Professional VISUALLY	0-7645-3421-1	$39.99

For visual learners who want an all-in-one reference/tutorial that delivers more in-depth information about a technology topic.

The *Visual*™ series is available wherever books are sold, or call 1-800-762-2974.

Outside the US, call 317-572-3993